The

American Christian Review

(Vol. 2, 1857)

Edited by
Elder Benjamin Franklin

Charleston, AR:

2021

The American Christian Review, Vol. 2, 1857, is republished by Cobb Publishing, 2021.

Cobb Publishing

704 E. Main St.

Charleston, AR 72933

CobbPublishing@gmail.com

www.CobbPublishing.com

(479) 747-8372

ISBN: 978-1-947622-59-3

CONTENTS OF VOLUME II, 1857,

A Discourse on the Regeneration,	257
A Discourse, by Elder J. A. Clarke,	161
A Few words for Mr. Ford,	157
A Generous Proposition,	381
A Sermon, by William Gilpin,	198
Acknowledgment of Missionary Funds,	253
Address, by Elder S. W. Irvin,	138
Address on Bible Revision,	173
An Elder and a " Trio of Editors,"	221
Anti-Revision Sermon,	312
Are We Disciples,	366
Bill of Grievances,	270
Bracken Association,	86
" "	109
" "	146
" "	184
" "	216
" "	242
" "	305
" "	280
Campbellism Aroused,	234
Campbellistic Theology,	193
Campbellism Unchanged,	379
Communication from Elder Johnson	27
Communications,	29
Communication,	61
"	94
"	251
Correspondence,	181
Death of Elder Johnson,	44
Debate with Rev. T. J. Fisher,	225
Discourse, by Elder Greene,	65
Discourse, by Elder Raines,	97
Discourse, by Elder Emmons,	129
Disappointment, Delusion and Deception,	371
Discussion,	112
"	146
Dialogue of Devils,	82
"	204
"	297
Editor's Table,	126
" "	63
" "	151
" "	130
" "	319
" "	223
Evidences of Christianity,	21, 46, 73
" " "	46
" " "	154
Excursion to Northern Illinois,	170
" " " "	220
Editor's Table,	382
Fore-Knowledge and Human Agency Again,	376
Gleanings From a Sacred Field,	19
God to be Found in His Appointments	374
How to be Saved—A Discourse,	289
Introductory,	1
Last Moments of Elder Johnson	67
Letter from Jerusalem,	123
Messrs. Ford, Fisher, Johnson & Co.,	346
Missionary Society,	49
More About Debates,	275
Mr. Ford in Trouble,	363
Not a Gentleman Nor a Christian,	361
Northern Illinois,	153
Obituary,	32
"	96
"	160
"	128
Obituaries,	224
"	288
Oskaloosa College,	308
President Fanning's Course,	340
Query,	246
Reminiscences of the Past,	252
Sectarianism Confessedly Wrong,	277
Sermon, by Eld. Hoshour,	33
Speculative Questions,	369
Spiritualism and Spirit-Rappings,	176
Spiritual Influence,	302
" "	313
Students on Hymn Book Avails,	315
Success of the Gospel,	32
" " " "	64
" " " "	96
" " " "	128
" " " "	162
" " " "	192
" " " "	255
" " " "	287
The Comfort of Love—A Sermon,	5
The Book of Job,	25
The Work of the Church,	120
The Heresy of Open Communion,	124
The Controversy on the Influence of the Spirit,	283
The Gospel of Christ—A Discourse,	331
The Christian Name,	247
The Disciples,	39
" " in Noblesville,	54
Throwing Dust in the Eyes of the Baptists,	168
The Necessity of Regeneration—A Sermon,	353
Tour to Illinois,	209
To the Brotherhood of Disciples,	352
To the Brethren in Kentucky	12
Upward Tendency—Reformation Not a Failure,	135
" " " "	186
" " " "	316
" " " "	349
" " " "	238
Visit to Kentucky	77

THE AMERICAN CHRISTIAN REVIEW.

VOL. II.   CINCINNATI, JANUARY, 1857.   No. 1.

INTRODUCTION.

Nation after nation rises, enters and occupies a place among the nations of the earth, falls and is only known in the faithful records of history. Generation after generation comes forth, enters upon the great theater of life, throngs the world for a little while, falls in death and passes into eternity. Upon an average, about once in thirty-three years, the whole inhabitants of the earth, or as many as are upon it at any one time; about one thousand millions; are carried beyond the reach of all missionary effort—beyond the reach of all repentance—all gospel invitations, and so many as are not saved, beyond all possibility of salvation. During the same short period, the preachers, missionaries, writers and professors of religion of one generation, are all borne where no mistakes can be corrected, and no amendment for wrongs done, or time trifled away, can ever be made. Taking off from this time eighteen years, for childhood, only leaves about fifteen years for the vast work of personal preparation for a state of boundless duration, in the pure and holy society of just men made perfect, the angels of God, Jesus the Mediator of the New Covenant, and God, the judge of all. It also leaves about the same length of time for the good and virtuous, those with the love of God in their hearts, and lovers of mankind, to make an effort to save our race. In this view of the subject, and no other can be justly taken, it will readily be perceived, that what we do must be done quickly. Those who do anything for mankind must engage in the work immediately and with energy. All who intend laying up a good foundation against the time to come—laying up treasure in Heaven, to which they can go, and upon which they can rely, when their temporal supports shall all fail, must commence the work immediately, persevere in it, and abound during the short space afforded them. There must be no delay, for there is simply time enough to do what must be done immediately, if done at all. Those who have never prepared to meet God, have still greater reason to enter at once upon the examination of the subject. With them every thing, to secure their eternal happiness, so far as their own action is concerned, is yet to be done. How short the time, in view of the amount to be done, and how carefully every moment should be employed by any person who has never been reconciled to God! What vast multitudes throng our streets, lanes and highways, who have never seriously thought upon, much less taken the elementary steps, to come to God, and who will remain in their present condition, unless arrested in their thoughtless career by those who have already tasted the good word of God, and felt the power of the world to come! What an everlasting reason we find here, for a most energetic, persevering, and godly effort to rescue them and bring them to God!

But when we think of putting forth an effort, in another volume, and in the pulpit, during another year, the solemn question comes up and thunders in our ears: *In what manner can an effort be made, acceptable to God, and that shall accomplish the greatest amount of good for man?* Here is the perplexing question for this generation. Anciently, when men were of one mind, spoke one tongue, were united, and their energies were concentrated upon one work, a great work—though a *wicked* work—the means the Almighty employed to thwart their designs and defeat their work, was to divide their tongues, confound their language and thus scatter them abroad over the earth. This means, too, proved entirely successful. It was easy to devise and put in execution means to defeat an united effort of men, though that united effort was in a bad cause, and scatter them. But when the Lord, in his great mercy and according to both his benevolent purpose and promise, was pleased to send the blessing of the gospel upon all nations, and bring the believers of all nations into one body in Christ, this confusion, or division of tongues, was a great obstacle. That which God had employed, and which had so well served the purpose to divide and scatter men, could not now but be an obstacle in the way of uniting them in one body. That confusion of language which had served the *good* purpose of defeating a united and concentrated effort, in a *bad* work—building the tower of Babel—now when the Lord would concentrate and combine the efforts of men in a *good* work, in one body in Christ, would lie directly in the way. The Lord saw this; and, at the commencement, by that stupendous and miraculous gift, the gift of tongues, removed the difficulty, by presenting the word of God to every man in his own tongue, so that all were lead to wonder that every man heard of the wonderful works of God in his own language.—His greatest and most wonderful of all supernatural spiritual gifts, was God's miraculous means of instantaneously translating the word of God into all languages spoken by men. Through this means, *one faith,* or *one religion* was given to all nations of the earth, in their mother tongue. To defeat this "one faith," which the Lord gave for the "one body," to which he had given "one spirit," and before which he had set "one hope," which he had placed under "one Lord," into which all had been baptized by "one baptism," all from "one God and Father of all," the enemy has confounded their tongues, confused their language, divided and disconcerted the people of God. They are not now scattered from a wicked, preposterous work, such as erecting the tower of Babel, by the hand of God, as in olden time, or we could say too: "It is a wise providence of God that we are thus divided;" but their language is confounded, their tongues divided—they are scattered and dispersed from the work of the Lord, by "Mystery Babylon the Great, the mother of harlots and abominations of the earth." One little party is found in one place, under one name and one faith, another little party is found in another place, marshaled under a different name, a different faith, etc., etc., till it is said there are hundreds of parties, not only that do not know what their neighbors believe, but nine-tenths of them do not know what is contained in their own creed; and, not one out of a thousand of them, can tell what the

INTRODUCTORY.

one faith," of the New Testament, or "the faith once delivered to the Saints," is.

What is to be done in this state of things? Does God intend this state of confusion to continue? Or, does he intend to restore to all nations one language? Does he intend the world to return to one faith? one religion? From present indications, the English language will certainly prevail largely over the earth. But the one faith, or one religion! What shall be done? What can be done? We have long since decided, that it is useless to think of doing any good for any man, or any set of men, who cannot be cured of this confusion of tongues. If a man has talked the language of Babylon so long that it has become a kind of second nature to him; if he loves it better than the pure speech of the true Israel of God; if he prefer mysteries and confusion to the clear revelations of God; if he has worshipped at Mount Gerazim until he prefers it to Jerusalem from above, the mother of us all, where the Lord's name is recorded, he is past cure; like the unbelieving Jew, in rejecting Christ, with his back bowed down always, or the miserably blinded and stupid Papist, given over to believe a lie, and incapable of ever having the mists dispersed from his eyes till the thunders of the Almighty shall summon him to the judgment of the Great Day.

We have, however, a command from Heaven touching this precise state of things, else all Protestant commentators have interpreted wrong. And if their interpretation, of the following passage is not right, we should be much obliged to any man who will tell us what it means"

"And I heard another voice from heaven, saying: ' Come out of her, my people, that ye be not partakers of her sins, and that ye receive not of her plagues; for her sins have reached unto heaven, and God hath remembered her iniquities." Rev. xviii. 4, 5. This command is certainly not obeyed, in simply coming out of the Romish Church, or any other, as some German infidels have done, without receiving anything better; but those who come out, in obedience to this command, must lift up their hearts and attention to their great Leader, in heaven, and hear his voice. He says"

"My sheep hear My voice; but the voice of a stranger they will not hear."

His voice commands all who hear him, to come out from all the confusion of tongues of the present age, and follow him and he will lead them by the fountains of living water and grant them to sit with him in the paradise of God.

The effort of Christians should be, and our efforts, both with tongue and pen, shall be, God being our helper, more directly than ever before, aimed at the one supreme end, the rescue of the people from the confusion of tongues and thoughts, now prevailing to such an alarming extent, and teach them how they can believe on, love and serve the Savior of the world, put themselves under him, follow him and put their everlasting trust in him. We intend, the Lord permitting, going into the matter more fully, making everything more simple and easy of apprehension than ever before. We intend while the preachers are explaining their doctrines, views, feelings, forms and ceremonies, to show in the most satisfactory manner possible, precisely what the Lord requires a man to believe before he can be received; precisely what he has got to do before the Lord will receive him; precisely what he is now to enjoy, as well as what he is to hope for in future, and precisely what he intends his constant practice shall be from his conversion, till the end of his race. We must simplify more than we have ever done before, keep nearer the feet of Jesus and his holy Apostles, and learn of them; in every respect, we must be like them, imitate them, adopt their very words and behavior. The matter is, how can we enter into the very soul of Christianity, in preaching, praying and singing; live and be more like the first Christians? How can we make the identiical same truths of the gospel move the hearts, spirits and consciences of men as they did when preached by the Apostles and first preachers of the word of life? How shall we preach Christ with such great power; present him in such an attractive manner, as to call the attention of the people to him and induce them to rally around him, and thus forget their petty strifes and disputes about men and the views of men?

Before we shall succeed right, we must make the Lord more especially our theme, fix the mind upon him and lead men to love him. This is not to be done by eulogies upon him, or his word, from the lips of men, who neither love, honor nor serve him. But it is done by the preacher himself, really loving him, referring to him in every instance, with awe, reverence and regard, that will show that the Lord has a place in his heart. Speak of the work as the Lord's work, his church, his people, his doctrine, his cause, which is the case, if we are under him. Let us have nothing of "Reformation doctrine," "our doctrine," much less of "our views," when speaking of what Christians believe. Let us have no "joining the Reformation," or "belonging to the Reformation," etc. We must preach precisely what the Apostles preached. When men believe what is preached, they will believe precisely the same those did who heard the Apostles—they will believe in the Savior. When they inquire what to do, they will mean, of course, what they must do to be saved, and enter the church of Christ, and we must always recollect, when we speak of them, what church they belong to. We must not forget that they have received him, his doctrine and his salvation; and that he has received them, and that they now belong to him. There is immense power in keeping the matter in this shape, both upon ourselves and the world. The cause and all being his, forms a direct issue between him and the unbelievers, and makes every man feel that the indignity done, in refusing, is done to *him,* for it is refusing *him* and *his* cause.

The question is not whether men will receive us, our doctrines, our views, our church, or "the Reformation," or "Reformation doctrines; but whether they will receive him whom the Father hath sent, love him, follow him, place themselves under him, obey him and trust in him forever. He is the center of all union, all love, and all piety. Upon him, all who love him, have received him and desire to follow him, being led by his voice, may unite. Having received him, been identified with him, as a matter of course, we receive all who have been received by him, are united with and love them, as members of the same family. When we speak of union, the question is not about receiving men, nor their views, but whether we can agree upon a leader, head, lawgiver or king. Jesus is the true Light that enlightens every man that comes into the world. He is the only divinely authorized head, lawgiver and leader. The question we have to urge upon men, is whether they will come under him. If they will, they should proceed, like young Saul, to ascertain of him, what he requires of them, before they can be received, pardoned and saved by him. When they learn this of him, and come to him, in the way he has appointed, or by doing what he requires, they are received by him, united with him and with all that belong to him, and, as long as they continue to love and obey him, no adverse power can separate them from him. He is our rock, the rock of our salvation—the foundation which God has laid—for union in "one *new* man," or one new church, one "building of God," one "house of God," in which dwells the "one spirit," given by the "one Lord."

Here upon the one rock—one foundation, which is Christ—in the one building or temple, in Christ, where all spiritual blessings are found, all the good, the pure and holy, may strike hands, unite, live in holy fellowship, while they continue in this world of sorrow and affliction, and after, be received up into glory, to dwell with their Lord and the holy society of the redeemed forever. Brethren, look at the vast numbers we have gathered into the one-fold, and take fresh courage, and let us enter upon the work with spirit and might for another year.

BENJ. FRANKLIN.

-----o-----

THE COMFORT OF LOVE—A SERMON.

BY ELD. JOHN ROGERS.

"Wherefore, if there be any consolation in Christ, any comfort of love, any fellowship of the spirit, any bowels and tender mercies, comfort ye my joy, that ye be like-minded, having the same love, being of one accord, of one mind."—Phil. 2nd chapter and 1st and 2nd verses.

The Apostle had just exhorted the Christians at Philippi to stand fast in one spirit, with one mind, striving together for the faith of the gospel. And the more effectually to enforce this oneness of spirit, of mind, and effort, so essential to their own Christian comfort, and progress, and the conversion of the world, he presents to them five distinct motives, or arguments.

1. The consolation in Christ.
2. The comfort of love.
3. The fellowship of the spirit.
4. The bowels and tender mercies, or holy sympathies of our religion.
5. The completion of the Apostle's joy.

Observe, the Apostle here makes an appeal to the Christian experience of the Philippians; for it is certain, if they had not realized the consolation in Christ, the comfort of love, etc., there' was no motive, no argument, in all this appeal to their consciousness. But allowing what is certainly true, that they, as children, were enjoying the consolations in Christ, the comforts of Christian love, the fellowship of the spirit, the bowels and tender mercies, spoken of then, these were so many distinct arguments or motives to unity of spirit, unity of faith, and unity of effort, the great end sought by the Apostle. Can anyone fail to perceive, in this argument for unity, its great practical importance? We may paraphrase the Apostle's argument thus" "Brethren, you know full well that there is unspeakable consolation in Christ, measureless comfort in Christian love, fellowship with God, and all holy beings through the spirit, bowels of compassion and tender mercy enjoyed by all the saints; you know, too, that without these, you are nothing. Just as highly, then, as you value your Christian consolations, and comforts, the pardon of your sins, your enjoyment of the Divine favor, your Christian faith, your Christian privileges, your hope of salvation from sin and all its fearful consequences, your hope of heaven, and all its boundless, inconceivable bliss, just so highly you must estimate that unity of feeling, of faith and practice, inseparable from these saving graces."

'Tis clear as a sunbeam, then, that this argument for unity, contains, in a nutshell, all the motive power of the gospel. Need I say that these motives to unity, presented by the Apostle, to the Philippians, are equally intended for us, and' adapted to promote the same unity among Christians of our times? Our purpose, however, is not to look at these motives, except in this general way, but to select the second, "The comfort of love," and make it the theme of our present discourse. We hope to find much in this to stimulate us to seek after, and maintain, oneness of spirit, of faith and practice, and much also to dispose the sinner to seek after the comforts of love. It is assumed in our subject that there is comfort in love, and surely this needs no proof. Nay, we assert not only that there is comfort in love, but that in its absence, there is not, in the moral universe, one particle of comfort. Where, O, where is it? And echo answers, Where! The poet has said, very truly—

"Love is the bond of union,
And where love reigns is heaven."

And we may add, just as truly, that love, sanctified, enlightened and directed by Christian principle, is the soul of all comfort, in God's moral universe. "God is love, and he who dwells in love, dwells in God, and God in him." What glorious declarations are these? and what a world of comfort do they contain for the people of God? Dr. McKnight says that, "according to Estius, God is essentially love, even as he is properly and essentially power, wisdom and goodness. But it doth not appear that the Apostle meant to declare what the essence of God is, but only to teach us that God greatly delights in the exercise of benevolence, and perhaps that his other perfections are exerted for accomplishing his benevolent purposes. The declaration in verse 8 and verse 16 of 1st John and 4th chapter, "that God is love," being made by inspiration, must afford us the greatest consolation, as it assureth us that all God's dealings with us proceed from love, and in the end will assuredly issue in our happiness, unless we refuse to co-operate with him. As God is love, and is wholly independent of the universe, which is his creation, he can only be moved, in his dealings with his intelligent creatures, by disinterested benevolence, to seek the greatest good, of the greatest number. O, is it not cheering, to believe with unwavering faith, that Jehovah is doing all that a God of infinite wisdom and goodness can do, consistently with his perfections and man's responsibilities, to save our race! And that, therefore, though clouds and darkness are round about his throne, though his judgments are unsearchable, and his ways past finding out, nevertheless his gracious purposes are being accomplished, and will be accomplished in regard to our whole race, in such a manner, as to bring the greatest revenue of glory to God, and, all things considered, the greatest amount of happiness to man. All this is fairly deducible from the glorious truth, the divine proposition, that "God is love." But we must never forget, as Dr. McKnight says, that if we are benefited, saved by the infinite compassion and love of God, we must co-operate with him, in the matter of our teachings of revelation, as well as the text I have just quoted, which says" "He that dwelleth in love, dwelleth in God, and God in him." And again, the Apostle says, "Beloved, let us love one another;" for "he that loves not his brother is a murderer, and ye know that no murderer hath eternal life abiding in him." ' Would the inspired Apostle exhort us to love one another and dwell in love, upon pain of eternal death, if it were not in our power, by the grace of God, to obey the injunction? Never! Certainly, never!

But we are aiming specially to illustrate and enforce the thought, that there is comfort in love. O! what unspeakable comfort in the thought that in cultivating love to God, our Father, and to man, our brother, God deigns to dwell in us, and grants us the privilege, the high and holy privilege, of dwelling in Him? What comfort in the thought of such heavenly companionship? To be permitted to hold communion and fellowship with the high and lofty One, who inhabiteth eternity, and to realize that he is our Father, and that all his infinite resources are pledged to protect us, and bless us, and keep us unto his eternal kingdom—what comfort in all this? Well, this is the comfort of love. But more: How full of comfort is the thought, that love has provided for us an everlasting home? "He that dwelleth in love, dwelleth in God." "Lord, thou hast been our dwelling place in all generations!" What a sublime—what, a soul-chastening and comforting thought that, in the midst of continual, and universal change, and decay, while one generation passes away, and another comes, Jehovah lives forever and ever, and is the home, the unchanging home, of his saints! Our homes here, our sweet homes, however hallowed by numberless associations, that touch the heart; however, loved, because wife, children and friends are there, alas! they will soon he desolate—will be sweet homes no more—for all of us will soon have gone down to the silent grave! How grateful, then, to our spirits, to know, that while all we love and hold dear on earth is passing away, we have a refuge in God—a permanent home?

Need I say, if we love God for what he is, for what he has done, is doing, and has promised to do, for his people; if we love him, because he first loved us, that this love is our greatest comfort—our highest happiness? That it causes us to delight in God, to cleave to him with all our hearts; to study his character, that we may know him; to study his will, that we may do it; to draw near to him in prayer, that he may draw near to us; to study his justice, that we may be just; his faithfulness, that we may be faithful; his forbearance and long-suffering, that we may be forbearing and long-suffering; his holiness, that we may forgive one another, as God, in Christ, forgives us. And that thus we may grow in grace, and in the knowledge of the truth, in the enjoyment and under the influence of the comfort of love.

So, if we love our Lord Jesus Christ, obedience to him will be our happiness—our comfort. To study his moral character, as our exemplar, our great model, who has left us an example, that we should follow his footsteps, will be the delightful, soul-improving and comforting employment of our lives. We shall contemplate, with great advantage and delight, our Savior's labors of love, and patience of hope; and under the influence of love, strive to imitate him. What a comfort, in this dark valley and shadow of death, this funeral vale, this sad express gloom, this land of apparitions, empty shades, where all is changing, is dying and passing away. O! what an unspeakable comfort, to know that we have such a leader—such a guide as the blessed Savior! That he is the root and offspring of David; that he has gone before us through this gloomy vale of life; has met all our foes, and conquered them for us; destroyed death and him that had the power of death, and made life and immortality clear, by his triumphant resurrection, and given us divine assurance, if we follow him and trust in him, that he will never leave us nor forsake us; and that in the end, he will bring us off conquerors, and more than conquerors! Jesus was anointed with the Holy Spirit and power, and spent his life in going about and doing good. He was manifested, says an apostle, that he might destroy the works of the devil.

The Savior's mission, then, to earth, was to do good, on the one hand, and destroy evil on the other. If we love him, then, it will be the greatest happiness and comfort of our lives, to do all the good, and destroy all the evil, in our power. The measure of our ability to do good and destroy evil, must be the measure of our duty. What a solemn thought! Let the religious state of our Christian families and churches be examined in the light of this truth; and how painful—how overwhelming the contrast! O, when will Christians learn that to do good, and thus get good, and destroy evil; that to do all in their power to promote their own personal purity, the unity and purity of the church, and the salvation of the world; that to shun the very appearance of evil, to avoid evil thought, as well as evil actions! O! when, I repeat, will Christians learn that this is the grand end of their Christian calling, so far as this world is concerned!—that love forbids the indulgence of any thought, or trains of thought; the speaking of any word or words; the doing of any deed or deeds; the engaging in any profession, or business, or vocation, the tendency of which is not to promote the good of all concerned. This is most palpably and unmistakably the teaching of the Word of God; and, if not the teaching of reason, it is clearly sanctioned by it. Reason, common sense, recognizes man as a social being, and as such, he must recognize, the rights and interests of his fellows, in the social compact. The very moment we concede that any member of society has a right to disregard the privileges and interests of his fellows, that moment we allow that everyone has a right to take his own course, and lie, and steal, and murder, and do anything and everything, which he fancies may promote his own interests! And thus, society would be at an end, and the race soon self-destroyed.

As certainly, then, as God has made man a social being, so certainly he requires him to love his neighbor as himself, and to do unto others, as he would have them, upon a change of circumstances, do to him. While the corrupt and profligate hate this doctrine, it is full of the comfort of love to the good. They can appeal to God, that poor, and weak, and unworthy as they are, they love his character, and want to be assimilated more and more to it; that they love his Word, and strive to obey it; that they love their brethren with a pure heart, fervently; that they love their entire race, and would not hurt a hair of the head of any human being; that they love their worst enemies as the creatures of God, and most sincerely pray that they may be made the friends of God and their friends, through Christ.

Unequivocally, in such a state of mind and heart as this, there is much comfort. Well, this, too, is the comfort of love.

But we have said that love is inseparable from all comfort, in the moral universe, and that, apart from love, comfort is not. And for proof of our position, in its affirmative and negative forms, we shall, in the light of God's Word, examine Heaven, Earth and Hell. Turn your eyes, then, to that bright world where God and holy angels, and the spirits of the just made perfect live, and what do you see? God, the center of the moral universe, the standard of moral excellence, who is the light and glory of that bright world, is love; and all who dwell in his presence are filled with that love by which God dwells in them, and they in God. The poet, therefore, has justly said—

"Love is the golden chain that binds
    The happy souls above;
And he's an heir of heaven who finds
    His bosom glow with love."

The Heaven of heavens, then, is love, and all its comforts are the comforts of love. There Death, the great enemy of our race, the embodiment, in its various phases, of all the ills that flesh is heir to, the offspring of sin, is felt and feared no more. There Sin, the parent of all evil, natural and moral, the maker of Satan and all his hosts, all his children, whether they belong to the world of spirits, or to this wicked world of ours, the maker of hell and all its fearful and endless fires—Sin, we repeat, has no place there. "God himself," it is written, "shall be with the redeemed there, and be their God. And God shall wipe away all tears from their eyes; and there shall be no more death, neither sorrow nor crying; neither shall there be any more pain: for the former things are passed away."

But why, O! why, no sin, no sorrow, no sickness, no pain, no crying, no tears, no separation, no graveyards, no death-scenes, no coffins, and winding sheets, and funeral processions; and why the perfection of happiness and comfort in that blissful world above? Because all its inhabitants are made perfect in love. There is, therefore, the absence of all evil, and the presence of all good; the absence of all discomfort, and the presence of all comfort; because love's work is consummated, and we may sing, in view of it, in the beautiful language of the pious and venerated Stone:

"What love has done, sing earth around;
    Angels! prolong the eternal sound!"

Turn we, now, from the contemplation of these blest scenes of permanent delight, full above measure, lasting beyond bound, to those dolorous regions, prepared for the Devil and his angels! How fearful and overwhelming the contrast! O, how oppressive to the sensitive, the virtuous mind, to look into a State prison, and see the wretchedness of its inmates; but how much more distressing to look into this great prison-house of the universe, where all the incorrigible and hopelessly lost of God's moral government, are being congregated, cut off from hope, from happiness and heaven, and doomed to eternal exile from God and all that is blissful forever and ever! O, ye saints and sinners, see! not only what love has done! but see! O, see! what hatred, what rebellion, what sin has done! Look! O, look into that everlasting fire, into which the Devil and the rebel angels have been cast; and into which the lost of our race are being gathered, there to be punished for their wickedness forever and ever; there with the rich man to be tormented in that flame! In the expressive, but slightly altered, language of the poet—

> "There to be banished from their life,
>   And yet forbid to die;
> To linger in eternal pain.
>   Yet death forever fly!"

There death reigns in its most fearful forms, amid the horrors of that dread abode! But why! O, why! no light, no life, no hope, no joy, but the absence of all that gives comfort, and the presence of all that gives pain, in that dread world of woe? Because their love is extinct in every bosom, and all is total depravity! Enmity to God, hatred, malice, revenge, and all those fiend-like passions, that characterize the lost, turned loose upon its inhabitants, as so many furies, to torment them forever and ever! Heaven is heaven, then, because it is full of love. And hell is hell, because love is an eternal exile; and sin and hatred, in every form, are eternally located, and their reign eternally established, there! The perfect comfort of heaven, then, is the comfort of love; and the perfect misery of hell, results from the absence of love.

We have seen, then, that in heaven all is perfect happiness, perfect comfort, because all is perfect love;—that, in hell, all is perfect wretchedness and despair, because no love is there!

Having now explored, by faith, the upper and the neither world, and found ample testimony to support our positions, let us to this world, where we may walk by sight, as well as faith, and see if it bear not a similar testimony. Here, according to the Word of God, and all reason, and all experience, and all observation and all history, there is a mixture of good and evil. Here there is much of happiness and much of unhappiness; much of comfort and much of discomfort. And wherefore, Because here there is much of love and much of its opposite; much of purity and much of impurity; much of wickedness and much of righteousness. And, therefore, precisely in the ratio of our love to God and man, will be our unhappiness, our discomfort.

Love is the great principle of attraction in the moral universe; while hatred is the great principle of repulsion.

Love attracts and conserves and comforts; while hatred repulses and destroys and makes miserable. Love unites us to God and to one another; while hatred severs us from God and one another. Love is the virtue of all virtues, the principle of all principles, in all true religion. Love is the fulfilling of the law; the end of the commandment. To implant deep in the human bosom this divine principle, and nourish it there, is the great end of the remedial scheme. Having love, therefore, we have everything; wanting love, we have nothing, and are nothing. Nothing will supply its place.

> "Nor gifts, nor tongues, nor fiery zeal,
>   The work of love can e'er fulfill."

Love is the more excellent way. Though we could speak with the tongues of men and of angels, in all the eloquence of both worlds; and though we had the gifts of prophecy, and could unfold all the mysteries of the future; had all the knowledge of the past and present dispensations of God's wisdom; and all that benevolence that would move us to give all our goods to feed the poor; and though we possessed that zeal for our creed, our party, that, rather than renounce it, we would give our bodies to be burned; yet, if we have not love to God and man, in the true sense of it, religiously, we are as sounding brass, or a tinkling cymbal—nothing; nay, infinitely worse than nothing.

Love includes in itself, in the apostolic sense of it, all the elements of goodness and greatness—of piety and holiness—of perfect happiness and comfort. Does not experience demonstrate that whatever of comfort falls to the lot of mortals here, is the offspring of love? The philosophy of religion, and, we may add, the philosophy of happiness, is taught by the disciple, whom Jesus loved, in this expressive sentence: "We love God, because he first loved us." This love assimilates us to him, who is love. It prepares us to delight in God and to be happy in his service. Love is happy in the presence of its object or objects. To walk with God, therefore, because we love him; to study his character, in the light of his word and works; to behold, as in a mirror, the glory of the Lord, is a most improving and comforting employment, and is to be changed into the same image, from glory to glory, as by the spirit of the Lord. If evil communications corrupt good manners, then, by parity of reason, good communications promote good manners.

He, therefore, who loves to commune with God, will know more of him, enjoy more of him, and be more and more like him, and, by consequence, more and more happy. Like David, he is glad when it is said, "Let us go up to the house of the Lord; for a day in thy court is better than a thousand. I had rather be a doorkeeper in the house of my God, than to dwell in the tents of wickedness: for the Lord God is a sun and shield; the Lord will give grace and glory, and no good will he withhold from them that walk uprightly." They who love God, and his house, like the ancient Christians, will not forsake the assembling of themselves together, as the manner of some is, who have lost their first love; but, knowing that all their comforts and progress depend upon love, they will, in their meetings, and in all their intercourse, consider one another, to provoke unto love and to good works. O, if Christians, in the higher walks of life, instead of plunging into the world and provoking one another, to conform to its foolish, extravagant and corrupting fashions, would be patterns of simplicity and plainness in manners, their dress, their style of living, their equipage; and especially in their benefactions for benevolent objects; how happy for them, for the church, and for the world! They would thus provoke one another to love and good works; and let their light so shine, that sinners, seeing their good works, would be converted and glorify our common Father in heaven! Yes, if Christians would live thus, they would enjoy the fullness of Christian comfort—a comfort which the world can neither give nor take away.

One more illustration, and we shall have done, on this branch of our subject.

Suppose a family, consisting of husband and wife, parents and children, brothers and sisters, all understanding the nature and obligations of their relations with one another; and all faithfully performing the duties growing out of their various relations. The husband loves the wife, the wife the husband, the parents the children, the children the parents; the brothers love the sisters, and the sisters the brothers. Is there not comfort here? Is not this, indeed, a picture of perfect domestic bliss?— nay, a picture of Heaven? This is the comfort of love.

We have seen, now, that in heaven there is perfect bliss, because perfect love reigns there; that in hell there is unutterable wretchedness and despair, the absence of all happiness, because sin reigns there, and love is an eternal exile; that in this world of ours we have much of comfort, because much of love. Let us now look a little at the other side of the picture. We appeal to experience. In the possession and cultivation of hatred, malice, envy, revenge, is there any comfort? Experience answers with an emphatic No! All just thinking persons unite in asserting with Solomon, that anger rests in the bosom of fools. Therefore, he who nurses his wrath to keep it warm—who allows these fiend-like passions to dwell within him, in the language of inspiration, is a fool, and is enkindling a fire in his own bosom, which will burn up all his enjoyment—which, unless it be extinguished by the means of Heaven's appointment, will burn to the lowest hell. He who hates his neighbor, is made unhappy every time he sees him; nay, every time he thinks of him.

To enforce this thought still further, let us suppose a family, from which all love is exiled. The husband hates the wife with perfect hatred, the wife hates the husband with perfect hatred; the parents hate the children with perfect hatred, and the children hate the parents with perfect hatred; the brothers the sisters, and the sisters the brothers. Need I say, what is self-evident, that in such a family as this there can be no comfort? What a misery—what a punishment, to be compelled to see and associate and live with the objects of our hate! We have here, then, a picture of hell, the most graphic and fearful. In view, then, of all our testimony in support of our positions, drawn from Heaven, Hell and Earth, may we not conclude, in brief, that the perfect bliss of Heaven arises from the congeniality of the tastes and employment of its inhabitants, and especially from the fact, that they all love, and adore, and serve the same God, and love one another with a pure heart, fervently? And, on the other hand, that the perfect wretchedness of the inhabitants of hell results from their enmity to God, the source of all bliss, and their enmity to one another, leading to endless criminations and recriminations?

In conclusion, permit me to make a few remarks, by way of application. We have seen that in heaven, all is perfect happiness; that in hell, all is perfect misery; that here, we have a mixed state, intermediate, between the perfection of the bliss of heaven, on the one hand, and the perfection of the misery of hell, on the other. And if there be a purgatory in the moral universe of God, for man, this world is that purgatory. For, unfortunately as is his condition as a sinner, it is cheering to know that here he may be purified, and fitted for the bliss of heaven. This world, we have intimated, is midway between heaven and hell. And, since the fall of our first parents, it has been the scene of a mighty conflict, between the armies of both worlds. The prize contended for, is man. The question at issue between the armies of God and Satan is, whether Satan, who seduced man from his allegiance to God, and led him into sin, shall continue to rule over him and drag him down to eternal death, to suffer the vengeance of eternal fire, prepared for the devil and his hosts; or, whether God, who made man, and preserves him, and has sent his Son to die to redeem him; and who has, therefore, the highest possible claims upon him, shall accomplish his benevolent designs, in delivering him from sin, and all its damning influences, and lift him at last to his own bright abode, where there is fullness of joy and pleasure forever more! O, how do the strifes and conflicts of earth, where the stakes are empire, glory, honor, and a sort of earthly immortality—are "gems, and monuments, and crowns"—dwindle into perfect nothingness, in comparison with this "conflict for ages," between Michael and his angels, and the Dragon and his angels, for the government of man! And how does this fearful conflict, which has been raging, and has been prosecuted, with various success, through the whole earth, for six thousand years—how, I repeat, does it heighten our conceptions of God's estimate of the worth of man? Would Jehovah, who made man, and knows him perfectly, set on foot a scheme of grace, which he has been developing and carrying forward by all the agencies of heaven, to its consummation, for six thousand years, to deliver man from sin and all its fearful consequences, if he were of little worth? Never!—certainly, never! Well did he, who died for man; who gave his Life a ransom for him; who bought him with his own precious blood, and knew his value by the price he paid for him—well did he say, What shall it profit a man, if he gain the whole world and lose himself? Not only does this fearful war, in the prosecution of which the magazines of heaven are being emptied, give us some just notions of God's estimate of the value of man, but it also gives us a clear and terrible view of God's estimate of the heinousness, the exceeding sinfulness of sin—its damning, man-ruining nature! Though the blessed Jesus was God's only-begotten and well-beloved Son—though he was the brightness of his glory and the express image of his person; yet, rather than sin should live and reign over and eternally ruin man, he gave him up freely for us all, that we might live, through him! O, if sin were that trifling thing, which many make it—that mere shadow of a shade—that nothing which modern Universalism makes it, would not the divine Father, infinite in wisdom, and goodness, and power, have spared his own Son the painful and ignominious death of the cross?

But the great practical thought, which, in conclusion, I wish to enforce, is, that in this conflict which is going on in our world, between the powers of light and darkness, the force of heaven and hell, the principles of truth and falsehood, man, as a subject of the moral government of God, a moral agent, cannot be neutral. He, says the Savior, who is not for me, is against me; and he that gathereth not with me, scattereth abroad. Says Paul, "To whom ye yield yourselves servants, his servants ye are, whether of sin unto death, or of obedience unto life."

Thank heaven! you cannot be forced into the service of Satan. You may yield yourselves up to his service, and lie down in endless sorrow; or, you may yield yourselves up to the service of the Lord Jesus Christ, and thus be made free from sin, and have your fruit unto holiness, and in the end everlasting life.

O, sinner! do you realize, then, that you are forming a character for an eternal state? And, that upon the character you form during your short stay upon earth, will depend your eternal destiny? That you are traveling the broad way that leads to eternal death? O, let me beseech you, as there is comfort and happiness only in the service and love of our heavenly Father, in Jesus Christ, our fjord; and as this service fits us for the highest usefulness, of which we are capable here, and for all that bliss of heaven hereafter; and as the service of sin makes us unhappy and wretched, and fits us only to be a curse to our race, and to ourselves here, and for all the horrors of eternal death hereafter—turn, O, sinner! turn from your evil ways! For, why will you die?

-----o-----

TO THE BRETHREN IN KENTUCKY. NUMBER II.

We endeavored to show, in our article of last month, that we were stagnating, under a compromise of monthly preaching, mutually gratifying to the ease and pleasures of preachers and people, but unscriptural and destructive of the elements of aggression and conquest by which the "kingdom" is to be established. We hear occasionally of protracted efforts, that revive in us the memories of the past. Though these are rather spasmodic, they serve as an index to show what might be done, under a steady and general system of evangelizing. Why do we not have, all over the State, every year or two, such meetings as have been held at Louisville, Winchester, Grassy

Springs, etc.? It could be done, if our able preachers would distribute themselves over the country, and devote themselves to the work.

But there is something of error as well as wisdom to be learned from the examples of our early history. The great error that the preachers committed in their missionary efforts in the past, was leaving their work half done. They brought, by protracted effort, scores in the church, organized them with inexperienced and untaught officers, and left them thus wholly unprepared to meet the issues of adverse circumstances. The great wonder is, that we find ourselves, now, so numerous and strong, as a people.

What course should an evangelist pursue? In the absence of wisdom and experience of our own, let us go to the oracles of God. They will never lead us astray.

We borrow our inductions from the examples and precepts of the Apostles. We find in their history, that they were accustomed to tarry and labor at one point until they had completed all that could be done by a reasonable expenditure of time and labor. A month—a week—three months—or a year—it mattered not—they tarried and worked, if they succeeded, or if they thought the occasion important. No periodical appointments, for every week in the year, interfered to break up their meetings.

Let us introduce some proofs. At Samaria, Philip, the deacon, had been preaching with success for some time. As soon as the news came to Jerusalem, the Apostles sent Peter and John to aid Philip in this work. They "testified and preached the word" there; but how long, is not definitely stated. (Acts, chap. 8th.) Paul and Barnabas preached at Antioch until they were driven away by persecution. But they soon returned to this point to finish their work; and in the conclusion of the 14th of Acts, it is said, "they abode some time with the disciples."

The Apostles often returned to the scenes of their labors. (Acts xv. 36.) Paul said to Barnabas, "Let us go again and visit our brethren in every city where we have preached the word of the Lord, and see how they do."

Paul promises a third visit to the Corinthians. (1st Cor. xii. 14 and xiii. 1.) But, why multiply cases? These facts are known to us all.

We gather from our readings, likewise, that the Apostles were not accustomed to hurry the appointment of officers. It was not until they had visited Lystra, Iconium, Antioch, etc., "*again,*" that they thought fit to "ordain elders." (Acts xiv. 21-3)."Lay hands suddenly on no man," Paul enjoins on Timothy. An elder or pastor must be "apt to teach," "not a novice," etc.; all conditions indicating time and opportunity for preparation. Even the deacons "must be proved" before appointed. (1st Tim. iii. 10.)

The Apostles were model evangelists. Their examples are singularly adapted to all ages and conditions of man. These examples, imitated with zeal, sacrifice and perseverance, will never fail to enlarge and establish our Lord's kingdom. Our pioneer fathers followed in these paths more closely than others have done. But we have said their work was not perfectly done. They too often hurried through their work, spending not enough time to exhaust their materials, nor to bring to bear all their means. They paid too little attention to the careful selection and proper training of men for bishops and deacons. They neglected to impress upon the converted, the necessity of rewarding their bishops with a sufficiency to relieve them from secular cares, and enable them to fit themselves as shepherds and teachers of the congregations. This last error involves matters of momentous interest. The written injunctions are, "Let elders that rule well be counted worthy of double honor;" "the laborer is worthy of his reward," etc., etc. Here is the law of God. Why is it not written in men's hearts? Is it because they have never heard it from their preachers?—or, is it because the sin of covetousness is there? It is useless to deny or resist this law. It is written in justice, and founded in truth; and sooner or later men must recognize it. Wisdom, bought by sad experience, will force us to do so. It is a law, controlling the affairs of man, and which cannot be ignored, that that which costs but little, is worth but little—is but little appreciated. A law which makes the thief—the gambler—the speculator, prodigal of his means. An elder must be "apt to teach"—must be "able to exhort and convince gainsayers." But how can he fill these conditions unless he learns and prepares himself? How can he learn and prepare himself, unless he has time and opportunity? To have time, he must be released from his labor. Then, the time lost thus, is his support—is worth money or bread to him. Who should supply that bread, or that money, but those who reap the benefit of it?

If the congregation have use for but one working day in the week of their elder's time, let them pay him one-sixth of a support for himself and family. If they need two days, pay him two-sixths. If they need his whole time, let them support him. And let the time thus paid for, be sacredly devoted to the interests of the church. The bishop should always be a reading man. He must study during the week what he wishes to teach on Lord's day, or else his speaking will be desultory, pointless, inapplicable and uninteresting. He should be able to attract, interest, impress and profit those who are of his flock, and, if possible, the outside community around him. He should occupy time in visiting the members in their families, comforting the sick and sorrowing, and righting all the difficulties and misunderstandings among the members, and exhorting all to a strict observance of worship, as well as a due regard to a full practice of Christian duty.

From these reasonings and proofs, we ask the privilege of suggesting some rules as a source of action to be followed in the labors of evangelists and pastors. We propose nothing arbitrary, but conclusions to be thought over and improved upon.

1. The evangelist should keep himself free from, and untrammeled by, pre-engagements. He should be prepared to seize any opportunity, favorable to a successful prosecution of his work.

2. He should be located in the field of his operations, so that he may be able to familiarize himself with the necessities of the community around him. Unfortunately, nearly all our best evangelists are congregated in a few wealthy counties in the interior of the State. There they have been retained as periodical preachers, for years; while in other sections the cause has been languishing for want of aid. Three or four of these, constantly in the field, would have done double the good, in the same territory, while the others, by spreading over the State, might have advanced the interests of Christianity to a condition of great prosperity.

3. He should visit a point, to labor one week or six months, as the occasion required. He should not depend altogether on his preaching, but familiarize himself with all around, both of the church and world. A distinguished and successful preacher recently said, "that he done more in this way than in the pulpit." He could thus gain the good will and attention of everybody. A preacher, by his sociability, should attract and attach all to him. We do not mean that he should preach on for six months, but that he should continue with the congregation until everything is set in order, and they are possessed of all the elements of prosperity and strength. Is it not a burlesque upon missionary labor, for a preacher to follow an appointment of long standing, begin a meeting on Friday night, and conclude on Monday, that nothing can be done, because he has made no converts? And is not the indignation of the members justly aroused,

when, sometimes about the latter end of the week, just at the time that an interest is deepening and widening in the community, the preacher announces that he must close the meeting, to fill his *monthly appointment* at some place? But, how often do such vexatious appointments occur?

4. In preparing for the conversion of souls (and no effort should be made for this purpose until the church is all right), and throughout the progress of the meeting, the preacher should have an eye to the qualifying of the elder for taking charge of the congregation, when he delivers them over to him. Or, if he is just constituting a church, he should be instructing the most suitable person or persons to this end. Is it right that he should cease his labors, under any reasonable length of time, until the congregation have officers with scriptural qualifications? The Apostles seem always to have selected the pastor from among the members, over whom he was to preside; and at this day there is scarcely a congregation that has not someone in it suitable, and who would not make a good teacher, with study and time for preparation. But he must be relieved from secular care, and furnished with books and other facilities.

5. The evangelist must go from house to house. He must teach the members their individual duties. To support and obey their elders; to worship God openly in their families; to sacredly attend worship on Lord's day; to visit the sick, the afflicted and the destitute; and "to keep themselves unspotted from the world." How often is it that the preacher "puts up" at some brother's, convenient, and visits no other place during a meeting of several days! To succeed, he must work!—work from the pulpit, and work from the social circle!—work upon the members, and work with the world!

6. The evangelist should introduce and impress the necessity for weekly prayer meetings. In the country these are most efficient in the families of the members. On every Lord's day he should teach the members to assemble with their children, at the house of worship, at some hour early in the morning or in the afternoon, to join in a Bible class and Sunday school. These offices effected, the elders taught their duty, and these collateral aids introduced in the practice of Christian worship, the evangelist may safely leave them for a year or two, to a healthy and sure prosperity and growth in grace.

7. The evangelist should be rewarded. Has he labored one, two, or four months? Let the church pay him in proportion. If he has labored one fourth of a year, and it will take eight hundred dollars to support his family, they should pay him two hundred—a little more would do no harm. They will find that one protracted effort like this will be worth ten years of monthly preaching; *for* which they pay this amount annually. And we can see no impropriety in the preacher conferring with some prominent members as to an adequate compensation. Most certainly should he thus confer with them, if the church does not award him an adequate support.

Having finished our suggestions as to the course to be pursued by the evangelist, we turn to the elder's or pastor's office, with the hope that we may be able to throw some light across the pathway of this servant of God.

1. The *shepherd of souls* has assumed important and weighty responsibilities—the care and preservation of his flock in their Christian pilgrimage. To comfort the afflicted; to warn the unwary; to exhort the lukewarm; to rebuke the presumptuous; to bring back the wanderer; to stand as sentinel over his flock, and keep off the enemy; to nourish them with spiritual meat and drink; to excite to Christian practice, and to interest all, in their spiritual welfare, should be objects of the deepest and most anxious solicitude with him. Almost tearfully we read the admonitions of Jesus to Simon, in John xxi.

What tenderness, what anxiety, is apparent in his words! He is soon to leave his nurslings to the dangers and vicissitudes of life. And as the thought crosses his mind, a wave of anguish and despair breaks upon his sorrow-stricken soul. He turns, in hope, to his chosen ones, and in notes of sadness and earnest entreaty, he appeals to one" "Simon, son of Jonas, lovest thou me?" "Lord, thou knowest I love thee!" answered Simon. "Then," said Jesus, "feed my lambs!" By the *love of Him,* he beseeches them; and repeats again and again. By the *love of Him,* O! shepherd of the present day, we beseech you, *"feed his lambs!"* Enter your work, then, with all the earnestness of a good and great purpose, with thoughtful prudence, and with devotional self-sacrifice. Think and read! Read the oracles of God, and think of the peculiar as well as common necessities of your flock; compare, meditate, reflect, and "thoroughly furnish yourself to the good work." You will then have answered the first requisitions. You can thus make yourself interesting. You will then be loved, obeyed and confided in.

3. The bishop should continue the practices which the evangelist has introduced; or, if these have not been introduced, let him begin them himself;—as visiting the families of his flock (and those out of it as much as he can), instructing in Bible classes, Sunday schools and conversation, as well as by lectures—holding prayer meetings at the house of worship, or at the houses of the members, as may be most proper.

4. His lectures should be mainly directed against the evil tendencies and practices in the society around him—not so sourly and censorious, as warning and exhortatory. He should throw across the pathway of the disciples, the moral and spiritual light of heavenly wisdom, that they may at all times clearly behold the distinctions of right and wrong. Let him lead them often to the fountains of divine love, and its sweet waters be freely quaffed, until they have grown loving and lovely, in Christian character and practice; for the heart grows willing in obedience, when permeated with heavenly love. Exigencies may arise sometimes around him, which will make it necessary and proper for the bishop to lecture upon first principles and doctrines; but these, in the main, belong to the service of the evangelist. Of these necessities he must judge.

5. He should watch the individual course of each member, as far as propriety will justify; especially that of the young convert, who is at the critical stage of his pilgrimage. He should seek to win him from his former affinities, and woo him by the gentle policies and arts of Christian wisdom, that violate no Christian principle, to an interest in and attachment to his new associations. He should let none wander far from the fold, before the gentle, persuading voice of the shepherd is heard, calling him back. No one of his congregation should absent himself from time to time, without his giving a good and satisfactory excuse.

6. He should be paid for his time and service. This we have clearly shown to be Heaven's law. He should confer with his congregation, and make known to them how much of his time will be required to study and prepare his lectures—how much will be required in visiting and keeping in order the general affairs of the church, etc. Let it be considered how much is necessary to support himself and family, with suitable economy, and his allowance be proportioned to meet all these circumstances.

7. Lastly—a bishop should keep himself as much as possible from the care of secular affairs. He should likewise avoid being drawn into the excitement of politics, and other collateral questions and issues sprung in the present day. These matters should be of no great interest to him; and he should know nothing of them, save at the ballot-box.

This system introduced into the churches, sanctioned, as we have reason to think, by the

laws of revealed wisdom, and prosecuted in all its detail of duty, with zeal, self-sacrifice and energy, will once more make us an aggressive people, moving and increasing both spiritually and numerically in all the elements of strength.

Some other causes for the spirit of indifference and lukewarmness which permeates Christian society now, may be introduced as of importance. One of these is, the bringing of the powers of the church of Christ to bear upon politico-moral or semi-religious questions of the day—such as temperance, slavery, Know Nothingism, etc. Such questions are single in their aims, and contracted in their range of ideas and operations; hence, like all one-idea questions, intensifying and absorbing in their influence and advocacy. They have undermined and exhausted the means and interests of Christianity to a vast extent, and yet so subtlety, that the relation between the cause and effect can scarcely be seen.

Does the reader ask, How? If the money expended by Christians in Kentucky, in building Temperance, Masonic and Odd Fellows' Lodges, and in otherwise aiding these causes and others similar, the amount would sustain evangelists all over the State, for years. But this is not all! Whatever labor and time, whatever interests have been expended by Christians upon these, have been done at the expense of our Master's cause, thus robbing the arsenals of Christianity, to fight in behalf of secular causes. But this is not all. Whatever of good may be done by, and in the name of such institutions, by Christians, is done at the expense of their religion, and their Master's reputation. Thus, the services of disciples in those matters, are a continual drain upon the resources of the church, and the intense excitement gotten up in the advocacy of them, neutralizes—by absorbing the general interests and zeal in Christianity—its predominance in society.

We can point to at least two churches in our

Vol. II., No. 1.—2.

own county, of our own people, which have suffered from these agitations. One of them was rent and divided by the pride of opinion on the subject of temperance. In the other, the elder was carried away with the same subject, so much as to neglect the congregation; and they are scattered to the four winds. This same elder is a fine teacher, and as such, was, once, one of the most efficient men in his sphere, we ever knew. Bro. Campbell showed again that wonderful sagacity and judgment, which has led him always to balance his conclusions at the center of truth, with almost unexceptional precision, when he raised a warning note against Christians identifying themselves with these equivocal institutions and issues.

Another element of detraction from the spirituality and aggrandizement of Christian character, throughout Christian society, is the pecuniary prosperity of the country for some years past. Instead of looking to the great Author of such prosperity, with gratitude, and becoming inspired with greater zeal, to greater good, as the means of good are enlarged in their hands, men have become, to a great extent, blinded in covetousness and absorbed in wild and hazardous speculations. O, Christian, cease this! If God has liberally bestowed upon you, of this world's goods, more than is necessary for your temperate use, it is for greater ends than self-preservation. You have a great mission, an individual mission, to perform. You must understand this mission from your sphere and attainments, and go to work for the glory of God and the good of man.   S.

ANOTHER NEW BOOK OUT.

We desire to keep our readers posted up in regard to the various book enterprises of the day; not only the *good;* nor confining our notices to the *indifferent;* nor merely to the *positively bad;* but we must occasionally call attention to the silly; the downright simple;

those containing the most dull, stupid and the lowest order of sophistry. One of this latter description has just fallen from the pen of a contemporary, whom we have had occasion to notice once in five or six months for several years past: one, too, who certainly loves himself, and would receive any notices kindly calculated to give him notoriety. The volume alluded to contains some four hundred pages; and, from its "dedication," we infer that it was intended for our notice, as well as that of the balance of mankind. The title reads as follows: "The Gallows, the Prison and the Poor House. A Plea for Humanity; showing the Demands of Christianity in behalf of the Criminal and Perishing Classes. By G. W. Quinby. Published by G. W. Quinby, 74 West Fourth Street, Cincinnati *(Star in the* West office)." The dedication reads as follows" "To the Humane, Benevolent and Hopeful of every sect, party and creed, Religious and Political, of every country and clime, who feels himself connected by the ties of a common origin and a common humanity, and to every other human being, who not only sees the wrongs of society, but has faith that they can be removed, this volume is respectfully and affectionately dedicated by the author."

From the title page and dedication of this book, one would be led to conclude that the lever and fulcrum had at last been discovered, by which the world is to be revolutionized, man blessed, and the millennium ushered in. This devoutly- to-be-desired and stupendous achievement is to be attained by abolishing capital punishment, making jails, penitentiaries and prisons, of every kind, more comfortable and desirable; really converting them into respectable boarding-schools, where good and wholesome religious instruction is daily imparted. Who of the "humane and benevolent," the "hopeful," of "one common origin and humanity," can fail to feel the mighty revolutionizing and reformatory influence of such a book, and the everlasting obligations of mankind to him, who has made the discovery, that man-slayers, murderers, thieves, liars and rascals of every grade, are henceforth to be deterred from crime, by wholly abolishing capital punishment, and converting prisons and all places of punishment into comfortable dwellings, boarding-schools and places of enjoyment and refinement ? Who would violate the law, in acts of violence and murder, knowing that he could not by any possibility be hung, that all the prisons were changed into places of comfort and enjoyment, and that for crime a man would be sentenced to one of these places of comfort and enjoyment, to receive religious instruction from some pious divine?

Reader, please not to style this book **a** gull-trap, humbug or delusion ? It is too transparent for any such designation. It is too stupid, its conception too dull and its meshes too silly, to deserve any such title. A man who could be trapped, humbugged, or deluded by such a book, must either desire such to be the case, or have too little discernment to be an accountable being. The idea of reforming men by an everlasting tampering, not only with the penalties of the law of God, but the civil law, the law of the land, can delude no man, only one who desires to be deluded, or one who is incapable of being a responsible and accountable being. The idea of reforming the world by turning hell into paradise, abolishing capital punishment, making prisons comfortable places of enjoyment and happiness, in its conception, quickening and birth, is precisely worthy of the inflated, self-conceited and stupid author of this book! It is a wonder the Almighty did not adopt his mild, comfortable and pleasant punishments, in the place of drowning the Egyptians in the Red Sea, strangling the antediluvians in the flood, burning the Sodomites in fire and brimstone, hewing down the Jews with the sword at the destruction of Jerusalem, as criminals, who, with Mr. Quinby, appear to be the principle objects of human or divine benevolence!

This book is adorned with several engravings, among which is the likeness of the author, set forth by *himself,* believing, of course, that mankind would be anxious to see their benefactor. We, as a matter of course, are grateful, for we never saw Mr. Quinby, nor need we now be at any trouble to see him, as we can have his picture. O, shame! Where is thy blush? Ridiculous vanity! A worm of the dust publishing *his own* picture!!!   B. F.

-----o-----

GLEANINGS FROM A SACRED FIELD. NUMBER II.

"What is man, that thou art mindful of him?—or the Son of man, that thou visitest him?"—Psalm viii. 4.

Man was created a thinking being; hence, the earth was formed and fashioned to engage his attention——to employ with interest and profit the stupendous faculties of his mind. And while he is engaged in surveying the almost boundless fields in matter and mind, in science and art, there is an unceasing progression in his wisdom and happiness, provided his soul is deeply imbued with the truths of inspiration—provided he is a *Christian student.* To him the earth is but the vestibule to a spacious mansion, well built, garnished and decorated for the peerless inhabitant below. To him there is an enchanting, beatific rapture—a sublime, subduing reverence in all things above, around, beneath. Even the violet, unobtrusively blooming on the bank of the murmuring rivulet, speaks to him in tones of bewitching eloquence, and utters lessons of invaluable wisdom. The forest, peopled with unnumbered happy warblers, breaks forth in songs of praise to God, melting the heart, ravishing the soul. The waste-like desert, the beetling crags, the towering mountains, the far-off rolling clouds, the deep, wild and changeless ocean, philosophically considered, unfold the wisdom and skill, the power and glory, of the Almighty Architect; and with a voice loud as seven-fold thunder, bid man tarry not by the wayside, but hasten on to that bright and blessed home, far beyond the dark and sullen river of death. The Christian student stands on a proud—a lofty eminence. He occupies the only position commanding the beauties and excellencies of earth and heaven. He occupies the only proper, the only enviable position, in the sight of good men, angels and God. His acute, penetrating eye searches the illimitable plains of earth, gathering and garnering up ten thousand objects of infinite worth and resplendence. He is filled with admiration in contemplating the various attributes of that incomprehensibly great and glorious Being, who fills immensity with his presence; who formed the exquisite flower, the strong oak of Bashan, the stately cedar of Lebanon; who brought into existence the smallest atom, the mightiest world; who is and will forever remain, the absolute monarch of this wondrous and magnificent universe of his own creating—of his own upholding. In humble confidence, the Christian student sweeps, with telescopic vision, the broad fields of space, numbering, weighing and fixing, in their proper orbits, the shining hosts that gem the vault of heaven. On the wing of thought he soars above the clouds and makes his home among the stars. He converses with them in language clear and unmistakable. His mind is enlarged; his soul expanded; his thoughts and feelings elevated and refined. He falls prostrate at the shrine of "him that liveth forever and ever," and, with cherub and seraph, exclaims: "Thou art worthy, O, Lord, to receive glory, and honor, and power; for thou hast created all things, and for thy pleasure they are and were created."

To the eye of him thus devoutly impressed, God is clearly visible in the formation of the atmosphere, the ocean, the earth; in the structure, projection and majesty of the suns, satellites and systems of infinitude. In the ever-changing varieties of nature, there are changeless beauties continually exhibited to him, and glories radiant with the smiles of Omnipotence. During the resplendence of day he is cheered by glorious prospects, and, with unfaltering step, unwearied energy, pursues the even tenor of his way. In the awfully solemn silence of night he communes with the spirits of the "mighty dead," and, torch in hand, lighted at the fires of heaven, fathoms the deep and dark recesses, and scales the dizzy heights of science, entwining around his brow the laurel wreaths of unfading purity and beauty. When merry Spring comes dancing by, and brooks begin to bubble and songsters to warble their stirring notes of love; when flowers awaken from their cold slumbers and lift up their drooping heads in joyous glee, to the warm sun, he beholds, with delight, the mysterious operations of Him, whose power and wisdom are infinite and omnipotent; when, "from brightening fields of ether far disclosed, beheld of the sun, refulgent Summer comes," arrayed in loveliness, and walking forth amid ten thousand objects of beauty, he calmly, yet minutely, marks the sure ways, devised by Providence, to obtain for man and beast the promised good—the bounteous feast. When somber Autumn comes on apace, bringing, in boundless luxuriance, the blessings of life, with clasped hands, on bended knees, he thanks "the giver of every good and perfect gift." When cold, and dreary, and desolate Winter appears, with repellent, haggard countenance, with his wild shriek, his low melancholy wail; when nought save desolation and death are to be seen, his mind is filled with serious reflections, and he is forcibly reminded that the strength and beauty, the glory and greatness of earth, are evanescent that heaven alone is secure from separation, death and tears.

But when he turns from the contemplation of matter to that of mind; from the lower orders of creation to the highest—that of man—mysterious, God-like man—he is forced to acknowledge, with the rapt bard of Israel, that he is fearfully and wonderfully made. He is only a little lower in majesty than the angels, and bears the imago and impress of God. Who knows himself, his weakness, his greatness? Who can unravel the mystic web of his own character? Who unfold the hidden, exhaustless riches of his immortal mind? The poet has graphically and appositely sung:

> How poor, how rich, how abject, how august,
> How complicate, how wonderful is man,
> Midway from nothing to the Deity!
> A beam ethereal, sullied and absorbed,
> Though sullied and dishonored still divine!
> Dim miniature of greatness absolute!
> An heir of glory ! a frail child of dust;
> Helpless immortal! insect infinite."

He can grasp a universe, and yet expatiate on an atom. He is at homo among the stars, and yet delights to philosophize on the death of an insect. He looks with observant eye on the great plan of all things, and at the same time scans the varied tints of the blushing rose. In the thronged city he is alone; in the desert surrounded by companions. In thought he goes over the trackless fields of the past, wanders over realms, once fertile and populous, but now deserted and lonely. He listens to the bewitching melody of the happy bard, and hears the thunder tones of the lofty orator and statesman. He muses in silence over the sepulchers of kings and subjects. He sees the last resting-place of poor, fallen man, and turns aside to weep over the sad spectacle presented.

"O, what a miracle to man is man!" There is only one volume in which his true character is portrayed; only one volume in which his origin and fearfully sublime destiny are distinctly and definitely revealed. That book is the will of Heaven to man. Within its sacred pages the Christian student finds, weighed in a balance, the pleasures and sorrows, the crowns and coronets, the principalities and powers of earth. He might, with the highest benefit and interest, meditate for ages on the wonders of this glorious volume. The libraries of the past furnish no such work. It stands alone. It is entirely unique and original. The purity and beauty, the argument and pathos, the tenderness and melting sweetness of its narrative, the simple, yet touching eloquence of its poetry, the majesty and power of its facts, the imposing grandeur of its amazing plan to redeem and purify and perfect man for the mansions of rest above, entrance, nay, bewilder the highest powers, the loftiest conceptions of puny man, clearly teaching him that the wisdom of God is as far above the wisdom of man as the heavens are higher than the earth. In taking a survey of the vast fields of inspiration, the student takes his stand with Moses, on the verge of time; a dark, unfathomed ocean is laying at his feet—the ocean of eternity. Myriads of worlds are thrown out into space. All are motionless. Silence, dread and awful, broods over all things. The Almighty commands all the bright orbs to commence their onward movement. Quick as thought, they begin their march. He stands in wonder and astonishment, listening to the sweet music of the spheres, as they roll in ceaseless majesty and harmony sublime. With David, Jeremiah and Isaiah he rises above the clouds, and looking far down the dark, rolling stream, identifies the son of the Highest; foreshadowed in visions prophetic, he perceives him laying aside his regal attire, leaving his father's realm, clothing himself in mortality and dwelling with man. He hears the enraptured shout of the angelic throng, and sees the shepherds as they fall prostrate before the heavenly messengers. The life and character, the death and sufferings, the resurrection and coronation of Immanuel, among the higharchies of heaven, pass in review before him; and when the deep foundation is firmly fixed, to exalt and forever bless the poor, wayfaring pilgrim of this cheerless world, he feels a joy beyond conception—beyond imagination.

With John, on the Isle of Patmos, he beholds the closing scene in the grand drama of human redemption. He beholds coming down from heaven the mighty angel, having a rainbow on his head, and standing with one foot on the sea, and the other on land. Slowly lifting his hand to heaven, he swears that time shall be no longer. Heaven and earth pass forever away. The new Jerusalem, the Holy City, with its jasper walls, gates of pearl, and streets golden and transparent, gloriously descends from God. On the battlements stand the tall spirits, that dwell in heavenly light. They lean upon their harps amazed at the scene transpiring; and when they perceive man redeemed, they attune them to strains lofty, and pure, and thrilling; and the vast city of God resounds with voices of angels—with anthems of praise.

W. C. R.

-----o-----

EVIDENCES OF CHRISTIANITY.
NUMBER I.

There is one difficulty in approaching the evidences of the Christian religion, that every writer, who understands the present state of things, must feel. That difficulty is, to secure the attention of those who are now avowed skeptics, or those in danger of becoming such. There is not the least danger of the main body of skeptics thinking too closely, reasoning too minutely, or criticizing too rigidly. No fear need be entertained of their putting our articles into the crucible of investigation and examining them too carefully. The trouble is that they will not think on the subject at all; will not read; will not investigate, or make an earnest and solemn effort to determine what is truth. Our fear is, that they will assume, without any deliberate thinking, reasoning or examination, that religion is all priest-craft, the Bible a fable, and Jesus an impostor, and then act upon this assumption as if it were a well-known and established truth. It is the easiest thing in the world, for the most ignorant, stupid and unthinking creature living to assume all this, and much more, and in all his coarse and uncouth allusions to the subject, speak of it as a matter of indifference, and declare in both word and action, that it is a matter of no consequence what course a man pursues. This is the reason we dread infidelity. It stupefies men into indifference, recklessness and sensuality. Under its influence, they will risk anything and disregard everything. It stupefies their sensibilities, disqualifies them for reasoning, or any fair and honorable investigation, in reference to the very point upon which, above all others, they should have the most indisputable certainty.

We lament this state of things, for when a man reaches it once, he is almost, if not entirely beyond the reach of the benevolent efforts of all the good to save him or confer any religious benefits upon him. A man who assumes a false position, in reference to the precise truth designed and the only truth having power to save him, and proceeds upon that assumption as if it were truth, and peremptorily persists in refusing to open the question for investigation, or to reason or think upon it at all, is in a most deplorable and hopeless situation. It is utterly out of the power of the best and greatest of human kind to do such any good. They are beyond the reach of remedy. But there are many who have not reached this thoughtless, stupid and indifferent state, who can be induced to think, reason, and make an honorable effort to determine what is truth. These we hope, by the Divine blessing, to benefit.

There is, however, an entirely different class of skeptics from those just alluded to; a class always thinking, reasoning, theorizing and scheming in idle speculations; roaming in immense and fruitless deserts, vast barrens and waste fields where nothing can ever grow. They float in thin ether, if not some times in pure vacuum, in vast, unknown and unknowable regions of pure fancy and idle imagination. They roam in everlasting inquisitiveness in the immense realms of intangibles and invisibles. They are variously styled in New Testament term-inology, "clouds without water," "wandering stars," "filthy dreamers," etc., etc. They spend their time, confuse themselves and shatter their brains, in explaining "degrees in glory," "degrees in punishment," "different spheres," "the possibility of holding converse with departed friends," "the origin of sin," "how God will overrule evil for the good of man and his own glory," "the origin of the devil, if there be any," or, "who made the devil," or, "whether he is a real being, or only a personification of evil," "whether God did not know when he created man that he would sin," "why he created man knowing that he would sin," "whether he did not know when he made man, who would be saved and who would be lost," and if he did, "why he created those he knew would be lost," "whether angels are a distinct order of beings from men," "whether we shall know each, other in the eternal state," "with what body the dead will be raised," "whether the righteous and wicked will rise at the same time," "where the spirit is between death and the resurrection," "whether it is conscious, or can exist separate from the body," "when the end of the world will be," etc., etc.

We have now an immense swarm of these idle dreamers; some of these have already reasoned themselves into the hallucination that they are in the New Jerusalem state, and that the Christian dispensation, or the mediatorial reign of our Lord Jesus Christ has passed away! These idle away their time, in discussing the ascension through the different grades of spheres which they imagine they shall eternally be attaining and passing through, with other kindred topics. Another class reason themselves into absolute fatalism. With them all the actions of men and the very thoughts that lead to them, are of necessity, and cannot be anything else! There is no praise of one class, or condemnation of another, for all do just what they do from an eternal necessity! Off at another angle, another party is found, theorizing upon the whimsical notion of human pre-existence, in which state, they think a consistent origin for sin may be found! Yet another class perceive that deep down in the Bible, where till recently none had ever penetrated, the doctrine is found, that at judgment, the wicked will be stricken out of existence, thus ridding them of the idea of endless punishment, which had previously given them much distress! Still another class of these, have rid themselves of the same distressing and annoying doctrine, by making the astonishing discovery, that there is no devil, no hell, nor punishment of any kind, beyond the present state, and, therefore, no danger of any endless punishment! Still another class became perplexed with these metaphysical reasonings, subtleties and theorizing, in things that they cannot help feeling conscious can have no possible beneficial effects upon mankind, and rid themselves of the entire concern, by making the discovery that all things come by chance, that there is no God, Savior, angel or spirit, and death is an eternal sleep! But we sicken at the effort of trying to describe the vain and idle speculations of all these "wandering stars," and shall proceed to something more tangible.

1. Skepticism has no foundation, no basis, no reality upon which to rest. It has nothing to build upon; no rock; no pillars of any kind. Nor has it any materials or builders. Nothing can be built without a foundation, materials and builders. Skeptics are not builders. Their work is merely *pulling down* old buildings. This is the reason they make so much show; their work is easy, requires but little skill and no goodness. Anybody can tear down, but it takes a workman to build. Skepticism is a mere negative, consisting wholly of denials. It affirms nothing, establishes nothing, and builds up nothing. It is a natural impossibility to build upon a mere negative. A system cannot, in the very nature of things, be built upon a mere denial—a mere negative. If a man would deny, repudiate and condemn all the foundations of all the houses in his city, or if he would go and tear his neighbor's foundations all down, it would give him no foundation for a house, but would simply put them in the same condition with himself—that is, *without any foundation.* In the same way, if infidels could successfully deny, disprove and overthrow the foundation of every system of religion in the world, it would lay no foundation for them, but would simply put the rest of us upon a level with them—that is, *without any foundation.* The work of all skeptics has been simply to tear up the foundation of Christians, and not to lay any foundation for themselves. Not a man in all the ranks of unbelief has ever presented any foundation or has any. Their entire clamor is against the Bible, but if they could expunge the Bible from the universe, they are no better off—they have nothing to stand upon.

2. Skepticism has no center of attraction, no gravitation, no great central pervading idea, drawing everything to one common center. A system must have a common center of attraction, holding it, in its revolutions, from flying into atoms. But skepticism has no pervading idea, doctrine or constitution, in which everything centers, around which everything revolves, with power to attract and bind. It consists simply in denials of what others believe. If the things which they deny were untrue, and should be denied, the denial of them is no foundation or center of attraction. Their denial amounts to nothing in their favor, but is simply unfavorable to others—destructive of the attraction binding others together. A million of the most unequivocal denials of the most absurd and preposterous

doctrines the world ever contained, forms no center of attraction, doctrine or constitution, in which is embodied and concentrated any principle of attraction that can bind in a system. Denying simply frees men and cuts them loose, in their own estimation, from that which they deny, or what others believe, but binds them to nothing.

3. Skepticism has no law, gives no advice, and has nothing in it about the characters of men. It does not say that a man shall, or shall not, have a good character; that he shall or shall not have a bad character. It contains no such words and has no such idea, or keeps up no such distinctions as good and bad. It says nothing about love and hatred, revenge and pity, covetousness and benevolence, vice and virtue, happiness and misery. It contains not one sentence touching all the relations in life, providing nothing for individuals, families or nations. It consists of one negative principle, viz: *The denial of the truth of the Christian religion..* Any man can see that there is no law in this. If they could succeed in this denial and show beyond all contradiction that Christianity is not true, it amounts to nothing. It is no law and accomplishes nothing in any way only to bring Christians upon a level with them—with *precisely nothing!*

4. Skepticism has no rewards for the good. It promises nothing in this world nor that which is to come. It holds out no rewards, no inducements of any kind for the good, in time or eternity!

5. Skepticism has no punishments for the bad, here nor hereafter. It contains no punishments for evil-doers—the profligate, dissipated, and corrupt; thieves, robbers and murderers. It knows nothing of crimes or punishments for crimes of any grade or atrocity.

6. Skepticism has no reformatory power. A denial, or a train of denials, even denials of error, can never restrain sinners nor reform men. The influence is simply negative. In the very nature of things, it cannot act positively. Denials, or negatives, require nothing, give nothing, and, as a matter of course, can produce no reformation. It is a negative system, if we may be allowed to call it a *system* at all, and in the very nature of things, its influence must be negative. It is like cold, which is simply the absence of heat; for the suffering in the absence of heat, is from want of heat. Skepticism is simply the absence of the heat of Christianity. Darkness is merely the absence of light, or it is the negative of light, else it and light could exist at the same time, in the same place. In precisely the same way, skepticism is the absence of gospel light, or faith. The soul without faith is empty, cold, dark, and hungry, suffering and perishing, for light, heat and food. Skepticism is no system, not a reality, substance or entity of any kind, but the absence of all these. To speak in general terms of faith, both Christian faith and all other faith, the absence of it, would be the absence by far of the greater part of all we know, or that may be known by man. There is nothing more certain than that a man who knows much, must believe much. Skepticism is not the possession of reformatory principles, but simply the absence of them. There is nothing that a man can be more conscious of, than that skepticism never did, and never can, make a man better. Inherently, there is nothing in it. It is the absence of something. The mere absence of faith, of religion, doctrine and principles, most indisputably can do a man no good, and can have no power to save' him in any sense. To speak of saving a man from starving by the absence of food, saving him from thirst by the absence of water, or from darkness by the absence of light, or from sickness by the absence of the only medicine that could save him, is not more absurd, than to speak of unbelief reforming man. Skepticism is not heat, but the absence of it; not light, but the absence of it; not faith, but the absence of it; not knowledge, but the absence of it; not medicine, but

the absence of it; not nourishment, but the absence of it. The skeptic is a man perishing with cold, while he is graciously offered the warmth of Christianity; groping in darkness, while the light of heaven is as free for him as the rays of the sun; starving, with an invitation to eat of the bread that comes down from heaven; dying with thirst, while God is holding out to him the water of life; a sick man, refusing to take an infallible remedy from the physician, simply exercising the power to reject all that could do him any good, resisting, refusing, denying and dying. B. F.

-----o-----

THE BOOK OF JOB;
IN THREE PARTS.
BY THE AMERICAN BIBLE UNION.

New York: 1856. Just received.

A handsome quarto, consisting of Three Parts:

1. The First Part contains the Common English Version, the Hebrew Text, and the Revised Version in parallel columns, beautifully printed, and on the lower part of each page the philological notes and authorities sustaining the changes made in the revision.

2. The Second Part contains the revision in paragraph form with marginal readings, and Explanatory Notes for the English reader.

3. The Third Part contains the revision in paragraph form, accompanied by the marginal readings, with no notes or authorities, and with nothing to break the continuity of the impression.

Part Second is accompanied by an Introduction addressed to the English reader explaining the argument of the Book. This is, without exception, the clearest exhibition of the character and object of the book that has ever been published, and throws more light upon the positions and purposes of each of the speakers introduced, and the general scope and design of the whole poem than libraries of commentaries and general criticisms. For that peculiar beauty which results from the happy combination of concentrated thought, terse expression, bold imagery, and the utmost simplicity of pure Saxon phraseology, it can hardly be surpassed in English literature. While both thought and diction appear to flow without effort, not an idea could be omitted or changed in its relations, not a word could be displaced, nor another added, without unhappily affecting the otherwise perfect impression which it makes upon the mind of the reader.

In respect to the revision itself, whoever compares it with the version generally known as that of King James, must be struck with its immeasurable superiority. It flows in the true measures of Eastern poetry, so far as they can be transferred to our vernacular. It exhibits clear thought and pointed remark, where the common version appears confused, obscured, or aimless. No lover of the beautiful and appropriate can read it without continued pleasure, and the Christian will be delighted to find in it lessons of instruction, which he never expected to discover in a book which has hitherto been regarded as one of the most obscure in the canon of revelation.

To prove the truth of these remarks, we shall contrast some specimens gathered cursorily from different parts of the book, printing the phrases from the old and new version in juxtaposition:

KING JAMES' VERSION.	REVISED VERSION
Let darkness and the shadow of death stain it;	Let darkness and death shade reclaim it;
neither let it see the dawning of the day"	neither let it behold the eye-lids of the morning.
Why did the knees prevent me ? or why the breasts that I should suck?	Why were the knees ready for me, and why the breasts, that I might suck ?
For my sighing cometh before I eat, and my roarings are poured out like the waters.	For with my food comes my sighing; and my moans are poured forth as water.

Is not this thy fear, thy confidence, thy hope, and the uprightness of thy ways?	Is not thy fear thy confidence thy hope; it is the uprightness of thy ways.
But he saveth the poor from the sword, from their mouth, and from the hand of the mighty.	So he rescues the victim from their mouth, and the needy from the hand of the strong.
And thou shalt know that thy tabernacle *shall be* in peace; and thou shalt visit thy habitation, and shall not sin.	So shalt thou know, that thy tent is in peace. and shalt visit thy pastures, and miss nothing.
The things *that* my soul refused to touch *are* as my sorrowful meat.	My soul refuses to touch! they are as food which I loathe.
Then should I yet have comfort; yea, I would harden myself in sorrow: let him not spare; for I have not concealed the words of the Holy one.	For it should still be my solace, yea, I would exult in pain that spares not, that I have not denied the words of the Holy One.
My brethren have dealt deceitfully as a brook, *and* as the stream of brooks they pass away;	My brethren are deceitful, like the brook, as the channel of brooks that pass away:
Which are blackish by reason of the ice, *and* wherein the snow is hid; What time they wax warm, they vanish" when it is hot, they are consumed out of their place.	that becomes turbid from, ice; the snow hides itself in them. At the time they are poured off, they fail; when it is hot, they are consumed from their place.
The paths of their way are turned aside: they go to nothing, and perish. but. what doth your arguing reprove ?	The caravans, along their way, turn aside; they go up into the wastes, and perish. but what does your upbraiding prove ?
Do ye imagine to reprove the words, and the speeches of one that is desperate, *which are* as wind?	Do ye intend to censure words, when the words of the despairing are as wind ?
Yea, ye overwhelm the fatherless,	Ye would even cast lots for the orphan,
Now therefore be content, look upon me; for *it is* evident unto you if I lie.	And now consent to look upon me; for I will not speak falsely to your face.
Return I pray you, let it not be iniquity; yea, return again, my righteousness *is* in it.	Return I pray; let there be no wrong, yea return; I yet have a righteous cause.
Is there not an appointed time to man upon earth?	Has not man a term of warfare on the earth
thine eyes *are* upon me, and I *am* not.	thine eyes will seek me, but I shall not be.
I loathe *it;* I would not live alway: let me alone; for my days *are* vanity.	I waste away; I shall not always live; cease from me for my days are a vapor.
I have sinned; what shall I do unto thee, O thou preserver of men ? prepare thyself to the search of their fathers;	If I sin, what do I unto thee, thou observer of men ? note what their fathers have searched out.
Because *there* is wrath beware lest he take thee away with *his* stroke: then a great ransom cannot deliver thee.	For beware, lest anger stir thee up against chastisement, and a great ransom shall not deliver thee.
If I be wicked, *I am* full of confusion; therefore see thou mine affliction.	I am accounted guilty; filled with shame, and the sight of my misery!
And that he would shew thee the secrets of wisdom, that *they are* double to that which is!	and would show thee the secrets of wisdom, how manifold is understanding;

In collecting these passages we have gone over only a small part of the book. Yet these are sufficient to show the complete change in the aspect of the poem which the revision effects.

Even where the meaning is not materially altered, there is a manifest improvement in the phraseology, which develops with striking effect the beauty of the inspired poetry.

We cannot forbear to invite attention to the simplicity and appropriateness of the Explanatory Notes for the English reader. They comprise a vast amount of the most interesting information and judicious remarks, in the least possible space. We have never read comments with which we were better pleased.

On the whole, we regard this revision of Job as one of the most valuable publications that has ever been issued, and we congratulate the Bible Union upon so praise-worthy an installment of the great work which it has undertaken to give to the world.

COMMUNICATION FROM ELDER J. T. JOHNSON.

The Reformation in which we are engaged has been developing itself since the year 1823. The Christian Baptist was the Pioneer. The grand object was to introduce, amongst Christians, a pure speech; the very language of the Book of God; and thus, to restore unity to the Body of Christ, in order to its purity and happiness, and the conversion of the world. In accordance with this grand, this noble, this sublime conception, and movement, the living oracles wore, in a revised form, presented to the world. From that time to this, the Reformation has been most bitterly and unsparingly opposed by all the existing parties. In despite of all this, its success has been unparallel in modern times. Notwithstanding the numbers, the wealth, the learning, the piety and other influences of the opposition, a great party has been established upon the foundation of Apostles and Prophets, Jesus Christ being the chief corner stone, and the Bible alone its Magna Charta.

Much has been accomplished; and much now remains to be done. *No one* is so foolish as to suppose we have reached perfection. But because we have not progressed as rapidly as some have anticipated and desired, their sanguine temperaments have become soured; and the dark side of the picture has been presented to the world, with scarcely a ray of hope, or a redeeming virtue. In all that we say and do, we should never forget that there is a tribunal before which we shall be summoned to account for the injustice we have done to others. For *myself I speak,* and here I say, that, in my judgment, I am associated religiously with as noble a band of people as ever lived. I am not blind to their deficiencies, their faults, and their imperfections. With all these about them, I love them; I have confidence in them; and look forward to the day when they will roll on the ball of this Reformation to Pisgah's summit.

Taking a bird's eye view of the field before us, what most prominently strikes the eye? Congregations have sprung up as by enchantment; the land has been dotted over with houses of worship; evangelists have been sustained in the field beyond any former example; schools, male and female, and colleges, are rising in every direction; liberal endowments have been made to Bacon's College, Bethany College, the Female Orphan School at Midway, the Educational Society of Kentucky, and to Bacon's College again, besides all the liberal, generous efforts *made and now malting,* in these United States. The failure to accomplish, or to reach that perfection which has been most anxiously desired and anticipated, has been variously accounted for, according to the different mediums through which we have looked, and the different lights to which we have resorted, as well as the different judgments, tastes, and temperaments which govern us.

In the estimation of some, ecclesiastical organization is the grand panacea to heal all our maladies. Our present hopeless condition, with them, is ascribed to our want of a grand, consolidated, ecclesiastical establishment to bring up the congregation to their duty, to try congregational aberrations, heresies, and errors; to ordain, and try Evangelists, etc., etc. Considering the amount of dissatisfaction that has been manifested, and the length of time consumed in the discussions that have appeared, it is astonishing that a plan has not been submitted, that we might consider it, and test its merits by the divine standard.

If there is a *divine plan* of organization it is our duty to submit to it without a murmur, or demur. If there is none, where is the criminality in permitting the matter to rest where the Apostles left it. Unless indeed, it can be shown that this duty has been enjoined on the successors of the Apostles. So far from this being the fact, the Savior most expressly grants to the Twelve the power to judge, and of course, to give laws to the Twelve tribes,

—yea, to the Christian world. We have the law of citizenship, and the rule of conduct for the citizen prescribed in terms plain and unmistakable. Organization is a first principle; and it appears to me too plain to doubt.

The congregation at Jerusalem was organized. It had its membership and officers, its elders and deacons. The Apostles were law-givers, and for a time, acted in a double capacity. But in a short space the congregation was prepared to act *in* and *of* herself.

All the congregations were formed and governed after the same model, and matters progressed under the same auspices, governed by the laws enacted by the Apostles, for centuries, with slight departures, owing to the corruption of the times.

The congregations selected and ordained their officers, and held them accountable for their conduct, and the officers always acted in conjunction or with the sanction of the congregation.

We had supposed, that the fundamental, first principles were plain; that they had been ascertained to a moral certainty. But if the judgments and opinions of some are to be relied on, we are wholly mistaken; it is all a delusion.

From the positions assumed by some of the brotherhood, a most serious question forces itself upon us. Can a congregation discharge its duty to the Great Head of the Church, without entering into an alliance with such a grand, ecclesiastical establishment as is contended for, I have thought, and I still think she can. And, indeed, I think I can point out congregations that have done vastly more in their independent position and character, than in their ecclesiastical relation alluded to. In one view of the subject, each congregation is independent of every other, and it should be so. In another view of the subject, all the congregations stand connected together, as if they were a unit.

In objects, aims, fellowship, and hopes, they are one. A congregation can put forth all its powers without connecting itself with any ecclesiastical body, such as is contemplated. But as a matter of expediency, an alliance maybe formed for a general, co-operative effort.

The congregational plan is the divine arrangement. It works best. It accomplishes the most good, by calling forth all the energies and resources of each congregation, and the least injury is the result. Were it not for the fact that men can injure each other in person and property, there would be no need of human government. Our associations would be formed in accordance with our views of right, and the characters we had formed. It would be the interests of all to cultivate the virtues in order to the greatest good, and the greatest happiness.

And, inasmuch as Christianity inflicts no pains or penalties of a personal or pecuniary character, congregational independence is the divine plan. It is made the interest of all to cultivate purity, and reform the world. These being the objects of all, and all being a holy brotherhood, they would, of course, associate as much as possible, and assist, in co-operation, in converting the world.

I am yet to learn that an ecclesiastical establishment, by its messengers, has the divine right to select and ordain evangelists, to sit in [judgment on evangelists, on congregations, and their difficulties; to try heresies, to declare fellowship and non-fellowship, etc., etc. Let us have a scriptural, matter-of-fact case, of such power and action. Where were such ecclesiastical bodies before the last half of the second century? They originated in Greece, in imitation of the leagues formed by the little republics as a barrier against the Asiatic hordes that were in the practice of invading and devastating their country. We have just dispensed with the American Christian Bible Society, as unnecessary, and we have resolved to center our energies and efforts in behalf of the American Christian Missionary Society, and I pray the Lord that each preacher and member of the Reformation may exert themselves in its behalf till we meet next October. Let each one collect and send on names as fast as possible that something may be done worthy of us as Christians.

J. T. JOHNSON.

-----o-----

Communications.

CHARLESTON, Coles Co., Ill.,
December 9th, 1856.

DEAR BRO. FRANKLIN:—Bro. Thomas Lockhart, of Indiana, has just closed a protracted meeting in this place of nine days continuance. During the time, he was assisted, two days, by Bro. A. D. Fillmore, of Paris, Illinois. The result was twenty-seven made the good confession, and were immersed in the name of the Lord Jesus. These, together with ten others, by letter, etc., were added to the church—making, in all, *thirty-seven* additions during this meeting. This was a happy season of rejoicing with us, and we trust a season long to be remembered to the praise and glory of God. At this time we need an able and good Pastor for our congregation—one that can ably hold forth the word of life, in its primitive beauty and simplicity, in order that the good work begun may be continued in this place, to the great glory of God and the salvation of the church.

Hoping then, through the fidelity and prayers of our congregation at home, and the interest of our dear brethren abroad, in our behalf, we shall have far more prosperous and refreshing seasons in the Lord, than in years gone by. I subscribe myself, yours in Christ,

JEWELL DAVIS.

-----o-----

PARALLELS.—In looking over my rambling remarks, when I came to the *Harbinger* and my *Age,* my mind recalled several parallel cases between myself and Elder a Campbell. In the first place, we were both born in the same year of grace; both born in the Presbyterian congregation; both sprinkled in our infancy; both became dissatisfied and were baptized by immersion; both left our mother church and attached ourselves to another branch, and both were expelled from that branch, and both are now members of what I truly believe to be the Church of Christ; the day that he first left Ireland for the United States. I was married on the Island of Nantucket, Mass.; both crossed the salt water to procure us wives; both had large families; both of our wives are numbered with the dead; both of us are now living happily with our second wives; both of us have traveled thousands of miles with our second wives in railroad cars, steamboats, and other conveyances, etc., etc., and in conclusion I have to inform you that I have not yet had the pleasure of seeing the face of Elder A. Campbell.

Please excuse the liberty that I have taken, and, as an Irishman would say, "ye need not read it unless ye have a mind to." Again farewell.

J. W. BROWN.

-----o-----

CINCINNATI, Ohio, Oct. 1st, 1856.

BROTHER EDITOR:—As a result of my late labors, I give you the following: Besides my regular engagements at Harrison, Ohio, where the *"Pole Evil"* seems so to affect the people that the efforts of the church and the power of the preached gospel appears to be paralyzed, I have found time, in the last two months, to hold meetings at Howard's Creek, Butler county, Ohio, resulting in one addition; at Cedar Grove, Franklin county, Indiana, during which there were five additions; and at Wilson's Station, Clermont county, Ohio, where large and attentive audiences gave ear to the truth, and we were happy in hearing two noble souls declare their confidence in the name of our blessed Redeemer, through whom, to God be all the praise, now and ever, amen.

Truly your Brother,

JAMES P. ORR.

MAYS LICK, KY., Dec. 22, 1856.

BRO. EDITOR Health and peace to you through Christ Jesus, our Lord.

You have, I perceive, lost from your list of Cincinnati ministers our excellent Brother, D. S. Burnet. He has gone to New York. I solemnly regret it; may the blessing of the Almighty rest upon him.

With the prestige of having fought and won many battles for the great Captain of our Salvation, to Bro. Burnet has been granted the heritage of many of heaven's choicest gifts and graces. To the accomplishments that adorn the gentleman and Christian, he unites an oratory which is at once enlightened, impressive, brilliant and persuasive. Besides this grand quality he is happily endowed with an excellent knowledge of the immortal oracles of heaven, and well he understands how, by the blessing of God, to apply them successfully to the head and heart, the feelings, sympathies, and consciences of his auditors.

Besides these noble gifts, his tastes for the holy war which, as a minister of Christ, he wages against sin, make the victories of the Cross his joy and chief delight. If success is the test of militant power, who will deny him the first rank in the army of the faith? Of those who contend against the powers of darkness few, perhaps none in the West, have given better proof of their evangelical prowess than he.

When a man has devoted the length and strength of his youth and manhood to the best interests of the church and the world; when he has, like Bro. B., successfully given himself to the work of the Lord, and the glory of our God, surely, he must be the object of tenderest regard; yea, of love; yea, of admiration with all God's people and all good men.

I go to Cincinnati now as formerly, but, alas! more than one element of ancient delight and splendor are withdrawn—gone, perhaps, to return no more. Sadness enthralls my heart. May the blessing of God be with our absent ones.
W. SCOTT.

Editor's Table.

EVIDENCES OF CHRISTIANITY.—Such is the title of a neat little volume from the pen of the beloved, widely-known and talented brother, "whose praise is in all the churches," James Challen, formerly of this city, but now of Philadelphia, Pa. This volume was kindly sent to us, but, through a mistake, we let some one have it thinking it was the "*Gospel and its Elements.*" But when a man has made the Bible his study for thirty years, and applied his energies to preaching during the same length of time, with much success, it is only necessary that the people know that he has produced a volume of this kind, to give it a passport to numerous readers. We shall have it constantly for sale at this office. Price and size the same as "The Gospel and its Elements."

-----o-----

HISTORY OF ENGLISH BIBLE TRANSLATION.—This valuable and ably written work, from the pen of Mrs. Conant, wife of the distinguished Dr. Conant, of the Bible Union and translator of the book of Job, can be had at this office, at the price of $1.25. No book that we are acquainted with is fraught with more interest to the friends of a pure English Bible.

AMERICAN CHRISTIAN REVIEW FOR 1857.—We have secured a fairer and finer quality of paper for our Magazine for the present year than we used last year. It is also printed upon type never before used, and, we trust, in its execution, it will compare favorably with any magazine in this country. We are determined to spare no labor in our power to make it meet the wants and expectations of its patrons. It may now be put down among the permanently established publications. Our encouragements are now superior to anything of the kind we have ever enjoyed. Truly are we grateful to the Heavenly Father and to those who love him for a generous patronage. May we be enabled to conduct it to the good of man and glory of God.

SERMON OF ELD. JOHN ROGERS.—We call especial attention to the sermon found in this number from the pen of Eld. John Rogers. This venerable brother has been an able and pious preacher more than thirty years, and imbibed much of the piety running through this sermon, from Eld. B. W. Stone, with whom he personally associated for many years. He is a brother of Eld. Samuel Rogers, who is still an older man, and who is also a patron of piety. These two men, and Eld. John T. Johnson, are, in our estimation, as near primitive evangelists as any we know. But they need no encomiums from us; the Lord knows the labor they have done and are now doing, and we trust he will yet spare them to do much more. Eld. J. T. Johnson has done much to enrich our pages; and we now have an arrangement with Eld. John Rogers, which will secure, we trust, the frequent aid of his able and accomplished pen.

THE MISSIONARY SOCIETY.—It is truly gratifying to learn with what great unanimity the brethren are taking hold of the Missionary Society. There appears now to be but one voice in relation to it; viz: *That it must be pushed with great power.* Many brethren are voluntarily making contributions for this great work, and from present indications we doubt not it will receive a liberal support. If the churches in general would make a liberal contribution once in three months for this work, thus affording all the members an opportunity of adding their mite, to the amount collected, the work that would be done would be cheering in the highest degree. Brethren, we must do what we do soon, for our time is short and our days will soon be numbered. O, let us make a manly and noble effort to save mankind. Let us love and strive to save those whom God loves and invites to his kingdom.

"THE FAMILY COMPANION."—Elder E. Goodwin's valuable new book of sermons, styled "The Family Companion," is obtaining a liberal circulation, and not undeservedly. It is a valuable book—a book calculated to do a vast amount of good. The variety in it gives a pretty full development of the Christian religion, in a simple, clear, and yet able manner, well adapted to the people at large. It is sound and strong, inculcating sentiments of piety, union and love, in a manner rarely to be found in any book of these times. This valuable "Family Companion" will be kept at this office, and can be sent by mail any place in the United States, postage pre-paid, for $1,20. By the quantity a liberal discount will be made.

"THE APOSTOLIC COMMISSION; A Discourse by Dr. S. E. Shepard, of New York." Such is the title of a decidedly able and valuable sermon, on the Lord's commission to the Apostles, now before us. In this discourse the Doctor throws down the gauntlet in the following words" "Authority for this change in baptism can be found nowhere but in the Papal Church; and as all Protestants reject that authority, and utterly repudiate all her claims of power to 'change times and laws,' there is an end to all rational controversy on this subject; and more especially as there is not a single passage in the Christian Scriptures which even intimated aspersion, nor a single case of sprinkling for baptism, in all the annals of the Greek Church, in all the length and breadth of her vast territory, from the time in which the first Greeks became 'obedient to the faith,' to the present time."

The change alluded to in this defiant passage, is that from *immersion* to *sprinkling or pouring.* This assertion is a plain matter of history. If it is not correct, no talent or learning is needed to refute it, only to find the passage in the Bible or the records of history that refutes it, refer to the place, read and transcribe. Who will try to produce a refutation?

By the way, this sermon is a splendid tract to circulate all over the land. Address Dr. S. E. Shepard, New York.

WHAT IS TO BE DONE?—In several latitudes it has been intimated that brethren will not subscribe to the *Review* till we visit them. This may appear reasonable to them; but there is one claim more pressing upon us than this, viz.: In those sections where *they have raised splendid lists of subscribers,* they have laid us under obligations that must be regarded, as far as our ability will extend. In one word, we go as far and wide as one man can go, and are certainly never idle. This is all that can be done.

APOLOGY.—We handed our former printer an obituary notice, written by Bro. T. M. Allen. It and several other documents were crowded out of the December number. We changed printers at the end of the year, and our former printer could not produce the obituary notice from Bro. Allen. We regret this, and will cheerfully insert it, if he will be at the trouble of furnishing it again.

CORRESPONDENTS.—Many brethren complain that we condense their communications, or do not insert them at all. To all such we reply, that this is unavoidable. We fill the *Review to* its utmost capacity every month, and then do not insert one-half. All obituary notices and reports of success must be limited to the smallest dimensions, or not be inserted at all. Sermons, reviews and essays, well written, upon themes bearing upon the interests of the cause and entering into the soul of the work of God, may be lengthy. We will do the very best we can, and show due respect to all.

COLUMBIA, MO.

Life members of the A. C. M. Society at Cincinnati:

M. E. Allen, Elder T. M. Allen, President W. W. Hudson, Professor G. H. Matthews, Professor S. Price, W. A. Buckner, A. Douglass, A. Haynes, N Carter, S. B. Victor, C. S. Stone, J. B. Harston, J. D, Brown, D. A. Park, T. J. White, J. Shannon, J. Haddon.

Brother Austin Bradford handed me $90.00 for the Bible Revision Association.

Caleb S. Stone appointed agent and collector here. J. T. JOHNSON

FRANKFORT, Dec. 17, 1856.

DEAR BRO. FRANKLIN"—Some sad errors have been made in printing my discourse, viz.:

Page 354, 17th line from bottom, left hand column, "dear" should be "clear."

Same page, 17th line from top, right hand column, "contrivance" should be "continuance."

Same page and column, 25th line from top, "mediation" should be "mediator."

Next page, right hand column, 9th line from top, "need" should be "heed."

Same page and column, 10th line from bottom, "circumstances" should be "circum-stance." Six lines below, "and *that* to be," omit "that."

Page 357, left column, 25th line from top, "appointments" should be singular.

Page 362, left hand column, 20th line from the top, is such an omission as wholly destroys the sense of a most important passage.

I shall be glad if you will correct these; and will you please say if the type has been distributed.

Very truly, yours,

P. S. FALL.

-----o-----

Success of the Gospel.

Brother J. T. Johnson, writing from Columbia, Mo., says:

"We have had a glorious meeting on hand here. Up to this time we have had twenty-four noble additions."

Brother B. Wharton, Fulton county, Indiana, says:

"The cause is advancing in the bounds of my labors. We have had, since June last, thirty-nine additions—thirty-two immersions and seven by commendation."

Within two months we have had eight additions at Point Pleasant, three at Union, Boone county, Ky., and some ten by baptism, by letter and from the sects, in Covington, Ky. Including the first Lord's day in December some eight additions, by baptism, by letter, reclaimed and from the sects, at Alexandria, Madison county, Ind. Including the second Lord's day in December eight were added by baptism, from the sects and reclaimed, at Union City, Ind.

LEXINGTON Dec. 8, '56.

BRO. FRANKLIN—I closed a meeting, of a few days, with the Baltimore Church last week, with eight additions, and with increased audiences. The church numbers about two hundred and fifty members. Among them are at least some seven or eight good speakers, of whom Brother Austin is the chief, and by their teaching and the general co-operation of the whole brotherhood they have continued to maintain the cause in the city, and also to plant the churches at Harford, twenty-six miles N. E., and also a small congregation at New London, in Pennsylvania.

In all Maryland the brethren could not name one evangelist who is laboring in word and doctrine, nor could they name more than five congregations, scattered over the State. What a picture? Is not Maryland and Pennsylvania a good field for Missionary effort by our Missionary Board? My spirit was stirred within me when I saw the want and cry for help.

It is evident that the small churches are unable to meet the demand, and I have never found the people more willing to hear the whole truth. It is a rich field for good and efficient evangelists, and I pray that laborers may be sent to their aid.

The young brethren and the sisters have charge at Baltimore, of a most interesting Sunday School, of some one hundred scholars in regular attendance. They have a morning and evening session every Lord's day, and great devotion to the work is manifesting rich results. I spent my time among them with much interest, and with an urgent appeal to return to their aid. May God speed the truth.

Yours truly,

G. W. ELLEY.

BOONE CO., Mo., Dec. 6, 1856.

DEAR BRO. FRANKLIN"—Yesterday evening I returned from Rocheport, where I had been preaching for seven or eight days, and obtained twenty-eight additions. There had been seventeen previously added to the church by the labors of our good and devoted Bro., J. T. Johnson, and others, making forty-five additions in all, since the meeting commenced. It was truly an interesting and glorious meeting.

Bro. Johnson has gone to the western portion of our State; and, while in Rocheport, I heard that he was conducting a successful meeting at Lexington.

Bro. Gaines was to be in Rocheport today, and I have no doubt will obtain other additions,

To the heavenly Father be all the praise.

Fraternally and truly yours,

T. M. ALLEN.

P. S.—I enclose you $1.00 for the subscription of Sister M.

Among the additions at Rocheport were three Baptists, one Methodist, and one Episcopalian. I took a copy of "Sincerity" and the "Union" move with me, and I have no doubt they contributed to promote the spirit of union that pervaded that community.

T. M. A.

-----o-----

Obituary.

QUASQUETON, IOWA, Oct. 23, 1856.

BRO. FRANKLIN"—It is with much sorrow that I record the death of my much-esteemed Bro., John H. Mowry. He died on the 21st of October, after an attack of typhoid fever of some fourteen days duration. He suffered very much, although he bore it with fortitude becoming a Christian. He had been a member of the Christian church some five years, and died with a well-grounded hope of immortality and eternal life beyond the grave.

As ever, your brother,   R. S. MOWRY

THE AMERICAN CHRISTIAN REVIEW.

VOL. II. CINCINNATI, FEBRUARY, 1857. No. 2.

THE DIVINE AUTHORITY FOR OBSERVING THE LORD'S DAY

A SERMON. BY ELDER J. K. HOSHOUR.

"The Son of man is Lord also of the Sabbath."—Luke vi. 5.

There are several absolute prerequisites to animated existence:—A substratum upon which it can be located; space to move in; food for subsistence; and *time* for the development of its endowments and the indication of its mission into this portico of being.

But, of all these, *time* has a paramount essentiality; for there may be substratum upon which existence could be located; means for subsistence; space for action; but, if time were wanting for development and perfection, all these would be useless.

Various definitions of time have been given. One philosophic definition is, that time is the general relation of things perceptible to each other, as to their origin, their continuance, and their dissolution; made cognizable by the succession of events. It has been called a narrow isthmus lying between the eternity past and the eternity to come. And one of no secondary position, in the domain of poesy, sings in the following strains" "From eternity's mysterious orb, time was cut off, and cast beneath the skies—the skies that watch him in his new abode, measuring his motions by revolving spheres—that horologe machinery divine;—days, months and years, his children play around him as he flies!" The divisions of time, natural and artificial, are, under any circumstances, *interesting;* upon which, however, we cannot now dilate—an enumeration of them must suffice.

The natural divisions are days, months, years and cycles; the artificial are seconds, minutes, hours and centuries. In this enumeration, you see the week is not included; for the reason that it is neither, strictly speaking, a natural nor artificial division—it is a *revealed division.* There is no motion in the natural world that indicates a septenary division; and the artificial are all expressed in even, not uneven, numbers.

The septenary division prevailed among the most ancient civilized nations of the globe—the Egyptians, Chinese, Greek, Roman and Northern Barbarian—indicative of one common origin, the primogenitor of our race, who obtained it through divine instruction.

When the heavens had been garnished with their respective luminaries; when the earth had been founded and made inhabitable; when the sea had been filled with its untold orders of sportive inhabitants; when the dry land had been replenished with its diversified departments of enjoying existences; when Eden had been hedged in and beautified by the hand of God; when the primitive pair, intact by pollution, had entered upon its luscious entertainments; when a new and unsullied creation had evoked the harmonies of the "morning stars," and elicited the "shouts of the sons of God," then the divine hand ceased its creative labors in this department of the universe—then was the seventh day blessed and sanctified, *and the Sabbath instituted!*

According to the instituted arrangement for this occasion, it has been assigned to me to discourse on the divine authority for *Sabbatical rest*.

The divine authority for the Sabbath, which means periodical rest, can, we trust, be made apparent from the revelation of God, as also from the divine threatenings against the violators of this institution, on the one hand, and from the constitution and wants of man, on the other.

To get at the origin and primitive circumstances of this institution, it is certainly, at present, not within my province to expatiate upon the divine existence, on the great probability, that God takes such an interest in the prosperity of his rational creation here, as to favor man with a revelation of his will; nor on the divine legation of Moses, who furnished the record containing a summary detail of the Sabbath; nor need I prove that the first three chapters of Genesis are to be taken literally, and not be considered a significant *myth*;—the divine legation of Moses and the literalness of his narrative, are looked upon, as conceded by you.

I am aware that it has been averred, that Moses spoke, in Genesis, of the Sabbath, by *anticipation;* and that the historian, writing after it had been instituted at Mt. Sinai, *there* gives the *reason* of the institution—that it did not exist prior to the egress of the Israelites out of Egypt, 2500 years posterior to the commencement of our race. This was the opinion of Dr. Paley, as discussed in his Moral Philosophy. It is readily admitted that the references to the Sabbath, during the patriarchal periods, are not very clear. Moses nowhere gives a professed history of the Sabbath; neither did he of the rite of circumcision. But still there are expressions scattered through his general narratives which serve as a way-mark to this matter.

It is said in "the *process* of time" Cain and Abel offered sacrifices to the Lord, literally at the *division,* the section, of time—that is, the hebdomadal section. They brought their oblations—they sacrificed on the Sabbath.

Noah entered the ark *seven* days prior to the flood. In the emission of the raven and the dove, his explorers of the laved earth, especially of the latter, he observed the intermission of *seven* days; and, in all probability, he left the ark on the first day of the Jewish week.

At the introduction of the manna among the Israelites, which was prior to the giving of the Decalogue, which contains the injunction, "*Remember* the Sabbath to keep it holy," Moses explained certain phenomena in relation to that food, in language which obviously indicates that the previous existence of the Sabbath was a known fact. In that case, he did not use the language of *injunction* in relation to the Sabbath, but of *explanation.* Nor did he, in any other of his narratives alluding to this matter, speak by way of *command,* until he furnished the summary of moral laws embodied in the Decalogue; and there the verbiage of the injunction is such as indicates the prior existence of the institution—"*Remember* the Sabbath to keep it holy."

In speaking, then, of the authority for

the observance of the Sabbatical time, we may well pause a little, right at this period of its history. We find it here a part and parcel of a code of laws in which the shrewdest jurists have never been able to find a flaw, to detect a deficiency or superfluity—a code in relation to which one of the most profound civilians, who thought he could successfully negative every claim of Moses to a divine mission, observed he could not perceive whence *its perfection came,* unless from the perfect Governor of the universe.

Is, then, the Sabbatical institution an indispensable *constituent of a complete moral, code, or system of moral laws?* Does it belong to the number of those laws or institutions which are *essential* to human happiness? Certainly. What are moral laws? I reply, such as tend to the elevation and happiness of moral agents. The supreme object of action, is happiness, which, however, lies only in the direction of moral actions. Complete happiness implies an easy and undisturbed *state* and *action* of all the powers and endowments pertaining to a rational, moral, and conscious existence. All laws, then, are moral that have a tendency to lead to such a consummation. Stealing is immoral because it interferes with the means of happiness of others—so is false testimony, adultery, etc.

The Sabbath belongs to the category of *moral laics,* because it stands inseparably connected with matters entering deeply into the temporal and eternal well-being of mankind; and as all the other laws included in the Decalogue are beyond abrogation by man—are of divine authority and of abiding obligation, so is that which pertains to the Sabbath.

The authority for the Sabbath is also seen in the divine admonitions to the Jews in relation to it, and the severe penalties inflicted by the Lord, on the violators of it. In Jeremiah xvii, 21-28, we have the following language: "Thus says the Lord, take heed to yourselves, and bear no burdens on the Sabbath day, nor bring it in by the gates of Jerusalem—neither carry forth a burden out of your houses on the Sabbath day—neither do ye any work, but hallow ye the Sabbath as I commanded your fathers, but they obeyed not, neither inclined their ears but made their neck stiff, that they might not hear nor receive any instruction. And it shall come to pass, if ye diligently *hearken to me,* saith the Lord, to bring no burdens through the gates of the city on the Sabbath day, but hallow the Sabbath to do no work therein; then shall there enter into the gates of the city, kings and princes sitting upon the throne of David, riding in chariots, and on horses, they and their princes, the men of Judah and the inhabitants of Jerusalem; and the city shall remain forever. But if ye will not hearken unto me to hallow the Sabbath day, and not bear burdens, even entering in at the gates of Jerusalem on the Sabbath day; then will I kindle a fire in the gates thereof, and it shall devour the palaces of Jerusalem, and it shall not be quenched."

Again, Nehemiah xiii, 17, 18: "Then I contended with the nobles of Judah, and said unto them: what evil thing is this that ye do, and profane the Sabbath day? Did not your fathers thus, and did not our God bring all this *evil* upon us and upon this city? Yet, ye bring more *wrath* upon Israel by profaning the Sabbath." An institution, the violation of which induces such fearful visitations as the Jews *have* and *are now enduring,* must have divine authority.

Again, the diversity of our endowments, physical, intellectual, and moral, makes it necessary for our happiness, to use the means originally designed to keep them in the best condition, and conduct them to an end allied to the great object of our existence—hence the necessity of rest for the body, and leisure and means of improvement for the moral and intellectual elements.

These means are embodied in the Christian

Sabbath. That our physical structure needs periodical rest is apparent to the commonest observer, in the succession of day and night. The shade of the night silences the melody of the grove—hushes the din of active life and allays the fervor of worldly pursuits. "Sleep, nature's sweet restorer," wraps the weary toiler in his mantle of forgetfulness until the birth of a new day. Is this periodical nightly rest adequate to restore the full measure of exhausted energy? A certain amount of nervous fluid is necessary to keep our physical man in an active and healthy condition. Nightly repose is insufficient to keep up the requisite complement. It has been repeatedly proclaimed from the tribunals of physiology, that to the nocturnal, the superaddition of other periodical repose is necessary for conducting earthy existence to the *good* which infinite wisdom has allotted to it. And from the same source, we are taught that no repose is so conducive to this end, as the septenary, or every seventh day. More *frequent* would be an excess adverse to the interests of social and civil life, and *less frequent,* inadequate for the proper restoration of wasted energies. France, in the reign of infidelity and terror, abrogated the Christian Sabbath, and substituted the decades, that is, enjoined cessation from labor every ten days. But experience and observation compelled the abandonment of that diversion, and imperiously demanded a return to the hebdomadal or weekly.

Experiments in continuous labor, disregardful of the Sabbatical recurrence, have clearly demonstrated, that weekly repose is essential to comfortable and protracted existence. It has been ascertained that among horses and other beasts of burden that were subjected to daily and incessant toil, four times the mortality occurred, that did among those that had weekly rest.

Of two thousand laborers, who had been induced by the offer of double wages for labor done on the Sabbath, on some public work, the majority became subjects of most afflictive diseases, in many instances issuing in premature mortality. In the late war, it was a matter of common observation, that when the soldiery had to labor incessantly, for, weeks on some fortification, disease and death were more abundant among them.

Unremitting labor breaks down the stoutest spirits, and extinguishes the most effective motives to exertion. Every individual compelled, by the force of circumstances, to labor without days of rest, finds the effect not only a decay of strength, but also the diminution of the aggregate amount of productive effort. Health, strength, genius, and all the functions of the mind and body, are inevitably prostrated by unremitting toil. He that labors faithfully six days, and rests the seventh, will, in a given time, accomplish more than if he were to labor without intermission during the whole period. The institution of the Christian Sabbath is exactly adapted to the organism of human nature. Like the recurrence of balmy night, it frees the mind from corroding cares, disenthralls the body from servile labor, and prepares it for returning efforts.

The Sabbath meets toiling man, and *exacts* rest. The plow must stand still in the field; the hammer must lie silent on the anvil; the hum and din of machinery must cease; the roar of the locomotive must be silenced; the merchant lock up his store; the judge descend from the bench; the politician leave the arena of fierce discussion; grateful stillness prevails in the hamlet, the village and the city. Wherever the Sabbath bell is heard, it checks the rush of earth's millions in their pursuit of the world, and cites them to the sanctuary, and to bow in the presence of the Lord their maker. The eager mind is forced to *pause* amid its selfish plans of pleasure and frantic schemes of wealth and aggrandizement, and is made to think of death and judgment, of God and his commandments.

The law of the Sabbath is not only written in the Decalogue, but is also most legibly inscribed in our physical constitution. But the needs of man extend beyond mere repose for the body. He needs leisure for the improvement of his higher endowments. He is a social being, as such made for social intercourse with his fellows, not in the low grounds of carnal indulgence, but under circumstances highly conducive to the elicitation of his benevolence, humanity, cordiality, and devotion; such social intercourse the Sabbath furnishes. So far as our social element requires the suspension of worldly pursuits, the Sabbath is adapted to the exigency. The conjugal, parental, and filial feelings are all cherished by the observance of the Sabbath. Freed from the cares and the labors of the week, the family collecting around the social hearth, forms a circle in which the tender and delightful feelings are enjoyed in the freshness of a new creation. In this enjoyment, the peasant is equal to the monarch. With his children at his knees, and the partner of his cares and loves by his side, he may enjoy a day of rest, no less refreshing to his heart than to his body.

Man's intellect, also, has wants which the Sabbatical institution can, to a great degree, meet. It has been questioned by some, whether the intellect is ever at rest. Well, suppose it is ever active, it certainly needs a change of thought. He who thinks upon but one subject, becomes a monomaniac—whether it be on money, on acquisition, on gratification, or any other of the common interests of life. The recurrence of the day of rest is calculated to recover man from any unbroken influence that may have fascinated him, especially if he is inclined to use the day according to its original intention.

Ceasing from labor, frequenting the sanctuary—placing himself under efficient and scriptural pulpit instruction, he may be disenchanted from earth's influences, and furnished with new subjects for his contemplation. The regular recurrence of the Christian Sabbath, and the benignity of its character, are well adapted to induce a preparation to meet it. Cleanliness, cheerfulness, moral and intellectual improvement, are the natural results of its appointment. The neat and well-arranged apartments of the home, the quiet and cheerful aspects of the family, and the intercourse of congenial and tranquil minds, tend alike to the improvement of the *understanding* and the solace of the heart. Nor does the intellectual nature of man stand in need of the periodical recurrence of the Sabbath.

Man is a moral agent—*sinner*—needs a preparation for the enjoyment of higher and holier circles than earth affords. He is the repository of a religious element which will manifest itself in some shape before its entire suppression within him—will manifest itself, either in blind superstition, wild fanaticism, or in enlightened piety. With the proper culture of this element of our nature, the Sabbath stands in close alliance.

Now, an institution that stands so signally connected with interests entering so deeply into the well-being of mankind, has undeniably a *moral complexion,* and must of necessity be included in a *complete code of* morals, such as the Decalogue, and is, therefore, like *all other moral laws,* of abiding obligation.

In view, then, of the primeval sanctification and benediction of this institution by the Lord—in view of its inclusion in the Decalogue—in view of the divine reprehensions to the Jews for their violation of it, and in view of its adaptedness to the physical and higher endowments of man, we cannot avoid to come to the conclusion that it is of divine authority to a duration commensurate with that of time itself. It is undoubtedly within the province of my assigned labor, on the present occasion, to speak of the authority for the change of the day of rest, from the seventh to the first day of the week. In our text, the Son of Man claims lord ship over the Sabbath, and consequently, we must look to him for authority for this change. There are about five thousand of our fellow professors, within the bounds of our Union, who do not admit any authority for this transfer. In this respect, they are extremely *unique*.

The considerations, or arguments for the transfer, are such as to command the acquiescence of the great majority of the Christian profession. It seems to have been included in the prophecies respecting the promised Messiah, that his rest, in the original Sabbath, should be glorious. The Psalmist predicting the rejection of Christ, and his yet becoming the head of the corner, as be indeed did, by his resurrection from the dead, says: "This is the day which the *Lord has made,* we will be glad and rejoice in it." Ps. 118.

The language of these passages indicates a new Sabbath, "a *day made by the Lord,"* hence, called the Lord's day. Accordingly, our Lord made special visits to his disciples on this day; on this day he founded his church; on this day his disciples met for worship and acts of benevolence, and on this day John was in the spirit.

The authority for this transfer is also attested by the current of ecclesiastical history. Ignatius, a companion of the Apostles, says: *"Let* us no more Sabbatize, that is, keep the seventh day, but let us keep the Lord's day, on which our life arose." Justin Martyr, who lived at the close of the first, and the beginning, of the second century, says: "On the day we call Sunday is an assembly of all who live in the city or country, and the memoirs of the Apostles, and the writings of the prophets, are read." Irenaeus, a disciple of Polycarp, the disciple of John himself, and who lived in the second century, affirms, "that on the Lord's day, every one of us Christians keeps the Sabbath—meditating in the law and rejoicing in the works of God." Dionysius, bishop of Corinth, who lived in the time of Irenaeus, says in his letter to the church at Rome: "To-day we celebrate the Lord's day, when we read your epistle to us."

Thus, my hearers, I have presented to you some of the points that enter into the reasons for observing Sabbatical time, and for resting on the first instead of the seventh day.

In the contemplation of what our predecessors transmitted to us, we come in contact with institutions and interests to which they attached no common importance. Some of these originated, in the course of divine Providence, from the peculiar circumstances of the race—others were the direct and positive institutions of the Deity. In following these up the stream of time we arrive at their respective origins—some running eighteen hundred years into the past, others fifteen hundred years beyond that period; but when we pursue the Sabbatical institution to its birth, we are brought to within a few hours of the commencement of our race itself. Venerable institution! Can it be possible that as long as the Christian revelation shall obtain in human society, this will ever be extinguished? No! It is too replete with benignity—too deeply rooted in the minds of the good and virtuous, ever to be supplanted by any other day! The American family will have a day of rest, a day of relaxation, and so long as Christianity is cherished in its bosom, *that day will be the Lord's day.* But like all the blessings of a benign Providence, it can be abused, and prostituted to ignoble purposes. It can be either a curse or a blessing to this great nation—a *blessing,* if heeded according to its intentions—a *curse* if diverted from its legitimate use. Our population is about twenty-five millions, of which fully one-half are in their minority, and in need of parental control. Let twelve millions of youths lose every seventh day, and *go* where they please, and *do* what they please, and who can estimate the amount of evil induced by their hebdomadal relaxation.

From early, habitual violations of this institution, have grown the most shocking enormities that have disquieted human society.

In view of this, should I not charge every one of you, from the wealthiest and most influential of you, down to the humblest mother in this assembly, to use the influence you have over any of your fellow pilgrims, for the sanctification of this institution! The honor of God—the prosperity of our common country, and the purity and the eternal well-being of your families, demand it!

-----o-----

THE DISCIPLES, OR CAMPBELLITES.

When this body of professing Christians took their rise nearly forty years ago, they were considered by the orthodox and evangelical churches as heterodox to a considerable extent. Mr. Alexander Campbell was the leader of the sect, and his teachings had unbounded sway, in shaping the principles and discipline of the new church. The Baptists, from whom they seceded, met them in the field of controversy, and so did most of the other churches of the country; yet among the Baptists there were many who, from their previous teachings, naturally became allied to the Disciples, as they officially call themselves. I have had frequent opportunities of learning their present condition in the West; and, according to the best accounts, they are advancing steadily in the direction of orthodoxy and evangelism. The leading issues on which they set out seem now to be given up, or not dwelt upon; and they seem to be drinking into the evangelical spirit of experimental religion, and adopting the orthodox}- of other churches. Even Mr. Campbell himself seems to be willing to leave out of the count of important points those things on which formerly he laid so much stress. Whether the opportunities of proselyting are now as numerous or as favorable to the new Disciples as at the first, I will not decide; yet it is certain that they do not now, to any extent, pursue this course in order to gain accessions to their numbers. The pressure of the orthodox churches on the Disciples has been very great; perhaps, indeed, irresistible. The force of truth outside of their enclosure penetrated into the very heart of their churches, and imperceptibly reformed them.

The case of Mr. Campbell's churches is one which teaches useful lessons. In their example we see the folly of substituting human novelties for the truths of God, or of putting the traditions and doctrines of man in the place of the revelations of God. Those new-fangled notions, sooner or later, wear out, and are abandoned by their most zealous defenders,

The history of these people teaches us, too, the great value of our evangelical and orthodox churches. The truths which they hold are great and must prevail in the end. God is with them; and it teaches a lesson to all when they see their neighbors, the Disciples, gradually shaped into the mold of the truth and influence which surround them.

Nor is error the less so, because it assumes that its positions are from the word of God. Pretensions to a divine origin is a very common source of the greatest errors; and this is as fully exemplified by the Disciples as by any other people. Let us all, however, rejoice that they are gradually coming to the knowledge of the truth, and let us all give them the right band of fellowship as soon as this can be done in consistency with the truth itself.—*Western Christian Advocate*.

-----o-----

REMARKS.

The writer of the above certainly writes with great ease. His production reads much like an oracle. He is so accustomed to assumption; mere assertion; that such a thing as proof does not enter into his head. How easy to produce editorial, for those who take naked assumption as they would an oracle from heaven, base assertion as the most profound and infallible argumentation! Let us take a deliberate look at the assumptions in this precious production:

1. He assumes, that the popular religious sects in this country are evangelical, or orthodox.

2. He assumes, that "the Disciples, or Campbellites," were heterodox some forty years ago.

3. That, in their early history, they laid much stress upon many things of a very erroneous nature, though he unkindly fails to inform us what they were.

4. That many of these things are not now pressed.

5. That they are now approaching orthodoxy, or evangelicity.

6. That this happy effect is from the influence of the orthodox churches around us!

7. That they are actually teaching, or drinking into experimental religion.

8. That the orthodox churches should, as soon as they can, extend to them the hand of fellowship.

9. That *he knows* what is orthodox, or evangelical.

10. That *he knows* when the Disciples teach and press the truths of Christianity.

We can but look upon this as a little the coolest assumption and impertinence our eye has lit upon! What a luminous divine! What are the specifications? "The Disciples are advancing steadily in the direction of orthodoxy and evangelism!" Can he tell what that direction is? He says: "they are drinking into the evangelical spirit of experimental religion!" Pray, Doctor, what does that mean? We doubt if all the prophets, apostles, evangelists and martyrs of the first century of grace were here, whether they could interpret such an expression. What saint in the whole kingdom of God, can tell how a people would "drink into the evangelical spirit of experimental religion?" Never, till we have something more intelligible than this, will either priest or people know the scriptures or the power of God. Such words will do to confuse and mystify, but can never enlighten.

But we are approaching orthodoxy!

Indeed! but in what? We should like to know where the change is. That we are orthodox, or evangelical, in the true sense, or in the popular sense, has been and can be again, sustained beyond all controversy; but wherein we are any more orthodox or evangelical than we were from the beginning, we are at a loss to conceive, save that we have in defiance of all the sects around us, accumulated in numbers, established ourselves as a body, and gained the attention of the commonwealth, so as to satisfy our opponents that we cannot now be put down. Even the *W. C. Advocate* now finds that our position is invulnerable, and, to ease the matter off, he perceives a great change—a most encouraging proximity to orthodoxy! and this gracious effect is attributable to the influence of the precious orthodox churches around us! What a happy thing to have such precious influences upon us from without! In this happy proximity to orthodoxy, on our part, the *Advocate* "sees the folly of substituting human novelties for the truths of God, or putting the traditions and doctrines of men in the place of the revelations of God." May he profit much by this lesson.

But since we are becoming orthodox and likely to have the hand of fellowship extended to us, we must post up the account, and see if we are worthy of such distinguished favor. Let us make out a brief epitome.

1. The Holy Scriptures contain all things necessary to salvation, so that whatever is not read therein, nor may be proved thereby, is not to be required of any man. Therefore, the Methodist Discipline is not required.

2. All scripture given by inspiration is profitable, for doctrine, reproof, correction and instruction, that the man of God may be perfect, thoroughly furnished for every good work. Therefore, the Methodist Discipline is not required.

3. God's written word is the sufficient and only infallible rule, both of faith and

practice. Therefore, the Methodist Discipline is not required and useless.

4. The Lord laid but one foundation, spoke of building but one church, which Paul calls one body, one new man, one building, one temple, one husbandry, one kingdom and one household, the habitation of God through the spirit, the residence of the Holy Spirit, styled the church of Christ, the church of God, church of the Living God, pillar and support of the truth, salt of the earth and light of the world, through which, according to the eternal purpose of God, the unsearchable riches of Christ was to be made known, according to the commandment of the everlasting God, for the obedience of faith among all nations. Therefore, the Methodist church is a human novelty substituted for the church of God, in which traditions and doctrines of men predominate over the clear revelations of Heaven.

5. The one faith of the New Testament, the faith once delivered to the Saints, the gospel preached by the Apostles, which they published that men might believe, is that Christ died for our sins according to the Scriptures, that he was buried and rose from the dead according to the Scriptures, or, as John the Apostle, expresses it, that Jesus is the Christ the Son of God, and is the faith and the only faith that can give life to a perishing and lost world, as well as the only faith ever preached in the days of the Apostles to convert and save sinners. The confession that Jesus is the Christ the Son of God, is the gospel in fact, the creed upon which the new convert is admitted to baptism and received into the church, and the only creed the persecutors anciently labored to induce the Disciples to deny. This is the only faith that any man now has a right to preach, or require men to confess before they are admitted to baptism or received into the church. This being the only creed the Disciples have ever made converts to, and not being the Methodist creed, we cannot see the proximity to the Methodist church.

6. When persons are converted to Christ, the Disciples teach them all things which Jesus commanded, as found upon the pages of the New Testament, as the only rule of faith and life. This not being the rule of faith practiced or enjoined upon the Methodist church, we are unable to see any proximity toward that establishment.

7. The Disciples practiced the one immersion of the New Testament, invariably, for the remission of sins, as commanded on the day of Pentecost, taught by John Wesley and other Methodist authorities. This one immersion, in certain cases, is required in the Methodist Discipline, practiced by Methodist preachers, and, as a matter of course, admitted by them to be right. In this we are certainly orthodox.

8. Sprinkling or pouring, for baptism, being always in doubt, from the first case practiced to this hour, and wholly unauthorized in Scripture, though practiced by Methodists, is not orthodox nor catholic.

9. Infant baptism being in doubt and dispute from the first account of it, not known to the Bible, nor any writing of the first century, is not catholic nor orthodox.

10. The Methodist Discipline, not believed, subscribed to, nor practiced by any party in Christendom but one, is not orthodox nor catholic.

11. The Holy Scriptures, being the only and the sufficient rule of the faith and practice of the Disciples, admitted by all but Romanists to be right, is orthodox, catholic and evangelical.

B. F.

Weak princes flatter, when they want the power To curb their people; tender plants must bend; But when a government is grown to strength, Like some old oak, rough with its armed ark, It yields not to the tug but only nods, And turns to sullen state.

THE BRACKEN ASSOCIATION OF UNITED BAPTISTS.

NUMBER I.

A copy of the minutes of the 57th Session of the above-named Association was sent me, as I was credibly informed, by Elder W. W. Gardner, a leading member of said body, and the writer of its very long circular letter, on "Restricted Communion." It was thought proper, doubtless, by Elder Gardner, that I should know the position of said body in reference to us, and all the rest of the religious world. Well, I acknowledge the receipt of the document, and present my thanks to the donor, as it gives me important information concerning the movements of the eight ordained ministers, and other delegates of the twenty-two churches, and some two thousand and two hundred members, of which said Association is composed; and also, an inkling of the movements of many "United Baptists," in various sections of our country. I shall proceed at once to pay my especial respects to said minutes, in all kindness and good feeling, but with "great plainness of speech."

The Association was held in this county (Nicholas), Ivy., "with the Mt. Olivet Church," embracing the first Friday, Saturday and Lord's day of September, 1856. It's minutes, constitution, rules of decorum, order of business, circular letter on "Restricted Communion," etc., make a pamphlet of some 40 pages octavo.

It appears from the minutes, that at the previous session of said body, Elder Gardner was appointed to prepare a circular letter, as above noted; and also, that a committee was appointed to "Revise the constitution, articles of faith, rules of decorum, and order of business of the Association." It is clear, then, that said body had on hands much more work than usual; and work, too, most fearfully responsible. For, to "Revise, correct and extend" a people's religious creed, is, I take it, a very responsible, if not a dangerous, undertaking.

In its preamble (see Appendix A.), to its works of revision, correction, etc., it says: "Whereas, it has been deemed right and proper, by the Bracken Association of United Baptists, to *revise, correct* and *extend* the constitution, *articles of faith,* rules of decorum, and order of business of said Association." The same "Preamble" states, that all the aforesaid revisions, corrections, and extensions of the articles of faith, etc., were "duly adopted and agreed upon by the unanimous vote of the Association."

It is worthy of special remark that, while in the preamble above named, ample provision has been made for future revisions and amendments of their "constitution and form of government," no provision has been made for revising, or in any wise changing their articles of faith. This, to me, is very significant, especially when taken in connection with what Elder Gardner says on page 37: *"We* (United Baptists), *hold the truth, the whole truth, and nothing but the truth!"* This is high ground for a Protestant, and especially for a United Baptist Protestant Association. And I cannot, therefore, persuade myself, although this assumption is made in the name of the Baptist Association, that even the majority of its members (I mean of the churches), will deliberately endorse it, for it is evidently Popish all over, and represents the Association in the very unenviable predicament, of wrestling with Pius the IX. for St. Peter's Chair!! This is very odd work for Baptists, who are such sticklers for civil and religious liberty; and, I apprehend, they will be worsted in the scuffle. The Church of Rome claims to be infallible, and as such claims to teach "the truth, the whole truth, and nothing but the truth and in harmony with this assumption, decrees that all Protestants are damnable heretics, living in mortal sin, and must perish everlastingly, unless they become reconciled to Romanism. And, therefore, the Catholic

Church claims the right, where it can be exercised with safety, of lashing heretics and pagans into conformity to their usages, by pains and penalties, even unto death. All this we expect from Catholics as in harmony with her claim to infallibility, and kindred claims. But by our highly Protestant Baptist friends, the claim to teach the truth, the whole truth, and nothing but the truth, sounds very strange in our ears! And do they, indeed, teach "the truth, the whole truth, and nothing but the truth!!" As a matter of course, then, they have arrived at perfection in Christian knowledge, and have no use for that exhortation of Peter, which requires Christians to grow in grace, and the knowledge of our Lord and Savior, Jesus Christ! And hence, perhaps, the reason why they have made no provision, in their late revision, correction, and extension, of their articles of faith, for any future correction of said creed. For, if, since its revision, correction, and extension, it now contains "the truth, the whole truth, and nothing but the truth," it would be ruinous to touch it. In the name of God, we say, hold on to it forever; and proceed forthwith to demonstrate to the whole religious world, your divine warrant for making said creed of 16 Articles; and that the quintessence of all Bible truth is contained in it! The moment you establish these positions, I pledge myself to join the United Baptists, and use my utmost endeavors to dispose all I can to do the same, and thus embrace "the truth, the whole truth, and nothing but the truth." What a glorious triumph this would be, over all religious parties!

The position assumed by the Association, forcibly reminds me of a "Dedication to the Pope," written by Bishop Hoadley, in the 18th century. He preached a sermon before George the I. on the words: "My kingdom is not of this world," in which he struck a blow at the High Church party, which almost drove them to madness, and which gave rise to the Bangorian controversy. He was the champion of civil and religious liberty, in his times, and the enemy of all tyranny, whether in Church or State. His "Dedication to the Pope," like his sermon before George the I., was intended to excuse the corruptions of the times. While, therefore, in that document his avowed object was to show to his Holiness, in cutting irony, how nearly they (of the Church of England), had approached to the glorious liberties, and privileges of the Church of Rome, his true object was, to expose the corruptions of said Church, by showing conclusively that she acted upon the same corrupt principles of the Church of Rome—the mother of harlots, and abominations of the earth. Said he: "The only difference which the most sharp-sighted among us can see between *you* and *us* is, that *you are infallible, and we are always in the right;* or, in other words, that *you cannot err, and we never do.* And, now (said the Bishop), we cannot but conclude, that the advantage is greatly on our side; for we have all the advantages of infallibility, without the absurdity of pretending to it, or, the more difficult task of proving a proposition so shocking to the human understanding."

So our friends of the Association have contrived to have all the advantages of infallibility, without the absurdity of pretending to it, or the more difficult task of proving it, for they "hold the truth, the whole truth, and nothing but the truth."

Unequivocally, the Church of Rome sets up no higher claim than this. It grieves us, therefore, to see our friend Gardner scuffling most awkwardly and unbecomingly, with the Pope for St. Peter's chair, with Elders Hunt, James, and others, begging for him.

What a strange sight! But other friends of the Association, I presume, do not mean to be Popish, or claim to be infallible. Their zeal for their "isms," and the tendencies of our fallen nature, have carried them away beyond Jerusalem into the territory of the Pope. Luther is reported to have said, that "every man is born with a Pope in him and Archbishop Whately has written a work entitled:"The errors of Romanism traced to their origin, in human nature." True enough! There is a downward tendency in human nature. "The flesh lusteth against the spirit." We may, , therefore, trace all the corruptions of true religion, in every age since the fall, as well as the corruptions of Romanism, to their origin in human nature; or, in other words, in harmony with Luther's truism, that all departures from, and corruptions of the truth, in all ages, may be ascribed to the influence of the old man, or the Pope, born with us. The ancient nations, under this influence, "changed the glory of the incorruptible God into an image made like to corruptible man, and to birds, and four-footed beasts, and creeping things." "Changed the truth of God into a lie, and worshipped and served the creature more than the Creator." The Jewish Commonwealth, or Church, under this same influence, made void the law of God, by their traditions. And, therefore, Messiah thus rebuked them:—"In vain do you worship me, teaching for doctrines the commandments of men." When we take into consideration, then, the tendencies of our nature, and the fact that our friends of the Association had a burning zeal for preserving, intact, the United Baptist Church; and that, in addition to all this, they were almost frightened out of their wits, at the report that had gone abroad, that they and the "Campbellites" were about to be united; and confident as they were, that such a result would kill off the "Baptist Denomination," it ought not, perhaps, to be thought strange that "the old man," for the time being, got the ascendency and drove them far away from home into Babylon. I hope, therefore, when they shall have time to reflect and get over their fright, they will right themselves. My sheet is full. More anon.

JOHN ROGERS.

-----o-----

A GREAT AND GOOD MAN FALLEN.

We cannot express the emotions of our heart, when the sad intelligence reached us, that Elder JOHN T. JOHNSON, whom we had so lately seen, from whom we had so recently received communications, some of which were just printed, had departed this life. When we last saw him, he was in apparent good health, full of life, cheerfulness, devotion and zeal for the great cause of humanity. In the last communications from him, he evinced that the work of the Lord was upon his soul. In the able and valuable discourses he preached in Covington, Ky., while with us, in October, he developed as much scriptural light, real genuine Christian spirit and piety, as any man ever did in our presence, in the same length of time. His noble bearing, kind and Christian, as well as gentlemanly deportment, with the most ardent love, won for him the approbation of all who were present at our Anniversaries. His whole being appeared engrossed in the great missionary work—the effort of the people of God to convert and save mankind.

We have been familiar with his reports of success, and reports of his success, made by others, for more than twenty years, and long have been anxious to know the secret of his success, but never had an opportunity to hear him, except in a single discourse, till the visit alluded to above. We, therefore, gave him special attention, and we are now prepared to say that we have never known a man who could bring the force and power of Christianity to bear upon a community, to better advantage, than he. He loved the Lord most devoutly, which appeared without an effort on his part. He loved all mankind, and entered the assembly with a zealous determination to make the best effort in his power to save man. He had strong faith, and was so identified with the Lord, the Bible, Christianity, the church and the people of God, that the work of the Lord was his element. For persevering industry, he scarcely had an equal among his preaching brethren.

Some twenty-six years ago, he gave up the practice of law for the Christian ministry, which we heard him mention with pleasure the last time we saw him. From the day he gave up the law to the end of his career of usefulness and happiness on earth, he was certainly one of the most laborious, untiring and persevering advocates of the faith of Christ the world contained. Nor did he ever appear to have a burden upon him, to repine, murmur or complain. With him the burthen of Christianity was light and the yoke easy. No glaring despondency found a lodgment in his heart; nor did any discouraging words escape his lips or pen. Onward and upward was the word, with him, in a career of happiness and usefulness, till the very passage over Jordan, where he entered Heaven's bright and glorious chariot, escorted by angels away to the midst of the paradise of God, while his memory is cherished in many thousands of the hosts of the children of God.

Many were the battles he fought, and numerous were the conquests over the enemy, gained through his noble efforts; but his last battle has been fought, his last trial is over, and the last victory won. We shall see his face no more on earth; hear his warning voice in the great assembly no more. The Lord took him. He rests with the fathers. As Jesus lives forever and ever, so shall he live. Blessed be God! we shall see him, and be with him, if we live as he lived. We lament his loss to the cause; we mourn that such an example for young men, in the ministry, should be taken from us; but, while we lament, our loss is his eternal gain.

He is with the Lord, whom he loved and served faithfully to the end. He is with many, brought to the kingdom of God through his instrumentality, and with all the pure and holy.

We tremble to see such men as the beloved and lamented JOHN T. JOHNSON fade! Where are the young men who will fill their places? Many young men are coming into the field; some of them very good; yet there are but few of them that seem to think of devoting themselves to the work—working for God, as he did. Where are the men who will traverse from State to State, from town to town, from city to city, from neighborhood to neighborhood, and incessantly preach the word of the living God as he did? Where are the men to inspire the brotherhood with such nobleness of heart, zealous perseverance for righteousness and moral excellence, as he did? We trust the Lord will give us such. To Him we must look for help.

Since writing the above, the following, from the Kentucky State Board, came to hand, which we cheerfully insert, that it may speak for itself: B. F.

-----o-----

LEXINGTON, KY., Dec. 29, 1856.

At a regular meeting of the Board of Directors of the Kentucky State Meeting, held on the above date, the death of Elder John T. Johnson was announced, and the following resolutions were unanimously adopted:

1. *Resolved,* That the meeting have heard, with deep regret and unfeigned sorrow, of the death of our highly esteemed and much-beloved Brother, Elder JOHN T. JOHNSON, lately one of our State evangelists.

2. *Resolved,* That this Board have especial reason to deplore the death of Bro. JOHNSON, from the fact of his having been connected with us, more or less, since our organization, as one of our most efficient, laborious and devoted evangelists, ready and willing to sacrifice ease and comfort, that the gospel

might be preached and sinners converted to God.

3. *Resolved,* That in the life of Bro. JOHNSON, from the time he put on the Lord Jesus Christ, until the day he ceased from his labors, we have an example worthy of imitation, and to which all praise is due, especially in his cheerfully and promptly relinquishing his flattering prospects and growing influence as an American statesman for the cause of his Lord and Master, and that he might preach to perishing sinners salvation through the blood of the lamb.

4. *Resolved,* That in the death of Bro. JOHNSON, the cause of primitive Christianity, and the Bible alone as the only divinely appointed rule of faith and practice, has lost one of its ablest, fearless and most devoted advocates and defenders.

5. *Resolved,* That although we are called to mourn the loss of our venerable and much-beloved brother in Christ, yet we sorrow not as those who have no hope, but rather rejoice in the consolation that he died as he lived, a soldier of the Cross and a faithful follower of the Lamb.

6. *Resolved,* That the immediate relations of our deceased brother be furnished with a copy of these resolutions, and a tender of our condolence on this their bereavement; and that the *Millennial Harbinger,* the *Christian Review* and the *Christian Age* be requested to publish these resolutions in their respective papers.

OLIVER FARRER, Chairman.
JOSEPH WASSON, Secretary.

A SIMILE:—

Decrepitude steals on us with the secrecy of sleep
(No snow falls lighter than the snow of age. None with such subtlety benumbs the frame),
Till we forget sensation, and lie down Dead in the lap of our primeval mother.
She throws a shroud of turf and flowers around us, Then calls the worms, and bids them do their office;—Man giveth up the ghost—and where is he?

EVIDENCES OF CHRISTIANITY. NUMBER II.

There is no man of sane mind who cannot believe. It is as natural and rational for men to believe, under proper circumstances, as it is for them to think. No faculty possessed by a human being, is more readily, frequently and universally exercised, than that of believing. For a man to affect that he is so organized or constituted, that he cannot believe, is preposterous in the highest degree. There is no sane-minded human being so organized as to be incapable of believing. This is not only true, but a large portion of all the important and even business transactions pertaining to this life, are based in faith and by faith carried out. The man who ridicules acting upon faith, ridicules a large proportion of all the important actions and transactions in this world. Why does the speculator offer one dollar more to-day than he did yesterday per barrel for flour? Because he believes the news he has received, of an advance in some other market. Why does that pork dealer advance the price one dollar per barrel? Because he believes the news of an advance in some other market. Why does that trader refuse that bank bill? Because he believes the statement in the detector, that it is under par. Look through the various departments in life, business transactions and all, and see what a vast amount of it is done by faith. All business men are daily and hourly acting in matters where thousands of dollars are involved, upon faith, and acting with great confidence too. Look at that man at the post-office, opening a letter and reading! In a few minutes you see him stopping quickly and closing an engagement, involving thousands of dollars! What is he acting upon? Faith in the letter just received and read. Look at that other man, waiting for a dispatch. Presently he receives and reads it, In a few minutes he is waiting the arrival of the cars. As the cars approach, you notice him eyeing the passengers as they come out of the train. Presently he rests his eye upon a man. In the next moment the man is arrested! What is he acting upon? Faith in the telegraphic dispatch he had just received. Thus, we perceive men are constantly acting upon *faith*, in all the affairs of this life.

Is it possible that men who are thus constantly, and without hesitation, acting upon faith, will have the assurance to apologize for their unbelief in matters of religion, by saying they cannot believe? It, will also be observed that the men thus acting are not merely a few credulous and thoughtless persons, but business men of all classes—men of the first order of mind, thus showing that they *can* believe, and *do* believe, in matters of great importance, and thus demonstrating that they can believe in matters of religion, as well as others, if they will but give a candid attention to the evidence. The same faculties of the mind exercised in believing the news of the day, political, commercial, or of sickness, health, or accidents, etc., are exercised in believing the divine testimonies, The same mind that believes the testimony of men, is exercised in believing the testimony of God. The difference in the effect produced upon the human soul, by divine testimony, or divine faith, from that produced by human testimony, or what is purely human faith, is not that the same mind, or the same faculties of the mind are not exercised in both cases, nor is it owing to the difference between divine and human testimony; but the difference is in the things believed—the difference between divine and human things believed. Heavenly things believed would, beyond all dispute, make a different impression from that produced by the belief of earthly things, however true they might be. A mere earthly truth, even if proved by divine testimony, could produce no more than an earthly impression; but a heavenly truth, if proved by earthly testimony, would produce a heavenly impression. The same mind that understands and believes that there is an advance in the flour market, believes that the Lord rose from the dead, but the effect produced by the faith in one instance is very different from that produced in the other-instance; not because different powers are exercised in believing; nor because the testimony differs; but because the things believed differ.

The relation a thing believed sustains to the believer, is the main cause of its effect upon him. Robert Owen, who professed to have read and traveled forty years, without being able to find any evidence of the truth of Christianity, has lately become a believer in Spiritualism. How is it, that he is so slow to believe in one case, but so ready to believe in the other? The reason is to be found in the relation these two things to be believed sustain to him. The belief in modern Spiritualism involves nothing, requires nothing and promises nothing. It is merely a speculative subject for vain and idle curiosity, placing no man under any new obligations who believes it. It is a very suitable thing to catch a man of a perverted mind and heart; one who has rejected Jesus, resisted the testimonies of the Holy Spirit, and despised the Bible during an earthly pilgrimage of many years, which God has mercifully and graciously granted him. But the fact that Jesus of Nazareth is the Son of God—that he is divine—that he is alive and lives forever and ever, is a fact sustaining a different relation to time. It is not a speculative fact for idle curiosity; not a mere theme for empty, cold and unfeeling hearts; for idle, confused and wandering brains; but a fact, intimately connected with all mankind; a fact, in which the destinies of all men are involved; one, too, bearing upon the lives and conduct of all men. Here is the reason that many are so slow to believe this, the greatest and most important of all the facts presented for the belief of mankind; it *requires a holy life*.

A strange feature truly is it, in men, that they should prefer to believe that which requires nothing, proposes nothing and promises nothing, to that requiring the purest life, most exalted character, and ennobled feelings, promising the approbation of the Almighty now, and eternal joy in the world to come!

In entering the evidence of Christianity we are anxious to determine precisely what it is that skeptics deny. It is not that there was such a person as Jesus of Nazareth; for all skeptical writings and conversations abound in references to him, as a real person. Nor is it that he was the author of the Christian religion, for all skeptics refer to him as the founder of Christianity. Nor yet do skeptics deny the location where Christianity had its rise. Nor have they denied the time when it rose. If then, they admit that there was such a person, that he was the author of Christianity, that he lived where the Bible says he lived, and at the time when the Bible says he did, what is it that they deny? Nor is it the account the Bible gives of the customs of ancient times, the reference to the governments of the world, their location and boundaries, the different rulers or civil officers incidentally mentioned, the institutions of the various countries alluded to, the cities, towns, villages and hamlets mentioned; the "certain waters," rivers, lakes and seas, incidentally introduced, nor yet the geography of the country, so far as found in the sacred canon; nor is- it the reference to the various streets, lanes, roads and highways, that skeptics deny. Nor is it the moral lessons, the purity of life, the uprightness of character, the love to all mankind, love to our neighbor as to ourself, the requirement to do unto all men as we would have them do to us, caring for widows and orphans, the aged and infirm, the poor and needy, found in the Bible, that skeptics deny. What, then, is it that they deny? If they admit all this, what is it that they are opposed to?

The trouble is, *its claim to divine authority*. They prefer to regard the Bible as a good old book of *advice,* in which is a convenient place for a family record, and wish the privilege to quote a proverb of Solomon, an expression of David or John the Apostle, with the understanding that they receive what *they* think good and wise and reject the balance. Strip it of all claims of divine authority and they have no further war with it. Hence the efforts of skeptics have been to strike the idea of divine authority out of the Bible. But the war upon the subject has been conducted in a most unwise and injudicious manner, on the part of many who are sincerely and honestly friends of the Bible. At sometimes they have apprehended that it devolved upon them to defend all the views and doctrines that the party to which they belong, think can, by some hook or crook, be proved by the Bible. At another time they apprehend that they are bound to understand, fully explain and show the relevancy of every expression of the whole Bible from the beginning of Genesis to the end of Revelations; answer every objection, explain every difficulty and fully clear up and dispense every doubt started, stereotyped, iterated and reiterated from Paine down to the beardless skeptic of nineteen years, who speaks of "contradictions" in the Bible. But this, we undertake to say, no Christian is under the least obligation to do. We are not to infer, because the astronomer does not tell us what gave the earth its momentum as it whirls upon its own axes, or its momentum in its mighty circle around the sun, in the first place, that the existence of these revolutions is to be questioned. The fact that these revolutions exist may be believed and confided in rationally, by him who cannot tell where the momentum comes from, or give the immediate cause of it, or could not answer many other questions of a similar nature. Indeed, many points be mentioned, that he might not only be unable to explain, but that might appear to him contradictory, and he might still consistently believe in the revolutions most confidently. The revolutions of the earth he may know to be a settled matter, but those things that he cannot explain, or that appear contradictory to him, he doubts not are things that he does not understand, for the lack of a more widely extended horizon or expanded information. He attributes the difficulty to his want of information—his ignorance, and not to an actual inconsistency or absurdity, in the solar system.

The same is true of the Bible. We have never had the vanity to think that we could explain every difficulty, solve every question, or clear up every hard place, or reconcile every apparent incongruity; but in the place of thinking that there are real difficulties, unanswerable questions, or real irreconcilable incongruities, we doubt not, if we had the information, every difficulty could be removed, every question could be answered, and every apparent incongruity cleared up. We have such incontestable evidence of a divine foundation—infallible and immovable bases for the hope of all nations, that we stand upon that as fixed. All besides stands upon this, and till this rock is removed, no side questions, irrelevant points, or remote reasonings can depreciate our confidence in the everlasting source of comfort and hope for mankind.

But we cannot present this rock fully now, and the exact issue between believers and unbelievers; but we must close the present article by inquiring why any man should be opposed to Jesus Christ, the Bible and the Christian religion? What reason can any man give for such opposition? No man believes that the Lord Jesus Christ ever made any human being worse. No man sincerely believes that the Bible makes any person worse; or that the Christian religion does any

Vol., No. 2.—2.

harm to any one of our sinful race. No human being solemnly believes that any harm could result from the universal prevalence of pure Christianity, as set forth upon the pages of the New Testament, throughout the world. All men, upon cool and deliberate reflection, must be satisfied, that if all peoples, nations, tribes and tongues of the earth, were fully under the power and influence of the Bible, mankind would be infinitely blessed by it. Not a skeptic in the world can give a reason for his opposition to the Lord Jesus and the Bible. O, that men knew Jesus! O, that they possessed his spirit and temper! O, that they would love him and be blessed by him!

B. F.

-----o-----

MISSIONARY SOCIETY.

Our esteemed and worthy brother, C. L. Loos, who has spent a year in our city, as evangelist in the Church, corner of Eighth and Walnut streets, so profitably and so much to the satisfaction of all, so far as known to us, and who was made Corresponding Secretary of the Christian Missionary Society, has seen fit to leave his position here, for what he conceives to be, under all the circumstances, an opening of Providence for more extended usefulness, as President of Eureka College, Illinois. May this prove, as he, no doubt, conscientiously believed it would be, a wise and prudent change on his part, and may the field of usefulness open to him according to his expectations and moral worth. Though we believe all here were desirous for him to have remained with us, and reluctantly yielded for him to leave, we are confident that he goes with the kindest wishes for his happiness and fullest confidence of all the holy brethren here.

His resignation, as Corresponding Secretary of the Missionary Society, has perplexed the Board somewhat, as changes here have an unhappy influence upon the interests of the Society. The Board, accordingly, corresponded with the President, Elder A. Campbell, and received suggestions from him. Acting upon these suggestions, the Board appointed us Corresponding Secretary, *pro tem.*, in the place of Bro. C. L. Loos. We have accepted the appointment, and shall enter into the work as fully and faithfully as possible, and do all for the Missionary cause in our power, till such time as some brother shall be agreed upon to take the position permanently.

The Bible and Publication Societies being discontinued, and the brethren in the Anniversary, in this city, in October last, agreeing, with great unanimity, to concentrate our energies upon the Missionary Society, is a proceeding, so far as we are informed, that meets the wishes of the brotherhood at large with more favor and general approbation than any move of the kind that has ever been made among us. Many fruits are coming up from different sections of country that speak louder than words. Holy men of God have volunteered, asked brethren for donations, obtained members and life-members, without retaining one farthing for their trouble. The lately deceased and lamented J. T. Johnson, did noble work of this kind, reports of which were in type in our office when the sad intelligence of his death reached us.

In the same manner, churches and individuals can act, if they prefer it, without any expense of agents, making their contributions for the Missionary Society and Sending them voluntarily. But we would remind any who think of the *expense* of agents, that we intend, as far as possible, obtaining preachers who are good missionaries, and as they pass through the country, have them preach, strengthen the brethren and make most devoted and godly efforts to convert sinners and advance the cause. We do not wish them to pass as mere tax-gatherers, but as missionaries— evangelists, doing the work of evangelists, and at some appropriate time, at each place, present the missionary cause and kindly and affectionately request the brethren to make a donation for the work. In their private intercourse obtain life-members and donations, without any of the old-fashioned labored speeches on contributions, or any of the offensive references to penurious instances that have occurred in sundry places.

This Society is now about as simple an arrangement as we can have for general, and especially foreign, missionary work. It will now be conducted on the score of the very best economy. All but a very small fraction will go directly to the object designed by the donors. From the spirit manifested in regard to it, we can see no reason why we may not do a great and good work by means of this Society. Brethren, what do you say of this work? Are you favorable to it? It is the most simple and safe arrangement that could be made, professing no authority over churches, interfering nothing with their independence, government or officers in any way; but an arrangement simply of combining means so as to concentrate your efforts upon important points remote from, and out of the reach of, single churches or individuals, in usual local operations.

Things are now taking, we think, a rational and proper form. The Bible Union is the great Translating, Revising Bible Society, doing precisely what we desire in the Bible cause. The Missionary Society is a medium for us to operate through, as a general body, throughout the nation in such works as single churches or individuals cannot do. The State Missionary Societies open the way for the voluntary contributions to be combined, united and concentrated in sending the Word to destitute regions, and penetrating important points, as single churches or individuals could not do. If the brethren generally make a moderate contribution to these objects, two or three times in the year, besides what they do in their churches at home, it will certainly be a means of great good.

We have only definitely fixed upon one mission yet. We allude to the Jerusalem Mission. Dr. Barclay, we trust, will, in a short time, be prepared to return to the ancient city. But we have no idea of stopping at this. We ought, before this year expires, to have at least two missionaries sent to England, and one to Australia. If this can be accomplished, as it can with perfect ease, if the brethren generally will make but a reasonable effort, in the ' place of embarrassing us at home, it is precisely the work to keep up an interest. Brethren, let us hear from you as extensively and frequently as possible on the subject. The Lord help us all to do all in our power to save the perishing millions of our fallen race!

All communications on the subject, applications for agencies, enquiries, contributions, etc., should be addressed: "Benj. Franklin, Cor. Sec'y, Cincinnati, Ohio," and they will be promptly responded to. B. F.

-----o-----

INDUSTRY IN THE MINISTRY—ITS SUPPORT.

6

BROTHER FRANKLIN—Dear Sir: I have been a reader of the *American Christian Review,* edited by you, and can truthfully say, I have read it with profit and pleasure as a general thing; some articles, it is true, I could have wished had slept in obscurity, or had been more carefully dressed in the beautiful garments of Bible truth and sober reason by their authors before they asked their publication in one of our deservedly popular journals. I still, however, had the consolation of believing that none of the less excellent essays were calculated to do harm. I felt, therefore, no disposition to complain, and not the least desire to trouble you or your readers with my thoughts or criticisms on any subject, until cast my eye on an article in the December issue, headed: "Industry in the Ministry—Its Support," which I feel disposed, in the spirit of Christian courtesy, to review, and I wish you distinctly to understand, we agree—at least, I felt pleased until you commenced writing under figure 4, and I ask you to re-examine the essay embracing the introduction, and what you write under figures 1, 2, and 3, and reconcile, if you can, the two parts of your own piece. In the first part you admit the well-being of the church requires a certain class of men to devote their whole time to the preaching of the Word, and that such preachers ought to receive an adequate support, and to withhold it is to crush the ministry and destroy the church. In short, you admit all that sober reason could ask, or the Word of God require, of preacher or congregation, and write like B. Franklin until you commence writing under figure 4, and there, my dear brother, you make a sweeping expression which, if true, will paralyze all said before, viz: "Not one word is said in the Scriptures about a plan of ministerial support, for the good and valid reason they had no plan for any such object and needed none." My dear brother, does the Sacred Record sustain you in this assertion? If it does it is extreme folly to talk about support, or think about it, because every sane mind knows nothing can be done without a plan. But the mystery to me is, how a man can read the letters of Paul and fail to see a plan, and words enough spoken about it, to make him understand, not only that they had one, but a law, a positive law; hence, the regularity of their operations. He exhorts the brotherhood by all the love of Christ, exhibited in his becoming poor that we might become rich, to encourage their liberality, but commands, with apostolic authority, each man to bear his own burden. By comparing the 16th chapter of 1st Corinthians with the 6th of Galatians, I think an unbiased mind will arrive at the following conclusions:

1st. The first Christians all had a plan, a law for the support of preachers. God was its author.

2d. It was so plain all understood it.

3d. Such a plan would now, among us, be called the ad valorem system.

My dear brother, all the bargaining, chaffering, bartering and settling prices, so much complained of by you, were common occurrences among the first Christians, and had the sanction of the Great God Himself, who, by the statute of the old law, had said, "Thou shalt not muzzle the ox that treadeth out the corn," and hereby prepared our minds to respect and venerate the new law, which has ordained, "that they who preach the gospel shall live of the gospel." Brother Franklin, why did you select the "making a piece of railroad" as your comparison? Is it because it is a modern invention? But is it any more a matter of barter or contract than other labor? Certainly not. And here is an important matter: you overlook all the kinds of labor then understood, which all required the same sort of bargaining, chaffering, etc. The Holy Spirit has used, as illustrating the apostolic plan, plowing, sowing, feeding sheep, planting a vineyard, overseeing or managing: and not only shows by comparison, but by positive assertion, that price was agreed upon (for you will agree that a full definition of the word hire is price agreed upon), and a barter entered into, by which they who preached the gospel lived of the gospel.

You then proceed to make a comparison about doctors and lawyers, as if these professional men, or some of them, lived just from the hap-hazard gifts of the people, when you know such a thing was never thought of. Such reasoning (if you think I ought so to misname it), may deceive and mislead your thoughtless readers, but certainly it can have no effect other than to disgust an intelligent mind. After giving a fair description of a preacher, you advise him to go wherever he can find work, say nothing about pay; you add, the Lord will put it into the hearts of his people to supply his wants, and that there is not one of such preachers who has the least trouble to find a place or pay, unless his manners are so untoward as to be repulsive. My experience confirms what you say about place, but teaches me a very different lesson about pay. I have seen the great and truly accomplished B. W. Stone, with all his popularity, twice driven by pecuniary wants to stop evangelizing and go to teaching school. I once, in the company of B. F. Hall and my father, after having traveled precisely on your principles three months, in Indiana, planting churches, or building up such as had been planted, with good success, yet when we started home we just had money enough to feed our horses one night and pay our ferriages; we ourselves had to ride ninety miles without eating. My experience does not differ from my reading. Who, that has read the life of Wesley, can hope to be sustained without system or arrangement, when that great and good man, before he got his societies organized, had sometimes, after faithfully preaching to large admiring congregations, to make his dinner on a few blackberries for want of a shilling. My dear brother, the old Christian preachers, while they recommended your plan to others, they lived it themselves, and if you would just show your faith by your works, it would convince you much sooner than I can. Do you cease editing a paper, for which you require a stipulated price in advance, and when you go out to preach, instead of going to the rich and well-organized churches, as you have been in the habit of doing, take your own advice, go to every nook and corner, say not a word about money, and you will soon come to your sobered senses, or the demon of fanaticism is not one of the kind which goes out by fasting. You will soon learn that you are but flesh and blood and not able to work miracles, and that God will not work one to save those from pain who depart from reason. Your brother in hope of immortality.

WILL F. MAVITY.

REMARKS.

We feel truly waked up and refreshed by the above. We have met with no document "pitching into" us after this sort for a long time. Still, after recovering somewhat from the first shock and looking over the matter a little coolly and deliberately, as our brother should have done before his attack, we find the damage done much less than one at first would have supposed. Upon all we have said of *Industry in the Ministry,* the main point in the article complained of, our brother has made no attack. Nor has he made any assault upon our remarks upon the *Support of the Ministry.* Indeed, his attack touches but two points, as follows:

1. Our inconsistency, in first preaching that the ministry must be supported, and then, that there is no *plan* and that chaffering, bargaining, etc., is wrong.

2. He insists that there is a plan; that chaffering, bargaining, etc., is right, and he attempts to prove it by Scripture.

As to inconsistency, we think no one will perceive it, for it is only based upon his assumption, that the ministry will certainly not be supported without a plan. But this is precisely the point to be proved. We do not admit any such assumption. We have not said, and do not intend to say, one word against the support of the ministry, for as we said before, the ministry must be supported. Indeed, one objection we have to the continued discussion of plans, is that it is directly in the way of the support of the ministry. Plans and discussions of plans support no ministry. It is a great cry and no wool. When it is in a brother's heart to give Bro. Mavity five dollars, what plan does he need to do it? But our brother arrays some illustrious examples to show that we are mistaken, but he must first prove that this deficiency originated from their denying that there is any plan, or from the lack of a plan. It was not the lack of *a plan,* in either the case of Wesley or Stone, that caused them to lack support, but it was the fact that liberality was not established in the hearts of the people, or perhaps, in some instances, to the fact that their brethren had not wherewith to give.

As to there being any plan in the New Testament for supporting the ministry, except for the disciples to give as they dispose in their hearts, no man has been or will be able to find anything of the kind. We know of no intimation that the weekly contribution was ever appropriated to the support of the ministry. But since Bro. Mavity guesses at our preaching for rich churches, we beg leave to inform him that such is not the fact. We were preaching in a town where there is no church at all, when We wrote the article complained of, upon the principle we recommend, and were well supported in doing so. The REVIEW is a different thing, as we have to pay out a large amount of cash for paper, printing, etc., yet we give away many copies in the course of the year.

As to stipulating the amount, or giving some reliable assurances to a brother for a certain term of labor, we have no uncommon squeamishness; but as a matter of prudence and propriety, the less is *said* and the more *done* the better. As a general rule, the nearer the preacher will trust in God and the generosity of the brethren, the greater the good that will be done. We need not look for generosity from the brethren, unless we show them that we have confidence that they will be generous. Preaching plans, setting forth schemes, making contracts—so much preaching for so much money, and all that kind of thing, makes no one any more willing to give. Precisely in proportion as we make men better; more like Jesus, and fill their hearts with love to God and love to man, will they abound in every good work. I am still as certain as I can be of anything of this kind, that what is wanting is to go out into the field and work, not without support, for this is impossible; but without perplexing our heads about plans of supporting preachers. It is not *plans* of supporting preaching that we need, but the support *itself.* We do not live in such a time, nor under such circumstances, as Wesley, nor yet such times and circumstances as B. W. Stone; nor do we discard the idea, as they did, of men receiving a support, a liberal and competent support. All we discard is, empty plans and schemes that have no support in them, but simply do for men to talk over who are never ready to do anything upon any plan. All, or nearly all, the plans we have had amount to but little more than excuses for men not willing to do anything, either with or without a plan. In one word, we want more preaching and better support for preaching. In order to obtain this, let preachers go out into the field, and if they are able, do about twice as much work, and let the brethren give them about twice as much support, and they will all be much happier and double the amount of good will be done. Let empty *plans* and *schemes* go to the moles and bats, and all the empty talk about them go with them, and let us go at it and do the work.

This is the organization we want; both preachers and churches that will work. All the plans and schemes of organization that we have had, or that brethren want, are as empty and powerless as they are inefficient and useless. They neither preach nor support preachers. Men must preach and the brethren must support them. Let the preacher and the brethren where he goes make their own arrangement, and then we shall be satisfied with it. For conscience-sake, do not try to support a preacher *upon plans or schemes,* and by all means, let not preachers think of building up churches by *plans or schemes,* for they will neither preach nor pay preachers. We do not wish to cut Bro. Mavity, nor any other brother, out of one dime of his support, but would much rather add to it, but we would rid him and others of empty plans that have no *support* nor preaching in them. We need *work,* on the part of both preachers and people—more work and less scheming, and when we have this the cause will prosper. Brethren, remember the preachers you have in your midst, men of God and men who work for the Lord and for you, and see that they lack for nothing.

It may be found expedient to have some simple missionary arrangement in each State, with a board, to penetrate destitute portions of country, in addition to the general Missionary Society in this city, for Home and Foreign Missions.   B. F.

-----o-----

RECONCILIATION AMONG THE DISCIPLES IN NOBLESVILLE, INDIANA.

We are truly thankful that we are able to announce a complete reconciliation among the Disciples in Noblesville, Ind. On December 24th, the committee, to whom all matters of complaint were referred, met, and the investigation commenced and continued seven days, and, as announced by the committee, was, as we think, most happily and satisfactorily settled, and the brethren all united. Many developments made during the investigation, many things said and done, were of a somewhat exciting nature. In the very nature of the case, many things were personal, yet the whole proceeding was orderly, the brotherhood and spectators respectful, in such a high degree, as to reflect much credit upon the moral character and general deportment of the community. Indeed, we think, considering the state of things, and the exciting nature of the examination, we have rarely seen more evidence of a well-informed community, good deportment and moral worth. There were certainly many valuable brethren on both sides, and we regard it as a mercy of the Lord that, peace and harmony are again restored among the children of God in Noblesville.

In this case, we have another evidence of the power of the gospel upon the hearts of the Disciples. Love to God and scriptural procedure, will accomplish the work among all who are *Disciples* indeed. On this occasion, the committee met with a determination to settle the matter, restore peace and order, without the loss or dishonor of one. This, we think, was achieved; and we never saw greater subordination, on the part of any set of brethren, than appeared to prevail on all hands. Thanks be to God for the evidences of his love, in this great work! May God bless and keep all these dear brethren in peace and love to the appearing and kingdom of Jesus Christ.

Never before have we met with anything so calculated to endear the Christian Ministry to us. Here was Eld. John O'Kane, who has traversed several of the Middle States largely, contending for the faith against the most wily opponents the truth has ever had in this country, both publicly and privately, preaching, baptizing and building churches, for more than thirty years, usually lively, cheerful and sometimes jocular, but now grieving, solemn, and mourning over the condition of these brethren. Never shall we forget the solemn and appropriate prayer he poured forth to Heaven, in the private room, before lying down, on the night before the investigation commenced, Bro. Pritchard and myself alone with him; and confident I am that God heard him. None but one whoso life has been spent in winning souls to Christ, can present brethren, who are dearer to him than his life, and who have fallen into confusion and discord, before the Lord as he did. O, that brethren could know and appreciate who their friends are, who love them, and would suffer to any extent, the Lord might require, for them! how differently they would feel and act.

Long have we appreciated the labors of this great and good man, and well have we known his worth to the cause. But his ardent love for all those brethren, his impartiality, faithfulness and desire to save all, sustain truth and righteousness, and his godly and manly course, in the whole matter, endeared him to us more than ever. The Lord be with him, support and strengthen him, in his noble and manly efforts in the work of the Lord! He is now fully out upon the primitive evangelical plan. In the Lord, who has sustained him in his long and useful ministry, he is putting his trust, going forth wherever an effectual door is opened, believing that in due time he shall reap, if he faint not; and, we trust in God, he will find open hearts to receive the truth, bring many souls to the kingdom of God, and an open hand among the brethren to supply his wants. Among a people like the brotherhood, in such a land as ours, an old servant of God like he is, should know nothing of want. Remember, he is an *old* preacher, one of the *working* men, spending and being spent for the work of God. Let not brethren, who abound in the goods of this world, but who withhold from him, and others like him, a full and liberal support, dream of heaven, happiness and the joys of the New Jerusalem. When he shows his generosity, by leaving his family, incurring expense in traveling, laboring faithfully in efforts to build up the cause and winning souls to God, let brethren show their generosity, in a liberal, manly and generous contribution, and thus let us have generous preachers and brethren.

Bro. L. H. Jamison was also present some portion of the time, and deeply interested in the success of our effort to restore peace and order among the brethren. He also has spent a large portion of his life as a minister of the word of God, and gathered many precious souls to the Lord Jesus. We were truly happy to learn that he has given up his position in the University, for what is evidently more congenial to him, as a preacher—*the work of an evangelist;* the most noble work in which one so competent as he can possibly engage, among all the pursuits known to men. That Bro. Jamison is an accomplished, able and powerful preacher, is as well known to the thousands who have heard him as any truth we could utter. We do hope the Lord will give him strength, open to him an effectual door, and that the brethren will not fail, in a single instance, abundantly to supply his wants, and that his days may be filled with usefulness and happiness.

Bro. Geo. Campbell was also with us, full of his characteristic love, devotion and zeal for the good of man and the glory of God. He is consecrating himself to God as but few men are, getting in years, with but a small competency of temporal things. We fear that many brethren sin in reference to him, in withholding liberality from him. We do not fear this from what we have heard him say; for he would not complain, if he had not more than half food or raiment. No people will prosper in religion or be prepared for judgment, who neglect such men. Brethren, remember such men while you have them with you, and think of their worth. Think how many are falling—such men as S. S. Church, John T. Johnson and A. Miller, and do your part by those you have still with you.

We cannot go on to mention others, but must suffice it to say, that we are greatly encouraged, our heart is enlarged, and we believe such an opening for good is now at hand as we have not known for years. Preachers are going into the field, in the Lord's name, in the good old evangelical spirit and power, and the Lord will grant them such a response as they have never heard. O, that we may have faith and zeal, love and good works, that will commend and carry forward the work and cause it to bless mankind! Let us go, in the spirit of true missionaries, with hearts filled with love to God and man, making mighty efforts to save man, knowing that the days are evil and the time short in which we are to labor. B. F.

To the brethren in Indiana and elsewhere, be it known, that the middle wall of partition between the brethren in Noblesville, Indiana, is broken down, and the two bodies have become one. Praise the Lord! The undersigned met in Noblesville on the 24th of December, 1856, as a committee mutually chosen, and remained in session for seven days and nights, hearing and carefully considering the matters of complaint among the brethren, and are now happy to say that, through the blessing of God, our labors resulted in a reconciliation of the parties, so that the two bodies, before we left, merged into one, and, through their respective officers, publicly declared their willingness to forget and forgive the past, and to live and love as brethren. We would advise our preaching brethren to visit Noblesville, assuring them that they will find an interesting band of Christian brethren in this place.

ELIJAH GOODWIN, Chairman.
JOHN BOGGS, JOHN YOUNG,
OVID BUTLER, GEORGE CAMPBELL,
JOHN O'KANE, B. FRANKLIN.

-----o-----

APOLOGY.—Success of the Gospel, a communication from C. D. Hurlbutt, with many other important documents, were unavoidably crowded out of this number. We left home at an early period, and had arranged everything before many of these documents came. We never can publish even a tithe of what comes to hand. We do not say this because we are out of patience, but as a reason for the non-appearance of many things.

CHRISTIAN PSALMIST.—We have this work for sale here, in both the superior and common binding.

DISCUSSION ON REVISION.

The interesting discussion on the Revision of the Holy Scriptures, through the columns of the Louisville *Courier,* between James Edmunds and Dr. Bell, on the part of Revision, and a committee of five clergymen, appointed by a Congress of Clergymen, for the purpose, in the city of Louisville, Ky., is still in progress. We take pleasure in laying the following before our readers, as a kind of specimen of the present state of the affair. By the way, we have made arrangements to have this discussion constantly for sale at this office. The following article speaks for itself:

B. F.

THE REV. MR. DENISON'S SPEECH.

An ancient English traveler, Herbert, published a book of travels in 1634, devoted to Africa and Asia, of which a copy belonged to Dean Swift. The Dean's copy is yet in existence and contains this criticism in it, in his handwriting: "If this book were stript of its impertinence, conceitedness and tedious digressions, it would be almost worth reading, and would be two-thirds smaller than it is. 1720. J. Swift." It strikes us that a similar stripping of Mr. Denison's speech at the meeting he called for invoking the charities of the public, for a distribution of the Bible to Hotels, Hospitals, Work House and Jail, might leave it clothed in a few tolerable rags. We are unable to imagine any one good motive that could have animated Mr. Denison on that occasion, an occasion that should have roused all the noblest powers of a Christian mind to philanthropic and benevolent efforts for blessing the destitute with the word of God.

The managers of the Society, under whose auspices the meeting was called and who published the noble and excellent themes that were to be discussed, did not place Mr. Denison on their published programme for the perpetuation of the deed upon which we are trying him. The trustees of the Church, to whose courtesy Mr. Denison was indebted for permission to enter the house on that occasion, gave him no warrant for his conduct. Neither the cause of Revision, nor the friends of that cause, have ever manifested the least desire to make war upon the benevolent enterprise in which the Louisville and Vicinity Bible Society is engaged. So far, indeed, are we from any such desire that the objects of that Society command our warmest sympathies and approval. We should rejoice to see that Society able to place a copy of the Bible in the hands of every human being that needs it, and that can be induced to make use of it. We endeavor to show our faith by our works. The Society, upon receipts, equal to $937.58, from eighteen churches and from various individuals, have given away, during the past year, ninety-two Bibles and one hundred and seven Testaments, while *a single congregation* in this city, devoted to the cause of Revision, which Mr. Denison regularly sneers at as "another little concern on the corner of Walnut and Fourth," have given away, in the same time, one hundred and eight Bibles, of King James' version, upon the voluntary contributions of the members. Does that look as though the friends of Revision were antagonistic to the objects of the Louisville and Vicinity Bible Society. Why should Mr. Denison attempt to involve that Society in one of his own miserable controversies?

In this state of case, what could have warranted Mr. Denison in sowing dragon's teeth, where there were peace and a strong tie of sympathy? What good spirit on earth could have prompted his outrages upon the Bible Union and the Revision Association? What excuse can he muster to his service for the desecration of the interesting services of a Bible meeting on a day that Christians consecrate to the worship of Jesus Christ, of a church whose courtesy he was indebted for the opportunity of speaking, and of a pulpit that is not his own? It belongs not to mortals to delve into the recesses of the human heart for the motives that stir it to its iniquities, but we may learn something of these secrets, by looking at the acts of a man, and the only rational view that we can take of the animus of Mr. Denison on the occasion alluded to, is, that he was overflowing with long-pent-up malice, that hungered and thirsted for revenge. Of the truth of this view, we think our readers will be satisfied when we develop the speech of the reverend gentleman. And if the exposition we make of Mr. Denison shall enable him to root from his heart, malice, that source of unnumbered wrongs, our labor would be a blessing to him. Peter admonishes Christians not to use their liberty as a cloak for maliciousness. That dreadful passion taints everything it touches, darkens the avenues of reason, poisons the atmosphere of contemplation, and the faculty of speech, is easily stirred into action, and when astir dries up and withers justice, truth and righteousness. These are not the ornaments nor the weapons of the Christian. The living element of his character is expressed in that sublime and immortal declaration. "He is free, indeed, whom the truth makes free." Nothing but truth can give freedom to human thought and action, and enable the human soul to return to the image of its maker.

The profound and bitter hatred which Mr. Denison exercises toward the cause of Revision and all its friends, is precisely the kind that good, righteousness and holy efforts have always received for attempts to throw light upon the word of living truth. Wickliffe and Tyndale and Frith were hunted down as though they had been wild beasts, for the crime of attempting to translate the Scriptures into English. When Capellus wrote a work against the divinity of the Hebrew *points* and another for *various lections* in the Hebrew text itself, he excited as much of an uproar in the Reformed Churches as though he had professed Atheism. He was charged with making infidels! When Erasmus performed his illustrious labor in printing the text of inspiration for the first time in the language in which it was written, Lee and Stunica hastily rushed into the position now occupied by Mr. Denison, toward Revision. They abused, calumniated and vilified Erasmus as though he were a monster in crime. He also was thus making infidels, according to these saintly adversaries, who never seemed to imagine the infinite nourishment that wickedness could draw from their labors and example, rather than from the calm, learned and righteous acts of Erasmus. The names of Erasmus and Capellus are now embalmed in the memories of all who love the truth of God. But in keeping with the conduct of the enemies of Capellus and Erasmus and all in every age, who, like them, have undertaken to remove rubbish from the words of God to man, Mr. Denison, in his speech at the First Presbyterian Church, announced that the Revision Association and Bible Union were producing similar effects, and that he was personally cognizant of the fact. In all decent logic, it is considered that when a man is so hard pressed, that he has to bring his personal experience to bear upon an opponent, that he has completely broken down in argument, and has run dry of facts and truth. We shall not attempt to bring our personal experience to bear in opposition to Mr. Denison's, although we could surprise him with some facts on this subject, for which we could furnish localities, names, and all other requisite evidences. Nor shall we give his statement a contradiction, for it is not only not worth it, but it is beneath contempt. This appeal to personal experience is quite a favorite movement with Mr. Denison. In his discussion on Baptism, in which his Greek was foundered, he boldly asserted that he had known instances in which Immersion had destroyed life, as if he had never heard of instances in which faith in Jesus Christ had done the same thing.

Mr. Denison claims great superiority for Protestantism over the Roman Catho lics in urging the study of the Scriptures among the people, but he, and all who join in that cry, might learn some useful lessons from some of the Catholic clergy in these matters. Bishop Kenrick has made a noble revision of the New Testament, alike creditable to his fidelity and his scholarship, and in it he urges all Catholics to study the word of God for themselves, in order that each individual may learn the mind of the Holy Spirit for himself. The Bishop's revision is an invaluable contribution to the study of the life of Jesus Christ, of the founding of Christian congregations, and of their instruction in all spiritual matters. Its appeals to the Greek text are numerous. And when Stunica ran to old Cardinal Ximenes (to whose noble labors the world is indebted for the Complutensian text of the New Testament), and in the very spirit of Mr. Denison, with horror springing from his eyes, Stunica informed the Cardinal that Erasmus had anticipated the Complutensian text, that noble prelate administered a lesson to Stunica, by which Mr. Denison might profit, in his thoughts about Revision. Ximenes replied to him: "I would that all men might thus prophecy (referring to Num. xi. 29): *produce what is better, if thou canst; do not condemn the industry of another."*

In the commencement of Mr. Denison's notorious speech, he seemed to have a singularly accurate appreciation of the character of the labors he was about to perform. He was somewhat apologetic, and remarked that "if his audience should find themselves *bored* with his subject, they might enjoy the consolation of knowing that there was another congregation in the city equally bored." He did not seem to reflect that that congregation also had its consolations; first, that it was not bored with the punishment upon the audience before Mr. Denison, and secondly, that it was not tricked into the infliction, by false pretences. The ornamental fringe with which Mr. Denison graced this part of his opening referred to President James Shannon.

With great dignity he said that the newspapers had announced one day that Professor or President Shannon, (he thought that was the name, as though *his* contempt might annihilate that gentleman), would make an address on Revision, on a subsequent day, it was announced that he had been requested by the Revision Association to deliver an address that night; and again, on Saturday it was published that a number of gentlemen, who were unable to hear the address of Thursday night, had requested him to address them on Saturday night. And with a delicate sense of propriety, Mr. Denison said he did not know whether there had been three addresses, or one discourse and failures. Now common honesty should have taught him, that if he knew nothing on the subject, to keep silent, but when it is remembered that Mr. Denison could have ascertained truth instead of calling up trains of figments, the character of the animus that inspired him is evident.

From this pleasant exordium, Mr. Denison branched off into an attack upon the Revision Association. Throughout the whole of his speech he seemed to adopt Dugald Stewart's definition of the office of language, slightly altered for this occasion. Mr. Stewart said, "the office of language is not so much to convey ideas as to call up trains of thought." Mr. Denison's course seemed to add, "such as I desire." He, therefore, undertook to make his audience believe that "the little concern on the corner of Walnut and Fourth streets," as he, with supreme dignity, called the rooms of the Revision Association, "was engaged in making translations of the Bible!" There is not a shadow of reason for this calumny, more than that it suited his views to utter it. No word has ever been uttered by the Revision Association to give a pretext for any such fabrication, nothing has ever been said or done to justify the representation.

But Mr. Denison could not have loomed out more largely upon this gross deception, if he had had documentary evidence before him to sustain his averments. Upon this false predicate he fairly boiled over, and he turned to Professor Stuart Robinson, and asked him if he believed there were, on this Continent, six scholars capable of doing justice to these matters, in comparison with European scholars. We are sorry to learn that Professor Robinson, who is himself a scholar, thought that there were not more than that number. Now, we think that the Presbyterian Church alone, has more than that number of Biblical scholars in America, who are fully equal to any six Biblical scholars in Europe. The "train of thought," which Mr. Denison desired to call up is, if this is the meager condition of American scholarship in point of numbers, how contemptible must be the efforts of "the little concern on the corner of Walnut and Fourth?" But how little did the audience think that Mr. Denison ranks as *one* in this scarce American scholarship. We think we can establish his claim.

In his book, entitled, "Unitarian Views, Reviewed," he quotes a passage from King James version, and says, *"or* as it should be translated and punctuated, 'whose are the Fathers, and of whom (according to the flesh) Christ, who is over all God, blessed forever.'" He adds: *"in vain will other constructions be put upon this verse.* The Greek as it stands is confirmed by all the manuscripts, all the ancient versions, and nearly all the fathers." Now, if Mr. Denison is able to re-translate and punctuate one verse of King James' version to such a degree of perfection that all the Biblical scholarship of the world can see it in no other light than that in which his version presents it, what is to hinder him from re-translating and re-punctuating the entire New Testament? We confess that neither the Bible Union, nor "the little concern on the corner of Walnut and Fourth," has any scholar employed who can make translations that can have "no other constructions put upon them," than such as the translator gives. If Mr. Denison can as perfectly satisfy the Committee on Versions, of the Bible Union, respecting his perfections as a reviser, as he seems to be satisfied himself, he can easily get a profitable contract and obtain the entire control of the revision of the New Testament. We hope he'll try. There is one thing that we are a little at a loss about. His construction is gained by punctuation, and, with a Hellenistic sweep, he says, "the Greek as it stands is confirmed by all the manuscripts all, the ancient versions, and nearly all the Fathers."

Now, neither the ancient manuscripts nor ancient versions had any points for punctuation, and we are at a loss to understand how they can give countenance to the construction, that defies all criticism. But we have some serious questions for Mr. Denison. Where did he see all the manuscripts, or all the ancient versions? And where did he acquire the art of reading the ancient manuscripts, for a man may be a great Greek scholar, without being able to read a verse of the ancient manuscripts. And if he condemns King James' version in a single verse, as improperly translated and punctuated, is he not unsettling the minds of the people as to what the Bible teaches? And if an immaculate construction of one verse can be obtained by re-translation, by a new punctuation, and a comparison with "all the manuscripts, all the ancient versions, and nearly all the Fathers," may not all the verses of the New Testament be made equally immaculate by the same process? And is it not a matter of solemn, imperative duty on the part of all who love the Holy Oracles to attain this desirable result? And if it is, what becomes of Mr. Denison's warfare on revision, and of all his "tedious digressions" in his speech, while talking of the excellence of King James' version, on which he has himself affixed the seal of condemnation? Out of thine own mouth do we condemn thee.

After the onslaught on the Revision Association, in that majestic style, that classic, tasteful and beautiful language, and in that elevated dignity that characterized every movement of his speech, after building up his calumny as to the translating labors of the Revision Association, Mr. Denison asked: "Can an eagle be hatched from a duck egg?" We shall answer that question when we come to examine some of his broodings over Greek words and classic literature. If an eaglet does not come, Mr. Denison must determine the character of the egg.

We must reserve to another occasion our examination of the remaining statements, charges and follies of Mr. Denison. A large portion of his speech was a rehash of the matters he used in "the Discussion," and on which he was fully answered then, so fully, indeed, that while we have distributed thousands of that work, Mr. Denison has never ordered a copy of it for any of his friends. Indeed, he flattered himself that probably not ten persons present at his Sunday night exhibition had ever read the discussion, thus showing the low estimate he placed upon the solicitude of the public to know what he had to say in behalf of the Bible in common use. We shall not again notice any of these matters thus disposed of, but confine our future remarks to Mr. Denison's new criminations against the friends of Revision. On each of those, we shall meet him fully.

JAMES EDMUNDS,
T. S. BELL.

Revision Association Rooms, Louisville, corner of Walnut and Fourth.

-----o-----

Review of Eld. J. B. Jeter, by M. E. Lard, with an introduction by Eld. A. Campbell, is advertised upon the cover of the *M. Harbinger*. We shall give it a more extended notice as soon as we receive it. We hope this will be a valuable book.

Communication.

CARLISLE, IVY., DEC. 8th, 1856.
DEAR BRO. FRANKLIN:—The December No. of the REVIEW is received, and I have read it with special interest. Bro. Fall's Sermon on the question: "Can we infallibly know the gospel when we hear it?" is an admirable discourse—clear, forcible, pointed, logical, and infinitely better than all, it is scriptural; and allow me to say, it is death to sectarianism, in all its protean forms. It is every way worthy of its learned, talented, and Christian author, and will, doubtless, be read with much pleasure and profit by all lovers of the simple truth as it is in Jesus. It ought to be scattered broadcast among the religious sects, and studied in the light of God's Holy Word, and not through party-colored spectacles. May God help us all to know the saving truth, and follow it whithersoever it leads! It has been a growing conviction of my mind for some years, that, as a people, we are becoming too compromising. The tendency of poor, fallen human nature is always downward—we love ease, we love peace and quiet, and, alas! too often sacrifice truth and purity in the name of a spurious charity, and to secure an unholy peace! "Charity," says the holy apostle, "rejoiceth not in iniquity, but rejoiceth in the truth." "The wisdom from above," says the apostle James, "is first pure, then peaceable." Let us by all means, then, have fervent charity, but let it be that heaven-born charity that mourns over evil and labors assiduously to correct it—to destroy it: that charity which rejoices in the truth, and labors to promote its triumphs. Let us see to it also, that we seek peace and pursue it: that we follow peace with all men; but in the mean time

it behooves us to be certain that we *"seek, pursue and follow peace,"* only in the way of purity and holiness. The peace of fiends, of counterfeiters, of cut-throats, of pirates, may be secured by the sacrifice of purity. But the peace of God, which passes all understanding; which keeps the minds and hearts of God's people, can only be fully enjoyed in connection with truth and purity. We have no doubt that among the religious party there is much of wisdom, much of goodness, much of true virtue, and much of genuine piety. But to recognize them in their distinctive sectarian and schismatic characters, as churches of Christ, battling for their party names, and platforms, would be a burlesque upon the nature and design of Christianity, and prove that Christ is divided against himself, Paul to the contrary, notwithstanding! I am happy to believe that the various religious denominations, despite the ignorance, superstition and violent prejudices, in certain quarters, are, upon the whole advancing in religious knowledge and feeling, and thus making advances towards the Bible, the only infallible rule of faith and manners, the only true basis of Christian union and communion; and the only means under God, of curing our schisms. Indeed, any other position than this, on our part, would be suicidal to our cause. For, unequivocally, if all the parties have a divine charter for their existence as such, then have we been very wrong, as a people, in opposing them as sects; and they have all been just as wrong, in opposing us and one another. Nay, more: in such warfare against them, and in all their warfare against one another, *we and they* have all been found fighting against God! We ought, therefore, if this is true, to make haste and publish to the ends of the earth, that we retract every word we have ever spoken or written against them; and that from our hearts, with deep penitence, we ask our God, and our justly offended brethren, to forgive us, and solemnly promise, before heaven and earth, never, in like manner, to offend them again. We ought at once to claim to be an evangelical sect among the sects; to take an independent stand among the religious parties of the day, assume a party name, publish to the world our party creed and system of ecclesiastical government, as soon as we can agree upon them, and have done with our war upon human creeds, and names, and parties forever.

But, on the other hand, if the position we have taken against all sectarian names, and creeds, and churches, is the true position (as the writer most confidently and strongly believes), then we may not cease our efforts until Jerusalem be made a praise in all the earth; till the church, torn into fragments and scattered in the dark and cloudy day, shall come up out of the wilderness, leaning upon her beloved, fair as the moon, clear as the sun and terrible to her enemies as an army with banners. Till she cease from man, whose breath is in his nostrils, we may not hold our peace, day nor night; but must continue to cry aloud, and spare not; to lift our voices like trumpets, and show God's people their transgressions, and the house of Jacob their sins. My half-sheet is full.

J. ROGERS.

-----o-----

Much is being said in reference to publishing the life of Eld. John T. Johnson. Nothing is yet determined as to whom this work will devolve upon. We know but little as to the opinion of the brethren touching a proper person for this work. We have spoken of Elder John Rogers to many brethren, not one of whom have made the least objection.

Power will intoxicate the best hearts, as wine the strongest heads. No man is wise enough, nor good enough to be trusted with unlimited power: for whatever qualifications he may have evinced to entitle him to the possession of so dangerous a privilege, yet, when possessed, others can no longer answer for him, because he can no longer answer for himself.

Editor's Table.

HISTORY OF ENGLISH BIBLE TRANSLATION. This valuable and ably written work, from the pen of the distinguished Mrs. Conant, wife of the learned translator of the book of Job, employed by the Bible Union, can be had at this office. No book that we know is at this time of more importance to the friends of the English Bible. Price $1.25.

"THE FAMILY COMPANION."—Elder Elijah Goodwin's new book of sermons, styled *"The Family Companion,"* is obtaining a liberal circulation, and certainly very deservedly. It is a valuable book—a book calculated to do a vast amount of good. The variety in it gives a pretty full development of the Christian religion, in a simple, clear, and yet able manner, well adapted to the people at large. It is sound and strong, inculcating sentiments of piety, union and love, in a manner rarely to be found in any book of these times. This valuable *"Family Companion"* will be kept at this office, and will be sent by mail, postage pre-paid, to any place in the United States, for one dollar. By the quantity, expense of transportation paid by the purchaser, a liberal deduction will be made.

DISCUSSION ON REVISION.—This valuable, spirited and able discussion, by Edmunds and Bell, of Louisville, Ky., on the part of Revision, and a Committee of Clergymen, appointed for the purpose by a Congress of the Clergy of Louisville, in the opposition, will be constantly for sale, on the most moderate terms, both wholesale and retail, at this office. We most heartily recommend this work, and hope it will obtain an extended circulation. The friends of a pure version of the Bible, and of the light, have a most signal triumph in this work.

THE "MILLENNIAL HARBINGER."—This is the oldest periodical published by the brotherhood, being the successor of the *Christian Baptist,* which contained the first seven year's work of Elder A. Campbell, now President of Bethany College, of Virginia. We utter but the deliberate and simple conviction of our mind, when we say that we believe the pen of the editor of the *Millennial Harbinger,* Elder ALEXANDER CAMPBELL, has made the greatest religious impression upon the human race of any man of the nineteenth century, and that his pen is still wielded with great power. He is also assisted in the editorial department by Elder R. Richardson, who commands one of the first literary pens of the day, and is certainly also strong and sound in the faith. Elder W. K. Pendleton, who holds a keen, pointed and able pen, is an assistant editor of the *Harbinger.* No one among us can doubt that *the Harbinger* is an able and most interesting publication, and that it is doing good service to circulate it as widely as possible. Address A. Campbell, Bethany, Brooke county, Va.

THE "CHRISTIAN RECORD."—This well-known and ably conducted monthly magazine is edited by Elder James M. Mathes, of Bedford, Indiana, and published by Bro. J. M. Tilford, Indianapolis. Bro. Mathes is one of our ablest and best men, and we hope he will meet with success equal to his merit.

THE "CHRISTIAN EVANGELIST-"—This is one of the well established Monthlies, well conducted and well patronized. Bro. D. Bates, the editor, is one of our safe and reliable men, who has, through manly and faithful perseverance, established and sustained his publication in a new country. His address is Fort Madison, Iowa.

AGENT FOR THE MISSIONARY SOCIETY.—Elder John Rogers, of Carlisle, Ky., has accepted an agency for the Missionary Society, in all his travels in Kentucky, and we hope—indeed, from what we know of the brethren in his State, we feel assured—that they will enable him to make such a report as shall speak in their praise and redound to the glory of God.

THE "GOSPEL ADVOCATE."—This ably conducted and neatly printed monthly publication, is edited by the highly accomplished and gifted President of Franklin College, Tennessee, Elder T. Fanning. It is not only an ably conducted publication, but one that is attracting much attention, by its bold stand against all innovations, worldly policies and human isms of every grade. Address Elder T. Fanning, Franklin College, Tennessee.

THE "CHRISTIAN INTELLIGENCER."—This valuable religious newspaper is issued once in two weeks, and edited by our able and long-tried Brother, Elder C. L. Coleman, of Richmond, Va. This paper has done good service for the cause for many years, and is still an able advocate. We hope it may receive a liberal support.

"CHRISTIAN SYSTEM."—This book has been, and still is, one of the most useful of the many valuable works written by Bro. Campbell. A new edition, with additions, will soon be ready, which we will furnish at one dollar per copy.

ERRATA.—We are deeply mortified to find in Bro. John Rogers' Sermon the following errors in printing: Page 5, in text, read *comfort* for "complete." Same column, 7 lines from bottom, *Christians* for "children." Page 9, 4th line from top, *nether* for "neither." Same column, 8th line from top, after the word *us*, insert "turn." At the close of the same paragraph, after the word man, for "will be our unhappiness, our discomfort," read *or our want of it, will be our happiness or unhappiness.* Page 11, 9th line from top, for the word "For," put *But.* Same page, 11 lines from bottom, for "conflict of ages," put *Conflict of Ages.*

In Bro. R.'s article in this No., p, 43, 2nd column, 9th line from top, for "excuse,"—*expose.* Same column, 3rd line from bottom, for "begging"—*aiding.* Page 44, 2nd line, for "isms"—*ism.*

In our notice of the death of Bro. Johnson, page 45, 1st column, 24th line from top, for "glaring"—*gloomy.* Same page, 2nd column, 8th line from top, for "fade"—*fell.*

Success of the Gospel.

CENTRALIA, Ill., Dec. 26, 1856.

BRO. EDITOR:—In order to redeem my pledge, I proceed to state that we held a two days' meeting at Antioch, closing last Lord's day, resulting in one confession and one addition from the Baptists. In this portion of that part of Illinois called Egypt, our preachers are rather scarce, yet we have two in Centralia, brethren M. L. Wilcox and J. A. Williams, "workmen that need not be ashamed."

Having been engaged in improving a raw prairie farm during the year that is now closing, I have only found time to preach about one hundred discourses. At the few protracted meetings I have held, and others at which I have assisted, there have been some twenty or thirty additions.

I hope during the coming year to have more time to devote to holding protracted meetings. The plan I have found productive of most good, is to hold a ten days' singing, and have preaching every night, I can instruct a class to read music in the *Christian Psalmist* by teaching from two to four hours per day, for ten days; and singing hymns at night to the tunes we learn in the day, the singers acquire confidence, and the music in the congregation is greatly improved. We generally attend to the baptisms late in the afternoon, and repair immediately to the chapel to engage in worship. Thus the attention of the audience is kept concentrated on the objects of the meeting, and the more good effected.

Although such a plan of labor is very exhausting to the teacher, yet as I can do the most good thus, I have concluded for, and during the coming year, to hold myself ready to answer the calls of congregations desiring to be instructed in church music, and have a protracted meeting at the same time. From my residence near Centralia, I can, by railroad, reach almost any point in our Western country in a few hours.

I prefer to teach in the *Christina Psalmist,* because it has been before the brotherhood nearly ten years, the music and hymns in it are acceptable to the brethren generally, as shown by the fact that they and the public have purchased from twelve to thirty-five thousand copies per year since the first eighteen months of its existence, because the plan of notation takes up so little room, giving more music and hymns on a given surface of paper than any other system of notation, and because there are more persons in the congregations who will and can learn on that system, and hence, as our traveling preachers have remarked, there are more singers, more singing, and better church music in congregations where the *Christian Psalmist* is used than in those where it is not used.

Yours in the good hope,

S. W. LEONARD.

BUCHANAN, MICH., Dec. 25th, 1856.

DEAR BRO. FRANKLIN We have just closed a series of happy meetings in Buchanan, resulting in *twenty-four* accessions to the Christian congregation. *Thirteen* were added by confession and baptism, *four* by letter and relation, *three* from the Baptists, *three* from the Methodists, and *one* from the Tonkers. Eld. Wm. Lane and Wm. Anderson, two indefatigable servants of God, were the chief speakers most of the time. The audiences were far the most part large, and profoundly attentive to the close of the meeting (of some seventeen days continuance), and we feel confident that a deep and lively religious interest has been awakened throughout this entire community. Efforts here made to arrest the progress of the truth by a few sectarian bigots and parasitical demagogues, who have grown so wise that they have discovered that *immersion* is not required in *cold weather,* and that baptism is a non-essential command. Such men are wolves in sheep's clothing, infidels, who have stolen the livery of heaven to serve the devil in, serving not the Lord Jesus, but themselves, ever seeking to please men, that they may secure the honors of the world, disregarding the mandates of heaven, without God and without hope in the world. But the word of God is not bound. The truth is destined to triumph and over all prevail. To the Lord be all the praise.

WM. M. ROE.

THE AMERICAN CHRISTIAN REVIEW.

A DISCOURSE-- BY ELD. A. B. GREEN.

SUBJECT—**What are the dangers to which the cause we plead is exposed?**

An apostle once said: "Look to yourselves, that we lose not those things which we have wrought, but that we receive a full reward." 2 John, i. 8. We cannot make the language too emphatic: *"Look to yourselves,"* etc.

Paul once said to the elders of the church at Ephesus : "Take heed to yourselves, and to all the flock, over which the Holy Spirit has made you *overseers,* to feed the Church of God, which he has purchased with his own blood." The reason assigned is: "Of your ownselves shall men arise, speaking perverse things to draw away disciples after them."

Moses and the Prophets, Jesus and the Apostles, were ever cautioning the faithful to take heed lest there should be in any of them an evil heart of unbelief, in departing from the Living God. And well they might do it, since there has no great good been offered to humankind, but some ambitious man has sought either to counterfeit the good, or professedly to make an improvement upon it, and thereby turn the public mind from the good first offered, and center it upon the imposition offered by himself. And it must be confessed, that Quacks are not more common in the medical profession than in religious matters. Hence, the necessity of looking to ourselves, lest we loose the things we have wrought. A caution signifies danger.

The fact that sin entered even *Eden,* and so strongly grew with the growth of man, that in 1656 years there was found but *one* righteous family on this green earth, should serve to alarm us for the fate of a cause so dear to all the interests of man. Again, when we look at the simplicity and purity of the gospel, as it fell from the lips of the inspired Apostles of the Son of God, and hear them beseeching the brethren in the name of the Lord Jesus, to all speak the same thing, to be of the same mind, and of the same judgment, and then look at the host of party names and unscriptural officers, such as Popes and Cardinals, Bishops and Prelates, Presiding Elders and Class Leaders, etc., etc., it becomes us to give heed to the admonition: "Let him that thinketh he standeth, take heed lest he fall."

But in enumerating the dangers that threaten the cause we plead, I confess that I feel an embarrassment that I cannot well overcome. We are such frail beings, and take such partial views of things, and are so local in our views and feelings, that one sees a danger where another sees only a favorable omen. And I doubt very much if several persons of equal judgment were called upon to speak of threatening dangers whether they would all speak of the same things.

True, there are things common to be spoken of by all, the want of which exposes the cause to much neglect, and therefore to great delay in being published to the world, such as the want of a more efficient Eldership, or an Eldership wholly devoted to the interests of the cause, and who make it their business to take care of the flock. The universal want of more Preachers also, is not only a common topic of conversation, but is awakening the brethren, not only to pray the Lord of the harvest to send forth laborers into the field, but to enquire what are the duties of the churches, that they may be furnished with those who shall be qualified to go forth to the world to proclaim the glad tidings of salvation to man.

But we are surrounded with evils, and *they are in our midst,* that will cripple that Eldership, and prevent the judgment of that ardent young man, pledged to plead the Savior's cause, and convert his talent and piety even, into uses not connected with the Christian ministry, and thus divide his mind, and turn the ardor of his soul away from the one thing needful. I wish, therefore, to speak, not of wants, but of evils that are calculated to mar our peace, destroy brotherly love, and devotion to God, and cool our zeal in pleading the cause, and so divide our efforts that we shall not be found *striving together* for the faith of the gospel, and thereby bring the cause into disrepute, and make it a hiss and a bye-word among men.

The first of all evils, therefore, to be guarded against is this feeling of security that says: "There is no danger. We are not going to give up the faith, nor make a creed, nor run into sectarianism. We have seen the folly of such things."

This feeling of security has been the ruin of empires. That great city, Babylon, once said in her heart: *"I am,* and there is none besides me; I shall not sit as a widow, neither shall I know the loss of children." Isa. XLVII, 8. Yet in an unexpected moment fell, devoted to destruction for her pride. Ancient Israel, also, thought there was no danger, when they had learned the power of God to deliver, and saw the weakness of the Gods of Egypt to save. But strange to say, they were secure out of the sight of Egypt before they were seen dancing around their Golden Calf!

The ancient Christians, also, when they learned the gospel of Christ, and saw the weakness of human philosophy, were led to say with Peter: "Lord, to whom shall we go? Thou hast the words of Eternal Life." But the Apostles were not dead, before philosophy and vain deceit had so eclipsed the gospel in the minds of many, that Paul was led to say: "Brethren, I am afraid of you, lest I have bestowed labor upon you in vain." And who can read the history of the church from that day down without feeling the necessity of watching unto prayer?

But I pass to a second evil which is in our midst, and whose withering influence has long been felt to our sorrow. It is that old Athenian spirit, that is always seeking or telling some new thing. It is a spirit that is ever ready to run after everything that comes up, to investigate it. It feels perfectly competent to judge of all doubtful matters. When rebuked it meets you with this Scripture: "Prove all things, and hold fast that which is good." It is a spirit that is generally quick sighted, but not far-sighted. It views everything on the run, and frequently has a smattering of everything, but a sound understanding of nothing. I have known some churches, and many brethren, so drunk with this spirit, that they died for the want of an appetite for the bread of life. It is a restless spirit that lives only on excitement, and the many "hobbies" of the present day afford it ample sustenance, and it lives and thrives beyond measure. A few examples in our past history may serve to illustrate in some degree its baneful influence.

Some years ago the subject of capital punishment began to be discussed in many of the newspapers, and of course, in all of our debating clubs, by both men and boys. The question finally found its way into the church, where a few preachers, and many "laymen," became wise beyond measure. Their eloquence made some of our church walls ring, and their fame took wings and flew through the papers the length and breadth of the land. To awaken the church to take hold of the matter, we were told there was no great evil in the land, but the church was responsible for it. And many a time have I been accosted thus: "Why don't you *preachers* come out on this subject? You occupy the ears of the people one day in seven, and can do more to revolutionize community than any other class of citizens. But instead of that, the *pulpit is drunk*! and opens not its mouth against this relic of heathenism, that hangs a human being by the neck as you would a dog, until he is dead! And none but those whom you call sinners, are found pleading for the abolition of this inhuman barbarity. Why is it, that the church is always behind the times, and the world ever taking the lead in all the great efforts of reform?"

Such was the vaunting style of these self-styled reformers, who are ever seeking to make a tool of the church to accomplish all their ends.

By-and-bye Washingtonianism came up, and the people *en masse,* men, women and children, hastened to sign the pledge. Whoever refused his name, was christened a wine-bibber, and, guilty or not guilty, he must bear the reproach. To keep pace with the times, preachers and people, sober men and drunkards, must pledge their names together, henceforth and forever, to live sober men. So high did the excitement run at one time, that on a New Year's evening I recollect hearing a clergyman say, in a temperance meeting: "I have always thought that the Lord designed to reform the world from drunkenness by the gospel, but I am now satisfied that he has reserved this honor for the Washingtonian Society, and henceforth I shall regard a membership in this society as a stepping-stone to a membership in the church!"

Such was the interest taken in the temperance reform, that church doors were thrown open, and whoever would lift his voice in favor of temperance was invited to occupy the sacred desk. Preachers were frequently called upon to open the meeting by prayer, and often the amen was scarcely pronounced before some vulgar witticism from the mouth of the orator, created such an uproar of laughter and feet stamping, as made the godly man fear for the abuse of the sacred desk. But he was taught to console himself with the thought, that perhaps the end justified the means, and so things passed on without rebuke.

At length, however, the rudeness indulged in, and the unhallowed influence that was exerted, called for church doors to be closed, and then began the "mad-dog cry," down with the churches, they are opposed to temperance and every benevolent scheme, and their communion wine is but the stepping-stone to a drunkard's grave, etc. I need scarcely add, that many a professor lost his balance, and slid back to the world to save his credit, and find purity and benevolence.

But that which makes these things doubly dangerous, is the humiliating thought that the people, as a mass, are becoming more and more an excitable people, and these themes of excitement take deeper and deeper root every year, and the Demetriuses with their craftsman, who are occupied in making shrines for the party, are ever busy in calling their councils, and passing their resolutions, and thus awakening an enthusiasm that finds no rival this side of the uproar at Ephesus, in their praises of Diana.

Closely allied to these things is a third danger, to which I must invite attention. Yet I almost feel that I shall be considered as treading on forbidden ground to do so. Nevertheless, it is duty to say, there is danger in these times of forgetting the dangers that threaten the *church,* for the dangers that threaten the *country.* Yes, *of forgetting sinners before God, for sinners in Congress!* Concerning the church being political in its mission, as well as religious, I have nothing to say at present, lest my words be construed to mean what I would not design to teach. But I may say, there is great danger in considering ourselves equally wedded to Christ and to Caesar, of forgetting the greater for the less, and giving Caesar a far greater portion of our energies than we do Jesus Christ.

A preacher, not long since, as his custom was, took the *Lord's day* to speak of our *national sins,* said he "felt much more like a politician than he did like a preacher." The thought struck me, that the feeling was a natural one from the course he pursued. I will confess, however, that when I see a preacher take the Lord's day to preach a new President, instead of "Christ, and him crucified," and tell the people how to vote, instead of calling on them to repent and turn to God, and thus lead the people to forget the right of Jesus Christ to rule, for the right of the people to rule; I am led to enquire whether He who raises up kings and puts them down at pleasure, has ever asked this favor at his hand.

Connected with this I mention another circumstance. Some time since, a preacher of some note called me, and with great earnestness asked me if I saw a notice in the papers of an "indignation meeting" held in his town not long before? On telling him I had not, he began to speak much in its praise, and especially to commend the brethren for their zeal, and spirited resolutions offered on the occasion. I confess I could not help the thought of Jesus and the Apostles recommending to the churches the propriety of holding indignation meetings, to detest the wickedness of the "Powers that be."

I fancied that I saw the church at Jerusalem assemble, with Peter at their head, who told them that the church was responsible for all the evils in the land, and said it was the duty of the church to show herself first and foremost in every good work, and Rome must be reformed, or it would soon be blotted out as a nation. To arouse them to action, he referred them to Caiphus, whom he called a wily old politician, always studying expediency that he might save a sinking cause, although he could save it only at the price of innocent blood, and referred them to the unjust trial of Jesus, as a fair specimen of his dishonesty and intrigue.

There was Herod, too, whom he called the "emissary of Satan," and said the public must know, that we Christians detest such characters, and that we will trample under foot his unjust authority.

Yes, and there is Pilate, too, a perfect "old dough-face," wholly unworthy of the confidence of the people, who, for fear of losing his office, condescended to the mean and contemptible act of signing the death warrant of the Son of God. He told them it was time that Christians were awake, and show to the world that such men in authority were wholly unworthy of any respect from a Christian community, and recommended that the clergy throughout all the land send in their protests, in the name of God and suffering humanity, to their legislative halls, against their wicked enactments and ungodly rulers, whom they placed in authority over the people, and closed by saying, let it be known that from henceforth, correct political views shall be considered essential to Christian fellowship.

I had to give but one more stretch of imagination, to see Constantine stepping forth, wearing the imperial crown, and holding up the Cross, in token of the triumph of Christianity, and the Pope soon was seen following, wearing the wedding ring of Church and State, saying "Millennium has come, and the Saints of the Most High possess the kingdom." But alas! as I looked and saw them wed, I saw also that the Church had proved herself a *Harlot*.

Permit me here to add, that if this spirit of "pious indignation," "holy wrath," and "contemptuous love," that brothers each other with the near and endearing appellations of "tories," "doughfaces," and "emissaries of Satan," is not among the evils that threaten the spirituality and life of religion among us; it is because great grace will rest upon us to keep these furnaces of Nebuchadnezzar from leaving the smell of fire upon our Christian garments. But I forbear, lest perchance I may bring down some of its withering rebukes upon my own head.

But there is a fourth evil, that is found everywhere in this day of "progression." I name it *Korah, Dathan and Abiramism.* It is a sort of wild democracy in the churches, that says to the Elders: "Stand back, you take too much upon yourselves, since all the congregation is holy, as well as you." One half of the church difficulties that I have become acquainted with, have grown out of this spirit of insubordination. It refuses submission to the elders, and calls in question their right, as well as their qualifications, to judge in their case. So strong a hold has this spirit gained, that it has destroyed the confidence of the elders to act in their official capacity in many instances. Hence the cry, all over the land; "the inefficiency of our Eldership." I care not how well qualified our eldership may be, if this spirit is permitted to reign, we might as well have so many Egyptian mummies set up for elders, as men bearing all the qualifications given by the Apostle Paul, for the elders cannot act where this spirit reigns.

As much as we may need a more efficient eldership, we need far more a disposition to obey those who have the rule over us, who watch for our souls as those who must give an account to God. Also, a greater degree of that charity that thinketh no evil, and that brotherly love that esteems others better than ourselves. And less of that self-love that has so often characterized us, in publishing the weakness of our brethren, the length and breadth of the land, in the ungodly newspapers of the day, to justify ourselves and show that we are righteous. This Korah, Dathan and Abiramism, if not subdued, will make us tremble yet.

But I pass to a fifth evil that endangers our happiness, and the prosperity of the cause we plead. Because of its selfishness, I shall call it *Absolemism.* It is that aspiring spirit that seeks to be the greatest in the kingdom, and cannot bear the idea of a superior. Ourself, our church, our city, our section of country, is all that can be seen by it, that is of any value. This spirit is venerable for its age, and found a lodging place in the hearts of the Holy Twelve, and when cast out, was as restless as that unclean spirit, that wandered through dry places seeking rest, and found none until it returned to the place from whence it came. And then, fearing a second expulsion, took seven other spirits worse than itself, to assist in carrying out its object.

I would that I could here add, that our preachers and editors have never fostered its soul damning influence. But alas, it must be confessed that we have had our full share of this class. But we hope, under God, that the evil is passing away. But we need to take heed to ourselves and watch as well as pray, for it is evident that this demon is among us yet.

But I must not dwell upon this evil too long, but pass to a sixth evil, the legitimate offspring of the preceding evils. *It is a distaste for all religious reading,* unless it partakes of the same exciting and novel character of these spirits by which they are actuated. It will account for the few that take a religious paper. Magazines of literature and trash are often seen upon our center tables, but no Ladies' Christian Annual. Agricultural and political news may be seen hanging upon the farmer's line, but no *Millennial Harbinger* or *Christian Age,* or anything touching the spiritual interests of man. Parents may often present their children with richly bound books, but they are not of the character of "Harvey's Meditations among the Tombs." No. Under the influence of these spirits there is little love for quiet solitude, to meditate upon the wonders of Divine Grace, or to converse with those who love to talk of Jesus only. And when you invite them to take a walk with you to the garden of Gethsemane, their eyes become heavy with sleep, as did the eyes of Peter, James and John. And it's hard to make them sensible, of what the Savior endured, when he said: "Now is my soul exceeding sorrowful even unto death." And their eyes are held, that they see not the anguish of his soul, that starts the sweat from every pore, and they hear not that soul stirring prayer: "Father, if it be possible, let this cup pass from me." No, for such food they have no relish. To stand at the foot of the Cross, with the beloved John, and gaze upon him who bore our sorrows and carried our grief, is a painful task. Yet how important to make us pure in heart, and rich in good works, and fill us with the true spirit of devotion to God and the interests of the Redeemer's Kingdom. I would that I could dwell upon this for an hour, but time forbids.

I will now consider the seventh and last evil to be discussed at present, which is not general, but deserves a notice here. I confess, however, that I scarce know what to name it, whether to call it a spurious Elijahism, or a religious Hypochondria. It is certainly a spirit of discouragement that sees nothing only on the "shady side." Like Israel, when they came to the Red Sea, it forgets that God is on the throne, and has not strength to add to its faith courage, for it sees nothing but death and ruin hang over the churches. It gives up the idea that the gospel is ever going to take the world, and says there is no use of preaching to sinners, we must right up the churches on the point of order. This reformation is all wrong, and must be reformed. We must have a more "efficient eldership," and better regulations about supporting preachers. The churches must be awakened to the subject, to educate young men, and thereby qualify them to take care of the churches. It cannot be expected that our farmers and mechanics can feed the lambs of the flock. But we want young men of learning and talent, that can meet and stop the mouths of gainsayers.

A timorous captain at sea might as well say to all on board: Our vessel is rotten, and we are just ready to be dashed upon an iron bound shore, and unless you can construct a new vessel there is no hope of safety. Such language would paralyze the whole crew, and fill them with despondency and destroy all courage to act.

And how many young converts, as well as old ones, too, who were weak in faith, have become discouraged and said: I started too soon. I thought all was right and the vessel good, and the pilot skilled in steering safely into-port. But alas, it is all a mistake.

Brethren, I don't like to hear such preaching. Neither do I like to bear their doleful strains, when they sing the churches desolation. It is not the language of either faith or hope, but the language of Israel: "Why are we brought out into the wilderness to die?"

The alarm, in my judgment, is needless. True, there are dangers, many and great. Dangers that must be guarded against. But I fear the evil workings of these evil spirits of which I have spoken far more than our want of a knowledge of order, or of educated young preachers, who will be tempted to cater to the will of these spirits, to secure employment and become popular in the world. If these spirits can be cast out, order will be brought around and preachers of the right kind will gradually be supplied. But maturity cannot be expected in a day.

When I think that we have, with only the Bible in our hands, struggled and fought our way out of sectarianism and infidelity, and when few in number, have met in the private chamber, and in the school-house; yes, and in the grove, with a stump for' a pulpit, and the trunk and branches of a tree for seats, where our unlettered farmers and mechanics have preached to us the word of life, and have made sectarianism quail before them, and infidelity to turn pale and lay down its weapons at the foot of the cross. When I think that the mouths of gainsayers have been stopped, and in spite of their Sanballads and Tobiases, we have built meeting-houses, and colleges, and seminaries of learning, and the old Jerusalem gospel gained a foothold that has astonished the world, and led it to court our favor, and the learned man with his creed to come and ask our advice; I say when I consider these facts, shall I give up in despair, and say that the gospel has lost its power? And when we look at the good accomplished, shall we now cry out that this Reformation is all wrong? No. We began in the right place and with the right armor, and with the right weapon, "the sword of the spirit which is the word of God." But there is a little too much of that spirit which once troubled Israel—a desire to be like the nations around us, that we may have a popular standing in the world, and reach out and shake hands with those in high stations.

Brethren, I am, and ever have been, for a *learned ministry*. But I assure you, that I am foreign from thinking that a knowledge of the languages, or the arts and sciences of the day, will ever qualify a man, young or old, to feed the lambs of the flock with the sincere milk of the word, *unless he keep himself free from one and all of these unclean spirits, of* which we have been speaking. It may gratify him to embellish the gospel, and dress it up to look pretty, and thus please a fashionable audience, and lead the people to love and admire the preacher, instead of Jesus Christ, whom he professedly preaches. But these things are neither good nor profitable to men.

Two or three years ago, a preacher at the south became so possessed with this spirit of despondency, that he had no rest day nor night. He could see nothing but the desolation of the churches, and he began to cry aloud and spare not. "Something must be done to save the cause. We must have a learned ministry, and the brethren must be more liberal in sustaining preachers, or the cause must go down, for carnality and selfishness reigns triumphant, and a spiritual death is in all the land."

On inquiry, it was found that he was a learned man, and had a high salary, but his congregation, when weighed in the balance, was found equally wanting in the one thing needful. Brethren at the north took advantage of the admission, and said that slavery lay at the bottom of all the difficulty. But the same complaint of a spiritual death, is now made the length and breadth of the land, and the same remedy is proposed as a cure. But the remedy proposed will never eradicate the disease. But while I might speak of the want of more of an effort to raise up and sustain preachers, I would rather commend the brethren to the articles of Bro. Errett on this subject, as they are published in the *Aye,* and commend themselves to a careful reading. But it strikes me as being unwise to be discouraged on account of the illiberality of the brethren or a want of disposition to do what they think is right. For the churches certainly have made great strides in liberality, by way of supporting preaching at home, and in sending missionaries abroad, as well as giving great sums to the Bible Union, and other benevolent institutions. True, I think there is room for improvement, but I think the churches are growing in these matters as fast as could be expected.

But the difficulty is here. One church is possessed of the *Athenian spirit,* and seeks a preacher that will gratify and foster it. And that church will have that preacher, if he is to be found and money can obtain him. Another church is troubled with *Korah, Dathan and Abiramism,* and they will have neither preachers nor elders that will not let them do as they please. With them the voice of the people is the voice of God. A third is troubled about *sinners in Congress,* and will not consent to a preacher that will not make *National sins* the burden of his preaching. But these spirits, if they can be gratified, will be liberal and submit to any form of order, that will best promote that in which they feel the most interested.

But permit me to say, that these several spirits cast out of the churches will leave them like Mary Magdaline, when dispossessed of the seven demons that haunted her, the meek and humble followers of Jesus Christ, and favorably situated for triumphing over every other difficulty spoken of, for then, *Faith, Hope and Love* will reign.

But brethren, I incline to think that casting out of these spirits will, in many instances, require *fasting and prayer,* together with "strong crying and tears." We cannot do it by holding conventions, nor passing resolutions. But the preachers first, must become more one idea men, and that one idea must be Christ and him crucified, and know nothing else among the people if they would make the churches such. We must lay aside all thought of pleasing God and pleasing the people. Popularity for either the preacher or the cause is out of the question. He who seeks it, seeks it at the peril of the cause of Christ and his own soul. Some-one has said:

"O popular applause, what heart of man,
Is proof against thy sweet seducing charms?
The wisest and the best, feel urgent need
Of all their caution, in thy gentlest gales,
But swelled into a gust, who then alas,
With all his canvass set, and inexpert,
And therefore heedless, can withstand thy power?"

In conclusion, let me say, we cannot reform the world, nor the brotherhood, by the wholesale. We must approach them individually, and whatever spirit we find supplanting the spirit of Christ, seek to cast it out. It will require a strong nerve, a steady hand, and a perseverance even to the end, to accomplish it. We must, therefore, be men of faith, and consider that the Lord reigns and although the cause has passed through many a fiery ordeal, yet it is destined to arise "fair as the moon, clear as the sun, and terrible as an army with banners." "For great is the truth, and mighty above all things, and will prevail."

Let us then, seek the favor of him only whose approbation is heaven gained, eternal life secured, and undying bliss beyond the grave our sure reward. Let us contend only for that faith that was once delivered to the saints, and let us cherish that hope that serves as an anchor to the soul, sure and steadfast, that enters to that within the vail, where the forerunner for us has entered. And may that charity, which hides a multitude of sins, and suffers long, and is kind; that envieth not; that vaunteth not itself; is not puffed up: that behaves not unseemly; that seeks not her own; is not easily provoked; and thinketh no evil, be ours. And to HIM, who is able to keep us from falling, and present us faultless before the presence of His glory, with exceeding joy, be the glory, and majesty, and dominion, and power, both now and forever. Amen.

-----o-----

Ye lightnings, the dread arrows of the clouds!
Ye signs and wonders of the element!
Utter forth God, and fill the hills with praise!

EVIDENCES OF CHRISTIANITY.
NUMBER III.

The man who advocates skepticism should, to be consistent, have something more to stand upon than his *doubts* of the truth of Christianity, because his doubts may arise from his lack of information, or his own mere instability of mind. In the very nature of the case, doubts imply uncertainty; and it is preposterous and absurd in the extreme, for a man to advocate anything of which he is in doubt and uncertainty. His doubts might be regarded as a reason for neutrality and inactivity, but certainly no reason for advocating the precise thing involved in doubt. Before any man can, with any reason or propriety, advocate skepticism, his doubts about Christianity must be removed: he must, in his own mind, come to absolute certainty; because his doubts of the truth of skepticism must be of precisely the same number and magnitude as his doubts of Christianity. While he doubts Christianity, he also just as much doubts skepticism, and he never can know skepticism to be true till he can know Christianity to be false. He must be certain that Christianity is false, before he can be certain that skepticism is true, and he must be certain that skepticism is true before he can consistently advocate it.

We mention this point for the purpose of cautioning men how they run into skepticism and advocate it; and we entreat of them to hear a few words before they further go. We insist again that they should have the most absolute certainty, because if they make a mistake here, they will find it the most fearful and momentous mistake in the power of man to make. In all enterprises where there is great risk there should be the probability of great gain. But if skepticism be called an *enterprise,* it is certainly one involving the greatest possible risk—the liability, in case of a mistake, to the most fearful and overwhelming dangers to which man can be exposed. This risk, this exposure to the most dreadful consequences that could result to man, in case the skeptic should find himself mistaken, he ventures, without any possibility of gaining anything if his position should prove true. No skeptic has been able to prove that any good could possibly come to him, or any of the race, even if his doctrine could prove true. It amounts to nothing good, for any of the human race, for this world or that which is to come, even if true. The true state of the case is, that if the skeptic makes a mistake he sinks everything in ruin; and if he could prove right, he cannot by any possibility gain anything, in time or eternity. He risks everything without the possibility of gaining anything. For this cause he should have infallible certainty before he receives or advocates skepticism.

How infinitely different is the position of the believer! No skeptic ever has, or ever can, show that he risks anything in believing. His faith cannot do him any harm; it cannot injure either his usefulness or happiness. No skeptic ever has, or ever can, show that, by believing, he exposes himself to any danger, even if he could be mistaken, in this world or that which is to come. We appeal to all skeptics everywhere to point out to us, even if they could prove right in the end, what danger we are exposed to by believing! Suppose we persist in believing to the last breath, as well as opposing skepticism with our dying words, and skeptics could prove right in the end, what will befall us more than other men? Not a man in the world can show that any dangerous consequences can follow. The Christian risks nothing in any event. If right, his choice is the richest treasure—the brightest gem in this universe. He gains all things; is an heir of God and joint heir with Christ. His is a rich and unfading crown of glory and honor. But if it were possible for him to prove mistaken, he is even then as well off as any skeptic in the universe. Skepticism has nothing for the man that believes it, any more than for the man who opposes it. The fact then, that the Christian is safe—infallibly safe—that no serious consequences can befall him on account of believing, is an additional reason why a man should hesitate, pause and reflect most seriously, and have the most indisputable certainty before he receives or advocates skepticism.

For the sake of reasoning as safely as possible, while looking at the issue between Christians and skeptics, the one class affirming the truth of Christianity and the other denying it, we start the question whether the certitude on each side can be anything near equal. We claim that the certainty on each side bears no comparison—that on one side, the utmost height that can be attained is doubts, misgivings, and distrusts. On the side of unbelief, confidence is destroyed, confusion reigns, uncertainty prevails, and all is thrown into perplexity. "It is a leap in the dark." There is nothing reliable. The soul is left without a support, wavering, wandering and floating without a basis. Hence, in nine cases out of ten, in the decrepitude of old age, in declining years, in dangers, in solemn circumstances and approaching death, skepticism vanishes from the minds of men and they repudiate it. Precisely at the time when more than at any other period in their history, they needed a rock, a foundation, a resting place for the soul, all has disappeared and they find themselves sinking, hopeless and despairing, in the midst of thick clouds and gloomy darkness. This shows that there is no settled conviction, no established principles in the soul—in a word, *no certainty.*

How infinitely different the state of the Christian! In his declining years, in the decrepitude of old age, in dangers, in sickness and approaching death, that which he had believed in health, spoke of, relied upon and trusted in, now that he is evidently approaching his great and solemn change, becomes more deeply and still more deeply fixed in his soul. The solemnities of dangers, sickness and death, impressing him with the certainty that he must soon leave the world, presses the rock of God more closely to his heart, and he more tenaciously than ever holds on to his confidence, Here is something that looks like certitude! That which will comfort and support the spirit of the dying, when the world is receding, when all earthly comforts are powerless, when time is closing down the thick curtain, when life is failing and eternity, with all its solemn realities, is heaving into view, is unquestionably that of which the soul is certified, if there can be certainty in anything in this universe. No man who believes Christianity through the main career of life, so far as known to us, ever denies and repudiates it in death. It is, however, we claim, a fact, on the other hand, that nine-tenths of all skeptics, some time or other, before they die, repudiate and renounce their unbelief. But no man who believes Christianity, through the career of his life, at death renounces it. An instance of this kind we have never known nor heard of. This shows that there is a certainty on one side that does not exist on the other. No man, with this before him, can think the certitude on each side equal. The certitude preponderates infinitely in favor of Christianity.

In the very nature of things, upon their own hypothesis, skeptics never can prove to a *certainty* that they are right—that Christianity is false. Upon their own principles, they never can *know* Christianity to be false. The reason why they never can know this, or prove it, even if it were so, is that in order to escape the arguments of Christians, they repudiate the only testimony to which they could appeal as evidence in the case. They discard the testimony of history, the testimony of books, the testimony of men, and all records that reach back far enough to be witness in the case. The only means of information by which any question of antiquity can be known, any point decided, or anything shown to be true or false, they repudiate and discard; thus not only placing themselves beyond the reach of any argument to convince them that Christianity is true, but equally beyond the reach of any argument to prove it false. They dread the books of antiquity, such as histories, biographies, and commentaries. They shun and spurn the writings of the ancient fathers. Indeed, they have but little relish for old books, written either by friends or enemies of Jesus, for they all, of every grade and date, are interwoven with statements, references, dates and admissions of one kind or other, militating against the unbeliever, causing him to totter, and reel, but rather strengthening the believer. If they open the records, books, histories, biographies and commentaries of ancient times, with those of more modern date, as well as the writings of the fathers, they find the testimonies all on the other side; hence they repudiate all testimony of this kind. To what, then, can they refer for evidence to prove that Christianity is false? They acknowledge no source of information, by which they could know Christianity to be false, if it were false, and therefore, in the very nature of the case, they never can know it to be false or prove it to be false. The most they ever can attain is doubts and uncertainty, for two reasons: 1. They reject the only testimony that can throw any light on the subject; 2. It is an utter impossibility to know anything to *be* so, that is *not so*. The Christian hypothesis is the only correct one; Christianity is true, and no man *can know it to be false*. All skeptics are in uncertainty, doubts and confusion. They never can, in the very nature of the case, attain to anything more than wavering, want of confidence, fears, apprehensions and distrusts. They can neither know themselves to be right, nor others to be wrong. Their whole course can only destroy confidence, create distrust and confusion in the public mind. Their advocacy simply unsettles, darkens and involves the world in hopeless uncertainty, without clearing up or establishing anything. Theirs is a system of darkness, confusion and uncertainty that can benefit no one of the human race in any event, and, if they are mistaken, will involve all under its influence in ruin.

Is there no certainty in history? ancient records? in ancient books? in all books? Is there no certainty of any fact in antiquity? Certainly there is. We are as certain that there was such a man as Alexander the Great, as that there was such a man as General Washington, and as certain of either as that there is such a man as James Buchanan. We are as certain that there was such a man as Nero, as we are that there is such a woman as Queen Victoria. Who feels any doubt that there was such a man as Pontius Pilate? Such a man as Julius Caesar? No one ever thinks of doubting that there were such men. Who doubts that there were such cities as Jerusalem, Rome, Corinth, Ephesus? No man who has ever read. Why has the world come to such a unanimous agreement in reference to these places and men? Because the unanimous statements of all writers, in all books, both ancient and modern, furnish a chain of concurring and corroborative testimony, from ancient times to the present, which produces as much certainty in the mind as we have of anything we know. We are not more certain of what we have seen with our own eyes. Nor is there anything of which we can be more certain, than we are of numerous things which have come to us upon testimony of this kind.

We have simply mentioned this kind of testimony, not to elaborate it now, but to set the mind of the reader in motion and to open the channel of evidence to him that we are about to enter into.

In our next we shall define the proposition more explicitly, and show how the proof is to be applied to it. We never can appreciate evidence without the exact issue before the mind. The whole Bible bears upon one single proposition, which it has been pointing to from the first prophecy ever uttered to the final amen of the sacred canon. That is the proposition that men are required to believe, and which we shall endeavor to develop and sustain in these papers.　　　　　　　　　　　B. F.

-----o-----

LAST MOMENTS OF J. T. JOHNSON.

BOONE Co., Mo., JAN. 1, 1857.

BRO. FRANKLIN:—Although you have received the painful intelligence of the death of our dearly beloved Bro. J. T. Johnson, of Kentucky, yet I take the liberty of sending you the following extract of a private letter from Bro. Allen Wright, of Lexington, dated the 25th of December, 1856. Believing it will be read with interest by the numerous friends and relatives of that great and good man, it is sent for the purpose of being used as you deem proper. Bro. Wright says:

"DEAR BRO. ALLEN:—Your kind letter of the 18th inst. came to hand to-day, and I pen you a few lines in reply. Our fears, my dear brother, have been realized, and our beloved Bro. Johnson is no more. He died on the 18th inst., 15 minutes after six o'clock, P. M. Who can estimate the loss the cause of truth has sustained in the death of J. T. Johnson. But our loss is his eternal gain. With subdued and sorrowful hearts, we must submit to the will of Him who doeth all things well. Bro. Johnson arrived at our house of worship on the 4th Lord's day of November, just as I had commenced a discourse to quite a full house. I with pleasure gave way, and he addressed the people from the latter part of the 8th chapter of Romans. He continued his efforts for two weeks at nights, and sometimes in the day.

"On the evening of the 1st Lord's day inst., he gave his last discourse to an overflowing house, announcing an appointment for the following night, but was attacked on Monday evening and never entered our house again until borne there by six of his brethren. I had the mournful privilege of standing by his bed-side for eleven days and ministering to his wants the best I could, and at last to close his eyes. His attack was severe, and some sixty hours before his death, he had hemorrhage from the bowels, and it was evident he was sinking rapidly. Bro. H. M. Bledsoe told him, that he felt it to be his duty to inform him, that it was believed he must die in a few hours. He replied: "I did not think that death was so near, but let it come." Bro. B. asked him if he had any fears as to the future. He answered: "None, none whatever; I have lived upon Christianity, and can die upon it." He then spoke of Christ as a sacrifice for sin. Some twelve hours before his death, he sung in a low tremulous voice, a verse or two of the song, 'O, when shall I see Jesus.' At another time, he called for us to sing, 'O, land of rest for which I sigh;" naming the page 413 where it stands. Bro. Duval and myself sung it for him, and he participated in it the best he could. It seemed to me, Bro. Allen, that the old saint must have opened his eyes in paradise, without realizing that he had passed the ordeal of death.

"During his efforts here the weather was very inclement, but, nothing daunted, he hung on, determined to accomplish something for the cause of truth, and I think exhausted himself more than he was aware of. He had excited a great deal of interest, and there had been twenty-two additions up to the time of his attack; I have immersed three since, making twenty-five in all. He spoke several times in his efforts, of his daughters frequently writing to him: "Come home father, you will die some day, and not one of your children present to close your eyes." And so it was; but I thank the Lord, as he died from home, that his way was directed amongst us, where there were so many of his old brethren, and some who had never seen him—myself among them—that were permitted to show their esteem for him, by all the kindness and attention that Christian affection could bestow. He was always rational when spoken to, and was often preaching, exhorting, singing, etc. Thus he died as he had lived, showing the truth of the saying, 'The ruling passion strong in death.'

"His place will be hard to fill in our ranks. Bro. Allen, I am gloomy in my feelings, when I see so many of our able and excellent preachers falling in death, and you and I must soon follow. May we be prepared for that solemn hour.

"Bro. Palmer, hearing that Bro. Johnson was in Lexington, came down to see him. I saw them meet in our church, and 0! what a cordial greeting. But the old saints will meet no more until they meet in heaven. When the meeting closed here, Bro. Johnson and myself were to go to Independence; he wanted me to spend a month with him in upper Missouri, and I had determined to do so. He seemed to have formed an attachment for me, and would call for me during his sickness when I was absent. He also often spoke of you, and desired greatly to see you. He wrote to you by his son Victor, who returned home before his father's sickness, requesting you to come up, and assist in the meeting.

"We buried him in an air-tight metallic coffin, with a view to his children removing his remains to Kentucky, if they so determine. Bro. McGawey was with him two or three days before his death, and remained until his burial."

Thus passed the pilgrim days, and closed the earthly mission of one of the purest and best of men, and one of the most successful Christian ministers I ever knew. This is a sad, sad affliction, and truly can I "weep with those who weep" for him.

I thank the Lord that I was permitted to be with him so much just preceding his death, and while I sorrow at this mournful event, I nevertheless rejoice in the belief that I have one more friend in Heaven. Lord grant that I may be ready to meet him in "that land of rest."

Affec'y your Brother,

T. M. ALLEN.

-----o-----

VISIT IN LEXINGTON, KY.—ELD. THOS. SMITH.

During our very agreeable and pleasant visit in Lexington, Kentucky, we made the acquaintance of ELD. THOMAS SMITH, extensively known as one of the pioneer preachers and great and good men, in the work of the Lord, in Kentucky. He has now arrived at a good old age, and, by a paralytic stroke, has been disabled from preaching. Indeed, it is with great difficulty that he converses in private. He and his worthy and venerable companion are now comfortable and happy, in the estimable family of their son-in-law, Mr. Hamilton, in Lexington. We had truly an agreeable, instructive and interesting time with this aged couple, who now keep the New Testament near-by them, and make it the man of their counsel, while in their declining years, they look to Heaven, and lean, with the most implicit confidence, upon him who gave it, as their everlasting trust and supporter.

Many interesting and instructive considerations group around such patriarchal men as Eld. Smith, a few of whom God has still left with us, but whom, in his providence, in the ordinary course of events, he must soon take to himself. How good it is to be with them, to look upon them, think of their lives and look forward to their prospects, thus witnessing the power and consolations of the religion of Jesus Christ as exemplified in them and sustaining them to the last. We live in "the last days," when *old men,* no matter how great and good they may have been, are forgotten, neglected and passed by—when men are "without natural affection, unthankful, unholy." This must not be the case with Christians. We must remember these holy men, remember their works, and draw lessons of instruction from their lives. In the place of doting upon, lauding and spoiling our young men, who should now be persevering in their studies, labors, and examples of diligence in the work of the Lord, thus gaining favor with God and man, we should give due respect to the aged and infirm, comforting, strengthening and encouraging them. They are precious in the eye of God, have been precious gifts to us, and have made us what we are.

As to our young men, it is not yet time to decide upon their merits. They are yet to be proved. Many of them will slip and fall. The race is yet to run. Their sacrifices are yet to be made. Twenty years will tell the story, so that all men can see who of them are great and good men. It is useless to tell how talented, how learned and great a man is who has done, is doing and not likely to do anything great or good. The true measure of a man is his works. If they are great and good, he is a great and good man, and his greatness and goodness will generally be awarded to him by men and will certainly be awarded to him when God shall render to every man according as his works shall be. It is utterly out of the question for men to be inflated with the idea of greatness, who never do anything great. "By *their works,*" says the Lord, "you shall *know them.*" This is the infallible test—the divine test.

The venerable brother and father in Israel, whose name stands at the head of these remarks, gave us a sketch of an illustration of the present parties and their position in reference to their creeds, used by him in a debate, which we know would be interesting to our readers, and profitable, especially to young preachers, if we could present it. We cannot recollect it so as to pretend to anything more than the plan in general, without the particulars, which we will endeavor to sketch.

The supposed case ran in something like the following:

A day was appointed for representatives of all the parties to meet in one body, and the Lord was to meet with them. At the appointed time all were present. The Lord was the chairman, and explained the objects of the meeting as follows:

"When I was about to suffer for the world, I prayed for them who should believe on me, that they might be one, and when I was about to leave them, I admonished them to love one another. When I went to heaven, I gave them one spirit, united them in one body and set before them one hope. I also gave them one faith, and one baptism, by one spirit into one body, and taught them that I was their one Lord and that there was one God and Father of all. I also gave them the word which my father gave me—the law of the Lord, which is perfect—the perfect law of liberty.—to perfect the man of God and thoroughly furnish him to every good work. While they continued under this simple arrangement, they prospered, loved one another and honored my name among men. But I find you now divided, with different names, different churches, different faiths, and different laws. My house is set at variance throughout the world. I have, therefore, called you together to have you give your reasons for your present positions and creeds. I shall, therefore, call you by name, in turn as you sit around me in a circle.

"John Baptiste Purcell, stand up and state your reasons for your position and creed."

Purcell.—Master, we understood you to teach that Peter was the rock upon which the church was to be built, and from the keys you gave him and your language to him, we understood that he had power to remit and retain sins. From your command to him to feed your sheep—to feed your lambs, with many other things you said to him, we inferred that you made him Universal Pope, or Father.

As he died, and you declared the gates of hell should not prevail against the church, which we understand to be built upon him, as the rock, we inferred a succession from him down to your present Vicegerent, most holy Pope Pius IX, now in the chair, in the eternal city. We also understood his Holiness, Pope Peter, to teach that the ignorant and unlearned wrest the scriptures to their own destruction. We also infer that Holy Mother Church is infallible, from your requirement, to "hear the church." We, therefore, have piously taken the scriptures from the common people, who might "wrest them to their own destruction," and put them in the hands of holy doctors, authorized to expound them in due order. All Protestant heretics, who will not hear our most Holy Lord God, the Pope, who watches for their souls, will not hear Holy and Infallible Mother Church, but reject unwritten tradition, which we understand you require us to receive as divine authority, we anathematize; and we also call upon God, who created them, Jesus who died for them, the Holy Ghost, sent to reprove the world of sin, all the holy angels, the holy and blessed Virgin Mary, and Mother of God; the holy prophets, apostles and martyrs of Jesus, all the holy saints, with the entire army of the heavenly host, to anathematize them, from the crown of their heads to the soles of their feet, in all their parts, and sequester them from the threshold of the church of the Living God. Such is our zeal for Holy Mother Church, the oldest church, the only true church, the unchanging and infallible church. Here, Master, I stand, upon Peter the rock, under his Holiness, Peter's successor, and your visible representative on earth, Pope Pius IX, Arch-Bishop of Cincinnati.

Jesus.—That is sufficient. Take your seat, sir. N. L. Rice, stand up, sir, and state your reasons for your position and creed.

N. L. Rice.—Master, we have read your holy word, and, in meeting the gentleman who has just spoken, with all identified with him, we have felt it our duty to protest against the absurdity of Peter, your apostle, being the rock upon which the church is built. We believe that saying of St. Paul, that "other foundation can no man lay, than that which is laid, which is Jesus Christ." We also protest against all of his "unwritten traditions," as unauthorized. That we might understand ourselves, and be understood by others, as well as glorify your holy name, an assembly of our wise men have made this "blessed book" (holding up the Confession of Faith), in which we have protested against all "unwritten traditions," in the declaration, that "the Holy Scriptures contain all things necessary to salvation, so that whatsoever is not read therein, nor may be proved thereby, is not to be required of any man." Thus, you perceive, our position is declared and defined as we understand you to mean in your written word.

We have also found the doctrine of God's Eternal Decrees clearly taught in many passages in your most holy word, but not collected together, nor stated so concisely and explicitly, as we, in our wisdom, think it ought to be. We have, therefore, stated what we understand your meaning to be, in a concise form, which statement is received as the doctrine of our church, upon this point. We have found this article of great value, as it not only defines our understanding of what you mean, but keeps Armenians out of the church. In this way, this book has been of great value to us.

We also protest against the Romish doctrine that the Pope can "remit and retain sins," in the sense in which he pretends; but we have declared, in the Confession, that "church officers can remit and retain sins," in *our* sense of remitting and retaining sins.

In these, matters, we believe we have the doctrine of scripture; but for the sake of enabling all men to understand us, and having it in a more convenient form and better adapted to our church, we have stated what the scriptures mean, not only upon the points mentioned, but upon all other matters, in our Confession of Faith; or, in other words, we have set forth what we understood you to mean. Indeed, we have satisfied ourselves, that men cannot agree about what you mean in the New Testament. We, therefore, have set forth your meaning in a short, concise and simple form, that all may understand it. This Confession, we think, contains precisely what you meant, and when we believe and practice it, we think we are believing and practicing precisely what you intended. We have everything in this book that we think essential, and receive all who will unite upon it. As to the name, we think that is a matter of but little consequence, and, as we are favorable to the presbyterial form of church government, we call ourselves *Presbyterians*.

Now, holy and blessed Master, we protest against all the unwritten traditions of Rome, the pretense that Peter is the rock, and declare in favor of the all-sufficiency of the Holy Scriptures. We have examined these scriptures, ascertained what we think you intended, and have stated it in a concise form better adapted to all, than in the form as you originally set it forth in the New Testament. Blessed Master, as we have set forth in this book precisely what you meant, and nothing else, we entreat that you would set aside Arch-Bishop Purcell, for building upon another foundation, taking the scriptures from the people, and substituting tradition for them. We also beg you to set aside the Methodist Discipline, the Baptist creed and all others, as none of them set forth precisely what you meant, and decide in favor of the Confession of Faith, as it contains exactly what you mean. Believing that we are right, we fellowship those only who unite upon the Confession, though we admit many are Christians who do not believe it, and will not unite with us.

Jesus.—We have heard you sufficiently; take your seat, sir. Dr. Elliott, stand up and state your reasons for your position and discipline.

Dr. Elliott.—Blessed Master, we protest against Arch-Bishop Purcell's unwritten traditions, against his doctrine, that Peter is the rock, the doctrine that the Pope can "remit and retain sins," or that "church officers can remit and retain sins," as declared in the creed so extolled by Dr. Rice. We also protest against the doctrine of "God's Eternal Decrees," as set forth in the Presbyterian Confession of Faith, and we think the Doctrinal Tract of Father Wesley, in refutation of that doctrine, and the expose of it by Bro. Foster, which has lately appeared, have completely nailed it to the wall. But, blessed Master, we found that many did not understand your meaning clearly, and, in order that we might be understood we have set forth, in this blessed little book (holding up the Discipline), in twenty-five articles, our doctrines which, we think, precisely what you mean, in the New Testament. Most adorable Master, this book has been "founded upon the experience of a long series of years, and our observations upon ancient and modern churches," and Father Wesley says, speaking of our general rules, "all of which we are taught of God, to observe even in his written word, which is the sufficient rule and the only rule both of our faith and practice." Not only so, but that we show proper respect to your most holy word, we have inserted in our fifth article that great protestant statement, that "the Holy Scriptures contain all things necessary to salvation, so that whatsoever is not read therein, nor may be proved thereby, is not to be required of any man." We think we have what you meant set forth in this book, more brief, simple and easy to understand, than it is in the Bible; and we infer from our great increase, that you have abundantly blessed us, and that you intended that the M. E. Church should fill the whole earth. We entreat of you, therefore, that you approve of our book of Discipline and sanction our position as a church.

Jesus.—We have heard you sufficiently; take your seat, sir. J. E. Graves, stand up, sir, and state your reasons for your church and creed.

J. R. Graves.—Blessed Master, we protest against the Arch-Bishop, his creed—in one word against Rome, as the Man of Sin—the Mystery of Iniquity—Anti- Christ. We protest against Presbyterianism, and Methodism as offshoots of Romanism. We have turned our attention to your blessed forerunner, John the Baptist, whom God sent, and who first baptized. He preached the Baptist doctrine, founded the first *Baptist* church, and gave us our Scriptural name—*Baptist.* He established immersion in going "down *into* the water," "baptizing in Jordan," "baptizing in Enon because there was *much water* there." That all men may know what Baptist usage is, Regular Baptist doctrine, and understand the Regular Baptist Church, we have set forth what we understand you to mean, in Scripture, in the Baptist creed, in a very brief, concise, and simple form. Master, we have no other doctrine in our creed, than that contained in your word; but we have the meaning of that word set forth in a more concise, brief, and simple form than that in which you gave it, more convenient and easily apprehended. This summary contains the Regular Baptist doctrine, and all who receive it, we receive, and those who reject it we refuse to communicate with, as they are not of the "same faith and order." Blessed Master, we desire you to approve the Regular Baptist doctrine and creed, as what you meant in the New Testament.

Jesus.—We have heard you sufficiently; take your seat, sir. John T. Johnson, state your reasons for your position and creed.

Vol. II., No. 3.-2.

John T. Johnson.—Master, we understand you to mean precisely what you have said, in your revelation to us. We have carefully attended to your own most holy teachings, especially your prayer to the blessed Father, just before your great sufferings for our sins. We notice, that in that prayer you say: "The words which thou gavest me, I have given them." And, in the commission you gave the Apostles, you commanded them to preach the gospel to every creature—to teach all things whatever I have commanded you. We find also, that you say to the Apostles, that it shall not be you that speak, but the Holy Spirit shall speak in you—that your apostle Paul says, we speak not the words which man's wisdom teaches, but the words which the Holy Ghost teaches—that a mighty curse shall befall any man, or even an angel, who shall preach any other gospel, or even pervert the gospel of Christ—that the plagues of the Book of God shall be added to any man who shall add to the things written in that book—that if any man shall take away from the words of that book, God shall take away his part out of the book of life, and out of the holy city, and out of the things written in that book. We also find, in your most holy word, that you declare that if any man shall be ashamed of you, and of *your words,* that you will be ashamed of him before your Father and the holy angels. We have also found your declaration, that heaven and earth shall pass away, but not one jot or tittle of your word shall pass till all be fulfilled. This word, we find, you declare to be quick and powerful, and sharper than a two-edged sword—that it is spirit and life—that it will judge us at the last day. We find too, in holy scripture, the declaration that you have given us all things necessary to life and godliness—that all scripture given by inspiration is profitable for doctrine, reproof, correction and instruction, in righteousness, that the man of God may be perfect, thoroughly furnished to every good work—that he who hear these sayings, which the sacred historian has recorded from your lips, and does them, shall be like a wise man—that he who hears these sayings and does them not, shall be like a foolish man—that if any man shall do your word, he shall know of the doctrine whether it be of God. These and many other expressions, blessed Master, in your most holy word, cause us to fear and tremble at the idea of the least departure from your pure law as you gave it at the beginning.

We also find in your solemn intercessory to the Father, that you entreat that all who believe on you, through the word of the Apostles, may be one, as yourself and Father are one, that the world may believe. In many other parts of your word, we have learned that you require us all to be one—perfectly joined together, in the same mind and in the same judgment—that there be no divisions among us—in one word, that you require union among all the children of God. Blessed Master, we have thought much upon these things and prayed much in reference to them; and that we might not be offensive to our brethren who differ with us, we have tried to rid ourselves of everything that has not your authority; but your holy word, we have refused to give up. We are satisfied that union never can be had upon any of the platforms that gentlemen have presented upon this floor, or anything else in this world, than your holy word. But we cannot see why all who are disciples indeed, may not unite upon your own blessed word, receive it as their doctrine and the man of their counsel!

We know that we are weak and erring creatures; we have concluded that if there is any safe course for us, it is to receive precisely what you have said to us, do precisely what you have commanded, and hope for what you have promised. We, therefore, take your word—your blessed gospel, your holy doctrine—the whole of it, no more, no less, in your own precise words, as you gave it, as near as we can understand it, as the man of our counsel, and our directory to a better world. We prefer your own statement of *your meaning,* to that of any of the gentlemen that have spoken. We try to speak of your followers in New Testament style, as Christians, Disciples, etc. We also speak of the church as the church of God, church of Christ, temple of God, God's building, etc. Blessed Master, wilt thou be our Leader? Let our faith be in thee, and thy word be our guide.

Jesus.—Thou hast this: That thou holdest fast my name, and hast not denied my faith. Be thou faithful until death, and I will give thee a crown of life.

We have not used the same names mentioned by father Smith, except the name of Bro. Johnson, nor have we confined our remarks to the same points, but we are indebted to him for the plan.

Many important matters came to our notice, while in Lexington, that we thought of speaking of, but the length of this article forbids it now.   B. F.

-----o-----

DIALOGUE OF DEVILS.
NUMBER II.

Present *Diabolos, Apollyon, Lucifer* and *Diamonion.*

SUBJECT.—The most successful method of subverting and defeating the word of God and the mission of Christ.

Dialolos.—It is common in distinguished deliberative bodies, like this, to read the minutes of the previous meeting, but we will dispense with that old form, and hear reports of success.

Diamonion.—I have been out practicing among the people, most worthy *Diabolos,* upon your wise suggestions, made at our interesting meeting, a month ago. I am truly astonished at the results of following your sage counsels. You suggested, you know, that it would be silly and imprudent, in the extreme, to oppose many things that we know to be good and true; that in cases where the truth and goodness of a position are well established and popular, we must not deny it, but subvert it by means of some insidious stratagem. Well, sir, I have been experimenting in a case of this kind, that I will state, if it will be in order.

Diab.—It will be in order. Proceed.

Diam.—Well, sir, the sons of God assembled, with a great multitude, and I also was in the midst, though no one saw me, or knew of my presence, and—

Lucifer.—How did you avoid being perceived?

Diam.—There is not the least trouble in that. The image, or picture-makers, have invariably represented devils with frightful horns, terrifying tusks, and fearful claws, with dangerous fangs in their tails. So long as nothing of this kind is seen, the people never suspect that a devil is near enough to know anything that is transpiring.

Apollyon.—There cannot be any trouble on that score, for many people do not believe there is any such being as the devil in the universe.

Diam.—True, there are men who talk so, but you will perceive that they have not been led to this state of mind by directly denying that there is a devil. The way I have effected this state of mind was, to lead some men who would put on as much appearance of sincerity as possible, and in the place of denying the existence of the devil, preach that Judas was a devil, Peter was a devil, the Roman government was a devil, and all violent diseases were devils—that *devil* is the mere personification of evil, as men call it. But while I have gulled a certain class of men thus to preach, and thus to believe, and have seen such preaching produce tremendous laughter, among ignorant and wicked men, there are many that will never be caught in the meshes of such a net.

Apollyon.—You are right, most worthy Diabolos; and there are some few who will suspect a devil of being present, if in the sleeve of the most saintly looking worshipper in the assembly, though wrapped in silks and satins, and a gilt-leaved Bible in hand; or, if hid, in the folds of the prayer-book, or under the black robe of the clergyman. Rest assured, you must be on the lookout for these, for they will suspect you, unless well secreted. Indeed, these are apt to call upon the name of Jesus, to disarm and cast out every unclean spirit, fearing that some devil might be present, though they have not the slightest hint that one is about.

Diab.—You had as well be guarded, for you will find many that will suspect you, unless you are well concealed. Respecting those who preach that there is no devil, and believe it; you need give yourselves no trouble about them. They are certainly sufficiently blinded, and surely enough deluded, and will inevitably precipitate themselves, with all who can be influenced by them, into perdition, without any further attention from us. If you please, *Diamonion,* proceed with your report.

Diam.—I was going on to say, that I attended a great meeting, where a simple-hearted, plain man preached to an immense concourse of people. I tried to divert his course, distract his attention, or in some way defeat his power. His theme was the love of Christ. He dwelt upon the ruined and lost condition of man—his helpless and irrecoverable state, without a Savior! He then proceeded to dwell upon the great love of God—that he so loved the world that he gave his only be gotten Son, that whoever believeth on him might not perish but have everlasting life. He showed here that *perish* is the opposite of *life,* and that Jesus came to save man *from, perishing* and give him *life.* He dwelt much upon his sufferings, and with great effect upon his audience, as many were in tears. I trembled and fled, but resolved to defeat this preacher. But how was this to be done? The preaching was not only good and true, but what perplexed me was, that *everybody knew it to be good and true,* and I could not deny it. Many were almost ready to confess Christ. What was to be done to defeat this work?

I, therefore, resolved upon my plan. As I walked away, no one suspecting me to be anything short of a saint, I joined in with the general opinion and expression, touching the sermon—that it was *good* and *true,* though I hated it from the bottom of my heart, if such miserable beings as we are can be supposed to have hearts; and determined to make an effort to defeat it. In a few days I found a preacher to my liking, and had an agent of ours to engage him to preach at the same place, on the same subject. The time came, the preacher was ready and the audience large. I was in a conspicuous place, not to oppose, but to aid; not to tremble, but to laugh; not in my proper character and name, of course, but as a *Christian!* All eyes stared at the preacher, while he put on as sacred and solemn an appearance as was possible for such an one, and read the sublime words:"God is love." He now looked over the audience with such an air of consequence, wisdom and piety, that I feared he would overdo the thing; but I saw presently that it was an old art with him, and that he had full confidence that he could conceal the sophistry and do the work effectually. He set out by extolling the love of God to man. He eulogized the love of God, wrapped the subject in a great multiplicity of high- sounding words, and soared aloft in most eloquent strains and touching heights. I never heard so many eulogies upon the love of God, and upon God himself, nor such a combination of words and phrases from any man. He appeared unable to satisfy himself in language in describing how *good* God was, and when he had come as near as possible making his hearers believe, that the only attributes the Almighty possesses are love and goodness, he raised to his tiptoe and emphasized at the top of his voice, that so *good* a God—a God who is *love,* could not inflict upon any of his creatures endless punishment!

When he had concluded his sermon, he offered a tract I had engaged him to prepare for occasions like this, containing—"One Hundred Reasons for being a Universalist," for five cents each. In a few moments all the pious part of the congregation, in deep mortification, appearing confused and defeated, walked away. Some twenty wicked men and boys crowded round the preacher and bought his tract, and walked away laughing. Some infidels, as they walked away, said: "Anything can be proved by the Bible, and religion is all priest craft." Thus, you perceive, I have succeeded in defeating the word of God and mission of Christ, without directly denying either, in this case.

Diab.—You have acted your part admirably in this instance. This case illustrates the great principle of operation for mischief in these times. These are days of progress, and we must keep up with the times. But you must remember this: No stratagem will accomplish the work in all cases. This one that you have adopted that has been so efficient, and that you have reason to be proud of, will only delude a certain class; and, what you are bound to admit, too, a class very little disposed to be religious. But you will find that many will see the sophistry and the deceitfulness of the agent you employ to use it, and turn from both with the utmost disgust and contempt.

Luc.—What shall we resort to when this proves a failure?

Apol.—I have been acting upon a principle many centuries, that works admirably. Ever since Wickliffe, Tyndale, Coverdale, Chillingworth, Luther, Calvin, Huss, Wesley, etc., have made such an ado about "the Bible and the Bible alone," I have been engaged in an effort to defeat them, and had great success. I, therefore, beg leave to set forth my plans of operation.

Diab.—Proceed, sir; that is the great matter to be accomplished, and anything promising success in that work is precisely what we want.

Apol.—Well, sir; one move I have made, with delightful success in that direction, was to infuse the idea into the minds of the clergy, that their doctrine should he set out explicitly, in a brief epitome, or series of articles of faith, declaring wherein they protest against Borne, wherein they protest against heresy, and precisely what they believe.

Diamon.—I do not perceive how you ever succeeded in introducing a position in such direct contradiction to that popular sentiment, exhibited by the clergy, with such great power against the church of Rome, that the Bible, and the Bible alone, is the religion of Protestants.

Apol.—I had but little trouble in accomplishing that work. I had those I employed to do this work, to maintain that the brief, or epitome, was the Bible doctrine, condensed and concentrated into a small space, so that it might be easily comprehended. In the second place, to make the masses of the people believe that there was no innovation and no danger in the adoption of such a creed, I had them to insert at an early period in the creed, that the holy scriptures contain all things necessary to salvation, so that whatever is not read therein nor may be proved there- by, is not to be required of any man, as an article of faith, or requisite to salvation. This, they thought, covered over everything and made all safe.

Diamon.—But did they not perceive that these briefs, or epitomes, did not contain a tithe of the Bible doctrine? and did they not perceive, that every argument you could invent for this epitome was founded in the wicked assumption, that the Bible, and the Bible alone, is not sufficient? and that this attempt was to supply this deficiency, thus clearly implying that their leading position against Romanists was, in their own estimation, false?

Apol.—I kept this out of view, pretty much, and covered it up with many fine words, touching the usefulness of such a brief, to promote unity, peace, harmony and love, as well as to show all men what they believed, and covered it all over by saying, these articles are all taught of God even in his written word, which, as Mr. Wesley said, "is the only rule and the sufficient rule both of faith and practice."

Luc.—But could they not see, that if "God's written word was the sufficient and the only rule of faith and practice," that your epitome was a fifth wheel—that it was useless—nay, worse, that it contradicted the statement that the word of God was *sufficient?*

Apol.—No sir; they never saw this, but supposed- it was a most benevolent and wise arrangement, and would be a great advantage to the cause of God! You must not forget, that I did not employ ignorant men to do this work, nor wicked men, but the wisest and best men in the world; and I induced even these to think that this arrangement would be a great blessing to them. When I had once established the precedent, that one class of good and great men had the right to set forth such a brief or epitome of what they understood to be the doctrines of the Bible, the way was clear for another, and another set of men to do the same, until the land is filled with these briefs, or epitomes, set forth by bodies of men, both learned and unlearned, of the most contradictory nature, and thousands of men engaged in trying to prove the one which is the center of the little party to which they belong, and trying to disprove all others, by the Bible. In this method, I have succeeded in setting them at war, variance and hatred, thus engrossing their time and energies in proving *their* doctrine, pulling down and devouring their neighbors, while infidels laugh at their silly efforts to prove so many contradictory theories by the Bible. In the mean time, the Lord Jesus is not preached, the word of God is not maintained, and the world is thrown into confusion upon the whole subject, to such an extent that a man is considered ostentatious who will attempt to tell what the truth or the right way is.

Diab.—Gentlemen, these are interesting reports, and I am sorry that time fails to furnish an opportunity to hear all of you; but it is now time for us to adjourn for another month. Meantime let us profit by these suggestions, and make an effort, knowing that our time for working ruin is short. By the way, there are new influences at work, of a most powerful and overwhelming nature, that we must counteract, or our cause will suffer. A new set of Bible-men, Bible Revisionists and Bible Translators, with more learning, greater facilities, more zeal, more power and influence than any we have ever dealt with before; in a country of free institutions, free presses, free speech, and all other facilities for filling the world with the Bible and calling the attention of all mankind to it in a new and most powerful manner, have appeared. That silly laugh, attributed to us, supposed to be written by Dr. N. L. Rice, which we never had, is all turning the other way, and all the agencies we have yet employed to oppose revision, have proved abortive and fruitless.

REPORTER.

-----o-----

BRACKEN ASSOCIATION OF UNITED BAPTISTS.
NUMBER II.

In the close of our first No. we noticed the fright which the Bracken Association has taken, at the idea of a union between them and the "Current Reformation." We propose now to notice the evidence of this alarm, and the awkward predicament in which it has involved this Association. On page 5th of the Minutes, we learn that Elders Gardner, Hunt and James, were appointed to prepare "suitable Resolutions to be presented this evening." In accordance with this appointment, on page 6th, the following, among other resolutions, is introduced:

On motion of Eld. John James:

Whereas, The erroneous impression has been made, that there is virtually no difference between the Baptists and the current Reformation, and that the two denominations are rapidly blending in one; and

Whereas, There are *natural differences* between us and them on important and fundamental *doctrines*; therefore,

Resolved, That we distinctly and emphatically avow our belief that said Reformation holds, and is propagating *radical and destructive errors,* and that a union between the two bodies, at present, would be disastrous to the cause of true religion, and suicidal to the Baptist denomination; and, therefore, we would cordially recommend to all our brethren and churches, "Campbellism Examined and Re-Examined," by Dr. Jeter, of Richmond, Va., as a candid and truthful exhibition of the *doctrinal differences* between the denominations.

Here it is distinctly avowed, that union with us would be the ruin of the Baptist denomination: nay, more, that, as a denomination, to countenance and further such union would be to commit the fearful sin of self-murder! Clearly, then, these Elders are greatly alarmed at the mere thought of such a fearful result. And to prevent their good Baptist brethren everywhere from laying violent hands upon themselves, they distinctly avow, that, while "they teach the truth, the whole truth, and nothing but the truth," we teach "radical and destructive errors." That, therefore, as a matter of course, if their people unite with us, they embrace a "body of death," and must die in that embrace!

Well, gentlemen, as you have taken it upon yourselves, as guardians of the Baptist faith and order, to make against us the serious and fearful charge of teaching "radical and destructive errors," before the whole world, you will not think hard of being required to prove your charge, or take it back. Come, then, brethren, (we suppose you will allow us to use this freedom, as you say you esteem many of us as "Christian brethren"), we hold you bound as honorable men, as men of principle, as Christian men, by every consideration that ought to influence true men, to sustain your charge, or take it back. As Christians, you can have no interest in violating the 9th Commandment—in bearing false witness against your neighbors. On the other hand, if the fearful charge you have made against us is true, you owe it to yourselves, your people, to us and to the world, to make it good. On your own account, as men of truth, you must prove it. You must prove it to your brethren, the United Baptists, or they may unite with us on the word of God alone, and thus kill themselves as Baptists! As the servants of the Lord, you must prove it to us, for you are required to have compassion on the ignorant, and on them that are out of the way—in meekness and patience to instruct those who are in "destructive errors," that they may recover themselves from the snare of the devil, and thus avoid eternal perdition. Finally, Christian duty and benevolence require you to prove it to the world, lest we lead them into our "destructive errors," and they be lost forever. Clearly, then, brethren, you have taken upon yourselves great responsibilities—high obligations. And, we may say of you, as you have said of us, with a slight difference: "You may neglect your duties, but cannot escape your obligations." By every motive, then, that ought to influence Christian teachers, you are bound to make good your charge, or take it back as publicly as you have made it, and acknowledge you have done us great wrong. To hold and teach "destructive errors," is as dangerous a condition as we can conceive. And could we believe that the charge made against us by a few persons belonging to the B. Association, was believed by the whole denomination, we would feel it infinitely more than we do. But we are sure it is not, as we shall show before we have done. Come, then, brethren, let us compare notes—let us reason together.

What are our "destructive errors?" We believe:

1. That the books of sacred scripture, commonly recognized by Protestants, contain the entire word of God; a complete revelation of the will of God to man.

2. That "God alone is Lord of conscience, and hath left it free from the doctrines and commandments of men."

3. That "those things which are necessary to be known, believed, and observed, for salvation, are so clearly propounded and opened in some place of scripture or other, that not only the learned, but the unlearned, in a due use of the ordinary means, may attain unto a sufficient understanding of them;" and that "nothing at any time is to be added to scripture, whether by new revelations of the spirit, or traditions of men."

4. That "the infallible rule of interpretation of scripture, is the scripture itself.

5. That "the Supreme Judge, by whom all controversies of religion are to be determined, and all decrees of councils, opinions of ancient writers, doctrines of men, and private spirits, are to be examined, and in whose sentence we are to rest, can be no other but the Holy Spirit speaking in the scripture."

6. That the word of God does not recognize the Pope of Rome, or any privileged class of men in the church of Christ, as the depositories of the truth, and as the keepers of the consciences and faith of Christians.

7. That the right of private judgment is inalienable, and forms the basis of personal responsibility; that, in matters of religion, we must call no man Father, or Master; that the Bereans were more noble than the Thessalonians, because they heard the word with all readiness, and searched the scriptures daily, whether the things presented by Paul were so; therefore, many of them believed.

8. That, to us Christians, there is but one God the Father, of whom are all things, and we in him; and one Lord Jesus Christ, by whom are all things, and we by him; and one Holy

Spirit, by whose influences, extraordinary and ordinary, we have all saving truth and saving grace. "Holy men of old spake as they were moved by the Holy Spirit." The Apostles spake as the Holy Spirit gave them utterance, and God bore witness to the truth of their utterances, by signs and wonders, and divers miracles, and gifts of the Holy Spirit, according to his will. So that we may say, that all divine truth with its proofs, is from the extraordinary influences of the Holy Spirit. And as all those ordinary influences of the spirit, received by faith, by which we are led to repentance—brought to the Cross, to look on him whom we pierced, and mourn as one mourneth for an only son—by which we are made new creatures——created anew in Christ Jesus—filled with love, joy, peace, long-suffering, gentleness, goodness, fidelity, meekness, temperance; so we may truly say, that all we have, and are, and hope for, is of grace, is the result of divine influence. "Not by works of righteousness which we have done, but according to his mercy he saved us, by the washing of regeneration, and the renewing of the Holy Spirit."

1. That, on account of the sin of our first father, we are all fallen and doomed to death. As in Adam all die, even so in Christ shall all be made alive. We think that what we lost in Adam without our agency, we gain in Christ without our agency.

2. That our whole race has become alienated from God by wicked works—dead in trespasses and sins, and doomed to perish without divine aid.

3. That God so loved the world, as to give his only begotten Son, that whoever believeth on him might not perish but have everlasting life. Come then, brethren, what *destructive errors* do you detect in these items of our faith and opinion? But our sheet is full. God willing, we shall prosecute our review next month.

JOHN ROGERS.

THE RISE OF THE CURRENT REFORMATION IN KENTUCKY.

On the cover of *The Christian Repository,* for February, edited and published in Louisville, Kentucky, by Eld. S. H. Ford, we find, as the first item in his list of enducements, or as he styles them: "Substantial attractions," he promises his readers: "The Rise of the Current Reformation in Kentucky; its internal history; the struggles and divisions in the Baptist churches to which it gave rise; the gradual development of its principles, and the lives of the principal actors in the exciting drama." This proposition might have been made by one desiring and intending peace, love and joy in the Holy Spirit. It does not purport to be a direct and open proclamation of war; but results frequently follow the procedure of men which they did not intend or expect. Men frequently intend things, too, which they do not ostensibly set forth. But we stop not now to speculate upon the designs of Eld. Ford, whether they may be good or bad. Leaving all this out of the question, we doubt exceedingly the necessity of the history he proposes at this crisis. It is as clear as sunbeams, that the result cannot be promotive of peace, harmony or good will, let the intention be what it may. There is no more love, peace and good-will between the Baptists and Disciples now than the New Testament allows, and the proposed work will certainly not be productive of any more. To start back now to look over the ground anew, to see where provocation for complaint lies, we fear, will turn out like the following:

An old gentleman and his lady, who lived rather a quarrelsome life, agreed on a Christmas morning, that they would cease their wrangling for a year, which they did. When the year had passed off, the old gentleman observed:

"Well, my dear, we have lived one year without a quarrel."

"Yes," replied his lady, "and the last quarrel we had, *you begun it.*"

This was contradicted, and hostilities reopened and the former disagreeable state of things followed. This, we fear, will be the result with Eld. Ford's history.

We should like to know of Eld. Ford, if he thinks it desirable, for peace and the good of man, to have all the unpleasant things that occurred during the time to which his history is to refer, spread out anew and investigated. Would it not be infinitely more profitable to read the Bible, study the rise of Christianity, with most solemn prayer, for a better understanding of the will of God, for more of the mind and spirit of Jesus, love, joy and peace in the Holy Spirit? We say, would not such a course be transcendently more for the good of all parties, for the cause of Christianity, and the glory of God, than resurrecting the dry bones of contention, many of which have not had sufficient substance upon them to keep a hungry saint from starvation for many years? Would it not be better to throw a mantle over the rash steps taken, such as excluding as good members as the Baptist church contained, for no offence except commemorating the Lord's sufferings and death with the Disciples, than to spread them out before the world anew? Can these matters be spread out afresh without a renewal of hostilities? Does Bro. Ford desire this? or can he think of pursuing the course he marks out without such a result? He must know that he cannot. We put it to him, to decide whether it is better to have peace or war. We are for peace. If Bro. Ford is for war, and forces us into it, what follows is the result of his choice, not ours. If he thinks the Baptists have anything to gain by such a course, and will pursue it, in opposition to all our expostulations and entreaties for peace, *on him* rests the responsibility, *not upon us.*

If Bro. Ford proceeds, we will publish *every word* of his history, if he will publish *as many words* in reply. What do you say, Bro. F.? B. F.

-----o-----

EXCURSION TO NORTHERN ILLINOIS.
NUMBER I.

Residing amid the din of political strife, and in a community permeated with the offensive odor and ruinous fluid of a mammoth distillery, the ineffable disgrace of any civilized region, and desirous to enjoy a balmier and healthier atmosphere, at the kind invitation of a Christian brother, I set out, per railroad, from my home, on the 10th day of October, for the higher and purer latitudes of Northern Illinois. On the evening of that day I found myself at Pond, on the Illinois Central railroad. The town is small and the accommodations poor. I stopped at *a semblance* of a hotel, with the express stipulation, that I was to have a "downy bed of ease," as my uncarnal physical man protests against all indurated mattrasses. My host conducted me to an upper chamber, which no plasterer ever "graduated," and which, consequently, will never be guilty of suffocating any of its inmates, especially the multipeds.

I committed myself to my stipulated couch with an unconfined anticipation of a full fruition of the balmy reign of "nature's sweet restorer." But what a frustration of all this! The bed "ruffians" commenced an invasion on my poor and weary tenement, and after marching and counter-marching, animated, it seemed to me, by the music strains of a brass band sojourning on the opposite side of the street, *en route* to a democratic mass meeting on the next day, some thirty miles from Pound, they extracted no small portion of my already too reduced sanguineous fluid! And an hour before day, the proprietor of brandy and bugs extracted fifty cents out of my pocket for reclining and picking, not sleeping, three hours and a half, on a *substratum,* any constituent of which possessed scent sufficiently pungent to keep all volant bugs from tender melon vines, if placed in proper proximity to them. Such establishments passing for hotels are sheer humbuggings!

Next morning we progressed to Decatur,

the county seat, I believe, of Lacon, where we awaited the arrival of other trains, and breakfasted. Having to wait an hour or so, I endeavored to catch the "tone" of society in that community. The sounds I heard and the sights I saw, soon convinced me that if the exponents of the locality that presented themselves were not absolutely pro-slavery, they were unmistakably pro-liquor. The morning service at the shrine of Bacchus was thronged and earnest. Such jingle of *glasses,* not *"horns,"* such ingurgitations of disease and death is not every where witnessed! What was specially, painfully ominous to the patriot's heart in the spectacle, was the juvenile appearance of the worshippers, or rather, of the *victims.* The incense of tobacco accompanied the service, ascending in lingering volumes.

Society is an orchard full of fruit trees, some young and some old, some sound and some decayed. Liquor dealers are a hapless sort of entities, whose fated mission into the world seems to be, to hack some of these trees down for *their subsistence.* Many of them, from outside pressure, cry out: "We sell not to drunkards," which, in truth, means, we apply not our *glittering* axes to the old or decayed trees, but to the young and the sound. This is the "excelsior," aye, the acme in their mission of death. O, if it is fated that you must cut down for your living, trees that should bear fruit for affectionate wives and dependent children, cut the old and already riven ones, but spare, O! spare the young and thrifty, the glory of the orchard, and the hope of society! O, ye legislators, make laws that will strike the glittering implements of destruction from the hands of these hordes of *interior* "ruffians" and drive them back into the *state of* industry, and availability in their respective communities! Amen. Let every Lutheran, every Methodist, every Disciple, every Presbyterian, every Baptist, and every other Christian patriot, say amen and amen!! More anon.

S. K. HOSHOUR.
Pleasant Hill, Ia.

MISSIONARY SOCIETY.

CINCINNATI, OHIO, Feb. 10,'57.

BRO. OLIPHANT—DEAR SIR: I have just risen from a perusal of your valuable *Christian Banner,* which I always esteem a pleasure. I have for several years considered the *C. Banner among the safe and sound* publications, and wished it great success. But your strictures upon the Missionary Society, addressed to Bro. Loos, are so perpendicular that they lean a little the other way. I am as far from innovation as yourself, but when I speak of innovation, I do not mean innovation upon some of our own customs and usages, nor those of the days of the Christian Baptist, but innovations upon Christianity, or the usages and customs of the first followers of Christ. It amounts to nothing, that we have not been advocates of a missionary society, nor any plan of this kind, nor that we have been doing little in this way. The simple question that we should settle is the question, whether *it is right.* If it is, in itself, right, I am for it, no matter what our previous practice may have been; but if it is, in itself, wrong, I am against it.

I would be as clear as you, my dear sir, of encroaching in the least upon ancient precedent, or Bible authority. But I have thought upon this matter much, and searched the New Testament with great care; and, as now advised, cannot see any departure from Scripture, or ancient usage, nor any danger to the cause, in such an arrangement as our State Missionary Societies, or our general Missionary Society in this city. I have tried to simplify the question and look at it from different points, and can look at it from no quarter where I can see anything dangerous. Still I am willing to take one more look at it. Let it stand out as if we had never thought upon the subject before:

1. The gospel is clearly revealed, elaborated, and set forth upon the pages of the New Testament, so that we need no society, convention, council, conference, synod or assembly of wise men to decide for us, what we shall hold, or what we shall preach.

2. Each church is an independent community, fully authorized to interpret the Bible for itself, preach it, attend to its own discipline and government, as well as receive and exclude members.

3. The church has a mission from God to convert the world, or "disciple all nations."

4. Certain matters are clear matters of revelation; or, in different words, there is a clear province for explicit revelation. Here nothing may be added to, or taken from.

5. Certain matters are clear matters of human prudence and discretion; or, in different words, there is the clear province for the human understanding, or for human discretion and prudence.

6. It is not a question for the human understanding, whether the gospel shall be preached in all the world; whether the church shall labor to disciple the nations. This requirement is a matter of clear revelation.

7. Revelation nowhere names Bro. Oliphant to preach, the territory where he shall preach, the amount or kind of support he shall have; that he shall publish the *Christian Banner,* etc., etc. Nor does it in any place name your humble servant to preach, to publish the A. C. Review, books, tracts, etc., etc. The same is true of all the other editors, publishers and preachers. Nor does revelation decide where we shall build churches, who they shall employ to preach, where they shall preach, what amount of support they shall have, etc., etc. These, and an extended catalogue more of the same kind, are matters for the human understanding, for human prudence and discretion. Our Missionary arrangement is of this category. It is simply an arrangement of the brethren for preaching the gospel beyond the reach of an individual congregation, and for no other purpose, and just as legitimate, perfectly and properly in the range of our province, as Disciples of Christ, as publishing our periodicals, our own arrangements for preaching at home, or merely publishing books, tracts, etc., etc.

The Missionary Society, and our State Missionary Societies, are like the Bible Union, simply arrangements of the people of God for doing works that individuals, or single congregations cannot do. They are creations of brethren, supported by their voluntary contributions, for certain objects, and can only exist by their will and support. Every man employed by them, is a messenger of the brethren, "called and sent" by them to do a certain work. It has no authority over anybody, except those employed by it, for carrying forth its work, but is under the authority of the brethren who arranged it, and its perpetuity is dependent upon their will.

The brotherhood are generally becoming well satisfied with the shape things are assuming, and, I trust, a greater unanimity is about to prevail among us in all these matters. The Lord direct us!

With kindest regards, I am respectfully yours, BENJ. FRANKLIN.

Eld. D. OLIPHANT, Brighton, C. W.

DIALOGUE ON JUSTIFICATION.

Between a Baptist Preacher and a Disciple.

Preacher.—I agree with you on the mode of baptism and the *subject,* but I think that you lay entirely too much stress on its *design.* I cannot go with you there.

Disciple.—I do not see that we lay more stress upon it than our Savior and the Apostles did. We teach what they do on the subject, and I do not see how we can do that and lay too much stress upon it; or be in error.

P.—I think the Bible shows very plainly that a man is justified by *faith* without baptism. Our Savior says: "He that *believeth* on the Son *hath* everlasting life." If this is so—and it cannot be controverted—then the man who believes on Christ is justified by that faith, before he is baptized.

D.—I admit the truth of the passage as much as you do, and believe as strongly what is really taught in it. But I cannot understand it to exclude baptism. You might, in the same way, exclude repentance, and have a man justified by faith *without that!* You know it is well said, that "a good rule will work both ways." If you leave out baptism, you must, by the same rule, leave out repentance too. This would make havoc of the Bible. But to proceed with the passage, can a man have eternal life in this present state of existence?

P.—That is what the scriptures say: "He that believeth on me hath eternal life," as I before quoted. The believer is represented as having it—as being already in possession of it, and, of course, as being in a justified state. 'The issue is between you and the words of the savior. I hope that you will not attempt to deny so plain an assertion as the one I have quoted.

D.—I told you that I fully admitted the truth contained in it, but I cannot see any relevancy in it to the point between us, or how it can be made to apply to it. I think you certainly don't understand the apostle, or you would not make the application you do of the passage. The apostle Paul represents the Romans as seeking for eternal life, and says: "What a man hath why should he hope for?" If they already have eternal life, in the sense you seem to contend for, why are they represented as seeking and hoping for it?

P.—Paul does not say they were seeking for eternal life. His language is, that God will render "to those who seek for glory, honor and immortality, eternal life;" and we know that the apostle does not contradict himself.

D.-You are wandering away from the point. Paul speaks of them as seeking for immortality, and I cannot see any difference. It looks too much like a quibble. The passage is easily understood. We are told in the Bible, that God speaks of things to come as though they were; and there is a difference between being in possession of eternal life, and the enjoying of that life. All true Christians have the principle of eternal life in them; but cannot enjoy it in this world, as they have to be born from the grave first; as when a person believes on Christ he receives spiritual life, but cannot enjoy it until he is "born of water and of the spirit." I think this fully explains the passage.

P.—I think that you are wandering off from the point yourself, for we are on justification, and you have gone off on being born from the grave, and being born of water, etc. Let you Campbellites start where you may, you always get to the water before your are done. It is water! water! water!—water all the time!

D.—We are used to hear the like of that; and it is a. very good "come off," when pressed for argument. That is the very place that I want to get you at—to the water—to baptism, and as it is the place at which you started, I think that you ought not to talk as you do about it. Will you please answer me this question: Were the three thousand on Pentecost justified before they did what Peter commanded.

P.—[He made no reply to this.]

D.—Does not John say, that "many other signs truly did Jesus in the presence of his disciples which are not written in this book; but these are written that you might believe that Jesus is the Christ, the Son of God; and that believing, you might have life through his name?" Is not this the same life spoken of in the first passage—in the one you first quoted? and which shows that a man is not justified by faith, in the sense for which you contend. And if not, please tell me by what?

P.—But John says nothing about baptism there. He says it was "through the name" of Christ; and that is what we believe and teach.

D.—Here another question comes up—where do you find that name? Did not Peter tell the penitent believers on Pentecost, when they enquired what to do, to "repent and be baptized, every one of them, in the name of Jesus Christ, for the remission of sins?" Here you find the name of Christ connected with baptism, and we have no authority for separating them. "What God hath joined together let no man put asunder." And did not Ananias tell Paul to "arise, and be baptized, and wash away his sins, calling on the name of the Lord?" How will you get around these passages?

P.—I will admit that the Jews were commanded on Pentecost to be baptized for the remission of sins, or in order to remission, but it was their sins in crucifying the Savior; as when Peter had convicted them of that, they then cried out and asked what they should do; and he told them to repent and be baptized for the remission of these. And as to Paul's case, it was his sins in persecuting the church, that Ananias told him to be baptized and wash away.

D.—Well, I am truly glad to hear you make these admissions, for these were sins of the darkest and most aggravated character; and if they could thus receive the remission of these, in baptism, certainly they could and did receive the remission of all their past sins. You can make no distinction. And even admitting your interpretation of the passage, you cannot, according to it, have the believer justified by his faith before he is baptized, since he is not really justified until all his sins are forgiven!

P.—[Again he can make no reply.]

D.—Are we not taught that Christ "came to his own, and his own [the Jewish nation] received him not; but to as many as received him, to them gave he power to become the sons of God, even as many as believed on his name?" Now can a man have this eternal life, of which you have been speaking, and not be a son of God?

P.—No, he cannot.

D.—How was it, then, that he had the power of becoming a son when he believed?

P.—He had the power to be baptized.

D.—That is enough—we will cease our conversation for the present. You have admitted all I contend for, and that is sufficient.

J. R. H.

-----o-----

DISCOURSES ON CHRISTIAN EVIDENCE.

BELOVED BRO. FRANKLIN:—The following paragraphs contain reflections so valuable, that I cannot refrain from their transcription. I hope they may prove to be "words fitly spoken," which are, as Solomon tells us, "like apples of gold in pictures of silver."

If discourses on Christian Evidence are to be a profit to any, there appear to be one or two preliminary conditions in the choice of a subject, now needful to be observed, which, failing to observe, we shall, of sure consequence, fall wholly short of those ends of usefulness which we desire. And first, a work of Christian defense will be marred, if the subject which we select be one upon which none of the great and decisive issues of the mighty conflict between truth and error depend; as when in jousts and tournaments a knight touches the shield of some feeble adversary, passing by and leaving the stronger and more accomplished unchallenged. For thus it is with us, when we go off upon some minor point, which, even were it plainly won, would leave us in no essential degree the better, nor an adversary the worse; which he might yield without being dislodged from his strongholds of unbelief, without even feeling them less tenable than before.

Or again, it will be to little profit that we deal with hindrances to men's belief which once indeed were real and urgent, but of which the urgency and reality have long since departed; if we take our stand in some part of the battle-field from which the great turmoil of the conflict has now ebbed and shifted away; or conjure up phantom forms of opposition, which once indeed, were living and strong, but now survive only in the tradition of books, and at this day practically weaken no man's faith—disturb no man's inner peace. This, too, were a fatal error, to have failed to take note of that great stream of tendency, which has borne us amid other shoals, and near other rocks, from those among which our forefathers steered with manful hearts the bark of their faith, and of God's great mercy made not shipwreck of that faith among them all.

Or, once more, Christian apology fails in its loftiest aim, when it addresses, not the whole man, but the man only up on one side, and that not the highest, of his being; when it addresses, not the conscience, the affections, the will, but the understanding faculties alone. How often do we meet in books of Christian evidence, the attempt made to substitute a logical or mathematical proof of our most holy faith for a moral one; to ascend to that proof by steps which can no more be denied than the successive steps of a problem in geometry, and so to drive an adversary into a corner from whence there shall be no escape. But there is always an escape for those that in heart and will are alienated from the truth. At some stage or other of the process they will successfully break away, or even if they are brought to the end, they remain not with us long. And we may thank God that it is so, for it. is part of the glory of the truth that it leads in procession no chained, no unwilling captives—none that do not rejoice in their captivity, and share in the triumph which they adorn. It is not, therefore, that arguments which address themselves to lower faith of man's being, than the highest are to be rejected—but only their insufficiency acknowledged; that they of themselves will never introduce any to the inner sanctuary of the faith; but can only lead him up to the doors. Most needful are they in their place; most needful that Christianity should approve itself to have a true historic foundation; that as a fact in history it should stand as rigid a criticism as any other fact; that the books which profess to tell its story should vindicate for themselves an authentic character; that the men who wrote these books should be shown capable and credible witnesses of the things which they deliver; that the outworks of our faith should be seen to be no less defensible than its citadel. But, after all, the heart of the matter is not there; when all is done, men will feel in the deepest center of their being that it is the moral which must prove the historic, and not the historic which can ever prove the moral. That evidences drawn from without may be accepted as the welcome impresses, but that we can know no other *foundations,* of our faith than those which itself supplies. Revelation, like the sun, must be seen by its own light; being itself the highest, the ultimate appeal with regard to it cannot lie with any lower than itself. There was, indeed, a sense in which Christ received the witness of John, but there was another in which He received not witness of any man, only his own witness and his Father's. Even so is it with his Word and his doctrine. There is a witness which they can receive of men; there is also a witness which no other can yield them than themselves. Affectionately yours m the Lord.

CHAS. D. HURLBUTT.
Steamboat Prairie Rose, Dec. 17,'56.

ERRATA.—On page 67 for "*drunk*" read *dumb.*

-----o-----

Communications.

PHOENIX POST OFFICE, BUTTS CO., MD.
DEAR BRO. FRANKLIN:—Enclosed you will please find two dollars for the current and coming year of the REVIEW—sent me, I presume, at the request of Bro. G. W. Elley. All the numbers from July to November, inclusive, came safely. So far, I find in it much to admire, instruct, strengthen and comfort; would that as much could be said of the many whose aim it is to enlighten us on the great subject of human redemption. If we have not attained to the full assurance of understanding, it is not for the want of books, The body is in more danger from too much eating and too much drinking, than the mind is from too much reading. There is, however, a thousand times more reading

than there is of thinking. Too much reading is to the mind not very much more to be approved, than too much eating and drinking for the body; its tendency is to weaken rather than strengthen; still we must eat, nothing can be done without it; and so must we read, nothing can be done without it. But as there are more who eat than work, so are there a thousand times more who read than think. The legitimate object of reading is to help a man to think, and for this a little at a time, of the right sort, is all he needs. How refreshing it is to follow a mind that understands itself and is able to enlighten and instruct those for whom he labors. But, Oh! what accumulated masses await their certain doom. "To the moles and to the bats." One can but feel a sort of inward, inexpressible something—call it what you may—in being in full fellowship with a community whose teaching, preaching and writing has done more to instruct and enlighten the mind on the great subject of human redemption, than any other people since the days of Peter, John and Paul. In no language is there to be found a production of human intellect and genius so full of correct thought—so easy *of comprehension by the common mind*—in such perfect harmony with the "Philosophy of the plan of salvation" as the "Christian Baptist." The same thing, in a remarkable degree, is true of the writings of our most able and distinguished men; would that of such there "were a thousand times as many more than there are," for it is for us but to lift our eyes and see that the harvest is great and the laborers few. May the great Lord of the harvest send forth strength out of Zion to help us as a people to fill up our calling and mission in bringing back the minds and hearts of our contemporaries to a knowledge and enjoyment of the gospel, as given to the world by its great Author through his own chosen Apostles. Had we known of your being at "Beaver Creek" in time to have reached you, certainly your return home without visiting Baltimore, could not have been, if any effort on our part could have prevented it. Bro. Elley, I presume, will keep you advised of his labors in our city; so far we have had four confessions, and the prospects for good are very encouraging. Yours most truly and affectionately. GEORGE AUSTIN.

"The days of our years are three score years and ten; and, if by reason of strength, they be four score, yet is their strength labor, and sorrow; for it is soon cut off."

BRO. FRANKLIN:—A short time since, I went some distance to see an old mother, in Israel, who has been blind for many years, and is at least ninety-one years old. She, and her daughter, who is near seventy, live together. They are Israelites indeed. I have known them for more than a third of a century. Frequently, in the lifetime of the head of the family, I preached at their house. They have a comfortable home, and two servants to help them; and might live more free from care, by boarding with some of their friends. But they prefer their loneliness, that they may have a better opportunity to commune with their God. and their own hearts. They say their neighbors are kind, but when they come to see them few of them have anything to say of God, of Christ, or the things of religion. Said the dear old woman, "their talk is all about the things of time and sense, and these things (said she) do me no good, they are all not worth a thought."

How true! And what a rebuke of the worldliness of the church! I enjoyed the evening with them highly, singing for them the songs of Zion, and talking with them concerning the kingdom of God, and the name of Jesus; and uniting with them in prayer, evening and morning.

They seemed overjoyed with our interview. Ah! thought I, how much more blessed are these humble and pious women, in the midst of their plainness and simplicity, than Presidents and Emperors, and Kings, and Queens, and Nobles, and Senators, and Judges, and Sages, and the vast multitudes that no one can number, who, throng the great thoroughfares of wealth, of pleasure and fashion, and seek their happiness from this world! While all those who look upon the outward appearance, would esteem the condition of our aged and humble sisters most unfortunate. He who sees not as man sees; who looks on the heart, and sees the spirit of true devotion to Him burning there, says, to such will I look, and with such will I dwell, who are humble and of a contrite spirit, and tremble at my word. So true is it, that what is highly esteemed among men is an abomination to God, and what is highly valued by Jehovah, is an abomination to the devotees of this world. Of man's "miraculous mistakes," this is the sum, the laying up for himself treasures upon earth, rather than treasures in heaven—the laboring all his days for the meat that perishes, rather than for the meat that endures unto eternal life. O, God! let thy people be my people, let their God be my God—where they live, let me live, and where they die, let me die! For a day in thy court is better than a thousand in the courts of earth—in the circles of pleasure and fashion. I had rather be a door-keeper in the house of my God, than dwell in tents of wickedness. For the Lord God is a sun and shield; the Lord will give grace and glory, and no good will he withhold from them that walk uprightly.

Our aged mother said to me, in her conversation, that she was the first person whom B. W. Stone ever immersed. It is known that after he and his co-laborers broke off from the Synod of Kentucky, in 1803, and took their position on the Bible alone, and the New Testament especially, as the only basis of union for the church of Christ, for some years the war waged between them and their opponents upon the questions of human creeds, Calvinism, &c., and that it was not until 1807 their eyes began to be opened upon the subject of baptism. Our old sister was baptized then, in 1807.

JOHN ROGERS.

Success of the Gospel.

ILLINOIS.—Bro. J. S. Sweeny, Waverly, Jan. 13, writes:"There have been three additions to the saved in the bounds of my poor labors, since I wrote you last."

INDIANA.—Bro. Jackson Dobbins, Reynold's Station, Jan. 25th, writes: "In August last, Bro. Geo. Campbell held a meeting here, resulting in eight additions. And this month we have had five more."

Bro C. W. Harrison, Feb. 5, writes: "A six days' meeting continuing over the first Lord's day, in Feb., held at Hamilton, Ind., resulted in 19 additions—16 by immersion—mostly young persons.

MISSOURI—Bro. C. P. Arbuckle, Linn Creek, Jan., 1st, writes: "My labors, during 1856, were mostly within Dallas, Camden, and Miller counties, and resulted in 170 additions. Brethren Davis, Glass, and Satterfield have assisted me."

KENTUCKY.—Bro. J. H. Walton, Germantown, Jan. 30th, writes: "Bro. J. A. Brooks, held a meeting here the 1st of this month, when two intelligent young ladies were baptized. Bro. Brooks bids fair to make an able evangelist."

Our meeting at Lexington, Ky., continued over two Lord's days, the 2d and 3d in Jan. There were 15 additions.

At Flemingsburg, Ky., Saturday, Jan. 31, we commenced a meeting which continued several days with good results. Nineteen were added to the congregation.

Many of the incidents connected with both of these meetings, render them among the happiest times of our life.B. F.

Ohio.—Bro. R. B. Henry, Lafayette, Jan. 12, writes: "We have had 15 additions and 2 reclaimed, recently, through the labors of Bro. T. M. Bernau of New Paris, Ohio.

Feb. 11th, 1857.

BRO. FRANKLIN:—I have just closed a meeting of twenty days, in Clermont county, Ohio, which resulted in 17 additions (fifteen by immersion). A general interest evinced in the vicinity.

THOS. J. MURDOCK.

-----o-----

Obituaries.

DIED, in Noblesville, Ind., at the residence of her son-in-law, J. M. Mallery, Jan. 21st, 1857, Mrs. ABIGAIL EMMONS, aged 78 years, wanting six days.

She made a public profession of her faith in Christ, was immersed, and joined the Baptist Church in Swanton, Vt., April 7th, 1816, and remained in this connection till the Spring of 1832; when, with her son, F. W. Emmons, she. united with the church at Wellsburg, Va. In the fall of 1834, she came with him and family to Noblesville, and was one of the original members of the church in the "current Reformation" here—or, rather, joined it after its formation, early in the winter of 1835, of which she continued a member till her death. Mrs. Emmons was a worthy woman, possessed of a vigorous mind, and of established Christian principles. Her weary pilgrimage has ended in hope, through Christ, of everlasting rest.

DIED, on the night of the 11th of January, at the residence of her father, in Hamilton county, in the 18 th year of her age, Amanda L. Truman.

Our loved sister who has been so early called from us, made a profession of Christianity and was baptized into the communion of the Christian Church, at the age of fifteen, and from that period her life was that of a model Christian. Ever foremost in the Sabbath school, ever present in the sanctuary, and in the home circle or among friends, ever wearing the "ornament of a meek and quiet spirit, which is, in the sight of God, of priceless value." Disease, for many months preyed upon her, yet she murmured not. Long before her departure, she expressed perfect willingness to leave this world, although her youth, affection for friends, and a desire to lighten a mother's cares, while raising a large family, of which she was the eldest, caused her, at times, to wish to remain, but to the will of her Heavenly Father, whether to live or die, she expressed her entire resignation. Her faith in her God, and in his blessed promises, grew brighter and stronger, so that at last, when Death, with his icy touch, benumbed her frame, and caused the damp, cold sweat to gather upon her forehead, she calmly asked, "is this death?" and, when told that she was dying, she shrunk not, but welcomed him as the messenger to waft her blood-washed spirit to a happier home. R.

DIED, on the 11th of October, 1856, at New Bloomfield, Calloway county, Mo., in the 49th year of his age, DANIEL M. WHYTE, after a few days illness. He obeyed the gospel in 1850, and has ever since been a zealous and worthy member of the church of Christ, at Bloomfield. Bro. Whyte was a generous and- noble man—a warm and devoted fried of Bethany College, and liberally assisted in the endowment of the Missouri chair, in that Institution. He gave near $2,000 to the education of a young Brother, who was several years at Bethany, preparing for usefulness in the Redeemer's cause. Indeed, he was ready for every good work, and long will he be remembered as a philanthropist and a Christian. He was an affectionate husband, a warm and devoted friend, and useful citizen; well may his sorrow-stricken wife, numerous relations and many friends mourn his loss to them. Much more could be said in praise of Bro. Whyte, but I know you can't insert long Obituaries. T. M..

THE AMERICAN CHRISTIAN REVIEW.

A SERMON.
On the Life, Character, and Death of Eld. John T. Johnson.
BY ELD. A. RAINES, PARIS, KY.
Your fathers where are they? And the prophets, do they live forever?—ZECHARIAH, ch. 1: 5.

Our brother Johnson is dead. He departed this life on the 18th of last December, at fifteen minutes after six o'clock, in the evening, at the residence of Bro. Thos. C. Bledsoe, of Lexington, Missouri. His disease was pneumonia. It was violent and painful; but he was abundantly sustained, by the favor of God, in patience and resignation, and died full of the hope of a blissful immortality!

BRETHREN AND FELLOW-CITIZENS!—I present myself before you to-day, feeble and unworthy as I am, to address you on the life, character, and death of our departed brother. I do not wish, however, to be considered as the mere eulogist or panegyrist of Bro. Johnson. He was too rich in religious principle, too brilliant in moral character, too irreproachable in life, too exemplary in all good works, to need an eulogy at my hands. I stand here to point you to his virtues, to his excellencies, to his noble deeds, not that you may admire only, but that you may imbibe his spirit, and copy his example.

We have often heard objections to the language of praise, as used in the pulpit, in application to deceased persons. This practice cannot be too much reprobated, as to encourage sinners to the belief, that living, if not dying, in sin, they may be converted on a death-bed, and reach heaven as certainly as if they had consecrated their days to the service of God. Giving due praise to the genuine. Christian, is as different from that fulsome and sinful flattery which we sometimes hear in funeral sermons, as light is different from darkness, or the rectitude of God from the puerile vanities of earth. Paul, who determined to know nothing but Jesus Christ and him crucified, praised his brethren, living and dead. And was not this knowing, or making known, Christ and him crucified? What have we that we did not receive? Whence has the Christian his graces and virtues but from Jesus? Are they not all fruits of the Holy Spirit? And are not the Spirit, and all the Spirit's fruits, gifts of the love of Jesus—benefits made accessible to us through the bloody passion, and most cruel death of the Son of God? We consider therefore, the excellencies of Christians to be the glory of Christ, and of Christianity!—for what other system ever purified, elevated, adorned, glorified human nature and human character, as Christianity has done? We shall, therefore, in giving you the characteristics of our brother, consider that we are preaching Jesus, and giving the most effectual testimony of which we are capable, to the divinity and excellency of the Christian religion!

We proceed now, to the brief consideration of the solemn words which we have selected, rather as a motto than a text: "Your fathers, where are they? and the prophets, do they live forever?" This passage suggests to our mind the mortality of man, the transitory and evanescent nature of all terrestrial things!

"Your fathers, where are they?" Gone to the narrow house appointed for all the living—whelmed beneath the dark cold waters of death—numbered with the pale nations underground—departed to that undiscovered country, from whose bourne no traveler returns. Their love, and their hatred, and their envy are now perished, neither have they any more a part in all that is done under the sun.

> "Princes, this clay must be your bed,
> In spite of all your towers;
> The tail, the proud, the reverend head,
> Must lie as low as ours."

"And the prophets, do they live forever?" Their ashes mingle with the dust of all past generations. Death, the insatiate archer—the ruthless leveler—the remorseless destroyer—the relentless enemy of man, has thrown the good, in common with the bad, into one vast, promiscuous ruin. There the dust of enemies embrace! The murderer and the murdered, in each other's arms repose! The persecutor and the persecuted, the oppressor and the oppressed, the master and the servant, sleep together, the long, damp, deep, dark sleep of death! The thunders of heaven—the artillery of earth—the giant tramp of armies—the convulsive throes of earthquakes, upheaving earth, and ocean, and mountain, cannot disturb their slumbers! Nought but the voice of the Archangel and the trump of God!—the summons: *Awake ye dead, and come to judgment!*

But there shall be a resurrection of the dead, both of the just and the unjust. On that bright morn, the righteous, a bright and happy band, with crowns on their heads and palms in their hands, symbols of victory, shall stand on the banks of deliverance and sing: *O! death, where now thy sting! O! grave, where now thy victory!*

In that bright band will be congregated all our righteous fathers. And the patriarchs will be there, and the true prophets will be there, and the apostles will be there, and the martyrs will be there—a great multitude that no man can number, having washed their robes, and made them white in the blood of the Lamb, will be there;—and in that cloud of witnesses, that constellation of worthies, we hope, with a steadfast and joyful hope, to meet our Bro. J. T. Johnson, shining as the brightness of the firmament, and as the stars forever and ever!

CHARACTERISTICS.

We approach now, not without trepidation, the characteristics of our brother. We feel that this is a difficult task; and it is, especially so, in the case of Bro. Johnson. He was a man, and a preacher, *sui generis*—a perfect *original!* I shall not, however, attempt to sketch the minor traits, or lighter shades of his character, but those, only, of the more bold or prominent class, leaving it to a more accomplished scribe, in a biography, or otherwise, to supply the deficiencies. We say, then:

That he was a man of great physical or natural courage. We shall give but one incident in proof of this position. We could give many, but as physical courage is not necessarily a Christian characteristic, one may suffice. He was at Fort Meigs at the time at which it was besieged by the British and Indians. He was sent out with a detachment—whether as commander or not we are not prepared to say—to drive the enemy from a certain position, and to spike his guns. This was an exceedingly perilous enterprise. It was bravely executed, however, and the detachment returned victorious to the Fort. I asked Bro. Johnson how he felt during that rencontre. He informed me, that until after his return to the Fort, he was insensible to fear—that during the engagement he had no apprehension, for a single moment, that he might, by any possibility, be penetrated by a ball! This instance is as good as a thousand, to prove the sterling bravery of our brother; for what he did in this instance, he would, on precisely the same principle, have done in a thousand, or if you please, in ten thousand other instances!

2. *Great moral courage.* This attribute manifested itself most unequivocally whenever Bro. Johnson was subjected to the pressure of a formidable, sectarian opposition. You might, then, see it in the glance of his eye, in the expression of his face, in the movement of his arms, and in all his gestures; but, especially, might you hear it, in the intonations of his voice, in the energy of his speech, and in the pungent significance of his words. By the same figure of speech, by which one of old was said to breathe threatenings and slaughter, might it be said that our brother breathed moral courage. Hence, under his preaching, the despondent was nerved with hope, and the moral coward became valiant for' God and the truth. "Would I be a coward," was one of his strong, and frequent appeals; and often he would say: "Before I would compromise away the Christian religion, or any part of its truth, I would lay my neck upon that table and have my head chopped off with a broad-axe" And I verily believe he would have done it! I doubt not that he would have followed truth to the martyr's stake, or to the mouth of the cannon! When he was engaged in fervent exhortation, he often reminded me of some great captain, haranguing his troops, and inspiring them with his own fearless and indomitable spirit—urging them onward to deeds of noble daring and to victory! This characteristic will receive further illustration and proof from that which immediately follows.

Large conscientiousness. His parents, and numerous relatives, were persons of wealth, and of high respectability. He moved, from his infancy, in what is termed the higher circles. He was bred to the law, and became a popular practitioner at the bar, commencing his practice before he had gotten out of his minority. Twice he represented his congressional district in the lower House of Congress. He served several sessions in the legislature of Kentucky. Taking, therefore, his position in society, his family patronage, and his deserved general popularity, his prospects were most brilliant in the departments of both law and politics. Just at this point he became a professor of religion, and joined the Baptist church. In a few years after, he imbibed the sentiments of Bro. Campbell, and became a preacher of the gospel, and an advocate for that which has been vulgarly dubbed Campbellism. These views were exceedingly unpopular at that time. Meanwhile his fortune had been swept from him, in consequence of his generously loaning his name to others as security. These were circumstances to try a man's soul. Why did he not continue to identify himself with some popular religious party? By preaching an unpopular gospel, he could certainly not have calculated to better his circumstances, in a pecuniary point of view. Why did he not continue the practice of law? This is a highly respectable and lucrative profession, from which he might have derived not only a competency, but also wealth. We have the answer in one word—*conscientiousness!* His conscience dictated that it was his duty to preach the gospel, and he had the moral courage to run, in pursuance to its dictates, in the pathway of duty, he counted wealth, and fame, and pleasure, and all worldly good, but refuse that he might win Christ—that *his* might be the excellency of the knowledge of Christ Jesus, our adorable Redeemer. Indeed, I have been told, by very respectable authority, that from his boyhood, he was highly honorable and conscientious. These practical facts—not a tithe of what might be adduced—may suffice to prove, not only the moral courage, and conscientiousness of our Bro. Johnson, but serve as an exhibition of the moral sublime, in the religious career of that great and good man, in the faith, and hope, and love of the gospel, in putting under his feet the pomps and vanities of the world, and living wholly for Christ, and the salvation, present and eternal, of his fellow men.

4. *He was a lover of men—a great Christian philanthropist.* The ardor and perseverance with which he engaged in all plausible Christian enterprises, abundantly sustain this proposition. Take, if you please, the question of Christian union; never did his heart glow with love more intensely—never did he speak more eloquently, than when engaged on this subject. He knew that to "endeavor to keep the unity of the Spirit, in the bonds of peace," and to be perfectly joined together in the same mind and judgment, avoiding all divisions, are Divine commands. He knew that the union of all Christians was the subject of an impassionate petition of our Savior, in his valedictory prayer. He felt that the spirit of Christian union is "the spirit of power, and of love, and of a sound mind"—leading to a golden era, for which all the godly pray, and against which the mere sectarist vents all his envenomed hate. He knew; he felt; he acted. Hence we find him, not long after he had become a preacher, a co-operant with Bro. Stone, another philanthropist of the highest order, in bringing about a union between the Christians nicknamed Newlights, and the Reformers, as they were sometimes called. This union was happily consummated; and glorious, already, have been its fruits on earth; a glory to be perfected only in heaven.

Shortly after the consummation of this union, we find Bro. Johnson appointing a general union meeting, at Lexington, Kentucky, to which all the religious parties were invited, especially the clergy, to investigate the principles of Bible union. I need not, I presume, inform my auditors that the clergy were very scarce at that meeting. Wounded, and bruised, and ready to die, as, perhaps, they esteemed us, and greatly needing their learned assistance, Catholic and Protestant, for once of one mind, in at least one particular, like the priest and the Levite, passed by on the other side! Nay, more; some of them warned the people, in some of the public prints, not to attend our meeting. Sagacious gentlemen I verily, I say unto you, you have your reward! But a large number of persons did attend, and we had a glorious meeting. We discussed, among ourselves, the principles of Christian union—worshipped and rejoiced together, and were greatly edified.

Sometime after this, a Kentucky State Co-operation was gotten up for the purpose of evangelizing destitute portions of the State. Bro. Johnson took hold of this enterprise with a strong hand; and his voice was heard in most sections of our country, in bold and moving advocacy of the claims of those who were perishing for lack of knowledge.

Next came up for our sympathy and patronage, the Female Orphan Asylum. This institution was most congenial with his philanthropic spirit; and most manfully did he bend himself, during many long and laborious years, to the work of endowing the Midway Orphan School. For the Jerusalem Mission, too, belabored and prayed, and rejoiced in every intimation that it might ultimately prove eminently successful. And the revision movement was greatly benefited by the thrilling appeals which he often made in behalf of a pure version of the scriptures. He greatly aided, also, in making up our State fund for the purpose of educating pious young men for the Christian ministry of the word. In short, he *"abounded* in love and in good works," and "diligently followed after every good word and work." We fear, that in these respects, we shall not shortly look upon his like again!

5. *His energy, industry, and perseverance were untiring.* Day and night, Spring, Summer, Autumn and Winter, he was in the field. He usually preached twice a day when engaged in protracted meetings, which, if successful, he often continued for weeks, and at the close rested no longer than until an opportunity presented for another meeting. He seemed not in his proper element unless engaged in preaching the gospel. His hope was large, and hence he but rarely became discouraged, no matter how limited his success, or dark his prospects. If he failed of success at one place, he was certain that he would have it at the next; and so he went on conquering and to conquer! His course was always onward and upward. I have never known him to despond. Wherever he went he inspired hope, and confidence, and courage. He was happy himself, and made all happy around him. He felt strong in the Lord, and in the power of his might, and imparted his strength to others. He never cut the sinews of the church's strength, by murmuring and grumbling, and preaching, instead of Christ, the phantasms of dyspepsia, or the hallucinations of Hypochondria. He was a great recruiting officer of the Great King, and was highly endowed with the rare faculty of inspiring the soldiery of the Cross with the noble attributes of his own rare and mighty spirit. "Whatever his hand found to do, he did it with his might; knowing, that there is no work, nor device, nor knowledge, nor wisdom in the grave" The language of his life was: "I must work the work of him that sent me into the world, while it is day, for the night cometh, in which no man can work." These characteristics account, to a considerable extent, for his unparalleled success in preaching the gospel.

6. *He possessed largely, the self-denying or self-sacrificing spirit.* We have already referred, under another head, to his having put away from him, law and politics, and ease, and the probable fame and affluence which might have accrued from his former profession and pursuits, for Christianity and the ministry of an unpopular gospel.; This is a sacrifice that few—perhaps not one in a hundred thousand, would make; indeed, in this money loving, and luxurious age and country, the powerful tendency is, from the laborious life of the gospel minister—his poor pay, and little fame—to a vocation compatible with indulgence in the lust of the flesh, the lust of the eye, and the pride of life. But add to this, the intensity of Bro. Johnson's domestic feelings. He was one of the kindest of fathers, and a most affectionate husband. Hence, even in the pulpit, his thoughts and his affections were always clustering around, and intermingling with, the domestic circle. He said more, I presume, in the pulpit with regard to the domestic relations, than all the other preachers in Kentucky. And yet, for Christ and the gospel, he became almost an exile from home. This must have been felt, both by himself and his family, to have been a very great sacrifice. I will relate here, one incident, which will portray more vividly, than any amount of dry details could do, the feelings of our brother in regard to his own domestic sacrifices, and those of his family. He was, some years ago, preaching at Cane Ridge, and telling of the sacrifices that his wife was making in consequence of his being the greater part of his time from home. Here he became much excited, and as if filled with the enthusiasm of some mighty conception, placing himself on tip-toe, and his eyes upturned to heaven, and his finger pointing to that land of rest, he said, from the fullness of his large heart; "If I ever reach that glorious world, and find but one crown there, I will say, *give it to my wife! give it to my wife!!*" There shone the bright, serene, warm, generous, magnanimous soul of J. T. Johnson!!

He was, pre-eminently, a pure minded

man. He exemplified, or illustrated, as fully as any brother within my acquaintance, the beatitude of our Savior—"Blessed are the pure in heart, for they shall see God." As much as I have been with him, by day and by night, I cannot recollect that I ever heard an impure word or sentence from his lips. He was not only a Christian, but a gentleman—a gentleman in the true intent and meaning of the term—not such a gentleman as any tailor might make—but the production of good breeding, and the refinements of Christianity. He was instinctively a modest man; and looked with a holy horror upon everything vulgar or obscene. He had, too, a high sense of honor. I could have entrusted my property, my reputation, my life, in his hands, without the smallest disquietude. He was emphatically a good man. An eminent statesman told me, only a few days since, that he had been long acquainted with him, and considered him one of the best of men. And, from another source, I have learned, that when he was in Congress, he was reputed as one of the purest of its members. Hence, he was unsuspecting—some say credulous. He intended no evil himself, and, therefore, could not easily suspect it in others. Take him, all in all—his conscientiousness, his benevolence, his energy, industry, and perseverance, his self-sacrificing spirit, his purity of heart, purpose, and life—what an example for the young! But we must hasten to consider another characteristic.

8. *He possessed a strong and well-balanced mind.* Hence, he never ran into doctrinal extremes. he was no idealist or ultraist. He was essentially practical in all his pulpit exhibitions and in all his religious views. Being the strenuous advocate of a religion of facts, he poised himself upon those facts, and through a ministry of a quarter of a century, kept his balance true. His eye was steadily fixed on the glory of God and the conversion of souls. He saw a completeness—a divine fullness in Christianity, without any human additions or embellishments, and he was satisfied with it; and, was, hence, beyond the glitter and glare, the bewildering and seductive influences of religious speculations. What would convert the sinner, what would perfect the saint, what would ameliorate the condition of man what promote the interests of Messiah's kingdom, were, with him, the all engrossing considerations.—But had he a powerful intellect? We judge of causes by their effects! Who impressed the community more than he? Who made more converts than Bro. Johnson? Who effected as much as he, in all the departments of well doing? Can these be achieved without tremendous mental and moral power? But it has been said he was a scattering preacher! This, however, determines nothing as to mental or moral force! A bomb scatters—but with what a resistless force! He took aim at all sorts and sizes of sinners—a motley scattered foe! Fortified, as he was, in the center of Christianity, he hurled the missiles of truth to all points of the moral compass. Wherever there was a sinner, in that direction sped a fire pointed arrow. He aimed at effect, not system! at beautifying souls, not his sermons! at glorifying- God, not himself! Or, by another figure, we may say, that as a sower of the word, he scattered the seed of the kingdom, broadcast in the gospel field; and rich, and glorious has been the harvest!

Religion, the Christian religion, was with our brother, the fundamental idea. It was the radix from which sprang all his plans, pursuits, enterprises; the axle around which revolved all his thoughts and feelings. Hence, he had no plans of worldly aggrandizement; and, although he had been once deeply immersed in politics, he seldom lisped a syllable on that subject. Religion had formed a magnetic nucleus in his soul, powerful in the attraction of all virtue and truth, and in the repulsion of all sin and falsehood. This element had gotten fully the mastery of his mind. He saw, he heard, he felt, he spoke only in reference to this idea. It gave coloring and significance to the whole universe of matter and mind. It constrained him to see God in everything, and everything with reference to God. It made the material universe, but the scaffolding of the house not made with hands, eternal in the heavens. This is the highest Christian accomplishment—the result of unfeigned faith, steadfast hope, and love divine shed abroad in the susceptible and confiding heart. In this he was an imitation of the Savior. Jesus, in all the walks of life, gathered good from every object, whilst his soul repelled the evil—walked among the works of nature, and the busy scenes of life, making every object, and every circumstance the messenger of his instructions. Does he inculcate the doctrine of Providence, and utter a warning against distrustful care? The lilies, the ravens, the sun, the rain, and even the little sparrow become mediums of religious impression. Are little children brought to him? He takes them into his arms, and beholds in them a resemblance to the inhabitants of the heavenly world, and inculcates humility. Is he athirst? He is reminded of the water that endureth unto everlasting life, of which a man may drink and never thirst. Do an immense multitude follow him for the loaves and the fishes? I am the bread that came down from heaven—labor not for the meat that perisheth, but for that meat that endureth unto everlasting life. Do his disciples contemplate a beautiful vine or a luxuriant vineyard? I am the true vine, my Father the husbandman, you the branches, your good works the rich and beautiful clusters of this heavenly vine. Are they in the neighborhood of a sheepfold? You are my sheep, I am the good shepherd; the good shepherd giveth his life for the sheep. This characteristic is apparent in the whole of Christ's teaching, especially his parables; and, as out of the abundance of the heart, the mouth speaketh, indicates, both with respect to Bro. Johnson, and him who spake as never man spake, the mastery of the religious element. As it was with Bro. Johnson, so it should be with all Christians; especially, with those who minister in word and teaching.

It has been thought by some that he was uncharitable towards the sects. He certainly handled them, frequently, with great plainness, and sometimes with apparent severity. But this is not necessarily uncharitableness. He believed that all religious error is more or less pernicious; and, hence, in the ratio in which he loved the souls of those whom he believed to be in error, in just that proportion did he hate their errors, and put himself in opposition to them. He had too much boldness, honor, and independence to cry peace, peace, where he knew there was no peace. His organization was such that he could not but look with burning scorn upon the hypocrite. Hence, he gave the willfully ignorant no quarters; but cherished the kindliest feelings, for the sincere seekers after truth, in all denominations. In scores of instances, I have heard him declare himself on this subject; and cannot mistake, when I say, he was noble and magnanimous in all his battles against sectarianism; always charitable, and at the farthest remove from bigotry.

The following, from Bro. Burnett, will be acceptable:"He pleased and attracted generally; he repelled but few. Head and shoulders above every other peculiarity, was his zeal. His religion was a sentiment, not a creed; a sentiment which assumed the force of an all-controlling instinct. Sinners never thought of arguing with his preaching, as they would with a doctrine. Each one simply enquired: 'Shall I submit, or shall I defy him, and the gospel he proclaims?'

"Can my reader see J. T. Johnson now? Bland, yet fiery; powerful, but never gross; seeking to please no one but God; yet gratifying his audience; really possessing very strong love of approbation, still peculiarly self-sacrificing; half his discourses without real or apparent method, but at the same time full of points that pierce and hold fast like Roman javelins—in other words, without a point and yet all point—sincere and direct. His preaching was unequal at different times; seldom smooth and regular, or harmonious, yet at times there were passages that, like strains of wild music, filled his own soul and carried away his audience. At all times, everyone felt that he was earnest, and insensibly caught his spirit. Men of all ranks crowded to hear him, and generally every eye was riveted upon him. His simplicity and directness disarmed criticism, and the resistance with which one fortifies himself against ordinary eloquence, vanished like snow before the sun. Here was the hiding of his power. The heart of his hearer was open at once. The *suaviter in modo* cost him no effort. His liveliness out of the pulpit was no more natural than his gravity in it. All these qualities made him "great before the Lord."

HIS DEATH.

Bro. H. M. Bledsoe says: "I am not disappointed to find that the death of our beloved Bro. Johnson has produced a deep sensation in Kentucky, as it did here, and as doubtless was the case throughout the length and breadth of the land, wherever the deceased was known; and he was well known in most of the States and Territories ; indeed, wherever there were brethren his name was almost as familiar as 'household words and it may truly be said of him, that his " praise, in the gospel, is throughout all the churches." There is, perhaps, but one other in our ranks, whose death would produce a deeper sensation ; and he was second to none in devotion to the cause, and was, perhaps, equaled by none in zeal and self-sacrificing labors. I fear, my brethren, that we shall never look upon his like again in this probationary state. I know that we are prone to exaggerate and over estimate the character and services of those who have passed the boundary of time, who have been regarded as benefactors or philanthropists ; but, I do not feel that there is any such danger in the case of our deceased brother. His character and disinterested labors are above all praise. A Christian is said to be 'the highest style of man!' What, then, shall be said of him, who was not only a *Christian* but a Christian philanthropist and benefactor. It may truly be said of him, that he went about doing good! None were too exalted, or too humble, to be the objects of his labors and of his kind solicitude. None could associate with our brother, without feeling that the tone of his moral sentiments was elevated, the compass of his benevolence enlarged, and his spiritual enjoyments increased."

From a committee, at Lexington, Mo., we have the following:"He left Cincinnati at the close of the Convention, in October, for Missouri, purposing to traverse the State to its Western border. After preaching with marked success in Columbia, Fayette, and Rocheport, he arrived in this city on Lord's Day, the 23d of November. From the steamboat landing he proceeded immediately to the church, filling the brethren with surprise as he unexpectedly entered the door. Upon the urgent solicitation of Bro. A. Wright, who had just commenced a discourse, he addressed the congregation then assembled: and from that time he continued his labors uninterruptedly for fifteen days, speaking the greater part of the time twice a day, and also visiting much, from house to house, instructing, exhorting, and admonishing the brethren and sisters, and others—devoting himself to the work with an earnestness, energy and success that astonished the whole community. The result was twenty-four additions to the church, and such an awakening of the entire community as has not been witnessed here for many years. On Lord's Day night, the 15th day of his labors, he preached to a crowded audience, and announced as his theme for the following night 'The Word.' After leaving the heated room and walking a few steps, he drew his coat around him, and remarked that he felt rather cold. The next morning he was understood by a gentleman of this place, to complain of slight indisposition; but later in the forenoon of the same day, when advised by some of the brethren to take care of himself, that they were fearful he was exposing himself too much, he replied, that he was accustomed to go through heat and cold, and that it never hurt him, and that he had never felt better in his life. In the afternoon, at the house of Bro. Bledsoe, he was taken with a severe pain in his side, and it very soon became so intense that he was compelled to lie down on the bed from which he never rose. He received the most assiduous attention from numerous brethren and sisters, and the most skillful service from Dr. Cooly, and three or four consulting physicians, but, notwithstanding all, the disease gradually increased in violence, till the day of his death. He seemed, however, to a considerable extent, insensible to pain. For a great part of the time he was delirious, but during the whole period of his illness he had but one theme. In his rational moments, he was exhorting and admonishing those around him, and even during his delirium he was preaching and exhorting. When it was thought, a few days previous to his death, that his dissolution was near, in accordance with the wish of his physician and other friends present, Bro. H. M. Bledsoe informed him that it was believed that his death was nigh at hand. He replied 'I did not think that it was so near, but let it come.' He was then asked whether he had any doubt or fear in reference to the future, to which he replied: 'No, not the least; I have lived by Christianity, and I can die by it!' When asked whether he had any message he wished sent to his children, he replied: ' None, except that they live godly lives, and meet me in heaven!' The day before his death, when a female friend approached his bed, he grasped her hand and said: ' In a few days more I shall be at home in Heaven.' he made many other remarks, during his sickness, too numerous for this communication, all full of hope and love, which made a deep impression on the minds of those around him. The triumph of his death was complete; and we feel that it was a religious privilege of the highest order to stand around his bed."

"I will add," says Bro. Bledsoe, "a few additional items, that may not have been detailed, such as struck me with force at the time. When he was aroused from the state of stupor, in which he lay the most of the time during his illness, for the purpose of communicating to him the fact that his death was believed to be near at hand, he spoke distinctly of Christ as ' a sin offering,' showing that that was the ground of his hope and confidence; and as he sank back into a state of repose, he was heard to murmur: ' the sufferings of Christ,' relying, as he doubtless did, on those sufferings and the shedding of his most precious blood, as the ground of his acceptance with God, without the shedding of which, we are told, there is no remission. He would sometimes indulge in a soliloquy like this: 'How rapidly we are passing away!' He would often commence a favorite hymn, and with the assistance of some of the brethren present, would very distinctly sing almost, if not an entire song. Upon one occasion he requested those around him to sing from the 413 page of the Christian Hymn book. This was particularly a favorite hymn with him, as he several times sang it during the meeting whilst in health, and most appropriate were its sentiments to his own case. The brethren, as requested, turned to the page designated and sang it. And he, with surprising strength and distinctness of voice, sang the entire hymn with them, and seemed to enter into, and enjoy its sentiments. This was not more than a day or two before his death. And after the hand of death was sensibly upon him, at the request of a good Methodist sister, who was present, and who was often to see him during his illness, the same song was again sung, by a number of brethren and sisters, in a low plaintive tone, standing around his bed, evidently much to his gratification; as, to the concluding line he responded, in a low, rather indistinct, but audible whisper or undertone, 'And so we must,' or 'ought.' These were the last utterances of this great and good man; and in the connection in which they were spoken, and under the surrounding circumstances, were most appropriate and significant. I feel, to adopt the language of one of old, and say: 'May my last end be like his.' Thus gloriously and triumphantly has passed away one of nature's noblemen, rendered pre-eminently so by the Divine grace. But he has gone from the active field of his labors to his reward, to that house of many mansions, which the Lord has prepared—that city which hath foundations whose builder and maker is God."

Thus has the mighty fallen! A tall cedar of Lebanon lies low in the dust! The charter oak has numbered its days, and been removed! How deep the solitude that remains! *"Man goeth to his long home, and the mourners go about the streets."*

A TRIBUTE.

He is dead! He lived as he died, and died as he lived, a Christian. No more shall we see his face—no more hear his voice in this vale of tears. He has gone from his labors to his reward—from his trials to an infinite weight of glory!

He was truly a soldier of the cross—his weapons, not carnal, but spiritual, mighty, through God, to the pulling down of strongholds. Brave in his country's battles—braver in the battles of the Great King! His was a spirit that never quailed!

Too true, too honest, too noble to be the vehicle of cowardice—kind, magnanimous, generous, confiding, self-sacrificing, energetic, indefatigable. His like we shall not shortly see again!

Twenty-five years did he wield the sword of the spirit; and many are the hearts of the King's enemies which he pierced with that Jerusalem blade of heavenly make and temper. Truly he "did the work of an evangelist, and made full proof of his ministry." Day and night, Spring, Summer, Autumn, and Winter, he was in the field; and great is the number of his converts: With these—when this world's audit shall approach—he will shine as the brightness of the firmament, and as the stars, forever and ever!

He was a philanthropist—a Christian philanthropist—but by way of eminence, the orphan's friend. In almost every section of our State, his plea has been heard in advocacy of the orphans. He had a heart that felt and bled for human woe—a soul deeply imbued with that religion which prompts to the "taking care of widows and orphans in their affliction." These, especially those of Midway, will rise up and call him blessed, and be set as brilliants in his crown of rejoicing forever more!

Farewell, noble brother! Often have we, shoulder to shoulder, and hilt to hilt, encountered the motley hosts of darkness. Often have we wept, and often rejoiced together, in the triumph of the gospel. Noble pioneer of apostolic Christianity, farewell! Others of your fellow-laborers will shortly follow! Our heads are whitening with age—our souls are ripening for glory—our treasures are increasing in heaven—our affections are withdrawing from earth—a short farewell till we meet where

"Congregations ne'er break up,
And praises never end."

A. RAINES.

Paris, Ky., Jan. 9th, 1857.

EVIDENCES OF CHRISTIANITY.
NUMBER IV.

In all controversies there must be some point where the issue is formed, so that all may see precisely what it is, or they never can know whether they believe or not. There is nothing men have such vague and indefinite notions about as religious faith. Before any person can be a believer, that person must know what it is that is to be believed. In the same way, before any man can, knowing what he is about, declare himself a *skeptic,* he must have distinctly stated in his mind, so that he may know precisely what it is that he does not believe. Many persons are strongly committed to a church, supporting it, defending it, and enraged if any person should utter a sentence against it, who know nothing of the doctrine and never saw the creed. Such persons know nothing about what they believe; or, rather, they do not believe anything. They have no faith. If you hear them giving their reason for their preference for their church, you most likely hear them speaking in idealizing laudation of the preacher, his pleasant manners, his eloquence, learning, talents, or what a great man he is; or probably of the service of the church, the class of attendants, their respectability; or probably their preference is founded upon the simple circumstance, that their friends belong there. All this class have no faith at all, nor should they ever be ranked with believers. They are merely worldly church-goers.

We cannot let this class pass with a single paragraph. There are too many deceived and deluded in this way, for us to let it pass in silence, or with a single touch of the pen. How can any man hold the faith of a church without knowing what that faith is? It is a self-evident truth, that no person can have a faith without knowing what it is. Yet it is as manifest as the noon-day sun, that nine- tenths of the popular church-members could not tell what their own articles of religion are if their salvation depended upon it. Many of them, who make loud professions and are so bigoted that they will hear nothing but their own party, never saw their own articles of religion or their own faith, and know nothing about it. In Popery, where the clergy are the keepers of the faith, this will do, but in a Protestant church, where personal justification is by faith, it is absurd in the extreme. If the declaration of Protestants, that justification, or salvation from sin, is by faith, or, as the New Testament has it: "without faith it is impossible to please God," for "he that cometh to God must believe," it is evident that faith is for all—for the masses of the people. All must have faith, or be lost, for "he that believeth not shall be damned." What shall we think of church-members who never saw their articles of religion, or the faith of their church, and who do not know what either is? Are they justified by faith, without knowing what faith is? or are they believers, without knowing what they believe?

Here, if we are not widely mistaken, is the ground of much unbelief. Many sensible people have friends in church; and they hear them talk, but from all they say, they never can learn what they believe, or, indeed, in many cases, they become satisfied that after all their professions, they do not know what they believe, or do not believe anything. From conversing with many of this kind, and becoming satisfied, as any sensible man would in a short time, that they are in confusion and do not know anything about it; they jump to the conclusion that all professors are in the same condition, and that the whole matter is an unintelligible delusion, and that there is no reality in any of it. The sooner the world is rid of all this kind of religion the better. It is deceiving those involved in it and preventing them from ever becoming rational believers, and driving away others unto skepticism. We claim something more rational than this, and shall, therefore, proceed to show what it is precisely that God requires a man to believe. When we shall determine this from the New Testament, we ascertain the exact point where the issue between the believer and unbeliever lies.

There is one alleged fact in the Bible that the whole volume points to, centers in and stands upon. This fact is referred to in a great variety of forms, but all these references to it amount to the same. All depends upon it. It is referred to as the rock, the foundation, the way, the truth, the life, the beginning and ending, the Alpha and Omega, the first and the last, etc.,

etc. This great fact was preached on all occasions, presented to the people, as that which must be believed, that upon which they were justified, or pardoned, which they believed and by which they were saved. It was not something, in a lengthy train of written articles, that the masses of the people never saw; that none but preachers knew anything about; but it was the first thing presented to every man, woman and child, for their belief, before they could be permitted to an ordinance or received as members. It was that great truth that the soul had to act upon, either in receiving or rejecting, on the very first interview with the primitive preacher. No man under the wide heavens can come to God without receiving from the heart that great truth. Upon it the issue of life and death turns. The soul that receives it shall live. The soul that does not receive it shall die. Over this truth the mighty battle was fought during the first age of the church. The disciples believed it, loved it and suffered all things for it. The enemies did not believe it, hated it, and persecuted all who adhered to it. Every person in the church knew the faith of the church, believed it and defended it. Those out of the church knew what the faith was and opposed it.

Let us take one look at the New Testament, and see if it reveals anything tangible for one to believe. Let us see if it reveals any great truth, person or foundation principle upon which the minds, hearts and souls of men can take hold and rest with unshaken confidence. At an early period, when our Savior enters upon his public movements, we see him approach John the Baptist and demand baptism of him. On account of his superiority, as a man, John, being an humble man, excused himself, saying: "I have need to be baptized of thee, and comest thou to me?" He did not excuse himself on the ground of his Divinity, or Messiah-ship, for in this sense, he says: "I knew him not;" but he, at this time, simply looked upon him as a superior man to himself; but hearing the Lord's requirement: "Suffer it to be so now, for thus it becometh us to fulfill all righteousness," he walked into the river Jordan with his Savior and Redeemer by his side; when he took the Lord in his hands and gently lowered him down till he was buried in the water, and then raised him to his feet. As they quietly walked up the bank of the river, they lifted their eyes and saw heaven open, and saw the Spirit descend and resting upon him. While attention was thus directed to him, a voice came from the Almighty Father, announcing: "This is my Son, the beloved, in whom I am well pleased." This announcement contains the proposition over which the battle is to be fought. Here is the question of life and death. Here is the issue for the nations of the earth to act upon. Those who receive this proposition, that *he is the Son of God, the beloved,* and act upon it, shall be saved; but those who reject it, shall be lost.

In the mountain of transfiguration, the Father repeated the same again, adding: "HEAR YE HIM." We shall only develop a sufficiency of passages to show that this oracle is the one upon which everything rests, in which everything centers, and which forms the issue between the infidel and the Christian. Paul says: "Other foundation can no man lay than that which is laid, which is Jesus Christ." In telling the Corinthians what he first delivered to them, which was certainly laying the foundation, he says: "Moreover, brethren, I declare unto you the gospel." What was the gospel? or what did he first declare unto them? He says: "I delivered unto you first of all, that which I also received, how that Christ died for our sins according to the scriptures; and that he was buried and that he rose again according to the scriptures." This is the gospel, not in promise, nor in detail, but in its great foundation fact. The fact contained in this announcement, as presented in one form or other, was that which all believed, to which all were converted anciently, which is called "the faith," and the fact upon which the great battle anciently was fought. Hence John, the apostle, says: "Many other signs truly did Jesus, which are not written in this book, but these are written that you might believe that Jesus is the Christ, the Son of God, and that believing you might have life through his name." Here is the same proposition, in different form. The entire controversy is over Jesus Christ. Is he the Christ, the Son of God? He asked the apostles, on one occasion: "Who do you say that I, the son of man, am?" Peter answered: "Thou art the Christ, the Son of the Living God." The Lord responded: "Flesh and blood hath not revealed this unto thee, but my Father who is in heaven." Here, then, is the -inevitable issue between the believer and unbeliever. The New Testament claims that God revealed from heaven the sublime oracle that "Jesus is the Christ, the Son of the Living God." Jesus himself said: "Upon this rock I will build my church." John says, he wrote that we might believe that "Jesus is the Christ, the Son of God." This is what the opposers denied and what the disciples believed. This is what the controversy with skeptics is about. Every objection they make must bear against Jesus. Our position is simply, that *he is the Christ, the Son of God.* There may be things in his teachings, in the New Testament or the Old Testament, that we cannot explain, or possibly that no man can explain, but that may be simply owing to our lack of information, and no evidence against his mission. There may be things that to us appear unreasonable, or contradictory, but which may be entirely reason-able and consistent if we understood them. There was a time when the Pope thought it inconsistent and unreasonable for men to teach that the earth revolved upon its axis, but its apparent unreasonableness and inconsistency to him did not disprove the fact. His difficulty existed wholly in *his ignorance,* and not in any real difficulty. In the same way, difficulties of skeptics, existing wholly in their ignorance, and not in reality, are not to be taken as objections to the mission of Christ.

We wish skeptics to understand that we do not propose to examine the Bible, verse after verse, and argue every verse in it nor do we ask them to invalidate each separate verse; but they must come down to the bottom corner-stone, and if they invalidate that, we will give up all the balance without controversy. Their objections must be against Jesus. In what, then, do they object to him? Let us inquire distinctly and in separate items:

1. Do they object to his life—his example? Was he not good and exemplary in all his life?

2. Do they object to his teachings? Did he not teach good morals? Were not all his teachings, in the various relations in life, good?

3. Were not his works of a good and benevolent character? To which of these do skeptics object?

4. Do they object to the claim that he was the Son of God? We presume that this latter is the trouble. It was for this claim that he died. It was for this claim the holy apostles suffered and died. It was for this claim all the ancient martyrs died. This is the claim we intend to vindicate in these articles. Jesus of Nazareth is a Divine Person? B. F.

THE BRACKEN ASSOCIATION OF UNITED BAPTISTS.
No. 3.

As our brethren of the Association have charged us with teaching "destructive errors," we had a right to demand of them the proof of said charge, without any statement of our views. But as we have no secrets in religion, and wish to know the truth, that we may be made free from all error in principle and practice; and as we esteem them our best friends who correct our errors, and direct us in the good and right way, we have determined to unbosom ourselves to our brethren, who "hold the truth, the whole truth, and nothing but the truth," that they may have all the means of detecting and correcting our destructive errors, and of leading us into the "whole truth" as it is in Jesus. We shall, therefore, proceed with the development of our views. We believe

12. That salvation is, ever was, and ever will be, of grace; grace in its incipiency; grace in its progress; and grace in its consummation. "By grace are ye saved." "The grace of God bringeth salvation." Not only do the scriptures everywhere teach that salvation is of grace: but even reason, enlightened by the Word of God, not only sanctions this decision, but proclaims, that from the nature and necessity of the case, it can proceed upon no other principle. Man being a sinner, can be justified only by favor. In view of law his mouth is stopped, and he is guilty before God, as is the whole world of sinners. If, then, sinners are ever saved, they must be justified freely by his grace through the redemption that is in Christ Jesus, as justification on the score of innocence, or merit is out of the question, so far as they are concerned.

13. We believe, most cordially, and teach that "He that believeth on the Son, hath everlasting life."

14. That "without faith it is impossible to please God; for he that cometh to God must believe that he is; and that he is a rewarder of them that diligently seek him." Faith is the great mainspring of religious feeling and action in man. We cannot, therefore, make one motion heavenward without it. Nor can we have one right thought, one right feeling, or perform one acceptable action, in religion, without it.

15. We believe that "God commands all men everywhere to repent," because all have sinned, and therefore "except sinners repent, they must perish."

16. That God has appointed a day in which he will judge the world in righteousness, by that man, whom he hath ordained to be judge of the living and dead. And that, by raising his Son from the dead, he has demonstrated that there will be such a judgment.

17. That sinners are required to confess with the mouth the Lord Jesus, and believe in the heart, that God hath raised him from the dead, in order to salvation.

18. We believe, with all our heart, that "He that believeth, and is baptized shall be saved." That sinners everywhere, to whom the gospel is preached ought to "repent and be baptized, every one of them, in the name of the Lord Jesus, for the remission of sins." That believing, penitent sinners, ought to "Arise and be baptized, and wash away their sins, calling on the name of the Lord."

19. We believe and teach most cordially, that faith, repentance, confession, prayer, and baptism, have no merit in them—are simply means of enjoying salvation—which is wholly of grace, through the redemption that is in Christ Jesus. That a thousand immersions in water, without faith, without repentance—without a "new heart," would only wash the subject of them to fouler stains,

That when persons have come into the church of God by faith, repentance, confession, and baptism, and have thus been made partakers of the Divine nature, they have only started, or fairly prepared to start, in the Christian race. Or, they have only enlisted, received the bounty, and put on the armor, the battle is yet to be fought—their election is yet to be made sure. And, that this may be done, they must, in the language of Peter: "Giving all diligence, add to their faith courage, knowledge, temperance, patience, godliness, brotherly kindness, and universal benevolence; for, if those things be in you and abound, you shall neither be slothful, nor unfruitful in the knowledge of our Lord and Savior Jesus Christ. If ye do these things you shall never fall; and so an entrance shall be ministered unto you abundantly, into the everlasting kingdom of our Lord and Savior Jesus Christ."

Here, then, Bro. Gardner, are some 20 items, in our creed, a longer one, or at least, one containing more articles than yours; and yet we are far from thinking it contains "the whole truth." Tell me, now, my good brother, where are the *"radical and destructive errors"* of our creed? Of course you do not understand me, as writing out an authoritative creed for our people, any farther than it presents the language and meaning of the Holy Spirit. And yet I hazard little in saying that very few, if any, of our brethren will object to anything I have written.

We propose now to notice, a little more particularly, some positions of the "Circular" on "Restricted Communion," written by Bro. Gardner. After disposing of the various Pedobaptist parties, and those immersed persons belonging to them; still the question recurs: "Why do you refuse to commune with the Reformers, or Christians, who immerse?" To answer this question, Bro. Gardner finds it necessary to divide us into two classes:

1. Those "Baptists among the Reformers who were immersed by our ministers."

2. "Those Reformers who never belonged to our churches, and who were *"baptized for the actual remission of their sins,* without professing a *previous* change of heart and pardon." The Italics are Bro. Gardner's. I confess I do not know of any among us who were baptized "without professing a previous change of heart!" Let this, however, pass for the present. We proceed to notice the disposition he makes of the first class, or those among us who were rightly baptized by Baptist ministers. What is to be done with them? O, says Bro. Gardner: "That's easily explained: They are not only beyond the limits of our discipline." Indeed! "Beyond the limits of your discipline!" How so, Bro. Gardner? O, says he: "They were justly excluded from our churches, on account of having embraced, or fellowshipped the errors of the current Reformation; and while we still love many of them as Christian brethren, we are bound to regard them as *excluded members in error,* and, as such, we cannot invite them to the Lord's table, without trampling on our own discipline, and becoming partakers of their errors."

Hold! my Bro. Gardner, hold! Do you say that those whom you love as Christian brethren among us, you have justly excluded from your churches? Well, then, according to your own showing, either your churches that did this, are not the churches of Christ, or, the churches of Christ have a right to exclude their own members, who are recognized as Christians, when excluded—Christians have a right to exclude Christians!! Which horn of this dilemma, Bro. Gardner, will you choose? Did the apostolic churches ever have occasion to exclude Christians from their midst? Certainly not. The very idea is almost or quite blasphemous. What! Christ *here,* against Christ *there!* Christ divided against himself! What! Some of Paul, and some of Apollos, and some of Cephas! You are carnal, says the holy apostle, and walk as men! All! my brother, what a tyrant is sectarianism! Tell me, I beseech you, did ever a church of Christ, under apostolic teaching, exclude a Christian from its bosom? You are constrained to answer, never, certainly, never! Whence, then, I pray you, have Baptist churches obtained the right to do, what apostolic churches never did, and never could do? Are we not yet in the mists of Babylon?

I supposed that the church of Christ was founded, and builded as a spiritual house, to be the home, the permanent home of the Christian, as God's habitation by the spirit. But if churches of Christ, or Christian congregations, may exclude living members, then where is the blessedness of the Christian state—

the permanency of the Christian's home? Aye, but says Bro. Gardner, if we invite them to the Lord's table, though we know they have been rightly baptized, because our ministers immersed them, and we are compelled to admit they are Christians, we trample upon our own discipline! That explains the whole matter. You are afraid of trampling upon Baptist law! But my brother, where is the law of Christ that justifies your course? Baptist law, or usage is nothing, nay, infinitely worse than nothing, if it conflicts with Christian law and usage. The good Lord help us to trample upon all human usages in religion that conflict with the truth, and keep the people of God apart; and hasten the time when Christians shall be one, as the Father and Son are one; that the world believe and be converted! In my next, I will notice what is said by Bro. Gardner, in reference to our people, who have never been members of the Baptist church. JOHN ROGERS.

LETTER TO T. J. FISHER—DISCUSSION.

REV. T. J. FISHER—DEAR SIR:—A short time since, I received a letter from several brethren, from Ghent, Kentucky, stating that you had been there, making some pretty serious assaults upon the Disciples, which drew out from them a proposition for discussion. In reply, they received from you a proposal, of which they sent me a copy, for a discussion of "the distinctive differences between the Disciples and Baptists," with any of the following: A. Campbell, W. Scott, L. L. Pinkerton or B. Franklin. My brethren in Ghent, have taken your last choice, and placed the matter in my hands. I, therefore, as yours to them contained no proposition, returned them the following, for your consideration:

1. Do the scriptures teach, that baptism, administered as the Lord intended, to a proper subject, is for the remission of past, or alien sins?

2. Do the scriptures teach that a Christian experience shall be related, evidence of pardon obtained, or any article of religion acceded to, other than the confession with the mouth, of the belief of the heart, that Jesus is the Christ, the Son of the Living God, on the part of the penitent believer, before baptism?

3. Are articles of religion, written by uninspired men, as bonds of Christian union and fellowship, detrimental to the progress of the Christian religion, and sinful?

4. Is monthly, instead of weekly meeting, for the commemoration of the Lord's sufferings and death, attended with other acts of Christian worship, according to ancient usage, or scriptural?

In reply, you send the following:

1. Baptists affirm it is right for us to pray for sinners. Disciples deny.

2. Baptists affirm it is right for sinners to pray for themselves. Disciples deny.

3. Disciples affirm that baptism is for the remission of sins to a penitent believer. Baptists deny.

4. Disciples affirm open communion to be scriptural. Baptists deny.

5. Baptists affirm that the saints will persevere through grace to glory. Disciples deny.

6. Baptists affirm the divinity of Christ. Disciples deny.

7. Baptists affirm the total depravity of man. Disciples deny.

8. Baptists affirm an experimental change of heart before baptism. Disciples deny.

Dear Sir—The enclosed propositions I will debate with the Rev. Ben. Franklin. There is no essential difference between him and myself in his 3d and 4th propositions. Yours truly,

T. J. FISHER.

Your closing remark, that "There is no essential difference between him and myself in his 3d and 4th propositions," is a clear reason for declining discussion on those propositions. If you grant that "articles of religion, written by uninspired men, as bonds of Christian Union and Fellowship, are detrimental to the progress of the Christian religion and sinful;" and that weekly instead of monthly meeting, for the commemoration of the Lord's sufferings and death, attended with other acts of Christian worship, is according to ancient usage, or scriptural," as a matter of course, we have no debate on those subjects. Yet, I think, it will perplex you to harmonize this concession with the practice of the Baptist church. This, however, is no matter of mine.

But, my dear Sir, why did you pass my 1st and 2d propositions so coolly? Why go on with such a parade of propositions, without making the slightest objection to, or mention of, these two propositions in any shape? Had you stated some good reason why you could not debate these propositions, there would have been some show of propriety in proposing others. I object to your course as not respectful and courteous.

But I object to your propositions, as follows:

1. No man doubts that it is right to pray for sinners; nay, more, for all men. There is no issue between Disciples and Baptists, whether it is right to pray for sinners, or all men.

2. There is no dispute between Disciples and Baptists, whether it is right for sinners to pray for themselves. We believe that proper subjects, believing, penitent sinners, should "arise and be baptized, *calling* on the name of the Lord," and that the promise of God is, that whoever thus *calls* upon the name of the Lord shall be saved, or pardoned. This proposition, as stated by yourself, forms no issue upon the *difference in* practice between the parties.

3. Your third contains nothing that is not in my first, and there is, therefore, no reason for substituting it for mine. You must make some valid objection to mine before there can be any reason for offering another.

4. Disciples affirm nothing about "open communion," or "close communion;" but below you will find what they affirm. Will you deny it?

5. Your fifth proposition, in its generous range, proposes to us to deny that "the saints will persevere through grace to glory!" We should be sorry to deny this of the whole of them. We trust that many of "the saints" will "persevere through grace to glory." Below you will find a proposition on this point, upon which we deny. Will you affirm it?

6. "Baptists affirm the divinity of Christ"!!! Indeed! What bold and daring men! Why they would affirm that there is a God, or a Savior, I presume! So do we affirm the divinity of Christ, as often, as strongly and as devoutly as Baptists.

7. Below you will find a proposition on depravity.

8. We affirm, and in our preaching produce, a divine change of heart, as much as Baptists.

I now present you the following:

1. Do the scriptures teach, that baptism, administered as the Lord intended, to a proper subject, is for the remission of past, or alien sins? Disciples affirm. Baptists deny.

2. Do the scriptures teach, that a Christian experience shall be related, in which the penitent professes to have obtained pardon, as practiced by Baptists before baptism? Baptists affirm. Disciples deny.

3. Do the scriptures teach, that in our efforts to convert sinners, as a part of the process in turning them to God, they should come to the mourner's bench to pray and be prayed for, as practiced by Baptists? Baptists affirm. Disciples deny.

4. Do the scriptures teach that any Christian, or follower of Christ, anyplace, where the Lord's table is spread, has the same right to partake of the emblems of the Lord's body and blood that he has to

be in the kingdom of God? Disciples affirm. Baptists deny.

5. Do the scriptures teach that saints can apostatize, fall from grace and be lost? Disciples affirm. Baptists deny.

6. Do the scriptures teach the doctrine of total hereditary depravity? Baptists affirm. Disciples deny.

The public will desire to know something of the grounds of the debate, if we have one; or the grounds of the failure, if we do not have one. I have, therefore, arranged this letter with an eye to its publication and preserved a copy for that purpose.

As Covington, Kentucky, is a central point, easy of access, and many of both parties reside in that community, I suggest that as the place where the discussion shall be held. Respectfully, yours, BENJ. FRANKLIN.

Cincinnati, O., March 3d, 1857.

REV. T. J. FISHER.

CARROLTON, MARCH 7th, 1857.

REV. BENJ. FRANKLIN—*Dear Sir:*—You say in your letter to me, that "I received a letter from several brethren from Ghent, Ky., stating that you had been there making some pretty serious assaults upon the Disciples."

The above charge is *not true,* and I challenge the proof and specifications.

In your communication you ask, why I passed your first and second propositions so coolly? A man of your discrimination, can certainly see that the substance of your 1st and 2d propositions was embodied in the 3d and 8th of mine to you. You say, "I object, to your course as not courteous and respectful." I intended nothing disrespectful or uncourteous.

Sir, as you and I cannot agree as to the distinctive differences, between the Baptists and Disciples, would it not be better to refer this matter to the Baptist church and society of Disciples in Ghent, or, if you prefer, to make your selection from the the following list of propositions I am ready to meet you, when we can agree upon the time and place:

Prop. 1st.—Do the Scriptures teach, that Baptism administered, as the Lord intended, to a proper subject is for the remission of past or alien sins. Disciples affirm, Baptists deny.

Prop. 2d.—Baptists affirm an experimental change before baptism, and that it is right to make confession of the same. Disciples deny.

Prop. 3d.—Baptists affirm that it is right to pray for sinners at the altar of prayer (not the mourners bench). Disciples deny.

Prop. 4th.—Do the Scriptures teach, that the saints can apostatize, fall from grace and be lost? Disciples affirm, Baptists deny.

Prop. 5th.—Do the scriptures teach the doctrine of total, hereditary depravity? Baptists affirm, Disciples deny.

Prop. 6th.—Baptists affirm Jesus Christ to be God, as well as man, Disciples deny.

Now, sir you have the propositions for discussion; three of them in your own language, three in mine. You say the public will desire to know' the grounds of debate, if we have one, or the grounds of failure, if we do not have one. In conclusion, permit me to say, the Lord willing, "This fellow," will debate certainly, unless the Rev. Benjamin Franklin, backs out. You suggest Covington as the place of debate. I have no objection to that place, provided, the Baptists and disciples of Ghent are willing, and likewise that the Baptists and Disciples of Covington desire it.

Yours Respectfully,

T. J. FISHER.

GHENT, KY., MARCH 14th, '57.

REV. FISHER—*Dear Sir:*—Yours of the 7th is at hand and three propositions are agreed to. This is right; for these three fairly embrace "the distinctive differences between the Disciples and Baptists." But I do not admire your course, in attempting to dodge the real issue, touching the other points. I preach that baptism is for remission of sins, and come forward and affirm it without equivocation. I believe that saints can apostatize, fall from grace and be lost, and come up to the work and affirm it, without hesitation. The doctrine of total hereditary depravity, I do not believe; and therefore, unhesitatingly deny it. You believe and practice calling sinners forward to the mourners bench, anxious seat, or altar of prayer, to pray and be prayed for as a part of the process in conversion, that they may obtain pardon before they confess Christ and are baptized into him; but, when it comes to affirming it, you modestly dodge, leave out the words, "as practiced by the Baptists" and simply affirm that "it is right to pray for sinners at the altar of prayer!!" Why not affirm what you practice? This you are now bound to do, or have it published to the world that you *will not do it.*

Again; you believe and preach, not only that sinners "must have an experimental change before baptism," but *evidence of pardon,* and that it is right to state that before baptism. This you also must affirm, or shrink from your practice.—Dodge it you cannot.

The proposition that "Christ is God, as well as man," I will debate, if you will deny. I believe that "Christ is God, as well as man"—that he is "God with us" that "in him dwells the fullness of the Godhead bodily"—that "he is the express image of the invisible God"—that "he who sees him, sees the Father," and have so preached for twenty years.

Why have you dropped the proposition on communion? I cannot let you off silently on that. You must defend your position, or show to your brethren that you are ashamed of it. Come, sir: let us look the subject square in the face. In addition to my three propositions to which you have agreed, I propose the following:

1. Any person in the kingdom of God, has the same right to commune, anytime, and any place, where the children of God are at the Lord's table commemorating the death of the Savior, that he has to be in the kingdom of God. Disciples affirm, Baptists deny.

2. Do the Scriptures authorize calling sinners forward to pray and have others pray that the Lord may convert them and pardon their sins, as practiced by Baptists, before they are baptized? Baptists affirm, Disciples deny.

3. Do the scriptures authorize the relating of experiences, in which the candidates profess to have obtained pardon, and give evidence of the same, before baptism as practiced by Baptists. Baptists affirm, Disciples deny.

Please answer soon and decisively, whether *"this fellow"* will defend what he preaches, or evade it, as I wish the whole to appear in the next issue of the A. *C. Review,* now in the hands of the printer.

I find, on arriving here, that the statement about your serious assaults upon the Disciples, *is true in the fullest sense,* and can be abundantly sustained.

The citizens insist that the debate shall be here. Respectfully yours,

BENJ. FRANKLIN.

COVINGTON, March 19, 1857.

REV. BENJ. FRANKLIN—*Dear Sir:* Yours of the 14th inst. is at hand. The three propositions in your own language, to which I have heretofore agreed, and which in your last you say, "fairly embrace" the distinctive differences between the Disciples and Baptists, I am still ready to debate. If these three "fairly embrace" the distinctive difference between the parties, and you say they do; what else is there to debate? What other issues do you wish to make? Now, sir, I am ready to meet you upon these, and beg that you do not "dodge" them. I am unwilling, however, that you shall take to yourself the privilege of fixing all the points of issue and terms of debate. And, sir, as you evidently intend to change or "dodge" the true issues in other points of debate, and attempt to trumpet your victory in an unfought battle through the columns of the "A. C. Review" (what is it?), and as we do not disagree upon the Divinity of Christ. I propose that you select two men from among the Disciples, and I will select two from among the Baptist, and these four select one from among the worldlings, and place our correspondence in the hands of these five persons, who shall settle the real points of difference upon which we are not agreed as issues in debate.

If, sir, you wish "to look the subject square in the face," you will not dissent from such a reference as I here propose.

When the points of debate are all agreed upon, and we meet at Ghent, I shall expect you to make out the specification and proof of the charge of my having made "serious assaults upon the Disciples" of that place. *This matter you shall not dodge.*

I now reassure you, the Lord willing, "this fellow" will debate, unless I am compelled to look the Rev. Benj. Franklin "square" in the back, as he ingloriously retreats.

Yours respectfully,
T. J. FISHER.

REPLY.

CINCINNATI, OHIO, March 21, 1857.

REV. T. J. FISHER—*Dear Sir:* Yours of the 19th is at hand, and I shall hasten to respond. I am truly sorry to find your courage failing you, when called upon to defend your practice. In your notice of your meeting in Ghent, in the *Western Recorder* of the 18th, you assert that "that abominable heresy of open communion had been practiced by some of its (the Baptist churches') most worthy members." Here, sir, is a proposition in your own unequivocal words. You affirm that some of the most worthy members, in the Baptist Church, in Ghent, are guilty of abominable heresy, in occasionally communing with the Disciples. I deny it.

You shall defend your position, maintained in that community, on this point, or let it appear to the people that you are conscious that you cannot. Your charge of heresy against some of the most-worthy members in the Baptist Church in Ghent, is not true. I deny this charge; and you shall defend it, or show that you had no confidence in it when you made it. Will you defend your pompous charge, as it stands, in your own printed words, in the *Recorder?* This you shall now do, or show that you were not sincere when you made it.

You shall also defend your precise practice, in bringing sinners to the mourner's bench, or altar of prayer, as a part of the process in conversion, or show your consciousness that you cannot do it. Come, sir, no cringing here. You know I have offered you a fair proposition, embracing "the distinctive difference" between us on this point; and you must now "face the music," or shrink from your own manifest practice, thus showing that you have no confidence in what you practice.

You preach, and so do all in this crusade with you, that the sinner must give in an experience, evidence of pardon, before baptism. This you shall also defend, or show that "this fellow" will not defend, before an opponent, what he will preach, where no one can reply. Come, sir, remember your pompous words: "I maintained Baptist principles with all the power I possessed "the old landmarks were reset." Come, sir, and "defend Baptist principles with all the power you possess," before the same people where you performed this great feat, in the presence of an opponent, or shrink from the task, showing that you know that it cannot be done.

Come, my dear sir, these propositions are agreed upon, and consequently it is desired that we *shall meet,* God willing. Take in the other three points also, and let us make clean work of it. You are now in for a debate, and you had as well be hung for an old sheep as a lamb.

I suggest, as the time, Tuesday after the first Lord's day in April; or, if that will not suit you, just one month later.

I also suggest that we be ruled by the ordinary rules of debate, each choosing one moderator, and these two selecting a third, and continue one day on each point.

   Respectfully yours,
    BENJ. FRANKLIN.

-----o-----

DIALOGUE OF DEVILS.
NUMBER III.

Present *Diabolos, Apollyon, Lucifer* and *Diamonion.* Subject—The most successful method of defeating the word of God and the mission of Christ.

Diab.—Let us now proceed with our reports, suggestions and counsels as rapidly as possible. We must be on the alert.

Luc.—Most worthy *Diabolos,* permit me to give you a short account of my procedure. You know we have been annoyed and harassed exceedingly ever since Luther's time, with a class of people who seem to think of nothing but pushing the Bible upon the people. This, you know, is exceedingly annoying to us, for therein we not only find an account of the condemnation of wicked men, but devils. Well, sir, I determined that I would defeat not only these Bible men, but the Bible itself. But the question was how this was to be done. The people all believed the Bible, and any man that would question its truth, or its goodness, would be called a simpleton or a devil. I had a deep and settled hatred of the Bible and all its friends, as you know we all have; but I did not dare to say it was not good and true. I, therefore, chimed in with the general expression, that the Bible was good and true, and that all should believe it. I discovered, too, that I could find no men who would deny its truth, right out, and boldly oppose it, as an old legend, fabulous dream, or Pagan imposition, except men of miserable lives, no influence and no responsibility. I, however, engaged a few of this class to stand about the doors of drinking and gambling saloons, attend balls, theaters, and many other such places, and, in their broad and vulgar manner, make the Bible a jest; but I never counted much on these, for they are so repulsive that demons would almost shudder at them.

Diam.—That is a fact, most worthy Lucifer. I have myself been almost repulsed and ashamed of some of the class you allude to. These overdo the thing to such an extent, that men shudder at their enormities. Still, they do their work, do it effectually, and not only go themselves, but send multitudes like themselves down to hell. But, sir, there is a different class of skeptics from this, that are doing us good service. This class are moral, respectful and still. They are more sensible than those and manage with more discretion. Many of them are not known to be skeptics. They generally have "Paine's Age of Reason," keep it secretly, read it when they are alone, or when one or two of their own sort are present and laugh over it. These scarcely ever mention Paine, or the name of any infidel writer, or that they ever saw an infidel book. But occasionally, I have led them to profess a great desire to become Christians, but in reading the Bible and meditating upon it, they have found this difficulty, that difficulty, or the other, which, when stated, is nothing but a retailing and peddling anew something from Paine's old infidel book. These will occasionally give some preacher one of his *serious* difficulties, about which he cares not one farthing, and request him to "clear it up to his satisfaction." The poor preacher and some of his unsuspecting brethren, are delighted, thinking that he is inquiring to know his duty. A sermon is preached to convince him, but alas! he coolly walks away, saying, "He never touched the case!"

Luc.—I concede, sir, that these do us much

service in the way you describe; but not one tithe of the work is done by them, that is done by others whom I have employed. I have engaged many good men, well-meaning men, and made them think they were doing the work of the Lord, and at the same time, had them rendering us the most efficient aid we ever had.

Diam.—How did you accomplish that?

Luc.—Well, sir, you know what trouble that despisable New Testament doctrine, that "the gospel is the power of God unto salvation to everyone that believeth," has given us. You know what trouble we have had with that old doctrine of the prophet, of "hearing with the ear, *understanding* with the heart, and being converted." You know well how we have been perplexed with the language of the New Testament, such as: *"Understandest* thou what thou readest?" "The good ground is the man who receives the word into a good and honest heart, *understands* and obeys it." "As I wrote before in few words, whereby, when you read, you may *understand* my knowledge in the mystery of Christ." "If our gospel be hid, it is hid to those that are lost, in whom the god of this world hath blinded the mind of them that believe not," etc., etc. Well, sir, I employed a class of men, believers in the Bible, and preachers, to assist me in defeating the doctrine contained in these and all similar passages, thinking at the same time, as those who persecuted the apostles, that they were "doing God service."

Diam.—I do not see how that was possible!

Luc.—I am aware that it looks incredible; but I nevertheless did it, and I have succeeded to such an extent that I now have thousands almost daily preaching that the "word of God is a sealed book"—"a mystery"—"a secret," and that it cannot be understood by any only the especially illuminated !!!

Diam.—But do they not know that the scriptures say, "These things are written that you might believe"?

Luc.—Certainly, they know the scriptures *say* so, but if they cannot understand them, they do not know what that means any more than other passages.

Diam.—But did they not see, that when the apostles preached to men, they heard it, understood it, and submitted to it?

Luc.—No, sir; I made them believe that all the effect was produced by some other agency, and not by the gospel at all; and in this way, have induced many to lose all interest in the gospel, and pretty much cease reading it. Indeed, I have succeeded with this deception to an incredible degree. I have positively had preachers quoting scripture to persons whom they declared could not understand the Bible at all—to prove to them that it was a sealed book: a mystery; to prove that they could not understand it, as if anything they could not understand could prove anything to them! I have thus led them to turn their ears away from the truth, and turned them into fables; and thousands of them now that will not hear the Bible at all, will shout over a dream, a "spirit ray," a trance, or a wrestle with the devil.

Diab.—But what do you do with those who will not believe your preacher, who says the Bible is a sealed book? You know there are many of this kind.

Luc—Well, sir; I have preachers employed who tell such, that it amounts to nothing if they do understand it, for it "is a dead letter"—that it is powerless—that it is simply lamp-black upon paper—that they must have some other power to turn them to God. In this way, I lead the preacher to cease preaching the gospel, which we know to be the power of God unto salvation to everyone that believeth, and induce him and the people to unite in calling upon God mightily to "send down converting power." In this way, I have set the gospel aside, as "the *mere* word," and lead many thousands to practice human substitutions and traditions, in the place of the clear requirements of heaven.

Diab.—But there are some that will

believe neither of these. They will maintain that they can understand the revelation of God—that it would not be a revelation if they could not understand it, and will maintain that it is the power of God. What will you do with these?

Luc.—Well, sir, I have a preacher standing ready for those who declare they can understand the Bible and that the gospel is the power of God unto salvation, who preaches to them the doctrine of total hereditary depravity—that they are so dead in trespasses and sins, as to be entirely powerless, and that they cannot do anything till they are quickened by irresistible power. Many will believe this, and, as a matter of course, wait for irresistible power to quicken them so that they can repent and believe. This I find very effectual. It lulls to sleep in carnal security, delightfully. The process is sure and the reasoning simple. The sinner led into the duplicity of this net, says to himself: "I cannot do anything, but simply wait the Lord's own good time; and if I die in my sins, it is not my fault, as I could not do anything."

Diab.—But you will find many who will believe none of this. What are we to do with them?

Luc.—Well, sir, I have engaged preachers who tell them that God unchangeably foreordained whatsoever comes to pass—that a certain number are foreordained to everlasting life, and a certain number to everlasting death—that the number thus unchangeably foreordained and predestinated is so definite that it can neither be increased nor diminished. This doctrine I have them argue from scripture, and I induce many to believe it. This, too, answers the same purpose as either of the former doctrines. It rocks men to sleep in carnal security delightfully. They say "If God, by the decree of election before the world, has made me one of the elect, I am safe; do as I may, I will infallibly be brought in and saved. But if I am of the non-elect, no matter how much I read the Bible, pray and cry to God for mercy, I cannot be saved." In this way, I keep thousands from attempting to serve God.

Diab.—But there are many who will not be caught in any of these snares. Is there any other stratagem for them? I want all the wisdom you have now. Our time for deceiving is short, and we must employ every moment.

Luc.—About the next stratagem is, to find suitable instruments such as I could name, with no conscience, no faith and faces of brass, to preach that all will be saved, no matter what their lives in this world. All who will believe this will soon set aside every ordinance of the New Testament, and turn the most fearful, solemn and momentous matters in the revelation from God to man, into ridicule, and soon despise every attempt to keep the commandments of God. This answers as a kind of whirlpool to suck down the lukewarm, cold, black-sliding, negligent, prayer loss and godless professors, to whom the yoke of Christ is a burden, spiritual things are insipid and the good things of the kingdom of God are loathsome.

Diab.—You are an apt scholar, most noble *Lucifer;* you are getting into the work pretty effectually. These have been most efficient agencies; but there are new phases of things appearing, that I am scarcely decided myself in reference to. The Bible Union is giving me much trouble. I thought when I engaged Mr. Judel, and succeeded in getting the influence of that good old man, Dr. MacClay against it, I would crumble it into atoms; but in this I was disappointed. I thought when I employed the five clergymen at Louisville against the Revision Association I should certainly succeed: but here I have been most sadly foiled. My instruments, in this case, too, proved most inefficient and unsuccessful, and are now exposed to the derision of the masses of the people.

Apol.—I hope you are not disheartened, most noble *Diabolos;* I think I see some indications favorable to our cause. I am employing some agencies among these Bible Union men, that I think will set them by the ears, burst them up and defeat them. I have alarmed some of the Baptists till the hair stands on end upon their head, with the idea that if they do not kick Mr. Campbell, and all identified with him, out of the Bible Union, they will lose their precious name, *Baptist;* lose their identity and be swallowed by the Disciples. This I am working to a charm. I have already worked the alarm, on this score, into Sirs Graves, Crowell, Ford, Sands, Jeter, and a host that move at their bidding, till they are deciding in all directions, that communion with Disciples, and all fraternal communications must be broken off.

Diab.—Do you think the great, good and wise men among the Baptists can be moved by such a simple panic as this? Why you must be ignorant of your work! Do you not know that the Baptists outnumber the Disciples three to one! and they be alarmed for fear the Disciples will swallow them down? Why do not the Disciples become alarmed for fear the Baptists will swallow them down?

Apol.—With all due deference to your superior knowledge, most worthy *Diabolos,* I beg leave to say, the reason why the Disciples are not alarmed is obvious. You know, and we all know, that the Disciples care for nothing in religion only what is contained in the clear revelations of God, when correctly translated. Thus you perceive that the Bible Union secures and maintains all that they are aiming at; and that they cannot lose anything. The men I have alluded to see this, and all that distinguishes them, as Baptists, from the Disciples, is in danger of being lost. The Disciples have nothing to distinguish them, only what is clearly found in the scriptures when correctly translated. In the Bible Union, therefore, they not only maintain and hold on to all they have ever contended for, but get the Baptists to help them. Why, most noble *Diabolos,* Sirs Graves, Ford, etc., have reason to be alarmed, when they see their own brethren in friendly "alliance" with the Disciples, and aiding them in translating the very name *Baptist* out of the Bible!!! There is not one thing about "Baptist principles," in the Bible Union. "Baptist usage," too, is not mentioned, nor is there anything there to secure anything but truth, the whole truth, and nothing but the truth—the Bible, the whole Bible, and nothing but the Bible, correctly translated into all languages, for all people, thus embracing all that the Disciples have ever contended for, and nothing more, and the 'Baptists aiding them in the work! Baptists, sir, have reason to be alarmed and they will be alarmed, and break up the "alliance" sure. I have already set the work in motion.

Diabolos.—Most worthy *Apollyon,* your reasonings are weighty. I do believe there is something in your suggestions. I see now the meaning of "resetting the old landmarks," maintaining "close communion," and the doctrine set forth by Mr. Crowell, on "the order of Conversion," in the February number of the *Christian Repository,* that love to God is first, repentance second and faith last. I think you are right: that a muss is coming and the "alliance" will be broken up. Let us keep an eye to these matters till our next meeting. Meantime, leave no stone unturned in an effort to set the Disciples and Baptists at variance.

REPORTER.

-----o-----

THE WORK OF THE CHURCH.
NUMBER I.

For what purpose was the church organized here upon earth?—or, what was, and is, the business, duty, and work of the church? The business, duty and work of the church was, and is, to convert the world of mankind to Christianity, or, to the belief and obedience of the gospel. See the commission given by Christ to his Apostles:"Go ye into all the world, and preach the gospel to every creature. He that believeth and is baptized shall be saved; and he

THE WORK OF THE CHURCH.

that believeth not shall be damned. Teaching them to observe all things whatsoever I have commanded you. And lo, I am with you always, even unto the end of the world." The above commission defines the business, duty and work of the church. What organization or institution, religious, political, civil or social will not be more or less effected by the influence of the church, when she is faithfully acting out her work? Who, then, from the beggar to the monarch on his throne, is not interested, deeply interested in the work of the church? At the very threshold of the subject, we are met by a serious question. Has the church succeeded in her work? This question may be answered by asking and answering another. Has she converted the world to Christianity? Who will take the affirmative? If she has not succeeded; in her work, what has been the cause of her failure? The answer to two or three questions may shed some light upon the cause of her failure. For the organization and government of His church, Christ, by his own teaching, and by the teaching of his Apostles, gave a chart, or constitution and laws, called the New Testament. Has she, from her first organization to the present time, faithfully acted in accordance with the true spirit and purport of her chart, or constitution? Has Christianity failed to effect the object for which it was sent into the world?—or, has the church failed to act it out? Would the church have failed to convert the world if she had acted out genuine GOSPEL Christianity? The failure is either in the conduct of the church, or in the inefficiency of the chart or constitution and laws given by inspiration. The church has departed from the spirit and purport of her constitution; or, then, inspiration could not introduce a process by which the world could be converted, even if faithfully acted out by the church. Who will affirm the latter? After an appeal to the main principle contained in her chart for the conversion of the world, let truths and facts decide. What, then, is the main or foundation principle contained in her constitution, upon which she was and is to act, that she may convert the world? Every theory, system or argument has, for its foundation, one main principle, which constitutes its efficiency or power. Hear Christ, in the 17th chap, of John: "Neither pray I for these alone; but for all them also which shall believe on me through their word, that they all may be one, as thou, Father, art in Me, and I in thee, that they also may be one in us; that the world may believe that thou hast sent Me." From the above quotation, we are plainly given to understand, that the oneness, or union of the Apostles amongst themselves, and the oneness or union of all that should believe on Christ, through their (the Apostle's) word, was to be the means, principle, power or agent of the church, in converting the world.

Is professed Christianity united? Let him who will, affirm. If all professed Christianity were united, and acting out genuine gospel Christianity, would the church fail to convert the world? From what Christ has said, the conversion of the world would infallibly follow the oneness or union of Christians. Who can enumerate all the jarring, warring, jangling and antagonistic religious sectaries now extant? All, then, have not been converted in accordance with the true spirit and purport of her constitution. The church then, has, honestly, but ignorantly; or, wickedly, and knowingly, departed from the true spirit and purport of her chart. As the oneness of Christians was to be the converting means of the church, will the world ever become converted till professed Christians become united? As union or oneness was to cause the world to believe, what will disunion produce but unbelief? And what is unbelief but infidelity? What then, are those religious organizations called churches, which are not exclusively the organizations of the New Testament, but departures from the true spirit and purport of her constitution? Are not such organizations, or churches, counterfeit, spurious, and anti-Christian? Churches *"on their own hook?"* The influence of their divisions directly tends to infidelity. Will such churches, with all their preaching, missionary efforts and zeal without knowledge; enthusiasm, fanaticism, animal excitement and *"steam of the flesh,"* ever convert the world to gospel Christianity? Will anything but obedience to gospel Christianity ever take them to heaven? Are not their efforts more to convert the world to party organizations and peculiar doctrines than to gospel Christianity? Before the world can be converted to gospel Christianity, our present religious infidelity, or infidel religion, must, itself, be first converted. J. M.

-----o-----

A LETTER FROM JERUSALEM.

We have before us a letter from our dear Bro. M. T. Diness, dated Jerusalem, January 30th. Bro. Diness is one of the converts to the ancient faith, made through the labors of Dr. James T. Barclay, while a missionary to Jerusalem, and now himself a preacher and missionary. Though he has been long left by that man of God, who was the instrument, in the hand of the Lord, in bringing him to the kingdom of God; and much of the time without a single disciple to stand by his side, he ceases not to stand up alone, in the city where the prophets stood, where the Holy Twelve stood, and where the Lord stood—in "the city of the great King," and preach the gospel as it was at the beginning, in Jerusalem. Here is something noble, courageous, and manly; a man almost without any assistance from his brethren, far separated from them, without friends, fighting, not 'with carnal weapons, but spiritual; mighty, through God, to the pulling down of strongholds; battling against most fearful odds, for truth, for righteousness, for God.

O, how it must have comforted his heart, when he heard that the beloved Bro. Barclay, who is nearer his heart than any other man on earth, was making arrangements to return to him! What a cheering thought to him, that the missionary family shall return; and the little band shall again sit at the Lord's table, near where he hung on the cross, for the sins of the world, and commemorate his death and sufferings. I long to see the day again, when we at the Lord's table in Cincinnati, and everywhere else in this country, can reflect that we have a faithful little band in Jerusalem, near the very spot where the Lord first spread the table, gave thanks, and broke the loaf, also gave thanks and poured out the wine; engaged in celebrating the scenes of Calvary. Shall we? O, can we know that we have a man there; a good man; a man of God, holding and preaching the pure faith of Christ; and begging—humbly, solemnly and earnestly entreating us to send Bro. Barclay to him again, and assist him, and not make an effort in his behalf? Come, brethren, we appeal to you in the name of Him who died for your sins—who, though he was rich, for our sakes became poor, that we might be rich; come, let us make an effort, simultaneously, throughout the extent of the churches, for Jerusalem, and cause that word which once sounded out from Mt. Zion, went forth from Jerusalem, and thence to the uttermost parts of the earth, to return again and bless the inhabitants of that land.

Brethren, you are in the midst of your friends, surrounded by brethren, with the Bible in your houses, and the word of the Lord faithfully preached, not only to yourselves, but to those around you. You are enjoying the worship of God, the ordinances of the New Testament, and the light of heaven. Your children are surrounded by the gracious influences of Christianity, Christian parents, and Christian associates. Do you ever think of the poor, ignorant and degraded multitudes who

who have never heard of the name of Jesus? Be you ever think of our Bro. Diness, alone in a land of ignorance, superstition, and sin, standing up for righteousness, for truth, and for Christianity; in a mighty, noble, and manly effort, to return the word of God to the nation that was instrumental, in the hand of God, in sending it to us? Be you feel no interest in sending Dr. Barclay and family again to their work in that land? Look, we entreat of you, at the mighty sacrifices made by the first converts to Christianity, all Jews, to send the gospel to the Gentiles! Look! O, look! at their incessant zeal, perseverance, and labor, in spreading Christianity among all nations, and see how the Lord blessed them, and through them blessed the Gentiles. And now shall we, who are the subjects of such inestimable blessings, forget and make no effort to bless those whom God made the instruments in blessing us? They believed in the promise to Abraham—"in thee shall all the nations be blessed"—waited for it, and when it came, received it joyfully—embraced it, and, at immense labor and sacrifice, sent it forth to all nations and kindreds of the earth, and thus blessed us. Shall we now, who have received the blessing, forget the nation through whom this blessing was conveyed to us, now that they have fallen? Let us love Israel, if not for their own sake, now while in their apostate and fallen condition, for their work's sake, while they were in the faith, and for their father's sake, and let us make an effort to return a blessing to them, in making them know their King, David's son, God's Son, and their Messiah. O, let us arouse to the importance of saving all nations, and an effort in the Lord's name for all mankind.

Brethren, we entreat of you, that you unanimously unite in doing something in this good work. Let congregations contribute from $5 to $50, and send it to us, for this work, and immense success will attend the effort. Let individuals, where they are not convenient to a congregation, or the church does not act in the matter, contribute any sum, and send it to us, and due acknowledgement will be made; and let us have the outfit for Dr. Barclay in two months from now. Let us not think of stopping at this, but have other missionaries in the field. B. F.

-----o-----

BACON COLLEGE.

Bro. Franklin:—It is, perhaps, known to some of your readers, that we are making a vigorous effort for the full endowment and reorganization of this Institution. But little has hitherto appeared in the public prints in regard to it, for the simple reason, that we purposely avoided the usual policy of enlisting the services of the press, to give notoriety to the movement, until we had accomplished some-thing worthy of the attention and approbation of the brotherhood. The time has arrived, when we can speak of it publicly, and with some pride and satisfaction.

Suffice it to say, that unlike former attempts to build up Bacon College, this is no spasmodic or abortive effort; but, after a long and deep conviction of the importance of the work, we have quietly and earnestly begun it, and are firmly resolved to prosecute it to a glorious consummation. Here in Kentucky, in the heart of the Reformation, in the midst of a noble brotherhood of fifty thousand to stand around it, and foster it, we intend to build up an Institution of learning, which will meet, in a satisfactory manner, the wants of our young men throughout the West and South. We are, indeed, laying firmly and surely, the foundation of a first-class University, to be commensurate, in its organization and its provisions, with the demands of our age, and the wants of the church; and destined, we hope, to become a pillar of our cause, and the glory of our State. The special details of that organization, or the particular features of the enterprise, we do not propose to give in this communication. The character and magnitude of the work will be developed as it progresses. But we will say, that with a pecuniary basis of not less than *three hundred thousand dollars* we hope to build up an educational system worthy of us as a people.

To this end, I have been laboring diligently during the past year, and, with the Divine blessing, intend still to labor, so long as my brethren stand by me as nobly as they have hitherto done. The wonderful success which has so far attended our efforts is an evidence of their unanimity and liberality, and is an earnest of the munificent endowment which they seem determined to give. I will here state a few facts. We have already increased the amount to $150,000 of the most solvent and available subscriptions that we have ever known raised by any people for any purpose, and have as yet canvassed only eight counties of the State. We take no subscriptions for a less amount than $100; some forty of these subscriptions are $1,000 each; a hundred of them $500 each; and the average of the whole about $300 each—an important fact as regards their reliability.

As further evidence of the unanimity and cordiality of the brethren in the movement, I would say, that in the county of Woodford I obtained in two weeks $17,000, and in the county of Fayette $25,000; and I did not find a half dozen persons who refused to give when asked. This effort was made, too, just a few months after one for the Orphan School, by which $20,000 were raised for it, mostly in these same counties. The names of the donors and the amounts of their subscriptions—which we desire to publish soon—are such as give character to the movement, and inspire confidence in its success. In a word, the spirit which they are manifesting, as I progress, is indicative of a determination, on their part, to accomplish, in a worthy manner, a great and good work.

But the chief object of this communication is to state, that in accordance with a resolution of the Board of Trustees, a meeting of the subscribers and friends has been called, to be held the first Wednesday in May next, at Harrodsburg, to which we desire to call the attention of the brethren generally. The Board feel that the proper investment and management of the endowment fund—the first installment of which is due at that time—and a full and thoroughly digested plan of organization, such as will meet the wants of the brethren, are matters of great importance; and, for the perfecting of which, they desire the aid and counsel of the friends of the enterprise. They therefore earnestly invite the attendance of all such. We are authorized to state that some prominent brethren of this and other States will be present and address the meeting.

Yours truly,
JNO. B. BOWMAN.

-----o-----

THE HERESY OF OPEN COMMUNION.
CARROLTON, KY., Feb. 9, 1857.

BRO. ROBINSON:—I have been preaching for the last ten days to the Baptist Church in Ghent, Carrol county. The pastor is Elder Johnson, a pious, useful, talented and zealous minister of the gospel. The church was in a cold and distracted condition. That abominable heresy of open communion has been practiced by some of its most worthy members. I advocated Baptist principles with all the zeal and power I possessed. Thanks to God, the old landmarks were reset; peace, order and harmony were restored to the church; the prayers of the faithful were answered, and truth owned and blessed of God. Ten were added to the church by letter and baptism.

This is quite a flourishing body of baptized believers. The citizens are kind and hospitable. May the smiles of heaven rest upon the

church and community, is the prayer of
Yours, in Christ,
T. J. FISHER.

-----o-----

REMARKS.

This refreshing little item of intelligence we find in the "Western Recorder" for February 18th. It is so remarkable, that we thought it due the author and our Baptist brethren, to give it a more extended circulation. We are now in the favored town of Ghent, Ky., where this remarkable work was done, and are well satisfied that more interest still might have been given to the account, by stating more minutely some of the particulars. For instance, the extent of the "abominable heresy of open communion," it appears, was much greater than would be supposed from the above. In the place of saying, "that abominable heresy of open communion had been practiced by *some* of its *most worthy* members," it might have been stated that it had been practiced by *all of its members,* both "most worthy," and least worthy! It might have been stated, with all due respect for truth, that "Elder Johnson, a pious, useful, talented and zealous minister of the gospel," as recognized by Rev. T. J. Fisher, was not only not a member of the Baptist church at Ghent at all, but not a member of the Baptist church *any place,* nor *any other church* on earth, and he and his lady were two of the accessions spoken of above. The whole church, therefore, were guilty of "that abominable heresy of open communion," with this "pious, useful, talented and zealous," preacher, called "pastor," during a space of some two years, while *he did not belong to any church!* Not only was this whole church guilty, of "that abominable heresy of open communion," with this pastor, not a member of any church for some two years, but they authorized him to administer the communion, preach to them, and act as their pastor, while not a member of any church!

Well, says the reader, that was "abominable heresy, and I think Rev. Fisher did right in exposing it." Reader, please not be misled. This case was not the "abominable heresy," in the eye of Rev. Fisher at all. He made no ado about this case. This most manifest and glaring disorder was not what vexed his righteous soul at all. This same Elder Johnson was heart and hand with him in opposing the "abominable heresy of open communion!" Do you inquire what the open communion practiced and complained of was? Why, sir, it was simply that "some of its most worthy members" were in the habit of communing with the Disciples. This was what the trouble was!! But "peace, order and harmony were restored!" Upon what terms. Did these *"most worthy* members" confess their "abominable heresy?" No; but persisted in declaring that they were right, at the same time consenting to desist the practice, if thereby *weak* brethren were wounded! This was "conquering a peace," "resetting the old landmarks," restoring "peace, order and harmony!!" In answer to "the prayers of the faithful," "peace, order and harmony," have been restored, by those "most worthy members," maintaining that they were right in "that most abominable heresy," of communing with the Disciples, but that they might not offend their *weak* brethren, such as Elders Johnson, Fisher, Ford, Graves, etc., they would desist the practice!!! And then, to cap the climax, the pastor, who had preached to them for some two years, and communed with them, while not a member of any church, with his lady, join the church, of which he was pastor, and thus make two of the ten additions, in Elder Fisher's crown of rejoicing! All this, too, was done by the effort expressed in the pompous declaration: "I advocated Baptist principles with all the zeal and power I possessed."

How infinitely different all this from the

spirit of Christ! In the place of establishing some old human landmarks, and wicked sectarian bars between the children of God, who live neighbor to each other, know each other and have full confidence in their profession, to keep them from worshipping together, the Lord said to them all: "By this shall all men know that you are my disciples; if you have love one to another." "These be they who separate themselves, sensual, not having the spirit." "We know that we have passed from death unto life, because we love the brethren." "Love is of God." "God is love." "I pray for them," says the Lord, "that they may be one." God have mercy upon all the good and honest under those who only scatter and rend the children of God asunder, who are only hirelings and not the shepherd of the sheep! B. F.

-----o-----

Editor's Table.

The Music of the Foot-fall.
"His very foot has music in't,
As he comes up the stair."—BURNS.
TO MRS. T. SR.

There is music in the foot-fall
  Of those we love to greet;
And echo answers in the heart,
  In murmurs low and sweet:

For it whispers *he* is coming,
  Thy sunshine draweth near;
And melting in that radiance
  All shadows disappear.

Oh! holy lights of home love—
  The gentle influence given,
To smooth the stormy path of life,
  And lead us on to heaven!

And blessed is the loving ear
  That listens, not in vain
For the music of the foot-fall,
  And the heart's sweet answering strain.
Dec. 23,'56.   M. F. M.

CHRISTIAN SUNDAY SCHOOL JOURNAL.—This valuable and almost indispensable little sheet has been conducted for the last year by Bro. H. S. Bosworth, alone. Seeing the importance of the continuation success and prosperity of this publication; and our office joining the office of Bro. Bosworth, so that we can with very little trouble, we have consented to take charge of it with him, and make an effort to extend its circulation, and still more fully meet the wants of Sunday Schools. The First No. of the new volume will be issued early in May, under the new arrangement. Please send in the subscribers as early as possible, that we may know how large an edition to print. All letters sent to our address for this purpose will receive strict attention:

TERMS.
Single copy, -----------$ 35 cents.
Three copies,-------------   1 00
Four copies, to one address,....1 00
Twenty-five copies…………...5 00
105 copies………………….. 20 00
                    BENJ. FRANKLIN.

WE call attention to the article of Bro. Bowman, found in the present issue, touching Bacon College. This speaks for itself. Where has the like of this been done? Where has a man started and proceeded quietly, and steadily onward, and obtained an endowment for a noble institution of learning, in a few short months, of $50,000? Among what people has any man laid aside his worldly avocations, gone quietly along and done such a work? Nowhere! nor has the like been done by any people. There is a heart and a nobleness in the brotherhood, for which we have reason to be thankful to God, which will respond when properly appealed to.

BIOGRAPHY OF ELD. J. T. JOHNSON.—Bro. John Rogers, sr., has been mentioned by some of us as a suitable person to write the life of Eld. J. T. Johnson; but learning that Bro. Johnson, himself, had mentioned Dr. L. L. Pinkerton, as the man for this work, we hope he will proceed with it. His accomplished pen, can, and no doubt will do the subject ample justice. The public are anxious for the life of this great and good man.

SUCCESS OF THE A. C. REVIEW.—We have been so engaged this year that we have not thought of saying anything of the success of the "Review;" nor have we now time to say anything more than that we had more subscribers renewed and new ones obtained on the first day of March, than we obtained all last year, and still they come. We thank God and take courage. Some few snarlers, men of one idea, and some even without one idea; with only one eye, to see one side of a subject, one ear to hear one side, have made a fine effort to depreciate our list, because we would not let them dictate to us, what we should think and what we should publish, on the subject of Slavery. But they are the last men, who should say one word about freedom of press, speech, or any other freedom, for they are the most absolute despots (*despotes* is the word translated *master* in the New Testament) and tyrants we know, so far as they have any power. They have done their utmost upon us, with both tongue and pen, as well as withholding and inducing others to withhold subscription, and all without the least provocation, except that we could not see through their spectacles, and would not become a tool to aid in a scheme that has not one scriptural, tangible, practical idea in it.

SERMON OF ELD. A. RAINES.—We bespeak for the Sermon of Bro. Raines, in this number, upon the death of Bro. Johnson, a careful reading. It will do any pious persons heart good, especially any person who loves good men, and takes pleasure in their memory. It is an able and affectionate sermon.

He has printed off a large edition in tract form, so that any persons not subscribers to the Review can obtain it. Price per hundred; a less number in the same proportion. Address, Eld. A. Raines, Paris, Ky. It will be also for sale at this office.

ACKNOWLEDGMENTS OF MISSIONARY FUNDS.—

	Pledged.	Paid.
Job Hastings, Martinsville, Ind.,		$3 00
Unknown, Lexington, Mo.,	1 00	
M. V. B. Devetell, Indiana, Pa,		3 50
Miss Fannie Baker, residence unknown,		1 00
T. C. Ross, Sparta, Ky., Life member,	$20,	5 00
T. J. Brown, New Liberty,	25,	
Jesse Lindsey, Ghent, Ky.,	20,	5 00
Mrs. Lucy Craig, Madison, Ia.,	20,	5 00
H. J. Foster, Ghent, Ky.,	20,	5 00
Hubble Foster.	25,	
Wm. McClure,	20,	5 00
Levi McCann,	20,	5 00
Z. Carpenter, Fisherville, Ky.,		4 00

The above Life members were obtained by a slight effort during our protracted meeting in Ghent, Ky., without saying one word in public on the subject.— During the meeting three valuable additions were obtained to the church.

-----o-----

CAMPBELL AND RICE'S DEBATE.—Bro. C. D. Roberts has obtained the plates for this valuable work, with the copyright, and it will soon be for sale at this office. Our Presbyterian friends soon got tired of their great victory, let it fall dead and go out of print. But it will now very soon be resurrected and doing its work of benevolence, throughout the world. Orders may be forwarded immediately. Price $2.

BEAUTIFUL PICTURES.—We have for sale, at this office, what good judges call " the best likeness of Eld. A. Campbell, ever taken," and one equally good of Eld. James Challen. Price of each 25 cents.—They can be sent by mail perfectly safe.

GENERAL AGENTS FOR THE A. C. REVIEW;.—Eld. J. D. Seaton is to make an extended tour over the principal parts of Missouri, as an agent for the Christian University in that State, and is an authorized agent for the A. C. Review, in all his travels. May this excellent brother have a prosperous journey and do much good for the Saviors cause!

CORRESPONDENTS.—We have valuable addresses from F. W. Emmons, S. W. Irvin, C. D. Hurlbutt; with valuable articles from G. W. Elley, Z. P. Goodman, and many others with which we shall do the best in our power, inserting as fast and many as possible.

MISSIONARY SOCIETY.—We have some sage suggestions before us touching the Missionary Society, such for instance, as that there are other Missionary fields nearer home, promising more than the Jerusalem Mission. This is a poor consolation now. Before the meeting, in October, we tried to obtain as full an expression as possible. At the anniversary meeting, venerable brethren, such as A. Campbell, W. Scott, and J. T. Johnson, were present, besides a number of others not so venerable in years but long in the faith. Such, for instance, as Raines, Henshall, Barclay, Pendleton, Pickett, Ayres, Pettigrew, Wiley, Bernau and others. In the presence of these, many of them participating in the discussion, right or wrong, without a dissenting voice, was to make the Jerusalem mission permanent, by sending Dr. Barclay back as soon as the outfit could be obtained. This the Board is now confined to, and compelled to make the first item in the work. What can it amount to for brethren to make suggestions about other fields, till we secure this outfit, unless it be to prevent brethren from doing anything?

MISSIONARY SOCIETY.—The Board of the American Christian Missionary Society, at its meeting 3d February, 1857, passed the following resolutions:

Having heard with the most profound regret of the death of our Vice-President and agent, and much beloved Brother, John T. Johnson, we feel it to be our duty to express ourselves in sympathy with that feeling of sadness that fills the church, at the loss we have sustained in the death of our gifted and laborious brother. We feel that his weary travels, his privations from home, his undying ardor, and energetic defense of Christianity, for many years, reminds us very forcibly of that labor of love which distinguished the great apostle of the Gentiles. His loss to this Society is very great, as we know that his labors in its behalf were of the first importance.

Wherever he went, he urged upon his brethren the true missionary spirit; and such was the Christian unction of his speech, and the pathos of his love for sinners, that he made them feel, as he felt, the necessity for sustaining the great work of missionary operations. Sorry are we that his voice has been stilled, but we bow in reverent humility to "our Father who is in heaven," that "doeth all things well." We tender to the members of his beloved family our most profound sympathy in this their painful bereavement, praying that they, with us, will appropriate to our hearts the rich and precious promises of that Christianity "that he had lived upon, and upon which he died."

-----o-----

Success of the Gospel.

OHIO.—Bro. Benj. Lockhart writes:

Jan. 10, at Oxford Holmes county, I held a meeting which resulted in nine additions. Next—at Waynesburg, Stark county, Jan. 23, resulting in thirteen additions; and at Manchester, Summit co., Feb. 6th, seventeen were added to the congregation. Bro. Jno. Sinclair, assisted at this place.

MARYLAND.—Bro. G. Elley writes: Baltimore, March 12:—During the last week we have had three additions, with a good feeling in the Church and community.

IOWA.—Bro. B. F. Snooks, Indianola, Feb. 2d, writes:—At our last meeting we received three by letter and one by baptism. The cause of Christ is prospering here.

PENNA.—Bro. C. J. Berry, of Connelsville, Pa., Feb. 26, says: "At Bethel, 5 miles from here, twelve were immersed, and a decided improvement has taken place here.

KY.—We are informed that at a protracted meeting at Petersburg, Ky., principally through the labors of Bro. B. Vawter, some 35 were added.

NEW YORK.—A letter just received from Brother Burnet, reports two valuable additions to the church in New York city.

PARIS, ILL., Feb. 17th, '57.

BRO. FRANKLIN:—Since my last letter, we have had the labors of Brethren Wright and Lockhart, of Ind., each a few days. The brethren were much edified by their teaching, and fourteen were added to the congregation. We praise the lord for his abundant favor, and pray its continuance.

A. D. FILLMORE.

DEAR BRO. FRANKLIN:—We have just closed a highly interesting meeting in Pipestone. We delivered at this place some twelve discourses; and though the weather was, for the most part, very miserable, and the roads as bad as we ever saw, yet the audiences were large and profoundly attentive. There were fifteen accessions to the Christian congregation in this place; eight by confession and baptism, three from the United Brethren, and four reclaimed. Since my last report, the saints have been led to rejoice in the salvation of sinners at Brownsville, Little Prairie Ronde, and Paw Paw, At these three points, under the conjoint labors of Eld. William Anderson and the writer, about thirty have been added to the Christian church. We do not recollect ever to have seen more Christian love and zeal than was exhibited on the part of the saints in our recent meetings. There are many noble and truly devoted brethren in this section of country, who are faithfully toiling for "the better land." We never more richly enjoyed the comforts of love with the people of God than at our recent meetings; indeed, we have had much to refresh and encourage the way-worn Christian pilgrim in this vale of sin and sorrow. May the Lord preserve us all in the way of life everlasting. Wm. M. ROE.

PIPESTONE, Mich., Feb. 24, 1857.

-----o-----

Obituaries.

NICHOLASVILLE, Feb. 10, 1857.

BRO. FRANKLIN.—By special request, it becomes my melancholy duty to announce the death of our beloved brother in Christ, A F. Davis, who died at his residence in Nicholasville, Kentucky, January 17, after a short but painful illness of eight days, which he bore with much Christian fortitude. It was the writer's painful duty to witness his last sufferings, but it was pleasing to observe his entire resignation to the will of God, and the confident hope he manifested of a glorious resurrection with the just. Bro. Davis was thirty-seven years old, and a member of the Christian church some fifteen years prior to his death. It is pleasing to note that, being thrown upon the world a penniless boy, by industry, economy, and a strict observance of the Christian precepts, he accumulated an independence, and secured the love of the pious and just.

Bro. Davis leaves a wife and three children to mourn his loss. But why should they mourn, with the consolation of the scriptures before them? Though a temporary loss to them, it is his eternal gain.

J. M. S.

THE AMERICAN CHRISTIAN REVIEW.

VOL. II. CINCINNATI, MAY, 1857. No. 5

CHRIST'S TERMS OF DISCIPLESHIP.

A DISCOURSE, BY ELD. F. W. EMMONS.

"So likewise, whosoever he be of you, that forsaketh not all that he hath, he cannot be my disciple."—LUKE XIV: 33.

When the subject of religion is introduced to persons out of Christ, in private or in the social circle, and its importance pressed upon their consideration; it is not unfrequently that they reply, "I know that it is important—I would be a Christian if I could—I would give all the world if I were a Christian."

Now, this reply seems to be made with all sincerity; and we lure no reason to doubt, that many, and, perhaps, the most of those who thus answer, are sincere, and really think, that it is not owing to any unwillingness on their part that they are not Christians. But when the subject is still further pressed, and they are told, that everything has been done for their salvation that could be done, and that can, consistently, be done, on the part of God; that he has given his Son to die for them; that the testimony of his love has been recorded by many witnesses, and confirmed by the demonstrations of the Holy Spirit; so that "it is a faithful (*credible*) saying, and worthy of all acceptation, that Christ Jesus came, into the world to save sinners, even the chief;" when the willingness of God to save, is set before them in the most striking passages of his word, "Have I any pleasure at all that the wicked should die? saith the Lord God, and not that he should return from his ways and live?" "For I have no pleasure in the death of him that dieth, saith the Lord God; wherefore, turn yourselves and live ye." When the willingness of Christ is exhibited in his inviting language "Come unto me, all ye that labor and are heavy laden, and I will give you rest. Take my yoke upon you and learn of me, for I am meek and lowly in heart, and ye shall find rest to your souls for my yoke is easy and my burden is light." When, still further, they are pointed to the garden of Gethsemane—to the bar of Pilate—to the hill of Calvary—to the Cross—and to the dying prayer of Jesus for his enemies, and for them: "Father, forgive them; for they know not what they do,"—and, to complete the argument, Paul is quoted: "But God commendeth his love towards us, in that while we were yet sinners, Christ died for us there are but few (and none, I think, who are truly candid and sincere), who have aught further to reply in justification of themselves. No, the unwillingness, the fault that we are not Christians, is all ours and on our own part. And if we think that we are willing—that we would give up all, we are deceived. It becomes us, therefore, to examine our hearts anew, and strive to enter into life through the strait gate; "for many," said our Lord, "shall seek to enter in, and shall not be able."

"So likewise, whosoever he be of you, that forsaketh not all he hath, he cannot be my disciple."

This text propounds our Lord's terms of discipleship.

It will be the object of this discourse, by explanation and illustration, to lay these fully before you; and then, by appealing to your best judgments and consciences, to enforce a compliance on your part with these terms.

Our text is addressed to sinners—to persons out of Christ, without God and without hope in the world; and our discourse shall be addressed to such. We would preach to you the gospel. We would point you to the Lamb of God, who taketh away the sins of the world. We would exhibit to you Christ, as "the chiefest among ten thousands, the one altogether lovely." And O! that His love might enlist your best affections, and His reasonable commands your best obedience in all things!

Is it an *easy* thing to become a Christian?

"It is easy," say some. "It is as easy as to will and to execute anything else, which God requires of us." "It is hard—it is difficult," say others, "to become a Christian; we must be created anew in Christ Jesus—we must be born again; and for this, we are dependent on the Spirit of God."

We assent to both these answers. It is easy—it is hard. It is easy for all, under certain circumstances; it is hard for all, under others. It is easier for the young, than for the middle aged and old. It is easier for the poor than for the rich; for our Lord has said. "That a rich man shall hardly (or with difficulty), enter into the kingdom of heaven." And, again he said: "It is easier for a camel to go through the eye of a needle, than for a rich man to enter into the kingdom of God."* The disciples being astonished at these words, Jesus answered again: "Children, how hard it is for them that trust in riches to enter into the kingdom of God!"†

Here we have a clue to the difficulty—"for them that *trust* in riches." The poor have less to cling to, and bind them to earth, than the rich. But this, only by the bye.

The question, the great question before us, is not whether it is hard or easy—difficult or not difficult, to become a Christian or disciple of Christ; but *what are his terms of discipleship?* The answer of the text is, we must give up all—we must forsake all.

Now for an explanation and illustration, that will make this matter plain. How are we to forsake all?

In the foregoing context, we have some specifications of what and how. "If any man come to me," says our Lord, "and hate not his father, and mother, and wife, and children, and brethren, and sisters, yea, and his own life, also, he cannot be my disciple. And whosoever doth not bear his cross and come after me, cannot be my disciple."

A parallel passage to this, and which explains the word *hate* in it, is found in Matthew 10:37-39. It reads: "He that loveth father or mother more than me, is not worthy of me; and he that loveth son or daughter more than me, is not worthy of me. And he that taketh not his cross, and followeth after me, is not worthy of me. He that findeth his life shall lose it; and he that loseth his life shall find it."

It hence appears, that the import of *"hate,"* in our context, is simply *to love less*. To come to Christ and become his disciple we must love father and mother, with all other relatives and friends, and our own life also, *less* than

*Matth. 19: 23, 24. †Mark, 10: 24.

other relatives and friends, and our own life also, *less* than we love Christ. In other words, he must be enthroned in our affections; and all that we do, must be done in subserviency to His will. "Son! daughter! give me thy heart," says God—"thy whole heart." Till this is given, we do not come to Christ—we cannot come to him. We may ask; but he will not hear us. We may knock at mercy's door; but He will not open to us. And why not? Because God and Christ are infinitely lovely—because, from the relations which they sustain to us, they cannot require anything less of us, than that we love them with all our heart, with all our soul, with all our mind, and with all our strength.

Our first parents, before the fall, loved God thus Holy angels have thus loved, and continue to love him thus, from the beginning. In this, therefore, consists the apostasy of man and of fallen angels, that God is dethroned from their hearts; and that they love and serve the creature more than the Creator, who is over all and blessed forever. We repeat, therefore, that to come to Christ—to become a disciple of Christ, the great work to be effected in us and by us, and by the Spirit of God, is the dethronement of self and the enthronement of God and of Christ in our affections.

This great work is to be effected in us; and it is to be effected *by us, and by the Spirit of God.*

We say not by ourselves first; but first by the Spirit of God. How by the Spirit of God first? We answer: By the Word of God. which is the *sword* of the Spirit, by the Word of God, which is the *revelation,* of the Spirit. By this word we are taught the being and perfections of God—we are taught that we are his creatures—we are taught our relations to time and to eternity—we are taught that God so loved the world, as to give his only-begotten Son. that whosoever believeth on him should not perish, but have eternal life. By this Word, given and confirmed by the demonstrations of the Holy Spirit, are we enabled to believe and come to Christ. Hence, said our Lord, in answer to the question, "What shall I do, that I may work the work of God? This is the work of God, that ye believe on him whom he hath sent."

To come to Christ, and become a disciple of Christ, we must come to God, and exercise repentance towards God. To come to God, we must believe in his existence and rewarding goodness. For, "he that cometh to God," says an apostle, "must believe that he is, and that he is the rewarder of all them who diligently seek him." We must believe the gospel of the love of God in Christ—that God is in Christ, reconciling the world to himself, not imputing to them their trespasses. We must believe all the testimony, which God has given of his Son,; and receive him cordially, as our prophet, priest, and king.

It hence appears, that the first act of our agency in coming to God and Christ, is an act of *faith.* This is the gift of God, and is produced in us by the Spirit of God, through the word of truth. "Being born again," says Peter, "not of corruptible seed, but of incorruptible, by the Word of God, which liveth and abideth forever. For all flesh is as grass, and all the glory of man as the flower of grass; the grass withereth and the flower thereof falleth away; but the Word of the Lord endureth forever. And this is the word, which by the gospel is preached unto you."*

Faith is the first act of our agency—the first step, that we take or can take, in coming to God and the Lord Jesus Christ, because by this we set to our seal—(or, affix our seal to the divine testimony)—that God is true. "Without faith, it is impossible to please him."

Again: By faith we receive Christ, and are enabled to become the children of God. "But as many as received him," says John, "to them gave he power to become the sons of God,

---

*1 Peter 1: 23-25.

even to them that believe on his name."† By faith we stand; by faith we live; by faith are we justified This, in all the subjects of it, is a living, energizing principle—the spring and source of all holy exercises. "With the heart man believeth unto (or into) righteousness," says an apostle.‡

Faith is an exercise, which begins with the understanding, and ends with the heart. It comes by hearing; and the hearing, which produces it, is by the word of God. It has been said, and truly said, "I cannot believe at will—I must believe according to the evidence." There is, therefore, no merit in belief, or demerit in unbelief, only in so far as one or the other results from a proper attention, or want of attention, to the testimony which is given to produce faith. Such, however, are the evidences of the divine mission of Jesus of Nazareth, and of the truth of his gospel, that no man *can* examine them, as the importance of this subject demands, without believing. Therefore, said our Lord: "If I had not come and spoken unto them, they had not had sin: but now have they no cloak for their sin."* Again, said Nicodemus: "We know that thou art a teacher come from God; for no man can do these miracles which thou doest, except God be with him."† And, therefore, says our Lord again: "He that believeth not is condemned already, and the wrath of God abideth on him;' and, finally: "He that believeth not, shall be damned." The reason is obvious. We receive the testimony of men, and the testimony of God is greater; and in slighting the testimony of God, and in disbelieving it, we make God a liar. "He that believeth on the Son of God," says John, "hath the witness in himself; he that believeth not God, hath made him a liar, because he believeth not the record that God gave of his Son."*

† John 1; 12.
‡ Rom. 10: 10.
*John 15: 22.
†John 3: 2.
*1 John 5: 10.

How Heaven daring, and obnoxious to divine wrath, the attitude of the unbelieving, impenitent sinner! But, important as is *faith*, it is only the first step, and by which alone, no sinner ever did, or ever could, come to Christ. There is no "forsaking"—no "giving up all," in faith. To do this, there must be an act of the will. We remark, therefore, that the second step is *repentance towards God*.

Except ye repent, ye shall all likewise perish." "And they went out and preached that man should repent." "That repentance and remission of sins should be preached in his name among all nations, beginning at Jerusalem." "Men and brethren, what shall we do? And Peter said unto them, repent."

Repentance is that exercise of the heart and will, by which we give ourselves up to God—by which we turn away from all iniquity and turn to holiness—by which we give up all, and forsake all for Christ's sake. It results from faith, which works by love. Its immediate antecedent is an apprehension of the goodness of God, and of our own sinfulness and vileness, and a godly sorrow for sin. "Now I rejoice,"* says Paul to the Corinthians, "not that ye were made sorry, but that ye sorrowed to repentance: for ye were made sorry after a godly manner, that ye might receive damage by us in nothing; for godly sorrow worketh repentance to salvation, not to be repented of; but the sorrow of the world worketh death."

No person can truly believe the testimony, which God has given of his Son, without having his heart affected, to some degree, by the love of God. At the same time he must begin to see and feel himself a sinner, and begin to sorrow after a godly manner. But godly sorrow is not repentance. It goes before—it leads to it. Godly sorrow is but a feeling of the heart. A person, therefore, who stops here, may grieve for days and weeks and months, and never find relief. We must repent.

*2 Ep. 7: 9,10.

And repentance, as we have already defined it, is an exercise, not only of the heart, but of the will.

The language of repentance is: "Here, Lord, I am, a miserable sinner—deserving thy wrath—unworthy of thy favor; but have mercy upon me! I cast myself at the feet of sovereign mercy. I *give* myself up to thee, without reserve. *Take* thou the throne of my affections. I *would*, and *will*, be thine forever; and though thou slay me, yet *will* I love thee. I *will* serve thee and obey thee. Accept of me, and have mercy upon me for the sake of Jesus Christ, thy well-beloved Son!"

This is forsaking and giving up all. And every sinner that thus comes to Christ will find mercy. Heaven will smile. It ever has smiled on an offering like this. That load of guilt is now removed. For darkness, there is light in the Lord; and for the spirit of heaviness, there is joy unspeakable and full of glory. The heart is now renovated by divine grace. "Old things have passed away; behold all things are become new." Now can the sinner say: "Christ is *my* Savior. He has loved and died for *me.*" Now can he pray, and say: "God is *my* gracious Heavenly Father."

"Faith," we said, "is an exercise, which begins with the understanding and ends with the heart;" and "repentance is an exercise, beginning with the heart and ending with the will." By faith and repentance, therefore, the whole mind of man—the spirit and the soul—are subjected to God.

And yet, to complete discipleship—to make us citizens in the kingdom of Christ on earth—to entitle us to the name and relation of sons and daughters to the Lord Almighty, there is another step. It is called in our context, *a bearing of the Cross,* and *a coming after Christ.* "And whosoever doth not bear his cross, and come after me, cannot be my disciple." It is elsewhere called. "*a confessing of Christ before* men"—"*a taking of his yoke upon us*"—a *confessing with the mouth to salvation.*" In other words, IT IS A SCRIPTURAL PROFESSION OF OUR FAITH IN CHRIST. It is an act of the whole man—body, soul, and spirit. It begins with a confession of Christ with the mouth, and ends with a baptism into him—a burial and resurrection, by which we put him on. "For ye are all the children of God, by faith in Christ Jesus," says Paul to the Galatians. How? "For," he adds: "as many of you as have been baptized into Christ, have put on Christ." "But, can I not be a disciple of Christ, and make no public profession of faith?" says one. We answer: In simply believing and repenting, there is no bearing of the Cross, or coming unto Christ. "And whosoever doth not bear his Cross, and come after me," says Christ, "cannot be my disciple." Again, he says, "Whosoever shall confess me before men, him shall the Son of man confess before the angels of God. But he that denieth me before men, shall be denied before the angels of God."* Not to confess Christ, we virtually deny him.

Again: In his commission to his apostles to make disciples, this public profession of faith is enjoined: "Go ye, therefore, and teach (disciple, or make disciples of) all nations, baptizing them." "Go ye into all the world and preach the gospel to every creature. He that believeth and is baptized shall be saved; but he that believeth not shall he damned." †

Christ's terms of discipleship are now fully before you. We proceed, therefore, *to enforce a compliance with these terms.* Come and let us reason together.

I remark, first: That all, who hear the gospel, ought to comply with these terms, and become the disciples of Christ, because they are most reasonable.

God is our Creator. We are creatures; dependent on him for life, for the air that we breathe, for the food that we eat, and for all the enjoyments and blessings of life. Christ has died for us. It is, therefore, the right of God and of Christ to require our subjection to all their co-

* Luke 12: 8, 9.

† Matth. 28: 19, and Mark 16: 15, 16

mmandments.

How various and abundant the divine revelations! We have line upon line, and precept upon precept, of divine instruction—of testimonies of the divine goodness. And all these testimonies have been confirmed to us, by signs and wonders, and other miraculous attestations of the Holy Spirit. It is credible, therefore, all that He requires us to believe. Why not believe Him? Why not yield a ready and willing assent to the testimony, which God has given of his Son; and receive him, at once, as our prophet, priest and king, and put our trust in him? Why, I repeat it, should we not do so?

And having departed from God, the fountain of living waters—having enthroned self in our affections, and loved and served the creature more than the Creator; how reasonable it is, that we should repent—reform! That we should turn and return to Him, with all our hearts—that we should give Him the throne, which belongs to Him, and humble ourselves at His feet! Is not this reasonable? Why *not repent,* therefore? Every one of you, repent. "Cast away from you all your transgressions, whereby ye have transgressed; and make you a new heart and a new spirit; for why will ye die?"*

And let us bear the cross, too, and come after the Savior. He bore a heavy cross of wood for us. He carried it till he sunk under it, and then he was nailed to it, and died on it, a most cruel and ignominious death, for us. And shall we not confess Him before men? "I beseech you, therefore, by the mercies of God, that ye present your bodies a living sacrifice, holy, acceptable to God, which is your reasonable service."†

I remark secondly: That these terms of discipleship, should be complied with, because *there is no other name, given under heaven and among men, but the name of Christ Jesus, by which we can be saved.*

"I am the way," says Christ, "the truth and the life." "If you believe not that I am he, ye shall die in your sins, and whither I am, ye cannot come." "He that believeth not shall be damned." "Except ye repent, ye shall perish." And, "he that denieth me before men, shall be denied before the angels of God."

I remark thirdly: That we should close in and comply with these terms of discipleship; because *they are proposed for our happiness.*

"And you shall find rest to your souls," says Christ. Every disciple has known, and knows, this is true, from, experience. "Then Philip went down to the city of Samaria and preached Christ unto them. And the people, with one accord, gave heed to those things which were spoken by Philip. * * * And there was *great joy* in that city."* "Then Philip opened his mouth and began at the same scripture and preached unto him Jesus. And as they went on their way, they came unto a certain water; and the Eunuch said: Sec, here is water; what doth hinder me to be baptized? And Philip said: If thou believeth with all thine heart thou mayest. And he answered and said: I believe that Jesus Christ is the Son of God. And he commanded the chariot to stand still; and they went down both into the water, both Philip and the Eunuch: and he baptized him. And when they came up out of the water, the Spirit of the Lord caught away Philip, that the Eunuch saw him no more; and he went on his way *rejoicing.*"* And again: "If there be, therefore, any *consolation in* Christ, if any *comfort* of love, if any *fellowship* of the Spirit, if any bowels and mercies," says Paul to the Philippian Christians, "fulfill ye my joy, that ye be like minded, having the same love, being of one accord, of one mind."†

*Ezek. 18. 31.
†Romans 12: 1.

*Acts 8: 5, 6, 7.
*Acts 8: 35-39.
†Phil. 2: 1, 2.

Yes: there is consolation in Christ—there is comfort of love—there is fellowship of the Spirit. Would you, therefore, be happy, my friends, come to Christ. Believe on him—repent—obey him. Come now. "Behold now is the accepted time! Behold now is the day of salvation!" In the world, all must have tribulation; but in Christ there is peace. "Great peace have they, that keep thy law," says the Psalmist, "and nothing shall offend them." Their peace is like a river; and their righteousness like the waves of the sea. The Christian is happy here, in this world; and, in the world to come, he shall inherit eternal life.

I remark fourthly, and finally: That we should comply with these terms of discipleship; because *we must all stand before the judgment seat of Christ.*

"The former times of ignorance," we are informed in a discourse of Paul, "God winked at;" but "now he commands all men everywhere to repent. Because he has appointed a day, in the which he will judge the world in righteousness, by that man whom he hath ordained, whereof he hath given assurance unto all men, in that he hath raised him from the dead."*

Now, if there were any such thing as escaping this appearing—if we could sustain ourselves in being without God—or, if when we should call on rocks and mountains to fall on us and hide us from his presence, they would obey us, and we so escape; we might have some show of reason or excuse for neglecting this great salvation. But now we have none—No: *none.* And if we neglect it, we *cannot escape* the penalty threatened against the finally impenitent—death, the *"second death"*—an *"everlasting destruction"* and *"banishment,"* from the presence of the Lord and the glory of his power; when he shall be revealed from heaven "in flaming fire, taking vengeance on them that know not God and that obey not the gospel."† For the decree has gone forth, and will not be revoked, "That at the name of Jesus, every knee shall bow in heaven and on earth, and under the earth; and every tongue shall confess him Lord, to the glory of God the Father."† All must bow, willingly or unwillingly. "Whosoever falls upon this stone"—this Rock of ages—"shall be broken"—humbled, changed, regenerated and made a new creature; "but on whomsoever it shall fall, it will grind him to powder." "O, kiss the Son," therefore, "lest he be angry, and ye perish from the way, while his wrath is kindled but a little. Blessed are all they, that put their trust in Him."

*Acts 17: 30, 31. †2nd Thess. 1: 8.

-----o-----

UPWARD TENDENCY—REFORMATION NOT A FAILURE—MISSIONARY WORK.

The effort we have made, and are now making, at reformation, can never prove a failure upon any ground, unless it be that we have not moral courage enough, as the Disciples of Christ—have not sufficient integrity to the great principles of the gospel, to which we have pledged ourselves, to maintain them against the mighty torrent of opposition from the various ranks of bigotry, prejudice, and partyism, together with the combined influence of unbelief and sin. The position we occupy can never fail. While the holy prophets live and speak in their writing; while the preaching of the apostles, their lives, miracles and martyrdoms, live in the memory of men; while Jesus lives, and the throne of the Almighty, upon which he sits, stands unmoved the position we occupy cannot fail. The gospel will live and he who believes it shall never die. The men who believe the gospel, who love it, and hold on to it—keep the faith, press it to their hearts, love and reverence him who gave it, will live co-existent with the years of God. They will never fail; their lives, in this mortal state, will fail; but tiny, at the same moment, will triumph. They are not in any doubt and uncertainty, in calling upon

*Philip. 2: 10, 11.

their fellow man to return to the faith as it was at the beginning. They have no fears that they are wrong, or that they can possibly be mistaken, in making the best effort in their power to determine precisely what the ancient faith was, separating it from everything else, and maintaining it before the world. They know they are right in this. In one word, they believe the gospel, maintain and defend it, and nothing else. It is the system they believe, maintain and defend and nothing else. They may not understand everything contained in it, as others who have other systems, do not understand everything in their system; but the system itself we know to be right, infallibly right and that we are infallibly right in maintaining it; not because we understand everything contained in it; but because we know the author of it, and know him to be Divine—infallible. We know him, love him and regard him; therefore we know that what proceeds from him is infallible, and love it and regard it.

We occasionally see, from men called brethren, a kind of fling at something they call "The Current *Reformation.*" Then, again, some one of the same class makes an allusion, in derision, at something he calls "The Ancient Order of things." Another of the same sort, makes a hit at what he sneeringly calls "The Disciples' church." Many other expressions of a similar kind may be selected, showing settled uncongeniality, deep-rooted hostile elements, painful grippings, malignant feelings, poor, sickly perversity and opposition. These are hobbyists, idolizers and oppositionists. There is but one thing certain about them, and that is they are certain to be in the opposition, in the negative, pulling back and discouraging. They do not speak of the cause as if they were identified with it; but as if it belonged to somebody else.—They do not speak of it as if they had any responsibility in it. In their estimation the responsibility is all upon others.

They are not responsible, have neither part nor lot in it, and if any misfortune to the cause occurs, they stand ready not only to publish it, but to magnify it, and cry out, in self-complacency and exultation, "I told you so," "I knew it would be so," etc., etc. Some of these are traversing the country, claiming fraternity with the Disciples and support from them; and at the same time cannot pass through a single community without manifesting their deep settled and malignant opposition to the principal measures and men among us. Their mission is to institute, infuse and perpetuate a set of petty annoyances, strifes and contentions among brethren. They build up nothing, advance nothing, and exercise none but a negative influence. Even the hobbies which they adore and idolize, they do not *carry* and *push* through the world: but have the hobbies to *carry* and *push them* into notice.

There are several classes of these hobbyists, with their various hobbies, each man of them, however, only having one, which, with him, is the center around which everything revolves, and the touch-stone by which everything is to be tried. Even the Bible itself, must come before each man's hobby, be tried by it, and compelled to testify in favor of it, or be rejected as not from God! Mention a State mission to one of these, and the first thing that enters his head, is the question, will it support my *beau ideal,* which *I expect to support me?"* If it will make that the center of its revolutions and attractions and make itself auxiliary and subservient to that end and thus declare itself, I am for it. Present the claims of the Missionary Society, and another replies "Will it become auxiliary to my center of attraction, and thus strengthen the hobby, that is carrying me into notice?" If it will it can have my gracious smiles, good will and approbation. If not I am down upon it and down upon all that are in favor of it. However good men may sympathize with these several classes of persons, pray for them, and wish them well; one thing is inevitable, and that is, that so far as the work of God is concerned, they are unavailable. Whatever talent, influence and means they possess cannot be brought to bear upon anything that is simply the work of God; that has an eye singly to the Divine authority and the glory of God. If you will not allow them to make the cause of God and the work of God subservient to their ends, they will not touch a finger to it. On the other hand they will throw themselves back in the harness exert all the negative influence in their power, and if possible, sink the cause. You may explain it as you please, excuse on the ground of honest mistakes—or make it the deliberate design to retard and oppose; we shall have no controversy here, as it matters nothing to us about the intention. We do not have to try them, judge them, nor punish; all we are concerned with is the simple fact they are not available, and we need not count anything upon them. Their entire power and influence, we must understand distinctly, are to be incessantly in the negative.

They may object to State Missions, the English, Australian or Jerusalem Missions, or any others that may be suggested; but cannot any man, with the least discrimination, see as clear as sunbeams, that on the part of all that class of men who build up nothing, do nothing in any way, have no success in anything, but are simply, as far as they think prudent to risk it, eking out their inharmonious feelings, it is mere cant? Who are the men that encourage the people of God? Who are they that strengthen and inspire the churches with love, zeal and harmony? Who are they that restore peace, order and good will among the saved, and increase their numbers? Who are they now, that are gathering men into the fold of Christ? Look over the land, brethren, and you can see who they are. They are the men who are doing the work in the churches at home, and all around on every side. They are the men who are pushing our State Missions, the Foreign Missions, Bible Revision, and every other good work. These are the man to whom we must look for the promotion of the cause. The other class may preach their hobbies till doom's day; but no success will follow; no love will be infused; no good will inspired. All that class of preachers will die; their preaching will become insipid; the churches will die under their influence, and their candlestick will very soon be removed out of its place. You might as -well think of keeping the life, power and spirit of the Christian religion in active exercise, by preaching the eternal decrees of Calvinism, the empty ceremonies of Episcopalianism, or the superiority of the Methodist church polity, as by preaching any one of a half dozen hobbies that some brethren are now trying to ride into notice. The breath of life cannot be breathed into them.

In the kingdom of God the Lord is the center. He said, "I, if I be lifted up, will draw all men to me." "As Moses lifted up the serpent in the wilderness, even so must the Son of Man be lifted up, that whoever believeth on him should not perish, but have everlasting life." The great apostle to the Gentiles, after giving a brief summary of side considerations, and many of them weighty, in his situation, says of them all, "I count all things but loss for the excellency of the knowledge of Christ Jesus my Lord; for whom I have suffered the loss of all things, and do count them but refuse that I may win Christ."—Phil. 3: 8. Again, said this man of God, "I determined to know nothing but Christ and him crucified." He would not be drawn aside from the center of attraction in the kingdom of God. In the close of his elaborate letter to the Corinthians, among whom many distracting annoyances were operating, and in reference to those who disturbed the peace and love of the church, he declares that "If any man love not the Lord Jesus Christ, he will be accursed when the Lord comes."—1 Cor. 16:22. "Whoever hateth his brother is a murderer; and ye know that no murderer hath eternal life abiding in him."—John 3: 15. Again, says the holy apostle, "These be they who separate themselves, sensual, having not the spirit." James 1:9. The Lord says, "By this shall all men know that you are my disciples, if you have love one to another."

From him who thus teaches, we are not to be drawn aside, whether we precisely agree upon every side question, or the manner of procedure in reference to it or not. By him we must stand forever more. To him we must pay supreme homage. This can only be done by standing firmly upon his precise teachings, as far as poor imperfect creatures possibly can, and putting our everlasting trust in him. The cause is now progressing, its prospects brightening, and its way opening beautifully in almost all directions. The good, the reliable, the faithful and working men, are gathering up afresh, combining and accumulating strength, which will be expended upon the armies of the enemy around with tremendous effect. Let every man who can lift a Bible speak a word, or give an expression of countenance, for the Lord and for his work do it; do it with earnestness, spirit and power; do it with strong faith and determination, and it will tell upon the world for good in ages to come. Let us make an effort, united, energetic and mighty, in the Lord's name, for his cause; and let the effort continue while the Lord shall give us life, and exhort the brethren to push it onward with our dying breath. To his name be honor and power everlasting.

BENJ. FRANKLIN.

-----o-----

The beginning of strife, is as when one letteth out water: therefore leave off contention, before it be meddled with.

Address by Eld. S. W. Irvin,
OF POPLAR PLAINS, KENTUCKY.

LUKE 6: 36.—Be ye therefore merciful, as your Father also is merciful.

Christians are commanded to be imitators of God as dear children. They are called upon to imitate Him in what He is, and in what he does. Is God holy? He has said, "Be ye holy, for I am holy." Is He pure, absolutely, eternally, unchangeably—it is said, "Blessed are the pure in heart, for they shall see God." Is He continually manifesting Himself in active benevolence to his creatures, it is said: "Be ye therefore merciful, as your Father also is merciful."

We cannot grasp the full idea of Godhead, because we cannot comprehend the infinite. Watts has well said:

"Reason may grasp the massy hills,
    And spread from pole to pole;
But Lord thy name our nature fills,
    And overloads the soul.
In vain our haughty science swells,
    For nought is found in Thee—
But boundless inconceivables,
    And vast eternity.''

"Such knowledge is too wonderful for me," said the Psalmist, "it is high, I cannot attain unto it. Whither shall I go from thy spirit, or whither shall I flee from thy presence. If I ascend up into heaven, thou art there; if I make my bed in hell, behold thou art there. If I take the wings of the morning and dwell in the uttermost parts of the sea, even there shall thy hand lead me, and thy right hand shall hold me. If I say, surely the darkness shall cover me, even the night shall be light about me. Yea, the darkness hideth not from thee, but the night shineth as the day; the darkness and the light are both alike to thee."

Our imitations of God must be like our comprehensions of Him. We cannot grasp the immeasurable attributes of God, but we can know enough of Him to love, and wonder, and adore; and we can only imitate His mercies as the creature can imitate the Creator. As the heavens are higher than the earth, so are his ways above our ways, and his thoughts above our thoughts. We gradually approximate toward the object of our affections, and hence love to God is the foundation of all our benevolence, as indeed of all our morals. The moral law was founded upon this fact. The first and great commandment is, hear, O Israel! "Thou shalt love the Lord thy God with all thy heart, and with all thy soul, and with all thy mind, and with all thy strength." Out of this flows the second commandment, which is like the first. "Thou shalt love thy neighbor as thyself." "Upon these two," said the great Redeemer, "hang all the law and the prophets."

But what is the basis of our love to God? It is not that his ways are above our ways, or his thoughts above our thoughts. It is not that he spake and it was done; that he commanded and it stood fast. Not that by his word he garnished the heavens, or hung the earth upon nothing. Nor is it that he charges his angels with folly, or that in his sight the heavens are not clean. Indeed, the wisdom, and power, and holiness of God only seem to separate him infinitely from all his creatures. We feel that we are ignorant, and weak, and sinful, and hence unworthy of his notice or his care. But when we are made to realize that God is love; that notwithstanding our unworthiness he loves us, and makes us the objects of his care; that while we are so forgetful of him, he has never forgotten to be gracious; that while we were rebellious, he so loved us that he sent his Son to die for us, we feel that, notwithstanding his infinite exaltation, he pities us in our weakness, sympathizes in our sorrows and cares for us in our low estate. How true it is that we love him because he first loved us.

How great, how overpowering, is that love? and how astonishing are the mercies by which it is manifested? In the discourse from which our motto is taken, our blessed Lord, in commending the love and mercy of God to our imitation, commands us to love our enemies, and do good and lend, hoping for nothing again, and says our reward shall be great and we shall be the children of the Highest, for he is kind unto the unthankful and the evil.

Suppose one of us should find on the highway a man homeless, and destitute, and starving, and should provide the outcast with a home, and all the comforts of life; suppose he was perfectly destitute of gratitude, and, day by day, while he feasted upon our bounty, he would turn upon us no look of recognition, but would receive all our favors as if we were his debtor rather than benefactor; suppose he would wound the hand that fed and clothed him, and saved him from death, and return us enmity rather than love. What would be our feelings towards such a man as this? We might pity him—a sense of duty might impel us to save him from perishing—the love of God might prompt us even to treat him kindly, but we could only love him as a duty; our unsanctified nature would spurn such a man from our roof, and it would be difficult for us to look upon him without loathing. And yet, our Heavenly Father not only created us in his image, but feeds us, day by day, upon his bounty, and where is our gratitude of heart—our thank offering—our daily recognition of the hand that fills our mouths with good things, and makes our cup to run over with blessings? He is kind even to the unthankful. he causeth his sun to rise on the evil and on the good, and sendeth rain on the just and on the unjust. If the divine compassion ceased even here, we might well be overwhelmed with the long suffering and tender mercies of our Heavenly Father.

But in this he commendeth his love toward us, that while we were enemies Christ died for us. "He who spared not his own son, but freely gave him up for us all, how shall he not, with him also, freely give us all things?" "Behold what manner of love the Father hath bestowed upon us, that we should be called the sons of God." "Though he was rich, yet for our sakes he became poor, that we, through his poverty, might be rich." He went to Gethsemane—he went to Calvary for us. Let us draw near, and while we gaze upon the sinless sufferer there let us remember his words, "Be ye therefore merciful as your Father also is merciful."

God is denominated the *Father of mercies.* Are we to infer from this that as the sun is the fountain of light, God is the source from which all love and mercy flows. That our dark, cold hearts must be illuminated by his light, and warmed by his love, before we are capable of deeds of love and mercy to our fellow creatures. This was the secret of Paul's earnest missionary labors. "I am debtor both to the Greeks and to the barbarians, both to the wise and to the unwise, so as much as in me is I am ready to preach the gospel to you that are at Rome also, for I am not ashamed of the gospel of Christ, for it is the power of God unto salvation to every-one that believeth it, to the Jew first, and also to the Greek." Paul had been at enmity with Christ. In his condition, he called himself the chief of sinners. Yet God had loved him—Christ had died for him—though, in his own estimation, he was the least of all saints, because he persecuted the church of God, yet a dispensation of the gospel had been committed to him. For this overpowering love he felt that he could make no suitable return. That he could only show his gratitude to God by loving his creatures, and by striving to extend the blessings of the gospel to those for whom Christ died. Hence his self-sacrificing life in preaching among the Gentiles the unsearchable riches of Christ.

It was the love of God, as manifested in the gift of his Son, that led Judson, and Martyn, and Harrite Newell to India; that led Cox and Cross to their pilgrim graves in Africa; that led the interesting Barclay family to the Holy Land, and is continually leading weary pilgrims on Missionary journeys round the globe. One and all they could say, with the great apostle, "The love of Christ constraineth us." 'Twas this that moved the heart of Howard to leave his family and home, and suffer the privations and toils he endured, for the poor and needy and oppressed of Europe.

A young and delicate female has just finished her mission, in our country, traveling from State to State, of the Union, appealing in person to our legislatures in behalf of the insane. And what think you is the plea with which she has moved so many hearts, and inspired them with sympathy for those children of misfortune. She points first to the Cross of Christ, and then to the howling maniac; and says, Pity them, gentlemen, for the love of God. Be merciful as your Father is merciful. Her potent eloquence has moved the legislatures of nineteen States to carry out her regulations in the erection and management of hospitals for the insane. She is now gone to Europe to carry into effect there the same benevolent plans in which she has been so successful here. May God smile upon her efforts, and may his good angels guard and direct her in her mission of mercy. This lone and delicate woman, moving over the world with the love of God in her heart, is better than a queen—greater than a conqueror. Her name will be spoken with tears of gratitude when "Caesars laurels fade," and Napoleons victories are forgotten.

"O many a spirit walks the world unheeded,
   Who when this veil of flesh shall be laid down,
Will soar aloft with pinions unimpeded,
   And wear its glory as a starry crown."

These missionaries and philanthropists are mentioned with grateful reverence. I love and honor them, one and all. They are the true "immortal names that cannot die." Important is their mission, and great will be their reward. They have poured the oil and wine of sympathy into many a wounded heart. They have stood like ministers from heaven in the damp, dark dungeon, and proclaimed liberty to many a groaning captive, and spoken peace to many a howling maniac.

But while we cannot all imitate the extended benevolence of Howard or Miss Dix, yet there is a broader and deeper channel in which our Christian sympathies may flow. Go with me to the bedside of a dying Christian mother; she is a widow; she is poor; she has struggled long and hard to provide for the necessities of herself and the interesting daughter by her side. As that daughter holds her emaciated hand, or soothes her fevered brow, they are mutually meditating on the hour that will so soon separate forever the mother and the child. Approach and commune for a moment with that dying saint. She tells you that she has long since made her peace with God; that Jesus has made her "dying bed feel soft as downy pillows are." Whence, then, her agony of soul? Her thoughts are of the future. When she is gone, the wide world has no home that her child can call her own. Where can she go, and what will be her destiny in this cold, unfeeling world? Will she wander homeless and friendless, through many a devious way, to an untimely grave? Shall she find her way into some lordly mansion as a menial servant, to drudge out her life without love or pity, with no sympathizing breast upon which to lean her head, and weep away her sorrows? Shall she become a victim to one of those human harpies that sometimes devour the innocent? Or shall want drive her to infamy? No wonder that her mother's heart should fail her and that she cannot die in peace. Suppose one could approach that mother and tell her that the church of Christ had provided a house for her daughter—a happy, lovely home, where she had treasures to supply her wants, and friends to protect and love and train her up in the nurture and admonition of the Lord, and qualify her for a useful and happy life. Would not a mountain weight be taken from her heart? Would not her grateful soul break forth in the language of old Simeon:—Lord now lettest thou thy servant depart in peace, for mine eyes have seen thy salvation.

Such an institution is the Female Orphan School, at Midway, Kentucky. It is all that could be desired as a home for the homeless orphan girl. But it is not only a home, it is a school of the highest order—a true home-school, where the pupils enjoy all the advantages of a liberal and thorough education, in connection with that practical domestic training which is so necessary to qualify them for usefulness and happiness in life. It is especially designed to qualify, as many as possible of its graduates, for teachers and governesses, in families and primary schools.

Will you reflect for a moment on the influence of females on society, of mothers on their families, of teachers on their pupils, and then tell me the amount of good this institution is destined, in the providence of God, to accomplish, when it is thoroughly endowed, and when, year by year, it shall send forth its graduated inmates, refined and chastened by a thorough and Christian education; their hearts warm with the love of God, and burning with the desire to manifest to others that divine philanthropy which has been extended to them. The best patrimony a young man, or a young woman, ever enjoyed, is the influence of an enlightened, God-fearing, and affectionate mother. Next to this, in importance, is a teacher qualified, in head and heart, to complete the education the mother has begun. Education with me is first, and last, and mid-most. Fill a boy's head with the right kind of knowledge, and his heart with the right kind of principles, and you have done enough. You will have furnished him with the elements of manhood and it is then safest, and best, to permit him to weave the web of life for himself. If you could give him the wealth of Astor, or the fame of Napoleon, you would injure rather than benefit him by the gift. You would deprive him of all incentives to personal effort. He would have no laurels to win "in the world's broad field of battle."

No motive to be himself "a hero in the strife." The world's great names were none of them received by inheritance. They all won their palms and laurels for themselves. So must it ever be. Train and educate your boy properly, and then lead him to the field, but let the battle depend upon himself. This is the only way to make him useful, or honorable, or happy. It is idleness that leads to vice, and that drowns so many of our young men in destruction and perdition.

And in order to this education, especially in our own State, we need nothing so much as properly qualified teachers for families and primary schools. What can the College do, when our young men are spoiled, both in head and heart, before they go to College. Train your son at home, until he feels the importance of knowledge—the value of character—the dignity of virtue, and you have nothing to fear from any well-regulated College. If you fail to do this, you need not send him abroad to be ruined— you have ruined him at home. In this home-work, what instruments of good these homeless orphans may be made! What a blessing to themselves, and to the entire community! Ah! if I could approach the lordly mansion of the wealthy; or the bedside of the dying miser, and make them feel how much good they could accomplish, by donations or legacies to this institution, how happily might they learn, that it is more blessed to give than to receive. "Write this upon my tombstone," said a dying Christian. "Let my children read and remember it. *What I gave, I have—what I kept, I lost.*" "He that giveth to the poor lendeth to the Lord." That which is given to the Female Orphan School is safely and permanently invested.

When the donors are sleeping in the grave, their money will not be buried with them. When all they have hoarded up shall have passed from them forever, that which they have given to this institution will still be theirs. While the government shall last, it will bear a part, in wiping the tear from the widow's eye, in giving the outcast a home, and in qualifying and sending abroad missionary teachers—true Sisters of Charity—to honor God and bless mankind. As God has prospered us, let us give to this institution. Let us give cheerfully, liberally, and future generations will rise up and call us blest.

I cannot avoid here quoting a passage from one of the charity sermons of Angel James. "My fancy," says that eloquent and godly man, "has sometimes presented me with this picture of a faithful Sabbath school teacher's entrance to the state of her everlasting rest. The agony of dissolution is closed, the triumph of faith completed, and the conquering spirit fastens to her crown.

"Upon the confines of the heavenly world, a form divinely fair, awaits her arrival. Wrapt in astonishment at the dazzling glory of the celestial inhabitant and as yet a stranger in the world of spirits, she inquires: ' Is this Gabriel, chief of all the heavenly hosts; and am I honored with his aid to guide me to the throne of God?'

"With a smile of ineffable delight, such as adds now beauty to an angels countenance, the mystic form replies; Dost thou Remember little Elizabeth, who was, in yonder world, a Sabbath scholar in thy class; dost thou recollect the child that wept as thou talkedst to her of sin, and directed her to the Cross of the dying Redeemer? God smiled with approbation upon thy effort, and by his own Spirit sealed the impression upon her heart in characters never to be effaced.

"'Providence removed her from beneath thy care before the fruit of thy labor was visible. The seed, however, had taken root, and it was the business of another to water what thou didst sow. Cherished by the influences of heaven, the plant of religion flourished in her heart, and shed its fragrance upon her character.

"'Piety, after guarding her from the snares

of youth, cheered her amid the accumulated trials of an afflicted life, supported her amidst the agonies of the last conflict, and elevated her to the mansions of immortality! And now behold before thee the glorified spirit of that poor child, who, under God, owes the eternal life on which she has lately entered, to thy faithful labors in the Sunday school; and who is now sent by our Redeemer to introduce thee to the world of glory, as thy first and least reward, for guiding the once thoughtless, ignorant, wicked Elizabeth to the world of grace. Hail, happy spirit! Hail, favored of the Lord! Hail, deliverer of my soul! Hail to the world of eternal glory!'

"I can trace the scene no further. I cannot paint the rapture produced in the honored teachers bosom by this unexpected interview. I cannot depict the mutual gratitude and love of two such spirits, meeting on the confines of heaven; much less can I follow them to their everlasting mansion, and disclose the bliss which they shall enjoy before the throne of God. All this, and a thousand times more, is attendant upon the salvation of a single soul. Teachers, what a motive to diligence!"

True enough! What a motive for diligence in the Sabbath school; and may we not add, what a motive for diligence, and liberality, in our support of the Orphan school, and in every other means by which we may befriend the hapless orphan and point, or lead, it upward, to those happy mansions, where such may be our ineffable reward.

I have invited your attention, beloved friends, to this theme for practical purposes, this afternoon. We have on our church book the name of a sister A, _____, who, during the life time of her husband, was a resident of our village. For some years she has not lived in our immediate vicinity, but she still claims to be a member of this congregation. I am not personally acquainted with her, but I am told she is a worthy Christian. You know her history. She had seen better days, but was left, at her husband's death, in hopeless poverty, with six daughters, the oldest of which is now but eleven years of age, entirely dependent upon her for support.

She struggled on, as best she could, to keep her family together. I need not refer to the self-denial, and privation, and toil, she must have endured within the last four or five years. Anxiety and privation, and toil, have at length undermined her constitution, and for some months she has been prostrated on a sick bed; since then she has been dependant on her neighbors for support. Unable longer to keep her family together, it has become necessary to find them a home elsewhere. What can she do? She has no kind friend, or generous relative, to whom she looks for help, and she shrinks from the thought of sending her tender daughters among strangers. For this some have blamed her. I honor her for it. She has a mother's heart, and heaven pity the helpless girl, thrown, without a mother's care, on the cold charities of the world, and dependant on strangers for a home.

The school at Midway offers the only retreat to which she is willing to resign her children. If they were there, and she is to live—she could live contented; if she is to die—she could die in peace. At her solicitation I have written to the trustees, but they have already more beneficiaries than the endowment will support, and the congregation at Midway has already gone beyond its means in providing for those to whom they could not deny admission. They cannot therefore take these children entirely as beneficiaries. But I have the promise of the trustees that the two oldest shall be admitted to all the advantages of the institution on condition that we defray their actual expenses for two years. The sum demanded for this purpose is two hundred dollars. This then is the practical question I have called you together to consider, and in reference to which, in a few moments an answer will be expected.

This is a heaven-favored community God has given you enough and to spare. Will you then of the abundance with which he has blessed you, furnish the amount I have just named, and by so doing provide those innocent girls with a home, and place them beyond the reach of want.

What a happiness was that of Job. "When the ear heard me then it blessed me; and when the eye saw me it gave witness to me. Because I delivered the poor that cried, and the *fatherless-,* and him that had none to help him. The blessing of him that was ready to perish came upon me, and I caused the widow's heart to sing for joy. I put on righteousness and it clothed me, my judgment was as a robe and diadem. I was eyes to the blind, and feet was I to the lame. I was a father to the poor and the cause that I knew not I searched out." By imitating the benevolence of Job, let us cause the heart of another widow to sing for joy; and years hence when these children shall have enjoyed the advantages of that noble institution, they may return to us the cup of blessing which we this day hold out to them. Elevated, and refined, and Christianized, they may come again into our midst as intelligent graduates, in the maturing bloom of womanhood, to thank with full hearts those who befriended them when friends were so much needed.

Beloved friends this work will be done—it must be done! These orphans have no home—unless they have a home in our hearts; they have no friends if we fail to befriend them. But while I feel that the work will be done, it is desirable that it shall be done net by a few individuals, but by the entire community. Let the poorest, and the youngest bear a part in this work of faith and labor of love. And that we may act in such spirit as shall call down the blessing of our heavenly Father on the deed, let us turn our thought to him, who was rich and for our sakes became poor, that we through his poverty might be rich.

Who left the bosom of the bather, and the songs of angels, and the joys of heaven, to be a stranger and a pilgrim in the earth; to be despised and rejected of men, Foxes, said he have holes, and the birds of the air have nests, but the Son of Man hath not where to lay his head—*Hath not where to lay his head.* How similar was his condition to that of the little strangers who have come to-day into this Temple consecrated to the Man of Calvary. They hold up their feeble hands, in the name of Christ, and plead for a home, for they have not where to lay their heads.

How often have we thought of the immaculate and sinless Savior, as with weary feet he wandered up and down in the earth; opening the eyes of the blind, unstopping the ears of the deaf, raising the dead and preaching glad tidings to the poor. How often have we thought, that had it been our privilege to have lived while he was upon the earth, how gladly we would have ministered to his necessities. If we had found him hungry, how gladly would we have fed him; if naked how gladly would we have clothed him. Or, have we not often thought, had he come to us a stranger, how gladly would we have taken him in, and shared with him the hospitalities of home.

But are we sure that we would have dealt thus with our dear Redeemer? Are we sure that we would have been more pitiful than the cruel Jews, who often left him with no roof but the starry sky—no bed but the earth—no pillow but the rock, where

> "Cold mountains, and the midnight air
> Witnessed the fervor of his prayer!"

Let us not derive ourselves on this subject, but in the light of one of his own inimitable parables, let us examine our hearts, "and bid conscience tell us plainly now, what it will tell us then." I quote from the 25th chap, of Matthew:

When the Son of Man shall come in his glory, and all the holy angels with him then shall he sit on the throne of his glory; and before him shall he gathered all nations; and he shall separate them one from another as a shepherd divideth his sheep from the goats: and he shall set the sheep on the right hand, but the goats on the left. Then shall the King say unto them on his right hand, Come ye blessed of my Father inherit the kingdom prepared for you from the foundation of the world. For I was hungry and ye gave me meat; I was thirsty and ye gave me drink; I was a stranger and ye took me in; naked and ye clothed me; I was sick and ye visited me; I was in prison and ye came unto me.

Then shall the righteous answer him, saying: Lord when saw we thee hungry and fed thee or thirsty and gave thee drink? When saw we thee a stranger and took thee in? or naked and clothed thee? Or, when saw we thee sick, or in prison and came unto thee? And the King shall answer and say unto them: Verily I say unto you, inasmuch as ye have done it unto one of the least of these my brethren, ye have done it unto me.

Then shall he say, also, unto them on the left hand; depart from me ye cursed into everlasting fires, prepared for the devil and his angels; for I was hungry, and ye gave me no meat; I was thirsty and ye gave me no drink; I was a stranger and ye took me not in; naked and ye clothed me not; sick and in prison and ye visited me not. Then shall they also answer him, saying: Lord, when saw we thee hungry, or thirsty, or a stranger, or naked, or sick, or in prison, and did not minister unto thee? Then shall he answer them, saying, verily, I say unto you, inasmuch as ye did it not to one of the least of these, ye did it not to me. And these shall go away into everlasting punishment; but the righteous, into life eternal.

Christ then is in our congregation today, in the person of these little orphan girls. He is hungry, shall we feed him; He is naked, shall we clothe him: He is a stranger shall we take him in? These children have an eloquent pleader in their behalf. Inasmuch as ye did it unto one of the least of these, ye did it unto me, is the language of him who died for us.—With his words ringing in our ears, shall we close our hearts to this appeal? *Can we, dare we, close* our purses to it, and then go *up yonder* and be judged by him who has said: Inasmuch as ye did it not to one of the least of these ye did it not to me.

But I do you wrong—your earnest attention, and sympathizing tears abundantly attest, that you have hearts to feel for these homeless little ones, and that you only wait an opportunity, to bear each one his part, in the discharge of this sacred duty. He that giveth only a cup of cold water, in the name of a disciple, shall not lose his reward. For myself, I do thank God, that he has put it into my power today, to unite with von in this delightful work. May it be done with cheerful hearts and willing hands, that heaven may smile upon the deed. And may the God of mercy smile upon those tender orphans, in the new and happy home, to which we are about to send them. May he so bless them there, that they may be qualified for happy and useful lives—and may finally come back willing and prepared to care for and instruct their sisters—to be the stay and comfort of their mother in her declining years, and to make us all feel and realize as we ought, that it is more blessed to give than to receive.

-----o-----

CARROLTON MARCH 30th, 1857.
REV. BEN. FRANKLIN—Sir:—Your last communication is at hand. I regret that necessity compels me to reply to such a document.

Permit me to inform you that I am a Kentuckian, a gentleman, and, I hope, a Christian. I hope, hereafter you will not address me as if I were your humble vassal, and *you* my lord paramount.

I have somewhere read of an animal that put on a lion's skin, but his speech betrayed him

In relation to the propositions for debate. I have offered everything that is fair and honorable—as our correspondence will show. I will debate the propositions agreed upon already, and others that may come up during the debate. Sir, as you have not accepted my propositions, I am willing to place our correspondence in the hands of an Atheist, an Infidel, and a Universalist, and let them decide the points of difference between us. *Deo volente,* I will meet you on Friday before the first Sunday in June, in the town of Ghent.

Moderately, respectfully, yours,
T. J. FISHER.

REPLY.

CINCINNATI, O., APRIL 7th, 1857.

REV. T. J. FISHER:—Dear Sir:—Owing to my absence, yours of March 30th could not receive attention till now. Your new affirmative proposition, that you are a "Kentuckian, a gentleman, and you hope a Christian," as it contains nothing about "Baptist principles," I shall decline debating, as not a vital question to *me*. I am willing that the public shall render a verdict in that case without debate.

I am after you as a *Baptist.* It is *your practice as a Baptist,* that I challenge you to defend. It is your practice of demanding an experience, containing evidence of pardon before baptism; of calling up mourners or seekers, to pray and have others pray for pardon before baptism; and your pompous accusation against some of the *"most worthy* members" in the Baptist church in Ghent, that they are guilty of "abominable heresy," that I challenge you to defend. Will you do it? or let it go by default? Can you back out from this, and ever again, as you did in Ghent, pray for sinners to be pardoned before baptism; demand evidence of pardon before baptism; and publish that some of the most worthy Baptists are heretics?

The proposal to refer forming propositions to Atheists, Infidels, and Universalists, is simply ridiculous.

Hoping that at the time and place mentioned by yourself, I shall meet a "Kentuckian, gentleman and a Christian," and debate the three questions agreed upon, I am yours,
BENJ. FRANKLIN.

-----o-----

THE BRACKEN ASSOCIATION OF UNITED BAPTISTS.
No. 4.

Having shown, in our last number, the absurdity of the ground upon which our Baptist brethren, exclude from their communion that class of our people, who were once members of the Baptist Churches, and whom they still "love as Christian brethren,"—we have a few words to say, before we leave this branch of the subject, in reference to the *very liberal proposition,* made by the Association, to said portion of our erring brethren, as a means of bringing us together, as one people at the Lord's table. Here then is the proposition: "If they [our people who were once members of Baptist churches, and were baptized by Baptist ministers] renounce their errors and repent of their sins, and return to the fellowship of our churches, we will gladly receive them; and then, and *not till then,* can we consistently commune with them."—p. 29.— There now, brethren, isn't that clever—very liberal indeed? True, you have been justly excommunicated from the only true Church on Earth—the only church that teaches "the truth, the whole truth, and nothing but the truth yet, thanks to the great liberality of the Association yours has not been the fatal, "the greater excommunication," from which there is no deliverance. Hold up your heads, then, brethren, there is yet hope! you have only to renounce your errors, in repudiating the sectarian name Baptist—and in adopting the name Christian, the family name of all God's people, under the reign of Christ. You have only to renounce your still greater embrace in teaching baptism "for the remission of bins," and cordially embrace the Baptist dogma, that baptism is for the remission of sins; you have only to renounce all these, and all other errors you hold, and sincerely repenting of all, and singular, the many and grievous sins you have committed against the Baptist churches, return to them, and embrace the "whole truth as they teach it," and they will gladly receive you, without re-baptism, and commune with you!! O, how benevolent, and kind? You may yet find a place in the bosom of the true church, and not die "justly excluded from her, and therefore doomed to eternal perdition!" And yet, I apprehend, after all this exhibition of sympathy, and this ardent desire to restore that class of our people to the bosom of the only true church, upon the very easy and scriptural terms proposed, that, nevertheless, such is their perversity, and utter inability to appreciate the great favors proposed, that they will die in their sins against the Baptists churches, "justly excluded from them." We propose, now, to notice the disposition the Association makes of the second class of our people, thus described, on page 29 of the Minutes. "But as respects all those Reformers, who never belonged to our churches, and were *baptized for the actual remission of their sins,* without professing a *previous* change of heart, and pardon, no intelligent Baptist regards them as *baptized at all,* if indeed converted."

How deeply humiliating to know that this sentence was written by Eld. Gardner, and endorsed by Elders James, Hunt &Co.! For, we hold the preachers especially responsible for it.

Come, brethren, tell me, before God, are you not profoundly ashamed of it, and ashamed of yourselves as authors and endorsers of it! If you are not, the Lord have mercy upon you; for I am sure you ought to be.

Was there evermore falsehood included in fewer words?!

This is very plain talk, but God knows I write more in sorrow than anger. Indeed, I am conscious of none but the kindest feeling toward these brethren. But the time is past when they may hope to misrepresent ns with impunity. We are too well known—our views are too well understood. What do you mean, brethren, when you speak of those among us who were baptized "without professing a previous change of heart?" Do you mean to revive and propagate against us, the stale, but foul charge that we do not require a change of heart, in order to baptism? We supposed that all. respectable opponents had long since become ashamed to make such a charge. Or did you intend by the language quoted, to make upon that portion of the community under Baptist influence, the impression that we rely simply upon water, without any internal change; and still leave open to yourselves a back door through which you might escape, if cornered? Did you intend to be able to say, if the worst should come, and we should absolutely deny (as you must have known we would), that any of our people were ever baptized without professing a previous change of heart, that then you did not mean us? This were very disingenuous; nay, more, it would defeat the whole argument for rejecting us from the Lord's table, based upon our want of a change of heart—our want of conversion. There is, then, no escape for you by this door. But, if we were even disposed to allow such an escape, it would really avail you nothing. You are making an argument to justify yourselves in excluding our whole people, from what you term "sacramental communion and to do your work the more thoroughly, you include us under two classes—the first, embracing all those, who were once Baptists, and the second, all the rest, unless, indeed, you intended to except a third class, with whom you are disposed to commune.

This, however, we presume you will not pretend to have done. You intend, then, to have the world understand you as saying, that all those among us, who were baptized for the remission of their sins, were not only baptized without a change of heart, but without even *professing* such a change!! And, hence, you very justly conclude (if your premises were true), that we are not baptized at all!! This is too bad. If you sincerely believe this foul slander against our people to be true, then you are chargeable with an amount of ignorance of which we never esteemed you guilty; nay, more, an amount of ignorance which would seem almost, if not altogether to exclude the idea of guilt, or responsibility in any case. But, on the other hand, if you knew better, then we will not characterize your offence, but leave you to settle the account with the public, your own consciences, and your God. With great self-complacency, Eld. Gardner, in the Circular of the Association, in which he is vindicating Baptist usages, says: "Well, the Baptists believe in fair and honest dealings"—and "have a conscience void of offence both toward God and man," p. 33. This is very well; for certainly it is the duty of all to deal fairly and honestly, and have a good conscience. But how Elder Gardner and his co-laborers can have a good conscience, and realize that they have dealt honestly and fairly with us, we confess we cannot imagine, and are curious to know! What, sirs!—raised in our midst, acquainted with our writings, and familiar with our preachers and preachings from your youth up, and yet coolly appeal to God, that you have a conscience void of offence, toward Him, and us; that you have dealt fairly and honestly, in representing the great body of our people, as having been baptized without even *professing,* or being required to profess a *change of heart!!* O, shame! where is thy blush! The Lord judge between you and us! We make our appeal to the Searcher of all hearts, and say with Paul, "We are made manifest to God," and are happy, thrice happy in the consciousness that he knows we are innocent of the foul charge brought against us, by the Elders of the Bracken Association. And. we further say with Paul, "We trust also, that we are made manifest in your consciences." That is, that the less sectarian and better portion of the members of even the Bracken Association, and of Baptists everywhere, will (notwithstanding the efforts of a few of their brethren, by misrepresentation, to ruin our religious standing and influence) still regard us as most cordially repudiating the doctrine imputed to us, and most firmly believing and most zealously teaching the doctrine of a *new heart*—a *change of heart,* as an *indispensable prerequisite* to baptism!

And, that thus manifested in the understandings and consciences of the more intelligent, and less sectarian portion of our Baptist brethren, as not guilty of the foul charge made against us, they will rebuke their erring brethren sharply, that they may learn better manners, in future. O, it is humiliating and mortifying beyond expression, that a very large portion of that largest and very respectable religious denomination, occupying, in some respects, positions similar to our own, should, nevertheless, join in with our most reckless and bitter opponents in bringing against us charges the most foul, the most offensive, the most untrue I Lord, what is man! We had a right to hope for better things from Baptists. Well, they have thrown down the gauntlet, they have broken the peace, they have declared war—their generals, from Dr. Jeter to Elders Ford, Graves, Gardner & Co., down to their corporals, have been and are still marshalling and mustering their forces. Already they have given us specimens of the character of the war they are waging; and from these we may expect the worst. The rules of civilized and honorable warfare are to be repudiated, and the Jesuitical principle, that "the end sanctifies the means," seems to be adopted. Well, sirs, be it so. You will find us with our armor on, ready to fight the battles of the Lord—ready to repulse your attacks; and although we will not condescend to retaliate, or render evil for evil, you will find us always ready, and willing, and able to defend the truth of our positions, or honorably abandon them; and, if need be, occasionally "to carry the war into Africa." Sirs, your older men ought to remember, that a quarter of a century ago, you waged against us a most unjust, unmerciful, and unsuccessful war when the Current Reformation was in its infancy; and if you greatly weakened your own hands in that conflict, and strengthened ours, and therefore found it necessary to draw off your forces from the open field, and adopt the wise policy of fighting, what you called "Campbellism," by letting it alone, can you reasonably hope to succeed against us now? True, since you have introduced that policy, and adopted a simpler and more scriptural method of presenting the gospel, you have regained your lost strength, and added greatly to your numbers and influence in Kentucky and elsewhere. And now, flushed with success, and confident in your numbers and strength, and believing that the Reformation is on the wane and almost ready to die, you seem to think that by one mighty effort, you can crush out its life, and bury its dead carcass, and have done with the trouble of it. But, sirs, we warn you, that you have undertaken a perilous work. You will find, to your cost, if I am any prophet, that you are rousing a giant, that is not dead, but sleepeth.

More next month, the Lord willing.

JOHN ROGERS.

-----o-----

GREAT MISSIONARY MEETING.—For the convenience of the brethren of the great North-West, a General Missionary Meeting has been appointed at Macomb, McDonough county, Illinois, commencing Wednesday, May 27th. Come, brethren, from all over the North West, and let us have the greatest gathering we have ever had. Men of the world leave their homes, business, and lose their time and spend their money, for worldly purposes. Let us have a great meeting of holy men of God. We hope to be present.

BENJ, FRANKLIN, Cor, Sec'y.

Dialogue of Devils.
NUMBER IV.

Present *Diabolos, Apollyon, Lucifer* and *Daimonion*. Subject—The most successful method of subverting and defeating the word of God and the mission of Christ.

Diab.—Gentlemen, I am delighted with your ready adherence to my suggestions and the success that has attended your movements. If you please, proceed immediately with reports, suggestions, or whatever lies in our course, that ran in any way aid in our work.

Apol.—I have a device, that I desired to lay before this honorable body, that I have succeeded with admirably. I find that I can turn it to good account, in the propagation, maintenance and perfectuation of any false doctrine I wish to infuse among the people. My plan is simply this: I select my men; always, as a matter of course, the best, most talented, and influential I can command. I impress them, by dreams, visions, apparitions and imaginations, to believe that they are immediately called and sent, as the apostles and prophets, to preach—that they are inspired to speak under the infallible influence of the spirit of all wisdom. I now have many of this kind, to which I have added another large class, consisting of men who make the same pretensions, but know it to be a base pretence; and after keeping these two classes of men in this train of thought, and training them for their work a few years, they will not regard anything in the Bible; any utterance of prophet or apostle; of the Holy Spirit, nor of the Lord himself.

Luc—How do you turn these to account in our work?

Apol.—Well, sir, I send them out with the zeal of apostles, one class honestly thinking and preaching: "Woe is me if I preach not the gospel;" and the other class repeating the same for a pretense. I have them all to proceed as follows:

1. They set forth and establish, as far as possible, their divine call to minister in holy things, under the direct, immediate and infallible influence of the Holy Spirit.

2. That any man who is not thus called and sent has no right—nay, that it is sacrilege—for any such to preach, and that no man can hear such without being partaker in their presumption and sin!

3. That the *"common* people" cannot understand divine things—can never know the meaning of the Bible, or obtain the inestimable blessings therein contained for man, without hearing his called and sent ministers.

4. That, as a matter of course, all who do not hear these men, thus specially called and sent, will be doomed to bottomless perdition.

5. That when they rise to speak, they are merely the instruments in the hand of God—that they have not meditated what they will say—nay, more, that they do not know what the Lord will utter through them; but whatever the spirit shall reveal to them, they will honestly proclaim!

Daim.—But, sir, how do you induce any man of common sense to give the least credence to such preposterous, unfounded and bare-faced pretensions?

Apol.—There is not, sir, the least difficulty about that. I have these men to assume a solemn appearance, at suitable intervals turn up the eyes toward heaven, and quote the words; "How beautiful are the feet of them who preach the gospel of peace and bring glad tidings of good things and again: "How shall they hear without a preacher, and how shall he preach except he be sent."

Luc.—But if they cannot understand the Scriptures, how do they know what that proves, when he quotes it to them?

Apol.—That is perfectly easy and simple. They know what he is aiming to prove, or what he quotes it for, and when he "who is called of God as was Aaron," who can "discern spiritual things," unfolds the mysteries and reveals the deep things of God, touches a passage of Scripture, it becomes perfectly transparent, clear as crystal what the preacher means, and it is easily and readily taken for granted that such is the meaning of the Lord! It would be preposterous to think the Lord meant anything different from his ambassadors whom he had sent!

Luc.—I admit, sir, that if we can procure such men as you describe, and beguile the people to believe them, admit their claims and hear them, as speaking for God—as God's ministers, his witnesses and rulers, that they would be good instruments through whom to infuse whatever ruinous and destructive errors we please. But will not some of those men, of whom you know there are still a few, whom we never could control, deny their claim, show that no ether gospel can be preached, without incurring the curse of heaven—that revelation is complete—that nothing can be added or taken away—that if a man cannot understand the inspired prophets, apostles and the Savior, uttering the precise language of the Spirit of all wisdom, he could not understand any man now, however called and sent?

Apol.—It is easy generally to repel these. Those I employ, claiming to be specially illuminated, claim to discern spirits; and they pronounce all such unregenerate, not born again, and quote the words: "The natural man receiveth not the things of the spirit, neither indeed *can he know them,* for they are spiritually discerned"—"The wind blows where it listeth, and thou hearest the sound thereof but canst not tell whence it comes nor whither it goes"—that "we have the spirit of God, and the spirit searcheth all things, yea the deep things of God"—"how can he preach except he be sent?" In this way, I confound the people, and keep them listening to my called and sent preachers, preaching all the errors and ruinous nonsense imaginable.

Luc.—But what is to be done when a man, as one I have heard, points out the conflicting doctrines, wranglings, disputings among your "called and sent preachers," and shows clearly that God never sent men who have not the unity of the spirit and who speak not the same thing?

that God is not the author of confusion, but of peace? that God is one, and that there could not be but one doctrine from him?

Apol.—When men, such as you mention, and I know there are a few such, who give us great annoyance, start such reasonings as you allude to, among the people, viz That if they were of God, they would all speak the same doctrine, be of the same faith, of the same mind, in love and union, I am aware that it is a little perplexing; but I open a way for escape as best I can. At one time; when a little pressed with stub, I suggest, to quote the words: "Judge not that you be not judged"—and proceed to admonish them that all this argument, investigation and talking about the mere letter of Scripture is wrong, and confront them with the words:—"Where is the wise"—"the disputer of this world"—"the wisdom of this world is foolishness with God," and again: "The Lord knoweth the thoughts of the wise, that they are vain"—"he taketh the wise in their own craftiness"—"he hath chosen the weak things of this world to confound the mighty," etc., etc.

Luc.—But some of these men you have thus deluded, preach that Christ died for all, and others maintain that he only died for a part. Now when such clear and manifest contradictions are preached, I should think the people would see it.

Apol.—Well, sir, I admit that there are some few who occasionally see such palpable contradictions. But I have managed to repel the mass of these. I aim as near as possible always to have someone present, or to follow in a discourse soon after, and maintain that we cannot see alike; that we differ in our features, our customs; that we are better off separated and do more good than we could do united; that it is a wise providence of God that we are divided— that division has the same happy influence as competition in business; and that the Scripture says: "Let every man be fully persuaded in his own mind," and again: "as your faith is, so be it unto you"—that "we all have the right to worship God according to the dictates of our own consciences," etc. etc.

Luc.—But, how do you get the people to receive such palpable absurdities? Will they not see that you contradict the Bible in the most explicit terms? Do they not know that Jesus prayed that "they all maybe one"—that he taught them that "by this shall all men know that you are my disciples, if you have love one to another," and that Paul most solemnly beseeches all Christians to "be perfectly joined together in the same mind and in the same judgment, and that there be no divisions among them?" Do they not know that Jesus taught, that if even Satan's kingdom be divided against itself, it cannot stand?

Apol.—There are some few who know this, preach it, and give me much trouble: but I manage to keep their influence down to a considerable extent. You must bear in mind that, when the people once grant that those employed by me, are "called and sent of God," the trouble is over. These preachers only have to pronounce anything false, and the question is settled. They only have to declare a man not orthodox, and he is defeated, though he preach like an angel of God. If they know of a man quoting the prayer of Jesus, that *all who believe may be one,* they raise the cry, that he denies the divinity of Christ, does not believe in the influence of the spirit, and is not sound in the faith—that his doctrine is dangerous, destructive to piety and that he is unregenerate and wholly unenlightened in divine things. This, with many people, is an end to all controversy. Besides, if we can induce people once to depart from the truth, divert their minds from it, and loose the love of it, God will give them up to believe a lie—give them over to strong delusion, that they may be condemned. When they reach this point, they require no more attention from us, but will pursue the even tenor of their downward course to impenetrable night. They will not hear Jesus nor the apostles, neither holy men of ancient nor modern times, nor would they hear if one would rise from the dead. I have thousands of these so under my influence, their hearts so separated from the love of God and their souls so chalice to all that is contained in the Bible, that they would sooner their children, or dearest friends, would live and die without any profession of Christianity, than that they should believe in Christ with all their heart, repent of their sins, confess the Savior with their lips, be baptized solemnly in his name, thus simply submitting themselves to God as they did in the days of the apostles. They will be more excited, manifest more opposition and hostility to see their friends become Christians, according to the New Testament, than to see them become infidels.

Daim.—You are right, most noble *Apollyon;* I know this to be so. This not only can be, but *is* carried out with mighty success. Why, sir, I know of scores that will leave the house, in rage and fury, if they hear any man insist that men must believe precisely now what they did in the days of the apostles, to become Christians—that the faith must have the same effect upon their hearts—lead to the same acts of obedience, the same promises, and inspire the same hope. I know thousands that we have so blinded, that nothing makes them more miserable, than to hear a man maintaining that we should be Christians, as they were in the days of the apostles—simply Christians—no more—no less—that we must be the same, be called the same, and nothing else, than as found in the New Testament.

Apol.—Now you talk sense; why, sir, I have many now under the influence of this delusion so far that they believe in this supposed call to the ministry, and believe every word of those supposed to be called, and will pay no kind of respect for anything in the word of God. I have had these men, professing to be called, preach to them things not mentioned in the Bible, and for which they could give no more authority than a Romish priest can give for counting beads or worshipping relics. Why, sir, I have actually had them to stand up on the Lord's day, and in the name of the Father, and of the Son, and of the Holy Spirit, sprinkle water upon the face of an infant, for a religious rite, and not a man mention that there is no such rite in the Bible, from first to last, nor anything like it! This I consider decidedly the greatest achievement in all our efforts at deception. In this way, we get them into church before they know anything about the church, God, the Savior, the Holy Spirit, or anything divine. In this way, we get rid of regeneration, a change of heart and the love of God and get them into the church without conversion, being born again, or any reconciliation to God. In a short time, in this way, we shall have a church of sinners, under the delusion, that they are in the kingdom of God! These we keep in many instances, under this delusion to the day of their death without any conversion to God.

Luc.—That is doing our work finely, unquestionably; but I am not sure but I can mention some things that excel that, in defeating the Bible and the mission of Christ. Why, sir, I have lead some of these "called and sent preachers" to leave the pulpit, close the Bible, leave it behind them, declare that they never knew a sinner converted by preaching the gospel, that the letter killeth, but the spirit giveth life; and that they were going into the work to convert sinners. In a few minutes sinners who desired to be converted were called for and commanded to bow their knees. The gospel, "the power of God unto salvation"—the "incorruptible seed, the word of God," by which men are born again, with preaching to sinners and pleading with them to turn to God, are all thrown aside; and in a few minutes I have the whole assembly, both preachers and people, in one united clamor of deafening cries to heaven, to send down converting power—to send down grace—to pour out the spirit and convert sinners! Thus I have, on numerous occasions, had them to set aside the word of God, the plain cases of conversion recorded in the New Testament, all the examples God had spread before them; and, in their prayers, face the God of all grace, and tell him that the church was willing, anxious and laboring for the conversion of sinners; and that the sinners themselves were seeking God with all their hearts—and the pleading now appeared to be to get God willing to convert and save them!

REPORTER.

-----o-----

Excursion to Northern Illinois.
NUMBER II.

In my previous number I conducted the reader to Decatur, the county seat of Lacon, Illinois, where the passengers of the various trains breakfasted and "changed cars." Leaving Decatur and passing through a somewhat campaign country, I finally arrived on Saturday, at four P. M., at Polo, on the Illinois Central, Ogle county, a town two years old, with a population of nearly one thousand, and decidedly wearing a business aspect. Here, the son of Bro. John Hammer, two years beyond his majority, but so youthful in appearance that one would readily place him two or three years on this side of that period in human life, received me into his carriage, and in an hour after entering it I found myself at the hospitable abode of Bro. J. Hammer, whom I had not seen for a number of years. A quarter of a century ago, Bro. H., his amiable consort, and myself, were fellow citizens in a theological city built about three hundred years ago, by Martin Luther and his coadjutors, somewhere between Babylon and Jerusalem. It was the first city built on the road between those two points. It is at times said, even by my brethren, that the Protestant sects constitute "Babylon." That is a mistake. Protestantism is *not* Babylon. The papacy is Babylon. The term Babylon, in the New Testament sense, does not denote *confusion*. It primitively signified the country and power, in and under which the Jews were, for seventy years, kept in such bondage in which they could not worship God according to the ritual of Moses. In virtue of the decree of Cyrus, the pious and patriotic Jews returned to Jerusalem, the sacred metropolis of the nation, then in a state of desolation. It was the spot where the worship of God could be performed according to the institutes of Moses. Now it was one thing to be beyond the precincts of Babylon, and quite another to be in Jerusalem. There was a considerable distance between the two points. So there is a considerable distance between the spiritual, or rather metaphorical, Babylon, for there is not much spirituality in it, and the Jerusalem that is from above, which the apostles of the Lamb, filled with the holy spirit of wisdom, built on the brow of Mt. Zion. The smoke and filth of metaphorical Babylon became so thick and intolerable that Martin Luther proposed migration beyond its environs. He aimed for Jerusalem, and made no inconsiderable advancement towards the point of his destination, and probably would have arrived there, had he not had so many dukes and nobles, of tardy locomotion, in his moving columns, or had he lived a fifth of a century longer. But when he had made three-fourths of the journey, he died in the *encampment*—and his successors inhibited any farther progress. What was then in the encampment became stationary and spread out *laterally*. Indeed the encampment was soon transformed into a splendid city, walled in with ponderous volumes. The geographical position of this Lutheran city is not yet fully determined among theological geographers. Some of them, among whom is Rev. C. Buck, author of the Theological Dictionary, locate it *nearer* Babylon than any other city on the road. That is *not* so; at any rate, the Lutheran city in which Bro. H. and I resided was not so located. I am aware there are now three cities of the same name; the *symbolic,* the *moderate,* and the *expurgated,* but none of them is nearer to Babylon than others—their populations have probably retained some of the *customs* of Babylon, more markedly than those of some of their neighboring cities. The reader, of course, understands that there are many splendid and populous cities built along the road from Babylon to Jerusalem, some more and some less contiguous to the former place, under the names of Episcopalian, Lutheran, Presbyterian, Methodist, Quaker, etc.

The official men of some of these cities are men of lore, and of great personal dignity. Many of the inhabitants are men of great moral worth, and commendable exponents of practical Christianity. The cities have the divine luminary within their precincts, but the glass of their lamps is somewhat colored and tarnished, and the lamp posts are too high—which cause that hardly a moiety of the light in the volume reaches the masses of the cities.

Water is also very scarce in these cities—their inhabitants get it only by *sprinkling,* and not in tanks and pools;—in one of them, the Quaker's, there is no water at all, nor any melody to enliven its staid citizens! They quench their thirst by pneumatic inspirations! All these cities lie *east of the Jordon,* which must be gone through, on the highway from Babylon to Jerusalem. Moderate Luther city, to which Bro. H. and I belonged, was originally built with a goodly portion of materials, of apostolic make, in Jerusalem, but some planks had been prepared at Rome. They are known by their gnarled and dark surfaces. The city is eligibly situated—has a tolerably moral population—the suburbs, mostly inhabited by *foreigners,* need considerable reformation—so much so, that some of the better citizens have earnestly prayed for a "second Luther." Living in the city is tolerably good—and its official orders are respectably compensated. Bro. H. was born and raised in it. I and his mild consort had been indenizened. During the last nine years of my residence there, I was one of its "public advocates." Bro. H. rendered no mean services in its musical department.

We both were on good terms with the citizens of other towns on the road, and often visited them, but never *ate* with them. Indeed, it is notable that though there is apparently much amity between the populations of these various cities, they even now seldom eat with each other. Inspecting closely the Scriptural topography of Jerusalem, we became convinced that Luther city, in its location and customs, did not *exactly* correspond with it, and after making some explorations beyond its walls, westward, we emigrated, and following the apostolic chart we located, as we verily believe, in Jerusalem, that is, on the *unmixed apostolic basis.* I emigrated three times seven years ago—Bro. II. twice seven. From this point we frequently visit Luther city, but the inhabitants do not seem to know us very well; some treat us hospitably, others receive us coldly—some not at all. The cause of this latter conduct is not easily conjectured. Whether it is that we have *outgrown ourselves,* or a suspicion that we might describe Jerusalem too vividly to some of the citizens and stimulate them also to emigrate, I cannot say.

More anon,

SAMUEL K. HOSHOUR.

-----o-----

Evidences of Christianity.
NUMBER V.

Our happiness does not consist in possessing senses or faculties, but in exercising them. They are simply avenues through which enjoyments are obtained, or benefits conferred. Merely possessing the sense of seeing is no enjoyment, and confers no benefit. The enjoyment is found, and the benefit derived by the *act of seeing,* or by *exercising the sense* of seeing.

But it should be remembered, that a man might have the sense of seeing in its utmost perfection, and never see anything, He might be born with good eyes in a dungeon, be kept there, and die there, without ever seeing anything. In this case the sense of seeing would afford no enjoyment, and be a source of no good to him. He had as well have been born without eyes. Three things are essential to seeing. 1. Eyes, or the sense of seeing. 2. Objects to see, or that which the sense of seeing can take hold of. 2. Light, through which the eye communicates with the object, or reaches it. But even after the Lord has created eyes to see, and light, as the telegraph wires through which vision may be transmitted, and all the innumerable objects to be seen, a man may never see much, because the *will* has a vast deal to do in his seeing. He may live to an old age and die without ever seeing a tenth part of what is inscribed, in his own mother tongue, upon the pages of the Bible, simply because he *will not read it*. He may never see the principal rivers, lakes and seas; the villages, towns and cities; counties, states and territories; not because these objects do not exist, nor for the want of light, nor because the Lord has not given him eyes capable of seeing all these things; but because he does not *will* to bring himself in the proper proximity to them to see them. Having eyes does not compel him to see; hence the Lord speaks of some, "having eyes, but see not." The will has a mighty control over what a man shall see, and what he shall not see. He who sees much must make an effort to see. He must not deny the existence of objects that he never saw, when the reason he never saw them is simply that he would not go where they can be seen, and look at them.

In precisely the same way three things are necessary to hearing. 1. There must be an ear, or the sense of hearing. 2. There must be sound to be heard. 3. There must be the medium of the atmosphere to bear the sound to the ear. As in the case of seeing, the enjoyment is not in possessing the sense of hearing, but in exercising it. A man with a perfect ear, kept where there is no sound, would no more enjoy hearing than if God had endowed him with no such sense. The will too, has an immense deal to do with hearing. It determines what the man will hear and what he will not hear. The will decides where the car shall go, what sound it shall come in reach of, and what it shall not. The *will* just as much determines what a man shall hear as it does what he shall eat. A man can decide that he will swallow deadly poison, and the result is that it will kill him. A man can decide that he will hear the light, chaffy, simple, foolish, or the devilish, and the result of the poison he swallows is not more inevitable than the result of what he habitually hears. He will, in the very nature of the case, inevitably partake of the nature of what he hears. Show the books a man reads, the conversations and addresses he habitually hears, and you can read what kind of a man he is. He is just like what he hears and reads, and delights to hear and read, and he is that of choice, or because he wills it.

As in the cases above, there are three things necessary to believing. 1. The faculty of believing, or credulity. 2. That which is to be believed, or the truth. 3. The means to convey the truth to be believed to the mind, to the understanding, or the faculty of the soul that accredits truth, There is no enjoyment in the mere possession of credulity, or the ability to believe; nor is there any benefit derived from it. The enjoyment is in, and the benefit derived from, the exercise of the faculty. The speculator may have a large amount of produce in market; the truth may exist that there is a splendid advance in price, and he may have the faculty to believe; but he is too negligent to procure and read the news and, therefore, remains ignorant of the advance. His having the faculty to believe did him no good, nor was the fact of the any use to him. Why? Because, he decided not to seek the information—not to put himself to the trouble to know the truth, and this, as a matter of course, deprived him of both the enjoyment and benefit. The ability to examine testimony, to accredit it, or confide in it, must be exercised, or it affords no enjoyment and confers no benefit. Here is precisely where accountability arises in reference to faith. We have, in our previous articles, shown that all men of common endowments, or common sense; to speak more plainly, possess the faculty of credulity, or the ability to believe, and daily exercise it in reference to a thousand things all around them. We have sufficiently demonstrated the great fundamental, foundation, or central truth, in which is embodied all other religious truth, and that upon which everything else rests—the greatest of all facts ever revealed to mortals in the flesh—that Jesus of Nazareth, who was crucified and laid in the tomb of Joseph of Aramatheia, rose from the dead, ascended into heaven, is seated upon the throne, a Prince and a Savior, to grant repentance and forgiveness of sins—that he is divine. This is the grandest, most stupendous and benevolent of all facts in this universe. In it is our all for all the countless ages that lie beyond the narrow limits of this short life time.

This overwhelming fact comes not within the reach of any of the five senses. We did not see Jesus rise from the dead. We did not hear him speak. We did not handle him. Nor did he ever come in reach of either of the other senses. How then is the fact of his Messiahship, his divinity, or his resurrection, to roach the soul? How is the soul to be assured that Jesus rose from the dead?—or, which is the same, that he is *divine?* There must be a means of communication from that which is to be believed, and the human heart, or understanding, which believes it. There must be a telegraph-wire with one end connected with the fact to be believed, and the other end with the heart that is to believe, through which the fact can be conveyed. The wire is the divine testimony concerning Jesus of Nazareth. That testimony reaches from him in whom we are to believe, and to us who are to believe. Through it the fact comes to the soul, and becomes a part of our consciousness as much as what we see and hear. But notwithstanding all this, the human will has much to do. Although God has endowed one man with credulity, or the ability to believe, just as much as any other man around him; given the same fact to believe, and the same evidence, he may refuse to use his eyes in reading it, his ears in hearing it read or spoken of, his understanding in considering it, or his heart in believing it. Every man has the power to hear nothing but what is idle, fulsome and worthless, in itself; and, as nothing can rise above its fountain, the effect upon his heart must be of the same nature of that which he hears. If a man determines that he will spend his time in a dungeon, he will never see, though God gives him good eyes, creates beautiful objects to see, and plenty of light. If a man prefers darkness to light, he can find dark and dreary recesses, where he can no more see than if God created him without eyes. God does not force him to go where the light is, nor to open his eyes and see.

God has created man with credulity, or the ability to believe; he has graciously given us the truth, that Jesus is the Christ the Son of the living God, to believe; with the divine testimony that incontestably proves the truth. But he does not compel any man to read the testimony, to hear it read, to examine it, try to understand and appreciate it. He lays it before the world, and demands of the nations to hear it. It is like all the other blessings God has afforded man; it must be sought, inquired after and received, or do men no good. Men may be none the better of its ever entering into the world. It may be that God has created a rich mine of gold in some part of the earth. One man seeks all the information he can obtain in reference to it. becomes satisfied of its richness and accessibility; he makes a proper effort and obtains a fortune. Another man, with equally as good endowments, treats the whole question with indifference to it. Without examining the testimony, he pronounces all delusion, humbuggery, a chimera, and ridicules it, and the man that seeks information, or inquires into it. What good will the gold mine do him? None whatever. So far as he is concerned the gold mine might as well never have been created.

But, it fares infinitely worse than this with him who treats with indifference the pearls of Jesus Christ. He who prefers the darkness of this world to the light of the Son of God, turns away his ears from the holy and lovely lessons of the benevolent Redeemer, refuses to inform himself in reference to HIM to whom God requires all nations to be attentive, incurs a responsibility for which he will certainly answer at the most solemn tribunal. He who turns his back upon the Lord of heaven and earth, when we would call attention to him, not only looses or forfeits the benefits proposed through him, but incurs censure for indifference, ingratitude and disrespect, if not contempt of his Creator and merciful Benefactor. God has created him with a heart to believe, given the truth and furnished the testimony to convey it to the understanding, and holds him responsible for the exercise of his abilities. Come, then, dear reader, and let us fix our minds upon Jesus of Nazareth, and carefully consider his claims upon our attention. The whole question is about him. What do you think of him whom we claim as the Savior of the world? Do you love him and those like him? Or are you opposed to him?

B. F.

-----o-----

Work out your own salvation with fear and trembling; for it is God who worketh in you both to will and to do of his own good pleasure.—PAUL.

A FEW WORDS FOR MR. FORD.

Mr. Ford, editor of the *Christian Repository,* a Baptist monthly, published in Louisville, Ky., April number, page 257. speaking of Mr. Campbell, says: "In his long and laborious life-struggle, almost every subject embraced in the divine oracles has at one time or other come under his review; and his utterances have ever awakened the most painful suspicions of his skepticism, or hostility to what was the basis of real orthodoxy in one and all of those ecclesiastical centers."

We have tried for several years to think that Mr. Ford would be useful, in making an effort to enlighten mankind, promote peace, love and union among the children of God. It is true, we did not think so from anything we saw in him, or from him; but, from his connection with Mr. Waller, whose heart was so enlarged, and whose being was so ennobled, by an expanded acquaintance with the Christian oracles, we had reason to look for something better than a little, selfish, partisan feeling. But in this we have been lamentably disappointed. The sentence quoted above is unquestionably the most deserving of a prompt, decided and general rebuke from an enlightened Christian community of any sentence that has come under our notice in the last ten years. Is it possible that a miserable, sickly, peevish, and unlovely feeling, is to dethrone all that is noble, kind and inviting in those who might otherwise in some degree be useful? Has it come to this, that a narrow, morbid, schism-engendering and schism-loving disposition, is to lead comparatively young men, with only moderate information, or ability, so far to forget all that is reasonable, just and becoming, as thus to speak of a venerable man of God, who has made as able, enduring and effectual a defense of the Bible, *the basis of all that is really orthodox,* as any man now on earth?

Who is he that thus speaks of a hoary-headed veteran, who has consecrated every power God has given him to the defense, propagation and perpetuation of Christianity, in the same original purity as God gave it, in a "life-struggle," forming a span vastly greater than from the birth day of Mr. Ford to this hour? How came he to be competent; whence his qualification and authority to sit in judgment, and thus pass sentence upon a venerable man, three-fourths or four-fifths of whose writings he never read, and this day no more comprehends than an infant? Whence came he by the divine right to charge upon him skepticism in the basis of all real orthodoxy and hostility to it? When did he ever give evidence that he knew what the basis of real orthodoxy is?—or, where is the evidence that he is not skeptical? Not in his kindness, loveliness, nor in his efforts to promote "the unity of the spirit, in the bond of peace." Not in any respect shown to aged, faithful and devoted men of god. Not in the fact that "almost every subject embraced in the divine oracles has at one time or other come under his review." No; much of the truth contained in the Bible has never obtained the slightest attention from his pen, passed under his review, or found a place in his "Repository." Much of the plain teaching of "the divine oracles," he has entirely different from the simple statement in the New Testament, as, for instance, the "one baptism," "into one body," "into Christ," "for remission of sins," he calls the door into the Baptist church. Hence he teaches that a man must have remission of sins, be in Christ, in his body, before baptism, and then he baptizes him into the Baptist church. The Lord's Supper, which the Lord gave to all the children of God—all the disciples—his followers or people, he complacently gives to the Baptists—those "of *our* faith and order," and, as the Calvinists say, the Lord did by the non-elect, "the rest of mankind he *passes by*."

To sum up the whole matter, his kingdom is a Baptist kingdom, his principles Baptist principles, and his universe a Baptist universe. It has never occurred to him that the Almighty ever had anything in view, in sending the Savior into the world, more than the establishment of the Baptist church, Baptist usage, or "*our* faith and order." Though he has become a great historian—an *author* in history, his horizon has never extended beyond a Baptist Association, or something called the "Current Reformation." The heroes that figure in his history were all Baptists. The mighty galaxy of ancient worthies, cloud of witnesses, holy men and benefactors of mankind, marshaled, brought in mighty procession before us, and glorified, in his history, were all Baptists. In his eye, "the Israel of God," and Baptist church, are almost synonymous. In his luminous history, Cora, Dathan, and Abiram, were B. W. Stone, R. McNamer and David Purviance. His Julian, Pilate and Caiaphas, are A. Campbell, John Smith and John Rogers. His kingdom of heaven begun with Roger Williams, and his "unwritten tradition" is "Baptist usage." There we imagine we see our historian standing upon his Baptist observatory, with a Baptist telescope. He looks above him and he perceives that the precise center of the canopy is plumb over his head! He turns his telescope back, and his horizon extends precisely far enough to take in all the Baptists. He turns it forward, as well as to the right and left, and the result is the same. Never having been or seen beyond his circumscribed horizon, it is not strange that he should consider that the extent of the spiritual universe, and endeavor, by publishing a history of it, to enlighten the balance of mankind and make them as wise as himself.

'The ennobling, expanding, and elevating truths of the New Testament, have never extended his horizon so as to bring the kingdom, the law and the work of God definitely before his mind. He has never thought of such a thing as Christianity being a distinct and complete system, in itself. That little circle of ideas in which he lives and moves, and has his being, called "Baptist principles." Is no more comparable to Christianity, than a mole-hill is to the globe. The little kingdom set forth in his history is no more to be compared with the kingdom of God, set before all nations in the New Testament, than an isolated colony compared with the Roman Empire. The difference is as great as the statement of Mr. Waller, that Alexander Campbell *is* ORTHODOX, compared to that of Mr. Ford, that he *is* NOT. The former statement was from a mature, well-informed and unprejudiced mind, as well as a absurd and deliberate judgment; the latter merely the exponent of circumscribed, sectarian and bitter feeling. The former will be regarded, and the latter go for nothing.B. F.

----0-----

Editor's Table.

WHY DID YOU STOP MY REVIEW? YOU KNEW I WOULD PAY."—Thus a good old friend and brother addresses us. In answer, we reply, that our terms are *cash in advance*, plainly printed on the cover, every month, and they *mean exactly what they say*. We know the brother was good for the pay, and if we had thought of him, and our terms had been of that kind, we should not have doubted if we had sent him the Review, but he would have sent the pay. But in all cases we must know that persons *desire to subscribe*. This they can let us know by sending the subscription price and ordering the Review, when it will be sent to them with kindest thanks.

Some years ago, there was much trouble to know how many religious periodicals we ought to have. We were then, and are now, well satisfied that if every man that thinks he is called to the editorial chair, would call for votes in actual advance paying subscribers, the note of the brethren would soon decide the case to his utmost satisfaction. We determined to test our *call* in this way, and expect to stick to it. If brethren do not feel interest enough in publications to subscribe and pay in advance, in a majority of instances they will neither read them nor pay for them, if sent on credit.

But few calls have been made for the poor this year. If brethren will send us the names and address of about one hundred worthy persons, who are unable to pay, we will take pleasure in sending them the Review.

BACON COLLEGE.—In our notice of this noble enterprise, by some slip of the types, we are made to say $50,000 instead of $150,000, has been subscribed. We had marked out our course to attend the meeting of the friends of this institution; but the Lord has opened an effectual door in another direction, for us, where it is manifestly our duty to be present. We regret that we cannot be with the men of God who will be at Harrodsburg on Wednesday before the first Lord's day in May; but we cannot without letting an opportunity for good pass, such as does not open to us but once in a great while. The Lord be with them and enable them to act harmoniously and do all things in love. Our heart is cheered with the encouragements that surround us, and we thank God and take courage.

SERMONS.—We have some valuable sermons groaning for utterance, and for the sake of making room as fast as possible, we have two sermons at one session, this month, which, we are aware is a little out of the customary course of things, especially since the twenty-five and thirty-minute sermon preachers came upon the rostrum. But our readers will bear in mind that we have not been screwed down and laced into the straight-jacket-system, that bolsters pretenders of religion upon cushions, to hear a dandy with buttered and honeyed lips, talk prettily thirty minutes, call it "the sermon," and hear a tune on an organ, and return under the delusion that they are "serving God." These poor, little, sickly, fainting creatures, are nothing, doing nothing, and amount to nothing, except to fritter down and obliterate every trace of the pure and holy teachings of our Lord Jesus Christ. But this only by way of apology for two sermons at once.

REVISION ASSOCIATION.—The Anniversary of the Revision Association will be in Louisville, Kentucky, commencing on Friday, May 18th. The delegates to represent the Bible Union at the Anniversary are:

Rev. John Francis, New Brunswick; Rev. Dr. S. E. Shepard, New York; Rev. D. E. Thomas, Benjamin Franklin, Ohio.

Success of the Gospel.

MD.—BALTIMORE, April 5.—Bro. G. W. Elley reports 8 confessions during the two weeks previous.

TEXAS.—MIDWAY, March 17.—Bro. J. A. Clark reports 3 confessions at Lost Prairie School House. Bro. C. desires the brethren of his State to know that they can command his services at any point within his reach.

IOWA.—INDIANAPOLIS, March 19th.—Bro. B. F. Snook reports 9 additions at that place. Four by confession and immersion the same hour of the night.

ILL'S.—ROCK ISLAND CO., March 24.—Bro. Wm. G. Reynolds, writes: While on a visit to Iowa, I was privileged to hear a series of discourses from Bro. Warren an able preacher of the Gospel. The meeting resulted in 11 confessions, all were buried with Christ in Baptism, while the thick ice of Cedar river was broken to prepare for them a watery grave. I saw some young females get out of their carriages, lay off their bonnets and shawls and go down into the icy flood, come out praising God. A church of 20 members was organized before I left.

WAVERLY, March 16th.—Bro. J. S. Sweeney reports thirty-two additions to the Disciples in the bounds of his labors since last report. Thirty-one at Waverly (this was a glorious triumph), one at Franklin.

IND.—NOLENSVILLE, April 1st, Bro. H. St. John VanDake, reports as the result of a three days meeting at Eagle village. Seven additions, six by baptism.

OHIO,—CALIFORNIA, March 29th.—Bro. Thos. J. Murdock reports a meeting at Woodville Clermont county, which resulted in 5 additions to the church by baptism.

LAFAYETTE, March 24th.—Bro. R. B. Henry reports seven new additions at that place, making 23 in all since Christmas. Bro. Burnau was the preacher, and labored with an energy and zeal becoming the great cause in which he is engaged.

AKRON, Summit county March 29th.—Bro. W. S. Grey, reports 4 valuable accessions to the cause of Christ at Ashland, Ashland county.

CINCINNATI, April 13th.—On Lord's day, the 12th there were 6 confessions at the Clinton street Meeting House in this city. Brethren Geo. W. Rice, and Wm. P. Stratton were the laborers. The prospects are fair for greater increase.

Obituaries.

DIED, of consumption, in Madison, Ind., on the 10th of April, 1857, in the 33d year of her age, sister MARY C. DUBOIS, wife of Mr. J. D. DuBois, and only daughter of Bro. Jas. Orr, of Cincinnati, Ohio.

As a wife, a mother, a daughter and a disciple of Christ, she was beloved most by those who knew her best.

She put on Christ by baptism in her sixteenth year; was a member of the Christian Church since that time, and died as she had lived "in the Lord." She was calm and entirely composed; resigned and full of faith and hope in her Redeemer, during her sickness, which was protracted nearly three months and often very painful.

I need not repeat the many words of encouragement and exhortation which fell from her lips in the presence of her family and friends till the very last moment of her life. In particular, she was anxious that her sufferings should not be magnified, for, with Paul, she reckoned that the sufferings of this present time are not worthy of comparison with the glory which shall be revealed in us.

May her life and triumphant death impress all our hearts to faithfulness and unwearied perseverance in the Lord.

"Who would not wish to die like those
 Whom God's own spirit deigned to bless?
To sink into that soft repose,
 Then wake to perfect happiness."
                                J. H. L.

DEAR BRO. FRANKLIN:—I have just received a letter from Bro. Allen Wright of Lexington, dated, Feb'y 18th, 1857. He says: "I have just heard that Bro. N. W. MILLER died, at Pleasant Hill, last Saturday or Sunday. A gentleman informs me that Bro. Miller went to Pleasant Hill to hold a meeting, and was complaining of pain in his head, with which he had been much afflicted, and took Morphine—he repeated the dose, and soon died. He was to have been buried at Independence to-day. I have not learned the particulars, but fear the report is true!

Bro. Miller was the son of our venerable Bro. Abm. Miller of Calloway county—was a graduate of Bethany college, a ripe scholar, and an able preacher, and has been suddenly cut down in the commencement of a life of usefulness, and great promise for good in the Christian ministry. I have known him from a child and it gives me pleasure to bear testimony to his intellectual, moral, and Christian worth.—Bro. Miller had married the amiable step-daughter of Eld. F. R. Palmer, Miss Shanks, and leaves her in the morning of life, with an infant, to mourn his loss. May the Lord be gracious to her.

Affect'ly your brother,

March 7, '57.   T. M. ALLEN.

BRO. FRANKLIN:—It becomes my painful duty to inform you of the death of sister MARY POLLOCK, wife of Dr. J. S. Pollock of this place. Her sufferings were severe, yet she bore all with Christian fortitude. She trusted in the merits of the Redeemer, and her confidence in him remained unshaken. She died the death of a Christian.

                                J. C. IRVIN.
Bowerville, O., March 26.

Passed to a brighter world on the 17, of Oct. 1857, ELIZABETH HILL, wife of S. C. Hill in her 22d, year. Ever bright and cheerful while with us, and now gone and deeply lamented by all, her earnest pleadings, with all to obey the Gospel in all things, showed her love for the cause of Christ.   S.

THE
AMERICAN CHRISTIAN REVIEW.

VOL. II.   CINCINNATI, JUNE, 1857.   NO. 6.

MISSION OF THE HOLY SPIRIT.
A DISCOURSE, BY ELD. J. A. CLARKE.

"Now we have received, not the spirit of the world, but the Spirit which is of God, that we might know the things that are freely given to us of God. Which things also we speak, not in the words which man's wisdom teacheth, but which the Holy Spirit teacheth, comparing spiritual things with spiritual."—1 COR. ii. 12, 13.

Great confusion and error exist in the minds of the religious world concerning the work and office of the Holy Spirit—from which many of the Disciples themselves are not wholly free. I cannot, of course, expect to free the mind from all error on this subject, in a single discourse—if, indeed, I could do so at all; yet I may be able to lead to a train of investigation and thought that may result in seeing the truth with some clearness.

There is too much disposition to consider the Spirit abstractly. Abstraction is the source of many a religious error. The Spirit is not presented to us in the Bible in the abstract. We can know little or nothing of it in this light. In its work and office, we find it intimately connected with the word of God. In the Bible they seem joined together; and what God has joined, let not man put asunder. The first account we have of the Spirit of God, is in the first of the book. "The Spirit of God moved upon the face of the waters; and God said, Let there be light, and there was light." Here we have an account of the Spirit operating—and that physically, too—yet there is no effect apparent, until God *said*. By the word of *His said*. By the word of His power darkness is dethroned in her chaotic reign, and light breaks forth upon a new-born world. He *spake,* and it was done.

When the Spirit of God was sent to Moses, we find it accompanied by the word. The desired effect could not have been produced without. When Moses saw the flame in the bush, he could not, without the *word* of God, have comprehended anything about it. He might have imagined, dreamed, guessed and felt the balance of his days, and still he would have been in darkness—darkness as great as that upon the face of the great deep, till light broke forth by the word of God. Moses could not have understood that he was chosen as a servant of the Almighty, nor have known anything concerning his mission to the Israelites. The burning bush gives him no instruction, but commands his attention. But when he hears the words, "Moses, put thy shoes from off thy feet; for the place where thou standest is holy ground," he begins to receive instruction. When informed that it is the God of his fathers that speaks, and that he is required to go into Egypt, and bring forth the children of Israel, he comprehends the Lord's requirements. When he goes, with powers of inspiration, to Egypt, he is instructed what to say. His mission would have been fruitless and unmeaning without. He might have appeared in Pharaoh's court and before the Israelites; east his rod upon the ground, and it become a serpent—take it up in his hand, and it become a rod again; cast his hand into his bosom, and it become leprous—cast it into his bosom again, and it become sound; yet, if he had spoken no word, it would all have been as unmeaning to the Egyptians and Israelites as the wild freaks of a maniac. Throughout the Bible we find this same indispensable connection between God's Spirit and his word. Let another instance suffice. When the Spirit descended, on the day of Pentecost, with its rushing mighty sound, and its tongues like fire, there was no understanding of what or why it was, until Peter, with the words of inspiration, told them that this was a fulfillment of what had been spoken by the prophet Joel, and that Jesus, who had wrought mighty miracles among them, and whom they had with wicked hands crucified and slain, had boon raised from the dead and exalted to the right hand of God; and that it was he that shed forth that which they heard and saw; that he was both Lord and Christ. Then, the matter was understood. With this connection of Spirit and Word, we can comprehend all that God designs us to know, and thereby be fitted for all that God requires us to do. By the Spirit *alone*, we comprehend nothing. By *imagining* that we have the Spirit, we are, if possible, worse than ignorant and blind. Suppose those dreamy imaginings of a distempered brain, those excited animal impulses were the operations of the Spirit of God;—what do they teach? What sensible thought do they communicate? There is no word of instruction accompanying. How do we know it is an approval from God? How do we know it is not a condemnation? It is worse than vanity to suppose that the Spirit of God has any part in producing such feelings or delusions.

There is another fact necessary to be borne in mind, in order to a proper understanding of this subject. God, in different ages of the world, chose special servants, and specially qualified them to do special work, for general good. Such were Moses, the Prophets and the Apostles. Other men were not endowed like this class. How the Spirit operated upon them, and what were their peculiar feelings and impressions, is not for us to know, nor is it necessary for us to inquire. We cannot expect to be similarly affected, or be recipients of any such special gifts.

Bearing the foregoing in mind, let us now view the Spirit in some of its most important works, in its different missions to our world; for we find that it was sent on different and distinct occasions, and each mission or occasion was attended with a distinct work, belonging exclusively to that case. To apply the work of the Spirit in one case, to another, wholly foreign and distinct, would be doing violence to the order of Heaven's arrangement, and produce serious and calamitous confusion. The first account we have is the mission of the Spirit in creation. There it moved on the face of the great deep. The object of that mission was accomplished, and there was no further necessity for its work in that matter; nor of *that* work in any other matter. Since the works of creation were brought forth and pronounced good, we hear no more of the Spirit moving upon the face of the great deep—that work was finished. We have an account of another mission of the Spirit, in God's chosen servant Noah. The object was to preach righteousness, and warn a wicked world of the just judgment that awaited them. The Spirit, through Noah, strove with the antediluvians for their reformation. God, with long suffering, waited with them during the whole time of building the ark. He had warned them, saying, "My Spirit shall not always strive with man, for that he also is flesh; yet his days shall be an hundred and twenty years."

Gen. vi. 3. At the close of this period of time the ark was finished; Noah ceased his preaching; the Spirit strove with the people no longer; they repented not, and were destroyed. This mission had a special work—to instruct Noah, and warn the antediluvians; and this work belonged exclusively to that mission. We have no right to apply it to any other case. We do not *now* need, nor expect to see a Noah warning people of an approaching deluge as a punishment for their wickedness. Nor have we any authority to use the *language,* specially applicable to that case, as applicable to a mourners-bench excitement— telling the poor deluded subjects of such an imposition, that God says to *them,* in *that* case, "My Spirit shall not always strive with man."

The next mission of the Spirit, to which I would direct your attention, is that through God's special servant Moses. This was also for a special work—for the redemption, welfare and happiness of the children of Israel. Moses was supernaturally qualified for the work. He went to Egypt, and to the haughty Pharaoh made known his mission; presented his credentials in miraculous works, which no uninspired man could do. Asks that the Israelites may be permitted to depart and worship the God of their fathers. Failing to persuade, he, by the mighty powers of the Spirit, forces the relentless tyrant to give up his prey; guides his brethren out, sustained by the high hand and outstretched arm of the Almighty; divides the waters of the sea; passes through safe, beyond the pursuit of the enemy; calls bread from heaven to feed them in the wilderness; smites the flinty rock with his rod, and produces a fountain of pure water, sufficient to supply the wants of his vast host. The works of the Spirit in this mission, were also applicable to that case alone; no other occasion demanded them. They are not to be transferred. We cannot now expect a Moses, or any one with his powers, miraculously delivering people from temporal bondage; passing them through the sea; feeding them with bread from heaven; and quenching their thirst from a moving rock. That work was long ago accomplished, and with the occasion it ceased.

There was also a mission (or mission) of the Spirit to the Prophets. They were properly qualified, and did their work—applicable to the several occasions requiring it, and finished their labors. We cannot expect to see any one now endowed like them. Their work is not to be done over again.

The Spirit was sent on a mission to John the Baptist. This mission was to prepare a way for the Lord. This work was accomplished, and the labor belonging to that mission ceased. We do not now hear the voice of one proclaiming in the wilderness, saying, Prepare the way of the Lord. The time for that ceased long ago. We can expect, *now,* no such qualifications as John had.

During John's ministry, Jesus appears before the world, claiming to be the Son of God; he of whom Moses and the Prophets spoke. He comes attended with all the particulars, in his birth and life, foretold by the prophets; but the Father deems it proper not to rest the truth of his claim upon these alone. Therefore, he sends his Spirit upon another mission: Jesus went to John, and was baptized. Having arisen from the water, the heavens were opened, and the Spirit of God descended like a dove, and rested upon him, and a voice from heaven proclaimed, "This is my beloved Son, in whom I am well pleased." The object of the Spirit's mission on this occasion was to testify, beyond dispute, that Jesus was the Son of God. As though a father should lay his hand upon his son's head and say, This is my son. There was no mistaking the person. The Spirit, in a *visible* form, pointed him out; and God said, *This* is my Son. We of course, cannot expect to see the Spirit laboring in that mission now as it did then.

It was also necessary to give unmistakable proof of the extent of Christ's authority. Moses and Elijah had till now been reverenced as lawgiver and prophet. It was difficult for the Jews to conceive of any whose authority should be greater. Hence the necessity of another mission of the Spirit. The Savior repairs to a mountain with three of his witnesses. Moses and Elijah appear, and talk with him. He is enwrapped in glory to the view of his Apostles, who then seem desirous to remain there, and honor him *equally* with Moses and Elijah. They would build a tabernacle for each. But here, in the presence of these two, whom they revered as their lawgiver and their prophet, God gave them to understand that they must regard the authority of his Son as superior to that of his servants. Said He, "This is my *Son:* hear *him.*" We cannot *now* expect such visions, or such a voice. That work was finished on that occasion. The supreme source of instruction and information in all these matters is now found in the volume of inspiration. They happened for our benefit, and they are written for our admonition and instruction.

The being thus authenticated as God's Son, came to earth for the salvation of man; to redeem him from sin and death, and befit him for a residence in heaven. In order to do this, it required a government different from any that had previously existed. A kingdom, over which the Son of God should reign. This must be ushered in, sealed with God's authority and approbation. It was, therefore, necessary that the Spirit should be sent upon another mission. We see, then, the Apostles of Christ awaiting at Jerusalem the promise of their Lord. A vast concourse of Jews (the best judges in the world of these evidences) is assembled in the city from every nation under heaven. It is Pentecost; the feast for celebrating the giving of the law of Moses on Mount Sinai. Suddenly there comes a sound from heaven, as of a rushing mighty wind, and it fills all the house where they are sitting; and there appears cloven tongues like as of fire, and rests upon the Apostles; they are all filled with the Holy Spirit, and begin to speak with other tongues, as the Spirit gives them utterance. This is noised through the city. A vast multitude of Jews, citizens and strangers rush to the spot. They are amazed and confounded. What does it mean? This strange sight? These strange sounds? These ignorant men of Galilee, speaking in the various languages of the earth, as fluently as if they were their own mother tongues! What does it mean? Peter explained it: This is a fulfillment of the prophecy of Joel. This prophecy relates to the Son of God, and to the setting up of his kingdom. That Jesus, whom God attested and approved by miracles, and signs, and wonders, in your presence, and whom you have taken, and by wicked hands have crucified and slain, has arisen from the dead, and is exalted to the right hand of God in heaven. It is he who sheds forth this which you now see and hear. He is above all authority, and has full power to grant repentance and remission of sins to Israel. What overwhelming evidences were these to the Jews. They revered the occasion of the giving the law of Moses. The law of Christ comes upon the same day— Pentecost. The law of Moses was given from Mount Sinai, amid thunderings, and lightnings, and voices from heaven. The law of Christ is proclaimed from Mount Zion, amid a rushing mighty sound, flaming tongues, and living words breathed by the Spirit of God. What stronger evidence could be asked? What more could be given? It was enough. Thousands are pierced to the heart; and gladly seek relief and protection from heaven's King—the Son of God. This mission of the Spirit, like all others, had its object—the ushering in of the Reign of

Heaven, with a full, clear proof of the sanction of God. That object being accomplished, there was no further necessity for the work of that mission; it ceased. There was another mission similar in character, and the same in kind as this: The descent of the Spirit at the house of Cornelius. The Jews had been furnished, on the day of Pentecost, with sufficient evidence that they should now submit to the Reign of favor instead of the law of Moses; but always having esteemed themselves the especially favored people of God, to the exclusion of all others, nothing short of a miracle, as great as that which accompanied the setting up of the kingdom, could convince them that the Gentiles were entitled to reception and equal privileges with themselves. Hence the necessity of the Spirit falling on the Gentiles at the house of Cornelius, like it bad done on the Jews at the beginning. Peter could not now refuse to receive them; the Jews could interpose no objection. None could forbid water that the Gentiles should not be baptized, who had received the Holy Spirit, as well as the Jews. This mission broke down the wall of partition between the Jews and Gentiles, and made them one in Christ. This being done, the work of that mission ceased. We cannot *now* expect to see it still doing. There is no necessity for a descent of the Spirit, like that on Pentecost, and consequently we cannot expect it. God never does a thing which there is no necessity for. How worse than vain, then, those prayers, which we frequently hear, for the Lord to "send down a Pentecostal shower." Such people know not for what they are praying. How confused the ideas of some religionists with regard to the teachings of Scripture. Often do we hear the prayer boisterously vociferated, for the Lord to baptize the congregation "with the Holy Ghost and with fire." What an awful petition to the throne of heaven! They know not what they ask. Let such persons reflect a moment. Where do they find this baptism of fire spoken of? By John the Baptist, in Matt. iii. and Luke iii. The baptism of the Holy Spirit and that of fire are both spoken of in connection, and in the same sentence. If, therefore, the Spirit is meant literally, fire is meant literally; but we cannot conceive of any other than a literal baptism of the Spirit; consequently, the fire baptism must be literal. The context also shows this: "Whose fan is in his hand, and he will thoroughly purge his floor, and gather his wheat into the garner; but he will *burn up the chaff* with unquenchable fire." Read Matt. iii. 11, 12. In Acts i. 5, Luke tells us, in the Savior's own language, that the baptism of the Holy Spirit was to be "not many days hence;" but no mention is made of the baptism of fire at that time. "Not many days hence," the Spirit descended at Pentecost, and the disciples were baptized in it. But the baptism of fire is still reserved for "the day of judgment and perdition of ungodly men." So shall it be at the end of the world; the winked shall be cast into the furnace of fire. See 2 Pet. iii. 7, and Matt. xiii. 48-50. Who, that understands the Scriptures, can help shuddering at the utterance of such prayers?

There is one other mission of the Spirit to which I ask your attention:—The mission to the church. The Savior told the Apostles he would send them another comforter, which should abide with them forever; which should bring all things to their remembrance, and guide them into all truth. See 14th and 15th chaps, of John. This comforter was to remain with the Apostles forever, in the same sense that Christ tells them he will be with them "always, even unto the end of the world." Matt. xxviii. 20. This mission of the Spirit was to establish and confirm the first converts in the faith; and to command the attention and secure the faith of all, in every station of life. If it failed to do this, the cause was in the stubborn, rebellious will of the people, and not in the means instituted to instruct, convince, and save them. This mission was confined to the days of miracles. "The gifts of the Holy Spirit" were common to all the disciples, in the days of the Apostles. Some had one gift and some another. The Corinthians came short in no gift. The gifts were conferred by the imposition of the Apostles' hands. No others could confer them. When Philip preached at Samaria, "the people gave heed to those things which he spake, hearing and seeing the miracles which he did. For unclean spirits crying with loud voice came out of many that were possessed with them; and many taken with palsies, and that were lame, were healed"—and "they were baptized, both men and women." Acts viii. Philip, though he had such miraculous powers, could not confer upon others the same gift. He was not an apostle; and the Apostles only could bestow these gifts. Therefore, that these converts at Samaria might receive the Holy Spirit, Peter and John were sent from Jerusalem, who prayed for them and laid their hands upon them, and they received the Holy Spirit. From the nature of the case, it will be seen that these things had to cease. The Apostles only could confer miraculous power. Those upon whom they conferred it could exercise it, but could not bestow it upon others. When, therefore, the Apostles were all dead, there was no power to confer it; and when all had ceased to live upon whom they had conferred it, these gifts could be exercised no longer. Paul also informs us, 1 Cor. xiii., that these things must cease. "Whether there be prophecies, they shall fail; whether there be tongues, they shall cease; whether there be knowledge, it shall vanish away." Each had his respective gift, in order to the performance of his respective part. These different parts, together, formed the grand whole. This being done, the work was finished; and that character of labor ceased. We now have it complete in the living oracles—the New Testament. Instead of sending up to Jerusalem about any matter of instruction; or awaiting until Paul, Peter, James or John sends us a letter, we apply direct to the volume where their labors and instructions are compiled. Here we have *all things* that pertain to life and godliness; all that is "profitable for doctrine, for reproof, for correction, for instruction in righteousness; that the man of God may be perfect, thoroughly furnished unto *all good works."* No one, of course, expects these miraculous gifts now. When Peter replied to the vital question of the Pentecostians, in which he promised the gift of the Holy Spirit, he had reference to these miraculous powers, or else he meant the principle or nature of the Spirit. In the former sense, we cannot now expect it; in the latter, all Christians have it. It cannot be possible that any man now possesses the Spirit otherwise than in its principle or nature. I am unable to see how anyone can be possessed of the Spirit in person, without being able to perform miracles; or, in other words, I cannot see how anyone can possess the *physical* presence of the Spirit, without being able to exert the physical power of the Spirit. I cannot separate the two. A man's physical presence I cannot separate from his physical power. How he can be physically or bodily absent from his moral presence, I can understand very well. No servant of God, that the Bible informs us of, claimed to possess the Spirit without being able to prove his claim by a spiritual work.

The Spirit now dwells in the church by its moral presence, through its word—and in no other way. Physically or personally it is not here; or, if it is, we cannot know it, which amounts to the same thing to us. It is said of some of the ancient servants of God, that though dead, they yet speak. Then we have their moral presence. Let me illustrate my meaning. Washington's Farewell Address breathes the spirit of Washington. When we read it, and come under its influence, we then have the spirit of Washington. In like manner, we now have the Spirit of God, and in no other way. All those passages of scripture which refer to the disciples having the Spirit have reference to it in this sense, or are applicable to the age of miracles. "If any man have not the Spirit of Christ, he is none of his." And what was the Spirit of Christ? "Love, joy, peace, long-suffering, gentleness, goodness, faith, meekness, temperance."

The animal impulses, blind imaginations, distempered dreams, and mourners-bench excitements, which are now claimed as the workings of the Spirit, are as far from the operation of the Spirit of God, either morally or physically, as earth is from heaven. It is worse than a delusion. There is neither the operation of the Holy Spirit nor Christianity in it—nor even reason or common sense.

That we may view this subject from another stand point, I would remind you that the Scriptures allude frequently to the spirit of the world, and the spirit of Christianity. They allude to the spirit as a principle, disposition, or frame of mind. It is said of John the Baptist, "He shall go before him in the spirit and power of Elias," Luke i. 17. "But he turned and rebuked them, saying, You know not what manner of spirit you are of," Luke ix. 55. "The true worshippers shall worship the Father in spirit and in truth," John iv. 23. "Now we have not received the spirit of the world, but the Spirit which is of God," 1 Cor. ii. 12. "If ye receive another spirit, which you have not received, or another gospel, which you have not accepted," 2 Cor. xi. 4. "Walked we not in the same spirit?—walked we not in the same steps," 2 Cor. xii. 18. "In time past you walked according to the. course of this world, according to the prince of the power of the air, the spirit that now worketh in the children of disobedience," Eph. ii. 2. From these and similar passages of scripture, we are authorized to speak of the Spirit of Christ, of the Spirit of Christianity, of a holy Spirit, without meaning a *mysterious* presence and indwelling of the Holy Spirit in person. We are allowed to distinguish between the Spirit in person, and its moral influence. Between *moral* and *physical* feelings and influences. Between the Bible as a guide, comforter, and supporter, and some mysterious abstraction, independent of the Bible. Between the clear teachings of the Bible, and the beclouded superstitions and delusions of self-styled orthodoxy.

We may be in the Spirit, however, and not be always altogether right. To be fully right, we must be fully taught. Take the case of Apollos, for instance: He was instructed in the way of the Lord; and, being fervent in the spirit, he spoke and taught diligently the things of the Lord, knowing only the baptism of John. And he began to speak boldly in the synagogue: whom, when Aquila and Priscilla had heard, they took him unto them, and expounded unto him the way of God more perfectly," Acts xviii. 25, 26. So, we may be fervent in spirit, pure in mind and right in object, and still be in error. We may "have a zeal for God, but not according to knowledge." It is essential, then, that we be properly taught, and then be fervent in spirit, and we are sure to be right. We should not only have a holy spirit, by which we can heartily exclaim, Abba, Father; but we should, in all things, be led by the teachings of the Holy Spirit. "There is therefore now no condemnation to them which are in Christ Jesus, who walk not after the flesh, but after the spirit." "For they that are after the flesh, do mind the things of the flesh; but they that are after the spirit, the things of the spirit," Rom. viii. 1, 5.

What a heaven-fraught theme is the Spirit's labors and influences for man. There is nothing of earth about it. Through a long line of Patriarchs and Prophets, this heavenly Instructor and Comforter points us to the Lamb of God, that takes away the sin of the world. When the heavens are bowed, and the Savior stoops to earth; this same swift winged messenger of light, joy and power, heralds the glad tidings to the fallen sons of Adam, and bids them look up and rejoice. When, by wicked hands, the Savior in bleeding agonies expires upon the cross, the Spirit takes its everlasting flight from the now no longer sacred temple of such a wicked nation, shakes the earth to its center, and shrouds the universe in gloom. But soon returning to our lost, sin-benighted world, with the arm of Omnipotence, he breaks the bars of death, and brings forth from the confines of the tomb the Son of God, to life immortal and glory ineffable. Summons a convoy of heavenly messengers, and conducts him, in triumphal procession, through the vast universe of the worlds—familiar scenes of his previous glory and power—to the portals of eternal bliss and universal dominion. "Lift up your heads, O ye gates; and be ye lift up, ye everlasting doors; and the King of glory shall come in." All hail, the great Emanuel! Let angels prostrate fall. Bring forth the royal diadem, and crown him Lord of all. He is exalted to the right hand of the Majesty on high, as Lord of lords, and King of kings. Let all the hosts of heaven worship him. But man is not left in ignorance concerning these things.

Hark! what sound is that? 'Tis the same bright Spirit of the skies, hastening, with a sound as of a mighty rushing wind, to bear the news to man: Rejoice, O Earth, the Lord is King! That Jesus, whom you slew, is the Son of God. He has arisen from the dead. He has ascended to his Father. He now sits enthroned in glory. He invites you to come up and sit with him. You despised him—you put him to a cruel death; but his sufferings are over. He is willing to forgive you—he is willing to receive you. Was ever love like this? Look to the Savior and live. This heavenly invitation is not confined to that particular time and occasion. We find the same heavenly messenger accompanying the Apostles, instructing, strengthening, and building up the first converts.

And in living, burning oracles, we have his mission of love and mercy now.

"How precious is the Book Divine,
　By inspiration given!
Bright as a lamp its precepts shine,
　To guide our souls to heav'n."
　　MIDWAY, MADISON CO., TEXAS,
　　　　July 3rd, 1856.

-----o-----

THROWING DUST IN THE EYES OF THE BAPTISTS.

"We sometimes hear very good brethren and sisters, after hearing preachers of the modern reformation, say that their doctrine is sound. They told us, they say, that they believed in repentance, in faith, in the operations of the Spirit. And they also say, that they don't believe that baptism will do any good, unless the person baptized believes on Christ. And thus from what the Reformed preachers say, many Baptists take it for granted that they hold to orthodox doctrines—that they preach a work of grace upon the heart—advocate repentance and faith—and contend for the work of the Holy Spirit upon the heart of man. Now, we have a word or two to say about this apparent orthodoxy of our Reformed friends. And in saying it we are not to be understood as waging any war with them. But we want our people to know where they stand. Nor are we to judge many of their evangelists and local preachers by what Mr. Campbell writes in the 'Harbinger.' We know that many years ago they preached doctrines that were considered so heretical that they and the Baptists could not live together, and as a consequence, they divided and split to pieces many of the best Baptist churches in Kentucky. In that conflict the best Baptist preachers of that day were directly arrayed against them. Among those in Virginia who were most celebrated, were Elders Semple and Broaddus. In Kentucky, Elders Waller, Noel, Black, and others, now dead—and Elders Dillard, Vaughn, Black, and others among the living, were engaged in that conflict. Now, what is remarkable, the preachers among the Reformers will get up and tell their believers that they glory in preaching the doctrines which they advocated at that day—that they have never changed—and yet our brethren have the dust so thrown into their eyes, that they can see no difference whatever between the doctrines of the Baptists and the Reformers. We think the time has come when the Baptist ministry are called upon to change the mode of their operations. And when they will have to indoctrinate their members more intelligently. We can't see why the preachers among the Reformers should try to sugar-coat their doctrines. Why don't they preach them fully, boldly, and intelligently?

"We trust the day is coming when all these matters will be better understood than they are now. The truth is, the Reformers, according to our notion, make baptism necessarily to salvation."—*Western Recorder*.

REMARKS.

The above is from the "Western Recorder" of Louisville, Kentucky, which in the time of the much lamented Waller, was, so far as the West was concerned, *the organ* of the Baptists. But we are not certain that the "Tennessee Baptist" is not now *the organ,* and the *Letter exponent* of the Baptists in the West, and he probably has the largest circulation of any Baptist periodical west of the mountains, if not in The United States. In the time of Mr. Waller, the "Recorder" was vastly different, in its manly strength, its general bearing, and especially in its spirit. It has now retrograded till it is scarcely one whit superior, in ability, spirit or common courtesy to the "Tennessee Baptist." It now appears ready to catch at the lowest prejudice, the most stupid bigotry, or manifest partisan spirit, as capital out of which to manufacture a spirit of opposition among the Baptists. We know not who the writer of the above is, save that he is someone who figures in the "Recorder" quite conspicuously; but this we know, that the editor must be hard pressed for material for his columns.

The caption of the foregoing is ominous,—"Throwing Dust in the Eyes of the Baptists." What calls out such a caption as this? Why, sir, the time is come when Baptists are not to be trusted; not to be allowed the right to do their own thinking; when they are not to have the liberty to decide for themselves upon what is orthodox! Baptist writers have lost confidence in the intelligence of their members; and find it necessary to inform the poor creatures—"the common people," who hear the Disciples, and pronounce what they hear "orthodox," that dust is thrown into their eyes! Baptists are not to be allowed the "right of private judgment," till they learn better than to hear in such a manner as to decide that The Disciples are orthodox. No matter if they do hear them preach the most unfeigned faith, the most godly repentance, the most pungent, thorough and divine change of heart ever preached, and precisely the same baptism into the name of the Father, and of the Son, and of the Holy Spirit, as practiced by Baptists themselves, they must not think it orthodox; or, if they cannot help but think so, they must not say so, without liberty from some of the keepers of the faith!

Who are these Baptists, thus accused of their own brethren—public writers, with having dust thrown into their eyes? or, in simple and unfigurative language, thus accused of ignorance in saying the Disciples are orthodox?—or, are they not as well informed, pious and noble as any in their ranks? Are they to be published to the world, as poor, weak, gullible creatures—with dust in their eyes, because they decide, when they hear the truth, from those they know to be good men, that *it is the truth?* Who are they that are thus treated? John L. Waller, L. L. D., was one of the men that dared to think, say and publish to the world that Mr. Campbell was orthodox! Thousands of other Baptists say the same, and are as well satisfied that it is true, as they are that the Baptists are *orthodox*. Are these now all to be told that they are simpletons, with their eyes filled with dust, by such writers as the one that penned the foregoing article, and published to the world as "abominably heretical," if they commune with Disciples?

The "Recorder" "can't see why the preachers among the Reformers should try to sugar-coat their doctrines!" He asks, "Why don't they preach them fully, boldly and intelligently?" This is lamentable indeed! Why do not the Disciples come out and preach some errors, so that Baptists can see that they are not orthodox? Cannot someone accommodate this writer, in his extremity, so much as to deny faith, repentance, a change of heart, or spiritual influence, that Baptists may be able to show that we are not orthodox? This practice of preaching nothing but plain and manifest truth, as it is in Christ, is "throwing dust into the eyes of Baptists," and they, without the consent of their would-be spiritual guides, are pronouncing it orthodox! Horrible! What is to be done? "The time has come when the Baptist ministry are called upon to change the mode of their operations." That will not do, my dear sir. "The *Regular* Baptists" cannot *change!* That would be *irregular!* That would be equivalent to admitting that their "mode of operations" had been wrong. "The Baptist ministry" never gets wrong in "the mode of its operations!" If Baptist scribes do not cease this kind of writing, they will fill the Baptist church with fear that the Disciples are about to devour them—swallow them down. There must be something some place that is alarming these Baptists scribes. We beg in behalf of this affrighted brother, that brethren do not "sugar-coat their doctrines," so as to throw dust in the eyes of any uninformed Baptist that may be present, without any spiritual guide with him, or the Baptist ministry will be compelled to *change* the mode of their operations!   B. F.

-----o-----

EXCURSION TO NORTHERN ILLINOIS. NUMBER III.

In my second, I conducted the reader to the residence of Bro. John Hammer in the vicinity of Polo, on the Illinois Central Railroad, Ogle county. According to previous appointment, I was to preach next day (Lord's day) at a spacious school house on his premises, where it was anticipated a large assembly would be present. But the clouds disburdened themselves all day in copious showers, so as to compel us to remain within doors. The day being wet and gloomy, my physical and inner man were in a somewhat moody condition; and, of course, my intercourse with the inmates of Bro. H.'s elegant mansion was rather taciturn and pointless. However, towards noon, a brother who resides about twelve miles from Bro. H. arrived, having traveled all that distance through incessant rain. This Bro. told me that he first realized an interest in me, by reading my series of "Observations on things east of the mountains," which consecutively appeared in the columns of the *Christian Age,* when it was yet under your editorial control, some three years ago, and in which I expected to lay these numbers of my Illinois Excursion before its respectable readers—but, owing either to a degeneracy in my style of writing, or to the superior and more refined tastes of its present editors, my articles could gain no admittance into its *expurgated* columns.

It would greatly assuage my disappointment in that respect, if I could *now* believe that the want of *dignity* in the style of my numbers one and two was the real cause of their exclusion. If that was the real cause, then I must obtain from some spectacle repository, optical glasses of no common magnifying power, to discry a commendable consistency in the course of the editorial trio of the *Age*. For observant readers of that sheet have, no doubt, perused paragraphs in its professedly guarded columns, much more meager in dignity than any in the communications I offered them. Let facts be submitted. In one of the numbers, of the forepart of December ultimo, we had the announcement that a celebrated race-horse had been imported by a lover of turf sports, and that an enterprising Kentuckian had procured, in the same shipment, a heifer at the insignificant rate of $6500! How do race-horses and heifers stand related to the gospel? But, I have another morcean from the columns of its issue of the 17th of February, which badly quadrates with the professed purity and gravity which its editors so scrupulously guard. Here follows its last moiety. It is an African preacher's search after a tree for a certain purpose, furnishing also an illustration of the depravity of human nature: "I spied," says the sable preacher, "a tree suitable for de purpose, and I raised de axe to cut into de trunk. It was a beautiful tree! De branches reached to de four corners ob de earth, and raise up high to de air above, and de squirrels hop about in de limbs like little angels flopping deir wings in de kingdom ob heaven. Dat tree was full ob promise, my friends, just like a great many of you. Den, I cut in de trunk, and made de chips fly like de mighty scales dropping from Paul's eyes. Two, three cuts I gave dat tree, and alas! it was holler in de butt.

"Dat tree was much like you, my friends, full ob promise—full ob promise outside, but *holler in de butt!*" Certe Homer aliquando dormiunt—surely the Homers sometimes sleep, else such nugatories could not find entrance into their sacred enclosure!

But let us return from this deviation. On Monday evening I preached in the place where I was to officiate the day before. The audience was respectable in number and appearance. I discoursed to them on the Christian race, based on 9th chap, of 1st Cor. 24-27. The congregation was attentive to the teaching on the occasion. Some of the non-professors, men of sense and moral character, professed to relish that kind of teaching, *because it was scriptural!*

On Tuesday Bro. Hammer conveyed me to Mt. Morris, a beautiful village, about five miles from his residence, situated on an interesting swell of an extensive prairie region. In this town, the Methodists have a fine college edifice and a flourishing school.

I was introduced to Prof's Harlow and Pope, whose urbane and cordial demeanor could not fail to make a favorable impression.

Here I also found a number of my old acquaintances and friends from Maryland, among whom I was wont, a quarter of a century ago, to preach the gospel. At their solicitation I consented, that arrangements might be made for me to preach on the following evening in the chapel of the new and spacious college edifice.

Mt. Morris is so named after a distinguished bishop of that name in the Methodist Episcopal Church. In the founding of this town, a principle was adopted which might be safely and beneficially used in the location of new towns and cities anywhere, namely, that whoever purchases a lot, and at any time sells liquor on it, shall forfeit said lot—it shall revert to the corporation of the town. The place is, of course, clear of all liquor nuisances. How advantageous would such regulations be to towns, if universally adopted!

In the afternoon we went to Oregon, the seat of justice of Ogle county, and sojourned with Sister Seister, a worthy Disciple, originally from Maryland. The courthouse, at that time, was the place of resort on account of the trial of a man who had murdered a fellow-citizen—the act was committed under the influence of liquor, in proximity to a "saloon," *alias* a gate-way to hell.

It was a matter of suspense whether the culprit would be convicted of homicide or murder of the first degree. We mingled with the throng and had a good opportunity to note the legal and judicial magistrates of the occasion—talents were moderate, dignity medium.

At the most moderate estimate that trial will cost that county some thousands of dollars—an expenditure incurred by the tolerance of the liquor traffic and circulation, within its limits! Is it not every patriot's business to oppose this nefarious interest?

In this hall of justice I was introduced to Rev. Bower, pastor of the Lutheran Church of that place, who, from dictates of propriety, invited me to his house, but carefully avoided conversation on religion and church occupancy. His "outer man" is rather diminutive, and his "*inner*" somewhat compressed by a sectarian incubus. As the community was entirely absorbed in the "trial," and as those who are under the ban of heresy, have no other place to preach in but the courthouse, I left Oregon without addressing its citizens.

On Wednesday we returned to Mt. Morris, and sojourned with my hospitable old friend Mr. Shearer, formerly from Maryland.

In the evening I met a respectable audience in the College Chapel, composed mostly of old acquaintances from the State of Maryland, who, by their emigration to Northern Illinois, had most evidently improved their worldly circumstances—many of them having become wealthy. I congratulated them upon the occasion of our once more enjoying together the privileges of the sanctuary. Knowing that my audience was composed of those who occupied diversified positions relative to the Christian profession, and desiring to benefit them by presenting such truths as could not be construed into a sectarian interest, and knowing that they had become rich in temporalities, and having seen the havoc which rapid worldly prosperity has had upon the spiritual interests of Christians, I deemed it profitable to call their attention to the consideration of the following passage, "Charge them that are rich in this world, that they be not high minded, nor trust in uncertain, but in the living God who giveth us richly all things to enjoy; that they do good, that they be rich in good works, ready to distribute, willing to communicate, laying up in store for themselves a good foundation against the time to come, that they may *lay hold on eternal life.*" 1 Tim. vi. 17-19. The cardinal thoughts presented on this passage, were, first, Who are rich?—those who can command the necessaries and conveniences of life, and have still something to spare—such rich men belonged to the primitive church, consequently the early Christian profession was not composed of an uninfluential and ignorant rabble, as infidels sometimes insinuate; that the community of goods among the first Christians was a local and not a universal institution, otherwise there could have been no rich men among them; that riches do not necessarily exclude from heaven, but they that "trust" in them cannot enter. Secondly, reasons were assigned why the rich should not be high-minded, because riches are talents entrusted, for which men are *responsible*—our talents are our abilities to make ourselves felt for good in human society—that the rich have that ability, and therefore responsible; because, the rich dare not eat more than those who have a competency, unless at the hazard of their health and life, nor put on more than two coats—a thing which the man of competency may do,—can occupy but one room, and one seat at one time, which the *poor* man can do; because, riches make themselves wings to fly away, therefore those wings should be frequently cropped by liberal distributions to the needy; because, riches have no influence over the lofty intelligences in the higher spheres, nor over God the arbiter of our final destiny! Thirdly, to be *rich in good works* was earnestly insisted on, because that kind of wealth gives us dignity in all the circles in which we may mingle in the interminable future of our existence!—that by distribution for the alleviation of wants, and a promptitude in participating in the promotion of benevolent enterprises, they were laying up treasures for *"themselves,"* and not simply for their children, as is wont to be; that the rich *cannot lay hold on eternal life, unless they are liberal with their means of doing good* in this sin-stricken world. These truths were felt by many of my hearers, and it is hoped they are permanently lodged in their hearts. The liberality which that community displayed in the erection of spacious college edifices, and the support of available schools, were adverted to, and I presume it was well received. After the dismission of the audience, Prof. Harlow gave me a cordial shake of the hand, with the remark, that I had done that community a good and opportune service on the occasion. More anon.

SAMUEL K. HOSHOUR.

-----o-----

ADDRESS ON BIBLE REVISION.

The following extract is from an Address written for the Revision Association, in Louisville, on the first and second days of May, but not delivered. When we saw the shape of things, we delivered an extemporaneous speech.

B. F.

MR. PRESIDENT:—No man can work profitably in any department in the vineyard of the Lord without the constant realization that *it is indeed the Lord's work;* nor will any man, where such is not the case, apply to the Lord for his gracious aid, with full assurance of faith. To engage in any great religious work rightly, prosecute it properly and insure success, there should be a deep and settled conviction that *it is the work of the Lord.* This point should be fixed in the mind, established in the soul, and decided so as to be beyond all question. When this is the case, we can come to God, in full confidence, believing that when we ask the Divine aid, we ask according to the will of God, and that God will hear us. That the principal men in the Bible Union have, from the beginning, acted under the settled conviction that they are engaged emphatically IN THE WORK OF GOD, is as manifest to the observer as any other feature in the whole procedure. If they are right in this—*if it is assuredly the work of God*—it cannot be overthrown. This principle was admitted, stated and urged by a reasonable man, though not himself identified with the work of the Lord, to pacify the open and fierce opposers of the apostles, when first revealing Christianity to mankind and converting thousands. He urged, if the work is not of God, it will come to nothing; if it is of God, you cannot overthrow it. The enemies then were not willing to leave the matter to such a mild course; but determined to interpose the most violent opposition. Though this opposition was from a malignant and wicked spirit, designed to break down and destroy the work of God, divine Providence so overruled it for good, that their opposition greatly strengthened the divine testimony demonstrative that the work was of God.

In the same way, in placing a guard over the dead body of Jesus, when he lay in the tomb, though done by enemies, and in opposition, served a great and good purpose, in completing the chain of divine testimony. With this vigilant opposition, their careful precaution, and perfect arrangements, they had the means of detecting any possible imposition. The circumstance that the great fact laying at the basis of Christianity, and we may now say, of the Bible, that the Lord rose from the dead, which forever establishes his divinity, occurred at the precise time and place when and where the enemies were making a sufficient effort to have detected any possible imposture, is now of immense value to us, in assuring mankind that the work was of God. The effort they made, at the precise time and place, and for the special purpose of detecting or preventing imposture, would have done it, if there had been any imposition. In this way the Lord makes the wrath of man praise him.

The apostasy of the infidel Julian, and his opposition to Christianity, though wicked in itself and aimed to destroy it, and he justly punishable for his opposition, is now an additional evidence of the divinity of the Bible. He was once in the church, knew the doctrine, and was well acquainted with the whole premises. He lived sufficiently early to have a full history from the beginning; and, consequently, the best means in the world for opposing. He, like most men who become apostate, became a bitter enemy. He was a man of great power and immense energy, and spent his full force in opposition. But he never shook the Bible, nor the foundation of the faith. He had abundant means to have detected imposture, if there had been any. He was able to have overthrown the faith, if it had been of man. He could have shown it to be *human,* if it had not been *divine.* But how much did he impede the progress of religion? How far did he succeed in extinguishing the Bible? His effort to impede it was simply sufficient to show that man could not stay the Almighty hand that moved the vast work onward. His effort to put down the Bible, serves, in our time, to show how puny the arm of man is, when lifted against the Book of God. The Bible still lives; its influence spreads, and its work progresses in great power, among the nations of the earth, while he is measure- ably forgotten.

These early struggles of the Bible against its bitter and virulent opposers, with its mighty triumphs and glorious achievements, demonstrates with great clearness and power, that God was with it. But another train of enemies, loss honorable, more insidious and greater in power, whose history is more clearly and fully written in the prophetic Scriptures than any other, come upon the stage, and, in a systematic, persevering and protracted effort, extending over a span of more than a thousand years, to wrest the Bible from the hands of those for whom God gave it, furnish to the thinking man a fuller, clearer and more perfect demonstration, that "the hand that gave it is divine," than all that had gone before. How wonderful it is, that "the Man of Sin," whose character, stealthy course, and entire work are so graphically depicted upon the pages of the Bible, and his certain perdition there so legibly inscribed, should continue his protracted struggle through the long cycles of so many generations, among so many nations, to wrest the Bible from the people, without recognizing his description in that Book! How wonderful and overwhelming too, that the combined, systematic and giant power of this the greatest human organization ever on earth, for so many ages to put down the Bible and wrest it from the people, should have failed. Such efforts would have annihilated any other book in the world. But the Bible lived in defiance of all these efforts, and appears only to have been accumulating strength to burst forth in greater power upon the immense population of our times upon the earth.

Think of the numerous manuscripts of the living oracles, silently in their resting-place, where, by Divine Providence, they had been laid for safe-keeping, till the midnight of the dark ages should pass away, and which the finger of God, in modern times, has directed his servants to bring forth. Look at the immense variety of works, preserved by our Heavenly Father, all throwing light upon antiquity. Lay this along side of modern art, learning and science, with the innumerable facilities now in the hands of good men, aiding in purging away all impurities and corruptions from the Word of God, and restoring it to the nations in their own mother tongue; and then say, whether Divine Providence is not in it? What other book since the beginning of time has been thus guarded and kept?

If this book is an imposture, "a cunningly devised fable," why have not its opposers established that fact long since, and passed it by as a Pagan legend? Why did not Julian, with other ancient infidels, or the giant and learned infidels of France and England, in modern times, put the question to rest, and demonstrate to the world that it was fabulous?—or, rather, why were they excited by it? Why did they not let it pass with indifference? Why could they not rest? Why cannot skeptics now rest? Why the listless, belligerent and opposing malignity of all apostates? Why not pass it off as an old fable, a witch story, or tale of fortune-telling? Because the spirit of the Book itself, the divine nature in it, takes such a hold upon our spirits, that we cannot let it rest. God is in it, warring against sin, evincing his glorious power and divine nature in all its parts. The struggle over the Old Testament, beginning more than three thousand years ago, and that over the New, commencing almost two thousand years ago and lasting to the present time, with an overwhelming majority in the opposition, all the time, and its having a stronger hold on the world now than ever before, not only evinces that man cannot put it down, but that God has been with it from its earliest incipiency. Could it have stood, with the weak defense of one family alone, against the combined powers and opposition of all the nations of the earth, from the calling of Abraham to Christ, if God had not been with it? Could Abraham and his descendants alone have kept the sacred oracles, first during a space of near five hundred years, in the form of unwritten tradition, or from the calling of Abraham to Moses, or the giving of the law, at Sinai, and in manuscript from then to Christ, with all the new acquisitions from the prophets, in opposition to the combined and numerous hosts of all the Pagan nations of the earth, if God had not been with them? The idea then, that a new order of men, without learning, any superior talent, worldly means, influence and beginning, with but a small number, should take the sacred deposit in hand, combine the Jewish Scriptures and add to them the Christian Scriptures, keep the whole, and transmit them from generation to generation, till they reach our time, in defiance of the opposition of all Judaism, Paganism and infidelity, without the special care, of Divine Providence, is preposterous in the highest degree! A greater absurdity could not well be imagined!

When we turn our attention to the times of Wickliff, and see how few and feeble the friends of the Bible were. Infidelity abounded in all directions. A bigoted, blinded and unregenerate priesthood, sustained by a band of civil rulers, as ungodly as themselves, boasting of the imperfect Scriptures which they bad, sometimes declaring them *letter* than the inspired originals, opposed Wickliff with every power, and never ceased their hostility till he was persecuted unto death. This great and good man, however, infused once more a desire for the pure Word of the Lord. This could not be obtained without pure versions. The subject of translating became an all-absorbing question. Wickliff, Tyndale, and young Frith were the great soul of this important and most essential movement gave it the energies of their lives, and sealed their testimony with their martyrdom. This work grew regularly, advanced and produced translation after translation. All the English versions read, enjoyed, and for which so many thanksgivings and praises have devoutly ascended to heaven, have come from these great struggles. Can any man imagine that these feeble instrumentalities ever could have withstood the immense torrent of opposition, succeeded and established in the heart of the English people the desire for the pure Word of God, which lead to so many translations, if the

Lord had not been with them? Surely not. They were clearly in the right. They were for enlightening the world; and God who commanded the light to shine out of darkness; who anciently said, "Let there be light, and there was light;" who shined in the hearts of the Apostles, giving the light of the glory of God in the face of Jesus Christ, was with those holy men, or was with his own gracious work, of translating his pure Word into the language of the people—to "MAKE IT VERY PLAIN." Can any man have the shadow of a doubt that God was with this work? Lid not God hear the prayers of these holy men? In answer to their holy prayers, that the Word of God might be translated—made very plain—the Lord has given us the Holy Scriptures in our mother tongue.

No opposition can withstand God. The work that is of God cannot be overthrown. Giving the Bible to the world was of God. Making it very plain—interpreting it to those who speak another tongue from that in which it was originally written, is the work of God—the work of the Christian ministry. Their effort is, and should be, to interpret every word which the Lord has spoken—make it plain to all the people. Can there be any doubt but they are right in this effort? Is not the desire to have every word in the Bible correctly translated into our mother tongue, right? Is the effort to translate every word which God has spoken correctly into the English language, right? Are not the prayers that every word in the Bible may be correctly translated into the English language, and every language on earth, right? Will not the Lord be with those who thus pray? The Bible is divine, which is the same as to say, *that it is infallibly right*. The Bible is that which God gave us—his entire revelation to man. This is in dead languages, and must be translated into the languages of the earth, before the people can read it. The command to "preach the gospel to every creature"—"in all the world"—"to all nations," cannot be obeyed without translating. It is infallibly right to translate it correctly into every language in the world. Those honestly trying to do this, are infallibly right in their effort. Their prayers, that the Word of God may be correctly translated in all tongues spoken by man, are infallibly right They may err in the course they pursue, but there cannot be any error in their object—that which they are praying for.

The friends of this great and good work, then, should work with the full assurance that the work is the work of God; and consequently that God is, and will be, with them. They may pray, with full assurance of faith, that the Lord will hear them, answer their prayers and aid them in their work. The Lord is in the Bible Union. not providential hand has been clearly visible in it from the beginning.

-----o-----

SPIRITUALISM AND SPIRIT-RAPPINGS.
BY JOHN YOUNG.

Among the many surprising things of this stirring age, one of the most surprising is modern Spiritualism. When it was first alleged that sounds were made and tables moved without material causes, sober persons set the rappers down for insane or dishonest.

Although the adhesion of Judge Edmunds to the ranks of spiritualism, gave the matter notoriety and character, yet it produced little faith, as the common opinion seemed to be that the Judge was honest, but weak in mind, perhaps from hard legal study. In despite, however, of all the contempt with which it was treated at first, and all the hatred which has fallen upon it since, it did not sink before ridicule. This curious development has held on its way rejoicing, and now appears likely to become a permanent institution.

There are many, still, who affect to despise it so much that they will not seek for any information on the subject. This we think betrays moral cowardice on their part.

These persons have more faith in the allegations than they are willing to acknowledge.

If one or two traveling impostors, for the sake of money, were pretending to work miracles, we could safely afford to despise and look over their claim as we do the assertions of patent medicine discoverers. But in all the important towns and villages in the country, persons, upright and truthful in all the relations of life, testify to wonders seen and heard. The things are not done in a corner, but multitudes are eye and ear witnesses of the marvels. Then those wonders are certainly of the most astounding nature. Tables walk through rooms, marching. and counter-marching at the word of command, like things of life. Musical instruments breathe forth sweet melody without any visible performers. Hands without bodies pass round the room and salute the company by gentle squeezes. Pens become endowed with the *ictus scribendi* and make characters which puzzle the learned to decipher. Now we affirm that, when things as astounding as these are alleged to have transpired not far off, but even in our own vicinity, not under the eyes of a few but of thousands, we cannot any longer parry off the subject.

The age is, no doubt, a fast one, and prone to foolish excitements, but it cannot be that under all this there is nothing but knavery or insanity.

We have too great faith in humanity ever to believe that such largo numbers have conspired to deceive for nought, their fellow-citizens, and we know too much of the intelligence and sagacity of many of the examining committees, to believe that little girls could dupe them by an artifice.

That there is something singular in the matter, we feel confident, but then it is not so easy to find out what that something is. However difficult the solution of the mystery may be, we hold that that solution must be made. The investigation should be made fearlessly. It should be made impartially with only a love of truth before the mind, and it should be made speedily. That churches are losing members in large numbers through the Eastern States, seems to be admitted by the journals of the day. If, then, the stability of the church and the evidences of our holy religion are in peril, it surely becomes us to apply our minds to the matter, and furnish a solution that may satisfy the public mind.

If a man declares that he is altogether free from prejudice, he probably thereby shows that he knows little of himself. We will not do tins, but we affirm that if we have bias, prejudice or partiality on this subject, then we know it not. Should Spiritualism, with all its high claims, turn out to be true, we would indeed be surprised, but not displeased. To us it would be altogether a satisfactory affair to hold converse with the mighty dead. We would indeed thank God for it, and instead of upsetting our faith, we think it would be salutary to our drooping spirits. Yet, after giving, as we think, the weight to all testimony in its favor, we acknowledge that we are, at present without this hope in the world.

Then, should it appear that the true solution of this affair is a scientific one, we shall be well pleased. When new laws of mind or matter are discovered, the human family are more enriched thereby than when mines of gold are laid open to tempt man's love of wealth.

In this direction we look with strong confidence. We believe that, by the agitation of this subject, we shall become acquainted with a great force, operating in our mental and physical constitution, which has not as yet been developed in our philosophy.

Franklin and the Paris Committee rejected the experiments of Mesmer, but science is about to receive from that quarter a discovery of greater value than any made since Franklin ascertained the identity of lightning and electricity.

Believing, then, that spirit-rapping either

can now, or soon will be explicable, upon principles purely scientific, without the aid of miracle, we can most cordially bid it God speed.

We shrink not from it as the work of the Devil. We believe not in it as the work of Spirits.

But we say, let all rappers continue faithfully in their work, for we believe that they are simply performing scientific experiments, which, when once classified and their causes discovered, shall issue in great good to mankind.

One solution of the mystery indeed has been attempted, against which, perhaps, we entertain some prejudice. Many clergymen have delivered discourses, and some have published philippics, in which they declare that these are wonders wrought in our midst by the Devil. Now we were taught when a boy to entertain a sincere hatred towards his Satanic majesty, and we hate him still. Then to verily believe that he now has power to pull us about, to buzz in our ears, to spill our dinners off our tables, is far from a comfortable faith to us. We will not believe it. See what mockery falls upon the good men who tried the witches and their enchantments, in good New England. We pity the witches and despise the bigotry of these good men.

Now let us take care lest posterity thus mock our memory, and call us simpletons. It is an easy thing to quote passages of scripture, but whether these apply or not to the thing in hand, is a grave question. We think it would be very hard to find prophecies or passages about Demoniacal possession, so specific their character that they could lawfully be supposed to look exactly to the developments of this age.

The preacher can bring up a full array of texts, and hold up the most solemn threatenings in the Bible against the wizards who peep and mutter.

Now, if the hearers could be docile enough to take for granted that our present race of spiritualists are the parties referred to, all might be well. But at this point supposition must come in, for there is not a tittle of evidence in proof of such a strange assumption.

Some men have become insane through Spiritualism. But nervous, excitable people become crazy through religious revivals, through commercial panics, through Know-Nothing alarms about the Pope.

Spiritualism is no doubt doing injury at present, as it is carrying many away from Christianity; but this is partly owing to their own excitability and folly, and partly caused by the tirades of denunciation that have fallen from the sacred desk.

When upright persons see wonderful things which they cannot explain, they would gladly receive a reasonable solution if it were given in a friendly way, and continue good Christians as before. But when ministers charge them with imposture, or warn them that they are falling into league with the devil, when they are conscious of no wrong, it is not wonderful that they forsake these churches and cast their influence against a system that would rob them of their rights as free investigators.

Many infidels are undoubtedly using Spiritualism as an effective weapon against the church and the Bible.

Denunciation will not stop this, but whenever a satisfactory solution of the mystery involved in this thing shall be made, these men will find their arms paralyzed, and the foundations of Christianity shall stand firm as of old.

We write these things more by way of stirring up the right kind of careful and impartial inquiry into the matter, than for the purpose of offering a solution of our own.

We have, however, our opinion, and the public are welcome to take it for what it is worth. From all that we have read and seen of this matter, we hold that spirit-rappings is simply a new phase of mesmerism, in which the mesmerizer controls the mind and belief of the mesmerized circle who are seated with him by virtue of the electric current from his brain through the circle.

The passage of an acid or an alkali from one glass into another even through an intervening cup of pure water, without giving taste to the water, is a very mysterious result, yet the chemist exhibits it with ease by his galvanic circle. When metals leave their oxygen and journey to the negative pole of the battery, a remarkable motive power is thus operating before our eyes.

When a current of electricity, created by the action of acid water upon zinc, moves a machine with a thousand revolutions in a minute, we feel no disposition to deny to nature the forces which are thus operating before us. When we become even in a slight degree acquainted with these hidden forces that bind the atoms of all nature together, and especially operate actively in animal bodies, we are taught to wait upon nature, rather than deny to her powers which we may not understand.

A few passes by a magnet over iron will render that iron magnetic, and small pieces of iron will rush to the new formed magnet, and adhere to it with pertinacity. This has been successfully practiced by magnetizers on their fellow men. They make passes from the head downwards until the hand of the patient will follow theirs as the needle follows the magnet.

There is undoubtedly an electric or magnetic force in the human body by which one man can control the movements and actions of another, after the current has become established between them.

We suppose that most of those who deny this in the present day, are stubborn men who cannot believe even their own senses, and think their fellow men are gross deceivers.

The brain of man is certainly a great central battery for the production of the electric influence. It was long a question how the nerves conveyed sensations to the mind, and motions from the mind to other parts. Some thought the nerves were cords, effecting their work by pulling, but this could not be, for the nerve is a pulpy mass, and not a cord. Then animal spirits were supposed to flow up and down the nerves, but the medullary substance of the nerve is not fluid enough for this.

Physiologists, we suppose, now agree that the nerves are conductors of electricity. Hence, when the galvanic current is applied to the nerves of a dead animal, it will be convulsed and move as if endowed with life.

Mesmerism has only proved that these electric currents can pass beyond the nerves, and, by a transit through the air or the earth, can affect another person so powerfully that his nerves are controlled, and even the action of his brain influenced by the mesmerizer. That even the will and intelligence of the mesmerized person are under the control of the magnetizer is evident. I have seen a well-dressed, respectable man made to fall upon the floor and spread forth his hands to swim, at the bidding of his magnetizer, perfectly indifferent to the roars of laughter from a large assembly. This could not have been a trick, for men will not patiently allow themselves to be made fools of when they have their senses.

We take it, then, as true, that one man can control the mind of another by the electric current. Now, shall we, with these views, enter a spirit circle. The parties are seated around a table, the arms are pressed upon that table, and silence ensues. Why should the arms press upon the table, if not to establish an electric current from the body to the table? Perhaps the operator rises and recedes across the room and the table tips over and follows his movements. This is nothing more than what a magnet will do with small needles any time. Perhaps questions are asked, and the answer most likely discovers something known only to the asker. This, then, if it does occur, is nothing more than the mental sympathy or clairvoyance, claimed long since by the mesmerizer. Perhaps the arms of those sitting at the table are suddenly raised up, and then struck down on the table. This certainly indicates that a great nervous or electric force is moving in either one direction or another. But let greater stillness prevail; for lo! a piano utters its music without a human hand touching it. This music, is heard by all, if they are under the prevailing electric influence, but if they are proof against that influence they hear nothing.

Perhaps an invisible hand shakes hands with the company. Yes, but this is only when a skilful and well practiced mesmerizer is present, who has willed that their senses should be thus affected, and they are affected accordingly. But if the mind of the the mesmerizer is not in trim, no spirits will appear.

This was the case lately in the Court of Napoleon, Emperor of France. The Emperor gave audience to Mr. Hall, an American Spiritualist, who proposed to make spirits perform wonders. The first day appointed the mesmerizer's mind was not right, and he declared that he was too nervous—he could do nothing. On the next day his mind was elastic and the spirits waited on his call. The Emperor and his Court all testify that they shook hands with a spirit. But a Professor of the Soarbonne, who was present, believes that it was effected by the electric force of the operator controlling the minds and sense of the company.

I was myself present on one occasion when a table was made so heavy that no one out of four of us could lift the end of it from the floor, but a fifth person who was present could always lift it with perfect case. I explained the matter to myself, by supposing that his mind was not under the control of the operator, while ours had yielded to that control.

I hope that my preaching brethren who maintain it to be the work of the Devil, and my friends, the Spiritualists, will both pardon me for differing from their views.

My views of the matter happily relieve me from entertaining unkind thoughts of the operators in this thing. They are dealing with a power concerning which they confess that they know little, and as most things in America take a religious shape, they have unwittingly been carried into the notion that they have a new revelation, and, therefore, that they ought to found a new church. I believe they generally inculcate love, mercy and benevolence. These points I hold to be in accordance with true Orthodox Theology. Their spiritual church circles will soon pass away, but a great truth concerning the human mind will remain. Let us deal mercifully with men, for we are all prone to err, but let us fearlessly seek for truth, for it will stand forever.

-----o-----

REMARKS.

We have looked carefully over the foregoing, but must confess—whether it be ascribeable to bigotry, prejudice, or obtuseness—we are not any relieved, by the middle position set forth, but certainly without any evidence, by Prof. Young. He, it is true, would rid religion of Spiritualism. But how is he prepared to do this? The answer is, by separating it from all connection with departed spirits; by acknowledging the things done, and accounting for the strange phenomena upon scientific principles; or by assigning philosophical or natural causes adequate to produce the strange effect. He looks down from his lofty position with complacency, hailing the new-born *science,* "likely to become a permanent institution," with much joy, exhorting, "Let all rappers continue in their work;" but mildly and affectionately informs them that there is a slight mistake in their work, viz.: That their entire pretense of communicating with the spirits of the dead, or, as he expresses it, the "altogether satisfactory affair to hold converse with the mighty dead," for which he would "thank God," is without evidence, and he is left "without this hope in the world." On the other hand, the preachers who "bring up a full array of texts, and hold up the most solemn threatenings in the Bible against the wizards who peep and mutter," he informs us, are wide of the mark. All these, he assures us, have "not a tittle of evidence in proof of such a strange assumption," as that Spiritualists are the party referred to. These he sets aside with a dash or two of the pen and a back-band blow touching their "moral cowardice," without an attempt to refute their positions, or even evidence that he has read them. How are we to stand before one who bounds through such a subject as this, setting aside both the former parties in the premises, and setting forth a new position, at a few dashes of his pen, without a single argument against either of the positions he pronounces against, or in favor of the one he assumes?

But we must look at this new discovery! He says, "We hold that spirit-rappings is simply a new phase of mesmerism, in which the mesmerizer controls the mind and belief of the mesmerized circle who are seated with him, by virtue of the the electric current from his brain through the circle." This is the *belief,* or what the Professor holds! But this does not relieve us much, as it is simply calling the *same thing by another name.* Speaking, then, of spirit-rapping under the name of mesmerism, he proceeds to tell us what he has seen, as follows: "I was myself present on one occasion when a table was made so heavy that no one out of four of us could lift the end of it from the floor, but a fifth person who was present could always lift it with perfect ease." This is what mesmerism *can do.* The Professor enlightens us, then, as follows: "I explained the matter to myself, by supposing that his mind was not under the control of the operator, while ours had yielded to that control." That is. four of the company, the Professor one of the number, were mesmerized and one was not. Now lay this along side of the case be had stated just before, in these words: "I have seen a well dressed, respectable man made to fall upon the floor and spread forth his hands to swim, at the bidding of his magnetizer, perfectly indifferent to the roars of laughter from a largo assembly." Reader, what think you of the competency of this man, while thus dispossessed of his reason, to testify to anything that transpired while he was in this deplorable situation? Certainly he could give no testimony while thus literally and in the fullest sense "made a fool of." Yet Prof. Young, and the other three, who could not lift the table, were under the same influence—under the control of the mesmerizer, or mesmerized! Yet neither he nor any other one of the four mesmerized, nor the one not mesmerized, knew that they were mesmerized! If mesmerizers can thus "make a fool of" a man, can we receive his testimony concerning things that transpired while he was thus "made a fool of?"

The Professor continues: "But we say, let rappers continue faithfully in their work, for we believe that they are simply performing scientific experiments, which, when once classified and their causes discovered, shall issue in great good to mankind." What an acquisition to science, this stupendous art of dethroning a man's reason, throwing "a well dressed, respectable man" upon the floor, and set him to swimming for life, thus making a fool of him! What splendid discoveries!—interesting experiments! What a scene for "roars of laughter from a large assembly!" A pretty scene, this for "roars of laughter"—a man thrown into *insanity far* the time being! For all this laughing, and this wicked experimenting, sorrow, moaning and anguish will be the legitimate return. From it there will be no escape. How many! O, how many poor creatures have allowed themselves thus to be experimented with—yes, tampered with, and laughed over by a thoughtless rabble, and a heartless operator, under this most dangerous influence, again and again, till their reason for the last time departed, and departed to return no more! What reply does our brother make to this? He may say, it is weakness, but we shudder at his reply. It is this: "But nervous, excitable people become crazy through religious revivals, through commercial panics, through Know-Nothing alarms about the Pope." Is it right, then, to press and encourage these excitements, and produce more and more of the same results? Let him fear who produces these results, no matter by what means, and let him fear equally who encourages such experimenting, as there is no escape from the criminality in either case. Let every man fear and tremble who gives countenance to anything productive of insanity.

Prof. Young says. "Spiritualism is no doubt doing injury at present, as it is carrying many away from Christianity." How can a preacher of the gospel, and a Professor in a Christian University, then, say, "Let all rappers continue faithfully in their work?" How can he encourage them with the consolation, that they are "simply performing scientific experiments?" Will he, as Professor in the North Western Christian University, "perform scientific experiments," that will turn many away from Christianity?" But extenuating spirit-rapping, he says, "I believe they (rappers) generally inculcate love, mercy, and benevolence. These points I hold to be in accordance with true Orthodox Theology." Now we should like to know where this teaching comes from! Not from the "mighty dead," according to Prof. Young, for so far as hearing from them is concerned, he is "without hope in the world." Not from any spirit of revelation, for then "the true solution of this affair" would not be "simply a scientific one!" Where, then, does the teaching come from, according to his theory? From the operator, who produces insanity in a man, makes a fool of him, making him lay on the floor, trying to swim; who takes possession not only of the bodies of four men, so that neither of them can lift the end of a table from the floor, but can possess their minds, and make them think or say what he pleases. He makes the subject teach "love, mercy, and benevolence," which Prof. Young "holds to be in accordance with true Orthodox Theology." But he thinks their "spiritual church circles will soon pass away," and pleads that we "deal mercifully with men." The Lord knows when these dens of vice, called "spiritual church circles," will pass away, but not till they pass immense numbers into apostasy, others into the insane asylum, and many down to irremediable perdition. We desire to "deal mercifully with men," but we must not delude ourselves with the notion that we are dealing mercifully with them, when we are encouraging them to persevere in Spiritualism. If this is dealing mercifully with them, we know not how we would forsake, abandon, and give them up, to go speedily down to the most disgraceful ruin.

"The tree is known by its fruit," says the Great Teacher. The fruits of mesmerism, spirit-rapping, and all of the same category, have from the commencement been evil, and only evil, continually. Think, O man of God! of the vast number in the lunatic asylums, from its dreadful ravages! Reflect upon the number of orphan, or worse than orphan, children, robbed of their fathers or mothers, by the lamentable ravages of Spiritualism! Look at the desolation in character—the vast number of men and women who have utterly fallen, become utterly debased and corrupt, and tell if any man can estimate the ruin sent through the world by this loathsome and carnal thing! Look at the interminable licentiousness induced by it, and then say whether good men should encourage it! On the other hand, let any man point to any good it has ever done! I care not how much it teaches of "love, mercy, and benevolence," so long as its tendency is corrupting, sensualizing, and demoralizing. And that such is its demonstrated tendency, no candid and well informed man can deny without a blush. But, as Prof. Young pleads for mercy, in our dealings with spirit-rappers, we, in conclusion, submit the following:

1. If spirit-manifestations, spirit-rapping, or mesmerism, as you may choose to call it, is what it professes to be, it is to hold intercourse with the spirits of the dead—to communicate with the dead. This claim, we aver, is necromancy, and he who does it is a necromancer—"a consulter with familiar spirits," and no learning or ingenuity can evade it. The Lord says, "All that do these things are an abomination unto the Lord." Deut. xviii: 11-12. The severest penalty under the law of Moses was pronounced and inflicted upon any person convicted of this crime. Under Christ, it excludes from the kingdom of God.

2, If Spiritualists have had no communications with spirits, they have either been egregiously deluded, or are the most outrageous pretenders the world ever contained, and in either case are deceivers, deluding all under their influence; and, as such, should be rejected. It is self-evident, in this case, no matter whether the delusion is intentional or not, that all good people should avoid it. If it is a delusion merely, they are deceived and deceiving others, unintentionally; but if it is merely pretense, it is the most basely false and lying pretense that could be, resulting in many instances in leaving the Bible, the church, and their former associates, and entering a new fraternity, not having one feature in it except the most loathsome and degrading.

3. If it is simply, as Prof. Young thinks a natural cause, producing a natural effect, or simply mesmerism—in which the mesmerizer has complete control over his victim, so much so that he can prostrate him upon the floor, and make him attempt to swim, without being conscious that he is "made a fool of"—or make him lift at the end of a table without being able to lift if from the floor—possesses such absolute control over the mind as not to be conscious what is going on in one case, but perfectly conscious, and a veritable witness in another, it will certainly "go on its way rejoicing," and "become a permanent institution!" What a valuable institution it will be too! The operator possessing this power, is then prepared to victimise all susceptible of this influence, in any way he may desire. How easily he could empty the pockets of the poor dupe, upon the floor, trying to swim. How easily could he induce him to sign any instrument of writing, commit any forgery, swear falsely, or blow out the brains of any man the operator might desire to destroy. How safe our fair daughters would be in reach of men possessing such power!

But where has it been turned to any good account, or where can it be? Prof. Young does not inform us, and he will not—*he cannot*. Will he thus encourage that which he has not and cannot show to be productive of any good? We care nothing about the feats they can perform, no more than those that can be performed by gamblers, stage actors, or magicians, nor is any teacher of science under any obligations to investigate it. No man should allow himself to be "made a fool of by it."

We have one word to say about the "moral cowardice" of those who refuse to investigate spirit-rapping. There is one ambiguous expression in the foregoing article. Prof. Young informs us that he was taught to fear his Satanic majesty, the devil, in his early life, and adds, that he fears him yet. But the chaffy language that follows, is in a different tone and spirit from anything we find in the Scriptures in reference to that arch-deceiver. The same air of lightness, fearlessness. and indifference, pervades the whole piece. It evinces nothing of that deep, godly, and prayerful concern for either the church or the world, manifested in the whole lives of the Apostles and first Christians. But, on the contrary, he sympathizes with that reckless spirit that will run into Spiritualism in defiance of all expostulations. Now we deny either the right or the necessity to investigate every silly and useless thing that comes along. Nor can any man, that appreciates true science, true learning, and the real importance of institutions of learning, raised up by the donations of Christian people, to be disgraced with all the idle humbuggery of these times, under the name of *science*. There is a difference as wide as the poles between real science and modern humbuggery, and while a real scientific man has the courage to master the former, he has both the courage and manliness to repudiate the latter, and warn the unwary against it, as he would against the grossest corruption. B. F.

-----o-----

BRACKEN ASSOCIATION OF UNITED BAPTISTS.
NUMBER V.

From a misunderstanding of the term *regeneration,* as used by Bro. Campbell and others, in the beginning of our effort to introduce a pure speech, and a pure practice—to bring about the union of God's people, scattered in the "dark and cloudy day"—and from the want of proper caution and prudence on the part of some of our speakers and writers, we do not wonder that many honest persons innocently misunderstood us, and, therefore, innocently misrepresented us. But after the lapse of more than a quarter of a century—after a sufficient time has been given to allow the first great outburst of party feeling and prejudice to subside—after our preachers have been heard, and our writings read throughout the entire bounds of the Bracken Association, by all disposed to understand us, and do us justice, we confess we cannot conceive how Elder Gardner, and his co-elders, could allow themselves, in the year of our Lord, 1856, to send out in a grave historic document, the stale, foul slander, that our people, who were baptized for the remission of their sins, were baptized "without professing a previous change of heart." This is clearly the purport of their charge, or else their language is most ambiguous, and calculated to deceive. For myself I can say, I have been preaching Christ, in my humble way, and baptizing, from my boyhood, some thirty-seven years—that within that long period, I have immersed several thousands; yet, if *ever I baptized one of all that number who had not a "new heart"—a heart to love God and hate sin* (for all were required to profess it), then was I imposed upon—deceived. And I hazard nothing in saying, that every fellow-laborer in this cause, recognized by our people, can adopt the same sentiment in reference to his course in this particular. But we press this matter no further. It saddens our heart—it grieves us much to think that our neighbors, of the Bracken Association of Baptists, from whom, as *Baptists,* we had a right to hope for better things, should treat us so badly! We hope they will see their error, and yet do us justice. As much as lieth in us, we wish to live peaceably with all men, and especially with the Baptists. They have, doubtless, many great and good men among them; and I still think, upon the whole, both they and we are becoming more enlightened, and that we are approximating to each other, despite the efforts, in certain quarters, to prevent such a result. We have seen that those of our people who were baptized by the Baptists upon an "experience of grace," can all get back into the Baptist churches of the Bracken Association, by "renouncing their errors, and repenting of their sins," against said churches; that "then, and *not till* then, can we [Baptists] commune with them." (Minutes, p. 29.) To understand this whole matter aright, we must remember, that, in the Circular Letter of their Minutes, the Elders of the Bracken Association are making an argument to justify the Baptists in refusing to allow any of our people to commune with them, and by parity of reasoning—in refusing to allow any of their people to commune with ns. But I need not have said "by parity of reasoning," for the Circular leaves us nothing to infer. (See p. 27). Hear it: "Every Baptist, therefore, that *partakes* at the communion table of another denomination, and every Baptist church, that *welcomes* a member of another denomination to her communion table"—is guilty of the abandonment of the "*distinctive principles*" of the Baptists, and "becomes a *partaker of* the *errors* of others." That is plain enough! We may not commune with the Baptists, nor may the Baptists commune with us! But if, notwithstanding this Bracken- Bull, there should be intercommunion between some of our congregations?! What then? Let them be informed, if they are Baptists, that they are "guilty" of great inconsistency—of the "abandonment"—of "our *distinctive principles.*" "Let every pastor *explain and defend* the *practice* of our churches." But, says Bro. Gardner, to do the work effectually, not only must the pastor explain and defend our practice, but "Let every church *exemplify* the truth in her practice." This is plain. Let every church whose members violate Baptist law, in communing with any of our people, be dealt with, and, if possible, reclaimed from their error and sin in so communing; or, if they prove incorrigible, let them be excluded! And let every church put up a fence round its table, so high that none of our people, who "teach radical and destructive errors," will dare *"intrude* themselves" upon them! More of some matters here, under another head. Our object, in this paper, in the above references to the Circular, is to show, that it teaches, not only that all our people should be excluded from "sacramental communion," with Baptist churches; but, especially, and emphatically, that all Baptists who will recognize us as God's people, and commune with us, and persevere in it, ought to be—must be excluded from their "sacramental communion," and "church communion," though they may still hold "Christian communion with them," and "love them as brethren," though justly kicked out of their churches, as many such good brethren were more than a quarter of a century ago of whom the Circular says, "we still love many of them as Christian brethren!!" A rather unceremonious way of treating Christian brethren, Christ's brethren!! May He not say to such, in the great day, "Inasmuch as ye excluded these my brethren from your churches, you excluded me!!" Take heed, brethren, how you treat Christ's disciples! "Better have a mill-stone hanged about your necks, and be drowned in the depths of the sea, than offend against one of these little ones that believe in me." So teaches the Divine Master. But of the inconsistency of such a course we have spoken in a former number.

Having now seen the grounds upon which all our people are to be excluded from "sacramental communion" with the Bracken Association Baptists, and the terms upon which those of them who were once members of their churches, may get back into them—we wish now to see upon what terms, "all those Reformers, who were baptized for the actual remission of their sins, without professing a previous change of heart, and pardon," may be restored to their communion; or whether any terms are offered?! Alas! I fear we shall find no door opened for us! They have been kind enough to open a door to their quondam brethren, whom they justly excluded from their churches, for heresy in faith and practice, many long years ago, and have been pleased to state very plainly the terms upon which they may return, and be "gladly" received to their communion—"church and sacramental communion!" But there is no voice lifted in our favor—no door of the church opened to us! Why is this? Have we committed the sin against the Holy Spirit, that hath never forgiveness?! I hope not. Ah, say Bro. Gardner, James & Co., "No intelligent Baptist regards you as baptized at all, if converted." And, therefore, all those Baptists that commune with you, and allow you to commune with them, are a very silly sort of Baptists, great dunces indeed! This explains the whole matter of indifference in regard to us. The language of the Circular, taken together, amount to this: Those of your people who were once members of the Baptist churches, and who professed a change of heart, and pardon before they were baptized, have genuine conversion and baptism; but as to all the rest, you have neither conversion nor baptism at all!!" This is very liberal! Who dare gainsay it! For Bro. Gardner, who (with his co-elders) always teaches and speaks the truth, and believes in "fair and honest dealings," says, on page 36, "The fact is, the Baptists are the most *consistent* and *liberal of* all *others,* in their practice of communion!" Certainly they are!! Eld. Gardner says they are, and Eld. Gardner is an honorable man! Eld. J. James, and Hunt & Co., all say they are the most consistent and liberal of all people, and these are all honorable men. This matter, then, is disposed of. But still the question recurs—What is to be done with this class of our people, should any of them (as sometimes happens under peculiar circumstances), wish to join with Baptist churches? As a matter of course, as "they have not been baptized at all"— have not even "professed a change of heart," they must be converted, and immersed, and then, like any other aliens, they may be members of the only true, holy, infallible, apostolic, catholic church, which *teaches, and always has taught "the truth, the whole truth, and nothing but the truth!* But is this the course the Baptists generally take in such cases? Certainly not. I have heard of no such case in many years. I know of some who were received into the Baptist church, whose baptism was never questioned! And were it not that Bro. Gardner has declared it to be a fixed fact, that the Baptists are the most consistent of all people, I should say, there is a most glaring inconsistency here. What! Consistent for Baptists to take unbaptized, not to say unconverted, persons into their churches, and hold "sacramental communion" with them! I am positively tempted almost above that I am able to bear, to say this is inconsistent! But Eld. Gardner says the Baptists are the most consistent of all others, and he ought to know! Bro. Gardner allows and deplores the fact, that some of the Baptists are ignorant of the scriptural reasons for their practice, and "consequently are favorable to open communion." Go to work, then, Bro. Gardner, you and Elders James, Hunt & Co., and set your own people right upon this subject—and then bring up all our people who have united with you, that were baptized for the remission of sins, and immerse them again! Then let it be understood, that, hereafter, all of that class of our people that would belong to the Baptist church, must be re-baptized and reconverted, and our people will soon understand you, and I think it very likely you will contribute largely to the cause of pure, apostolic Christianity. In our next, we shall notice the charge of inconsistency brought against us, in regard to open communion. J. ROGERS.

-----O-----

UPWARD TENDENCY—REFORMATION NOT A FAILURE—MISSIONARY WORK.

We feel truly like thanking God and taking courage. The Lord says, "Return unto me, and I will return unto you." The Lord's people are returning to him, putting their trust in him and calling upon him. He is hearing them, blessing them, and extending his work among them. Blessed be his name forever and ever! "He will be with those who love him, and keep his commandments, to a thousand generations." A general unanimity of feeling, harmony and co-operation of action are obtaining, that will tell mightily for good in years to come. We have been corresponding largely with the brotherhood for fifteen years, but especially for the last two years. During this latter period, we have made every effort in our power to determine, as near as possible, where the lever should be placed to move the cause. We have ascertained as clearly, in our estimation, as anything of the kind can be determined, that the evangelical wheel needs the lever under it, to raise it, set it more effectually in motion, and keep it in motion. Evangelizing is, of all works, the work that must be done. No success attends, or ever can attend, the cause any place without the evangelist. The word of the living God must be faithfully, warmly and powerfully preached, both to convert sinners and build up saints. All the schemes in creation, or dreamed about, imagined and theorized upon, will avail nothing without the preaching of the word of God.

Thus all the more enlightened men among us feel, and to this point they are moving, and upon it they are bringing their forces to bear. Since we have been corresponding for the Missionary Society, we have felt the pulse of the brotherhood largely, and ascertained that there is a oneness of mind and feeling pervading the body—a concert of action obtaining, that must be followed by a result of a most cheering and encouraging character. It is now clearly understood, that it is not fine theorizing upon *the kind* of preachers we should have, that we need; nor do we need theorizing upon *the manner* in which the preaching should be done; but we need *preachers themselves,* who will go into the field and give us *living examples in the work*. We need men—not *angels,* but *men*—to preach the word of the living God to their fellow creatures; or, rather, we need the *preaching* from the men we have. We do not need that God should raise us a new set of men to preach, for the men we now have, after all the complaints that may be justly admitted, are the best men for this work on the Lord's green earth. We are neither to expect infallibility nor perfection in men; nor are we to conclude; because we see weaknesses and imperfections in preaching brethren, that other men do not have them. All men possess them. If you could look through the parties around us, and know them as you do the Christian communities with which we are identified, you would see sights that would astonish you.

There is but one remedy for us, as a religious body, as sure as we are human beings, and that is for both the preachers and private members we have, to buckle on the armor and go to work with every power which we possess. The decree has gone forth, and is as immutable as the purpose of God, that we must *work or die.* Theorizing about work will not answer the purpose, much less thinking how to avoid it. The work itself must be done, or we must die; and there is no way to get it done but to go at it and do it. The preachers we have must do the preaching. They are the only men we need look to. There are no others who know how to do it; nor are there others who have the disposition. We need not look to other men now living, who will do this work, for they are not to be found; nor need we wait for others to be raised up; for we may be gone to render an account of our stewardship before that shall be done. The preachers must go into the work, persevere in it and do it. To them the brethren must look; they are the men the brethren must urge and encourage. They must be admonished to quit their merchandise, shops and business of every description; brush the dust from the Bible and bring it to bear upon the world, as in days gone by. They must think of the value of the souls of men, or the Lord will call them to account. The accounts are coming in more encouragingly of the success of the cause than for a long time previously. We are in receipt of many letters from brethren, whose praise is in all the churches, of a most cheering character, in reference to the Missionary Society. Funds for this branch of the great missionary work are coming in, oneness of mind prevailing, and unity of action obtaining, for which we are truly thankful. Churches are making and sending up contributions, individuals are becoming life members, and the work is progressing finely. Brethren are taking hold of the State Missions with great earnestness and efficiency. Churches are also reviving in almost all directions. Many good preachers are cutting loose from secular pursuits and entering upon the work with great force. Cannot scores more be moved to do the same? Let us fix our minds upon the work and push it forward by every means which the Lord has given. What will it amount to, if we gain a little of the world for our children, but do nothing for them religiously? They have souls as well as bodies, and what an eternal mistake to do all for their bodies and nothing for their souls. What will all this mighty grasp for the world amount to, it we live and die without piety or devotion to God? What will it avail to be rich in this world, but poor towards God? What does it amount to for men to be enterprising in the affairs of this world, but without enterprise in religion? The notions of many men enlarge, their horizon extends, and they become truly great in all that is worldly, but the moment you present religion, you find them in all the little, narrow and circumscribed notions of a century back. They have not advanced one whit, ennobled their hearts or expanded their views in the least.

This is not the case with men awake in the cause of religion. Their minds enlarge, hearts expand, and souls are ennobled. They would disdain the idea of doing no more now, with the mighty facilities we have, than men did without these facilities twenty-five years ago. They are for doing something in religion bearing some proportion to the means with which the Lord has blessed us, and thus evincing that we are deserving of the times and opportunities bestowed upon us. The Lord help the children of the kingdom to be wise in their generation, and so to number their days as to enable them to to give a good account in the great day!

B. F.

-----o-----

Correspondence

LEXINGTON, MO., April 14, 1857.

BRO. FRANKLIN—Dear Sir:—I have received the *American Christian Review,* past and current volumes, and am very much pleased with the work. Its earnest and impressive style; the laborious and self-sacrificing spirit that it inculcates; and, above all, the humble, but confident reliance upon the Divine protection and support, and upon the fidelity and liberality of the brotherhood, too, which is manifested, meet my most cordial and hearty approbation.

Your essays upon evangelizing, and upon the ministry and its support, particularly that portion of the latter that insists upon the importance, indeed, the indispensable necessity of the adoption, by the churches, in their social and other meetings, such a course of instruction and training as shall bring into exercise, and cultivate, and develop the gifts and talents of the body, in order to the supplying itself and the world with efficient men to labor in the vineyard of the Lord; these are the means, and this the source, as you very justly remark, to which we must look for such men—laborious and self-sacrificing men; by whom alone the cause can be built up and sustained. If we fail to properly cultivate this field, and expect to obtain such men from any other quarter, or in any other way, such expectation is doomed to disappointment.

Great prominence was given to these views in the earlier periods of "the current Reformation;" indeed, they were considered as important characteristics of this Reformatory movement. Many, however, now seem disposed to lay but little stress upon them, and some to ignore them altogether, and thus build again the things which we labored to destroy. But you, my brother, I hope, will "cry aloud, and spare not, and show His people their transgressions, and the house of Jacob their sins." And I trust all will work together for good, for I have an abiding confidence that the great heart of the brotherhood is right.

Your position on the all-absorbing subject of slavery, I also approve. It is eminently conservative and just, and is precisely what the Scriptures teach in reference to it, pointing out the relative duties both of master and servant. It presents, as you say, safe, and, I think, the only safe ground upon which a Christian can stand, and should be acceptable in every latitude, both North and South, and would, if generally adopted, do more to mitigate the rigor of the institution, and to ameliorate the condition of the slave, than all the rhapsodies of all the abolition orators from Boston to Chicago. It would secure to the slave an amount of social enjoyment, and opportunities for religious instruction and improvement, which, under existing circum-stances, it is impossible that that class can have extended to them. For if they are permitted to meet separately, even for religious worship, no great time would, in all probability, elapse, before an abolition emissary would be in their midst, enticing them to run away, or exciting them to insurrection, resulting, possibly, in rebellion and servile war. Therefore, from an inexorable necessity, such meetings, as a general thing, have to be interdicted. And if you learn them to read, which many masters would like to do, so as to enable them to read the Bible, the abolitionist is ready with his incendiary publications, to excite them to discontent and insurrection. Before this excitement was gotten up, in many places the blacks were taught in Sunday schools, and many were taught at home, to read. But now, some of the States have prohibited their instruction in letters altogether. Then, as a means of self-protection, the master is often compelled to withhold privileges that he would cheerfully grant, and sometimes to adopt measures, the necessity for which he would gladly be relieved from. This class of men have done, and are now doing, more to rivet the chains of the slave, and make them more galling, and to perpetuate the institution of slavery itself, than any other; indeed, than all others combined. In many of the more northern slave States, and even in Virginia, public sentiment was evidently beginning to favor a system of gradual emancipation, connected with colonization, which, however, was arrested, and the subject indefinitely postponed by the pragmatic interference of northern abolitionists. The poor negro has much reason to adopt the trite, but not less true, adage, and say, "Save me from my friends." I doubt not, however, that many of the class referred to, are sincere and devoted philanthropists, and really think they are doing God's service in keeping up this agitation. But they are not more sincere than was Saul of Tarsus. Men often, however, with the best intentions, accomplish a work the very opposite of that intended, as has evidently been the case with the sincere of the class alluded to; but they are men of one idea, and can hardly be expected to take a comprehensive view of any subject.

Fraternally and truly, yours,

H. M. BLEDSOE.

-----o-----

FROM the liberality which says everybody is right—from the charity which forbids you to say anybody is wrong—from the peace which is bought at the expense of truth, may the good Lord deliver you!

CINCINNATI, April 22, 1857.

BRO. FRANKLIN:—I am requested to furnish for the REVIEW an obituary notice of the death of our beloved Brother in Christ, THOMAS S. HAYDEN, who died April 1st, in Nicholasville, Ky., after an illness of more than three years and a half.

During this long and afflicting period, the cheerfulness of spirit which he manifested was remarkable, when considering that he was fully convinced of his speedy dissolution, and that he was quite young (only thirty-three years of age), and never before chastened by the hand of affliction. It was his unshaken confidence in the religion of Christ, that enabled him to look on his approaching death with a smile.

Bro. Hayden embraced the Christian religion in his youth, and evinced both in life and at his death its salutary influence upon the heart. Blessed with much of this world's goods, he was liberal in his contributions to the great schemes of benevolence, as they presented themselves, looking for his reward in heaven.

Our Brother leaves a Christian wife and two small sons to lament his early loss. May the blessings of Heaven rest upon them; and may they lead lives of holiness, that they may be prepared to meet him in another and better world—to dwell together in eternal felicity.

J. M. S.

-----o-----

BENTONVILLE, IND., April, 1857.

DIED, at his residence in Fayette Co., Ind., on the 18th of April, 1857, Bro. S. H. SPRONG.

Brother SPRONG was already past the meridian of life; had been a professor of Christianity many years, and by his meekness and Christian-like deportment had secured the love of the pious, and gained a prominent place in the affections of all who knew him.

D. R. VAN BUSKIRK.

-----o-----

Editor's Table.

THE DEBATE.—On Friday before the first Lord's day in June, the debate between Rev. T. J. Fisher and the editor will commence in Ghent, Ky. This place is on the Ohio river, seventy miles below Cincinnati and twenty miles above Madison.

CORRESPONDENTS.—We must again apologize to correspondents. Many valuable and able documents, from brethren of the first distinction and standing, have been crowded out for months. Some of these complain. We are sorry for this, but we cannot help it, as the REVIEW will not afford space for any more. We are grateful to all these writers, and will do the best we can for them.

THE "CHRISTIAN SENTINEL."—This monthly periodical appears in new dress and much improved, as the vehicle for religious intelligence in Illinois. It is under the management of Bro. E. Burges, one of the former editors, and Bro. I. N. Carman, a graduate of Bethany College, and a talented preacher. We trust it will meet such patronage as these good brethren merit and the necessity for such a publication demand. It is published at Peoria, Illinois. Price, one dollar a year.

SUNDAY-SCHOOL LIBRARY.—This long-looked-for and very desirable work has been stereotyped, and the plates for fifty volumes have been finished, at a cost of some $2000. We are assured now, that brethren who have the matter in hand have contracted for printing and publishing an edition, and consequently that the complete Library of fifty volumes, nearly all written by brethren, will be ready in a short time. We are truly gratified that a work so much desired is shortly to appear, and we hope it will have a ready sale and extensive circulation.

LARD'S REVIEW OF JETER.—Mr. Jeter is a Baptist, and has issued a Review of something he calls "Campbellism," in a respectable sized book, which sells at one dollar per copy. It has been before the people some two years, and well endorsed by the Baptist scribes. Lard's book is of similar size, and consists in a critical review of Mr. Jeter's principal positions, and a clear statement and an able defense of the positions Mr. Jeter opposes. If he fails, in a single case, to state the positions of Mr. Jeter correctly, meet the issues fairly, and refute his antagonist effectually, we would thank any Baptist to show us where it is. For fairness, clearness and ability, this book is not excelled by any book we have seen. It will stand the test in all time to come. It's clear-minded author understood his work well; has performed it with a master hand; and to it we refer all who desire to know the difference between the blind guides of our time and an intelligent man under the clear light of the Sun of Righteousness, or between cloudy theories advocated by the Baptists and the clear light of the New Testament. For sale at this office. Price one dollar.

DEBATE—CAMPBELL AND RICE.—This elaborate work, consisting of 912 pages, octavo, or containing the entire correspondence preparatory to the debate and eighteen days discussion upon the Action of Baptism, the Design of it, the Proper Subject, the Administer, the Influence of the Holy Spirit, and the Tendency of Human Creeds, is now for sale at this office. The Presbyterians thought so little of it that they let it go out of print. The Disciples, with many others, were still calling for the work. Bro. C. D. Roberts, of Illinois, saw a notice of this, purchased the plates and the sheets, which the former proprietors had not enterprise enough to bind, and has had them bound, and they are now upon sale and going finely. Price two dollars.

"SUNDAY-SCHOOL JOURNAL."—Finding an increasing demand for this little sheet, by the solicitation of the former proprietor, Bro. H. S. Bosworth, we have engaged to assist him in furnishing the Sunday schools and children in general, a cheap and valuable paper. The first issue is now out, though detained a little, as it was difficult to obtain paper, as well as to determine how large an issue to make. The subscribers are coming in finely. We have issued about twice as large an edition as was issued last year, and think we shall have reason, in a short time, to enlarge the issue. We ought to circulate 20,000 copies of this paper. If we could do this, it could be enlarged and embellished so as to be equal to anything of the kind published. Brethren, make an effort, and thus aid us in circulating a good paper for children. For terms, see advertisement on cover.

BACK NUMBERS OF THE A. C. REVIEW.—We printed four thousand copies of the REVIEW last year, which gave us near one thousand extra at the end of the year. This year we are printing five thousand copies, which at present leaves us a considerable number over supplying our subscribers. These back numbers are all in good order, and selling almost daily. For the purpose of putting them in circulation as fast as possible, we have been giving all the back numbers of last year, and the current volume, for $1 50, or volume 1 neatly bound, and the present as issued at $2, From this time forward, any person sending $2 in advance, shall receive vols. 1, 2, and 3, unbound, or as issued, complete; or for $3 vol. 1 bound, will be immediately sent, vol. 2, bound, sent at the end of the year, and vol. 3 sent as issued, the bound vol. postage prepaid by us in all cases.

ACKNOWLEDGMENT OF MISSIONARY FUNDS—The following are monies pledged and paid:

	Pledged.	Paid.
Lucy Horne, Baltimore, Md		$25 00
C. D. Hays, New London, Mo.		5 00
Sarah Paul, Martinsburgh, Ohio		2 25
C. S. Stone, Columbia, Mo., on Bro. and Sister J. Shannon's L. M.		19 00
C. S. Stone, contributions		5 00
Priscilla Fisher, Powhattan, Ark		$25 00
J. Frank, Warsaw, Kentucky	20 00	5 00
Willis Peak,		10 00
Gen. J. Payne,		20 00
Mrs. J. Payne,		5 00
" L. Craig.		5 00
J. H. H. Nesslage, New York city	22 50	2 50
Thos. Loyd.	22 50	2 50
H. M. Bledsoe, Lexington, Mo., L. M		5 00
R. Milligan, Bethany, Virginia.		30 00
E. Bollinger, Emerson Mo., L. M		2 35
Eld. W. Mason, Eminence, Ky.		2 00
David Pettit, Freeman, Iowa.		1 00
Mrs. A. Campbell, Bethany, Va		20 00

-----o-----

"BEHOLD I BRING YOU GLAD TIDINGS OF GREAT JOY."

DEAR BRO. FRANKLIN:—Thanks be to God for the success of the gospel. Two years since, Bro. Vail and myself commenced preaching at Hugerford's Mills in this county, where the name of *Christian* was odious, while *Methodism* was all in all. We have labored there since with great results. About one hundred have been immersed, and have united on the "Bible alone," as the rule of faith and practice in life, and as the only foundation for hope in death. Many of the wealthiest of that vicinity have dedicated themselves and their goods to the Lord, and the church have erected a house of worship which tells, the world that God and his people are there. I am the first preacher of the gospel that settled in Rush county. Since my coming here I have immersed some sixteen or seventeen hundred persons, and been instrumental in budding up six churches that are doing honor to the cause. Give God the glory. I am growing old, and the weight of years admonishes me that soon I must lay my armor by and leave the field.

Your brother, G. C. MCDUFFIE.

April 20th, 1857.

Success of the Gospel.

EUREKA, ILL., April 18, 1857.

BRO. FRANKLIN:—We have just concluded a meeting of days, the results of which have been the joy and encouragement of the church. Thirty-three were baptized, a goodly number of which were citizens of this vicinity; the others students of the College.

CHAS. L. LOOS.

Including the second Lord's day in April, we visited Warsaw, Ky., and remained about a week. Some sixteen were baptized, and several others, who had been baptized, were added. During our short stay at home the week following eight were baptized on Clinton street. This work was wrought principally by the diligent and persevering labor of Bro. George Rice, who has mainly the charge of the church. Including the fourth Lord's day in April, we held a meeting with the brethren at Berea, Ky., during which four were immersed. We spent three evenings between the first and second Lord's days in May, with the little church lately built in Hamilton, Ohio, during which one was immersed and several united by letter and recommendation. From Lord's day the 12th to Wednesday, ten were added in Covington, eight by immersion and two who had been standing aloof.

MICHIGAN—*Buchanan, May* 1st.—Bro. W. M. Roe writes: We have just closed a twelve days' meeting at Vandalia, with very happy results. Bro. Anderson assisted. There was much opposition manifested by those more wedded to party than to Christ. There were twenty-five accessions to the congregation—fifteen by confession and baptism, seven were from the sects, and four by letters. About two weeks since, at Millbay, we had one valuable addition from the Methodist. And at a recent meeting at Paw Paw one soul was buried with Christ by baptism. "Glory to God in the highest."

KENTUCKY—*Dover, April* 16*th.*—We are informed that during two meetings held at this place by Bro. J. Brooks, the "church was much revived," and thirty-four added thereto.

INDIANA—*Union City.*—Bro. Thos. Wiley writes: We are laboring in the gospel ministry incessantly, and not without success. Between five and six months of this year's labor is done, and we have witnessed between sixty and seventy accessions to the good cause for which we plead.

Embracing the fourth Lord's day in April I held a meeting at home, Carmel, Randolph county, resulting in fourteen additions, thirteen by confession and immersion and one reclaimed.

ILLINOIS—*Emerald Point., Morgan Co.*—Bro. C. Rowe writes: We have had some twenty additions since New Years.

Bath, Mason Co.—Bro. Gowen writes: In January Bro. S. T. Galloway and myself held a meeting here, and organized a congregation of seventeen members; we had eight additions then. In February I visited them and there were nine more added. Some from the Baptists, but mostly by immersion. The Baptist unite with the Disciples in breaking the loaf, prayer, etc., and their minister, Eld. J. Dannels, co-operated with us.

Paris.—Bro. A. D. Fillmore, under date April 15th, writes: We have just closed a meeting here with twelve additions. Bro. Shocky was with us. The first Lord's day in this month there were six added to the congregation in Marshall, Clark county. The cause of our blessed Master is prospering in this part of our State..

OHIO—*Alliance.*—Bro. P. R. Dibble, April 16th, writes: I commenced a meeting in this place on Friday, March 6th, and continued sixteen days. The result of which was the organizing of a church of fifty-three members, of whom twelve were immersed, six from the Baptists, three from the Methodists, some from the old Christian order; the balance were Disciples who lived scattered through the town and surrounding country. On the 27th of March I commenced a meeting in Minerva, and continued till the 5th inst. There were eight who made the good confession, one reclaimed, and one by letter. On the 10th inst. I again commenced in this place, and am still continuing. There have thus far been two immersed and seven received by the right hand of fellowship.

MISSOURI—*Boon County.*—Bro. T. Allen writes: I have just returned from Huntsville, Randolph Co., where we reorganized the congregation with some new accessions. During my absence I had four confessions besides those at Huntsville: and a few weeks since I immersed two in my own vicinity—one the son of a Calvinist Baptist preacher.

IOWA—*Cedar Falls, Feb.* 16*th.*—Bro. T. K. Hansberry writes: Since I came to this place, last Spring, I have preached near one hundred discourses and immersed fifty persons. Religious prospects are flattering in this country.

THE AMERICAN CHRISTIAN REVIEW.

VOL. II.   CINCINNATI, JULY, 1857.   No. 7

CAMPBELLISTIC THEOLOGY.
BY ELDER JAMES CHALLEN.

The editor of the *Western Watchman*, St. Louis, as quoted by the *Baptist Watchman*, inserts in his paper the outline of a discourse of mine, recently preached in Washington city, on the Remission of Sins, with characteristic comments. These constabulary gentlemen—*Western* and *Baptist*—seem to have caught the language of their profession. Hear what they say: "But there is, in the good city of Philadelphia, a preacher of 'the water gospel' by the name of Challen," etc. Who this preacher is, I know not, as I know no one by the name of "Challen," who preaches "the water gospel." It must be some apocryphal person, created by the imagination of the *Watchman,* or someone who has assumed a name to which he is not entitled. I know one James Challen in this city, but I am sure he has never preached "the water gospel"—if, indeed, he knows what it is. He preaches "the gospel"—the gospel of the "grace of God," concerning the death, burial and resurrection of the Messiah; but never has he preached anything that can by implication be called "the water gospel." If, therefore, the editor of the *Watchman* refers to the above-named person, he has simply borne false witness against him; and this is a sin of no ordinary character.

Having transferred from the *Christian Age* the programme of my discourse in Washington city, on "Remission of Sins," I need not recall attention to it, but will refer the reader to my communication which contains it. I am glad that the *Watchman* has spread it before his readers. It will speak for itself. On the negative part of my argument he has nothing to say, but to express his astonishment at the ignorance of any one, who can confound remission of sins, with a change of heart—inward peace and joy—accidental passages of scripture, booked by the memory, such as "thy sins be forgiven thee"—the reception of the Holy Spirit. As he has expressed his surprise at such ignorance, so do I, and therefore deemed it necessary to expose it, which I accordingly did. But anyone who has ever heard an "experience" in the Baptist Church, of a candidate for baptism, knows that the above is a fair sample. It would pass count from "Dan to Beersheba" as genuine and true.

Let anyone (of good moral character) appear before either of the Baptist churches to which these "Watchmen" belong, and give evidence of a change of heart—of inward peace and joy—of *"experimental"* appropriation of the passage, "thy sins be forgiven thee"—of the reception of the Holy Spirit—and he would be regarded as justified, sanctified and saved. He would, without any hesitation, be recognized as a pardoned person. Indeed, the evidences of his "remission" would be overwhelming. Thousands have been immersed by the Baptists, with far less evidence than these afford. And yet the "Western" and "Baptist Watchman" repudiate it altogether! They cannot "conceive of a person so ignorant as to confound remission of sins with either of the things therein specified!" Well, we are glad to hear this, and entertain some hope that they will return to the good old paths of the Apostles, which persons were received to baptism, simply on the confession of their faith in the Lord Jesus Christ and repentance toward God. This we know is not "Baptist usage," but it is better—it is apostolic usage.

Having referred to my article in which I say "that the knowledge of pardon is communicated to the penitent believer by promise—promise recorded by the Apostles," and quote, as proof, "*He* that believeth and is baptized shall be saved;" "Repent and be baptized every one of you, in the name of the Lord Jesus, for the remission of sins—and in which I say that it is enjoyed by such persons "in the first constituted act of submission to his government in the ordinance of baptism,"—he adds, "This we take to be pure Campbellism in a nut-shell." This is too much honor for any man to possess. I am sure that Mr. Campbell does not aspire to it. Jesus said, "He that believeth and is baptized shall be saved," and Peter employed the language above quoted, before Bro. Campbell was born, by eighteen hundred years. It cannot be what the *Watchman* scornfully calls "the water gospel," for that cannot be contained in a "nut shell." This would better apply to the Paedobaptists, against whom the *Watchman* is so hostile. The water of *their* gospel could be held by a "nut shell" of very diminutive size; but not so with the water of the gospel preached by the Baptists, or the Christians; they require "much water."

But, in reply to this postulate of mine, the editor gives three marks of interrogation and one note of exclamation—a "no and denominates it "a miserable caricature—a sham"—gospel. And quotes the "anathema" of Paul over the head of anyone who so preaches it! "Let him be accursed," says the *Watchman*. Well, this is plain talk. The *Watchman* had better first ascertain who preaches "another gospel," aside from what the Apostle preached, before he thunders his anathemas. But I will not press this subject, lest I might be charged with the same presumption of which the *Watchman* is guilty. It is certainly a fearful thing to preach anything for "the gospel," not preached by the Apostles of Christ. We should like to test our claims on this issue in the pages of the *Western Watchman*.

Again, he says the gospel we preach "not only ignores but sets aside the agency of the Holy Spirit in preparing the soul to receive the forgiveness of sins." What a shameful perversion of the truth. The gospel itself is the ministry of the Spirit; it is both "spirit and life." It is the word of the Spirit; the sword of the Spirit. We neither ignore, nor set aside the agency of the Spirit, nor his word. He is the Spirit of wisdom and power. He proceeds from the Father, is given by Christ. He quickens the soul, convinces of sin. Testifies of Christ, guides into all the truth, dwells in the saints, and whom the world cannot receive. We are born of God, born of the Spirit—and yet the gospel we preach *ignores* the Spirit! And he adds, "According to this gospel, a man may obtain the remission of sins, without even so much as knowing whether there be any Holy Ghost." This last quotation may well apply to John the Baptist's gospel, which had no mention in it Spirit's reception; and whose converts. Paul reimmersed and laid his hands upon, that they might receive the Holy Spirit; but certainly cannot apply to those who "baptize the penitent believers in the name of the Lord Jesus that they may receive the remission of sins and the gift of the Holy Spirit. And who introduce at baptism all such persons "into the name of the Father, and of the Son, and of the *Holy Spirit.*"

But again, "It assumes that a man may be pardoned before he is renewed—without regeneration—without a new heart—without love to God." Is this true? Do we not teach the renewal of the spirit—contend for a change of heart—a new heart—love to God—begetting by the Holy Spirit—all that he scripturally understands or can understand by these terms, as prerequisites to baptism, and as the antecedents of pardon? But why pile words upon words, as in the above quotation. This is a common method with our adversaries; and is invariably done to hide the truth, or to render it ridiculous and odious, in the eyes of others. If a man's heart is changed by the belief of the truth, then is it renewed—it is a new heart—it is what the *Watchman* calls "regenerated." We will not fall out with him for a word. *And if such persons, previous to baptism, are pardoned,* then are our converts pardoned, in despite of any theory on the subject—pardoned as truly as are his, unless there are some special privileges given to the Baptist converts, in a change of heart, not guaranteed to those made by the Disciples. "Things equal to the same thing are equal to each other." But if it should appear that baptism has something to do, in the matter of remission, whilst we have decidedly the advantage of the *Watchman,* he may "ignore" a very important ordinance, and fail in preaching the whole counsel of God, in regard to the conditions of pardon. And in his own words, "This is" [may prove to be] "a perversion of the first principle of the gospel."

His remarks on repentance and faith, or faith and repentance, are not worth an observation; as we insist on both, with a strenuousness that he neither does or can, but we can hardly forbear a smile, at his "sort of belief on historic evidence." I wonder what *"sort* of belief" he or anyone can have, in Christ, without the "history," as given by the four evangelists. "These are *written* that you may believe that Jesus is the Christ, the Son of God, and that believing you might have life in his name." Take away the "history," the "written" records, and where would be his faith, or the faith of any one! The "history" always accompanies the Missionaries to foreign lands, and that faithfully translated. The faith of the heathen does not come without the "history"—never to them in the Hebrew or the Greek—nor in the English; but in the language in which they are born. Surely the labors of the American Bible Union, according to the *Watchman's* theory, are all vain—faith can be as well produced by an imperfect version as a perfect one; or without any "history" at all! Thus "making the word of God of no effect by *this* tradition."

"In the fifth place," he adds, "it perverts the ordinance of baptism. It makes baptism the means of obtaining the remission of sins instead of the token or symbol of past remission."

How baptism is "perverted (that is), misapplied, distorted, misstated, by those who administer it to such only, who believe with all their heart that Jesus is the Christ, the Son of God, and who give evidence of repentance and amendment of life, we know not. Some "other gospel" Beside that which was preached by Peter and Paul, must be found, to show that any other qualifications were necessary. I ask the *Watchman,* if he has ever immersed an individual in his life for the reason that Philip immersed the Eunuch—*"If thou believest with all thy heart thou mayest,"*—"I believe that Jesus is the Christ, the Son of God." I doubt whether he has ever done it; certainly it is not the practice of those with whom he is associated. Many of the St. Louisans, "hearing, believed and were immersed," would sound strangely in the ears of the readers of the *Watchman!* "What, without a Christian experience?"—would be the inquiry from a hundred lips.

But, says the *Watchman,* "It makes baptism the means of obtaining the remission of sins, instead of the token or symbol of the past remission."

We have seldom seen a more glaring "perversion" than this, of the views and practices of the Disciples; or greater ignorance displayed in regard to the design of baptism.

When or where have we "made baptism the means of obtaining remission"—"*the means.*" In other words, *the* condition—the only condition of pardon—"*the means of remission.*" Never. We urge the plea for remission, as he knows, on far other grounds. So far as the sinner is concerned, we demand of him faith in the Lord Jesus Christ and repentance unto life, before he is entitled to baptism—without these "means," his baptism will avail him nothing. In addition, we urge him to "arise and be baptized and wash away his sins, calling on the name of the Lord." A command (in good faith), without considerable travesty—the *Watchman* cannot—will not urge. According to his representation of our views, "baptism is '*the means*' of remission." This we deny; and affirm, that "faith, repentance *and* baptism are the means of remission."

Again, "Baptism" (according to our views) "is made the means of obtaining the remission of sins,"—so the *Watchman* affirms. Not so. The "obtaining" means of pardon is the blood of Christ. So we teach and so we believe. He does not use the word "obtain" in the sense of receiving and enjoying, but in the sense of earning—procuring. The meritorious means of pardon, or ground on which it is enjoyed, is the death of Christ. The means of enjoying and the means of bestowing a favor differ as widely as the poles.

But, according to the *Watchman,* baptism is "the token or symbol of past remission." This is simply his affirmation, and must be received on his authority, as he affords no proof in support of it, and can afford none. Baptism a *token* of *past* remission! That is, baptism is (in evidence), that the sins of the individual, has already been forgiven—a sign, seal and witness, that remission has already been enjoyed. In other words, it is a "symbol" of past pardon. Now this is certainly a new gospel. How unlike the one preached by Peter. "Repent and be baptized every one of you in the name of the Lord Jesus, for the remission of sins." To make this case apparent, suppose that when the three thousand asked "What shall we do?" Peter should have answered, "Be baptized—for the remission of your sins would not the *Watchman* have concluded that baptism alone was the means of remission? But, suppose he had said, "Repent—for the remission of your sins," would he not have said, that repentance is the only means of remission? But did Peter say either the one or the other? Did he not equally command both repentance and baptism for remission? Where two imperatives are used to secure a promised blessing, united by the copulative conjunction "and," who has a right to strike out one or the other of them, as the true condition of its enjoyment? If one of them—which? And, if one, why not both? No greater assumption of authority can be made than this. To suit the *Watchman,* Peter should have said—(and mark it; according to *his* theory, he by implication did say), "Repent for the remission of your sins"—and as a token of their past remission, "be baptized." Do the collocation of the words used, their grammatical construction, or the sentence itself, by any law of interpretation known, admit of such a meaning? The language is perspicuous, clear and lucid. It is as transparent as light; as compact as "arise and take up thy bed and walk." He arose, took up his bed and walked. The paralytic might have arisen and walked, but this would not have fulfilled the two commands—He must arise, and *take up his bed,* and walk. It is most certain, that if he had not "arisen," he could not have walked; though he might have walked, after he had arisen; but the actions required would not have been performed. It is doubtful with me, if the paralytic would have been permitted to "walk," if he had left his bed behind. He probably could not have arisen at all; or, if arising, he would have stood, immovable as a stone, if he had resolved to leave his bed untaken. Jesus would have known the thought of his heart, as he did those of the scribes and Pharisees present, and would have punished his obstinacy by refusing the favor. His bed would have been left behind, and him on it; not in proof of his *past* healing and remission, but of his perversity and disobedience.

But further, this dogma of baptism "as a token—a symbol of *past* remission," is a blow at the root of one of the most important items found in the gospel of Christ—that of the blood of Christ shed "for the remission of sins." Peter says, "Repent and be baptized—for the remission of sins"—*eis aphesin amartion;* and Jesus said, "For this is my blood of the New Testament, which is shed for many, *for the remission of sins"*—eis aphesin amartion. Now mark it. If baptism to the penitent believer, is a token—a symbol of his "past remission," then the blood of Christ shed, is a token—a symbol of past remission. In other words, the blood of Christ is not for the remission of sins, but a token, that without his blood, sins have already been forgiven. And thus, by a parity of reasoning—rather by this wicked sophistry, the blood of Christ is equally dispensed with, as baptism in the remission of sins. The formula in both cases is precisely the same.

But again, "It makes the remission of sins to depend on a mere outward form instead of the grace of God."

We would inform the *Watchman* that there are no "mere outward forms" in Christianity. If he regards baptism to a penitent believer as such, he needs to be taught "what be the first principles of the doctrine of Christ." To an unconscious babe, sprinkling, pouring or immersion, is a "mere outward form"—and so to an infidel. But it embodies the grace of God, as much as any other act does. Prayer, singing, breaking the loaf, etc., all have some outward form—but he need not be told that to the Christian, they are not bodily, but highly spiritual acts—and so of baptism.

But all this tergiversation about "mere outward acts," is simply ridiculous, if not wicked. Sometimes the merest insignificant acts, *under certain conditions,* are the mightiest engines, and most indubitable channels of conveying the greatest good and accomplishing the mightiest deeds. A man enters into a bank; he presents a cheque for three millions of money. (Such a cheque is preserved in the Bank of England now as a curiosity. It was drawn, I believe, during the French war). The clerk takes the bit of paper, looks at it, and refuses to pay the money. Why? Because a little, almost imperceptible mark is wanting in the signature of the name, which the owner of the money had agreed to make, and which the clerk does not discern. *It is pointed out, and the money is paid.* An army is ranged in order of battle. They stand perfectly motionless. *One blast, of the trumpet,* and the whole mass is in motion. Swords are brandished; troops charge; the battle is won; perhaps an empire is saved or lost;—all depending on that blast of the trumpet. Why? Because the commander had appointed that signal, *and the soldiers believed in him and it.* Napoleon places himself at a little wooden table, in the palace of Fontainebleau. In less than a minute, he scrawls a few black lines on a bit of paper. The whole French Empire, with its millions of subjects, millions of wealth, the destinies of

Europe, of innumerable generations, all change at once; just as the fate of an individual would be changed, if his own head could be cut off from his body, and another could be fixed on it. They pass from one master to another, by virtue of that little signature, attached to that little scrap of paper. Why? Because Napoleon has agreed that such signature shall be the sign of his abdication, and the allied sovereigns believe him. If either condition were wanting, the signature would be as worthless as any marks which a child scrawls on his first copy-book. A bit of wood on the top of a tower at Spit-head, will put a whole fleet in motion. Why? Because of a few little black marks, as big as a pin's head, the Admiral has received from London. It moves, because he has received by telegraph the little word "yes;" or stays, because he has received the word "no." The safety of Europe depends on that "yes" or "no." The turning of that bit of wood on the top of the tower, may decide the fortunes of an empire. How shallow, then, all such reasonings about "mere bodily acts." Recollect that all these little acts, on which so much depended, were but the signs and beacons of forethought, intelligence, and wisdom; the embodiments and expression of the councils of nations and of individuals.

But I will not dwell on the remainder of this weak and ill-tempered piece. Enough has been said to expose its sophistry, and every point of importance has been considered. Perhaps it would be asking too much of the *Watchman's* courtesy, to give it a place in his paper?

PHILADELPHIA, PA.

-----o-----

I would rather convince a man that he has a soul to save, and induce him to live up to that belief, than to bring him over to my opinion in whatever else besides.—LEIGHTON.

A SERMON.
BY WILLIAM GILPIN.

My Beloved Bro. Franklin:—You devote a portion of the REVIEW, I discover, to sermons. The following, by Gilpin, is not without its merits. There is a dignity in the style, a clearness in the conception and a comprehensiveness in the subject, that will make it generally acceptable and profitable. I therefore assume the pleasing task of its transcription, trusting that its transmission may tend, some time, to relieve editorial anxiety on the scarcity of matter more interesting in its character.   C. D. H.

"The kingdom of heaven is like a grain of mustard seed; which, indeed, is the least of all seeds; but when it is grown, it is the greatest of herbs, and becometh a tree; so that the birds of the air come, and lodge in the branches thereof."—Matt. xii. 31.

This short parable, and one or two others of the same texture, were intended to hold out the progressive state of the gospel. But interpreters, perhaps, in general, confine the meaning of these parabolic exhibitions within too narrow a period. They commonly consider them as exhibiting the propagation of Christianity from the commencement of our blessed Savior's ministry, till the time when Christianity shall obtain a footing over the earth. This period, no doubt, the parable before us includes; but, I think, it may reasonably be supposed also to include a more comprehensive one. It may begin earlier, and be extended farther. It may take in, I presume, the Whole history of the Bible; and connect the book of Genesis, with the Revelation of St. John. I shall endeavor, therefore, in the following discourse, to explain it under this comprehensive idea.

Without any harsh interpretation, I think, what the text calls the "kingdom of heaven," or the economy of the gospel, may be divided into four great periods—its *prophetic,* its *persecuted,* its *established,* and its *triumphant* state. We denominate each period from the *general cast* of the external circumstances, in which it is engaged; though these circumstances may blend together (as they often and certainly do) indifferent periods. In the mean time, real Christianity is, in all periods, we know, the same.

The prophetic state of the gospel commences at the fall of man. The grain of mustard-seed was then sown. The intimation of God's gracious design to recover man from the mischief of that sad event, was at first like the *least of all seeds*. An obscure prophetic hint was the only hope, on which the old world depended, aided by the mysterious rite of sacrifice; to which God never would have *had respect,* nor have distinguished its modes, if it had not been of his own appointment.

After the destruction of the old world, God separated to himself a particular family, as an instrument to prepare mankind for the reception of the gospel. In the economy of this family, which soon increased into a great nation, was displayed the most wonderful series of divine contrivance, in that system of types (historical and ceremonial), which were afterwards *realized* in gospel times. In the whole history of the world, we have nothing similar to this *sacred machinery,* if we may so speak. We trace the resemblance of it in no single analogy through the whole scheme of God's moral government. This shows it, I think, not a work in the common course of nature, but a miraculous interposition of Providence, contrived for some peculiar purpose.

Strange, no doubt, and whimsical many of these rites and ceremonies appeared to those, who viewed them superficially. But as the great scheme of the gospel dispensation began to open, and they were observed so connected with it in every part, the resemblance could not but have a great effect both on the pious Jew, and on the reasoning Gentile; and contributed greatly, no doubt, among other things, to bring over those large bodies of converts, of whom we read, on the first opening of Christianity.

After the *prophetic* state of the gospel, we arrive at its *persecuted* one. We still characterize each period, as I observed, by its *predominant feature.* In the fullness of time our blessed Lord appeared on earth. From the grand and pompous display of types, and prophetic notices, through so long a period, and dispersed by means of the Jewish economy and literature, through so many countries, not only the Jew himself, but many of the heathen also expected a prince of such power and greatness, as the world had never seen. The splendid court, the arrayed battalion, the triumphal chariot, the extended empire, were all to be the accompaniments of this potent monarch.

But it immediately appeared that the *kingdom of heaven* disclaimed all connection with the pomp and grandeur of the world. It was denominated the *kingdom of heaven* in very opposition to the *kingdom of the world.* This, however, was an indignity and disappointment, which the world could not bear. Its pride, its interest, and everything it valued, were offended. If Christianity opposed the world, the world immediately set itself to oppose Christianity. Persecution began. The blessed Jesus was the first victim. The disciple could not expect better treatment than his Lord. A succeeding generation arose; Christianity still disclaimed all commerce with the guilty world; and the guilty world in return still showed that it had the pre-eminence. The kings and rulers of the earth stood up, and took counsel against the Lord, and against his anointed.

As Christianity extended, the sphere of persecution was enlarged. It was not now carried on in the sparing and cautious manner of the first persecutors; when a wicked prince killed James, the brother of John, with the sword; and, because he saw it pleased the people, proceeded to take Peter also. But whole bodies of men were dragged to death—not only to death, but to extreme torture. A Christian and a martyr were in those days equivalent expressions.

In the mean time religion throve and flourished under all this violence. Then were displayed the Christian graces in all their purity and beauty. Faith, and hope and charity appeared with all their heavenly train of virtues—piety, humility, meekness, and perseverance in duty. Then were good offices returned for cruelty and malice. Then was an indifference to the world in every shape discovered—its allurements and its menaces were equally despised. None became Christians but from principle, and the hopes of religion showed themselves superior to the severest trials. The excellence of Christianity in the end prevailed. It overbore all opposition, and took it under their protection. It became *established* and *endowed*. This brings us to the *third* period of the gospel.

We should naturally suppose that the Christian church, now relieved from all its difficulties, would have united on one song of praise and thanksgiving; and that its several members would have shown their gratitude to God by the sanctity of their lives. But it is not common with mankind to be grateful to God, in proportion to his benefits. It is much more common to turn his blessings into wantonness. Thus it fared with Christianity. Being reconciled with the world, it immediately contracted an intimate friendship with it. In some places it was introduced to all the heathen superstitions, the Gothic ignorance, the barbarous, and immoral rites and customs, which prevailed; and with too many of them it closed. In other places, strange interpretations of scripture were taken up, monstrous heresies arose, and Christians quarreled among each other with the bitterest enmity, and on the most trifling grounds. As mankind grew more enlightened, Christianity made acquaintance with philosophy. Philosophy threw new lights on the old system of religion. The great truths of the gospel became offensive to the improved reason of man. Though Christianity was formerly at perfect variance with all the wisdom of the world, the wisdom of the world became now the criterion of a divine revelation. Men were not now to be imposed on like their simple forefathers. They were too wise to believe anything which they could not explain. Though the *works of nature* often puzzled them, they would allow no difficulties in *God's moral government*.

As it fared thus with the *doctrines* of the gospel, so it did with *precepts*. In early days it was said, that *he who was the friend of the world, was the enemy of God*. But this wholesome caution was soon forgotten. The wit of man was employed to make up a kind of fashionable religion. All the arts of reasoning were used to reconcile religion with expedience, and to explain with nicety how God and mammon might be served together. Indeed the connection became so close between Christianity and the world—the precepts of the former so modeled, by the latter, that it was not easy to distinguish and separate the several interests of these intimate friends. It was *real* Christianity no longer, *nominal* Christianity answered all the ends that were desired. In these mighty plans of ambition, in which the world formerly engaged alone, Christianity now united. Sometimes it raised a spiritual tyranny, domineering over the consciences of men; and calling *fire from heaven,* in opposition to every gentle precept of the gospel. Sometimes again thirsting after temporal dominion, it would lay waste whole countries by fire and sword. In private life, whatever schemes of dissipation and pleasure were going forward, though wholly opposite to the principles and simplicity of the gospel, Christianity was always ready to make one; modish fashions were everywhere adopted, instead of Christian virtues; and the fear of God gave way to the fear of the world. The gospel might talk, as it pleased, of the *narrow way to life,* and the *broad way to destruction.* That road which all the people took, must be right; and the shameless pastors of the church often led the way. In projects of trade also, to whatever length pursued; however made the vehicles of luxury and vice; to whatever objects extended, even the most inhuman and unnatural; in whatever wickedness involved, frauds, perjuries, breach of trust—it was all alike, Christianity never objected— never refused its warmest consent. Then again with regard to that great worldly code, the point of honor, Christianity at once entered into the spirit of it; and easily saw how very superior it was to the gentleness of gospel precepts; and how much more effectual, than the best of them, in the preservation of decorum among mankind. The text might cry, *If thine enemy hunger, feed him; if he thirst, give him drink.* These were precepts fit only for apostles and primitive Christians. Modern Christianity throws all these obsolete precepts behind; and, armed with vengeance, perhaps even for an indiscrete word, will rush with stopped ears to the murder of a friend.

Not but there are in this age, we doubt not, and have been in all ages, many who govern their actions by the sincere principles of the gospel; and would lay down their lives, if called on, in its defense, with the firmness of martyrs. God has never left himself without these faithful witnesses. In some countries also the truth of Christianity, no doubt, is more generally felt than in others. The fashions of the day are less adverse to it. But it must still be remembered, we characterize times by their binding features—of ours, I trust, the features are not overcharged.

How long it may please the Almighty, that this more corrupt state of our religion shall exist, we know not. We hold an opinion, however, founded on prophecy, that in some future period, after Christianity hath spread itself over this earth, it will exchange its corrupt state for a *triumphant one.* We formed our belief principally on the Revelation of John. This divine book (authenticated beyond cavil) holds out an amazing display of wonderful events— grand and sublime in the highest degree; and soaring beyond the capacity of men. The *seals,* the *trumpets,* and the *vials* have all been explained by various interpreters, and in various ways; but I doubt whether in any way, that is fully satisfactory. All interpreters make them, hold out the state of the church; but in their details they often lead us among the trivial events of civil history; which in many instances seem but little connected with the affairs of Christianity.

Indistinct, however, as these sublime, prophetic images may be, we are authorized at least to gather from them these truths—that after some great revolutions, and fearful events; some trying and purifying conflicts, which the church of Christ may have yet to undergo (though of what nature, or through what agency, we pretend not to explain), it will receive a form entirely different from that, in which it had over before appeared. All prophecies, yet unfulfilled, will now be complete. It will no longer be the *persecuted* church, it once was. It will no longer be the *corrupt* church it now is; but all offence of every kind being done away, the wickedness of the world, which hitherto had the upper hand, will be subdued under the excellence of Christian virtues. Then all that glory and all that happiness will take place, which we may conceive, when the principles of the Christian religion shall be divested of all worldly prejudices, all mischievous projects, and all wicked connections—when the whole Christian world shall be united in one great family, and join in praise to God, and universal benevolence to man.

We enter not into the niceties of this question, nor pretend to explain who are to be the partakers of the *first,* or who of the *second resurrection;* nor to decipher any of those wondrous images, which carry the imagination into vast, unknown and boundless regions. We go no farther than we seem fully authorized by the text; and though not so far as the interpretation of some learned men have led us, yet at least as far as that point in which all learned men seem to agree.

Here, then, we see the grand scheme of Christianity complete; of which the Bible, from one end to the other, is the great record. It opens with the origin of the gospel in the fall of man; and leading us through the Jewish history, as the vehicle of all those prophetic intimations, preparatory to Christianity, makes its first great pause at the opening of the New Testament. There the prophecies of the Old being realized, we are informed the gospel soon began to spread in the world; and as soon to suffer a state of *persecution.* For its full *establishment,* and wealthy endowment in a future period, we look into profane history; and we want no evidence but what our own times can furnish, of the *great corruption* into which it has fallen in these declining ages. Our holy record, however, leaves us not comfortless, but holds out to us still one period more—its *triumphant* state, in which all its difficulties being removed, it will assume its native glory.

I shall conclude with a few remarks on the principal uses which seem to arise from this extended view of the Christian religion.

In the first place, we have an answer to the objector's question, why did Christianity appear so late in the world? How does he know, that it is late? The world, for anything he knows, may yet be in its infancy. Christianity, we are assured, has many a hard conflict to pass through, before it arrive at that state, which itself is said to last a *thousand years;* and under that prophetic term, perhaps a much longer period. Christianity hath not yet overspread the face of the earth; which, we believe, from prophecy, it must do, before it arrive at its triumphant state. We have seen it in our day, making large strides in the East, and in the West. But though so much is done, yet more remains undone. Half the world is yet in darkness and ignorance. As learning and the arts of civilization spread, the light of the gospel, we doubt not, will spread with them. It matters not what instruments God employs; he can work with those, which seem most unlikely to forward his designs. The soldier with his sword, the merchant with his cargo, and the settler with his plough, all unite in promoting the schemes of God.

Besides, the objector should be aware, that some *preparation* to introduce the Christian religion was necessary. If Christianity had been introduced *earlier,* the grand proof from prophecy would have been in proportion *weaker.* It might be necessary also to show mankind from the miserable efforts of their own reason, how much a *heavenly instructor* was wanted; and, from the ravages of sin, how much they stood in need of a *Savior.* This, too, required time to effect. The ravages of sin, no doubt, still continue. But its empire, on the whole, is much repressed; and as to individuals, Christianity hath shown such numerous and illustrious shining characters, as never appeared under any other influence. In the mean time, with regard to the salvation of mankind, we have the best scriptural authority, that all men, who lived up to the lights they had received, both before Christ and after him, are saved through his merits. He is styled the *lamb slain from the foundation of the world.*

The *consolation* which this extended view of Christianity hath diffused, through all ages of the church, and many still diffuse, should be considered as another great use arising from it. While the grain of mustard-seed had yet spread little above the ground, the expectations of the patriarchs and holy Jews were awakened. They saw the glorious prospect far off, and waited with holy hope for the *consolation of Israel.*

The same idea animated the Christian in later periods of the church. It seems, indeed, to be often touched on by John in the Revelations; and is, perhaps, the best key to open, at least the *general intention,* of that mysterious book. In the persecuted period of the church, when all around was black and gloomy—when the sword was unsheathed, the fire kindled, and every engine at work to extirpate the gospel, the expiring martyr, with an eye of despondency, might have foreseen nothing but ruin to the cause in which he suffered, had he not been cheered by a prophetic ray, animating his breast with an assurance, that he was a holy victim, offered up in defense of that religion which was protected by the hand of heaven, and should exist to the end of time—and that the same good Providence which protected it would protect also his faithful servants, who died in its defense.

Again, the pious Christian, in these corrupt times of the church, when he sees dissipation and wickedness overbearing all things like a flood, and every appearance as if real Christianity were about to leave the land—when his spirit sinks within him at the dismal view—he is consoled by looking into future times, and there, in the visions of prophecy, seeing the holy religion he professes reviving with ten-fold brightness, and triumphing at length over all the impurities of the world.

Another use, arising from this extended view of Christianity, is giving courage, firmness, and modest dignity, to all the true professors of the gospel. They are the means, under Christ, to keep alive the holy flame of religion in this corrupt state of things. They are, as their Savior tells them, the *salt of the earth,* to preserve it from corruption, and may humbly consider themselves as carrying on the great scheme of redemption in union with Christ.

We trace an analogy through all God's works, as each individual undergoes a state of trial; so it seems does the church of Christ, as a general body. In early times it undergoes the harder trial of prosperity. Both, no doubt, are necessary to prepare it for the last great change, which awaits it. The Jewish religion, imperfect as it was, prepared the world for Christianity, and Christianity, in its present state, however defective, is a preparation, no doubt, for its future period. As then the holy confessors and martyrs of ancient times were the means of preserving the spirit of religion alive, under all its fiery trials, so are the pious professors of the gospel in these days of languor and indulgence.

Let them then consider, with proper humility, the situation in which they stand. Let them consider, that it is not less, but even more dangerous than that of the ancient Christians, inasmuch as the insidious friendship of the world is more dangerous to religion than its open violence. Instead of joining, therefore, in the corruptions around them, or even, by an incorrect behavior, breaking down the fences of religion, let its pious professors, especially its appointed ministers, stand up boldly in its defense. Let them consider the world as their greatest enemy. Let them keep it, as it were, at arms length, and not suffer it to close in upon them. Thus, by their firmness and example, may they show themselves to be humble instruments, in the hands of God, both of lessening the corruptions of the present times, and of preparing and leading forward Christianity to those wonderful events of its last great period.

Lastly, from the several periods of the gospel, taken together in one view, we draw a strong argument for its truth. Let us see how the comparison stands with any human institution. We select one of the most extraordinary. When an enterprising chief, at the head of a body of armed men, introduces a new religion, we confess it to be a very surprising event, as nothing is more difficult than to eradicate religious prejudices. Yet still we can account for this revolution on human principles. The subtle impostor, with great sagacity, adapting his plan to the circumstances of the times, told his followers, that the Jewish religion had been good at first, but on its becoming corrupt, it had been superseded by Christianity—that Christianity also had been good at first, but as it was now become corrupt, he had been sent from God to reform it. Such reasoning, in an age, and in a country where real religion was almost extinct (as we know it was, at that time, in the east) was specious. With equal subtlety, he strengthened his plan by retaining so much of the old religion as to make people believe they rather received an improvement of what they had before, than an institution wholly new. In this, too, he plausibly mimicked the process of Christianity from Judaism. At the same time, instead of the spiritual rewards of the gospel, for which his corrupt disciples had little relish, be promised a future state, replete with the highest degree of indulgence and sensuality, which was so agreeable to their manners, while fire and sword were threatened to those who opposed him—engines more terrifying than the distant penalties of the gospel. Though the revolution, therefore, introduced by this imposter, was a wonderful combination of art and force, and produced a singular phenomenon in the history of mankind, yet still it presents nothing but what may well be accounted for on human principles. But when we see a religion introduced with all the striking apparatus of prophecies and prophetic types—commencing at the beginning of the world, and not brought to perfection, perhaps, till the conclusion of it—successfully opposing, though violently persecuted, all the powers of the earth—and at length overturning everything that stood in its way, without worldly threat or allurement of any kind, but merely by its divine power, and the mild, yet forcible, persuasions of its own purity and excellence—when we see it afterwards assailed by the flattery and corruptions of the world; and though in many circumstances overpowered, yet in many instances rising superior to this trial also—when, instead of losing ground by these different attacks, we see it prevailing more and more in various parts of the world to this very day—and, finally, when we have assurance from prophecy (with which the course of its progress, hitherto, is perfectly analogous), that it will, in the end, prevail over the wickedness of the world, and display itself universally in its native colors—when we find such a combination of circumstances, all centering in one point, it is impossible to attribute so gradual, so complete, so wonderful a plan to any human means. The grandeur of the whole, and the amazing coherency of the several parts, are similar only to the great works of creation, and we cannot but acknowledge in them the hand of God.

-----o-----

DIALOGUE OF DEVILS.
NUMBER VI.

Present—DIABOLOS, APOLLYON, LUCIFER and DAIMONION. Subject—The Most Successful Method of Subverting the Word of God, and Defeating the Mission of Christ.

DIABOLOS.—Gentlemen, it has been two months since we met, and I am anxious to hear what you have been doing, or any suggestions you have to make.

APOLLYON.—I must confess, that I am miserably confused. Some of our best devices are likely to prove a failure, and I fear that our whole work will suffer an immense defeat.

LUCIFER.—I am of the same opinion. As an instance, showing this, you all know how many suggestions we made, and the special aids we afforded Mr. J. B. Jeter, in getting up and putting in circulation his *Review of Campbellism.* You know, too, that we thought something grand was achieved for our cause when we secured so many favorable notices of this book, and obtained such an extended endorsement from eminent men for it.

DAIMONION.—I am aware that we all aided in this work, and I thought were succeeding well. Nor do I see any reason still to doubt. The book has been in circulation more than two years, and, I think, the general opinion is, that it is unanswerable.

DIABOLOS.—Have you been asleep?—or idling away your time, without giving any attention to what is going on? Are you not aware that Moses E. Lard, of Liberty, Mo., a graduate of Bethany College, has issued a volume, reviewing the book of Mr. Jeter?

APOLLYON.—I am aware of this, and this is what I alluded to when I spoke of being confused. I know not what we are to do with this book. It exposes the sophistries we have induced Mr. Jeter to employ, disperses the mists and refutes his positions with such a master hand, that the people will certainly perceive it.

DIABOLOS.—You are right, most worthy Apollyon; the people will perceive that Mr. Lard's book contains a clear, masterly, most manifest and obvious exposure of Mr. Jeter's entire effort. I know not what is to be done about this book! I thought Mr. Jeter had covered up, mystified, obscured and involved conversion to Christianity in such confusion and darkness, and that such a number of ministers and writers had accepted and endorsed his effort, that the nearest approach the balance of mankind would make to Christianity would be to become *seekers,* or *mourners.*

APOLLYON.—That was my mind precisely. I thought that he had obscured the doctrine that "the gospel is the power of God unto salvation to everyone that believeth"—that "we are begotten again, not of corruptible seed, but of incorruptible, by the *word of God,* which liveth and abideth forever"—that "of his own will begat he us with the *word of truth,* that we should be a kind of first fruits of his creatures," and that men are "sanctified *through the truth,*" as clearly taught in scripture, so that men would discard it, repudiate it, declare it ineffectual, and from this time forward seek for and pray God to send down something better. But I despair of this now.

LUCIFER.—I thought Mr. Jeter put on such an air of candor and sanctimoniousness, that he would succeed with our former scheme of delusion, and that we should still be able to defeat all efforts at finding the way into the kingdom of God. But even the obscure passages, not clearly translated, quoted by Mr. Jeter to mystify and darken counsel, Mr. Lard takes hold off with a master hand, clears away the mysticism, disperses all obscurity from them, harmonizes them with the other Scriptures, and shows that they teach precisely the same. Even the passage, "Except a man be born again he cannot see the kingdom of God"—"Except a man be born of water and of the Spirit, he cannot enter into the kingdom of God"—"The wind bloweth where it listeth, and thou hearest the sound thereof and canst not tell whence it cometh nor whither it goeth, so is every one that is born of the Spirit," which you know we have had every ignoramus in the land quoting, without knowing what it meant, to blind the mind and obscure the way into the kingdom of God, Mr. Lard has taken up, purged the obscurities in translation from it, shown that it perfectly harmonizes with other scriptures, and teaches the same doctrine. I know not how we are to counteract this book.

DIABOLOS.—I thought, when Mr. Jeter came out, that through him we should succeed in leading the people to deny that statement of the apostle Peter, that "he" (Christ) "hath given us *all things* that pertain to life and godliness," and that we should completely subvert that old question of Scripture—"What more could I have done that I have not done?"—and that we should have the people in thousands, as in former years, seeking, mourning, grieving and failing to find. I thought, and intended to have the preachers blinded to all the answers the apostles ever gave those seeking the way.

I intended then simply to exhort seekers to seek on, mourn on, and agonize mightily unto God—that if he did not bless them now, he would soon or at some future time. In this way I intended to keep the fact out of view, that God had ordained any definite, explicit and clear steps for men to come to God. To invalidate all that God has done, keep it out of sight, I have advocated and had Mr. Jeter to advocate in his book, the doctrine, that God must do something over and above his word to save sinners. In order to do this, the most successful method I have found, is to set both preachers and seekers to praying for *something over and above the word,* and absorb them so in it, that this something over and above the word would become the all in all. The word is forgotten, or looked upon as of very little consequence, and the great struggle for this something over and above the word, without which no one can be converted, and which none but God can bestow, would become the all-absorbing matter. All would then cease warning sinners to receive with meekness the engrafted word which is able to save their souls. No one would admonish them that "God has commanded all men everywhere to repent;" to "Repent and be converted, that their sins may be blotted out; to "Save themselves from this untoward generation." The entire current would then be changed. The warnings, reasonings and expostulations with sinners would cease. The sinners, in this case, are represented as all willing, seeking, thirsting and panting for salvation. The preachers are doing their utmost for their salvation. The whole struggle now is with God, to get him to do what he has not done, what he appears unwilling to do—something over and above the word. This sets the gospel aside thoroughly, with all that Jesus has done, and leads the mind to something he has omitted to do, and which, if he does not do, sinners must be lost. In this case, if sinners are not saved, they are not to blame, for they are willing and seeking. Nor is it the fault of the preacher, for he is willing and doing all he can; but the fault is on the part of the Lord, who can do this something over and above the word, but will not do it!

APOLLYON.—I supposed that the Disciples were discomfited and defeated by Mr. Jeter's book, as they remained comparatively quiet for some two years, seeming to be letting the matter go by default. But I now perceive that they felt no alarm about it, but had the fullest assurance that they had men perfectly able to expose its sophistries, refute it throughout, not only to their own satisfaction, but to the satisfaction of all men of sense, and were simply waiting for it to obtain a good circulation, responsible notices and endorsement, and then gain a complete triumph in refuting it. Now the question is, what is to be done with this book? What course shall we direct Baptist preachers, scribes and editors to pursue?

LUCIFER.—I have directed an article or two to be published touching Mr. Campbell, his reception in New Orleans, and Mr. Lard's book, that I think precisely the thing. By some means Mr. Campbell was called upon to address the Young Men's Christian Association in that city. His great name called out a great audience, and in the notices of it in several Baptist papers, I have had them state that the audience was completely taken in—that his address consisted of an effort to show the catholicity of the name *Christian,* and thus justify his sectarian course in reference to the name *Christian.* In the same notices I have directed them to hold out the idea that Mr. Campbell is superannuated, and that he no longer thinks for his followers, and that the party have put foremost Mr. Lard to answer Mr. Jeter's book. This, I think, will defeat the whole thing.

DIABOLOS.—I have seen the notices you mention, but think you have done much worse for our cause than if you had said nothing. You present prominently two points decidedly favorable to Mr. Campbell, and calculated to give him conspicuity. In the first place, in one of those notices, you mention that the great name of Mr. Campbell and his widely extended fame as a lecturer drew out the largest assembly ever convened in that hall. This of itself tells mightily in his favor. The *opinion* of the writer of the notice, that the audience were taken in, amounts to nothing, only that the lecture did not suit *him*. This is no evidence how it suited the audience. In the second place, you mention that he dwelt upon the *catholicity of the* name *Christian!* Now this is a matter I dread. He made this tell with great power upon that great audience of intelligent people. How came the Association to be called the "Young Men's *Christian* Association?" What is the name *Christian* in such a conspicuous place for? Why was not the name *Baptist, Presbyterian,* or *Methodist* inserted, instead of the name *Christian?* For the simple reason, that the name Baptist, etc., is sectarian, but the name Christian is not. The name Christian is *catholic,* or what is worse for our cause, it is *divine,* and all can agree upon it. Nothing could have been more unwise in you than to have called attention to the name.

APOLLYON.—I agree with your wise suggestion, most worthy Diabolos, and further the notice of the fact that Mr. Campbell did not respond to Mr. Jeter himself, but confided this work to the hands of the graduate of Bethany, is all against our cause. The refutation is unanswerable, yet from a man measurably unknown to the world, and it must do infinite damage to our cause.

DIABOLOS.—I am ashamed of the notices of this book, to which you allude. They are calculated to make bad worse. My policy is to keep Baptist scribes from saying anything about it. Such notices as you say you have instigated, are precisely calculated to lead everybody to seek the book and read it. This is all wrong and unwise. The true policy is to keep still about it, and not let the good among the Baptists scarcely know there is such a book. If they see their preachers excited about it, referring to it in their sermons; find editorial notices, full of excitement and vindictiveness, they will never rest till they see it, and this will be ruinous to our cause.

APOLLYON.—I agree with you; but then, how are preachers, that are really excited, perplexed, and confused, to keep it penned up in their breasts? Do you expect Mr. Jeter to keep silent, with a book before him, showing his sophisms, false issues, manifest perversions, passages of Scripture quoted falsely, important words left out, as we know, *designedly* to cover the true import? The thing is impossible. The truth is, we have led on Mr. J. B. Graves, Mr. Crowell, Mr. Ford, Mr. Sands, Mr. Jeter, and many others, to make the attack, to enter the arena of war, and thus called out an expose of them, and now to command them to be silent, is out of the question. You might as well think of fastening up the fires of Ætna or Vesuvius.

DIABOLOS.—I know it is a little humiliating to compel them now to hold their tongues, but it is the best that can be done, and they must submit to it. They must put on a sufficient amount of affectation, to say they are engaged in a great work, and cannot come down. We must get them out of this debating, or our cause is ruined.

APOLLYON.—I would not regard the matter so much if none but the Baptists were to be effected by the new impulses set upon foot by this book, and other kindred books. But the whole arena is again thrown open; the whole question of conversion, remission, union, and all matters with which we were so annoyed years ago, are now to be discussed anew, and our cause is bound to suffer immensely. I know not what is to be done.

DIABOLOS.—I am now sorry that we instigated the Baptists to commence this war, yet I do not see how we could have done better, for if we had allowed them to proceed united in the Bible Union, and communing with Disciples, till all bitterness and party feeling had been done away, they would have carried everything before them. But probably we had better now let them proceed, for we had the lips of many preachers among the Disciples pretty much sealed, and they measurably ceasing the illustration, elucidation, and full development of the great principles lying at the bottom of their movement.

LUCIFER.—That is true, but the course we have pursued has simply aroused them; and, I find, that they have men in immense numbers, of splendid information, great talent, and any amount of resources, that are now entering the arena, and no power that we can command can stop them. After instigating this new- war, as we have done, I know not what is to be done. To require the Baptists now to be quiet, not notice this book, and affect that their work is too great to come down to it, cannot be made to take with the people. They will declare Lard's book unanswerable.

DIABOLOS.—That may be, but it is the best that can be done for our cause. Let us try that expedient, at least till our next meeting.

REPORTER.

-----o-----

CONVERTING INFLUENCE.

"There is an influence of the Spirit, internal, mighty, and efficacious, differing from moral suasion, but ordinarily exerted through the inspired word in the conversion of sinners—an influence distinct and above the truth."—J. B. Jeter. Lard's *Review of Campbellism Examined,* pp. 41-42.

It is presumed that the above contains a fair statement of the doctrine of spiritual influence, as held by those who believe in its operating in conversion independently of the word of God. But I trust there are many who suppose Mr. Jeter's statement, as above, to be true, who, did they pause to consider the consequences its belief involves, would no longer accept it as true. He says, "There is an influence in the conversion of sinners distinct from and above the truth." What is that which is distinct from the truth? Error is certainly quite? distinct from the truth, and has exerted a most disastrous influence in the world. This influence, too, is "internal and mighty," but it is in the children of disobedience that it is exerted, and never has resulted in their conversion to God. But this influence, he says, is "mighty . . . in the conversion of sinners." Who is willing to admit the mighty influence of error in converting sinners to God! Even Mr. Jeter would recoil from this conclusion. But is it not in his premises? It does certainly seem to be; for he says this influence differs from moral suasion, is distinct from, and above, the truth. Does not the Holy Spirit influence in conversion by moral suasion—by the truth? Mr. Jeter says ordinarily it does. But, "the Spirit exerts an influence different from moral suasion, or persuading to act morally. Can anyone seriously believe this? The Spirit does influence sinners to act "ordinarily through the inspired word." Is it only when it influences "differently from moral suasion, distinctly from and above the truth," that its influence is mighty and efficacious? Does not the truth act by "moral suasion?" But Mr. Jeter's spiritual influence acts differently from the truth! Influence is defined—first, Literally a flowing in; secondly, In a general sense, it denotes power whose operation is invisible, and known only by its effects.—Webster. Now, is not the influence of the truth invisible in conversion, and known only by its effects? Does not the Spirit influence invisibly in conversion, according to Mr. Jeter; and if so, how does he or anyone know that it influences differently from the truth, except by its effects? Is the difference in the effects in kind or degree? If the difference is in the former, i. e., in kind, then, in one or the other, the effect is not the conversion of a sinner to God; but if the difference is in degree, then there is no conversion through the inspired word, though Mr. Jeter says ordinarily they are thus converted, because it is this influence which differs from moral suasion, distinct from and above the truth, that is efficacious.

If this doctrine of influence is mighty, internal and efficacious, it is all that is needed to convert sinners. This being so, where is the necessity of the Holy Spirit convincing the world of sin, righteousness, and judgment, by *speaking?* Yet this is the way its influence is exerted, not only ordinarily through the inspired word, but in no other way, in converting sinners to God. It has operated internally, mightily, and efficaciously on sinners without converting them to God. Balaam furnishes one instance of Mr. Jeter's kind of influence, but it did not convert him. Num. xxiv. 13 and xxxi. 8. Caiaphas is mother example of the mighty influence of the Spirit of God (John xi. 49-51), but it did not convert him.

The belief of Mr. Jeter's doctrine is an influence, different from moral suasion, that is mighty, internal and efficacious in obscuring human responsibility, in excusing men for living in sin, and from which the only means of getting rid, is, to know that in the conversion of sinners the Holy Spirit influences always and "ordinarily through the inspired word." J. M. HENRY.

DAYTON, OHIO, May 20, 1857.

-----o-----

REMARKS.

Mr. Jeter's explanation of the influence of the Spirit, provided it is the influence that converts men to Baptist principles and actuates them afterwards, furnishes a clue to several things otherwise unaccountable. He insists that "there is an influence of the Spirit, internal, mighty and efficacious, *differing* from moral suasion." This "influence," he affirms, "is distinct from and above the truth." No wonder that a people should be somewhat wily, schismatical and factious, under an influence confessedly "*differing* from moral suasion"—"*distinct from,* and *above the truth!*" Here is a clear concession, that all the Baptists have been saying about holding "the truth, the whole truth, and nothing but the truth," goes for nothing. "The truth, the whole truth, and nothing but the truth," is moral suasion, and nothing more; but Baptists contend for and defend an influence "*differing* from this"—"*distinct from* and *above the truth!*" This is the part of *Baptist,* not *spiritual,* influence, that we do not believe in—that which "differs from moral suasion"—is "distinct from and above the truth."

This is a little the boldest heresy we have seen. It does not claim to be the truth of God, nor moral suasion, but "differs from moral suasion"—is "distinct from the truth," and claims to be *"above* it." We have no doubt that this Baptist influence "differs from moral suasion," and is "distinct from the truth," but we deny that it is *above* it! Jesus prayed that men should be sanctified *through* the truth, and the Apostle says they are begotten by the truth, and not something *above* it. B. F.

TOUR TO ILLINOIS—MEETING AT MACOMB.

On Monday, May 25th, we took cars for the General Missionary Meeting at Macomb, Illinois. Leaving at 5 o'clock and 30 minutes in the morning, passing Hamilton, Eaton, Ohio; Richmond, Cambridge and Indianapolis, Indiana, we reached Lafayette, Indiana, at 2½ o'clock P. M. Having obtained a ticket for the Wabash Valley road, we found that we were to wait here seven hours. Accordingly, we determined to look round a little. For this purpose, we walked out in town, and had proceeded but a little ways when we saw Elder John Longley, with his market-basket on his arm, standing talking with some gentleman. This old servant of God has been a preacher of the gospel fifty-three years, and has brought to the fold of Jesus more than three thousand souls. He looked us in the face, when we spoke to him, giving him, at the same time, a hearty shake of the hand, and said: "You are on your way to the meeting at Macomb." We told him we were. With deep feeling, he said: "Oh, how I long to see the brethren once more, but there is one difficulty in the way." I inquired what that was. He said, "The money to bear expenses." I told him to come ahead—that we would overcome that—that we would help him out, if it took the last money we ever saw. We walked on to his residence, when he presented the matter to his affectionate, worthy and Christian lady. Here was a hard struggle. She knew be desired to go, but that they really had not a dollar of their hard earnings that they could well spare. We can conceive the delicate position in which she stood, and recollect how distinctly she showed her desire that he should be gratified in going, while she showed that she knew not how to spare the money for expenses; but we cannot describe how she did it. She soon cheerfully yielded for him to go, and with her two fine daughters, every exertion was made to make all things ready and encourage him, with abundant assurances that everything would go on right till he would return.

At half past 9 o'clock, we set off down the beautiful Wabash Valley, in forty miles crossing the State line, for the first time, in the wide spread prairies of Illinois. Passing Danville, Ill., we reached Decatur at 4 o'clock in the morning, and found that eleven hours must be spent here for cars from the south passing north to Peoria junction. This was horrible! But it was immutable as the fates. Hungry and disgusting runners met us so thick and importunate to go to sundry hotels, that we could hardly get out of the cars. We concluded that we would hear none of them, but remain at the Junction House, which we did, though much of the time we could not get even a place to sit down. Finally the time was out, the train arrived and we set off; but, to our mortification, on reaching the junction, we found that we must remain there over night. This bitter, however, had its sweet. It afforded us a good night's sleep. On the morning of May 27th, we found ourselves scarcely in sight of timber. We could see cattle from three to five miles off. I was shown one or two houses that must have been ten miles off. Amid all this, however, we were restless, for the meeting was to begin this morning, and we were one hundred miles off, and that to be made on three different pieces of railroad.

At 9 o'clock we started for Peoria, Ill., and reached there in due time; waited three hours for connection, and passed to Galesburg, where we waited one hour, and took a southern train and reached Macomb after sun set.

The evening before, we passed Bloomington, one of the most beautiful towns, in the most beautiful country we ever saw. But in this pleasant town and country, as in old Eden, the enemy has long since sown the seeds of discord among the friends of the Lord, and immense injury to the cause and unhappiness to the children of God has, as a matter of course, followed. Wm. F. M. Avery figured largely in this disagreeable affair, but has now found a place in Kansas, where there is plenty of work congenial to his nature.

On the morning of the 27th, we passed Eureka, the new home of Bro. C. L. Loos, now President of Eureka College. A more beautiful country than this will be hard to find in the world. The good things of the world abound here. The cause of the Lord is upon a permanent basis. Education is on the ascendant. Bro. Loos is certainly at home here, and appreciated we trust, as his merits, deserve, Thanks to the Lord for such men and for such fields of usefulness as are opening to them.

On reaching Macomb, before we had stepped off the cars, we were seized by the band of Bro. I. N. Carman, formerly of Ohio, but now editor of the *Sentinel,* published in Peoria, Ill. In an instant more, we grasped the hand of Bro. John Stewart, with whom we formed an acquaintance, twenty-six years ago, in Henry county, Ind., and were introduced to his son Decatur, born several years since our acquaintance with his father, but now grown, pretty well educated, and making commendable efforts at preaching the gospel. We were introduced to many others immediately, whose names we cannot now recollect, but among them, Bro. C. D. Roberts, who took us into his carriage, and in a short time reached the residence of Bro. Twyman, where we were introduced to Sister Twyman and Bro. W. W. Happy, and afforded every kindness and comfort heart could wish.

In a few minutes we were in the Christian Chapel, where a large audience had assembled. Here we met brethren Parmer, Davenport, Taffe, Loos, Lindsey, Murphy, Lamphear, Reynolds, Perkey, Atkinson, Griffin, Major, and many more that we cannot now recollect. How good and how precious are brethren in the Lord! Able addresses were this evening delivered by brethren Happy and Lindsey. By these addresses, and meeting this army of brethren, we were greatly strengthened and comforted. As before mentioned, Bro. John Longley has been a preacher of the gospel fifty-three years, and Bro. Frank Palmer near the same length of time. They were well acquainted in former years. They are still both strong in faith, giving glory to God. How precious the meeting of these old servants of God!

On Thursday evening we met an hour before the time for the addresses, for prayer and exhortation. During this precious interview, Bro. Longley was called upon for a word of exhortation, when he responded in such an exhortation as none but one standing near two worlds—in one and almost in sight of the other—could give. The effect was most happy. A strange brother, not knowing that he had not money to take him home, but gathering from his remarks that he was poor, moved that a contribution be made for him, which was immediately done, while we united in one of the most joyful songs of praise to God, in which we ever participated. Some $33 was immediately contributed, to which more was afterward added, making near $40, and leaving him with more money when he returned home than when he left. Thanks be to God for his unspeakable gift! The addresses this evening, by brethren Loos and Lamphear, were able, instructive and in the right spirit, and did great good. An able address had also been delivered at 10 o'clock in the morning, by Bro. Atkinson, followed by appropriate and sensible remarks by Bro. O. E. Burgess, editor of the *Sentinel,* with Bro. Carman. At two o'clock, P. M., we were addressed at great length, and with much ability, by Bro. Apperson. We followed with a few remarks, explanatory of the Missionary Society, the Jerusalem Mission, and the probability of a Mission to Jamaica. Taken all in all, this was a happy day, and one long to be remembered.

On Friday, the 29th, brethren Bates and Johnson, from Iowa, had arrived. Brethren Piper, from Kentucky, and Russell, from Missouri, were also present; and, I think, during the same day, Elder M. Combs was seen in our midst. This was the first time we ever saw Bro. Bates, though we have been familiar with him for years, as editor of the *Christian Evangelist.* Bro. Bates is a safe and true man, and deserving of much esteem for his noble efforts in the cause. Elder Combs is an old soldier, whom we heard preach before we were in the faith, has fought many great and good battles for truth and righteousness. He is a little fearful of clerical domination—that Young America will run off with us; but we will try and rein him up a little and regulate him, and, we trust, it will be found that there is something noble in him. At 10 o'clock we addressed the audience at full length on the great work of converting the world, and were followed by Bro. Murphy, President of Abingdon College, with able and appropriate remarks.

Never did we witness more harmony among brethren, nor a better spirit. It is true, there were some local partialities about proper fields, or what fields should be first cultivated, but all were in favor of the great missionary work—or emphatically for the great commission, "Go disciple *all nations"*—"Preach the gospel to every creature." The benevolence of the meeting ran parallel with the love of God to man, the death of the Redeemer and the commission to the Apostles. We are aware that some men can speak with ineffable contempt of the idea of a body of people numbering not more than three hundred thousand, making an attack upon and starting out to convert the world. But we stop not to count men, nor measure purses, we proceed upon the principle that the cause is of God—that God is in it—that the Holy Spirit is in it—that divine power, the power of God for salvation, is in it. We look at the little band of one hundred and twenty present on Pentecost, who were commanded to preach the gospel to every creature—*"disciple* all nations," and who obeyed the command—never ceased till their sound went into all the world—till Paul was able to say, the hope of the gospel has been preached to every creature under heaven. The same God that commanded them to preach the gospel to every creature, commands us now to do it. and the same God was with them, as he promised, saying, "I will be with you always, even unto the end of the world," will be with those now commanded to preach the gospel to all nations. It is nothing but unbelief that leads the children of God for one moment to hesitate in enlisting in this great work. We *can,* if we *will,* go at the work, in the Lord's name, in his spirit and power, leaving houses and lands, wives and children, fathers and mothers, carry the ancient gospel again throughout the world—send it to every creature, and thus fill the earth with the glory of God. Shall we, in the Lord's name, and with his blessing, do this great work? We had just as well do something noble and great as linger along at a miserable, poor, dying rate. The Christian religion is, in its very soul and essence, a proselyting religion. Its mission is to disciple the nations; and whenever any member, or the church, loses sight of this, death must ensue. No round of sermons, prayers, songs and ordinances can keep a church alive when it loses the spirit of the great commission, and disrespects the authority that commands the gospel to be preached to every creature. No church that forms itself into a kind of Jewish synagogue, with a routine of ceremonies, merely for its own enjoyment and gratification, is worth anything to mankind, or ought to live. The Lord died for *the world.* The Apostles were sent to *the world.* The church is not for itself, as no man lives for himself, but for *the world.*

The preaching brethren at Macomb felt this, and though many of them have but a small pittance of this world's goods, some thirty-five or forty of them, at this meeting, put down $5 each, and pledged the same amount annually, simply for the General Missionary Society. Many other brethren contributed freely, and some three hundred and thirteen dollars was raised, and a considerable amount pledged. Bro. John Miller, of Eureka, donated three lots in that town, worth from two to three hundred dollars. Beside this, the brethren present decided that they would lay the matter at stated periods before the churches, and thus induce a systematic action in reference to this great work.

Though there were near fifty Illinois preachers present, we learned that there were more than fifty in that State not present. Bro. John S. Sweeney, of Waverly, Ill who has corresponded largely with us, and done much for us, was present, and many others whom we cannot now mention or recollect. Bro. Miller, a very amiable preacher, resides at Macomb.

On Saturday the rain was so incessant that we did not think there would be any meeting, and we spent the morning in writing. We learned, however, that a small congregation assembled, and were ably addressed by Eld. M. Combs. We met again, and were ably and agreeably addressed by Bro. W. Martin, at 3 o'clock. We addressed the audience at night. On Lord's day we addressed a dense audience in the Christian Chapel at half past 10 o'clock. The Methodists and Presbyterians cheerfully tendered their houses for brethren to address their audiences. Bro. Martin spoke in one house, and Bro. Apperson in the other. Bro. Piper, of Ky., spoke in one house, and Bro. Griffin, of Ill., in the other at night. We learned that large audiences were in attendance all the time. We spoke again in Christian Chapel at night. At the close, one lady confessed the Savior.

Here we took the parting hand with many, in many tears and much affection, whom we shall meet no more in this world.

"When we asunder part, It gives us inward pain, But still, we're joined in heart, And hope to meet again."

On Monday at 8 o'clock we took the cars for Abingdon, where we had agreed to stop and preach one discourse. In about an hour, we arrived, and were met at the cars by President Murphy, Prof. Reynolds, brethren Davis, Stewart and others, and spent a few happy hours with these distinguished brethren. Here a vast expanse of rich, beautiful and rolling prairie, with some skirts of timber is spread before the eye. Brethren Murphy and Reynolds have beautiful residences near town, and are very desirably situated.

After dining, we were shown the College building, a very respectable edifice, indeed, for a new country like this. From this edifice, without any exception, is spread out before the eye the most extended and beautiful landscape we ever saw. A considerable portion of a county can be seen at one glance from here.

At 4 o'clock, we addressed, in the College hall, a large audience, on the necessity of being born again. We were listened too with marked attention, during an address of more than an hour and a half, and, we trust, not without profit. We learned that several preachers, identified with sectarian parties, were present.

After tea, with a son-in-law of Bro. Davis, whose name we have forgotten, we were accompanied to the cars with many of these dear brethren, where we took the parting hand, entered the cars, passed to Chicago before sunrise next morning, over two hundred miles, and passing on *via* Michigan City, Lafayette, where we left Bro. Longley, and Indianapolis, we reached home at 1 o'clock Wednesday morning, thus making more than 1200 miles travel and attending these meetings, in some ten days. B. F.

-----o-----

SPIRITUAL INFLUENCE.

DEAR. BRO. FRANKLIN:—In the *Review* for June is a discourse by Bro. J. A. Clarke, on the Mission of the Holy Spirit, which contains sentiments that, with all love for Bro. C., I deem very untenable and very pernicious in their influence. I refer to column second, p. 166, and what follows, and especially to this sentence: "The Spirit now dwells in the church by its moral presence through its word—and in no other way." We are all in the habit of denying the charge so often made against us—that we do not teach that the spirit at present has any work to perform in the salvation of men—as a gross misrepresentation of our views. But when our enemies are able to turn to such sentiments as these, our mouths are closed; for, although we know that they are not the prevailing sentiment among us, to *them* it seems but a dodge for the occasion, to say so. I am not one of those who reject everything that I cannot fully comprehend and explain. I could do but little with the things of man with this rule, much less could I do with the word of God, with all its great infinities and profundity of wisdom. If I am much benefited, I must seek unto God with more humility. I presume Bro. Clarke will agree with me in this, and that he is not one that finds no profound mysteries in the Bible. Why then make the indwelling of the Spirit of God an exception?— Why subject it to rationalistic rules of interpretation? unless we are prepared to go out into the world and deny everything that will not submit to such rules.

I presume that those of us who think the Reformation is losing its moral power over the world, will find a solution of the problem, in the fact that, in those districts, where there is any ground for such fears, just such views of the work of the Spirit has prevailed.. A *merely logical* religion will *not* make men any better, else why does not simple moral philosophy arm men against temptation. Christianity has succeeded because it does not recognize man's intellectual as his highest nature, and has ignored the maxim that "to educate is to reform," but has dug deeper, and found a spiritual nature, and, by bringing it out in the warm sunshine of heaven, has made man strong against sin.

If Bro. Clark will look again at the reason Peter gives for promising the Pentecostians the gift of the Holy Spirit, he will see that it was because *the promise made by Joel was to them* as well as well as the Apostles. This is confirmed by turning to Joel and reading a little more than Peter quoted.

Now I submit to Bro. C. the following: Peter said the reception of the personal Spirit by the hundred and twenty was that which Joel promised. Peter and Joel both say that the promise extended to all the world, *and their descendants,* who should obey the gospel. Therefore, all who obey the gospel, are promised the gift of the personal Spirit.

Of course we understand in different measures. If Bro. Clark asks, Why, then, do not all work miracles: the answer is simply this, viz.: When God sent his Spirit to work miracles, it worked them; when he sent it to reveal truth, it did *that;* and when he only sent it to comfort the saints, it *comforted* them, and confined itself to the mission on which it was sent.

Many of the passages that Bro. C. has quoted as of so easy an explanation upon his theory, refer simply to the spirit of man, and not the Spirit of God. But there are some that he has not quoted that might be more difficult as well as some of those he has given. I submit that whatever spirit it was essential for the Roman saints to have (See Rom. viii. 9-11), was the identical Spirit that raised Jesus from the dead, and will raise us from the dead. If we are simply to have the disposition of Christ, then the disposition of Christ raised him up, and will be the agent that will raise us up. If we are simply to have the moral presence of the Spirit, then the moral presence was the active agent in his resurrection, and will be in ours; but if the personal Spirit is the active agent in the resurrection, then we must have the indwelling of the personal Spirit in order to be Christ's. See also 1st Cor. vi. 19: "Know ye not that your body is the temple of the Holy Ghost which is in you, which ye have of God, and ye are not your own?" II Cor. vi. 16: "For ye are the temple of the living God; as God hath said I will dwell in them and walk in them." Eph. xi. 22: "In whom ye also are builded together for an habitation of God through the Spirit." Let us humbly receive and rejoice in this truth, though we may not be able fully to comprehend it.

S. E. PEARRE.

REMARKS.

We have not preached a discourse on the influence of the Spirit for years; and, what is of vastly more importance, the Apostles never preached a discourse, or wrote an article upon that subject. When they would induce men to believe, they preached Christ crucified, buried and risen. When they would show men what to do, they preached the commandment of Christ. When they would inspire in the hearts of Christians the hope of the gospel, they preached the promises of Christ. When men believed the facts of the gospel, obeyed the commandments and hoped for that which was promised, they were happy and contented, without all these metaphysics *how* the Lord pardons, *how* the Spirit operates, *how* prayer is answered, etc. If we can learn *what* we are to believe, *how we* are to do what is commanded, and *how* confidently to hope for what is promised—in a word, *how we are to do the will of God*; and, having learned *how,* if we do it from the heart, the Lord will do his work, and do it right, whether we ever can tell *how* he does it or not.

Never did the enemy more successfully inveigle professors of religion and preachers, than by leading them off from the question *how* they shall do what the Lord commands to a dispute *how* the Lord operates by his Spirit upon the souls of men in their conversion and sanctification. Let the preacher preach Christ—preach the gospel faithfully, and when men believe the gospel, believe in Christ, and inquire what they must do to be saved, give them the answer of the inspired Apostles. Let the sinners do what the Lord commands—do it honestly and solemnly, in obedience to the Lord, and there is no danger but the Spirit will do his work, and do it right, whether we understand, or can explain *how* he does it or not. The difficulty is not that God does not do his work, and do it right, nor is it that the Spirit does not do his work, and do it right, but the difficulty is, that men do not do their work right, or do not do it at all.

The ministry is not sent to explain how the Spirit operates, nor to plead with God to do what they would represent him as having omitted, and what he would appear unwilling to do. He is willing to pardon sinners, ready to do it at any moment, and never failed to do it, in a single instance, where the sinner came according to his word. The Apostles plead with men—"Be ye reconciled to God"—"Save yourselves from this untoward generation"—and said, "We persuade men." But in this time of delusion and ignorance, the preacher frequently turns round and reasons and expostulates with God, as follows: "Now, Lord, we desire the salvation of these mourners, and have come here to pray for them. They desire salvation, and have come here to pray for themselves. Lord, thou knowest that neither they nor we can do anything. They believe, have cast themselves upon thee, and are seeking thy salvation. Thou hast promised, that those who seek shall find; that those who ask shall receive. These precious souls are seeking, and we are asking. Come now—come with power—come down with converting power—come with the Holy Spirit, and save these sinners." Who has not witnessed scenes like this in numerous instances? Who, too, does not know that nine-tenths of these who thus come and thus seek, go away without even professing pardon? and those who profess it, have not a promise of God, or any evidence that they have obtained it. Who is to blame for these miserable failures? Not the sinner, for he came and did, according to the representation, all that he could. Not the preacher, for he was willing, and did all that he could. Where shall we find the cause of the failure then? According to this system of things, the cause of the failure, was not on the part of the seeker, for he did all that he could, nor on the part of the preacher, for he did all that he could, but the cause of the failure was that the Lord would not send the Spirit to do what could not be done without him. This whole theory represents the failure to be on the part of heaven, and not on the part of man. This is as false as it is wicked and sinful. The fault is on the part of man in every failure. No sinner ever failed of salvation because the Spirit did not do his work, nor because the Lord did not do his work. All these failures, many of which leave persons in doubt till the hour of their death, are on the part of man, and generally the preacher, at that, who is experimenting upon a human scheme not containing one scrap of Divine authority. For this manifest departure from the practice of the holy Apostles, there is not a man in the world who can offer anything in the shape of a reason. What the Apostles told inquirers to do to be saved, pardoned or justified, is so plainly inscribed in the Acts of Apostles, that no man can be excusable who will give an entirely different direction to the inquirer, leading to a practice not mentioned in the Bible.

Preaching about *how* the Spirit operates never *causes* him to operate, much less explains to him *how* he should operate. God will operate right. The Spirit will operate right. The divine influence will be infallibly right. But what we fear is, that men will not operate right. Let us, then, preach to *men,* to be reconciled to God, to do God's will, to operate right, and let the preacher operate right himself. In doing this, we must preach the *gospel of Christ,* and not *our views* of spiritual influence, to save men. If men desire salvation, give them the commandments of God, and exhort them to obey them. If they do this, God, the Lord Jesus and the Holy Spirit, will do all things well. Believing in spiritual influence, and preaching it, is no evidence that a man has it, or that he will bring anybody else under it. Bringing the fruits of the Spirit is the only evidence that a man has it. Every pretender, even down to the infamous Joe Smith, preached the spirit, and claimed to have it, but none, only those who at heart love God and honestly keep his commandments, have it.

B. F.

-----o-----

BRACKEN ASSOCIATION OF UNITED BAPTISTS.
NUMBER VI.

In our last we showed that the Elders of the Bracken Association believe that the great mass of our people have neither been converted nor baptized, and that therefore all such persons, to become members of Baptist Churches, must be converted and immersed. And that, as a consequence, they are holding communion with some of that class among them, received from our churches, who have never been baptized at all, if converted! In this number we propose to examine a charge brought against us by the Association, in these words: "*But the Reformers are the most inconsistent of all others, in their profession of open communion.*" The italics are Elder Gardner's. After having shown, to his satisfaction, that, so far as the Evangelical sects practice "open communion," they are quite inconsistent, he adds: "But the Reformers are the most inconsistent of all others," upon this subject. "The Baptists (he adds) *could* practice open communion with far more consistency than the Reformers." How so, Bro. Gardner? Because, We believe that a person must experience a change of heart before he is a fit subject for baptism," pp. 32. But as we deny a change of heart, as a pre-requisite to baptism, we cannot practice open communion as consistently as you! You are determined, then, notwithstanding our uniform and constant denials, if possible, to make your people, and the world, believe that we are disposed to baptize persons without a change of heart, or even a profession of it! This is most contemptible! Again you say, in the next sentence: "Accordingly, we believe that our Paedobaptist brethren, *generally,* are truly *converted,* and need nothing but immersion, and union with a true church of Jesus Christ (the baptist Church, of course), to qualify them for the Lord's Supper." What, then, are the conclusions from these premises? Clearly these: The Paedobaptists lack two things to qualify them for the Lord's Table, namely, immersion and union with a true Church of Jesus Christ. But our people, who were baptized for the remission of sins, lack three things—conversion, baptism, and union with a true church of Christ! We have neither conversion, baptism, nor union with a true church of Jesus Christ, according to Bro. Gardner! This clearly is the charge against us, or there is no meaning in the Elder's language. This, too, we say, is most contemptible, because most false, as all know, who take the least pains to understand us, and do us justice.

But wherein appears the great inconsistency in our practice, in regard to communion? We may not be perfectly uniform, everywhere, in this matter; but, so far as I know, this is our manner. The table we spread is the Lord's Table, furnished with the bread and wine as the memorials of the broken body, and shed blood of Christ. "The cup of blessing which we bless, is it not the communion of the blood of Christ? The bread which we break, is it not the body of Christ. For we being many are one bread," or our unity as members of the one body is represented by the one loaf, and our joint participation of it: *"For* we are all partakers of that one bread." In the original institution of this ordinance, as recorded in Matthew xxvi. 26th, 27th and 28th verses, Jesus says to his disciples, having blessed the broad, "Take, eat; this is my body." And, having given thanks for the cup, "He gave it to them, saying, drink ye all of it." When the Corinthians had abused the Lord's Supper, by converting it into a sort of Bacchanalian feast, to correct that fearful abuse, he thus writes to them, 1st Cor. chap, xi.: "For I have received of the Lord, that which I also delivered unto you. That the Lord Jesus, the same night in which he was betrayed, took bread; and when he had given thanks he brake it and said, Take, eat; this is my body which is broken for you; this do in remembrance of me. After the same manner also, he took the cup, when he had supped, saying, This cup is the New Testament in my blood; this do ye as often as ye drink it, in remembrance of me. For as often as ye eat this bread, and drink this cup, ye do show the Lord's death till he come. Wherefore whosoever shall eat this bread, and drink this cup of the Lord unworthily, shall be guilty of the body and blood of the Lord. But let a man examine himself, and so let him eat of that bread, and drink of that cup." Here we have before us, in the language of Christ, and his inspired Apostle, a brief but clear account of the origin, the nature and design of this holy ordinance. What, then, are its teachings?

1. That it is an institution of Jesus Christ, having the seal of his Divine authority upon it.

2. That it was instituted for his disciples, for Christians, and no others.

3. That it is designed to show forth the Lord's death, as a sacrifice for our sins, and our trust in his precious blood for salvation, till he come a second time without a sin-offering, to save his people eternally in heaven.

4. That the obligation to attend to this ordinance, arises from the Divine command, "Take, eat—Drink ye all—Do this in remembrance of me;" and from the relation of his redeemed elect, saved people to him and his cross.

5. Persons may eat and drink unworthily, and therefore be fearfully guilty; not persons who have no standing in the church, for they, of course, are not alluded to, but persons who have professed the Christian faith, and submitted to the one Christian baptism. Thus it was at Corinth. And hence the Apostle says: "For this cause many are weak and sickly among you, and many sleep"—have been visited with death

for their abuse of the holy ordinance of the Lord.

6. None were invited to partake of this Divine Institution, simply because they were recognized as members of the church, but were exhorted to examine themselves, and so eat and so drink.

Now, then, in view of these positions, which are as clear as a sunbeam, we affirm that we have no right to invite any to this table, not even of the members of the church, or congregation in which we spread it. We have a right only to say, "It is the Lord's Table, furnished with the Lord's provisions, for the Lord's people; let every member examine himself or herself, and so eat and so drink." If, then, we have no right even to invite as such even the members of a Christian congregation, what have we to do with free, or mixed, or open communion? and, above all, what have we to do with the sects, schisms, or heresies of the times? Not one of these existed in the days of Paul, and not one of them can show a Divine charter for its being. Do you say this is a hard sentence? Not at all. There is not in it one word against the piety or Christianity of the members of these sects; for Christianity is something wholly distinct from, and independent of all these schismatic religions. This sentence therefore, is not ours, but the sentence of Divine Truth; nay, more, the sentence of the sects, pronounced against themselves. The Episcopalians say there are Christians beyond the precincts of Episcopalianism. Methodists, in all their seven or eight phases or parties, admit there are Christians outside of them all. So of all the Presbyterian parties, the Lutheran parties, the Baptist parties, and the entire catalogue of what is self-styled the Evangelical or Orthodox sects. But would these parties allow there are Christians beyond the pale of Christianity? Not they; for this were infidel.

You give it up, then, that there is no Christianity in your particular *isms,* and, as a matter of course, that God never made you—ever authorized your existence as sects. So far as you are Christians, simply Christians, you are of God; so far as you are sects, you are of men; "are carnal and walk as men." I shall never forget hearing a Presbyterian, who was trying to establish a Sunday School in a village, many years ago, remark, that the object of the school was not to make Presbyterians; and so say the Methodists, Baptists, Episcopalians. Their schools are not established to make partisans. But while these Evangelical parties would be ashamed to avow that their schools are gotten up simply to make persons members of their respective parties, would they be ashamed to let all the world know that they got up Sunday Schools to make Christians? Certainly not. You concede, then, that Christianity is something entirely distinct from *one* and *all* of your isms! Still, notwithstanding all these concessions, we would, by no means, admit that the Orthodox sects, generally see or feel the force of their own recognized admissions. Nay, more, they frequently make statements almost in the same breath, perfectly antagonistic; for instance—At a meeting conducted by one of the most numerous sects, at which there was a great amount of excitement, the preacher said, to this effect, if not in these words: "If we come here to make M, we pray God to defeat the object."

"As sinners, when I urge you to come to Christ, you will say—"You are so much divided among yourselves, we don't know where to go.'" "Why," said he, "instead of regarding this as a difficulty, you ought to thank God for the existence of so many parties, so many branches of the church, that all may be suited. We believe ours is the best way, but if you can't go with us, go with the Presbyterians, Baptists, Reformers—be a Christian, and join some branch of the church."

Here, in one breath, we are told by the preacher that he would be ashamed to be engaged in seeking merely to make persons members of his party or church, and yet in the next breath, that God has made all these sects, and that therefore we ought to thank him for them, because he has made them that we might all be suited!! This surely is confusion, fearfully confounded. What! admit that there is no Christianity in the distinctive peculiarities of the sects, and yet maintain that God is the author of all these antagonistic parties!—that God in Methodism, in its six or eight methods, is arrayed against God in Presbyterianism, in its half dozen or more phases! That God, in all the forms of Baptistism, is arrayed against God in Methodism in all its methods, and Presbyterianism in all its forms; and so of all the rest. How supremely ridiculous the thought; I had like to have said, blasphemous! What! Chris: divided against himself!! Then his kingdom cannot stand. Then he casts out devils by Beelzebub, the prince of devils! Why, sirs, this is to make Christianity little better than Paganism. What was the glory or the shame of Paganism? Was it not that it changed the glory of the incorruptible God into an image made like to corruptible man, and to four footed beasts, and creeping things, and fowls of the air? That its gods were

"Changeful, passionate, unjust,
Whose attributes were rage, revenge and lust?"

That the gods practiced all the vices that degrade and disgrace human nature? That, therefore, every sinner, even the most debased, could find a patron god whom he could most devoutly worship, as the Roman Catholics (whose religion is Paganism christianized, or Christianity paganized) have patron saints; and as our preacher claimed that God has made all the antagonistic orthodox parties, that every one might find a religion to suit his taste?! What superlative nonsense, to say nothing worse!

Alas! the history of the world but too clearly demonstrates that all false religions are corruptions of the true religion, and that they have originated in that depravity that loves darkness rather than light, falsehood rather than truth; that changes the truth of God into a lie; that caters to the corrupt hearts and lives of sinners, by making a religion to suit their tastes. But, for Protestants, in the midst of the nineteenth century, after conceding that there is no Christianity in their sectarian peculiarities, to stand up and proclaim that the infinitely wise and benevolent Author of the Christian religion, which consists in one body and one spirit—one hope, one Lord, one faith, one baptism, one God and Father of all; I repeat, to proclaim that the divine Author of this pure and holy religion, is, at the same time, the maker of all the schismatic religious systems of orthodoxy, falsely so called; and that he has constructed all these antagonistic systems, by way of suiting himself to the notions and tastes of sinners,—this, we say, is too bad—nay, it is abominable! In view of the facts, then, that God never made these parties—that they are self-made, self-named, and self-condemned, we know them not at the table of the Lord;—we only know Christians there, and admonish them to examine themselves, and so eat and so drink, in view of their personal responsibility to the great lawgiver, who is able to save and to destroy. As none of our parties existed in the days of the Apostles, as a matter of course, the apostolic churches never heard of *open, free, mixed,* or restricted communion, in our sense of these terms. A worthy membership in any one congregation of Christians, would be a passport to fellowship, communion, or membership, in any other Christian congregation, throughout the entire body of Christ. An evangelist of any one church, recognized as worthy, would be so recognized by all the churches of Christ everywhere. On the questions of communion, co-operation, etc., there was no trouble in those days. We are determined, therefore, by the help of God, to have nothing to do with these difficulties, which our schisms have made, contrary to the doctrine of Christ, but to labor to bring the people of God, who have been scattered in the "dark and cloudy day," amid the mists and smoke of Mystic Babylon, to stand together in the one body, with the one spirit, animated by the one hope of eternal life, trusting in the one Lord and lawgiver, by the one faith, having put on the one Lord, by the one baptism, and recognizing the one God, the Father of all in all, and with us all. More anon.

JOHN ROGERS.

-----o-----

EXCURSION TO NORTHERN ILLINOIS. NUMBER IV.

On the day after I preached in the College Chapel at Mt. Morris, I was conducted by Bro. H. to Brookville, Carrol county, Ill., where I filled an appointment made for me in the Evangelical Meetinghouse (Albright's), preaching in the German language. The audience was moderate in numbers—would probably been greater, had not a preacher of that order used some strong dissuasives from going, among the members of the congregation that worships there. Those that were present gave me unrelaxed attention Whilst I enforced the import of the 21st verse of the 7th chap, of the gospel by Matthew. The learning and doing the will of God in the present life were urged as indispensable in the preparation for a better life.

Brookville is located in the vicinity of Chamber's Grove, upon as fertile territory as the most aspiring agriculturist could wish—the prairie is pleasantly undulating, and skirted by a grove, that yields the requisite fuel and fencing, of the enterprising population of this attractive region. The inhabitants are mostly Pennsylvania Germans, whose industry and skill in agriculture is almost proverbial,—the improvements remind the visitor strongly of the appearance of Lancaster, Dauphine and York counties, Pennsylvania. In this measurably German community resides Bro. H. Hofheins, with whom I tarried over night, and who has everything good in the superlative. He has the best farm in his immediate neighborhood; the best park of domesticated deer; the best fruit I tasted the past year; the best trained family I saw during my tour; and the best arrangement in his newly erected mansion for home education. One apartment of his spacious domicile was especially constructed for a room of instruction. Whilst his Pennsylvania neighbors are tardy in the support of good schools, he is determined to have his family, consisting of a number of interesting daughters, thoroughly educated, under his personal inspection, by a well qualified teacher, or instructress, residing under his roof. "With him, wealth, without education, in its plenary sense, is but a means of low and gross enjoyment. May he meet with a full gratification of his educational aspirations! After enjoying the free hospitality of Bro. H. for a dozen of hours, Bro. Hammer conveyed me to the residence of the late Bro. G. Moffet, on the margin of Cherry Grove, some fourteen miles from Bro. Hofheins. Here we entered the "house of mourning." The once active proprietor of this well furnished house, had, two weeks before our arrival, gone to his "long home." Two months before, when my appointments were communicated to him, he expressed great satisfaction, intimating that the anticipated meeting would be very interesting to him. But alas! how precarious is human existence!—but a few weeks after this, he was attacked by the typhoid fever, and was interred two weeks before my arrival at his house. Bro. Moffet was a fair preacher—a man of great energy—acquired a great amount of property, of which he made liberal distributions for the advancement of the various significant interests of life. He enjoyed the confidence of society at large, and was universally esteemed. He left an amiable companion and five interesting children behind him, who have and are receiving liberal educations—are intellectually and morally qualified to act a profitable part on the arena of human life.

On Friday evening I preached at a spacious school-house on his premises, to a respectable auditory, on the Fear of the Lord. On Saturday evening, the audience was larger. The theme was Submission to God. On Lord's day morning, the house was crowded; the subject was the Promotion of "the truth." Great attention was given to what was said, and apparently good impressions were made. After service, I was accosted by a person who had not on his meeting-going clothes, with no common earnestness, to accompany him to his house, in sight of the place of meeting, and unite two willing hearts in the bonds of matrimony. As such cases seldom admit of postponement, I complied with his request, united the parties, being the four hundred and thirty-ninth pair that I have bound with the silken cords of Hymen—a circumstance that awakens no common reflections in my mind. I am afraid I never united that many to the Lord Christ, whom I profess and endeavor to serve. The betrothing of believing penitent and loving hearts to him, is, by far, nobler, in the eyes of all good beings, than numerous officiations at the hymnal altar.

At this school house, I delivered five discourses, all aiming more at the instruction and encouragement of the Disciples than gaining accessions to members.

On Monday evening, we returned to Bro Hofheins, and preached again in English, in the Albright meeting-house, to a very attentive audience, who undoubtedly learned that we are no such errorists as our opponents are wont to represent us.

With this I conclude my circuit through some of the loveliest regions that ever greeted my vision. My last discourse in the Commonwealth of Illinois was in the vicinity of Bro. Hammer's, on Domestic Education, based on the words of Solomon: "A wise son maketh a glad father, but a foolish son is the heaviness of his mother." All were attentive to the remarks made, and good seemed to be done. I now turned my face homeward, and, without suffering any great annoyance or calamity on my return, I arrived among my own—grateful to God for protection and comfort.

SAMUEL K. HOSHOUR.

-----o-----

AN ELDER AND A "TRIO OF EDITORS,"

BRO. FRANKLIN—*My Dear Sir:*—As the *American Christian Review* and the *Christian Age,* and their editors, have been on the most friendly relations, as far as I am aware, I was surprised to see in your June number a paragraph or two from an Indiana Elder, showing a feeling of hostility towards the *Age.* As the moans of this man have been heard before, the surprise is not that the paragraphs should have been written, but that they should have found admission into your columns.

What now is the occasion of the remarkable irritability shown by Elder Samuel K. Hoshour? Sometime last year he sent us for publication in the *Age,* number one of a series of articles. Upon reading the communication, we declined publishing it. That is all. Afterwards the article was printed in the *Review,* and we raise no question as to discretion here. You exercise your judgment as to what you shall publish—we do the same. But it seems that this is a questionable right; and, perhaps, some time ahead, when the rights of negroes and women shall have been settled, those of editors may come up for discussion. In the mean time, so far as the *Age* is concerned, we will assume that we have the right to exercise our discretion, be it much or little, as to what we will, or will not, publish; and no sneers from men of wounded feelings will be apt to change our purpose. The impression seems to be that we have used the Elder badly. We certainly had no such intention, and *we do not use him at all*. It is evident that if an editor has the right to decline a communication, its author has no right to take offense. Rights do not interfere. If we have not trespassed upon the rights of Elder Hoshour, he has upon ours. There is something wrong somewhere.

We would have been pleased, after having declined the favor of the Elder, to have had no further occasion to notice it; but the attempt has been made to *punish* us, and we are not allowed to be quiet. And now, since we have to face the music of the brass band, and the marching and countermarching of the bugs, let us, since we can't help ourselves, examine this rejected article with what patience, and what grace we may.

Will the reader turn back to page 89 of the *Review,* and examine the first two paragraphs of the Elder's article number one. It will be seen that Elder H. is on a tour, and, having reached a place called Pond, he says:

"Here I stopped at the semblance of a hotel, with the express stipulation, that I was to have a 'downy bed of ease,' as my uncarnal physical man protests against all indurated mattrasses." It ought to be suggested in favor of this poor landlord, that possibly the stipulations of our learned Elder are so elegantly and technically stated, as to be quite beyond his comprehension. To pass by the poetical "downy bed of ease," what could an obscure hotel-keeper—nay, what can anybody make out of an *uncarnal physical man's* protests? "Indurated mattrasses," too, would have required translation before it would have been understood that the "uncarnal physical" man's dislike was merely to a *hard bed.* But let us, for the present, pass by the door of the chamber, which no plasterer ever "graduated," and as the Elder *"progressed* to Decatur," we will *progress* to the next paragraph.

Here, says the "uncarnal physical man," "I committed myself to my stipulated couch with an unconfined anticipation of a full fruition of the balmy reign of 'nature's sweet restorer.'" This means, when put into plain English, that Elder Hoshour went to *bed expecting to sleep!*—unless the whole passage is modified by the word "unconfined." There may be some hidden meaning here, but we think that as the sentence was rather bare of verbiage, "unconfined" was thrown in merely as an embellishment; and, if we might say it, in our opinion, *coruscated* would have been a very nice word there. But to progress. "The bed 'ruffians'" commenced an invasion on my poor and weary tenement, and after marching and countermarching, animated, it seemed to me, by the music strains of a brass band sojourning on the opposite side of the street, *en route* to a democratic mass meeting on the next day, some thirty miles from Pond, they extracted no small portion of my already too reduced sanguineous fluid!" What have we here? "Bed 'ruffians'"—a personification—there is a most remarkable military evolution—there is an "invasion and what next?—blood, of course. But when, on a sublime occasion, the blood of a learned man has to flow, it is fit that it flow in Latin, and accordingly we have "sanguineous fluid!" Our recollections of the Iliad (the classic sneer of the Elder has brought Homer to view), are very much at fault, if, in all the wars of Troy, there is anything equal to the marching and countermarching of beg-bugs to the music of a brass band!

If we may be permitted to make the suggestion, we think there is a little more in this piece of fine writing than necessarily belongs to it. If the bugs *had.* to march, it was well enough to have music. We have no objection to the brass band; and though it may be an evidence of an over refined taste, we confess that we prefer the music to the bags; but whether the brass band was going (was *en route,* we mean) to a Democratic or a Whig meeting, or whether it was going or returning, or whether it was thirty or three hundred miles, the next day or any other day has just as much and just as little to do with part of the narrative, (i. e., the bugs and the marching), as whether the road they traveled was a mud road or railroad, whether the band went in a rail-car or a go-cart, or whether they went uphill or downhill, East or West, or any direction.

Time and space would fail us to note all the points in the first two paragraphs of this famous article. We have only to say it was not to our taste; we did not perceive that it would be of much value to the "respectable readers" of the *Age,* and we declined it. The author has taken the matter very seriously, and has, after nursing his wounded feelings through an entire winter, relieved himself as we see. He has, of course, a poor opinion of the *Age,* and sneers at its editors, but whether, when the merits of his own composition were to be decided, his own opinion, or that of at least three others, would be more likely to be correct, is a question which we wonder did not occur to so modest a man. We presume that a man who can quote Latin so freely, has met, in his readings, with the term *exparte.*

The Elder asks, in apparent triumph, what a certain "heifer" has to do with the gospel. He might as well have asked what it had to do with Astrology. The point is a false one. But does anybody suppose that that heifer, or even the negro, with his imagery, would have troubled the Elder, if his *bugs* had been allowed to creep into our columns? It is hardly worth-while to mention it; but we may explain that the specimen of African fancy (and we think it far preferable to the bed-bug narrative) was not selected for the *Age.* Our compositor "set up" the wrong side of a slip given him.

About the time Elder Hoshour was giving vent to his antipathy to the *Age,* the *Millennial Harbinger* was also expressing an opinion. Men will disagree in their judgments. The *Harbinger* says:

"THE CHRISTIAN AGE." * * * We have frequently expressed our high appreciation of its character under its present Editor, and find continually renewed reason to recommend it, as a family religious paper, deserving the general and cordial confidence and patronage of our brethren. We have been pleased to perceive and to notice, from the very first, the keen and delicate literary and spiritual taste and appreciation displayed in its selections, and the good sense and sound judgment and fervid spirit, which distinguish the matter and the tone of its original contributions. It is going on from good to better, and we sincerely trust it will be nobly sustained in the elevated stand which it is taking in behalf of our cherished work of religious reformation."

I am sorry, Bro. Franklin, to have had any occasion to occupy your space in this way. The *Age* is not the aggressor.

Fraternally yours,
H. S. BOSWORTH.

-----o-----

Editor's Table.

ELD. J. YOUNG'S article on Spiritualism, in the June number, should have been credited to the *Christian Record,* whence it was taken. Not knowing that it had been published, some brethren were sorry we had given publicity to it.

THE DEBATE.—By request of many friends, we have decided to publish an article of some length, containing a notice of our debate with Rev. T. J. Fisher, but we could not get room for it this month, and had to lay it over for another number.

MINUTES OF THE GENERAL MISSIONARY MEETING

We thought, at first, of abridging and publishing the minutes of this meeting; but on looking over them, we saw that it would be difficult to abridge them so as to give satisfaction, and, therefore, publish them in full in the *Age,* and inserted, in this number of the *Review,* comments upon the meeting that, we trust, will be more satisfactory, and, at the same time, afford us an opportunity to notice several resolutions passed at the meeting, and comment upon them.

BRETHREN HOSHOUR AND BOSWORTH.—We are sorry that a little unpleasantness has occurred between these good men. As Eld. Hoshour states, he has been an old friend and correspondent of ours, and when he presented the notes of his tour for insertion in the *Review,* without any hesitation, we inserted them. Knowing his age and experience, as well as his standing, we did not even read more than one or two of his articles till they were in proof. We supposed they were all written before they were presented to the *Age,* and knew nothing of the little hit at the *Age* for rejecting them, till we saw it in the proof sheet. We think no one will suffer to leave the matter precisely where it now is. We are on the best of terms with both parties, and hope to remain so.

"NATURE AND DURATION OR FUTURE PUNISHMENT" By DR. JNO. T. WALSH.—This is an able treatise, by Bro. Walsh, of N. C., published at Richmond, Va. The book contains an attractive and instructive introduction by which the reader is acquainted with the design and peculiarities of the book, and his mind prepared to consider the theme as presented in the body of the work.

The subject is presented in twelve chapters, divided into sections which, for convenience of reference and propriety of arrangement, renders the work, perhaps, the best popular treatise on Future Punishment extant. We will send this book at the publisher's retail price, free of postage; cloth 75 cts., paper 50 cts. We would say to our readers, and particularly our preaching brethren, send for a copy of Bro. Walsh's work.

"THE TESTIMONIES OF THE ROCKS."—This able work, the beatings of Geology on the "Two Theologies—Natural and Revealed, by Hugh Miller," by the kindness of Mr. Blanchard, No. 29 West Fourth Street, is upon our table. This is one of the most valuable scientific works we have chanced to lay our hands upon for some time. The author read the book of nature with sufficient care to perceive, and to enable him to show others, that it not only contains nothing contrary to what is found in the revelations in the Bible, but much to confirm and corroborate what is therein contained. He has gone sufficiently deep into the recesses of learning to find that all true learning is consistent with itself—that all true science is not only in harmony with itself, but with the Bible and its Author. He not only believed, but, we think, has shown conclusively, that nature—"the book of nature," so called—or the works of God in creation, agree with what he has revealed in the Bible.

A REASONABLE CALCULATION.—We make the following calculation, which, we think, is quite reasonable:

1. There are 1000 Christian churches at least, that could give for general missionary purposes, without any oppression, each $10 annually.
2. There are, outside of these, at least 2000 members who could give annually without the least oppression, $5 each.
3. There are, beside these, at least 10,000 members who could give annually, without any oppression, $1 each.
4. There are, beside all these, at least 40,000, who, without any oppression, could give 25 cts. each.

This would give us total amount annually of $40,000.

Any man can see that this would only touch a small proportion of the Disciples, and that, with anything like a unanimous contribution from the brotherhood, a sum four-fold larger than this might be also raised for State Missions, without being at all felt, or in the least interfering with church operations at home. The simple question is—Shall we, as a whole, try to induce a regular and systematic course of action, embracing the whole membership? or make no effort of the kind?

BENJ. FRANKLIN.

REVISED EPISTLE TO THE HEBREWS.—We are indebted to the Bible Union for this valuable work. The opponents of Revision have accused the Bible Union of holding back the portions of the Bible where *baptizo* occurs, because they dreaded to translate it *immerse*. But if they will turn to the letter to the Hebrews, revised, vi. 2, and ix. 10, they will find that the trouble is over. *Baptizo* is translated *immerse*. The opponents to Revision may bring their critical acumen to bear, whet their sword, enter the warfare and make the best defense against this invasion upon their practice the case admits of. The Bible Union is now prepared to hear, consider and test their strongest objections.

We are highly delighted with this work, and intend, when we have space, pointing out a few of the corrections in translation contained in it. Several of them are of high importance. It will certainly command the respect of scholars. We know not, however, why the old King James's "hath" is retained in it. We shall notice again soon.

Obituaries.

DIED, on the 5th of February, 1857, SARAH, infant daughter of Bro. George and Sister Elizabeth Williams, of Gibson Co., Ind.

"She looked into our world to see
  A sample of our misery;
She turned her little head aside,
  She shed a tear or two and died—
    Sweet babe."

E. SAULMAN

DIED, on the 11th of March, after a few days sickness, DIANNA A. ARBUNCKLE, wife of Elder C. P. Arbunckle, in her 43rd year. Her husband and eight children mourn her loss. She died as she had lived, a Christian.   H. CARNES.

DIED, on the 4th of March, after a protracted illness. Bro. WILLIAM COLLINS, late of Rush Co., Ind. He was one of the pioneers of that country. Bro. C. confessed the name of the Lord 21 years since, and lived a constant and devoted disciple of his Master, He lived to see six daughters bow to the King Immanuel; and in the hour of his death glorified his Redeemer. His death was a triumph, for with praise, prayer and exultation, he left for his eternal home.   MARY McDUFFIE.

THE AMERICAN CHRISTIAN REVIEW.

DEBATE WITH REV. T. J. FISHER.

According to promise, we now proceed to give some account of the discussion in Ghent, Ky. As announced, the debate commenced on Friday, 10 o'clock, before the first Lord's day in June. It lasted Friday, Saturday and Monday, with a session of two hours in the morning, three hours in the afternoon on Friday, but only two hours in the afternoon Saturday and Monday, and two hours at night each day. The audience was dense from the commencement to the close, there being many, much of the time, who could not get into the house, and many in the house who were compelled to stand in the aisles for the want of seats. The discussion was held in the commodious house of worship belonging to the Baptists, which they cheerfully opened for the occasion. Mr. Fisher chose Rev. Helm, a Baptist preacher of Covington Ky., as his moderator. We chose Eld. John Smith, of Georgetown, Ky., of whom our readers have been accustomed to hear some very interesting things for many years. These two selected some gentleman, whose name we have forgotten, as President, but, who could not serve, on account of sickness.

We therefore proceeded with two, and had no particular need of any others. They gave very full satisfaction, we think, both to the audience and to the parties.

A stenographer was present, as we understand, employed by Mr. Fisher, who told us that he had taken down every word. Mr. Fisher told us that he intended to publish the whole.

The correspondence was read by Rev. Helm, introductory to the discussion. The first proposition was then read, as follows: "Do the Scriptures teach that baptism, administered as the Lord intended, to a proper subject, is for the remission of past or alien sins?" As we have not even a note of the debate, we, as a matter of course, attempt nothing more than a statement of a few of the most important points, and to give specimens of the argument, with such comments as we deem expedient.

In our introductory observations, we explained at considerable length, that all we said of baptism was with the distinct understanding, as implied in the proposition, that it is administered to a proper subject. Administered to any but a proper subject, it is nothing, either in design or effect. We speak of it as an ordinance to a proper subject; not to one pardoned, but one who is a believer, a penitent, whose heart is changed by faith, who loves the Savior and wishes to obey him—one who believes in the heart in the Lord Jesus and has made confession with the mouth. To such a one baptism "into the name of the Father, and of the Son, and the Holy Spirit," "calling on the name of the Lord," is *for the remission of past or alien sins*. In the course of these explanatory remarks. we showed that to be cleansed from sin, pardoned, or saved from sin, the applicants must come to the blood of Christ, to the spirit and to the life of Christ—in one short sentence—that all spiritual blessings are *in Christ*. In Christ is the blood, the spirit, the life, pardon or salvation. Out of Christ there is no blood, no spirit, no life, no pardon or salvation. "In Christ," is in his body, his kingdom or his church. To enter into Christ, into his body, is to enter into a stale of justification. We should, therefore, make a careful discrimination between what is done *in* Christ and *into* Christ. Men believed in Christ, repented in Christ, prayed in Christ, and communed in Christ, but no man was ever baptized *in* Christ. Men were baptized "*into* Christ," but no man ever believed into Christ, repented into Christ, prayed into Christ, or communed into Christ, but men were "baptized into Christ."

An old preacher of our acquaintance, used to tell us, with much propriety, that there must always be an *into* before there can be an *in*—that no person was ever *in* any place, or state, without first entering *into* it. Men believed *in* the name of Christ, and did many other things in his name; but they never believed *into* his name, or did any other thing *into* his name, except to be baptized *into* the name of the Father, and of the Son, and of the Holy Spirit. Men believed *in* the death of Christ, but never believed *into* his death. What is the meaning of all this? The meaning of it is simply, that baptism is not something preparatory, or before entering into Christ, into his name, into his death, nor 'something done in Christ, in his body or church, after entering, but *the transition act* of entering *into* Christ. The faith that goes before repentance, change of heart and feeling, with confession, are all indispensable, but only preparatory to the change of state, and none of them the *act of transition* from one state to the other. It is, as has been stated thousands of times, and found in the libraries of all preachers of any note, *the initiatory rite;* or, as has been well expressed many times, in the controversies of the last twenty years, "the consummating act."

Faith changes, purifies or Christianizes the heart, or converts the subject in heart. Repentance changes, purifies or Christianizes the man in character, or converts him in character. But this is all simply a change *in* in the man, but no change in his relation or state. It is simply preparing the man to enter into a justified state, or a state of pardon. There is no forgiveness of sin in all this. There is no salvation of the soul from sin here. The salvation of the soul from sin, pardon or forgiveness of sins, is as distinct from all the preparation of heart and life, or all the change in the subject, as heaven and earth, as the work of God and the work of man. *Man* believes, repents, feels and confesses, but *God* pardons. No believing, repenting, feeling or confessing, saves the soul or pardons. It is God that pardons. Nor does baptism save the soul. It, too, is but the act of the creature; but it is the initiatory rite, consummating or transition act, where pardon is promised in the divine process. The candidate is baptized "*into* the name of the Father, and of the Son, and of the Holy Spirit." All the prophets bear witness of him, that through *his name* whoever believeth in him shall receive remission of sin. His is the only name given under Heaven and among men whereby man can be saved. When we come into his name there is salvation, or forgiveness of sins. As many as have been "baptized into Christ have been baptized *into* his death." In his death, his blood flowed to wash away sin. When man comes into his death, he comes to his blood that cleanses from all sin. When he enters the body of Christ, he comes to the life, to all spiritual blessings in Christ, to the salvation of our God.

This places pardon precisely where we find it in the divine process, as alluded to in the commission to the apostles, in their practice, and their allusions to it in their letters to the churches, in all of which there is not a case mentioned of *pardon before baptism,* or *one who had been baptized, unpardoned.* Let him invalidate this statement who can. The Bible is open before the preachers and scribes, and so are our columns open for a correction from any man who is able to make one. The Lord said, "He that believeth and is baptized, shall be saved." Here are two conditions—*belief* and *baptism.* They are in order to one object—*salvation,* or pardon. Other conditions may be shown besides these, in order to the same object, but certainly no man can avoid either of these two. The *faith* and *baptism* come first and then *salvation.* No fairness can avoid the conclusion, that these two conditions are in order to salvation. When the man of God came to Saul of Tarsus, with a commission from Jesus, to tell him what *he must do,* he placed the conditions before him in the following unequivocal words: "Arise and be baptized and wash away thy sins, calling on the name of the Lord." Here was a man who was already a believer, and a penitent, commanded to be baptized and wash away his sins. Baptism is the condition *required of this* believing penitent; and it is to "wash away his sins," or in order to pardon. No man can fail to see that pardon, or washing away sins, follows baptism, and is not before it. This perfectly accords with the expression of Peter, "the like figure whereunto even baptism doth also now save us." The baptism comes first, and is in order to the salvation.

We must now hear Peter a few days after he received his commission, and on the day the Holy Spirit came from heaven to guide him into all truth When he had delivered the first discourse, a multitude were pierced in the heart, and inquired, "Men and brethren, what shall we do?" He answered them, "Repent and be baptized every one of you, in the name of Jesus Christ, for the remission of sins and you shall receive the gift of the Holy Spirit." Here I find not simply the order, as in other places, baptism before pardon, but in the identical language of my proposition, "baptism *for the remission of sins.*" I am for taking this language precisely as it reads, in its most manifest import, without any interpolation or mutilation of any kind. Mr. Fisher, with all who agree with him, in their construction, to make the Scriptures harmonize with their doctrine, are obliged to insert an interpolation, in several passages, as follows: "He that believeth and is baptized shall *not* be saved." "The like figure whereunto even baptism doth *not* also now save us." "Arise and be baptized and *not* wash away thy sins." "Repent and be baptized every one of you, in the name of Jesus Christ, *not* for remission of sins." I can refer the gentleman to an instance in which a preacher, not a very honorable one either, nor one whose example should be imitated inserted that same interpolation in the word of God. God's word says, in the passage I alluded to, "You shall surely die." The interpolation made it read, *"You* shall *not* surely die." With the ruinous work induced in our world, by the insertion of this mischievous little word before their eyes, and with the declaration at the close of the sacred canon, that "if any man shall add to the words of the book of this prophecy, God shall add to him the plagues written in this book," and the language of Paul, "if any man perverts the gospel, the curse rests upon him," before their eyes, the Baptist Association, in their minutes, now undergoing the scathing review of Elder Rogers, declare before earth and heaven, that they "believe in baptism *not* for remission!" We strike out the interpolation—this word *not*—and maintain the commandment of God, as Peter gave it, "Repent and be baptized every one of you, in the name of Jesus

Christ, *for the remission of sins."* Such is a brief sketch of the argument on this point and some little comment.

But now for Rev. F.'s reply. Here, we confess, we feel at a loss how to give our readers anything like an adequate description of our opponent and his argument. We take it, however, that he was upon his very best behavior, and making his best effort to exhibit the "Kentuckian, gentleman and Christian." We are rather inclined to the charitable opinion, that he intended to be polite, genteel and keep in a good humor; and think that anything the audience saw that was otherwise, he did not intend should appear. But much allowance should be made in criticizing upon his course, or deportment, in the discussion. He is one of the most excitable creatures we ever saw. His self-conceit is enormous. He evidently thinks there is no other such a man as himself in this world. He is somewhat of a revivalist; perhaps as much so at least as any preacher in Kentucky. He makes some warm friends wherever he goes; and, we think, rarely fails to make some enemies; is indiscreet and falls into numerous improprieties. His mind is measurably undisciplined; his manner rude and uncouth, and his course neither lovely nor winning. He is pretty much unaccustomed to debate, though he claimed to have had two or three discussions. In his principal efforts he has been permitted to say pretty much what he pleased, without any rebuke, unless what came in private from some of his best friends. With this short outline, the reader will readily perceive how difficult it would be for him to keep cool, keep his seat, while his opponent was speaking, or conduct himself in a becoming manner while speaking himself.

As an illustration of this, he would frequently, when closely pressed, spring to his feet, contradict, object, or declare us out of order, though he did not at any time induce the moderators to call us to order. When speaking, as we supposed, to make his arguments strong and emphatic, he would turn to us, brandish sometimes his open hands, and sometimes his clenched fist, so near our face that we frequently felt the wind, and several times the tips of his fingers, and, what was not more pleasant, sprays of spit from his lips were distinctly felt in the face. But all this was evidently from excitement, lack of presence of mind, and not from bad intentions. He has acquired the habit, perhaps, in trying to appear earnest, of seeming all of a strain; his head and limbs all of a quiver, with the blood pressing all the veins in the neck and face as if they would explode, and his voice in an equal strain. He has got it into his mind that his descriptions are fine. We think he should have some credit here, especially in describing the horrible. It is questionable whether there are three men in a radius of one hundred miles of him, who can make the bottomless pit look deeper, hotter, blacker and more horrible than he. He declaimed several pieces rather finely, but gave no credit for them. But some of his attempts at poetical flights were most ludicrous and laughable bombast. Several of the young preachers present preserved some rare specimens of this kind, and can declaim them very finely.

But now for the argument or reply to our speech. His first objection, and a very serious one, was the awful consequences of the doctrine of "baptism for the remission of sins." If that doctrine be true, what will become of all who have not been baptized? Shall all the good people who have lived in all the evangelical denominations, and died without baptism, be lost. On this point he asserted, emphasized and repeated.

To this we replied, that there is nothing unreasonable in the requirement to be baptized, as all Baptists admit, and as their ministry have shown thousands of times—that any person can be baptized who desires to submit to it. All parties admit that it is a commandment of God and right. The main reason why there are so many who are not baptized, is that preachers have made this commandment of God of no effect by their tradition. It the preachers of the gospel were true there could be just as many baptized as believe. Nothing in this world causes so many believers to live and die without baptism, only the wayward course of preachers. Let them preach faithfully, and all that believe will be baptized, and then, if the baptized are saved, the believers will also be saved, and this will include all that either of us claim. Certainly unbelievers will not be saved. If baptism were something difficult, that but few could obtain, the case would be different. But such is not the case. All who desire to serve God, can easily be baptized, and those who do not desire to serve God, will not be saved in any event. Not only so, but we are not responsible for the consequence. We are not discussing the question how many or how few will be ultimately saved, or how many will be pardoned. God will decide that. The question with us is simply—Is baptism, to a proper subject, for the remission of sins?

Mr. F. objects, that baptism for remission of sins, makes salvation depend upon a second person. But if this is to be an argument, it is equally an argument against faith. Faith depends upon a second person. Faith comes by hearing. How can they hear without a preacher? You have the preacher that you may hear. If you believe when you hear, you have the preacher to baptize.

But let us look at his practice, and apply his logic. If men are saved by coming to the "altar of prayer," as he calls the mourner's bench, being prayed for, and telling an experience, what will become of those who have never come to the mourner's bench, and told an experience? Are they all to be lost? There are as many who never came to the mourner's bench, nor told an experience, as there are who have never been baptized. In that case, all in the apostolic day would be lost, for not one of them ever came to the mourner's bench, nor told an experience, as practiced by Baptists, nor was the like ever done for more than a thousand years after. But this only by way of showing how men would fare by their own logic. The simple question for us to determine is, *What is right?* I am for the right way, if none of us are saved. I am not here to prove that we are right, or the Baptists wrong. The simple question to determine, is, "Do the Scriptures teach that baptism is for the remission of sins?"

Mr. F. objected, that Simon, the sorcerer, believed and was baptized, but was yet in the gall of bitterness, and bonds of iniquity—not pardoned. In this case, he claimed a practical demonstration, that the doctrine we affirmed was not true. This objection is easily set aside; for, if, as some claim, Simon was insincere, and, consequently, was not pardoned, he was not a proper subject, and his *insincerity* was the cause of his not being pardoned, and not that baptism is not for remission. But we deny that there is any intimation that he was not pardoned. Luke does not make Peter say, "Thou art in the gall of bitterness," thereby implying that he had not been out of it; nor has he *"bonds* of iniquity," but simply *"bond of iniquity"*—but *one bond.* There is not any intimation in the case that there was anything wrong in his conversion. His offence was, that he proposed to purchase the gift of God with money, that on whoever he would lay hands, the Holy Spirit might be bestowed. Peter brings the charge against him in these words: "Thy money perish with thee, because thou hast thought the gift of God may be purchased with money." He exhorted him to pray God, if perhaps *the thought* of his heart might be forgiven him, and the last account the New Testament gives of Simon is, that he was entreating Peter to pray for him. There is no intimation that his conversion was not good, nor does anything appear against him, save the charge of *one wicked thought,* and when charged with that, he implored the Apostle to pray for him. If he had died then, without any more being known of him than appears in the Scripture account of it, and Mr. F. had preached his funeral, he would have told his friends that he had no doubt he had gone to heaven.

He objected that the thief on the cross was saved without baptism, which could not have been, if baptism is for remission of sins. But this objection amounts to nothing, for the reign of Christ had not commenced, and the terms of initiation were not published. The law of pardon, according to the New Testament, was not presented to man yet—not in operation. The thief was not under the law of Christ, but before the law was in force, he applied to the Sovereign, and was saved by a *special act,* for a *special case,* and not for an example of conversion for Mr. F. to preach from. Besides, it is not known that the thief was not baptized.

After much hesitation on his part, we induced Mr. F. to notice Peter's words on Pentecost. These words were to be taken in a declarative sense: Repent and be baptized every one of you, in the name of Jesus Christ, thus declaring the pardon of sins, which you have received. We cannot vouch that we have his precise words, but think we have the substance. It is humiliating to see the miser-able subterfuges, twistings and evasions of men to avoid the most manifest import of the clearest expressions in the Bible. How determined men must be on preaching error, when they will declare persons pardoned before repentance, rather than preach the simple truth! The Apostle here commands two things to be done for one object. One of these is to *repent*, and the other to be *baptized*. He would have men to repent—nay, have Peter command men, in the name of the Lord, to repent to declare that their sins were previously pardoned! Here is the doctrine that pardon is before repentance, or persons pardoned in impenitence, and commanded to repent because they were pardoned, or simply to declare that they were pardoned—an imperative reason for repentance truly! The Lord's reason for repentance is to obtain pardon, that men may not perish, and because God will judge the world in righteousness; and when he connects baptism with repentance, as in the sentence "Repent and be baptized," baptism is for the same purpose. "By one spirit we are all baptized *into* one body." The Holy Spirit leads all to be baptized into one body. No man who understands the Scriptures can say this is the baptism of the Spirit, for it is not initiatory. By it they are not baptized *into* any body. On Pentecost, the Spirit came from heaven, spoke through Peter, pierced the people in the heart, and when they inquired what to do, he directed them, or lead them to baptism *into* one body. We have now found where they were baptized "into one body," *"into* Christ," *"into* his death" and *"into* his name," and "for the remission of sins"—that "he that believeth and is baptized shall be saved"—that "baptism doth also now save us," and that a penitent was commanded to "arise and be baptized and wash away his sins, calling on the name of the Lord"—all evincing beyond all doubt, that when men are baptized into Christ—proper subjects—they are in his death, in his body, to his blood, his spirit, his life, his promise of pardon, and are saved from their sins.

Mr. F. objected, that Paul thanked God that he never baptized many, and while trying to make some show of argument, on this point, he declared and repeated it, that Paul never mentioned baptism to the church at Ephesus; and when he saw us take the Bible, he faltered and hesitated, and varied his statement, saying, "he never commanded it." We only allude to this to show his confession, that though Paul did mention baptism in his discourse (Acts xix.) to the Ephesians, and in his epistle (Eph. iv. 6), which he evidently knew; yet, in his bewilderment, he denied that it was mentioned. But we simply take occasion to remark, that Paul never thanked God that he never baptized many. In addressing some factionists at Corinth, he said, "I thank God that I baptized none of you," etc.; but what reason does he assign? because baptism is not for remission? No, but "lest any should say I had baptized in my own name." There were some there saying they were of Paul, but he had not even baptized them, or given them that much occasion for saying they were of Paul.

On Saturday, Mr. F. set out in the affirmative of the proposition: "Do the Scriptures teach the doctrine of total hereditary depravity?" The opening addresses were an hour in length. He labored hard, took some flights in the air, among the clouds, above both the air and clouds, among the stars, and beyond them, in open space; but much of the time no man could tell whether it was a Fourth of July oration, a fine declamation, or what, so far as anything contained in it of a distinguishing character was concerned. He aimed at the sublime, and certainly descended frequently to the ridiculous. One of his refined expressions of this latter class, was his imagery, to represent his opponent as out of argument, which was, that "he was out of soap." But we had to acknowledge that the Lord speaks of a refiner's fire and fuller's soap to purge wicked men—the sons of Levi. (Mal. iii. 2.) But the curiosity with us is, what effect a refiner's fire and fuller's soap could have in purifying total corruption. If man is nothing but corruption, or dross, when the dross is purged away by the refiner's fire, there will be nothing left, or when the filth is cleansed away by the action of the fuller's soap, there will be nothing left! Is there nothing but corruption, nothing but sin, in man? When the corruption, or sin, is purged away, there will be no man—nothing left!

But Mr. F. did, in the last five minutes of his hour, produce one passage of Scripture, and but one. That one was the following: "The whole head is sick, and the whole heart is faint. From the sole of the foot even to the head there is no soundness in it; but wounds, and bruises, and putrefying sores; they have not been closed, neither bound up, neither mollified. with ointment." Isaiah i. 5-6. This passage was simply quoted, and a few remarks made about it, without making any application. It was amusing to see the care with which Mr. F. would quote Scripture. We do not mean his care to quote accurately, or to give each passage its fair contextual import. But his studied care, where to commence a quotation, so as not to get proof that he did not want. He showed his skill particularly in this respect, in the above quotation. It is *man* that his proposition affirms to be totally depraved. He was careful not to commence at the third and fourth verses, where it is clearly seen that it was *Israel* that was spoken of, and not *man,* and not that Israel was *totally* depraved, or there would not have been one holy Isaiah, inspired of God, among them, to warm them of their sins. he was careful, too, not to begin at the fourth verse, where Israel are called "*children* that are corrupters;" for he knew that they could not corrupt that which is totally corrupt, nor did he desire to find the words, "they have forsaken the Lord," and "are gone away backward," for this would not only disprove the part of his proposition that affirms depravity to be *hereditary,* but show that they had themselves "*forsaken the Lord," gone away backward,"* thus refuting his other doctrine, that children of God cannot fall from grace. The Lord is here speaking of "Israel," "children," who had "forsaken the Lord," and "gone away backward." which shows that they had been with the Lord, or they could not have forsaken him, or gone away from him. The sores and bruises were not upon man, but upon Israel, children, and consisted in forsaking God, going away from him—their *own actions,* and not something that had descended upon them from their parents. We grant that Israel was in a bad condition, covered with bruises and putrefying sores, "the whole head sick, and the whole heart faint." But there is nothing *hereditary* in this. Not only so, but this whole figurative description implies something different from total corruption. The whole head of a body, totally corrupt, could not be *sick,* nor could the whole heart be *faint.* The idea of a mass of total corruption, being covered with bruises, putrefying sores, and, besides this, for it to be *sick* and *faint,* is preposterous in the extreme. What were these sores upon? What was it that was putrefying? not that certainly which was already putrid! What was it that was *sick and faint?* not that certainly which was dead, and wholly corrupt. Bad as this body was—Israel—it positively was not wholly corrupt, for God declares, verse nine, that he had left a small remnant, or they would have been like Sodom—that is, as bad as Sodom. But the Lord had left of this body, bad as it was, "a small remnant," on account of which they were not as Sodom, or not as bad, which could not have been said of them, if they had been totally corrupt. Sodom itself could not be worse than total corruption.

This being the only argument in his hour speech, in support of his affirmative proposition, we proceed to offer sundry arguments in the negative, in anticipation, as, for instance, the following:

1. If man is totally depraved—the whole race, in an unregenerate state, then all stand upon a level. There can be no degrees in that which is total; and if all men, in an unconverted state, are totally corrupt, all men are corrupt precisely alike; or all corrupt, one just as much as another; one man precisely as bad as another—that is, all just as bad as they can be. No man can be any worse than totally corrupt. The devil is no worse than this. Now, is this the case? Are not some men, in an unconverted state, better than others? We know, positively, that some men, and some children, in an unconverted state, are better than others. No man here believes, that a man who speaks truth, deals honorably, is benevolent, and moral, is as bad as a man without these qualities, though both may be unregenerate. That there is a difference, is one of the most manifest truths man can know. Yet there could be no difference if both were totally depraved. Both may be depraved, greatly depraved, one much more than the other, but neither totally. There is some good in both, but more in one than in the other. We never saw a man so bad that he had no good in him; but we have seen some that had very little.

2. The Lord makes a distinction among unconverted men, showing that some of them are better than others, thus refuting the doctrine, that all are totally depraved. In his parable of the sower, Matt. xiii., the Lord gives us six classes of unconverted hearers: 1. Wayside hearers; 2, Stony ground hearers; 3, Thorny ground hearers. Here we have bad, worse, and worst. The thorny ground is bad, the stony ground is worse, the wayside is worst. This makes three classes of bad. He then gives us the good ground, and explains what it is. It is the man who receives the word of God into a *good and honest heart,* understands and obeys it. Could the Lord speak of a man receiving the word into "a good and honest heart," knowing him to be totally depraved? The Lord never called a totally depraved heart *good and honest.* since the world was made. But the Lord divides this good ground into three classes, good, better, and best. It produces some thirty, some sixty, and some an hundred fold. Thirty fold is good ground; sixty fold is better, and an hundred fold is best. This classification is an eternal refutation of the doctrine of total depravity. There can be no such

classes, if all are totally depraved.

3. Paul divides men in an unregenerate state into six classes, in his caution for every man to take heed how he builds upon the foundation. (1 Cor. iii.) Having given the caution, he proceeds to speak of six classes of material that may be put into the building, three classes good and three bad. He styles them gold, silver, precious stones, wood, hay, stubble. Gold, silver and precious stones are good. Wood, hay and stubble are bad. Here, too, we have bad, worse and worst; good, better and best. Wood is bad, hay is worse, and stubble is worst. Precious stones are good, silver is better, and gold is best. Here, then, we find the same classification, among those to be converted, or built into the building, as the Lord himself classifies, which shows that all are not upon a level, or alike sinful, as would be the case, if all were totally depraved.

4. Paul says that "evil men and seducers shall wax worse and worse, deceiving and being deceived."(2 Tim. iii. 13.) If wicked men were totally depraved, they could not wax *worse* and *worse*. I defy any man to show how a man could grow any worse, who was totally depraved. The fact, then, that wicked men become worse and worse, shows beyond dispute, that they are not totally depraved. The devil does not become worse.

5. Mr. F. quoted, with much confidence, the words of David, "Behold, I was shapen in iniquity, and in sin did my mother conceive me," Psalm li. 5. But this language is speaking of *David,* and not of *man* in general. Mr. F., however, assumed, indeed he asserted, that what is true of David, as here set forth, is true of all men. It will be readily perceived that David is not speaking of the transgressions of all men, but of what he, verse 1st, calls "*my* transgressions." Below he says, "Wash me from *mine* iniquity, and cleanse me from *my* sin." Again, in the same connection, he says, "I acknowledge *my* transgressions, and *my* sin is ever before me." Is it not evident that he is here confessing and lamenting sin committed by himself? But hear him again, in the verse preceding Mr. F.'s proof text. "Against thee, thee only, have *I* sinned and done *this evil* in thy sight." The king evidently had his eye upon the great sin of his life, which caused him more bitter repentance than any other, and which afflicted his soul to the end of his life. In deep humiliation before the Lord, he was making most humble confession, in which houses the strong figurative expression, "I was shapen in iniquity, and in sin did my mother conceive me." He did not use this expression as an apology, that he had inherited his sinfulness, but as a strong and full acknowledgment of his sinfulness from his early life. It is like the expression, "They are estranged from the womb and go forth speaking lies." It sets forth early departure from the Lord, in strong terms, but teaches nothing of total hereditary depravity.

6. Mr. F. quoted, with as much confidence as any passage, on depravity, Eph. ii. 3: "Among whom also we all had our conversation in times past in the lusts of our flesh, fulfilling the desires of the flesh and of the mind, and were by nature the children of wrath, even as others." Here he emphatically declared we have the doctrine that we *are by nature children of wrath*. The argument here turns upon the word "nature." Is it *human nature* that is here spoken of?—or is it *man's* nature? If it is, and that is where the fault lies, man is not to blame for his sins. He did not make his nature, and cannot be responsible for anything wrong in it. But his *practice* or *custom,* he may be held responsible for. He has the ability to make it good or bad. Paul does not appear to speak disrespectfully of nature, Rom. i. 26. He says, "For this cause God gave them up unto vile affections; for even their women did change the natural use into that

which was *against nature.* "The sin was not in following nature, but changing the natural use and doing what was *against nature.* He does not blame them for going according to nature, but for going against it. Again, Rom. ii. 14, Paul says, "For when the Gentiles, who have not the law, do by nature the things contained in the law, these having not the law, are a law unto themselves." Reader, what think you of the Gentiles *doing by nature* the things contained in the law? In this case the Gentiles *by nature* were doing right. If this is human nature, it is not totally depraved, for those who go by it do right some of the time at least. If it were wholly corrupt, by it they would never do right. But, we presume, the truth is, that the word "nature" does not mean *human* nature in any of these passages, but is used simply in the same sense as in the following: "Does not even nature itself teach you, that it is a shame for a man to wear long hair?" (1 Cor. xi. 14). If *human* nature teaches anything about wearing long hair, it teaches that it is right, for nature makes it grow long. But human nature teaches nothing about wearing long or short hair. "Does not even *custom* itself teach you," etc. Gal. ii. 15, Paul says, "We who are Jews by nature and not sinners of the Gentiles." What does this mean? Jews by *nature!* Judaism was right before the gospel, and those who were *Jews by nature,* were right *by nature.* This *nature* was certainly not totally depraved, for by it they were right in some instances. They were Jews by *custom,* and not sinners of the Gentiles by custom. Some of them, even among the Gentiles, by custom or tradition, did the things contained in the law, and some of them *by custom* among the Jews, were children of wrath, even as others. This is the sum of the passage, and there is no total hereditary depravity in it.

The amount of the matter is, that the whole scheme of total hereditary depravity, belongs to a system of apologies for man's sins, and aims a death blow at all human accountability. The first step in this system of apologies for sin, is to prove that man's whole, nature is nothing but sin—total corruption; that he is so dead that he can neither hear, see nor believe the word of God, until quickened and made alive by some miraculous and irresistible power! Still, if man is not thus quickened and converted by this irresistible power, which is as much a miracle as creating the world, and which, of course, nothing short, of almighty power can do, he will be irrevocably lost!—he will be damned! For what? Because God did not exercise this irresistible power, and do for him what he could not do for himself! This doctrine, blur it over as men may, and call it *orthodox, evangelical,* or what you please, insults the grace of God, that brings salvation to all men, and the goodness of God, that inquires, "What more could I have done, that I have not done?" by declaring that he could have sent his irresistible power and saved those sinners who cannot come to him without it, and consequently are lost. This doctrine, in defiance of all the plastering over and most ingenious polishing of its most artful friends, contradicts the clear statement of the Lord, that "he is not willing that any should perish," in teaching that sinners are not converted, or regenerated, and consequently lost, because the Lord did not send his irresistible power, without which they could not believe, repent, be converted or do anything acceptable to God—could not by any possibility be saved! This is the foundation of that unwarrantable practice, that Mr. F. refused to bring into investigation, and knew he could not defend, of preachers, in the presence of an audience of the unconverted, throwing aside the gospel of the grace of God, ceasing their preaching to and exhorting sinners, in apostolic style, to be reconciled to God, save themselves from this untoward generation, repent and be converted, that their sins may be blotted out, and turn their addresses to heaven, expostulate with and implore the Almighty to exercise his irresistible power, without which sinners must perish! We allege, and let him call us to account who is able, that here lies the bottom root of all the systems of fatality found in all the different phases of unbelief and non responsibility of these corrupt times, and we had just as well go into the merits of it now as ever.

From this same corrupt root sprang the doctrine of infant damnation, traces of which are yet found in some creeds and standard works. Infants, it is maintained, have inherited a sinful nature from their parents, and must be regenerated, or lost. This was what gave rise to infant baptism. Mr. F., maintaining, as he does, hereditary depravity, makes infants totally depraved, and ought to be among the Paedobaptists, preaching infant baptism, in the company of Calvin and Wesley, both of whom believed in, and preached, infant regeneration in baptism. But the Lord said, of infants, "of such is the kingdom of God," and to adults, he said, "Except you be converted, and become as a little child, you cannot enter into the kingdom of God." Strange, indeed, if infants are totally corrupt, that Jesus should say to sinners, except you repent, and *become as a little child*—that is totally corrupt—sinful—just what they were now—before they could enter into the kingdom of God! This expression—"of such is the kingdom of God"—sets aside hereditary depravity, or the doctrine of infant sinners; for our Lord would not require sinful men to repent and become as infant sinners, in order to their entrance into the kingdom! Nothing can be more manifest than that Jesus recognizes *purity* and *innocency* in infants, or he could not have required sinful men to become like them, before they could enter the kingdom.

If human depravity is hereditary, unless it descends from the saints, it is strange that it did not run out when all the wicked were drowned in the flood, with their children! But the truth is, it is in bad keeping—exceedingly bad order—for Baptists to be talking of sins that descend from the parent to the child, whether in the flesh and blood, or in the spirit, for the same kind of argument maintains, with equal success, that grace descends in the same way from the saints, or believing parents, to their children. The same doctrine, both in theology and philosophy, that makes sin hereditary, makes holiness hereditary. Prove to me that a child inherits sin from its parents, and we will prove by all the same kind of logic, that holiness is inherited in the same way. So far as a man's sinfulness or holiness is concerned, or his privilege to the things of God, it matters not one iota whether he was born of a Jew or a Christian, a Mahometan or a Mormon. At birth he is the same to God, and his own actual personal conduct determines the case with him, and not his descent. It is just as good sense philosophy, and theology, to teach that holiness is hereditary, as that sin is. The new born infant is pure and innocent. It has the first action to perform, either good or bad. If it follows the Savior, it becomes a Christian. Before it has done either good or bad, or had ability to do either, it is neither a sinner nor a Christian, but simply a pure and innocent creature, needing nothing to prepare it for heaven, but the redemption of the body. He who teaches total hereditary depravity, if he believes his doctrine, believes that infants are not only sinners, but totally corrupt, and must find, or invent, a system of infant regeneration, not such as plants the word of God in a *good* and *honest heart,* that understands and believes, and is induced to turn to God; but regeneration, that converts a mass of total corruption into purity, without the word of God, or one word of teaching, any faith, repentance, experience, confession, or even the knowledge of the Deity! Such is some of the preposterous nonsense the doctrine of total hereditary depravity involves.

But, leaving all this, we hasten to sketch a

brief outline of the third day's work. The question on Monday was, "Do the Scriptures teach that the saints can fall from grace, and be lost?" As a matter of course, we affirmed that saints can fall. We claimed that all the expostulations, exhortations, and encouragements of the Lord and the apostles, are in view of the fact that Christians can fall, and started out with the admonition of Paul, "Let him that thinketh he standeth, take heed lest he fall." There can be no occasion for such admonitions if saints cannot fall.

1. We desired to make some further comments upon the case of Simon, the sorcerer, and therefore introduced him as one converted, and afterwards fell, and was lost. Mr. F. admitted that he was lost, but denied that he ever was converted. We relied upon the explicit statement of the commission, "He that believeth, and is baptized, shall be saved." Luke says, Simon believed, and mentions that he was baptized. Mr. F. said he was a hypocrite, that he only *pretended* to believe. We maintained that the historian did not say he pretended to believe; but that *he believed*. Before he was done with the case, he admitted that Simon was converted, according to our plan. This was sufficient; the man who preached to Simon was full of the Holy Spirit and wisdom, and his example, or his precedent, is good authority. The same was preached to Simon, that was preached to others, the same was believed, and the same process was observed. His turning out badly, is no argument against the manner of his conversion. But if, as Mr. F. has contended, justification is by faith alone, Simon was justified, for he believed. He, however, afterwards had a wicked thought, and, I presume, apostatized, and was lost. But, as I have had occasion to speak of Simon before, I shall not amplify now.

2. We presented the case of Judas Iscariot, who was among the twelve given to Christ, who was entrusted with all the others were, had given to him part of the apostleship and ministry, and who, by transgression, fell, and was lost. Mr. F. denied that Judas ever was a disciple, and contended that he was a wicked man from the beginning, and made more show of argument, touching this case than he did at any point afterwards. But still, we think, the show was remarkably poor even here, for he was with the Lord in all his counsels, at the communion, was put in the ministry, was made an apostle, and John xiii. 27, we read that "Satan entered into him," which implies that he was not in him before, and he, by transgression, fell and was lost. But since he contended that Judas never was a disciple, in the true sense, we invited his attention to Paul, whose claim to discipleship he will not question. He says, "I keep under my body, and bring it into subjection, lest that by any means, when I have preached to others, I myself should be a castaway." 1 Cor. ix. 27. Our question was simply, "Can the saints fall from grace?" Paul believed they could, or he would not have kept his body under for the purpose assigned—"lest I myself should be a castaway." He had not attained to such perfection that he *could not fall*.

3. We presented the following: "But when the righteous turneth away from his righteousness, and committeth iniquity, and doeth according to all the abominations that the wicked man doeth, shall he live? All his righteousness that he hath done shall not be mentioned; in his trespasses that he hath trespassed, and in his sin that he hath sinned, in them shall he die." Here is a clear case of the righteous turning away from his righteousness, and a clear sentence that he shall die. Mr. F. approached this passage with full assurance, that, at a single touch, he would demolish our argument. We confess that when we saw him turn to the passage with such an air of confidence, we thought probably he had reflected upon it, and would make some

plausible disposition of it. But to our utter astonishment, he informed us that the righteous turning away from *his* righteousness, was turning away from self-righteousness!!! This caped the climax! And, pray, what will become of a man if he shall turn away from *self-righteousness?* he shall surely die!—die for what? for turning away from *self-* righteousness! We had supposed the sooner a man turned from *self*-righteousness the better. But this is not all, for just preceding the verses quoted, we find the following But if the wicked will turn from all his sins that he hath committed, and keep all my statutes, and do that which is lawful and right, he shall surely live, he shall not die. All his transgressions that he hath committed, they shall not be mentioned unto him; in his righteousness that he hath done he shall live." This is the same righteousness that follows precisely two verses after. Ez. xviii. 21-24. According to Mr. F., self-righteousness will save a man. The man who continues in it *shall live*—the man who turns from it *shall die!* We never succeeded in getting his attention to this passage any more.

We argued the question at much length, from such passages as, "He that endures to the end shall be saved," which implies that he who does not endure to the end shall not be saved—"If ye do these things ye shall never fall "—"We should give the more earnest heed to the things which we have heard, lest we should at any time let them slip"—"If ye be circumcised, Christ shall profit you nothing; you are fallen from grace"—"It is impossible to renew them again to repentance"—"Lest any man fail of the grace of God"—"His part taken out of the book of life," etc., which the great length of this document forbids that we should elaborate. Mr. F. not only made no reply at all to the main body of our argument on this point, but declared that he would not follow us. This promise he certainly kept to the close faithfully, not only in not replying, but not even *attempting to* reply. His course from this out, was to quote certain passages, such as, "I will never leave you;" "I am able to hold you up;" "He who is able to keep you from falling;" "None can pluck them out of his hand," etc., etc., where no condition is expressed. But we showed, in reference to all this class of Scriptures, that the condition is always understood—that when certain blessings are promised upon condition, as in the following: "If you keep in memory what I preached unto you," 1 Cor. xv. 2. "If that which you have heard from the beginning shall remain in you, ye shall also continue in the Son and in the Father," 1 John ii. 24. "If you through the Spirit do mortify the deeds of the body, ye shall live," Rom. viii. 13. "If children, then heirs; heirs of God, and joint heirs with Christ; if so be that we suffer with him, that we may be also glorified together," the condition that they continue true, is always understood. Rom. viii. 17. Now when the Lord would encourage his children, by saying, "I will never leave you," it is with the condition distinctly understood, that they keep in memory what has been preached to them—that they continue in that which they have heard from the beginning—that they suffer with him, that they be glorified together with him—that they mortify the deeds of the body. God promised the Israelites Canaan, and from anything in the passage where the promise is found, no one would think of the promise being conditional. Yet a condition was understood, and breaking the condition—in having an evil heart of unbelief, in departing from the living God—was the cause of six hundred thousand, all able to bear arms when they crossed the Red Sea, except Caleb and Joshua, falling in the wilderness. The promise was understood to be conditional, but the condition is not expressed in the promise. Paul tells us, Heb. iii. 7-19, what they did that provoked the Lord, and caused him to swear in his wrath that they should not enter rest. God threatened to destroy Nineveh, and no condition is expressed in the threat; yet one was understood, and complied with, and the place was not destroyed. The Savior explains the matter in saying, "They *repented* at the preaching of Jonah." If they had not repented, they would have been destroyed.

The prophet said to Solomon, "If thou seek him (God), he will be found of thee; but if thou forsake him, he will cast thee off forever," 1 Chron. xviii. 9. The Lord says, Deut. xxxi. 16, "They will forsake me," and in the next verse says, "I will forsake them." There is not a promise in the Bible, in which this condition does not exist. It is always understood, whether expressed in every place or not, by a man who understands his Bible, that when the Lord says, "I will never leave you," that it is upon condition that you do not forsake him; for he declares if you forsake him, he will forsake you. These promises are precious to the child of God and comforting. It is strengthening and consoling to know that none are able to pluck the child of God out of his Father's hands, that he is able to hold him up and will never forsake him. But the intelligent Christian only thinks of claiming these promises while he abides in the Son and in the Father, continues in the things which he has heard from the beginning, keeps in memory what was preached to him and forsakes not God. But we cannot amplify.

We simply remark, in conclusion, that so far as Mr. F. is an exponent of any doctrine, it is merely a system of evasions of the manifest force of the gospel, and he would not get up a revival in seven years, were it not that he forgets and acts in direct opposition to all the positions he maintained in this debate. If his position touching baptism is true, that ordinance is as unmeaning a ceremony as ever was performed. He cannot tell what it is for. If his position on total depravity is regarded, there is no more use in preaching the gospel to sinners, than to the rocks; and if his position on saints falling from grace is to be regarded, there is no use in preaching to saints, for they can never fall. All preaching, paying men for preaching, with all human efforts, are idle or useless, as they can neither save saints or sinners, according to his doctrine.

But the gospel of Christ was preached among all nations, according to the commandment of the everlasting God, for the obedience of faith—was a savor of life to the believer, and of death to the unbeliever. May it, in its purity, prevail! Blessed be God, it will prevail.

-----o-----

UPWARD TENDENCY— REFORMATION NOT A FAILURE— MISSIONARY WORK.

WHEN Paul was about leaving the world, he cast his eye over the past, the present and the boundless future. Of the past he says, "I have fought a good fight, I have finished my course, I have kept the faith." Every preacher, just as much as Paul, should be able to say, at the close of his life, "I have fought a good fight." But, to be able to say this, the armor must be kept on, bright and in most vigilant use. This forcible and elegant figurative expression, does not describe a life of composure, ease, indolence, and pleasure. The allusion to the life of a soldier, implies hardships, toils, and fatigues; but especially the mention of his *fighting*, implies hard struggles. Never did a human being pass through more toils, hard struggles and sufferings for the kingdom of God, than this holy man; nor did any man ever, with more cogency, refer to his untiring, manly, and noble endurance for the righteousness which is by the faith of Jesus Christ. He could, with propriety, sing, affirmatively, "*I am* a soldier of the cross." He would appeal to his brethren, saying, "I bear in my body the works of the Lord Jesus." How like a man about to retire to rest, he would say,

"*I* have finished my course." He had gone through the toils, hardships, and sufferings of the day, finished his work, and was ready to retire to rest. Thanks to God, that there is a rest for such as he to enter!"There remaineth a rest for the people of God." Looking back to the time when stoned by the Jews, to the five times in which he received forty stripes save one, to the time when the Lord delivered him out of the jaws of the lion at Ephesus, his perils by sea and by land, among robbers and false brethren, with the immense labors of his life, besides the care of all the churches upon his soul, mentioned with tears, daily, in his fervent prayers before God, how comforting to know that his course was run, and that the endurance of these earthly toils was to be demanded of him no longer! How few men in our time know anything about endurance, toils, and sufferings! With such an example as this before us, we should blush to mention the little we do, the small amount we sacrifice or suffer for the name of Jesus!

He proceeds, "I have kept the faith." He had all the attractions of the world before him, to draw him from the faith, common to other men, and the intention of all the threats and tortures to which he was subjected, was to compel him to renounce the faith. But the power of all worldly inducements, all the threats, and tortures to which he was subjected, failed to induce him in the least to swerve from his integrity to the Lord Jesus. They all failed to move him, and when he was about to leave the world, in glorious triumph over them, in victorious language, he shouts, "I have kept the faith!" What an achievement! He had been true to Jesus Christ, constant and enduring, unmoved by persecutions, invulnerable to temptation, not deceived by the deceitfulness of speculators, metaphysicians, theorizers, and philosophizers, nor drawn aside by any of the foolish disputers of this world from the main issues of Christianity, and their bearings upon mankind, but had kept the faith, pure, uncorrupted, and maintained it as the Lord gave it to him. What does all this amount to? Has it any bearing upon another world? Has all that any connection with the mighty fortunes of the future? Hear him: "Henceforth there is laid up for me a crown of righteousness, which the Lord, the righteous judge, shall give me at that day, and not to me only, but unto all them also that love his appearing." Here we find what he has had in his mind from the beginning—*"a crown of righteousness."*

With this prospect before him, what kind of encouragement does he give young preachers? Let us hear him: "Godliness, with contentment, is great gain." That is certainly very encouraging. Concerning worldly prospects, he informs them, that "we brought nothing into the world, and it is certain we can carry nothing out." His conclusion, therefore, is, "Having food and raiment, let us be therewith content." Admonishing them against the love of money, which is the root of all evil, and pointing them to its destructive tendencies, he exhorts, "O man of God, flee these things, and follow after righteousness, godliness, faith, love, patience, meekness," As he had fought a good fight himself, and now realized the consolation it afforded at the termination of his course, he extolls it's men of God, "Fight the good fight of faith," and proceeds to give the solemn charge: "I give the charge, in the sight of God, who quickeneth all things, and before Jesus Christ, who before Pontius Pilate witnessed a good confession, that thou keep this commandment without spot, until the appearing of our Lord Jesus Christ." Again, says he, to the same class, "I charge thee, therefore, before God, and the Lord Jesus Christ, who shall judge the quick and the dead at his appearing and kingdom, preach the word; be instant in season; reprove, rebuke, exhort with all long suffering and doctrine; for the time will come when they will not endure doctrine; but after their own lusts shall they heap to themselves teachers, having itching ears, and they shall turn their ears away from the truth, and shall be turned unto fables." What a solemn charge this is to preach *the word,* or *nothing but the word.* In his charge, as collected from the different portions of his letters to Timothy, he appeals to God, Jesus Christ, the elect angels and the day when God shall judge the world, enjoining *preach the word.* What man, who has a heart that can be moved by an appeal, a solemn appeal, from a solemn man—a man whose life, in great power, showed him to be a most solemn, earnest and sincere man, an appeal to God, Christ Jesus, elect angels, the confession of Jesus before Pilate and the judgment of the great day, charging him to preach the word, fight a good fight and lay hold of eternal life, dare allow a thought of corrupting the faith, mutilating it, or perverting it in any way to enter into his mind? Better were it for a man that he had never been born than that he should corrupt, pervert or *detract from, the faith.*

What do you mean by "*the faith?*" "We all know that if we depart from the faith of Christ, we shall be lost; but the question is, *What is the faith?*" "The faith," with us, we wish it distinctly understood, *is that which is inscribed upon the sacred pages, in the clear revelations of God, in the Bible.* These oracles, we can maintain, in defiance of all contradiction and opposition, are revelations from God, genuine, true and veritable—revelations to the minds and understandings of men at large, beginning with the unregenerate, the unbelieving, and adapted to all classes to the end of the world—the last will and testament. But all claim to revelation outside of these, from the false apostles, rivals of the genuine *thirteen,* sent by Jesus, down by such as Mahomet, Ann Lee, Swedenborg, with all the pretenders to revelation and miracles in the Romish church, with the many deluded creatures among Protestants, claiming to speak by inspiration, with the entire retinue of Mormon apostles and Spiritualists, have been but a continued combination of pretenders, with some sincere, but deceived persons, the entire bearing of whose cause has been, and is still, to the subversion of the Word of God.

The faith of Christ, is faith in the *Divine Person* whom God has sent into the world, and "declared to be the Son of God with power, according to the spirit of holiness, by the resurrection from the dead." It is not faith in an idle, empty, and soulless theory, about views of men, their doctrines, regeneration, the influence of the spirit, repentance, or baptism. It is not faith in some theory of faith, some system of philosophizing upon faith, or speculations of the nature or kinds of faith. All the theorizing upon these themes, or any others, never made a New Testament believer since the world was made; nor did theorizing about regeneration ever regenerate any person. Many persons were made believers without hearing the word *faith* mentioned, much less any explanations of faith. Indeed, no person, so far as the New Testament goes, ever attempted to explain faith to men when trying to convert them. Nor did the apostles ever try, in all their efforts to bring men to the kingdom of God, to explain regeneration to them; nor could they, if they had attempted it, have ever regenerated any man by it. When they found unbelievers, they commenced in the most rational way possible, revealing to them the theme that filled their own hearts, that lay upon their souls, and was the center of all their thoughts. Let us have their example, that we may see how they preached to make believers. Let us hear Peter: "Ye men of Israel, hear these words: Jesus of Nazareth, a man approved of God among you by miracles, and wonders, and signs, which God did by him in the midst of you, as ye yourselves also know: him being delivered by the determinate counsel and foreknowledge of God, ye have taken by wicked hands, and crucified and slain; whom God hath raised up, having loosed the pains of death, because it was not possible that he should be holden of it." Acts ii. 22-24. Let us hear Peter open another sermon: "Ye men of Israel, why marvel ye at this? or why look ye so earnestly on us, as though by our own power or holiness we had made this man walk? The God of Abraham, and Isaac, and Jacob, the God of our fathers, hath glorified his Son Jesus, whom ye delivered up, and denied him in the presence of Pilate, when he was determined to let him go. But ye denied the Holy One and the Just, and desired a malefactor to be granted unto you." Acts iii. 11-14. "Philip began at the same Scripture, and preached unto him Jesus," and Paul says, *"I determined to know nothing among you but Christ, and him crucified"*— "God forbid that I should glory save in the cross of Christ." Christ was their theme, and they preached Christ to convert, regenerate, or save men, and not their views of regeneration. This is what must be preached now, in the simple and rational manner found in the apostolic practice. Preach the same now, in the same earnestness, love, and simplicity, as the apostles did, and men will believe it, whether we say anything about faith or not. Men everywhere, unless where they have been confused by blind guides, know how to believe, when truth is presented, as well as they know how to see when light is presented. Children, ten years of age, know how to believe, and how to disbelieve, and do believe and disbelieve, when matters are stated to them, with just as much readiness, and just as rationally, as the most profound philosopher in the world; and there is not a more irrational and useless thing in the word than theorizing, philosophizing, and explaining faith, to make believers. Let us come to the simplicity of the holy apostles of Jesus, and preach that which is to be believed, with earnestness and power, and

VOL. II.—No. 8—2.

men can believe it. The belief of it will also have the effect upon their hearts without any of the blind and stupid theorizings about *effects* of these times. Theorizing about effects, produces no effect, unless to lead people to believe in a *theory of effects.*

If a man is hungry, give him bread, and let him eat it, and the good effects will follow without a philosopher to theorize upon the effects. If a man is sick, give him medicine—the right kind, and the effect will follow. But by all means, unless you intend him to die, keep away a miserable, blind quack, who will deliver him a long lecture upon disease, and the effects of medicine, but not give him the medicine. In the same way, when the man of the world is hungry for the word of God, which brings Jesus—the bread that came down from heaven—to him, preach the word to him—the simple word, as preached by the apostles—and, if he receives it into a good and honest heart, it will have its effect, do its work, without any man to theorize upon the effects. When men are sick of sin, give them the medicine, as the Lord prepared it, and as the apostles administered it, and it will have the desired effect—cure all who receive it into good and honest hearts, without any theorizing upon the effects.

Buckle on the armor, you old soldiers of the cross, veterans in the King's army, men of God, who have fought so many battles, won so many victories, and done such a mighty work for mankind, in restoring a pure speech to the people of God, the simple gospel of Christ, or primitive Christianity, and built up such a vast number of churches, scattered so largely over the world, during the last thirty years, and decide whether this work shall be maintained. You know what this work has cost you, and what it is worth, and we appeal to you, to decide whether you will maintain it. We also appeal to that long list of noble young men, scattered so widely over the world, who have identified themselves with this cause, and have now entered upon such extended fields of usefulness, and are thus put in such a fair way for doing something noble for mankind, to know whether they intend to buckle on the armor and defend it! Shall we maintain the clear teachings of the New Testament, the manifest terms of induction into the kingdom of God, and expose those insidious attempts to darken counsel, obscure the clear light of heaven, muddy the waters of salvation, unsettle the minds of the brotherhood, throw everything into confusion, and create general doubts and distrust, making their appearance among us? We have received Christianity, become Christians, entered the church of Christ, and taken the law of Christ as the man of our counsel. Shall we keep the faith, continue in the things we have heard from the beginning? Yes, brethren, we know you will. There are thousands who will maintain the doctrine to the end, and with their dying breath. In the dying words of that noble soul, John T. Johnson, we "have lived upon our religion, and we can die upon it." We can maintain it, but we cannot give it up, we dare not give it up, we *will not*. We have preached nothing but the gospel, required no man to believe anything but the gospel, to be anything but a Christian—a Disciple of Christ—to submit to nothing but the law of God. All among us that are true, have believed the gospel, become Christians—Disciples of Christ, are members of the church of Christ, and under the law of God, and if they depart from this, they are ruined, will sink themselves, be miserable in this world, and lost forever. "It is a fearful thing to fall into the hands of the living God." "If any man draw back, my soul shall have no pleasure in him," says the Lord. Blessed be his name forever and ever!

B. F.

But to do good, and to impart forget not; with such sacrifices God is well pleased.

BRACKEN ASSOCIATION OF UNITED BAPTISTS.
NUMBER VII.

Eld. Gardner, in his letter on "Restricted Communion," page 17, says—"The Baptists, in common with all others, believe that an *error*, either in the mode, subject, or design of baptism *invalidates the* ordinance." This, I confess, is news to me. What! The Baptists and Paedobaptists agree that a mistake in the mode of baptism renders the ordinance void! And yet the Paedobaptists say, the mode is a mere unimportant circumstance—that the application of water to a proper subject, by a proper person, in any mode, is valid baptism, while the Baptists say, if there is no immersion, there is no baptism!? This is a strange sort of agreement. But, says Eld. Gardner, you Reformers have mistaken the design of baptism, and, therefore, you who were baptized for the remission of your sins, have no baptism! And to sustain him in this position, he makes a brief quotation from the Lexington debate between Mr. Campbell and Mr. Rice. I shall attempt no defense of Mr. Campbell, as he is able to defend himself. Still, I think, Eld. Gardner has put a construction upon Mr. Campbell's language which he would not endorse. But even if he would, what of it? It would simply be the opinion of a good and great man, from which we have a right to dissent, and from which our people do most decidedly dissent. Let Eld. Gardner and others who wish to know Eld. Campbell's views upon this subject, turn to the *Millennial Harbinger* for 1831, November number. They will there find a long article, headed "Rebaptism," in which he gives his reasons, at length, against a second baptism, because the subject, though a true penitent, and submitting to immersion in the spirit of true obedience to Christ, nevertheless did not fully understand all the benefits connected with the institution—did not understand it to be for remission of sins, as he afterwards believed. Mr. Campbell says (M. H. p. 483), "How a person who has been born again (of water and the Spirit), and entered into the kingdom of grace, can die in that kingdom, and be buried in that kingdom, and be born a second time into it, is not for me to explain. There is but one baptism, and but once baptism under the Christian King. Indeed I know not how any proclaimer of the gospel, how any intelligent disciple can presume to bury a living disciple, how he can immerse a believer a second time into Christ—into the name of the Father, and of the Son, and of the Holy Spirit. He must have received a new commission. The old apostolic commission authorizes it not. I know some will say that the candidates which they immersed a second time, did not rightly understand baptism the first time. Well, I am persuaded they did not understand it the second time; and shall they be baptized a third time? But did all the believers whom the apostles baptized understand their baptism in all its designs, meaning, and bearings? We presume not, else the apostles need not have written to them to explain it: ' Know you not,' said Paul to the Romans, 'that so many of us as were immersed into Jesus Christ were immersed into his death.' But did Paul command any one to be baptized a second time because he did not fully understand the whole import of his baptism? Did Peter command Simon to repent and be baptized again for the remission of his sins? If any person ought to have been re-baptized, it was this Simon the sorcerer. But no such idea is suggested anywhere in the New Testament." Mr. Campbell, I presume to say, does not think it would be necessary to re-baptize a pious Baptist who might wish to unite with us, though he had not been baptized "for the remission of sins," as we understand it.

But, says Eld. Gardner (Min. p. 20), "How unjust and unreasonable to criminate the Baptists on account of their restricted communion, when they cannot remove the barrier to mixed communion without the sacrifice of principle and conscience, while open communionists *can* do it without any such sacrifice, but *will not!* "Well, now, if this is the true state of the case, we may all, without any sacrifice of principle, be brought together and enjoy not only "Christian," but also "sacramental communion," and thus our schisms all be removed, and the great barrier to the union of the people of God, and the conversion of the world taken out of the way. If Baptists, as Eld. Gardner says, cannot remove the barriers to Christian union and communion, without a sacrifice of "principle and conscience," of course it would be cruel, nay, wicked, in others to ask it. And, on the other hand if, according to the same authority, Episcopalians, Presbyterians, Methodists, and all the evangelical sects, and the Reformers, can, without any sacrifice of "principle or conscience," bring about such union and communion, but, as Eld. Gardner says, *"will not,"* then, unquestionably, the blame and the guilt lie at our doors. We are keeping up divisions, contrary to the doctrine of Christ, and thus standing in the way of the conversion of the world, and must be incurring fearful responsibility! But how does Bro. Gardner make out his case? He begins by affirming that all the advocates of mixed communion admit, "that Baptist churches are true and regular churches of Jesus Christ." What does Eld. Gardner mean by this? That all sorts of Baptist churches—the General Baptists and the Particular Baptists, the Seventh Day Baptists, the Free-Will Baptists, and the bound-will hypercalvinitic Baptists, the United Baptists, and the two-seed Baptists, the Licking Dudley Baptists—that all these are true and regular churches of Christ?! Well, if he acknowledges those associated with Eld. Dudley, as regular churches of Jesus Christ, Eld. Dudley does not reciprocate the favor. In the minutes of their last Association. or some recent session of it, he takes the ground that those occupying the position of the churches of the Licking Association constitute the only true visible kingdom of Christ on earth—that while God has a people among other denominations, they are in Babylon, and of course ought to come out of her, and join their churches!!

But if the Baptists, in all their schisms and parties, are the only true and regular churches of Jesus Christ, what sort of churches are all the rest?! Untrue and irregular churches of Jesus Christ?! But whether the so-called evangelical parties among the Paedobaptists all concede that Baptist churches are true and regular churches of Jesus Christ, I beg leave to say, in behalf of our people, that we never have made any such concession, Eld. Gardner to the contrary notwithstanding. Nay, more, we have shown that all the evangelical sects, so called (the Baptists among the rest), concede that their Christianity is wholly distinct from, and independent of, their particular isms, inasmuch as each sect admits there are Christians outside of its pale, and, of course, independent of its ism. They are, one and all, too modern in their origin, too antagonistic in their spirits, creeds, names, organizations, and practices, to represent the original churches of Christ, perfectly joined together in the same mind and the same judgment, all members of the one body, inspired by the one spirit, animated by the one hope, having one Lord, one faith, one baptism, one God and Father of all, above all, with all, and in all. If the Baptists claim to have derived their name, and particular position, from John the Baptist, then they ought to remember that John died before the gospel church or kingdom was set up, and that Messiah said that although of them born of women, there had not arisen a greater than John, yet the least in the kingdom of heaven was greater than he. They ought also to know, that the New Testament knows nothing of Baptists or of a Baptist church or churches. It speaks of the church of God, in Christ Jesus—the churches of Christ, Christians, Disciples of Christ, etc., but never of Baptist churches or Baptists, and so of all the rest of the so called evangelicals. The Baptists ought to know, moreover, that to call their people Baptists is a clear misnomer, as the name given to John was official. He was called the Baptist because he baptized.

Well, but Eld. Gardner insists that Baptists are true and regular churches of Christ, maintaining and teaching the truth, the whole truth, and nothing but the truth; and that, but for the perversity of the sects, and the "Reformers," we might all be united upon the truth as it is in Jesus—that they cannot remove the barriers to such union, but that we, without any sacrifice of principle, can, but WILL NOT!! As to the orthodox sects, we leave them to make their own defense as best they can, and proceed at once to inquire, whether our cause admits of any satisfactory defense. Most certainly, if we, who have been pleading for union, the union of God's people on heaven's own platform, from our very birth, as a people, are ourselves in the way of such union, and *will not* remove the barrier to it, which can be done without any sacrifice of principle on our part, we must be very culpable, very wicked indeed!! Wonder if Eld. Gardner's memory is not a little at fault?! Wonder if when he penned the above charge against us, he thought of what he had written on page 29?! Or, if, when he wrote page 29, he thought of what he had written on pages 18,19-20?! The Elder tells us plainly, the terms on which we can have union and communion with them. "If they" (our people who were once Baptists) "renounce their errors" (baptism for remission of sins for instance), "and repent of their sins" (against the Baptist churches), "and return to the fellowship of our churches, then, and *not till then,* can we consistently commune with them." p. 29. All our brethren, then, who once were Baptists, but who were justly excluded from their churches for their errors and sins, can, according to the new divinity of Eld. Gardner, "without any sacrifice of principle or conscience," renounce errors which they are not conscious of holding, and confess, forsake, and repent of sins they have no consciousness of having committed, and thus remove the barriers to communion with the Baptist churches."

Is not Eld. Gardner a remarkable man?! But how may the rest of our people remove the barriers to union with the Baptists? O, says Eld. Gardner, that can be done very easily, without any sacrifice of principle or conscience whatever. The Paedobaptists lack two things to fit them to unite with us in communion and church fellowship, baptism and union with a true church of Jesus Christ, but you Reformers who were baptized "for the actual remission of your sins, without professing a previous change of heart"—lack three things, conversion, baptism, and union with a true church of Christ, and although I know you claim to have received gospel conversion, Christian baptism, and to stand connected with the church of God, in Christ Jesus, yet without any sacrifice of principle or conscience, you can renounce your conversion, repudiate your baptism, and your connection with the church of Christ, and seek after Baptist conversion, Baptist baptism, and Baptist fellowship and communion, and thus remove the barriers to Christian union!! Now, Eld. Gardner, don't you feel ashamed of this whole affair?! Ought you not to quit writing circulars? We did intend to say something on the creed question, as the minutes contain the creed of the Association, as "revised, corrected, and extended," by said body; but as the Baptists generally deny that they have any authoritative creed beside the Scriptures of truth, we shall say but little on this subject. We are as fully satisfied that all human creeds, as tests of Christian fellowship and co-operation, are unauthorized of God, and of evil tendency, as we are that "all Scripture given by inspiration of God is profitable for doctrine, for reproof, for correction, and instruction in righteousness, that the man of God may be perfect, thoroughly furnished to all good works." We are happy, therefore, in the Divine assurance, that the man of God, the church of God, is thoroughly furnished, in Scripture, with all the means of enjoying the right spirit, the right faith, the right practice—is thoroughly furnished with whatever is suited to bring glory to God, peace on earth, and good-will among men—with whatever is adapted to promote the purity, the unity, and prosperity of the church, and the conversion of the world, is, in one word, thoroughly furnished to all good works—all works of faith, labors of love, and patience of hope in our Lord Jesus Christ. But that human creeds, and the spirit that made them, and supports them on the other hand, have thoroughly furnished the church with the spirit of division and strife—of persecution and all bad works. Hence, in harmony with these views, the history of the church proclaims, that, during the first centuries, while the church recognized no creed but the word of God— while she had the spirit of God in her heart, and the word of God in her hand, she maintained her unity and purity, and triumphed over Judaism and Paganism, and converted the world. But as soon as she ceased to be animated by the spirit of the truth, and introduced human creeds, and made these tests of Christian faith and practice, the world converted her into an engine of state, and she was shorn of her unity, her purity, her power, and with rapid strides commenced her retrograde movement into Babylon, where creed-mongers and their votaries still live, striving about matters of opinion—questions which gender strifes of words, rather than godly edification, which is in Christ Jesus. We unequivocally deny that God has granted to any church, or council, or association of churches, the right to make a human creed in the ecclesiastic sense of that word. Let the advocates of creeds show that grant of power in the New Testament. The right, if it exist at all, belongs to all churches; but if all have this right, then God authorizes and approves all the multitudinous antagonistic creeds of Christendom, with all the antagonistic sects based upon them, and all the legitimate consequences flowing from these antagonisms. But this is impossible, as God can no more oppose himself than he can deny himself. Creeds, human, authoritative creeds, all proceed upon the assumption that the word of God is not sufficient: for if the word is perfect, thoroughly furnishing the church with a perfect rule of faith, why add an acknowledged imperfect one?! Such creeds are Popish, all over Popish, in their origin and tendency, and subversive and inimical alike to Christian liberty, Christian union, and Christian progress. If the creed embodies errors, they are stereotyped, and last while the creed is maintained. But the errors of the creed ought to be abandoned, and therefore ought never to have been adopted. But who dare abandon, with impunity, the creed Christ has given to his church?! If the creed contain less than that given by the head of the church, it contains too little; if more, too much; if the same, then it is superfluous. But who does not know that all human creeds, however long or short, contain both more or less than the New Testament—that they are as different from it in their structure, nature, and appearance, as the most ghastly human skeleton of dry bones, strung together with wires, is different from the most beautifully symmetrical living person. They are made up of mere abstractions, the notions, the deductions of speculative minds, while the teachings of the Scriptures are practical in their nature and tendency, all suited and designed to enlighten the mind, with a view to the purification of the heart, the conscience, and life from sin, and thus to fit us for the great purposes of our being here, and the happiness of heaven hereafter. Clearly, then, the church *will never, can never* harmonize upon any human schismatic creed. She must cease from man, whose breath is in his nostrils, and then she will be prepared to come out of the wilderness, (where she has been lost in the labyrinths of sectarian strife—in "The Conflict of Ages"), leaning upon her beloved, fair as the moon, clear as the sun, and terrible as an army with banners. In my next, I propose to show that considerable changes have taken place among the Baptists in the last twenty-five or thirty years, and that they are not all as uncharitable as the Elders of the Bracken Association. One or two more numbers, I think, will close my review of the Bracken Association of United Baptists.

JOHN ROGERS.

QUERY.

BRO. FRANKLIN—*Dear Sir:*—I have been a reader of your writings ever since you began to edit the *Christian Age,* and that was about my first reading, as I was then quite young. I have been very well pleased with all your sentiments which you have advanced. I have been very well pleased with the *Review,* and have, therefore, been actively engaged as your agent. I have not heretofore troubled you with queries, and I hope you will, therefore, comply with the request I am about to make of you. Please give me your views of the *"Baptism of the Holy Ghost and with fire."* Is it all past? if so, when was it consummated; and, if not, is any part of it past? The trouble with me is the fire. Yours, truly,

JNO. S. SWEENEY.

REMARKS.

This question has been so frequently discussed, and our space is so very limited at present, that we can say but few words in compliance with the above kind request.

We shall be as brief and concise as possible.

1. It is a fact that none but the good were ever baptized in the Holy Spirit.

2. It is a fact that two classes were present, and addressed in the discourse where the baptism of fire is mentioned—the disciples and others saying, "We have Abraham for our father," called a "generation of vipers."

3. Where these "vipers" were not addressed or alluded to, we find no baptism of fire.

4. In Matt. iii. 7-12, we find both parties present. In this passage the word fire occurs three times, as follows:—first, verse 10:"Every tree that bringeth not forth good fruit, is hewn down and cast into the *fire*."Second, verse 11: "He shall baptize you with the Holy Spirit and with *fire*."Third, ver. 12, "He will burn up the chaff with unquenchable *fire*." Now that these three passages are three figurative expressions, meaning precisely the same, we think no reasonable man can doubt. Each of these expressions applies, and is addressed, to the same persons. There is no trouble in determining that the "generation of vipers," who say "we have Abraham for our father," the "trees that bring not forth fruit," and the "chaff," are the same. In the first and third instance, the fire is unquestionably for the wicked. It would be remarkable then, if the fire in the second instance did not apply to the same persons. We have, first, fruitful and unfruitful trees, good and bad people, the one to remain in the orchard, the other to be cast into the fire; second, the baptism of the Holy Spirit and of fire, the former for the good, the latter for the bad; third, the chaff and wheat, good and bad, the latter for the garner, and the former for fire. No man would pray for the fire to come upon him that is to burn the trees that bring not forth good fruit, or that is to burn the chaff; yet he who prays that he may be baptized with fire, prays for the same fire. This fire is evidently not past, but the *gehenna of* fire for the ungodly. But the proofs we cannot give now.   B. F.

-----o-----

THE "CHRISTIAN" NAME.

BRO. FRANKLIN:—It is well known that our opponents frequently charge us with a want of charity, in assuming the name "Christian," to the exclusion of all others. They tell us we thereby *unchristian* all other churches. I lately made a reply to this objection which my brethren have requested me to publish, since they deemed it important that the objection be removed, that we may stand before the world in our true light. Bro. Lard has written well upon this point as indeed he has upon all others, yet it may be answered by an argument of another species which may be worth the while of our opponents to consider.

We have an *argumentum ad hominem* to which we invite the attention of those of our friends who charge us with presumption in our choice of a name. An objection is considered fairly answered when it is shown to lie with equal force against the party objecting. An argument is refuted when it is shown that it is equally potent when applied to those offering it. We will now show that the objection so often made to our only name is of this character. We have never claimed that our use of the name "Christian" or "Church of Jesus Christ" was either intended, or that it did *unchristianize* the rest of the world, yet this double charge is continually made upon us. We shall show that the name "Christian" does not exhaust all its meaning upon the Reformers, nor are all the members of Christ's church or body connected with our people. That all "Christians" *are* associated together is not claimed by any, but that they *ought to* be thus united is what we have ever contended.

But to our *argument*. Let us first examine the various names which a few of the sects have appropriated to themselves, and we shall see the real force of the above objection. Take for instance the name "Protestant Episcopalian." Now do these people assuming this name exhaust the whole meaning of the words upon themselves? Are not twenty other denominations equally *Protestant?* Yes, they acknowledge it. Then if they can use the name *Protestant* without thereby declaring all others non-Protestant, we may use the name Christian without thereby declaring all others un-Christian. Why not ? So of the other name *Episcopalian.* There are other Episcopalians beside them, if we mistake not. Is not the Church of England governed by diocesan Episcopoi (bishops)? Are not the Catholics and Methodists good Episcopalians? But they may say that they are *Protestant Episcopalians* because they *protest* against some things in the mother Church of England. But has not the Methodist Episcopal Church *protested* as much as they ? Yes, more. Therefore, whether we consider each part of the name by itself, or the whole as one complex thing, we perceive that the same objection against the name "Christian," lies with equal force against it. If, therefore, they can use their name without thereby *un-Protestantizing* and *un-Episcopalizing* all others, why can we not use the name " Christian " without *un-Christianizing* all others ?

We have examined the name of only one church, but the same remarks may be applied to several other names, for instance, "Protestant Methodist," so called because they *protested* against the office of diocesan bishops in the Methodist Episcopal church, from whose communion they sprang. But several other branches of the Methodist body have *protested* against the government of the church by such officers, and are therefore equally *Protestant*. So we might instance the name Congregationalist or Independent, which indicates no more a peculiarity of the body so called, than of the Baptists, and some others. Thus our opponents have been making an objection, which, if it have any force whatever, weighs equally against themselves, but which, in fact, is the most futile of all objections ever offered.

But it may now be alleged, that although there be Protestants and Episcopalians in other churches, as well as Congregationalists, yet there is but one body known as the "Protestant Episcopalian Church," but one known as the " Protestant Methodist Church," and but one known as the "Congregational Church," that is, when we use the word church in its general or generic sense. We admit it. We never yet heard it disputed. We also add that although there are Christians to be found scattered through the various sects of Christendom, yet there is but one body of Christ, but one Christian church, and this body is composed, not of our people alone, but of all the saints of whatever name. We do not, therefore, claim that the mass of our people complete the "Christian church," in its generic sense, neither does any other organization, nor do they all together complete the "general assembly of the first born," since there may be those who are Christians, and consequently in the kingdom of Christ, who are not connected at present with any of these organizations. That all Christians ought to be united in one visible body we believe, and therefore we have not ceased for many years to call upon all Christians to come together and be united in one, as the Savior prayed. All Christians are "in Christ," in his body, and are therefore members of " the household of faith, citizens of the kingdom, and made sons and heirs to the glorious inheritance beyond the skies." Why should they then allow their opinions to keep them apart? Why should the visible body of the church be longer dissevered, dismembered, and dishonored ?

Let us, before we take leave of this subject, look for a moment at the phrase, a phrase, a church of Jesus Christ, that is, a *church* used in accordance with its most common Scriptural meaning, denoting a Christian congregation, organized according to the grand model given at Jerusalem on the day of Pentecost. This is the Jerusalem church "which is the mother of us all." The true churches of Christ are the daughters of Jerusalem, they are not the daughters of Rome, nor of Geneva, nor of London, nor of Oxford, nor of Edinburg. We, therefore, do not hesitate in applying the name *Christian church* to a local congregation of the "saints and faithful in Christ Jesus," and do maintain, that if such an organization be built upon the foundation of the prophets and apostles, and "continue steadfastly in the apostles' doctrine, in fellowship, and in breaking bread, and in prayers," it is divinely entitled to that name. And how much more appropriate that name first given at Antioch, referred to by King Agrippa, and claimed by the apostle Peter in his first letter. Could Christians unite upon a sectarian name any more easily than upon a sectarian creed? Ah, why not take an inspired creed, a holy confession, and a Bible name? Let our friends know, then, it is for no want of charity that we have selected this name, but because we wish to unite with Christians of all denominations, we therefore throw away our human names, our human creeds, our human books of discipline, and propose to meet all who love our Lord Jesus Christ upon the good old apostolic creed and discipline. We meet you on the Bible, and not on any man's opinions. We have sacrificed all for this, come heal the wound in the body of Christ. May our dear Lord be no longer wounded in the house of his friends. Yours, in Christ,

H. C. PIERCE.

Cheneyville, La.

ONE often regrets saying too much, but seldom of saying too little.

LETTERS FROM AN INQUIRER AFTER TRUTH.
NUMBER I.

BRO FRANKLIN:—I would gladly avail myself of the privilege you were so kind as to afford me, to institute an enquiry into the religious views commonly held among us as a denomination; not by any means in a captious spirit, but in the utmost kindness, as my most ardent desire and prayer to God for my brethren is, that they may be saved.

And first, to show any necessity for my thus occupying your attention and that of your readers, I would, as a Baptist would express it, relate my "experience." Fifteen years ago I united from a Baptist church with the "Disciples." The motives which were prominent with me, were a sincere admiration of their pleas for *Christian union,* and for a return, both in speech and practice, to *apostolic Christianity:* pleas which yet seem to me to be very noble and very desirable. At that time, I supposed the teachings and views of the "Disciples" to be sound on the subjects of conversion, justification, and the Holy Spirit. In the letter which I wrote to the church of which I had been a member, I stated that the only matters of difference between the Baptists and Disciples were an opposition to creeds, and to sectarianism, and a belief that baptism was for the remission of sins, or, as I expressed it, and as I supposed was the teaching of the brethren at the time, *"the pledge* of an indulgent Father in heaven, that the sinner's transgressions *had been* pardoned."

Farther experience, however, convinced me that there were some very serious matters of difference. I found that the view generally entertained of the Holy Spirit's work was this, that it was simply the influence of the Bible upon the mind, and that there were no divine accompanying influences to increase its efficiency. I found the view of conversion to be, that it was a sincere belief that Jesus was the Son of God, and a profession of that belief in baptism; not requiring any new "birth of the Spirit, or "quickening" from God, in the sense generally held and taught by evangelical Christians. While, in regard to Christian union, which was the great attraction to me, I found the whole plea for it stultified by the teaching, that immersion was, in connection with faith and repentance, necessary for justification, or the pardon of sins, and consequently those who were not immersed were unforgiven, and, of course not Christians, and there were, consequently, no Christians outside of our own denomination, and the Baptists to unite!

And now, Bro. Franklin, I come to you as a scribe, supposed to be well instructed in the law, for assistance in my difficulties. Here is where I stand. I have an earnest love for the *"union of Christians,"* for the *"Bible only,"* as a guide in all matters of religious faith and duty, and for a complete restoration of apostolic Christianity; and in your pleadings for these things, I am, and shall be always with you, but I repudiate, with all my soul, these errors which ignore the Holy Spirit's work in conversion and sanctification, and that a sinner's forgiveness is based upon his immersion. And, now, what am I to do? Some of my brethren say, if you do not receive and endorse the views commonly held, you should leave; but you say, and I say, No; it is my duty to hold on to our broad platform, "the Bible and the Bible alone;" and if my brethren are wrong, help them to get right. And so, you have kindly offered me the use of your columns to state my difficulties. I appreciate your kindness and fairness, and could ask nothing more than this: an entire freedom to interpret the Bible for myself, and in meekness to instruct those that oppose themselves, if God may peradventure give them repentance to the acknowledgment of the truth, etc., etc.

So I shall write, with your permission, a few articles setting forth my understanding of the truth, and as my purpose is only to elicit truth, and not vain glory, I subscribe myself only,

Your Brother,

AN INQUIRER AFTER TRUTH.

REMARKS.

1. A few days ago we saw the writer of the above and cheerfully granted space for a few articles, but it certainly never entered our mind, that a graduate of Bethany College, a preacher, who was an editor a short time, and who has been united with the Disciples *fifteen years,* desired space "to institute an inquiry into the religious views commonly held by us," and that he had only attained the position of an "Inquirer after Truth!" But if his article is an exponent of the best light he has, our readers will readily grant that he has great need to "inquire after truth."

2. When he united with the Disciples, he supposed them sound on "conversion, justification and the Holy Spirit," but "further experience has convinced him that there Were some very serious matters of difference." Experience has been a slow teacher, to permit him to be *fifteen years* in finding this serious difference!

3. He found "the view of conversion to be, that it was a sincere belief that Jesus was the Son of God and profession of that belief in baptism, not requiring any new 'birth of the Spirit,' or 'quickening' from God, in the sense generally held and taught by evangelical Christians." We offer no argument now, but admonish him and all who agree with him, that we believe in the new birth—that a man "must be born again"—"born of the Spirit"—"quickened all from God, and expect to show that the "birth of the Spirit," "quickening from God" and influence of the Spirit by which men are brought to the Savior, according to the New Testament, are invalidated, subverted and set aside by his *new* theory, which has been upon the lips of sectarians for the past thirty years; and that he is now advocating something instead, not the "birth of the Spirit," "quickening from God," or the influence of the

Spirit of God at all. He shall not succeed in involving this subject in the dark.

4. He found "the whole plea for union absolutely stultified by the teaching that immersion was, in connection with repentance, necessary for justification or pardon of sins." Indeed!—and what is to be done? Shall we alter the Bible and disconnect baptism and remission of sins? No, sir; we must change the men who do not believe and maintain the plain teaching of the Bible, or show that they are opposed to it. We shall maintain the Bible whether men will unite upon it or not.

5. Not understanding, when he united with the Disciples, was, that baptism "is the *pledge* of an indulgent Father in heaven that the sinner's transgressions *had been* pardoned." He thought the Disciples held this, but he has found in *fifteen years* that he was mistaken! Why, then, does he state it as an item of difference between the Disciples and Baptists? The truth is, he commenced this confused and unmeaning sentence to state a difference between Baptists and Disciples, but closed it in an effort to show that he had not changed, but had misunderstood the Disciples; but told nothing different from the Baptists at all. But the design of baptism is *a, pledge* that sins *had been* pardoned! Then, when repentance is connected with baptism, as "Repent and be baptized * * * for remission," repentance, too, is *a pledge* that sins *had been* pardoned—had been pardoned before repentance, or in impenitence! Or when faith and baptism are connected, as "He that believeth and is baptized shall be saved," the faith has the same design as baptism. If baptism is a *pledge* that sins *had been* pardoned, faith is also a pledge that sins had been pardoned—pardoned before faith, or pardoned in unbelief; and they believe and are baptized for a pledge that sins had been pardoned before faith and baptism! Certainly, he has need to *inquire after truth!*

6. Several men have attempted to involve this cause in ruin who have been identified with it, but have only sunk themselves; and nothing will save the writer of the above from the same fate, only to cease his unwarrantable course, and maintain his integrity to the clear import of Scripture. In doing this, he would save himself, and those to whom he is dearer than life, of deep mortification and grief, and save the cause of Christ from being put to shame. We certainly do not wish to oppose him; but the cause must not be crucified and put to open shame. We have spent more than twenty years in this cause, of the main vigor of our life, and have been instrumental in bringing more than one hundred for each year to the fold of Christ; and we will not—we cannot, and be true to the Lord Jesus, see the seeds of discord and schism sown among them, and old sectarian notions foisted into the church, touching conversion, by those who have never built up the cause any place, or scarcely ever converted anybody, and be silent. Let those who claim a sounder system of conversion, convert, some, show us the better converts before they prate about the unsoundness of the work of other men. This is not a matter to be trifled with. The work of many of our older men, extending back over some thirty years; performed at great sacrifice, hard toiling, in many prayers and tears, is not to be trifled with by those who have never done scarcely anything, and they pass unrebuked. We can know no man after the flesh here, yet will be the first man to encourage our brother when he shall cease his wayward course. B. F.

-----o-----

COMMUNICATION.

Dear Bro. Franklin:—It has been sometime since I corresponded with you; perhaps not since your connection with the *Age* ceased. But I have been much pleased in reading the *American Christian Review* all the time it has been before us; and especially interested in some articles under the caption, *"The Reformation not a Failure—Upward Tendency."* I have been a preacher of what I believe to be, and call, the ancient gospel, for *many* years, and I think I am prepared with you to say, "The Reformation is *not* a failure; but, in my judgment, is now upon a more permanent basis than ever before.

We closed a meeting yesterday at *Otter Creek,* in this county, with *twenty-seven* additions to the congregation at that place. This was a triumph of the truth. Owing to business before the farmers at this season of the year, we only spoke in the evening. We spoke three evenings, and was joined by my son, Jno. S. Sweeney—with whom you are acquainted—who assisted us much by delivering three discourses in his usual style. We had an opportunity to speak but eight times *in all,* and our meeting was crowned with success as above. On Lord's day evening, when we met at the water to attend to baptism, I was reminded of "old times." We had about one thousand persons to witness the scene, the most of whom respected the occasion; but some made the old argument: whistling and singing "Old Dan Tucker," and laughing while we were attending to baptism. This we can "look over," knowing what allowance to make.

It may be proper to say, that nineteen of the additions were by confession and immersion, and eight took union with us upon the Bible, the whole Bible, and nothing *"distinct from* and *above* the Bible."

May God bless you, Bro. F., in the good work you are doing for his glory, the upholding of his cause *all over the land,* together with *all* who labor for this end.

Thine, in Christ,

G. E. SWEENEY.

Of Waverly, Ill.

Berean, Macoupin Co., Ill.,

July 15, 1857.

REMINISCENCES OF THE PAST.
BY ELDER JOHN ROGERS.

BRO. FRANKLIN:—I am now holding a meeting in Harrison Co., on Beaver, at the Republican meeting house, in the vicinity of which I preached at least thirty-seven years ago. I was then a mere boy, not yet twenty years old. I am now an old man. An entire generation, and more, has passed away since that period. The whole earth has been more than once emptied of its thousand million of inhabitants, since my first visit to this vicinity! What a thought is this! And what trains of thought does this awaken in a thoughtful mind! "Man dieth, he wasteth away, yea he giveth up the ghost, and where is he?" Aye, that is the great question. Where, oh where, are the millions upon millions that have gone to the spirit-land, since my youthful feet, with light and elastic step, first pressed the sod of Beaver, at the stand in the woods, just by the Cave Spring?! And echo, in mournful accents, repeats, Where! God only knows. This, however, we know from the word of truth: the good are in Abraham's bosom—are thrice blessed; the bad are with the rich man in hell. "The wages of sin is death, but the gift of God is eternal life, through Jesus Christ our Lord." Here, and about here, I used to meet the venerable, the learned, the smooth, the highly polished Christian gentleman, B. W. Stone, and hear him, in his own soft, soothing, earnest, and persuasive eloquence, preach Christ and him crucified to admiring thousands. Here, too, and often, about this time, I was permitted to meet and hear those holy, self-sacrificing, apostolic men—those sons of thunder, Reuben Dooley, and James Hughes, in their own fervid, stirring, heart-felt and heart-moving eloquence, preach the gospel of the blessed God. Eternity only will disclose the good accomplished by those men of God. They counted all loss for the excellency of the knowledge of Christ Jesus the Lord. They were men of but little education in the popular acceptation of that term, but they were deeply learned in the things of God—were graduates, with the highest honors, in the school of Christ, the school of experimental and practical Christianity They were plain, simple-minded, simple-hearted, and pre eminently *single-minded* men. They never thought of making fine sermons—of coming before the people with excellency of speech or man's wisdom. They preached *not themselves,* but Christ Jesus, the Lord, and themselves the servants of the people, for Jesus' sake. In the light of the Bible, in their closets, in their families, in all their conversations, in their journeyings, they studied God, and Christ, and man—life, and death, and judgment, with all their unspeakable realities, of eternal happiness and eternal misery. They came before their audiences, therefore, hiding themselves in the shadow of the cross, with their souls full of these great themes, and burning with an ardent desire to encourage and comfort the saints, and bring poor sinners to the foot of the cross. I shall never forget an anecdote, illustrative of the character of Father Dooley, showing his appreciation of the elevated and highly responsible position of a preacher of the gospel.

REMINISCENCES OF THE PAST.

At an early period, in the history of Ohio, not much short of a half century ago, a number of preachers of different religious denominations were members of the Ohio Legislature, and among them were two or more belonging to what was then called the Christian, or, more commonly nicknamed, the New Light Church. This church repudiated all sectarian names and creeds, as tests of Christian character and fellowship, and was seeking very earnestly for original Christianity, in faith and practice, and pleading for the union of all God's people, scattered in the dark and cloudy day of Popery and Protestant schisms, upon heaven's own platform Father Dooley was one of the pioneers in this great religious movement. Distressed to know that so many men, who claimed to be preachers of the gospel, and especially some of his own brethren had stooped from the great work of calling men to repentance, and urging upon Christians that purity of heart and life which Christianity requires, to mingle in the exciting scenes, and amid the corrupting influences of politics, he made a special mission to the capitol of the State, and getting the Legislators together, gave to his preaching brethren an earnest and most scathing discourse founded on the words of the angel to Elijah, 1 Kings, xix.: "What doest thou here, Elijah?" In his plain, heart-searching manner, he sought to convince them that they were in the wrong place, and engaged in the wrong work; that the work of building up the church of God—seeking after and promoting the unity and purity, and the salvation of sinners, is as much above the work of human legislators, as eternal things are above temporal; that their work being the highest and holiest of all works in which man can be engaged, is more than enough to engross their entire time and talents; and that, therefore, they should never stoop from the lofty eminence they occupy, to breathe the tainted atmosphere of party politics. How many preachers, as well as people, need to be warned against the dangers of political, partisan strife! How many preachers should remember the saying of the Master, "Let the dead bury their dead; but go ye and preach the kingdom of God!!"

During my visit to Beaver, I went to the house where old Father Robt. Snodgrass lived, a few hundred yards below the Cave Spring alluded to above. This was my usual stopping-place, when I preached on Beaver. Leonard J. Fleming, at my instance, made his first public prayer in this house. I shall never forget it. He and I had spent the winter of '19 and '20 in Georgetown, Ky., attending a school conducted by the venerable Stone. In the spring of '20, was ordained at Minerva, and commenced riding and preaching extensively, principally through the counties of Scott, Bourbon, Harrison, Nicholas, Fleming, etc. Leonard Fleming was determined, by the help of God, to be a preacher, and took his first tour with me, upon my extensive circuit, in 1820. He had never attempted to speak or pray publicly. He was a very pious young man in his 23rd year, but very diffident. On our first tour, we staid all night with Father Snodgrass, and in the morning when the family was convened for worship, I urged Bro. Fleming to take the books, and lead in the exercise. With much trepidation, he consented, and, turning his back to us all, he went through the exercises as best he could. I knew him more than once, during his first efforts in praying and speaking to become so embarrassed that he was obliged abruptly to stop. It was two or three years before he could make even a respectable exhortation. But his whole soul was in the work, and he persevered until he became an excellent preacher. He was plain and practical, both in and out of the pulpit. He was remarkable from his youth up. His father was wealthy—decidedly a man of the world—greatly devoted to the sports of training and running horses. Leonard, when a small boy, told his stepmother, he thought it was wrong to train horses on Sunday, and would sometimes absent himself from the house on Lord's day, to avoid doing what he believed was wrong. His mother prevailed on his father not to impose upon him what he was unwilling to do. This thoughtful and serious turn of mind, in Leonard, was by no means agreeable to his father. But all his efforts to turn his thoughts into a different channel, were abortive. Under the religious training of Father Stone and others, he became a member of the Christian Church, and turned all the energies of his mind to the study of the Scriptures, and the urging upon the church, and the world, submission to their requirements. His father, after he became of age, finding he was fixed in his purpose, and was evidently a good man, gave him a good farm, which he kept till his death. He never married. He traveled extensively, and for the most part sustained himself. He never tried to add to his property, but took care of it, and spent his income in doing good. Some twenty years of his life were devoted to the work of evangelizing. He was a good and true man; I loved him as a brother. He was a man of excellent sense, common sense; a good expositor of the Scripture; a safe, conservative Christian teacher. He died full of faith and hope, near old Union, in Kentucky, on the 22nd of July, 1840. "Blessed are the dead that die in the Lord."

ACKNOWLEDGMENT OF MISSIONARY FUNDS.

Mrs. R. M. Lemerit, Hibernia, Ohio, L.M., $ 5 00
Dr. L. Banks, Emerson, Mo., for Elder E.
    Ballinger, L. M.,......10 00
Mrs. P Fisher, Powhattan, Ark., L. M.,......25 00
J. H. H. Neslage, N. Y., for self and F.
    Loyd, L. M,......5 00
Mrs. M. J. Penny,......2 00
Mary Loudon,......1 00
Thos. Davis,......1 00
J. Wharey, Dyer county, Tenn.,......5 00

J. C. Redwood, for Virginia meeting,	374.50
Macomb, meeting, Illinois,	313 73
Church at Lexington, Mo., for A. Wright, and contribution,	33 27
L. Hunt, Whitesville, Mo.,	10 00
Church in Bloomington, Ill., by W. Hatch,	5 00
J. S. Maddox, Milton, Ky., bal. on L. M.,	5 00
Elder T. M. Allen, for sundry persons, Mo.,	96 00
Church at Princeton, Ill., Dr. R Howe,	5 00
Campbellsburg, Ky. (Desired the name not announced,	5 00
Elder J. O. Beardslee, by the hand of R. M. Bishop,	52 00
Total,	$953 60

-----0-----

Editor's Table.

ELDER ELI REGAL'S present address is Bayard, Columbiana county, Ohio.

PICTURES.—By the kindness of Bro. Challen, we are favored with two pictures, one of the North-Western Christian University, at Indianapolis, and the other of Eld. T. M. Allen, of Columbia, Mo. These are very fine pictures, both of which have appeared in the *Ladies' Christian Annual,* and may be had for 25 cents each by addressing J. Challen & Sons, Philadelphia.

NORTH-WESTERN CHRISTIAN UNIVERSITY.—This Institution, as our readers doubtless know, is located at Indianapolis, and, we are informed, is in a very prosperous condition. We understand that everything is going on harmoniously, that the Professors and friends of the Institution are in high spirits. The applicants for the coming session are numerous; it is thought as much so as can be accommodated.

We are informed that it is very desirable that more boarding houses should be established convenient to the College—that there is a fine opening for persons who wish to educate their children to keep a boarding house, and thus make a living, and send their children to school at the same time.

REVISED EPISTLE TO THE HEBREWS.—We were not a little amused with a well informed old preacher, not long since. In speaking of the Revised English Scriptures, he said the revisions had spoiled some of his best sermons. He said this in a playful way, but we shall all find our preaching pruned some little. But whatever is trimmed off, by correctly translating, we desire to have trimmed off, for nothing will stand the test in the last judgment only what is authorized by the original. We do not desire to appear there with a bundle of notions, only supported by errors in translation. But we desire to notice a few changes.

1. In the first verse, for "sundry times," we have, in the new, "many portions." This we simply specify as a difference, that the reader may reflect upon it, but one upon which we make no remark.

2. Verse second, for "by *his* Son," we have "by *the* Son."

3. Verse third, for "express image of his person," we have "exact image of Him."

4. Verse four, for "Being made so much better than the angels," we have, "having become greater than the angels." Though *krisson* is translated *better* or *best,* in every occurrence in the common version, it is manifest, that where it stands in contrast with *less,* as in the following, it should be *greater:* "The *less* is blessed of the *better."* This, as it is in the revised, is evidently the *less* is blessed of the *greater.* But, 1 Cor. xi. 17, it is used in contrast with *worse,* and evidently means *better.*

4. Verse sixth, for, "again, when he bringeth the first-begotten into the world, "we have, "when he again bringeth the first-born into the world."

5. Verse seventh, for "maketh his angels spirits," we have, "maketh his angels *winds."* We are at a loss to see why *pneuma,* translated *spirit* and *ghost* near four hundred times in the common version, should be translated *wind,* as it is here, in the revised version, or as it is in the common version, John iii. 8, or *life,* as it is Rev. xiii. 15. common version. We doubt its meaning *wind* any place in the New Testament.

6. Chap. ii. 16, for "He took not on him the nature of angels, but he took on him the seed of Abraham," we have, "He doeth not help angels, but he helpeth the seed of Abraham." This is an important change, and makes the passage harmonize with the expression at the close of the chapter—"to aid those who are tried."

Want of space forbids our extending our notice now.

ELDER W. JOHNSON OF GHENT.—Mr. Ford, of the *Christian Repository,* of Louisville, Ky., accuses us of making an unfair attack upon Elder Johnson. He is very careful not to let his readers see this attack, however, and the only specification he makes is, that we said "he was a member of no church." He demands that we take back this statement. This we cannot do, for we still believe our statement *strictly true.* Our statement is, that he was not a member of any church for some two years, and that he joined the church in Ghent during Elder T. J. Fisher's protracted meeting there, with which he had frequently communed, for which he had preached and of which he was called "pastor." when he did not belong to any church.

The only thing we have heard offered by any one as a reason for calling in question our statement, was that he had a letter and he was under the care of the church from which his letter was taken till united with another church. But was he a member of any church during some two years while carrying his letter in his any difficulty? Was it written in regular form, containing the usual words, "dismissed from us *when united with another church* of the same faith and order?"—or was not this important clause left out? If left out, what was the reason? Why did he *remain out of any church so* long? Would Elder Ford like to see a copy of this letter?

By the way, we have a question or two for Elder Ford. Why did he stop his "History of the Baptists" so unceremoniously? Why did he stop his "History of the Current Reformation?" Did the *Recorder* find the histories of Mr. Waller on the same subjects, after which he inquired so earnestly a few weeks ago? We should like to see these documents, to see how they would agree with those of Mr. Ford. It is said, great men are apt to *think alike.* And where did he find his authority for stating in his history, that there was a Baptist Church in America before the baptism of Roger Williams? Who established this Baptist Church, and where can we find an account of it, outside of Mr. Ford's history?

QUESTION BOOKS:—Many have inquired for Question Books for Sunday Schools, and we have heretofore paid but little attention to the subject, and recommend the following laid upon our table by Mr. Blanchard, publisher and book seller, Fourth street, South side, East of Walnut, and will be constantly on sale at this house.

1. Lincoln's Scripture Questions, with the answers annexed.

2. The Sabbath School Class Book, comprising copious exercises in the Sacred Scriptures.

3. Harmony Questions on the Four Gospels, for use in Sabbath schools.

By the kindness of the same gentleman, we have before us a neat little work, "The Christian Pastor—his work and the needful preparation," which contains some valuable thoughts, and will well repay a perusal.

COMBINATION OF PUBLICATIONS.—The reader will please see the notice on the cover of the combination of the *Age* and *Review.* These publications will be *one* after Jan. 1st, 1858. That one will be a weekly sheet, under our present name, *The American Christian Review,* and editorial control.

-----o-----

Success of the Gospel.

WE prepared a condensed statement of several interesting meetings we have attended for a former number of the REVIEW, which was crowded out, and which has been mislaid. We have to some extent forgotten the particulars, and, therefore, simply state that during our meeting at Republican, near Lexington, Ky., in company with Elder John Rogers, some twenty-four were added. In Rushville, Ind., with Bro. Daniel Franklin, ten were added. In Warsaw, Ky, sixteen were added. In the last two months more than thirty have been added in Covington, Ky. Brethren Vawter, Henshall and Brooks assisted much in Covington. Others have been added in sundry places, making our success better this year than ever in our life before.

At New Liberty, Ky., our Baptist brethren attended largely all the time, and when the audience increased beyond the capacity of the house owned by the Disciples, the Baptists cheerfully opened their house, greatly to our accommodation, some one of three of their preachers being present nearly all the time, reading the word of the Lord and praying for God's blessing upon us introductory to our discourses. A happier meeting than this we have never enjoyed.

KENTUCKY—*Lancaster, May* 18*th.*—Bro. A. Adams reports three additions.

Sharpsburgh, May.—Bro. Jno. A. Gano reports twelve confessions—and four at Harrodsburgh.

Since the above, Bro. Gano reports, that while laboring at Williamstown, during six days thirteen were convinced of the truth, and confessed the Lord in order to Baptism.

Chesher's Store, May 31*st.*Bro. Wm Horn reports thirty-nine additions as the result of his late labors.

IOWA—*Indianola, June 8th.*—Bro. B. F. Snooks writes: Since I last wrote to you, we have had six additions.

MICHIGAN—*Paw Paw, May* 25*th*—Bro. Wm. M. Roe writes: Since my last report, I have baptized five persons, and received one from the Methodists.

OHIO—*Greene Go.*—Bro. J. M. Henry writes: Embracing the 3rd Lord's day in May, Bro. B. K. Smith and myself held a meeting, resulting in two additions.

Bealsville, June 1st.—Bro. H. H. Lohmire reports forty-eight additions in all as the insult of meetings in his vicinity. Also Bro. Jno. Henderson report as the result of his labors since last fall, eighty four by immersion, and nine reclaimed.

Holmesville, July 1*st*—Bro. N. A. Walker writes: "Bro. J. J. Moss's debate with a Universalist at Blufftown, Ind., last winter, was one of truth's noble triumphs, resulting in the congregating of fourteen souls under its banner—one by immersion, and thirteen from the sects. This number was increased to near one hundred up to April 1st, by the labors of G. C. McDuffie, Wm. Dowlings, and myself.

Russelville, June 25th—Bro. Jas. White reports six additions by confession and immersion.

ILLINOIS—*Scottville June* 20*th.*—Bro. J. F. Hedges reports thirty-six additions during a meeting just closed, conducted by Bro. Jno. Sweeney.

Flora, June 15*th.*—Bro. H. Kinnaman writes:— Three were immersed here this morning.

MARYLAND.—Bro. Jno. O'Kane reports. that while preaching at Beaver Creek, Concord, and Baltimore, fifteen or twenty were added to the congregation.

MISSOURI—*Boone Co.*—Bro. T. M. Allen reports, as a result of a three weeks tour through the counties of Charlton, Livingston and Randolph, some fifty additions. Bro. A. has sent us a very interesting report of the trip, but we are unable to give it in full. Since the above, Bro. A. reports two additions at Bethany, Mo.

Salem, Dent Co.—Bro. Drennan reports seven accessions to the congregation.

INDIANA—*Noblesville, June 11th.*—Bro. H. St. John VanDake writes, that while attending the Annual Meeting in Lafayette Co., Ind., he witnessed twenty accessions. During his absence, Bro. Daniel Van Buskirk held a meeting with the brethren at Noblesville, and immersed nine.

Greensburgh, June 30th—Bro J. R. Lucas writes: That Bro. Wm. D. Moore, of Ohio, continued a meeting some ten days, which resulted in fifteen additions.

Cicero, June 4th—Bro. C. N. Harrison reports six additions in the vicinity of Eagle Village, Hamilton Co., Ind.

Vienna, May.—Bro. W. Hartley reports two additions at Lexington, Ind., on the Lord's 2nd day in May.

OHIO—*Morgan Co.*—Bro. John Bingman reports seven additions at the Winser congregation through the labors of brethren Henry White and Moody.

Belmont. Co., July 16th, 1857.—Bro. Jacob Hendershot writes as follows:—We have had a protracted meeting for six days past, closing last evening, held by Bro. John Henderson, which resulted in seventeen additions—fourteen by immersion and three reclaimed, one from the Baptists. Dear brethren, take courage, for the "gospel is the power of God unto salvation and the children of men that have been building upon the sandy foundation, have commenced digging for the Rock on which to build, and are removing the sand and rubbish—the doctrines and commandments of men—have found water, and that enough to bury them.

We quote the following from the July number of the *Millennial Harbinger.*

VIRGINIA—Bro. J A. Lipscomb, under date of May 20*th*, writes as follows:—Some eighteen confessions and four accessions from the Baptists, all of whom have been added to the church at Bethesda, Hanover county. Bros. Orvis, Ainsley and Dick were the preachers.

Bro. J. P. Wayman, of Glen Easton, Marshall Co., reports, June 5*th*, a meeting of some twelve days and nights, held at Beeler's Station, under the labor of Bro. T. J. Newcombe, of Portage Co , Ohio. The result was thirty-three additions—twenty nine by baptism, and four reclaimed.

Of the above number, there was one entire household baptized, all of which heard, believed, and confessed the Lord. Of course there were no infants.

Bro. Newcomb improved the intervals of the meeting in visiting from house to house, and speaking of the things pertaining to the kingdom of God.

MISSISSIPPI.—Bro. Phares, of Newtonia, writing under date of May 30, reports a meeting closed at Newtonia, with twenty-three additions. At this and other points, some forty more had been added previously, which had not been reported.

Bro. W. H. Stewart, of Cheneyville, La., labored with the brethren on the occasion, assisted by Bro. A. Ellett.

Obituaries.

DIED,—Mrs. MART HULL, consort of James W. Hull, and daughter of the late Eld. John Rush, died of consumption on the 19th of May last, near Tilton, Fleming Co., Ky.

The deceased was for many years a consistent and exemplary member of the Christian church, and was cheered and comforted throughout her protracted illness by the inspiring hopes and promises of Christianity. Affectionate and domestic, kind and conciliating in her character, she was devotedly beloved by her family, and universally esteemed by all who knew her; and by her pious walk and godly conversation, exerted a most salutary influence in recommending to others that pure and undefiled religion which enabled her to rejoice in tribulation and affliction, and to triumph in the hour of death. Gently, calmly, and hopefully, she passed away without a struggle or a moan.

So fades a summer cloud away,
   So sinks the gale when storms are o'er,
So gently shuts the eye of day,
   So dies a wave along the shore.

A large company of bereaved kindred and sympathizing friends assembled to pay the last sad tribute to her memory. It was truly a mournful occasion—but all felt that we were at the burial of a Christian and while depositing her lifeless remains in the cold charnel house—it was our glorious privilege to contemplate by faith—the flight of her ransomed spirit to that building of God, that house not made with hands, eternal in the heavens.   F.

DIED, on May 5*th*, 1857, Sister ANN PERKEY, wife of Bro. Daniel Perkey, in her 53rd year. She was a mother in Israel—a blessing to her neighborhood, and in her death her family and the church have sustained a loss which will be sensibly felt.

               C. W. HARRISON.
               Cicero, Indiana.

DIED, at Nicholasville, Lord's day May 10*th*, 1857, ALEXANDER C. DUNCAN, aged 70 rears He was an early settler in Kentucky. "He was an honest man." He lived and died a Presbyterian.

               SAMUEL L. DUNCAN.
June 8th, 1856.

DIED, of palsy, May 7th, 1857, Bro. JOHN COPPLE. Born in North Carolina, early emigrating to Indiana, he spent the last eighteen years of his life in Illinois. He was a member of the Christian Church from the year 1844 until his death.

THE AMERICAN CHRISTIAN REVIEW.

A DISCOURSE ON THE REGENERATION.
BY ELDER E. E. ORVIS.

"And Jesus said unto them, Verily I say unto you, that ye which have followed me, in the regeneration, when the Son of Man shall sit in the throne of his glory, ye also shall sit on twelve thrones, judging the twelve tribes of Israel."—MATT. XIX. 28.

"But after that the kindness and love of God our Savior toward man appeared, not by works of righteousness which we have done, but according to his mercy, he saved us, by the washing of regeneration and renewing of the Holy Ghost."—TITUS III. 5.

MUCH is said in this age of the world about regeneration, and about being *regenerated*—much that has no warrant in Scripture, and but little that has any. In the baptismal ceremony prescribed by the ritual of an orthodox and evangelical denomination, of very commanding influence, we commence reading an address in the following words:—"Dearly beloved, forasmuch as all men are conceived and born in sin, and that our Savior Christ saith. None can enter into the kingdom of God, except he be REGENERATE and born anew of water and of the Holy Ghost," etc. Now it so happens that "our Savior Christ" never said any such thing. Neither is the word "regenerate," or "regenerated," ever used by any sacred writer or speaker, so far as we are informed. The noun *regeneration* occurs twice—and only twice—that is, in the two passages above quoted; but the verb *regenerate* was never employed by divine authority.

Having found so palpable an error—and one so likely to lead to results highly injurious—floating upon the very surface of this subject, is it not incumbent upon us to investigate the whole subject with great thoroughness and particularity? Let us look a little farther.

What, according to the popular Protestant teaching, is regeneration? It is supposed to be a mysterious spiritual change—a change of heart—a change wrought within man. But Jesus says to the Apostles, "*In* the regeneration, when the Son of Man shall sit upon the throne of his glory, ye also shall sit upon twelve thrones, judging the twelve tribes of Israel." What a contrast! According to the teachings of Jesus, *the regeneration was something that men could be in.* But according to modern theological teaching, *the regeneration is something in them.* Both these ideas certainly cannot be correct. If "the regeneration" is something that men can be in, it certainly cannot be something in them.

The Scriptures very clearly teach the necessity of what is sometimes called "a change of heart"—a change of the thoughts, feelings and affections of the heart. No sensible reader of the Bible can doubt this.

But then this change is never called regeneration by any inspired writer; and therefore, never ought to be so called by uninspired speakers and writers.

What does the word "regeneration" mean, as used in the Scriptures? This question now demands our serious attention Let us take the first passage in which the word occurs, and thoroughly analyze it.

"Then answered Peter and said unto him, Behold, we have forsaken all and followed thee; what shall we have therefore? And Jesus said unto them, Verily I say unto you, that ye which have followed me, in the regeneration, when the Son of Man shall sit in the throne of his glory, ye also shall sit upon twelve thrones, judging the twelve tribes of Israel." In this passage there are three leading or prominent ideas:

1. The Regeneration.

2. The Son of Man sitting upon the throne of his glory.

3. The Apostles sitting upon twelve thrones, judging the twelve tribes of Israel.

These three things bear a very intimate relation to each other. The Apostles are to sit upon twelve thrones, judging the twelve tribes of Israel, at the same time that Jesus sits upon the throne of his glory, and these are both to be in "the regeneration." The parallel passage to this is found in Luke xxii. 28-30, and may assist us to understand this:—"Ye are they which have continued with me in my temptations. And I appoint unto you a kingdom, as my Father hath appointed unto me, that ye may eat and drink at my table in my kingdom, and sit on thrones judging the twelve tribes of Israel." The elements embraced in this text are substantially the same as in Matt. xix. 28.

1. What was there called "the regeneration," is here called a "kingdom."

2. What is there called Jesus sitting upon the throne of his glory, is here called having a kingdom appointed unto him.

3. And in this, as in that, it is said that the Apostles will sit upon thrones, judging the twelve tribes of Israel.

It is worthy of remark, that the common version of this text is rather obscure—more so than is necessary. Jesus says, "I appoint unto you a kingdom, as my Father bath appointed unto me;" from which a very natural inference would be, that there were two kingdoms referred to—one for Christ himself, and one for the Apostles. This, however, would be a mistaken inference, which the concluding portion of the sentence, even in this version, goes far towards dissipating, for it adds—"That ye may eat and drink at my table, in MY KINGDOM." It was in *Christ's kingdom*—not one of their own—in which the Apostles were to "sit on thrones, judging the twelve tribes of Israel."

From this text we learn an important fact—*That "the regeneration" and Christ's "Kingdom" are only two names for the same thing*. Now let us collate such antecedent facts as will tend to throw light upon this interesting theme.

1. Several of the ancient Jewish prophets had predicted that God would, at some future period of time, establish a government in this world; Isaiah and Micah portray it in glowing symbolical imagery, thus—"The mountain of the Lord's house shall be established in the top of the mountains, and shall be exalted above the hills." (Isaiah ii. 2; Micah iv. 1.) But Daniel says plainly and distinctly, that "the God of heaven shall set up a kingdom," etc. (Dan. ii. 44.) And the same subject frequently occupied the attention of the other prophets, down to the very last of the Old Testament prophets.

2. In due time a distinguished personage "*was sent from God,*" and made his appearance in the wilderness of Judea He was a preacher, and the burthen of his proclamation, addressed to his countrymen of the stock of Abraham, was—"*Repent ye, for the kingdom of heaven is*

THE REGENERATION.

at hand." (Matt. iii. 2.) This would naturally lead those who listened to the preaching of John to the conclusion, that those ancient prophecies were about to be verified.

3. But in a very short time Jesus of Nazareth, having been baptized by John in Jordan, "came into Galilee preaching the gospel of the kingdom of God, and saying—*"The time is fulfilled,* and the kingdom of God is at hand; repent ye and believe the gospel." What could those who believed this preaching think, but that the ancient prediction "that the God of heaven would set up a kingdom," was now to be fulfilled. Yes, "the time is fulfilled!"—the time appointed by the sure prophetic word—*"The kingdom of God is at hand."* (Mark i. 14-15.)

4. Very soon after this Jesus sent out his twelve chosen ambassadors with the following explicit instructions:—"Go not into the way of the Gentiles, and into any city of the Samaritans enter ye not, but go rather to the lost sheep of the house of Israel. And as ye go preach, saying—*"The kingdom of heaven is at hand."* (Matt. x. 5-7.)

5. Soon after sending out these twelve, he "appointed other seventy" evangelists, and thus commissioned them:—"Go not from house to house. And into whatsoever city ye enter, and they receive you, eat such things as are set before you; and heal the sick that are therein, and say unto them—*The kingdom of God has come nigh unto you.* But into whatsoever city ye enter, and they receive you not, go your way out into the streets of the same and say—Even the very dust of your city which cleaveth on us we do wipe off against you; notwithstanding *be ye sure of this,* that THE KINGDOM OF GOD IS COME NIGH UNTO YOU." (Luke x. 7-11.)

6. At the same time that these twelve Apostles and seventy disciples were engaged in making this proclamation—("The kingdom of heaven is at hand")—they were also to pray—"Our Father who art in heaven, hallowed be thy name; THY KINGDOM COME; thy will be done on earth as it is in heaven," etc. Thus they not only preached that the kingdom was "at hand"—had "come *nigh* unto" them; but they also prayed that it might come. With all this preaching and praying by men under the special guidance of the Savior, how could those who heard and believed this preaching, think otherwise than that the kingdom would be established *very soon!?*

Here is one series of facts. Let them be duly considered, while we proceed to record another series of equally important and interesting facts, naturally growing out of the foregoing, and which will immediately connect these with the theme before us—*the regeneration.*

When the Apostles, acting under the preceding commission, had visited and announced the approaching reign of Messiah, Jehovah's king, and had returned to him, Jesus took them and went into the retired district upon the coast of Caesarea Philippi, for the purpose of holding an undisturbed private consultation with them. Said he, addressing the whole twelve—"Whom do men say that I, the Son of Man, am?" And *they* (yes, they all) said, "Some say that thou art John the Baptist; some Elias; and others Jeremias, or one of the prophets." He saith unto them—"But whom say ye that I am?" This was asking too much; *"they"* could not, or would not, reply; Peter only had courage or intelligence sufficient to say in reply—*"Thou art the Christ, the Son of the living God."* And, therefore, in view of his bold and intelligent declaration, Jesus said to Peter—"Blessed art *thou,* Simon Barjona, for flesh and blood hath not revealed it unto thee, but my Father who is in heaven. And I say also unto thee, That thou art Peter (meaning a *stone),* and upon this rock (meaning the confession which Peter had made), I will build my church, and the gates of hell *(hades)* shall not prevail against it. *And I will give unto thee the keys of the kingdom of heaven;* and whatsoever thou shalt bind on earth shall be bound in heaven; and whatsoever thou shalt loose on earth shall be loosed in heaven." (Matt. xvi. 13-19.)

This is looking towards the organization of the kingdom, and clearly implies that the *King* will be absent from his dominion, and that the affairs of the kingdom will be administered by an agent, or by agents. "Keys" are the symbols of power and authority; and this address of Jesus to Peter was as much as to say—My kingdom is about to be set up; in the mean time I shall re-ascend to heaven; and I leave the keys in your possession; in my absence the government will be administered by you. I thus empower you to "*bind*" laws upon men, and to "*loose*" them from the observance of other laws; and all the acts which you thus perform here on earth I will sanction, seated upon a throne in the heavens.

2. But it appears that the other Apostles still, to a great extent, under the influence of carnal passions, were envious of Peter's distinction, and feared that he was about to be exalted to a leadership over them. After much private murmuring, they finally determined to inquire of the Master whether he intended to constitute Peter a Pope, Father, Leader, or Head of all the Apostles. "At the same time came the disciples unto Jesus, saying—*Who is the greatest in the kingdom of heaven?* And Jesus called a little child unto him, and set him in the midst of them, and said, Verily I say unto you, except ye be converted, and become as little children, ye shall not enter *into the kingdom of heaven.*"(Matt. xviii. 1-3.) He then continued to rebuke their unholy aspirations after preferment, and instruct them in relation to the approaching reign, until at the 18th verse he says to them all, as he had previously said to Peter *alone*— "Verily I say unto you, whatsoever ye shall bind on earth shall be bound in heaven; and whatsoever ye shall loose on earth shall be loosed in heaven."

Thus were the same powers and prerogatives that were at first bestowed upon Peter alone, extended to all the Apostles. The prior appointment of Peter only made him president of the apostolic college—like the foreman of a hoard of jurors. They are all, properly, vicars, vicegerents of Christ. This kingdom is about to be set up or established *on earth,* but as he will be in the heavens himself, these vicegerents of his are to set in order the grand elements of the new reign, and announce its laws among all nations.

3. In the next chapter (verse 28) he only reiterated the same assurances in other language—"Ye which have followed me, in the regeneration, when the Son of Man shall sit in the throne of his glory, ye also shall sit on twelve thrones, judging the twelve tribes of Israel." This only gave them one item of information which they had not before. It informed them at what time it would be their prerogative to *bind* and *loose* on earth as the vicegerents of Jesus—or as it is here expressed, to judge for the twelve tribes of Israel—viz.: "*When the Son of Man should sit in the throne of his glory.*"

Let the facts that we have now learned be distinctly kept in mind: The regeneration and the kingdom are the same thing; the kingdom was predicted by the ancient prophet; John announced that it was at hand; Jesus said "the time was fulfilled," and that the kingdom had come nigh unto them. He sent twelve apostles and seventy disciples to announce its near approach, through all the land of the Jews. He taught them all to pray that it might come. He appointed officers for its management; and finally informed them at what time they should enter upon the discharge of the responsible duties entrusted to them—"*When the Son of Man should sit in the throne of his glory.*"

Now let us attend to this specification of time. The "Son of Man," all admit, is Jesus of Nazareth. But what is meant by "the throne of his glory?" And when should he sit upon that throne? These are questions of thrilling interest just here. If we rightly understand these points, the whole subject is within our grasp—not without. There are two prominent ideas here for our consideration:

1. "This glory."
2. This throne—which is "the throne of his glory."

I. *The glory of Christ.* James calls Jesus Christ "the Lord of glory. "Brethren, have not the faith of our Lord Jesus Christ, *the Lord of glory,* with respect of persons'," James ii. 6. And Peter closes his second epistle thus: "But grow in grace, and in the knowledge of our Lord and Savior Jesus Christ. To whom be *glory* both *now* and *forever.* "Paul also calls Jesus "the Lord of glory," 1 Cor. ii. 8. These testimonies would seem to indicate that he had entered upon *his glory* previous to the writing of these Apostles. But there is still other testimony upon the subject.

Just previous to the death, burial and resurrection of Jesus, he prayed to his Father: "Father, the hour is come, *glorify* thy Son, that thy Son may also *glorify* thee." And again: "And now, O Father, *glorify* thou me, with thine own self, with the *glory* which I had with thee, before the world was," John xvii. 1, 5. And after his death, burial and resurrection, he himself said to two of his disciples, with whom he conversed as they went on their way towards Emmaus: "Ought not Christ to have suffered these things (his betrayal and death) and to enter *into his glory,"* Luke xxiv. 26. Hence the secret of godliness, according to Paul, was that God through Jesus "was manifested in the flesh; justified in the Spirit; seen of angels; preached unto the Gentiles; believed on in the world; *received up into glory,"* 1 Tim. iii. 16. Hence, also, Paul informs the Hebrews that he was "crowned with *glory* and honor," in consequence of having humbled himself even unto death. Heb. ii. 9.

How expressive are these facts. When about to leave this world he prayed to be "*glorified;* "after his death, burial and resurrection, he said it was necessary to suffer these things and "*enter into his glory;* " after his ascension his Apostles taught that he *had been* "*received up into glory,"* and that he had been "*crowned* with *glory* and honor."

II. That Jesus took a seat upon *a throne* immediately after his ascension up on high, cannot be doubted for a moment. Says Paul, Heb. viii. 1: "Now of the things which we have spoken, this is the sum; We have such an High Priest, who is set on the right hand of the *throne* of the Majesty in the heavens." Also, Heb. xii. 2: "Looking unto Jesus the author and finisher of our faith, who, for the joy that was set before him, endured the cross, despising the shame, and is set down at the right hand of the *throne* of God." These quotations show unequivocally that he was seated on *a throne.*

But was that throne "the throne of his glory?" Who can doubt it? Was not his being seated upon that throne and his being "received up into glory" synchronous events? Was he not "crowned with glory and honor," at the *same time* that he took his seat on that throne? It cannot be doubted for a single moment. Jesus was *enthroned* immediately after his ascent up on high—he was *set* or seated "on the right hand of *the throne* of the Majesty in the heavens." But not only was he enthroned; at the same time he was "crowned"—"crowned with glory and honor." Nay, he even then was "received up into glory," and "entered *into his glory."*So that at that time—his ascent into heaven—he took his seat "in the throne of his glory."

But some persons are disposed to object to this view of the subject, and now is perhaps the most fitting time to examine their objections. Everything in the understanding of this subject depends upon determining when Jesus took his seat upon the throne of his glory. That new age, called "the regeneration," should continue during the time that he should "sit in the throne of his glory," and during that same time the Apostles should "sit upon twelve thrones, judging the twelve tribes of Israel." It is, therefore, a matter of primary importance to fix, with entire certainty, the time when he commenced to sit upon that "throne of glory." Let, then, every objection to the position already assumed, be carefully and thoroughly examined.

First, It is objected that Jesus is not to "sit in the throne of his glory until his second coming to this earth, because he says himself: "When the Son of Man shall *come in his glory,* and all the holy angels with him, *then shall he sit upon the throne of his glory.*"To this it may be replied:

It does not follow because Christ shall "sit upon the throne of his glory," when he comes again to this earth, that he will not be seated there, on that same throne, for many centuries previous to that time. This passage does not say then shall he "be seated" or "take his seat" upon the throne of his glory. He may have taken his seat on that throne eighteen hundred years ago, and be sitting there now, and still sit there at the time of his second advent.

Secondly, But it is still objected that Jesus cannot be now seated upon the throne of his glory, because the throne referred to is "the throne of David;" and when he sits upon it, it will be in pursuance of the following prophecy, recorded in Luke i. 32-33: "He shall be great, and shall be called the Son of the Highest; and the Lord God shall give unto him the throne of his father David. And he shall reign over the house of Jacob forever, and of his kingdom there shall be no end." To this we reply:

1. It is exceedingly doubtful whether this prediction should be understood literally, as referring to the literal carnal "house of Jacob," and to that temporal and secular throne of David"—the veritable and identical throne on which the "sweet Psalmist of Israel," the poet king, sat and reigned over a portion of the descendants of Abraham.

2. But admitting, for the sake of the argument, that all this is to be understood literally; and that when Jesus *"comes in his glory,"* he will be seated on the throne of *David* literally, and will literally reign over the house of Jacob, it does not in the least affect the question before us. Jesus does not say that "in the regeneration he will sit in the *throne* of *David."* Even should he sit on David's throne, it does not follow that that was the throne intended by the phrase "throne of *his glory."* The throne on which he *"entered into his glory,"* would be *"the throne of his glory."* And he has certainly been seated on that throne ever since he was "received up into glory"—ever since he was *"crowned* with glory and honor, which is now more than eighteen hundred years.

Thirdly, It is objected again, that Jesus is now seated upon his *Father's throne;* that he has a throne separate from that of his Father, on which he is not now sitting, but upon which he will sit at a future time; and that this latter throne is the throne of his glory. In proof of which we are referred to Revelations iii. 21: "To him that overcometh will I grant to sit with me in my throne, even as I also overcame, and am sit down with my Father in his throne." To which we reply:

If it be true that the Father has one throne and the Son another, it will not follow that the throne on which Jesus now sits—the throne of his Father—is not the throne of his glory. The Father's throne could be the throne of his glory as well as his own; and it would be so if he possessed more "glory" on that throne than he would on his own. On the throne on which he now sits, his "subjects" are not confined to earth, and to the small portion of earth's inhabitants who have descended from Abraham,

THE REGENERATION.

Isaac and Jacob, as must be the case when he sits on *his* throne, if his throne is the "throne of David." He now has for his *subjects*, 1 Peter iii. 22, "Angels, authorities and powers." The throne on which he now sits—even though it be not his own—is the throne of his glory—of his superlative glory. He was "glorified" by being seated in it. His ascension up into it, is called receiving him up "into glory."

2. But Dr. Adam Clark very justly observes on this passage: "But Christ's throne and the throne of the Father is the same." And though the language of this verse may seem to intimate the existence of two separate thrones—one for the Father and one for the Son—there are good and valid reasons going to show that this would be a wrong conclusion, and that Dr. Clark is correct in saying that their throne is the same.

1. We can see no necessity for having more than one throne in the same kingdom, and it is clearly evident that the kingdom of God and of Christ is the same kingdom. "For this ye know, that no fornicator, nor unclean person, nor covetous man, who is an idolater, hath any inheritance *in the kingdom of Christ and of God,"* Eph. v. 5. Here the same kingdom is called the kingdom of "Christ and of God." Why should there be more than one throne in that kingdom?

2. But we are not left to settle this question by such inferences, however legitimately they may be drawn. We have explicit testimony. "And he showed me a pure river of water of life, clear as crystal, proceeding out of *the throne of God and of the Lamb."* And there shall be no more curse, but *the throne of God and of the Lamb* shall be in it," Rev. xxii. 1, 3. Here the same throne is called "the throne of God and of the Lamb," which settles the question that their thrones are identical.

These, if not all, are the principal objections to the position that Jesus ascended up from this earth, to be immediately seated upon "the throne of his glory."

And these objections are certainly invalid. Jesus may have *taken his seat* upon "the throne of his glory" long since, though when he comes to this earth again, he will then sit upon the same throne. And should he at that time, or after it, be seated upon the same identical throne on which David sat—the throne of the carnal house of Israel—which is certainly very questionable, still that could with no propriety be called "the throne of his glory;" for to sit upon that throne and circumscribe his reign to that fraction of humanity, would be the second time to forsake the "*glory* he had with the Father, before the worlds were." It would be leaving that *glory* into which he entered when he left this world. And the idea that the Father has one throne and the Son another is simply absurd, besides being directly opposed to those Scriptures which call the *same throne* the "throne of God and of the Lamb."

What, then, is the conclusion—the irresistible conclusion, in view of the premises before us? It is that when Jesus ascended up on high leading captivity captive—when he "entered into his glory"—was "received up into glory," was "crowned with glory," and was seated "on the right hand of the *throne* of the Majesty in the heavens," he then took his seat on *"the throne of his glory"*—the throne on which he enjoyed glory with the Father before the worlds were. This can scarcely be doubted by the most skeptical.

But if Jesus was then seated upon the throne of his glory, the *new age,* or regeneration, began then. Moreover, the twelve Apostles must then have been seated upon "twelve thrones, judging the twelve tribes of Israel." These apostolic thrones now demand our attention.

What did Jesus mean when he said to the Apostles: "Ye also shall sit upon twelve thrones, judging the twelve tribes of Israel?" Is this language to be understood literally or figuratively? And when was it to be fulfilled? In order to ascertain the true import of this language it is necessary to carefully separate the different ideas contained in the language, and examine, with the utmost precision, those separate ideas. What are they?

1. "Ye also shall sit upon twelve thrones."
2. "Judging the twelve tribes of Israel."

These ideas are perfectly distinct, though intimately connected. If, however, we can ascertain at what time they were to sit on the thrones, and what is meant by this, there can hardly be much difficulty in determining when they would exercise their judicial functions; and what is meant by it.

First, The thrones. If we have not been mistaken in relation to the time of Jesus taking his seat upon "the throne of his glory," we have already well-nigh settled the question as to when the Apostles would sit upon their thrones; for they were to sit upon their thrones at the same time that Jesus was to sit upon his. If when he ascended up on high and was invested with all power and authority in heaven and on earth—if he then took his seat upon the throne of his glory, at the same time the Apostles must have been seated upon their thrones.

We know, however, that the Apostles did not *literally* sit upon any thrones at that time. If the promise was then fulfilled to them, it must be understood figuratively, and not literally. Did anything occur to the Apostles at the time Jesus was received up into glory, and took his seat in the throne of his glory, that could with any propriety, even figuratively, be called sitting upon thrones? In answer to this question, let us consider a few facts which are already prominently before us:

I. What did Jesus mean when he said to Peter, "I will give unto thee the *keys* of the kingdom of heaven?" Is not the word "keys" used figuratively? And is not this language simply expressive of the fact that Peter was to be invested with power to act in his stead on earth, while he was seated upon his throne in the heavens? Two things are worthy of remark, in reference to this promise to Peter:

1. The time when he was to have these keys, was to be while he was yet on the earth.
2. But it was to be when Jesus was in heaven.

This is evident from what follows: "And I will give unto thee the *keys of* the kingdom of heaven; and whatsoever thou shalt *hind on earth,* shall be bound *in heaven,* and whatsoever thou shalt *loose on earth,* shall be loosed *in heaven.*" Peter was to do this binding and loosing *on earth;* Christ was to do the same *in heaven.* This was a promise to be fulfilled after Jesus left this world. It was to be fulfilled while Ire was in heaven, and his Apostles on earth. It is impossible that this shall be fulfilled in a kingdom—a merely fanciful kingdom—which some imagine is to be set up on the earth at some period yet in future; for then Christ will not be in heaven, but on earth. He will not then need—should such a kingdom ever become a reality—Peter or anyone else, as a vicegerent on earth, to bind and loose, in his stead. He could readily do in person all his binding and loosing. Besides, if he should come and establish a kingdom, such as these wild visionaries dream of, and Peter should really then have the "keys" of that kingdom, to bind and loose on earth, how would Jesus bind and loose in heaven, since he is not himself in heaven, but on earth.

No, no; that cannot be his meaning. He was himself about to be invested with all authority in heaven and earth, and the promise now made to Peter was designed to constitute him the embodiment of that authority, so far as earth was concerned—the agent through whom that power was to be unfolded. It is this, and this alone, that Jesus means when he says: "I will give unto thee the keys of the kingdom of heaven."

II. What did Jesus mean when he said to all of the Apostles, as he had previously said to Peter: "Whatsoever *ye* (not Peter alone, but ye all) shall bind on earth, shall be bound in heaven; and whatsoever *ye* shall loose on earth shall be loosed in heaven?" This was certainly conferring great authority upon them. What was the nature of that authority and when was it to be exercised?

1. "Whatsoever ye shall *bind* on earth." What can this mean, unless it is that whatever *laws* ye *bind* men to observe—whatever obligations ye impose upon men—these shall be ratified in heaven.

2, "And whatsoever ye shall *loose* on earth," *i. e.,* whatever obligations imposed by the law of Moses, or by any human authority, to which men have previously been, or considered themselves, bound—whatever such obligations as these, you "loose," or release men from, this also shall be ratified in heaven.

3. But *when* can the Apostles thus bind and loose, and their acts be sanctioned by Heaven's Lawgiver? Bear in mind that this language is a part of Jesus' reply to the inquiry, "Who is greatest in the kingdom of heaven;"and was spoken with the view of teaching that in that kingdom Peter will not be "greatest"—it is not he alone who is to bind and loose. These are prerogatives that will belong to all the Apostles in that kingdom. It was in the kingdom of heaven, therefore, that they were to exercise these functions of binding and loosing. And from the facts now before us, the following conclusion seems to be irresistible:

That when the kingdom of heaven was established on earth, the King—the supreme authority of that kingdom would be in heaven, while the Apostles as his vicegerents, would be his representatives, and the exponents of his authority on earth.

The fact that, *in that kingdom,* the Apostles would *bind* and *loose* ON EARTH, while the supreme authority of that kingdom, would do the same things IN HEAVEN, proves conclusively that the kingdom would exist on earth, while the king himself was in heaven. And this shows with remarkable conclusiveness that those who imagine that there can be no kingdom of heaven on earth, until Jesus—God's anointed King—shall return to this earth, are as much mistaken as they would be to call east, west, or rayless blackness, light.

Now that we understand what Jesus means when he says to Peter, "I give unto you the keys of the kingdom of heaven and what he meant when he said to Peter, and subsequently to all the Apostles, "Whatsoever ye bind on earth shall be bound in heaven; and whatsoever ye loose on earth shall be loosed in heaven," can we not readily understand what he means when he says to these same Apostles, in relation to the same period of time, "Ye also shall sit on twelve thrones, judging the twelve tribes of Israel?" Does he not mean by the latter precisely what he meant by the former? The authority which the Apostles were to exercise, in reference to the establishment of the government of Christ in this world, is thus fully and variously defined:

1. It is first defined by the symbol of "keys"—"I will give unto thee the keys of the kingdom of heaven."

2. It is next fully defined by assuring them that they will *bind* and *loose,* in such *a* manner as will receive the sanction of the supreme authority in heaven.

3. And lastly, the same authority is symbolized by thrones, in the declaration: "Ye also shall sit upon twelve thrones, judging the twelve tribes of Israel.

All that this language means, then, is that when Jesus was received up into his glory—was crowned with glory—was seated upon the throne of his glory—the twelve Apostles, as a body, would be his *vicars or vicegerents*. They talk vainly who speak of the Pope of Rome as the vicar of Christ; or who imagine that Peter was for the time being—and that his Successor has since been Christ's only vicegerent. This was an office to which all the Apostles were appointed. It is figuratively called—and the figure is a most beautiful and appropriate one—*sitting upon thrones.*

This apostolic authority is elsewhere spoken of, in language less figurative, but not less expressive of the great dignity and power with which they were invested. Jesus says, in his address to the Father, John xvii. 18: "As thou hast sent me into the world even so have I also sent them into the world." Again he says to them, "As my Father hath sent me, even so send I you. And when he had said this, he breathed on them, and said unto them, Receive ye the Holy Ghost. Whosesoever sins ye remit, they are remitted unto them, and whosesoever sins ye retain they are retained," John xx. 21-23. On another occasion, in allusion to their official dignity and authority, he said, "Verily, verily, I say unto you, he that receiveth whomsoever I send, receiveth me; and he that receiveth me receiveth him that sent me," John xiii. 20. And when he gave them their final commission, as recorded by Matt. xxviii. 18-20, the same principles are fully involved: "All power is given unto me in heaven and in earth. Go ye, *therefore, (i. e.,* go invested and panoplied with this authority) and teach all nations, baptizing them into the name of the Father, and of the Son, and of the Holy Spirit," etc.

To sit upon thrones, then, means neither more nor less than to act as the representatives of Christ, the anointed King on earth, while he occupied a seat upon the throne of the Majesty in heaven.

Secondly, "*Judging the twelve tribes of Israel.*" This embraces two distinct ideas that claim our attention: 1st, What is meant by the phrase "twelve tribes of Israel?" and, 2nd, What is embraced in the idea of "judging?"

I. Israel, or the twelve tribes of Israel, if used literally, would mean the whole of that portion of the descendants of Abraham which constituted the Jewish nation—all the twelve tribes which were founded by the twelve sons of Jacob, the grandson of Abraham. But the word "Israel" is often used in a figurative and more extended sense, as applied to Gentile Christians, as well as those of the stock of Abraham. When Paul, in his letter to the Romans, is endeavoring to show that though the Jew is benefited because he is a Jew—"much every way, chiefly because to him is committed the oracles of God" (iii. 2), still, as it regards acceptance with him, and the conditions of acceptance, "there is no difference between the Jew and the Greek;" he says: "Not as though the word of God hath taken none effect; for they are not all Israel who are of Israel; neither because they are the seed of Abraham, are they all children; but in Isaac shall thy seed by called. That is, they which are the children of the flesh, these are not the children of God, but *the children of the promise are counted for the seed,"* Rom. ix. 6-8. This clearly indicates that the word "Israel" is not exclusively applied to the lineal descendants of Abraham. It refers to the *"seed"* of Abraham; but, as here declared the "children of the promise?" Paul to the Galatians definitely answers this inquiry: "For ye (Galatians, Gentiles, not Jews) are all the children of God, by faith in Christ Jesus; for as many of you as have been baptized into Christ, have put on Christ. There (i. e., in Christ) is neither Jew nor Greek, there is neither bond nor free, there is neither male nor female, for ye are all one in Christ Jesus. And if *ye* (Galatians, Christians) be Christ's, then are ye Abraham's seed, and heirs according to the promise." Thus it is evident that those who are "Abraham's seed, and heirs according to the promise," are properly called "Israel," and that this designation embraces all good Christians, whether they belong to the carnal stock of Abraham or not.

Inasmuch as the word *Israel,* when used figuratively, as it is here by the Apostle, means true Christians, whether Jews or Gentiles, the phrase "twelve tribes of Israel," if used figuratively, would be intended to embrace *all* true Christians, since the twelve tribes literally embraced all of the carnal Israel. If this is the sense in which this phrase is used by the Savior, he gave them authority to judge for all Christians. If he used the phrase literally, then they were to judge for the twelve tribes of the lineal descendants of Jacob. The declaration interposes no serious difficulty, whichever be the true meaning of the phrase. But it is incumbent on me to state my reasons for supposing the phrase to be used figuratively, embracing all Christians, and not being limited to the carnal Jew.

1. We have already made it fully appear, that to sit on thrones, judging the twelve tribes of Israel, means substantially the same as to have the keys of the kingdom, with authority to bind and loose on earth. But this binding and loosing is not limited to any one particular nation. They were to bind and loose *on earth;* and all who yielded obedience to the laws which they bound upon them, were Christians, and by a very beautiful figure, might properly be called the "twelve tribes of Israel."

2. In point of fact, we find, by examination, that although the Apostles did judge for the twelve tribes of Israel, literally, they were not confined in their judicial labors to these twelve tribes, but actually judged for all Christians—both Jews and Gentiles.

II. *"Judging."* Some persons have understood the word "judging" to be synonymous with *"ruling"*—*"Ruling* the twelve tribes of Israel." There is no authority for this notion. A ruler may be, *ex-officio,* a judge, but the converse is not true. The idea of *ruling* embraces the idea of *judging;* but the idea of judging does not embrace that of ruling. The less does not embrace the greater; but the greater does embrace the less. Besides, the Greek word here rendered *judging* is the verb *krino*, which is never used in the sense of ruling, but in the sense of rendering a judicial decision; *Basiluo* is the proper Greek verb to rule or reign.

Have the Apostles ever *judged* the twelve tribes of Israel, or anybody else? Yes, they have judged the twelve tribes of Israel, and they have judged others also. In proof of which see the following Scriptures:

1. In Acts 15th, we have an account of a convocation of the apostles and elders, at which James made a speech, in which he said—"Wherefore my sentence is *(krino—I judge)* that we trouble not *them* which from among the Gentiles are turned to God," etc. This was judging both for Jew and Gentile; for it was judging or deciding how the Jew ought to act in reference to the Gentile.

2. The *judgment* of James, sanctioned by the Holy Spirit, met the approval of all the apostles and elders, and they wrote to the Gentile Christians accordingly. Hence we read, in the next chapter, an account of the travels of Paul and Silas. Acts xvi. 4: "And as they went through the cities, they delivered to them the *decrees to* keep, that were *ordained (krino—judged) of* the apostles and elders which were at Jerusalem."

3. Again we read, Acts xxi. 25, "As touching the Gentiles which believe, we have written and *concluded (krino—judged)* that they observe no such things," etc.

Here are three specific instances in which the identical word employed by Jesus in describing the functions of the Apostles, is used to describe what they did in the performance of those functions. "Ye shall sit upon thrones, *(krino) judging,"* says Jesus; and straightway the historian informs us that they *(krino) judged,* passed *"sentence,"* "ordained," "concluded" (as our translators have rendered the word). How could fulfillment of promise be more precisely noted. But if the word *krino* had not been used, on earth, a careful student of the Scriptures could not fail to perceive that what they were continually doing, after they were invested with power from on high, precisely came up to the import of that word. Were they not continually *judging,* ordaining, decreeing or deciding the laws of the kingdom, wherever they were, and whenever they preached the gospel, whether to Jew or Gentile? This was the specific idea embraced in the declaration—"Whatsoever ye shall bind on earth shall be bound in heaven; and whatsoever, ye shall loose on earth shall be loosed in heaven."

But it may be objected—"How could they judge "the *twelve* tribes of Israel," when ten of those tribes were lost? Lost! Who said they were *lost?* That when the Jews went up to Jerusalem, from their Babylonian captivity, but two tribes went up, while the others remained in captivity, or in dispersion, is clearly enough taught. But I know of no place where it is taught that they were ever lost. They Were certainly not so lost but what Paul must have known where they were, and found out what their hope was; for he told Agrippa what their hope was (Acts xxvi. 7). They were not so lost but what James knew where they were, for he addressed his letter "to the twelve tribes, which are scattered abroad, greeting." And in it he judged or decided for them. When the twelve Apostles first exercised their judicial functions—when they first bound, and loosed on earth—on the memorable day of Pentecost—they did so for "Jews, devout men out of every nation under heaven." Who dare say that all the twelve tribes were there represented? But whether each tribe was there represented or not, it is certain that what they there taught, judged or decided, was for "all nations," for "every creature," and would necessarily include the twelve tribes. It does not therefore Matter whether we understand the phrase *"twelve* tribes", literally or figuratively; in either case the Apostles actually did judge (*krino*) the twelve, tribes of Israel.

We have already shown, by several quotations, that the Apostles have (*krino*) judged. We shall take this as a settled fact, and shall make the best logical use of it we can.

1. The Apostles did, while on earth, exercise their judicial functions. But they had no authority to judge, until they were seated upon twelve thrones. Therefore they must have been seated upon twelve thrones while they were here on earth.

2. The Apostles were seated upon twelve thrones while, they lived on the earth. But, they were not to sit upon twelve thrones until Jesus was seated upon the throne of his glory. Therefore Jesus must have been seated upon the throne of his glory while the Apostles were upon the earth. We had however arrived at this conclusion by a different process. By direct Scripture testimony, we had learned that Jesus, was seated upon a throne, glorified—crowned with glory—was "received up into glory," etc. It is, therefore, a fact indisputably settled by clear Scripture testimony, that when Jesus left this world, he was immediately seated upon the throne of his glory. We may, then, take this as a starting point, and reverse our syllogistic process. Thus:

3. In the apostolic age, Jesus had taken his seat upon the throne of his glory. But when he was seated upon the throne of his glory, the Apostles were to sit upon twelve thrones. Therefore the Apostles must have been sitting upon twelve thrones in the apostolic age.

In the apostolic age, the Apostles were seated upon twelve thrones. But when they were seated on twelve thrones they were to judge the twelve tribes of Israel. Therefore they must have judged the twelve tribes of Israel in the apostolic age. Thus, do these two facts, clearly taught in the sacred record, mutually sustain and support each other. The school-boy who, by multiplication, proves the correctness of the process by which he has performed an example in division, can understand how these clearly revealed facts protect and uphold each other.

But we can now push our conclusions one step farther. It was "in the regeneration" that the Son of Man was to be seated upon the throne (or *in* the throne) of his glory, and that the Apostles were to sit on twelve thrones. Whenever, therefore, Jesus began to sit upon the throne of his glory, and the Apostles began to sit upon their twelve thrones, then that splendid era, called *"the regeneration"* commenced. We have also seen that what Matthew calls "the regeneration," Luke calls a "kingdom." Whenever the kingdom commenced, the regeneration commenced—for these are identical. The kingdom commenced when Jesus was *enthroned*—"crowned with glory and honor"—when he was invested with *"all power* in heaven and on earth"—when he became Lord, or Monarch of all—when angels, authorities and powers were made subject to him. Then began *"the regeneration;"* then the Son of Man was seated upon the throne of his glory; then the Apostles were (and it is a beautiful metaphor, expressive of their apostolic authority) seated upon twelve thrones, judging the twelve tribes of Israel; then they (and it is another expressive metaphor) were entrusted with the *"keys"* of the kingdom of heaven; then they were empowered to *bind* and *loose* on earth, and it should be bound or loosed in heaven. We thus conclude the first branch of our subject, and have no occasion to detain the reader long on the second branch.

The only other instance of the use of the word regeneration is Titus iii. 5:—"Not by works of righteousness which we have done, but according to his mercy he saved us, by the washing of regeneration, and renewing of the Holy Ghost."

The only point of inquiry in relation to this passage is the phrase, "washing of regeneration."

1. Does the word "regeneration" here mean the same as in Matt. xix. 28? Why not? There is no reason known to us why the word should not be understood alike in these two passages. Many who can see at a glance that this word in Matt. xix. 28, has no allusion to the new birth, so understand it here, and talk about the "washing of the *new birth."* As the word in the other instance evidently means the new age, the Christian dispensation, in contra distinction to the old Jewish economy, why does it not mean the same thing here? We know there was a bath or washing of the old age; we know there is one belonging to the new. Why does not the phrase "washing of regeneration" indicate the bath belonging to the new age, contra-distinguished from that which belonged to the old.

2. The word *louo* here rendered *washing,* is found in but one other instance in the New Testament, viz.: Eph. v. 26, "The *washing* of water by the word." Donnegan defines the word—"water for washing or bathing; a washing place; a bath." A *bath* or *laver*—i. e., the place where the act of bathing is performed—not the act of bathing itself—is undoubtedly the true idea of the word. "The *laver* or *bath,* of water by the word." "The laver of regeneration."

Louteer, another noun derived from *(louo)* the same verb, as *loutron,* occurs frequently in the Septuagint version of the Old Testament. This word is defined by Donnegan, "a vessel used for washing; a bathing tub." It will be noticed that these two words, derived as they are from the same root, are almost precisely synonymous in import. One signifies "a washing place—a bath," the other "a vessel used for washing." In fact, they both signify a place where the act of bathing is performed.

But whatever may be the precise meaning of the words *loutron* and *palingenesia,* it is admitted, by all biblical critics in Christendom, that the phrase "washing of regeneration" (*loutron palingenesia*) signifies baptism. It will also be conceded that the *"laver of brass," (louteera chalkoun)* which was placed in the outer court of the Jewish tabernacle, directly in front of the door of the first tabernacle, was designed to typify the Christian institution of baptism. Is it not true, then, that the "laver of brass," was the "laver" of the old age, or Jewish dispensation, and that baptism is the antitype thereof—is the "laver" of *the regeneration,* the new age, or Christian dispensation? This, it seems to me, is the true meaning and the real secret of Paul's use of the phrase.

This whole subject is now respectfully submitted to the study and reflection of those who read, study and think. Some of the views expressed may be considered *novel.* This I admit is no commendation, but is rather a suspicious circumstance. But it is not sufficiently suspicious to justify anyone in ejecting those views without an examination. The important question, after all, is not what is new, or what is old, but *"what is truth."* Let truth, like a precious gem, find a suitable casket in your very heart of hearts.

-----o-----

BILL OF GRIEVANCES.

BRO. FRANKLIN:—For twenty years past, I have been a careful reader of the sacred Scriptures; and being a portion of that time in rather indigent circumstances, and unfavorably situated to receive much assistance in my studies from brethren of high literary and biblical attainments, I have been compelled mainly to depend upon my Bible, to learn the ways of righteousness and peace.

I have, it is true, had greater privileges within the last few years past than formerly; but I still look to my Bible as the great source from whence we derive the knowledge that guides our feet into the path of righteousness and true holiness; and that will ultimately land us safely in the haven of everlasting repose.

I have also been a careful observer of passing events, and have for some years past read with much interest many different religious magazines; and have in this way received much useful instruction. Amongst other valuable documents, I have been a careful reader and a great admirer of your magazines, which were, and still are, hailed as welcome visitors, filled generally with substantial reading matter and encouraging religious news.

These periodicals, edited by yourself and sent forth to the world, show that you are an able defender of the claims of Christianity; but there are some things connected with your public labors recently, which have astonished me much, and caused me much regret, and upon which I deem it to be my duty to make some remarks; and I hope you will receive them kindly, consider them candidly, and give them a hearty response.

You doubtless remember that, in a private conversation in Union City last winter, I told you my honest convictions were, that your article, published in vol. No. 2nd of the A. C. REVIEW, under the caption, "Where is the Safe Ground?" would be hailed by the people of the slave-holding States, as favoring the institution of slavery. But you replied that you did not intend any such thing, and thought that such would not be the result.

Now, I ask, are not my convictions, as then expressed, clearly shown to be correct? They most certainly are. In the June number, current volume of the REVIEW, I find a letter from the pen of H. M. Bledsoe, Lexington, Missouri, correspondent of the REVIEW, that fully confirms the truth of my convictions, and clearly shows how your "Safe Ground" article is received and understood by brethren of the slave-holding States; that it is hailed and greeted, as establishing by the sacred Scriptures, the *relation* of master and slave, as well as pointing out the duties of said relation.

Yea more; a eulogy is thrown upon you, for having the nerve to do so. This writer says: "Your position on the all- absorbing subject of Slavery, I also approve. It is eminently conservative and just, and is precisely what the Scriptures teach in reference to it, pointing out the relative duties *both* of master and servant."

Now, according to this writer, as published by yourself, it is clearly seen that your "Safe Ground" article is understood to *mean* that the *relation* of master and slave is authorized by the Scriptures; and that slavery is indeed a Bible institution, and therefore "*eminently* conservative and just." Now, if this is not the sense in which your "Safe Ground" article is received in Missouri, as set forth by this Missouri correspondent, then I cannot understand him. This being correct, the case then stands thus: Your "Safe Ground" article is *understood to* sanction the *relation* of master and slave, and that this relation properly regarded, is eminently conservative and just, and is just the doctrine that should everywhere be preached on the subject.

Now, dear brother, to think of one with whom I have been acquainted and occasionally associated for many years—one that I highly esteem and dearly love, and one that I regard as being my superior in the labors of the Gospel ministry, taking a course that will influence and encourage men to cling to and practice, that which is fraught with as much sin and misery as any practice upon this sin- cursed earth, is indeed to me a source of astonishment and deep regret. And in saying this, I am conscious that I speak the sentiments of many of our brethren and sisters.

There is another item to which I will call your attention. On page 190, "Editor's Table," June number, current volume of the REVIEW, you say: "We must again apologize to correspondents. Many valuable and able documents from brethren of first distinction and standing, have been crowded out for months."

Now, Bro. Franklin, from the high and favorable opinion I have ever entertained of you, as a devoted, zealous and self-sacrificing teacher of Christianity, I could scarcely have been induced to believe that you would have allowed "*valuable* and *able documents*" from brethren of *first* distinction and standing," to be "crowded out" of your excellent paper, to give room for a pro-slavery letter; but such appears from your own showing to be the case. Now this is indeed to me a matter of astonishment and regret.

I will state, once for all, that I feel no disposition to impugn your motives; neither do I feel in the least disposed to speak in a disrespectful manner of your Missouri friend; but I feel a *deep* concern in regard to the influence—the destructful and sinful influence—that pro-slavery doctrine is having, and ever must have, while it is practiced, both upon the church and upon the world.

I have thought, for some years past, that you have been much more prompted in rebuking other evils of less magnitude than the sin of slavery. I have also seen, for some time past, that you would not publish an article, be it written by whom it may, rebuking the sin of slavery; but little did I think, till *now,* that you would suffer "*able and valuable documents*" *to be crowded out of the* REVIEW, to make room for a pro-slavery letter. Permit me, dear brother, to inquire what is the cause of this? Do you believe that slavery is right? Do you believe that the relation of master and slave, as practiced even by professors of Christianity in the slave-holding States, is right? If you do, why do you not come out and say so? If you do *not,* then why do you not speak out, through the columns of your paper, and let the public know where you do stand on this subject. The time certainly has come when public men will be regarded as favoring human slavery, so long as they refuse to show its sinfulness at least in the church.

It does, indeed, Bro. Franklin, seem as

though something must be wrong.

Now, dear brother, I am free to say that I solemnly believe slavery is wrong; that it is exceedingly sinful in the sight of God; and that it is the duty of every Gospel minister to fearlessly bear testimony against it, in ratio to its magnitude, as he would any other sin of this age. It is highly probable, however, that in doing this, some will meet opposition, and severe persecution; but what if they do! it is not for gospel ministers to stop and inquire whether they will or will not be persecuted; but the real question is, what is their duty? If, indeed, it can be shown, that human slavery is right—that it is taught in the Christian Scriptures, then we should not oppose and rebuke it; but if it is *not* right, if it can be shown to be in direct opposition to the spirit and teachings of the Christian Scriptures, then it should certainly be exposed.

When sectarianism crosses your path, you always appear ready and willing to meet and refute it. When Universalism or infidelity come in your way, you always appear ready and willing to meet their *ablest* advocates, and in a masterly, energetic and Christian manner, defend the truth. All this I believe to be right; and *all* should rejoice to know that these pernicious influences *can be met and refuted* by the holy Scriptures; but when slavery, with its train of attendant evils comes up, you appear unwilling to join issue. Here, again, I confess my astonishment and regret. Will you be so kind as to tell us the reason of this? Many good brethren think, from what you have written, that your article favors slavery, and they appear in suspense on the subject.

Now, dear brother, in conclusion. I will say, that if your mighty powers were brought to bear upon the sin of slavery—*the sin of the age*, it could not fail to have a mighty and powerful influence. In the language of your correspondent, let me say to you, "Cry aloud, spare not, and show the people of God their transgressions, and the house of Jacob their sins;'' and thus bear testimony against *the sin* of this age.

With kindest regards I am yours,
THOMAS WILEY.

REPLY.

The above, though the best among quite a number of articles upon the same subject, and from as good a man as has taken exceptions to our course, contains no attempt at argument; but, when separated from preliminaries, explanations and redundancies, amounts simply to the following items of complaint:

1. Our articles under the caption—"Where is the Safe Ground?" are understood to be pro-slavery by southern brethren, and, therefore, they are pleased with them.

2. We have allowed many valuable documents to be crowded out to give room for a pro-slavery letter.

3. We have not rebuked the sin of slavery.

Such is the sum of the complaint, and, as our brother appears deeply grieved, and thinks he speaks the mind of many others, we spread his complaint before our readers in full.

1. On the first charge, we plead *not guilty*. Not a man has quoted, or can quote, one sentence or one word, from the articles' in question, that *is pro-slavery*. Nor is there one word in the article of Bro. Bledsoe that is pro-slavery, or that interprets us to say or *mean* anything pro-slavery. Nor is there one word in his article about "establishing, by the sacred Scriptures, the *relation* of master and slave," alleging that "slavery is a Bible institution," or "authorized by Scripture," or any language equivalent to this. He does not give any expression as to the institution of slavery at all, whether he thinks it good or bad. But he does endorse our articles, in which we stated, in the most explicit manner, that Jesus and the Apostles did not institute slavery, and are not responsible for it, or any of its consequences!

The reasons attributed to him, by Bro. Wiley, for approving us, or any equivalent to them, are not found in the article at all, but are simply founded in suspicion. He assigns his reasons for his approval, with all clearness, which we will point out numerically, and see if Bro. Wiley can see them. They are the following: 1. Our "earnest and impressive style." 2. The "laborious and self-sacrificing spirit we inculcate." 3. "Above all, the humble, but confident reliance upon the Divine support and protection, and upon the fidelity and liberality of the brethren."

4. Our "essays on evangelizing." Each of these reasons, assigned by Bro. Bledsoe, are passed by Bro. Wiley without notice, and reasons assigned for him not mentioned by him at all! But with direct reference to our course, touching the slavery question, he gives the following reasons for his approval: 1. It is "eminently conservative." 2. It is just. 3. It is precisely what the Scriptures teach. 4. It presents safe and the only safe ground. Where does Bro. Wiley find one scrap of foundation for his reasons? The only word used by him upon which he attempts to hang anything, is the word "conservative." He does call our cause *conservative*. But there is neither pro-slavery nor anti-slavery in that word. There are many conservative men both pro-slavery and anti-slavery. Conservative men are safe men, peace men, not ultra or fanatical. They neither want church or state torn up. We are of this class. We have no confidence in ultraists, either pro-slavery or anti-slavery, as guides for either church or state. Where they go, ruin and desolation follow, to the extent of their influence. Bro. Bledsoe does not say, as Bro. Wiley represents him, that the relation of master and servant, or slavery, is conservative, but that our *course* is conservative.

2. We plead *not guilty* to the second charge also. Bro. Wiley and some others are so accustomed to suffering from *southern oppression*, that they find occasion for grief where no one else would think of there being any. He introduces this complaint with as solemn a preamble as if we had committed an offence that must inevitably destroy our fraternal relation forever. But when the matter comes out, the crime is that we have crowded out *many* valuable documents from distinguished brethren to make room for this one *short* pro-slavery letter, which, when carefully examined, *has not a pro-slavery word in it*. Every word in it, alluding to our course on slavery, is upon considerably less than one page! How *many* valuable documents could have been crowded out of *less than one page?* O Bro. Wiley, are you thus pressed to file a bill of complaints against one that has always esteemed you? Your own article, containing nothing but an effort to criminate your brother and impair his influence among those whom he desires to benefit, crowds out three times as much as the one complained of.

3. We have not rebuked the sin of slavery. Taking the language in the sense intended, which is the only way we have a right to take it, we are compelled to plead *guilty*. We have not, in his sense, rebuked the sin of slavery. For this, we have no secret reasons, and certainly are perfectly willing to be called to account. We have long since determined to pay due respect to the wisdom of God and not to be governed by the wisdom of man. If our brother will respect divine precept and example, we can go hand in hand; if he will not, we cannot go together. Will he and all of the same mind solemnly reflect on the following:

1. We must follow the example of Jesus and the Apostles without any evasion.

2. We must express ourselves in the New Testament language, especially in matters of difficulty, where men disagree, and in things of great moment.

In all the catalogues of crime, definitions of sin and flagrant outrage, mentioned in the New Testament, we find nothing called "the sin of slavery," or of the same import.

4. In the entire lives, labors and teachings of the Apostles, we find no instance of their rebuking "the sin of slavery," in Bro. Wiley's sense, thus giving us an example how it should be done. The charge that we have "*not* rebuked the sin of slavery," lies with equal force against the Apostles; and he who is grieved with us on this account, has equal occasion to be grieved with them.

5. The Apostles never attacked slavery, formed an issue with it, made a decision in reference to it, or gave their opinion of it, in their entire ministry. Let him invalidate this who can. Were they afraid of their popularity?—or persecution? Were they dough-faces? Let him blush that would think of such a thing! They feared God and yielded to the wisdom of God.

6. There is not a decision in the entire Christian code, determining slavery to be right or wrong. Such a decision is not found in the whole counsel of God to man. Therefore, the Christian preacher may declare the whole counsel of God without deciding the question, or even knowing whether slavery, in itself, is right or wrong. It is good to be wise, but *not above what is written.*

7. Christianity did not institute, authorize or regulate slavery, and is not, therefore, responsible for it or any evils or cruelties in it, or resulting from it.

8. Christianity does not directly abolish slavery, or any wrongs in civil governments. It only effects them in its general diffusion of light, justice, mercy and goodness, as its principles of universal benevolence are spread in the world.

9. Christianity gives directions to two classes connected with slavery, to which these must pay respect or forfeit their standing. These directions we must respect, and not subvert, or we forfeit our integrity to Jesus Christ. 1. The Lord gives directions to those in bonds, the most benevolent, merciful and gracious that could be given. He who is ashamed of these holy directions, ignores them and despises them, despises their Author. A mere specimen of these directions is all that we can give now. "Art thou called being a servant? care not for it; but if thou mayest be made free, use it rather," 1 Cor. vii. 21. "Let as many servants as are under the yoke count their own masters worthy of all honor, that the name of God and his doctrine be not blasphemed. And they that have believing masters, let them not despise them, because they are brethren; but do them service, because they are faithful and beloved, partakers of the benefit," 1 Tim. vi. 1-2. "Servants, be subject to your own masters with all fear; not only to the good and gentle, but also to the forward. For this is thankworthy, if a man for conscience toward God endure grief, suffering wrongfully. For what glory is it, if when ye be buffet- ted for your faults, ye shall take it patiently? but if, when ye do well, and suffer for it, ye take it patiently, this is acceptable with God," 1 Pet. ii. 18-20. These expressions decide nothing in regard to slavery, as to whether it is right or wrong, but simply decide the course to be pursued by those in bonds. 2. The Lord gives directions to those who have them in bonds, or masters, as follows: "And ye masters, do the same things unto them, forbearing threatening, knowing that your Master also is in heaven; neither is there respect of persons with him," Eph. vi. 9. "Masters, give unto your servants that which is just and equal, knowing that ye also have a Master in heaven," Col. iv. 1.

10. The Lord points out the duty of preachers as follows: "Exhort servants to be obedient unto their own masters, and to please them well in all things; not answering again, not purloining, but showing all good fidelity; that they may adorn the doctrine of God our Savior in all things," Tit. ii. 9-10.

11. In the following the Lord describes the

preacher who will not give these and similar instructions: "If any man teach otherwise, and consent not to wholesome words, even the words of our Lord Jesus Christ, and to the doctrine which is according to goodness, he is proud, knowing nothing, but doting about questions and strifes of words, whereof cometh envying, strife, railings, evil surmizings, perverse disputings of men of corrupt minds, and destitute of truth, supposing that gain is godliness; from such withdraw thyself," 1 Tim. vi. 3-5.

It will be noticed that these teachings say nothing in reference to the abstract question, whether the institution of slavery is good or bad, but simply direct the people of God connected with it what course to pursue. It is wiser, better and safer to follow these instructions than any of the vain rantings of pro slavery or anti-slavery men. Nay, the minister of Christ must follow these directions, or forfeit all claim to integrity to Jesus Christ. All we have said, and what Bro. Bledsoe said, relates simply to *the course to be pursued by Christians* and not to the discussion of the question abstractly, whether the institution is good or bad. That question Christianity does not discuss, is not responsible for and does not decide. That question the Lord and the Apostles left where they found it, as they did all the human institutions and civil arrangements among men, simply showing honest, peaceable followers of Christ how to serve God, whether servant or master; and, when done with the world, get to a state free from all the imperfect arrangements of this life.

In conclusion, we must say, though we think not such to be the case with Bro. Wiley, that much that has been said in reference to our course, is intended more to prejudice the brethren of the North against us, than through any benevolent feelings for the colored people. It is well known to those acquainted with us, both North and South, that, according to our ability, the colored people have no better friend than we are. To this we have given testimony in the most substantial manner in our power. We have been instrumental in bringing about thirty of them to the kingdom of God in the last three months. But Christianity is clear of the controversy about the institution—the mere question as to whether it is wise or unwise, good or bad. It decides no more upon it than upon the question of Democracy and Know-Nothingism. It instituted none of these things, decides them neither to be right or wrong. It is a party to no such questions. Jesus and the Apostles were parties in no such controversies. We stand with them, identified with none of these worldly strifes, and a party to none of them. We can show an honest man how to become a Christian, serve God and get to heaven, whether bond or free, master or servant.

We want no better evidence against the course pursued by those trying to bite, scratch and annoy us, to which class Bro. Wiley does not belong, than the spiritual desolation that follows them. They can destroy work done by other men, and pull down what others build; but they build nothing. Death follows in their train. There is not a wrangler on slavery, either pro-slavery or anti-slavery, in our knowledge, that is doing any good.   B. F.

MORE ABOUT DEBATES.

BRO. FRANKLIN—*Dear Sir:*—By the special request and earnest desire of the church meeting at Pine Flats, Indiana Co., Pa., I address you. I ask your attention, in the first place, to the statement of a few facts connected with the object of this communication.

At Pine Flats there was formerly a Baptist church—but whether it was through the neglect of their preachers, or the kind of materials that constituted the church, I do not know (perhaps it was both), but at all events the Baptist cause languished, and the church fell into decay. There were, nevertheless, some ardent, faithful brethren, who had become enlightened in the knowledge of the true gospel of Christ, and of the primitive order and worship of the church of God. These brethren desired to have the truth presented to the community in which they lived. To promote the object of their desire, they obtained the services of Bro. Darsie and myself to hold a protracted meeting, which we did. This occurred about eighteen months ago. The result of the meeting was quite a number of additions, and the organization of a church of about thirty members upon the foundation of the apostles and prophets, Jesus Christ being the chief corner-stone. This excited the jealousy and vindictive feelings of the Baptists, and from that time to the present they have pursued a systematic course of slander, defamation and falsehood, with the avowed purpose of crushing and wiping us out as a people. They have turned us out of the meeting-house which our brethren were instrumental in building. They have circulated all the vile trash of the opponents of Bro. Campbell, with that finished and minute production of Dr. Jeter!

In fine, they procured the services of a very distinguished preacher and orator, the Rev. Wm. Shadrach, D. D., who made his boast that he would wipe us out in less than a year, but his year has closed, and notwithstanding their persecution and abuse, the little church is as strong—as ardent and zealous for the truth as when they began. In all the trying circumstances in which they have been placed by the hatred and malignity of the Baptists, we have always treated them with the greatest courtesy, respect and kindness, that, if possible, we might soften their feelings, and win them to the truth as it is in Jesus, but all to no purpose; they only became more violent and abusive.

These things I only state to give you a slight knowledge of the whole premises, and a reason for the course we are pursuing.

The Baptists have accused us of teaching the sentiments and doctrines of Alexander Campbell, and other doctrines worse than Romanism, and subversive of the gospel, to all of which charges we of course demur, and emphatically deny. We asked them to give us a fair hearing before the community, but they have hitherto refused. Dr. Shadrach has pursued the same course in his labors of *love* and opposition to the cause of truth which we plead. On last Lord's day, he delivered himself in his usual characteristic style of abuse, charging us with holding errors of the most pernicious character, upon the work of the Holy Spirit, the design of baptism, etc.; the same old slanders with, which you are well acquainted. At the close of his sermon, Bro. Williams, one of the elders of the church, asked permission to say a few words, which was granted. He denied the charges made by the Doctor, and challenged him to come up to the proof of what he had said from the word of God. This, of course, he did not do. In a subsequent interview which some of the brethren had with him, he offered to meet one of our preachers in debate, *if we could get one six feet,* and discuss the differences between the Baptists and us.

The brethren have selected you to conduct the business upon their part, and wish you to open a correspondence with Dr. Shadrach, and see if there is a possibility of bringing him to a discussion of the points of difference. It would be very desirable and, I think, result in a great deal of good.

But I do not think he will debate with you or any other of our brethren. He could not do otherwise in the presence of so large an assembly than to declare his willingness to debate.

You will please let me know your mind upon the subject as soon as it is convenient.

The elders of the church at Pine Flats are Daniel Williams and Philip I. Arthurs, to whom, you can refer, if you should open, a correspondence with Dr. Shadrach. If you should have a debate, the brethren will defray all your traveling expenses and remunerate you for your time.

If you are disposed to engage in the matter, address Rev. Wm. Shadrach, D. D., Philadelphia, Penn.

Your fellow-laborer in the truth,
JAMES B. WYATT.
July 27, 1857.

REPLY.

We present the above as a specimen of what is going on in sundry places, as legitimate fruits of Elder Jeter's book. We are not anxious for debates, and have only accepted such as are prepared for and pressed upon us for several years. But it appears a little difficult to quit debating. As we become less inclined to debate, our opponents become emboldened. They can think of no reason why we should be less inclined to debate than in former years, except that which has so long deterred them from debate, viz., *a consciousness of inability to defend their cause*. For the enlightenment of some such man as this, we occasionally resort to religious discussion. As the above-named gentleman, in his own estimation, at least, is a *tall* man, a Rev. D. D., we inform him, that if he will discuss the *real issues or* differences between Baptists and Disciples, we will afford him every facility in our power. We, therefore, propose to question Baptist preaching and practice in the following items:

1. The cognomen, "Baptist Church," is unscriptural, and tends to schism or heresy.

2. The practice of monthly or quarterly, instead of weekly communion, as practiced by Baptists, is unscriptural and is destructive of spirituality, devotion and piety.

3. The practice of Baptists in debarring those from the communion whom they acknowledge Christians, is schismatical and heretical.

4. The practice of the Baptists, when persons come forward, inquiring what they shall do to be saved, in directing them to pray for God to convert them, and the preachers joining in these prayers, at the mourner's bench, anxious seat or altar of prayer, subverts the process of conversion taught and practiced in apostolic times.

5. The teaching of Baptists, that the Spirit of God, since the reign of Christ' commenced, ever converts or sanctifies men without the word, or the gospel, is a dangerous heresy.

5. The tendency of such books as the one written by Rev. J. B. Jeter, the "Iron Wheel," by Mr. Graves, and several Baptist periodicals, is heretical.

If there is anything in these items, ascribed to the Baptists, which the gentleman will not defend, he can specify what it is, and it shall be stricken out. He may, if he choose, make the same number of points of objections to us, allowing us the privilege of striking out anything we do not hold or defend; and we will meet and spend a week or ten days in the discussion of the points of difference. Will the Reverend gentleman let us hear from him soon?

B. F.

-----o-----

SECTARIANISM CONFESSEDLY WRONG.

THERE has been much discussion upon sectarianism within the last thirty years, and immense light has been elicited and great good accomplished. Still, some of the blind guides of these times will never see, till irresistibly forced, that sectarianism blights, strikes with death and sinks everything upon which it is inscribed. Many, however, knowing sectarianism to be ruinous, suicidal to everything upon which it is written, and neither catholic nor orthodox, having been long wedded to it, and loving it more than the bread of life, still cling to it as to life itself. In the place of inquiring, as they ought, "Who shall deliver me from the body of this death?" they are simply contriving how they shall hold on to the old sectarian bodies of sin and death. But contrive as they may, the breath of life cannot be kept in them. *Ichabod* is written upon them. The voice of heaven is against them. The voice of the people is against them. The voice of their own friends is against them. *Die they must.*

Why not call the American Tract Society, the Episcopalian Tract Society? the Methodist Tract Society? the Presbyterian Tract Society? the Baptist Tract Society? Because it is known that the seeds of death are in these names. There is enough poison, it is known, in any one of these names to kill the society. To put any one of these names upon it, would blast it forever. Why not call the American Foreign Christian Union, the Episcopal Foreign Union? the Presbyterian Foreign Union? the Baptist Foreign Union? Because it is known that there is death in these names. The poison in any one of them, it is known, is sufficient to kill the Union. If any one of these names were inscribed upon it, it is known it would blast it forever. Why not call the Sunday School Union, the Methodist Sunday School Union? the Baptist Sunday School Union? the Presbyterian Sunday School Union? Because it is known these names have no popularity, are partisan, and have the seeds of death in them. Any one of them inscribed upon the Sunday School Union would blast, kill and sink it forever. This they all well know. Why not call the American Bible Union, the Baptist Bible Union? the Presbyterian Bible Union? the Episcopalian Bible Union? Because they know the poison of partyism is in these names, and that it will kill everything upon which it is inscribed; because they know that these names have no popularity and would sink it. In one word, it is distinctly understood that any religious movement, designed to be general, or, which is the same thing, catholic, and obtain the general concurrence and co-operation of Christians, must not have any of these unpopular and prejudicial names upon it. They must be ignored and kept out of sight. How preposterous it is, then, to inscribe any one of them upon a servant of God, and thus compel him to encounter its poisonous, blasting and deathly influence, in all his honest efforts to serve God, through his entire life! Why not cut him loose from this dead weight, this miserable encumbrance, weighing him down, sinking him and destroying him, as they have done in the case of the above-mentioned enterprise? If it is wrong to fasten upon these enterprises a name known to be poisonous, blighting and ruinous, it is equally wrong to fasten such a name upon an individual, or a congregation.

The reason it will not do to call the Bible Union, the *Baptist* Union, is simply that the name *Baptist* is so unpopular, prejudicial and partisan, that every party in the land, except the Baptists, are opposed to it. The same is true of the names Methodist, Presbyterian and Episcopalian. Inscribe any one of these names upon it, and its fate is sealed. Every other party from that time forth is against it. It is therefore distinctly understood and agreed upon, that all these names must be kept off of every movement commanding general respect and co-operation. The reason is, that these names are barriers, known to be in the way of good and pious men, and that they must be kept clear, or we cannot get the co-operation of these good men! What must be the effect, then, when one of these names is fastened upon a man, only to bar off all those good men opposed to that name—and all are opposed to it except the one little party adopting it—from co-operation or participation in any good work with him? What can the effect be, when one of these names is fastened upon a church, but to bar off all opposed to that name? Why not, then, disencumber every individual and every church of every one of these unpopular, prejudicial and exclusive names, and call the church the Church of Christ, or the Church of God, and individuals, Christians or Disciples, as found in Scripture? No man has or can have any reasonable objection to being a member of the church of Christ, or the church of God; nor has any man any objection to being called a Christian or Disciple. Indeed, the question will be in death, Am I a Christian—a Disciple of Christ? Do I belong to the Church of God—the Church of Christ? No man objects, if in reality a good man—a Christian—to a work or movement because it is called *Christian*. No man disallows you to call him a *Christian*. Then, if all good people desire to do good in their day, let them disavow their prejudicial and injurious names, that serve no purpose only to bar good men from them, and be content with divine names and divine things.

Nor are the doctrines indicated by these names any more catholic, or general, than the names. That which is called Episcopalianism is believed by one church, and *one only*. All other churches oppose it—do not believe it at all. That something called Methodism is not believed by Baptists at all. That something called Presbyterianism is not believed by Methodists at all. It avails nothing to say that all those named believe a great deal in common. That which they believe in common is not Episcopalianism, Methodism, Presbyterianism, nor Baptistism, but simply *Christianity;* and that contains all the good, and does all the good among them. That which is peculiar to the party, makes the party. That which the party holds and practices, not held and practiced by other parties, is the occasion of the party; that which distinguishes it from others and is strictly *its own*. Nothing held in common makes the party, is peculiar to it, or can be claimed as its own. Strike out all that is held by the Methodists not held by any others, and though you would not have stricken out much, there would not be left one Methodist idea, or one particle of Methodism. But there would be much of Christianity left. Strike out of the Presbyterian confession everything not believed and practiced by any other party, and, though but little is stricken out, there is not one Presbyterian idea, or one particle of Presbyterianism left. In the same way, if all believed and practiced by Baptists, not believed by any others, was stricken out, there would not be one particle of Baptistism left; yet much of Christianity might be left.

This is all pretty well known by these parties, when they think of it. A presbyterian knows that Presbyterianism is not Christianity; hence he will admit that a Methodist, who does not believe Presbyterianism, can be a Christian; yet he knows that a man cannot be a Christian and not believe in Christianity. If a man can be a Christian and not believe Presbyterianism, but cannot be a Christian and not believe Christianity, then unequivocally Presbyterianism *is not Christianity*. If a man can be a Christian and not believe Baptistism, Baptistism is not Christianity—it is not the gospel—for a man cannot be a Christian and not believe the gospel. How many Christians there may be in these parties, we presume not to say; but they all concede that there are some. These are not made Christians by believing Methodism, Presbyterianism or Baptistism; for a man can be a Christian without believing any one of these, or else there are no Christians among Episcopalians who do not believe any of these doctrines; but many become Christians among Episcopalians who do not believe any of these doctrines; but they become Christians by believing in and submitting to the Savior of the world, as people did hundreds of years before these doctrines were born; or by believing what all these hold in common, and without which none can be saved. The Christianity, then, held in common by them all, which none can be saved without believing, is that which saves all that are saved among them; and that which is peculiar and constitutes the sect, which a man can be saved without believing, *never saved anybody and is useless*. It is not orthodox, not catholic, not popular, can never be agreed upon, and can only serve to prejudice the people against him who holds it and bar them from Him. Let us separate pure Christianity out from everything else, call it by its own proper name and unite with all who love it and him who gave it. B. F.

-----o-----

BRACKEN ASSOCIATION OF UNITED BAPTISTS.
NUMBER VIII.

BEFORE we proceed to the principal objects of this number, we propose to take another glance at Eld. Gardner's plan of union for the religious world. His plan is exceedingly plain, and upon the face seems very fair. It requires no sacrifice of conscience or principle. It simply requires, that we shall all become United Baptists! Now, however it may be with others, we have shown, that so far as we are concerned, a union with Baptists of any sort, would be a sacrifice of principle, of conscience, of everything. But for the sake of argument, suppose such a union were consummated, do you, Eld. Gardner, in your conscience, believe it would be *that union* for which the Savior prayed? Do you believe that apostolic Christianity would be restored in faith and practice? John the Baptist never established any church. He said, "I must decrease." And Christ, unquestionably, never established a Baptist church. Did he, Eld. Gardner?

1. We propose now to show, that considerable changes have taken place among the Baptists, within the last quarter or half century. When quite a youth, "seeking religion," as it was called, I attended the meetings of the Methodists, Baptists and others, who invited me, according to the custom of those times, to come up and be prayed for, and thus seek the forgiveness of my sins—the evidence of pardon. Nothing was more common among the Baptists and others, than for persons to be "seeking religion" for weeks, and months, and sometimes even for years, without finding it. Semple, in his history of the Baptists, speaking of the conversion of John Waller, p. 405, says: "His convictions were deep and pungent. He ate no pleasant bread, and drank no pleasant water for *seven* or *eight* months. He was almost in despair." My own experience was not much less protracted than that of John Waller. And many such, and some much more protracted, were very common twenty- five or thirty years ago. But are they common among Baptists now? Certainly not.

Not only was it common thirty years ago, for persons among the Baptists to be months, and sometimes years, "getting religion," or "getting through," but it was equally common for them to require those who had "got through" to give a protracted relation of their "experience." Some thirty-eight years ago, about the time I confessed my faith in the Savior, I often saw the pious W. Warder, and some of the prominent members of the Baptist church at Millersburg, sit for hours hearing the experiences of two or three persons. But now, in some places, the "Mourner's Bench" is dispensed with, and a few simple questions are asked, and the whole matter settled in a few minutes. This is certainly a considerable change. A correspondent of the *Religious Herald*, published in Richmond, Virginia, giving an account of a meeting held during the past year, says: "During this meeting, from day to day, broken-hearted sinners, in anxious groups, came with the inquiry on their tongues and in their hearts: Men and brethren, what shall we do? We who were their religious teachers and guides, did not tell them to sing on, to weep on, to read on; to think on, to fast on, etc.; but we exhorted them to believe on the Lord Jesus Christ, to repent and be baptized." In 1832, such teaching, according to the Rover decrees, was considered discouraging," if not "demoralizing." See *Millennial Harbinger* for '57, p. 209.

3. On the same page of the *Harbinger,* we have a quotation from A. M. Poindexter, of the Baptist church, in these words: "We come then to the conclusion, *that in the only commission in which a promise of salvation is made, it is connected with baptism."* We could quote many more authorities, but we shall introduce but one more at present in harmony with the quotation just made from Poindexter, to show that the Baptists are attaching more importance to baptism than formerly—that some of their most intelligent teachers are speaking and writing very much as we are. I allude now to S. W. Lynd, D. D. In 1855 he published a small pamphlet of 60 pages on the "Design of Baptism." We have read this little book with considerable interest, and all we have to say at present, in regard to its merits, is, that it does not exhibit that transparency, that straightforwardness we had a right to expect from Dr. Lynd's character for learning and piety.

On the one hand, he sees many of his Baptist brethren, in their untempered zeal to put down something they chose to call *"Campbellism,"* making almost nothing of baptism, and thus becoming the apologists of Paedobaptists, not to say their advocates. And, in his efforts to right them, he talks as we do, in Scripture language, teaching most clearly that God has established a connection between baptism and salvation, and we must not repudiate it. But anon, as if alarmed lest he should be suspected of heresy, of sympathizing with "Campbellism," he mystifies, and seems sometimes to reject the idea of the connection between baptism and salvation. It is not my purpose, however, either to show that the different parts of the work seem somewhat contradictory, or that they may be harmonized. I wish simply to show that certain portions of it clearly teach the truth in regard to baptism as we understand it; and thus, make good our statement, that our Baptist brethren are changing, and making advances in the right direction. On p. 13-14 of his book, entitled "The Design of Baptism," he says:"Faith, in the abstract, is simple belief, and in this abstract sense it never justifies a sinner. The circumstances under which it is exercised, give to it a saving character. It is the belief of a sinner who is enlightened by the Holy Spirit, through the word, who feels his lost condition, his entire want of righteousness before God, and his exposedness to everlasting ruin; who perceives a fullness in Christ to save him from sin and hell; a belief which contains within itself the element of the spirit of obedience and of holiness. Hence, in the New Testament, it is described by the apostle Paul *as a belief with the heart;* and by the apostle James, as *a belief which produces the fruits of holy living."* This is the language of Dr. Lynd, and this is precisely the truth in the case; and the truth, too, which from the beginning we have taught, and strongly urged. We know, certainly, that the faith "which contains not within itself the element of the spirit of obedience and of holiness," is not only useless, but worse than useless; "it is dead, being alone." But let us hear the Doctor again: "When we believe in Jesus as our Lord, we put ourselves under his government in the way which he has appointed—that is, by baptism. No saving faith can be exercised independently of this subjection, in those cases in which it is required. No part of the New Testament warrants a man in expecting salvation who does not come into subjection to the government of Jesus Christ in the way he has appointed—God granting him life and opportunity to put on Christ;" pages 14-15. Here I must say, with all emphasis, is the doctrine of baptism "for the remission of sins" as strongly presented as it ever was or is by those unkindly and most unwarrantably called "Campbellites." The Doctor says no man can exercise saving faith who does not subject himself to Jesus Christ, in the institution of baptism, God granting him an opportunity to be baptized. Unequivocally, then, if such an one cannot exercise saving faith without baptism, he cannot be saved or pardoned without it. This is what we mean by baptism for remission of sins. But let us hear the Doctor again, for we wish to extract all the heresy of "Campbellism," from his little book, and leave his Baptistism, his orthodoxy and mysticism for those who relish them: "We believe that immersion, and that only, is baptism; and we are persuaded that this is plainly taught in the New Testament. The opposition that is made by many to the revision of the common version, and their unwillingness to have the Greek word *baptizo* accurately translated by the most eminent scholars, shows that there is something wrong internally. To what extent this may arise from a heart not subdued to Jesus Christ, it is the duty and the highest interest of every person professing Christianity to investigate. To say that those who are not immersed lose no blessing in this world, would be to say more than the established order of divine laws will permit. The violation of any law, physical, moral or positive, will always meet its appropriate penalty, even when done by mistake or in ignorance. Even to say that, if saved, they will lose nothing in heaven, would not be authorized by anything we know concerning moral causes and their effects. It is very certain that the promise of salvation is to those who believe and are baptized. 'He that believeth and is baptized, shall be saved.' This is God's word. Let those who do not thus put on Christ, have all the trouble of meeting and explaining away the force of our Savior's words. Let their consciences meet it fully. Let them have the burden of reconciling their course with the declaration of the great commission. Shall we become the apologists of those whose action, if ever to become general, would obliterate from the inspired records a law of Jesus Christ? We may and ought to defend with holy zeal the doctrine of salvation by grace, through faith, and the fact that all who truly believe in Jesus Christ are justified and saved; but we ought not to apologize for any professor of religion whose faith has not in it the element of subjection to Jesus Christ. It would be as absurd to do this as it would be to suppose that the act of baptism *procures* salvation," pages 36-7 and 8. Here is language bearing on the question of the design of baptism as strong as any used among us. The Doctor says positively that those not immersed, even though it be through ignorance, will lose both in this world and the world to come; and that salvation is certainly promised to those who believe and are baptized. But, good Doctor, what salvation is promised to those who believe and are baptized? Not the eternal salvation, for you say truly that is promised to persevering obedience; he that endures to the end, shall be saved. It must mean, then, the present salvation, salvation from sin, the forgiveness of sins. But let us hear the Doctor once more: "We who call our- selves Baptists, are often more solicitous than Paedobaptists, to show that baptism amounts to nothing in salvation. And suppose we accomplish this *theoretically,* what is gained? Practically every man's interest in Christ must be tested by his character. We can never get clear of the connection which Christ has established. We can never repudiate the fact that salvation is promised to him who believes and is baptized. Whether we can understand it or not, it is a precious promise: 'He that believeth and is baptized, shall be saved.' Many have been afraid to teach this, lest they should impugn what are regarded, by all evangelical Christians, as cardinal doctrines. But more probably fear that others will charge them with making too much of baptism. [Most probably, Doctor, they are afraid of being called Campbellites!] This fear is absurd. [So we think.] The Bible declares a connection between baptism and salvation, not in mere allusions and figures, but in the great commission of the Son of God," pages 38, 40, 41-2. On page 47 the Doctor says: "The expression 'for the remission of sins,' would ordinarily indicate the same as the words, *'in order to* the remission of sins.' Professor Hacket, of Newton, who may be regarded as good authority, has translated, in the passage Acts ii. 38, the preposition *eis* by the words 'in order to.' In this, he adds, he will probably be sustained by the most distinguished scholars." On page 57 the Doctor says: "The wide-spread impression that there is no connection whatever between baptism and salvation, has no doubt greatly contributed to the indifference of many, as to their baptism, whether the act is sprinkling, pouring or immersing, or whether observed in infancy or upon a profession of faith. Jesus Christ is as much dishonored by making nothing of baptism, as he is by making everything of it."

Here, for the present, we close this number and leave our readers to ponder these few evidences of change in our Baptist brethren. JOHN ROGERS.

-----O-----

THE CONTROVERSY ON THE INFLUENCE OF THE SPIRIT.

IT appears more difficult at the present time to induce men to be content with simple Christianity, inspirit and practice, without any mixture with humanisms, than at any former period. The people have become so accustomed to leaning upon the human that they can scarcely conceive of the possibility of trusting wholly in the divine. We, as a body of people, have made wonderful strides in showing our neighbors of the sects, the schismatical tendency of all their creeds, the necessity of abandoning the whole of them and committing ourselves wholly to Christ, as our leader and instructor. But some of the controversies now going on show a wandering disposition, dissatisfied with the simple belief and practice of Christianity, as inconsistent with the unity of the Spirit and bond of peace as the adoption and maintenance of a human creed. After preaching the plain gospel of Christ, as the Disciples have done for more than thirty years, gathering some three hundred thousand souls to the fold of Christ, many of them from the contending parties around us and uniting them in the bond of peace and union, thus making ourselves felt as no other people have done in this century, a brother perceives where a slight mistake may have occurred. He becomes alarmed, looks upon all that has been done as nothing, and declares that nothing great and good will be accomplished till the evil is corrected. He just now perceives that there is danger of men resting their faith in *the word,* and not in the divine and glorious *person* revealed through the word. He thinks many are deceived, in relying simply upon the *word,* in the place of relying upon *Him* who gave the word. He now perceives the secret of there not being devotion, piety and zeal. It is found in the stupid mistake of believing *the truth,* in the place of believing in *Him* who is revealed through the truth.

This pretty little distinction is elaborated in many sermons, upon many pages, and upon a thousand tongues. The whole phalanx of *word-alone* men are now called to an account, and shown at great length, with profound learning and philosophy, that their stupid mistake has been, that they have believed the word, trusted in the word, relied upon the word, and preached the word, but lost sight of the glorious person of Christ, revealed through the word, and the Holy Spirit sent to be the Comforter of the saints. But no change follows all this wonderful discovery and very profound distinction.: No increase of piety, zeal, love or good works follow. No conversions of sinners follow any more than before, nor anything different, except contention, strife and confusion. On the other hand, here come the word alone men, accusing the former class with infidelity; or, at least, teaching doctrines tending to a rejection of the word, looking for something beyond and above the word, thus ignoring the word. These, too, now stand in defense of the faith, suffer for the truth, and sound the warning voice of dangerous doctrine! Some of the Disciples are on one side and some on the other, but the greater portion do not know what the controversy is about, but think there are good brethren on both sides. The only wonder with them is, that the parties should manifest so much irritability, use such severe and harsh language and appear so much alarmed. They can perceive no occasion for all this.

Where is the necessity of all this? When did an attorney ever find it necessary to inform the jury that the testimony was not the thing to be believed, but that that which was revealed through the testimony was what was to be believed. In what, except in religion, did any man ever think it necessary to caution the people that the *truth itself* is not what is to be believed, but that which is made known through the truth? Of what possible use can such metaphysical distinctions be to any human being? Did any man ever believe the truth of the gospel and not believe in him whom the truth of the gospel sets forth? Can any man believe the word and not believe him who uttered it? Can any man have confidence in the word and not have confidence in him who spoke the word? Is there such a thing as trusting in the word and not trusting in the author of the word? Can any man believe the word and not believe that which is revealed in the word? If you believe the testimony of a witness, do you not at the same time believe the witness and that which is communicated through the testimony of the witness? Can any man receive the word the Father gave Jesus, the word Jesus gave the Apostles, and the word which the Apostles by the Holy Spirit preached to us, and not believe the Father who gave the word to the Son? not believe the Son who gave the word to the Apostles? not believe the Apostles who gave the word to us? Can a man confide in the word the Father gave the Son, which the Son gave the Apostles and which the Apostles have given us, and not confide in the Father, the Son and the Apostles? Can a man confide in Jesus and not confide in his word? or confide in his word and not confide in him? Can a man confide in the Holy Spirit and not confide in his word? or confide in his word and not confide in him? Can a man receive the word of Jesus and not receive Jesus? Can any person believe the word of the Holy Spirit and not receive the Holy Spirit? Can anyone obey the word and not obey him who uttered the word? Can a man follow the word spoken by the Spirit and not follow the Spirit? Can a man be led by the word spoken by the Spirit and not be led by the Spirit? Are not all those led by the teachings of the Spirit, inscribed upon the pages of the Bible, led by the Spirit?

We put it to all those brethren engaged in this controversy, to produce an instance of one human being led by the teachings of the Spirit in the Bible, and not led by the Spirit; or one led by the Spirit. not led by his teachings in the Bible. "These things," says the Spirit of all wisdom, who guided the Apostles, or spoke through them, "are written that you might believe." Believe what? "That Jesus is the Christ the Son of God." They are not written that you may have a peculiar view of spiritual influence, but that you may believe that Jesus is the Christ, the Son of God. What are we to believe that for? "That you might have life through his name." Here is straight-forward work—no metaphysics nor speculations, but the plain truth to be believed and the object of believing it—that the believer might have life. The Holy Spirit comes not asking you to believe on himself, or some peculiar mode of his operation; but as a witness

INFLUENCE OF THE SPIRIT.

bearing testimony to Jesus. Hence Paul says: "The Holy Spirit also is a witness," and that no man can "call Jesus Lord, but by the Holy Spirit." At the Jordan, when the Lord was baptized and introduced to Israel, the Holy Spirit descended in a bodily form and rested upon him, thus indicating that all attention should be directed to him. When the Lord ascended to heaven, he sent the Spirit to the Apostles, to bring all things to their remembrance, guide them into all truth, inspire them, and thus through them spread out his entire testimonies upon the sacred pages, as left us from the bands of the four evangelists, that we might believe that Jesus is the Christ the Son of God, and that believing we might have life through his name. All this the Holy Spirit has done that we *might believe,* or to *enable us to believe.* Can we receive his testimony and not receive the glorious person of whom he testifies? or can we reject his testimony, without rejecting the glorious person of whom he testifies? Certainly not.

Shall we, then, confided in these divine testimonies of the Spirit, spread upon the sacred pages of the New Testament, that we *might believe* and set them before the world as sufficient to enable all men to believe? or shall we declare these testimonies of the Spirit insufficient, too weak and imperfect to enable the sinner to believe and maintain that the Spirit must come to the sinner and give him further evidence that his testimony, published eighteen centuries ago, believed by so many thousands and confided in by the holy martyrs even unto death, is true, and thus enable him to believe? Let any man who wishes to fall, question the all-sufficiency of the testimonies of the Spirit, set forth in the New Testament—testimony which we affirm to be complete and perfect—to which the Spirit himself forbids anything added or taken from. He who undertakes to depreciate this testimony, whether ignorantly or in unbelief, we care not what his design, weakens the gospel argument precisely to the amount of his influence, apologizes for the unbeliever, excuses him in his infidelity and strengthens his hands in sin. In the place of his being himself a believer in the testimony of the Spirit, he is trifling with it, creating distrust in the minds of others and subverting that which all admit to be the testimony of the Spirit of God.

There is but one safe course, and that is to follow the Apostles, preach the same truth preached by them, relying upon the same testimony upon which they rested as all-sufficient, and maintaining the self-evident truth, that *all men can believe it, when it is preached, and that they will be lost if they do not believe it.* This we are authorized to do, and this is all we can do. Even this can only be done by believers. Skeptics cannot do it effectually. But men who believe in Jesus with all the heart, can preach Jesus to others, with full confidence that they can believe in him also. They can bring all the testimonies furnished by the Holy Spirit, in the New Testament, before the mind of the unbeliever. But if these are not sufficient to enable a man to believe, they can do no more. The preacher may turn and preach to the sinner that these testimonies are not sufficient, and he must have assistance from some other source, but he cannot give that assistance and preaching does not make it come. If it does not come, who is to blame? Not the sinner; for he could not bring it. Not the preacher; for he could not bring it. Where lies the blame, then? The testimony the Spirit has given is not sufficient to enable the sinner to believe. He cannot obtain power to believe. The preacher has preached Christ and presented the testimonies of the Spirit, as found in the Scripture. But the sinner cannot believe till the Spirit comes and gives his testimony *efficiency.* The Spirit does not come. The man not only does not believe, but he cannot believe. Who is to blame? The Spirit, according to this very pious and spiritual theory, is to blame, because he did not come and do what he left undone when he gave his testimony, what neither the preacher nor the sinner could do, viz.: Give his testimony *efficiency.*

The difficulty in these times is not that the testimony of the Spirit, inscribed upon the pages of the New Testament, lacks *efficiency*, nor does the Spirit himself lack efficiency, nor does the Lord lack efficiency. The Lord, the Spirit, and the testimony are efficient, and do their work. The lack of efficiency is on the part of weak-minded and unbelieving or skeptical preachers and church-members. Let them become efficient, strong in faith, giving glory to God, and preach Jesus with great power, present the divine testimonies with full assurance of faith, and the work will go on. The Lord will do his work. The Spirit will do his work, and do it right. The testimony will do its work, and sinners will be saved. The trouble is to get the preachers to do their work, do it right, and thus operate rightly upon the world. Let us turn our attention more especially to men, and try and induce them to *operate right,* and all the balance will operate infallibly right. B. F.

-----o-----

Correspondance.

LEXINGTON, Mo., Aug. 7, 1857.

DEAR BRO. FRANKLIN:—I am much pleased with the REVIEW. To my mind it is sound on all the issues of the present erratic age. Moreover, it occupies the proper field, pleading for the great elementary principles of Christianity, while it does not ignore the importance of the disciples of Christ "going on to perfection." The old Jerusalem blade must be kept bright and wielded too, while there are sinners to be converted to Christ. When the time comes (should it ever come) when there are none to turn to the Lord, then may the " sword of the Spirit" be hung in the hall, or the gospel cease to be proclaimed, but not till then.

But I sat down to pen you a few items of intelligence in reference to the progress of the truth in our country. Sometime in February Bro. John W. McGarvey commenced a meeting in Wellington, and gained some five confessions. As the meeting promised fair, I was sent for. I went, Bro. McGarvey being compelled to leave. The meeting was continued a week longer and resulted in seventeen conversions.

In April Bro. McGarvey and Bro. Haley commenced a meeting in Richmond, and gained a few accessions;—both being compelled by former engagements to leave, the brethren sent for me again. I went and continued the meeting for some six days longer. That meeting closed with some eighteen additions.

On Friday before the first Lord's day in July Bro. Lard and myself commenced a meeting in Ray county. We constituted a congregation of Disciples—some eighteen or twenty strong—preached some ten days and gained ten confessions. Bro. Lard then came to Lexington and preached near one week; some three confessions and others added was the result.

On Saturday before the third Lord's day in July Bro. L. B. Wilkes, President of Christian Female College at Columbia, commenced a meeting at Union Meeting House in Pettis county, and continued the meeting till Thursday following with nineteen conversions. The meeting then adjourned till Saturday, during which time the brethren dispatched a messenger to me, bearing a letter, urging me to come forthwith. I accordingly set out for Union, fifty miles distant, and met on Lord's day morning brethren Wilkes, Hancock, and a crowded house. We continued the meeting till Monday week following. The result was glorious. About one hundred were added; some eighty-five or more by confession and baptism. Several of these disciples were among the best citizens of our country. The larger portion of the converts were youths and maidens. May the great Head of the church pour out his blessings upon these converts and preserve them to his eternal Kingdom. To the Lord be all the praise. Your brother in Christ,

ALLEN WRIGHT.

-----O-----

Success of the Gospel.

WAVERLY, ILL., July 29, 1857.

DEAR BRO. FRANKLIN:—I am very thankful that I am able to inform you that the glorious cause for which we, in our weakness, labor, is onward in "these parts." The gospel of Christ is telling powerfully in this part of Illinois. There seems to be a "general awakening" upon the subject of salvation. I will not say it seems to be, but there *is a mighty* "awakening" upon the part of the Disciples to the publishing of the ancient gospel to every creature.

Since I saw you at Macomb, I have had the pleasure to see over one hundred enter the church of God .for salvation. A large majority by confession and immersion, yet not a few who have hitherto been called "Methodists," "Baptists," etc.

I am pleased to see that the people are beginning to see it is better to be a *Christian* than anything else —that it honors Christ more to be so called. We preach no more "our church," "this branch of the church," "the reformation," etc., but preach to them Jesus—Jesus crucified, buried and risen—a mighty Savior. We endeavor to make the issue directly between them and Christ; then we can more confidently appeal to them for submission to him as the Christ.

I was very sorry to be compelled to leave Macomb before the conclusion of the meeting; but it was so, and probably for the better.

I have not, as yet, made a general effort in behalf of the cause of missions, owing to some local matters which seemed to forbid for a short time. But I have been, all this time, making known the nature, design, etc., of the General Society. The most of the brethren are "for it." In fact, I have to hear the first dissenting voice yet. I think about the 1st of October we will be able to tell, practically, how we stand upon the subject, and that, in my judgment, is better than *much* theorizing.

It is proper to say that, in this part of the State, we have had to struggle hard to make the different religionists sensible that we were in the community. But now, thank God, it is a fact no longer to be concealed. We have our heads clear above water, and can begin to look around and see what the gospel has done for us. And oh! how compatible with the spirit of the gospel to breathe out, "Go tell it to all nations."

May God bless you, Bro. F., in your mighty efforts in behalf of the true spirit of the gospel. You shall hear from us soon again.

J. S. SWEENEY.

COLUMBIA, MO., July 11, 1857.

DEAR BRO. FRANKLIN Brethren Wright and Lard had some four confessions at Antioch in Ray county, Missouri. Three of them Methodists. Meeting going on when I left.

J. A. SIDENER.

CADIZ; IND., July 18, 1857.

DEAR BRO. FRANKLIN The brethren feel greatly encouraged. Last Sabbath the Lord added one more to the saved. Mrs. Andrew Ricks, a very intelligent lady, came forward and made the good confession and was born again, Bro. G. W. Shortridge minister.

JOHN C. BECK.

CRITTENDEN, MO., July 12, 1857.

DEAR BRO. FRANKLIN:—Eld. Martin Scott preached for us to-day at the Pilot Grove Church and gained nine additions to the good cause—five by confession and baptism, and four by recommendation; one of the latter was from the Baptists. To God be all the glory. Yours truly,

W. S. BROWN.

LANCASTER, ILL., July 22, 1857.

DEAR BRO. FRANKLIN:—The good cause for which we plead is advancing in this county (Wabash). We immersed five at Lancaster on last Lord's day. Bro. Wm. Courter, the county evangelist, baptized seven on the second Lord's day; at the same time we had two additions at Lick Pearie—one by confession and immersion, and one reclaimed. We just now learned that there were twelve additions at Turner's school house on last Lord's day, under the labors of Bro Morgan. The Lord bless them all!

B. J. PAYNE.

BARNESVILLE, OHIO, July 26, 1857.

DEAR BRO. FRANKLIN:—This note is to inform you that Bro. Myers and myself commenced a meeting at this place about two weeks ago, and the result so far has been highly gratifying. Up to this date there have been twenty-eight additions, with an increasing interest.

This has always been a stronghold of Methodism, but the people have begun to *think* and ask questions, a sure indication of the triumph of truth.

Respectfully your brother in Christ,

W. L. MOORE.

RUSSELVILLE, ILL., August 8, 1857.

DEAR BRO FRANKLIN:—Knowing that anything relating to the success of the gospel of Christ will be interesting, I send you an account of a meeting held here on the 3rd Lord's day in July and Friday and

Saturday before, by Bros. Joseph Wolf and J. S. Howard, and the meeting closed on Lord's day evening and commenced again by Bro. J. H. Sloan on the Lord's day following, the result of both meetings being forty-three additions to the church—twenty-eight of the number confessing Christ and were immersed into his name.

Yours in Christ,
W. T. SHEPHERD.

LEXINGTON, MO., Aug. 15, 1857.

BRO. FRANKLIN:—Yesterday evening I got home from Dover. Their annual meeting which has been kept up for more than thirty days, closed yesterday morning. During the meeting there were eighteen persons who "heard, believed and were baptized." Brethren J. W. McGarvey, T. P. Haley and myself conducted the meeting.

ALLEN WRIGHT.

CLARKSVILLE, MO., July 31, 1857.

We have enjoyed some very "refreshing seasons" lately in witnessing the surrender of many to the claims of the gospel. I give the results at different places. At Paynesville five were added in June last; at Middletown, forty; at Indian Creek, eight. Bro. T. Ford assisted much at the two last named points. At Clarkesville brethren Smith, Haley and Grandfield closed a meeting with sixteen additions; and at Paynesville, Bro. Wiles has just closed with eleven more;—in all eighty within the last five weeks. May they all be enabled to live worthy of their high calling.

Truly your brother in Christ,
J. J. ERRETT.

CARLISLE, KY., Aug. 6, 1857.

On Thursday the 6th inst., we closed a meeting of a week's continuance at this place. Bro. B. Franklin was our speaker. He delivered thirteen discourses during the meeting, which were listened to by large and interested audiences. They were highly practical, bearing directly upon the great religious questions of the day. But he delivered *one* on the evils of schism, and the gospel plan of union, of great point and power, to a very large and profoundly attentive audience, embracing, it was said, two clergymen. Our 'meeting resulted in twelve accessions to our cause here; eight by confession and immersion, and four by letter and otherwise. The community was much interested, and could our meeting have been protracted, I think much more might have been accomplished. It was an unusually busy time, in the midst of oat and hay harvest, and what was more unfavorable, embracing our August election.

Bro. Franklin is becoming more and more efficient, both as an evangelist and an editor. May the Lord long preserve him to promote the union of his people and the conversion of the world!

JOHN ROGERS.

Obituaries.

DIED, in Millersburg, Bourbon county, Ky., on the 20th ult., and in the twentieth year of her age, Sister LUCY P., wife of Elder John I. Rogers. They had been married two years and nine months. She had come like a blessing or a joy into the family, and had only time to win all hearts and make them realize how necessary she was to their happiness, when they are called to mourn for her. How mysterious are the ways of God! But he doeth all things well, and all things work together for good to those who love him. We may mourn for ourselves, but not for her; for we know that she is happy. With an intelligent and cultivated mind and a pure heart, she embraced the Savior in the days of her youth and became an "Israelite indeed, in whom there was no guile." Those who knew her best loved her most; for she was remarkable for her retiring modesty, as well as for her deep and warm affection. Her most intimate friends alone can realize how much "they will miss her at home," or how deep are the wounds that have been made by her death.

Most deeply do we sympathize with the family in their afflictions. May God shield the little orphan babe, bless the husband and family in their bereavement and sanctify the affliction of all her friends, so that when called hence, we also may leave such hallowed memories behind us.   S. W. IRVIN.

DIED, in Fleming county, Ky., on the 7th of May, 1857, in the fifty-ninth year of her age, Sister MARY, wife of Jeremiah Hall. Without a moments warning, while attending to her daily avocations, she was prostrated by apoplexy, and in seven hours was a corpse. But although his approach was so unexpected, death did not find her unprepared. She became a Christian when only fourteen or fifteen years of age, and while she lived she honored her profession. As a daughter, a mother, a wife, a church-member, she was a model of Christian excellence. As a woman professing godliness, she had learned how to adorn herself with good works and to show piety at home. None more than she deserved the beautiful epitaph written by Solomon, for the woman who feared the Lord and guided her affairs with discretion: Give her of the fruits of her hands, and let her own works praise her in the gates. (Prov. xxxi. 31.)

DIED, on the 24th of July, a little more than two months from .the death of his mother, and after a painful illness of three weeks, THOMAS JEFFERSON, oldest son of Jeremiah and Mary Hall.

The deceased was in the twenty-ninth year of his age, and had been from his early youth a member of the church of Christ. Kind, amiable and affectionate, everybody loved him. He was much like his mother, to whom he was fondly attached. How soon he has followed her to the better land!

In the most tender sympathies of humanity do we condole with the bereaved family in their double affliction. . May God sanctify their sorrows.

S.W. IRVIN.

THE AMERICAN CHRISTIAN REVIEW.

VOL. II.   CINCINNATI, OCTOBER, 1857.   No. 10.

HOW TO BE SAVED---A DISCOURSE.

BY DR. B. F. HALL.

"What must I do to be saved?"—ACTS XVI. 30.

A SOLEMN and important question this, and one that calls for a serious, considerate answer, matured by a careful investigation of the sacred Scriptures with earnest prayer. It is a subject fraught with deep and abiding interest to the world, for with it is connected the present and future happiness of many souls. The answer that should be given to this thrilling question will depend upon several circumstances, which must first be considered.

Did the question refer to the *principle* on which salvation is offered, the answer would be, "It is of *grace*—the grace of God for "by grace we are saved;" Eph. ii. 8. Did the inquirer allude to the *procuring cause* of salvation, the answer would be, "*The blood of Christ,* which alone cleanses from all sin." Without this there is no remission.

The question before us, however, is one of *means*—means to be used by the sinner in order to obtain the salvation procured by the blood of Jesus, and offered to mankind on the principle of divine favor. "What must I DO?" "What must *I* do?" "WHAT must I do?"

But, considering the question as referring to means, still there are several circumstances which exercise a modifying influence upon the answer, which must be settled as preliminary to the investigation of the main subject.

1. Under what *dispensation* is the question asked? We need not inform the reader, that God has vouchsafed three dispensations of favor and mercy to fallen, sinful man—the *Patriarchal,* the *Jewish* and the *Christian.* Under the former two, God spake to the people by prophets; under this—the Christian or gospel dispensation—he speaks to us by his Son Jesus, and his inspired Apostles. Under the preceding dispensations, the terms of salvation were not the same which are required of sinners now. Faith, piety and obedience to God have always been the conditions of salvation; but the things to be believed, and the commands to be obeyed are, many of them, different now from what they were then. The Old Testament contains the terms of salvation to those who lived under the former dispensations; and, in order to be saved, they had to obey the laws given them. They were required, among other duties, to offer sacrifices of bulls and goats; to go up to

Jerusalem to worship, and to perform many ceremonies which are not required of us. Nay, the Apostle assures us, that if we were to do such things it would be apostasy from Christ and rebellion against his government. Heb. vi. 4-6; x. 26-29. And, again, the same Apostle informs us, that under the new dispensation God saves us by means which he did not require to be used under the old. Titus iii. 4-5.

The New Testament commenced after the resurrection of Jesus Christ. Hence what he said to the paralytic—"thy sins are all forgiven thee"—or to the guilty Mary—"go and sin no more"—or to the dying thief—"to-day shalt thou be with me in Paradise"—is not said to us. The conditions of our salvation are not contained in these instructions to those persons. I may go further, and assert that the conditions of our salvation or pardon are not to be found in the entire Old Testament, nor in anything commanded in the New prior to the resurrection of Jesus Christ. Perhaps, I should rather say, that Christ, after his resurrection, gave forth the law of his kingdom, in which are contained all things required of us to believe and do in order to our salvation. This is the gospel. It contains his address to every sinner under heaven. It is addressed to us and to all who have lived since the day of Pentecost, or who shall live until the end of time.

2. There is another preliminary question to be settled. What does the inquirer mean by the question—"What must I do to *be saved?*" What does he mean by the word *saved?* It does not always refer to the same deliverance. There are three things which, in the Scriptures, are called salvation. They are all *deliverances,* but they are not all the *same* deliverance. One is a deliverance from temporal evils; the second is a deliverance from past sins, and consists in pardon, and is enjoyed by all Christians in this life; the third has reference to the heavenly state, and is to be enjoyed after the resurrection. It will be perceived, at once, how materially the answer is varied by the import of the question.

3. "What must I do to be saved?" The answer to this thrilling question will depend also on the *condition of* the person who propounds it. Is he a saint or a sinner? a believer or an unbeliever? a penitent or an impenitent sinner? It will be manifest to all that the same answer would not be suitable to all these various classes of persons.

Whether one be rich or poor, bond or free, a Jew or a Gentile, is immaterial; for all stand in the same relation to the gospel, and God is no respecter of persons, and the same answer is suitable to all. It is equally true that the same answer is to be given to sinners of different grades—for there are different grades—even should there be ten thousand of them; for their character is the same, although it may appear in different shades.

The only thing that constitutes a difference in the subjects of gospel address, is *character. Of* these there are four classes, notwithstanding all are in the same state. These are all mentioned in the Bible, and are found in the Pagan jailor, the three thousand Pentecostians, Saul of Tarsus, and Cornelius, the Roman centurion.

We wish not to be misunderstood. By the word *state* we mean something different from character. Persons of very opposite character may be in the same state, and persons of the same character may be in opposite states. To be a citizen of this Republic is to be in a state of *freedom.* But in this state there are many different characters. *Life* is a state; so is *matrimony*. But there are very different characters in both. It is equally true that the same character may exist in very opposite states. There may be republicans in every government on earth. *Sin* is a state; so also is *justification*. Every person is in one or other of these states; hence everyone is either a saint or a sinner. But all persons in the sinful state have not the same traits of character;

for some are much worse, more sinful, than others. Some are the furthest possible removed from God and truth, while others approach nearer, and enjoy the twilight of the gospel—they "are not far from the kingdom of heaven." Some have scarcely a characteristic feature of a Christian, while others have many lineaments strongly marked. In drawing the portrait of a Christian there would not be the same amount of labor to perform in both cases. In one every line requires to be traced; in the other there is but the filling up.

We have mentioned four different characters all in the same state—the state of sin. All inquire what they must do to be *saved,* meaning thereby the *remission of their past sins.* Hence the answer to all, as far as it respects their state, will of course be the same, while the qualifications for this change of state may be very different. Each must seek the qualifications in which he is deficient. These are precisely the circumstances which vary the answers given in the Acts of Apostles by the inspired teachers, to those who propounded to them the question—"What must I do to be saved?"

Let us briefly examine these cases.

1. The first that presents itself is that of the *Pagan jailor at Philippi.* He was utterly ignorant of divine things. He knew nothing of God and of his Son Jesus Christ. It is even doubted whether he had ever heard of God's Messiah until Paul and Silas, for a work of benevolence, had received each thirty-nine stripes, and were then committed to the care of the jailor, who received a strict charge to keep them secure, and to have them ready for trial the ensuing day. The jailor thrust them into the inner prison. There confined—instead of meditating revenge upon the authorities which, contrary to law, had them beaten with stripes—and though under great suffering and agony, they prayed, and the Lord blessed them; and they raised their voices in songs of praise to his ever-blessed name. An earthquake shook the prison, and its foundations trembled; the massive doors flew open, and the irons dropped from the hands and feet of the prisoners. The jailor, awaking from his soft slumbers, by the strange noise in the prison, sprang up, and seeing the prison doors open, and supposing the inmates had fled, drew his sword, and would have killed himself, knowing that his life would be taken for the prisoners whom he supposed to have fled; but just as he was in the act of plunging the sword to his heart, the apostle Paul, inspired by the benevolence of the gospel, cried out at the top of his voice—"Do yourself no harm, for we are all here." The jailor, having called for lights, rushed in, greatly agitated, and fell prostrate before Paul and Silas, and, conducting them out of the prison, said—"O, sirs, what must I do to be saved?" They told him to believe on the Lord Jesus Christ, and he should be saved, and his family. The answer they made him was adapted to his condition as a Pagan, who had never heard of Jesus Christ, and who was entirely ignorant of the method of salvation. This answer was intended more to catch his attention and calm his agitated mind, than to furnish him with all the means of salvation through Jesus Christ. It had the effect intended; and as soon as they perceived that his attention was arrested and fixed, they proceeded to lay open before him the whole plan of salvation through a crucified Savior. So pleasing was the intelligence that he was not content to enjoy the instruction alone; he called up his whole family from their midnight slumbers to share the boon of heaven. When they were all assembled, Paul and Silas announced to them the word of God, and taught them the way of salvation through Christ. Luke, the sacred historian, says—"They spoke to him the word of the Lord, and to all that were in his house." The word of the Lord which they declared to the

jailor and his family was something in addition to what they announced to the jailor in their first address. Hence the gospel consists of something more than the words—"Believe in the Lord Jesus Christ, and thou shalt be saved." The apostle Paul, in another place, says the gospel consists of the following facts, viz.: "That Christ died for our sins, was buried and rose again the third day." Again, he told the Corinthians that he would declare to them nothing but Jesus Christ and him crucified. These facts he did not announce to the jailor in the first address; therefore, in preaching to him the gospel, he made known something more than that he should believe in Jesus Christ. Hence no person should imagine that telling the people to believe in Jesus Christ is preaching to them the whole gospel. They cannot believe by being merely told to do so. Facts must be presented, and evidence adduced, to enable them to believe. For faith depends upon testimony. All this Paul and Silas had to do before the jailor and his family could believe.

It is further manifest that they preached baptism to the jailor and his family; for no sooner had Paul and Silas preached to them the word of the Lord, than the jailor took these servants of the Lord to some place where he could get water sufficient to bathe their stripes, and he and all his family were immediately baptized. Now what could have put it into a heathen jailor's head to be baptized, unless Paul and Silas had preached it to him as a part of the word of God?

Christ told his Apostles to go into all the world and preach the gospel to every creature, and to announce that he who shall believe and be baptized shall be saved. They must, then, have preached baptism to the jailor and his family; for they could not otherwise have announced to them the promises of the gospel.

2. The second instance which we shall notice when the question is asked, "What shall we do?" is that of the three thousand, recorded in the second chapter of Acts. It was the day on which the great national feast was celebrated by the Jews, commemorative of the giving of their law upon Sinai. An immense number of Jews, from all parts of the world, and from among all nations, and of all languages, were assembled. The little company of Christ's friends were assembled together in one place. The Holy Spirit descended with a great noise, resembling that of a tempest. A lambent flame surrounded their heads in the shape of divided tongues and disappeared in their persons; and, being filled with the Holy Spirit, they began to speak in numerous languages, which they had never learned, the wonderful works of God. The report of this before unheard-of event spread with wonderful rapidity, and brought together a great multitude who were exceedingly perplexed to find an adequate cause for the phenomenon. Some could only ask, in astonishment, What can this mean? while others declared in derision that they were filled with wine. At this moment Peter, under the influence of God's inspiring Spirit, arose in the midst of the eleven other Apostles, and made the grandest and most sublime disclosures the world ever heard. He proved most clearly the Messiahship of Jesus from the Jewish prophets, and from what the twelve themselves had witnessed. He charged upon the Jews the horrid crime of murdering God's Messiah. The blood-stains were scarcely yet removed from their garments. Their hearts were made deeply to feel the guilt. Peter convinced them that Jesus was then alive and seated on the throne of the universe, and that the world was placed under his dominion. Terror-smitten and alarmed, lest the Messiah should take vengeance on them, and deeply impressed with a sense of their guilt, three thousand cried out, in the bitterness of grief, to Peter and the other Apostles, "Men and brethren, what shall we do?" We could not expect the same answer

to be returned to the question here that was given by Paul and Silas to the Philippian jailor. They had been convinced, by the lucid and overwhelming discourse of Peter, that Jesus was the Messiah, and that he was exalted to the heavens and was authorized to dispense pardons to rebel sinners. The apostle Peter did not tell them to believe, for they did believe already, that Jesus was God's Messiah. It was this truth that pierced them to the heart and made them cry out for mercy. He, therefore, directed them to obey the next commands which were necessary to their acceptance with God and their being received into the number of the disciples. "Repent and be baptized, every one of you, in the name of Jesus Christ, for the remission of sins, and you shall receive the gift of the Holy Spirit." They heard with joy the pleasing intelligence, and cheerfully complied with the conditions of pardon and salvation through Jesus Christ, and the same day they were numbered with the disciples of the murdered but now risen Jesus.

3. *The next ease is that of Saul.* He was a young man of gigantic intellect, finished education, and great energy of character and ardor in any cause he espoused. He had just completed his studies of the Jewish law, and was about to enter upon the duties of his profession, when the religion of Christ began to excite such a deep and general interest in Judea. Conscientiously believing it to be a heresy, he conceived it to be his duty to labor for its extermination. Accordingly he set out with his accustomed zeal to oppose the disciples of Jesus Christ. His first act was holding the garments of the young men who stoned to death Stephen, the protomartyr. His zeal increasing in the ratio of its exercise or indulgence, and his sensibility subsiding in proportion as his acts of persecution multiplied, he was soon prepared for the most horrid and unnatural acts of violence. Not satisfied with ordinary achievements, and unable to satiate his thirst for blood in his immediate vicinity, he applied to the chief priests in Jerusalem for letters of authority to Damascus, a city about a hundred and twenty miles distant, to bring bound thence to Jerusalem all who called on the name of Jesus. Men and women were equally the victims of his hate, and the only crime of which he pretended they were guilty, was that of worshipping Christ. How unnatural and blind is the spirit of persecution! It respects neither sex nor age, and makes no distinction between innocence and guilt. His hatred of Christians, and his determination to exterminate them from the earth, increased as he prosecuted his journey. He breathed out threatenings and slaughter against the followers of Christ, whose only crime was their attachment to Christ and devotion to his cause. As he approached the city of Damascus, about the hour of noon, when the orb of day rode in matchless splendor through the cloudless heavens, a light intense and greatly above the noonday splendors of the sun, shone round about him; and, under the weight of his insupportable effulgence, he fell to the earth, and, for the first time, suspected that all was not right with him. Paul was a most conscientious man, and the moment he began to doubt the propriety of his course in the honesty of his heart, he sought the way of the Lord and the path to heaven. Having witnessed the miracle, and very rationally concluded that it must be designed for some purpose respecting himself, and anxious to understand its import, he inquired, "Who art thou, Lord?" How greatly astonished must Paul have been when a voice responded, "I am Jesus whom thou persecutest." Until that moment Paul had not the most distant idea that Jesus was alive, much less that he was seated in the heavens and swaying the scepter of universal empire. Paul was not like many who, on obtaining a glimpse of light, close their eyes, lest they should be convinced of their

errors and compelled to abandon their present ground and suffer the mortification and brook the sneers and ridicule of the ignorant and debased, for having changed their religious sentiments, and perhaps suffer pecuniary loss for their honesty. Paul was honest. Having obtained a glimpse, he opened wide his eyes to gaze upon the broad sheets of heavenly light. The moment he discovered his error and learned that Jesus was the Messiah, he gave in his allegiance to him as king, and was eager to learn his duty and the will of Christ concerning him. "Lord," said he, "what wilt thou have me do?" Christ did not inform him what he should do, but directed him to the place where he could obtain the desired information. Why Christ did not directly answer Paul's question, is a very puzzling question to some minds; but it is easily answered when the divine procedure is once looked into. Christ's kingdom had already been set up. His officers were appointed, and each was acting in his proper place. The ministry of reconciliation had been committed to his ambassadors. It was their province to announce to penitent sinners the terms of reconciliation—the conditions of acceptance with God. He therefore directed Paul to the place where he could learn all that was necessary on this subject. It was the more fitting to do so, because a minister of Jesus Christ was to have something to do in his coming into the kingdom of Messiah. Paul, however, obeyed the command of Jesus to go into Damascus, where he was told he would be informed of all things he should be required to perform. Being unable to see from the intense splendor of the light he had seen, he was led by the hands of of his companions to Damascus. He waited and prayed three days. At length Ananias came in and, taking him by the hand, told him to "arise and be baptized and wash away his sins, calling on the name of the Lord."

Here the question arises—Why did not Ananias answer Paul as Paul himself subsequently answered the Philippian jailor? or, as Peter had previously answered the three thousand? The answer is easy. Paul was already a believer in Jesus Christ, and therefore could not consistently be called on to believe. The scenes he had witnessed on the way to Damascus had convinced him that Jesus, the Nazarene, was the Messiah. Nor could he be required to repent, like the three thousand on the day of Pentecost, because he had already repented deeply and sorely during the space of three days—the longest period we have an account in Scripture of any one being under repentance. Paul's heart and life were changed already. He now loved the Lord Jesus, whereas he once hated him. He deplored his wretched condition and deeply regretted having so long rebelled against Jesus Christ. But his state was yet unchanged. It was for the purpose of effecting this that he was told to be baptized.

The phrase "wash away your sins" is, of course, to be understood figuratively. As the body is cleansed by being washed in water, so is the soul purified from the defilements of sin, by faith in the blood of Christ, in obedience to the commands of Heaven.

There is one other case which we shall examine, materially different from all the preceding. It is the case of Cornelius, the Roman centurion. In the time of Cornelius, Judea was a Roman province. In this province Caesar had soldiers posted at military stations, among which was Caesarea. Cornelius was the commander at this post. Though brought up a Pagan, he embraced the Jewish religion—which, in all probability, he did while at Caesarea. Nor was he a mere nominal professor. So far from it, he became noted for his piety and alms-deeds. He was a pattern to the community in which he lived. All regarded him as a man of great piety and moral worth. The winds that blew chill and cold upon the poverty-stricken, but of the widow and orphan, wafted to them his name and told of his noble deeds of charity. They flocked to him in scores and gathered around his door in mournful, yet hopeful, clusters. He gazed upon them as they stood half-starved, thin-clad and weeping. Pity swelled his bosom, and his hand dealt out his bounties in great profusions. The angel of mercy with delight beheld his numerous deeds of charity, and flying up to God, spread the report of them through the realms of bliss, and the recording angel wrote them down in heaven. Thus was Cornelius esteemed on earth and approved in heaven. His prayers gave him audience with the Deity; and, together with his confident reliance on the word of God and his uniform righteousness, made him a favorite with all heaven. Accordingly, an angel was sent to tell Cornelius to send for Peter, who would inform him what he should do to be saved; for, with all his faith, piety and alms-deeds, he was still not saved. True, he was saved from the love and practice of sin, but not from its state. His heart was right with God, and his character, as far as it could be formed under surrounding influences, was such as God approved. But he was not in a saved state. And it was for the purpose of telling him how to get into this state, that Peter was to be sent for. Being sent for, he came. And what did he tell Cornelius to do to be saved? Did he tell him to change his conduct? To have given him such instruction would have been to tell him to change from good to bad. He could not tell him to be sorry for the past, unless he wished him to repent of noble and god-like deeds, which earth and heaven approved. Nothing in his character could have been altered for the better. All that yet remained, appertained to his state; and it was in respect to this that Peter instructed him. As baptism has respect to state alone, all Peter told him to do was to be baptized. He complied, unhesitatingly, with the divine command, and thereby came into the church of Jesus Christ, into the enjoyment of all its blessings and privileges.

We learn from the foregoing that sin consists in its love, practice and state; and that deliverance from the love of sin by faith in Jesus Christ does not constitute the whole process of the deliverance wrought for men by Jesus Christ in effecting their movery from sin. Faith saves them from the love of sin, but, of itself, it can do no more. It leaves them still under all the unholy influences appertaining to the sinful state. To leave them there, would be like converting the subjects of the King of Spain, or the Autocrat of Russia, to the principles of Republicanism, and then to leave them there, where they would more than likely return to their former principles; or, if they did not, where they would make no advances in knowledge and be of no benefit to others. The Christian religion is designed to place all its subjects under influences favorable to the formation of a character for the society of heaven, and in a field of usefulness to others. Hence the organization of the church state; and faith, repentance and baptism are all necessary to admittance into this state. Hence the inspired teachers of mankind, under the reign of favor, never stop short in their instructions of the church-state. They begin with the heart, and conclude with the state, as far as becoming a Christian is concerned.

We may learn, also, that persons of very opposite characters may be in the same state. The jailor, the three thousand, Saul of Tarsus and Cornelius were all in the same state before their baptism; but how opposite were their characters! The jailor was a Pagan; the three thousand were wicked Jews; Saul was a persecutor of the saints, and Cornelius was a devout worshipper of the God of heaven. All changed their state in the same way; by baptism. For this it was appointed, but for nothing more.

Finally, we are taught that it does not

require a long time for God to effect the process of conversion. The longest on record is that of Saul, and he was only three days a penitent; and that was occupied in qualifying him for the apostolic office. All the rest were effected in a few hours at most. And it appears that the jailor was changed from a Pagan to a Christian in the space of one hour. His conscience in the evening was so little disturbed that, after he had, as he supposed, secured Paul and Silas in the dungeon of his jail, he returned to rest and soon fell into a sound and refreshing sleep, from which he was awakened only by an earthquake and the uproar in the prison. The moment he heard the alarm, he sprang up and ran to the jail with sword in hand. Seeing the doors all open, and supposing the prisoners to have escaped, he was about to plunge the sword into his heart, when the voice of Paul prevented the horrid deed. How far, how very far, was he at that time from being a Christian! So far that he was in the very act of committing suicide. From that moment the current of his feelings began to change, and under the lucid and overwhelming exhibitions of the gospel of Christ by Paul and Silas, under the divine influence, in one hour he was a Christian. What a change! and how soon effected! God can soon do the work of conversion when the soul becomes willing; and it is effected by means of the word of the Lord. See the evidences of his change. When Paul and Silas were committed to his charge, all covered with their own gore, and suffering from the stripes they had received, and faint from hunger and thirst, without binding up their wounds or washing their stripes, he thrust them, unfed and with burning thirst, into prison, and turned the key upon them. Now, at the hour of midnight, he takes them to water and bathes their stripes, and is baptized, he and his whole family. He then brings them into his house and places food before them—then he and all his family express the joy they felt on believing in the Lord. The spirit of Christianity leads its subjects in the right path, imbues their minds with its principles, and excites them to noble deeds, without labored arguments and long persuasion. Such are the evidences of the jailor's conversion, and how short a time was required for its accomplishment. God's grace is the same now that it was then; and, sinners, you are as much the objects of divine regard as was the Philippian jailor. The gospel is still the power of God to all who believe in Jesus Christ. And if you will hear with the attention of the jailor and submit to Jesus with the same cheerfulness, you shall be saved as certainly as he, and in as short a time. How precious are your few, fleeting moments! Time is bearing you upon its rapid tide to a shoreless eternity. Hell or heaven depends upon the uncertainties of an hour. The jailor's submission to Jesus Christ decided his destiny; and it was done in a moment. Felix's rejection of the gospel announced by Paul decided his fate; and that, too, was the result of a moment. The crowd that listened to the discourse of Stephen little thought, perhaps, that the few moments which elapsed during that discourse fixed their condition eternally. This, my friends, may be the critical period with you.

"There is a tide in the affairs of men,
Which, if taken at the flood,
Leads on to fortune."

But, should that favorable period be neglected—should the tide once go out, it may never return to you. Then, we entreat you, embrace the present opportunity. Let it not pass unimproved. With the jailor, believe; with the three thousand, repent; and with Saul of Tarsus and the devout Cornelius, be baptized in the name of the Lord Jesus; and then, should you be faithful until death, an entrance shall be administered to you abundantly, into the everlasting kingdom of our Lord and Savior Jesus Christ.

All the above instructions, you will perceive, are adapted to sinners and that they are addressed to such.

When Christians are taught by the inspired Apostles what they must do to be *saved*—the word being used in the sense of remission of sins—for, alas! Christians do sin—they are told to repent of their sins and to pray for divine forgiveness. "If we (Christians) confess and forsake our sins, God is faithful and just to forgive us our sins, and to cleanse us from all unrighteousness."

When Christians are further instructed how they are to be saved in the sense of getting to heaven—of gaining the peaceful shores of eternal rest, they are told to "deny themselves of all ungodliness and worldly lust, to live soberly, righteously and godly in the present world, looking out for the blessed hope and glorious appearing of the great God and Savior Jesus Christ;" to "add to their faith, courage; and to courage, knowledge; and to knowledge, temperance; and to temperance, patience; and to patience, godliness; and to godliness, love or benevolence." And we are assured that, when this lovely cluster of Christian virtues grow and pervade the heart, the soul is neither slothful nor inactive in God's service. And those who possess these graces, will have ministered to them an abundant entrance into the everlasting kingdom of our Lord and Savior Jesus Christ. Thus Christians are exhorted to work out their own salvation with fear and trembling, assumed that God works in them to will and to do of his good pleasure. And they who thus live and labor, will, in the great day of the Lord, be accepted of their Redeemer. They shall enter his everlasting kingdom; they shall be saved with an everlasting salvation, and shall have right to the tree of life, that blossoms forever fresh and fair in the paradise of God.

CARLYLE says—"Make yourself an honest man, and then you may be sure there is one rascal less in the world."

DIALOGUE OF DEVILS.
NUMBER V.

Present—DIABOLOS, APOLLYON, DAIMONION and LUCIFER. Subject—The Most Successful Method of Subverting and Defeating the Word of God and the Mission of Christ.

DIABOLOS.—Gentlemen, it is now over three months since we have had a meeting. I have no doubt you have all been busy, as I have been myself; and, I trust, not without effect. I hope you will, therefore, proceed at once with any reports of success or suggestions you may have to offer touching our work.

APOLLYON.—I have been out preaching since I saw you, and, I think, have done a vast amount for our cause.

LUCIFER.—I should like to know what you have been preaching!

APOLLYON.—I have been preaching *charity*. My mission has been—1st, To preachers; 2nd, To hearers. I am preaching the doctrine that all men should have more charity. I lay down the doctrine, that there are good and bad in all churches, and that it is no difference what church a man belongs to, so that the heart is right. I maintain that whatever a man thinks right, that is right to him. The doctrine I advocate is, that the preacher should declare his honest convictions of truth and let other people alone. I also teach the people that, when a preacher makes any allusion to other churches, or the doctrine of other men, they should refuse to hear him, discard him and try to put him down.

LUCIFER.—But, I should think you would have them preaching every kind of doctrine and establish nothing!

APOLLYON.—Certainly; that is precisely what I aim at; it matters nothing what errors men imbibe, or maintain, so that we can keep their minds off from the truth. There is but one right way, but many wrong ways. We must not be choice about the wrong ways. It is but little difference which one of them a man follows, so that we keep him from the right way. It is but little difference what doctrine a man holds, provided he does not hold the truth.

DIABOLOS.—You are right, most worthy Apollyon, and there is wherein our work is easy. We need care nothing what a man believes, so that it is not the truth. Our work is to throw everything into doubt and uncertainty. To do that effectually, we must show that one way is as good as another—that almost any doctrine can be proved, and that nothing can be proved, and that people must have charity for all.

APOLLYON.—That is the principle precisely. When disputes arise between erroneous systems, we must be indifferent who gains the victory, be a little on both sides, declare both *evangelical* and *orthodox!* But if ever an issue between error and truth is formed, which we should avert as far as possible, we must be on the part of error and ever on the alert, with all the friends of error, declaring that it *is truth* and triumphing.

DAIMONION.—Gentlemen, what think you of debates? Do they serve a good purpose in defeating the truth?

DIABOLOS.—They do in some instances, when they are the right kind and in the right places; but most frequently they do our cause harm.

LUCIFER.—How can that be? Can the same thing be in favor of our cause and against it?

DIABOLOS.—It depends entirely on *the kind* of an issue, the *debatants* and the *place* of debate. I have instigated some debates that have done our cause great service, and others, again, I have known that did our cause much harm.

LUCIFER.—Can you give us some examples? Where would it be prudent in us to instigate a debate?

DIABOLOS.—Any place where truth and righteousness prevail; peace, love, order and prosperity abound; provided you start the *right kind* of a debate.

LUCIFER.—What kind would be the *right kind?*

DIABOLOS.—Well, sir, I will give you an example. In a church, in peace, harmony, love, prosperity and rejoicing in the truth, if I could, I would instigate a debate upon some unlearned question. I would lead Elder A. to propose the following: Is it right for Christians to join the Masons? Let him, then, remark that it must be either *right* or *wrong* for Christians to join the Masons. If it is wrong, those disciples who join, should be excluded from the church. It is, therefore, an important question, and the time is come when it ought to be settled. I have settled the question in my mind, continues he, that it is *wrong*—a crying sin—for a member of the church to join the Masons, and that it is my duty to rebuke this sin, to speak out. I can have no fellowship with error. Mr. B. agrees to meet him and debate the question. He, too, is in favor of speaking out, but he lifts his voice in favor of his brethren. He maintains that it is not only no harm for members of the church to join the Masons, but they have a perfect right to do so and can do much more good by joining the Masons than by remaining isolated from them. Let this controversy continue for a short time, between two of the influential members, and the church will divide, probably, about half and half. Some of the zealous opposers of the Masons will finally make a motion to exclude all the Masons from the church. In the course of this scramble, they will probably fill the members with hard feeling, wound each other by hard and offensive remarks, divide the church and call down the indignation of the Masons upon them.

LUCIFER.—I thank you, most worthy Diabolos, for your suggestions. I see now how we can work ruin in churches beautifully. We only have to divert the attention of the church from *her head,* and from *her own mission,* and induce the members to think that the church is an engine to be used as a kind of battering-ram to be brought to bear upon the evils that preachers may desire to put down.

APOLLYON.—That is the idea precisely.

In one community we must induce the preachers to bring the church to bear against Masonry and batter it down. No matter how insignificant the church may be, nor how uninfluential the preachers, we must induce them to form a direct issue with Masonry and try and batter it down. Where we have this kind of work going on, we must keep Masonry before the eyes of the preacher, keep him battling at it, till it recoils upon him and strikes from existence every particle of influence he had. In his zeal to put down a foe of his own choice, he forgets Christ, forgets the mission of the church, converts no sinners, makes no impression upon Masonry, only to repulse all under its influence. This is a beautiful plan of opposing the truth.

DIABOLOS.—We must be a little judicious, if we intend to be successful in our work. We must consider the place where we start mischief, and employ the most effective agents we can employ. The one you have alluded to, as an example, must not be resorted to in every instance. It will do the work effectually only in certain communities.

LUCIFER.—That is a fact. I never thought of that before. In a community where there are but few Masons and where Masonry is unpopular, it would not have the effect. In a community of this description, we should look round and perhaps we may find a large body of Odd Fellows. The members of the church are few, feeble and uninfluential. The preacher is an humble, ordinary and uninfluential man. If he loved Jesus, had him before his mind and *his* cause upon his heart, and, at the same time, would take into view the humble, sincere and honest persons before him, and preach the simple gospel of Christ, he might convert some honest souls and bring them to the kingdom of God. Now, to be successful in our work, we must lead such a man aside, decoy him into some inhospitable region, where his ship will be wrecked and sunk. To this end, it is good policy for us to make him feel that he is called and sent to preach against Odd Fellows. We must make him feel that, to be an Odd Fellow, is the next thing to the sin against the Holy Spirit—that it is *the sin* of the age—that he must rebuke this sin—that he must bear his testimony against it, and the whole church must bear her testimony against it.

DAIMONION.—That is the doctrine for us. I always know that I have a preacher safe, when I can decoy him off to engage in some such strife as that. It is easy, then, to bring the Odd Fellows to bear upon him, and they will soon extinguish him and his little party. A division will probably commence among the members, strife will ensue and general death and desolation will be spread all around. I have frequently amused myself, when I have had some poor fellow thus gulled, to see him struggle and toil for nothing. He would open the Bible, no matter where, and almost the first thing his eye falls upon is something directly opposed to Odd Fellows. Nothing else comes before his mind, his mission is for nothing else, the gospel appears to be for nothing else, and, if one could believe him, Christ came into the world for but little else besides to oppose Odd Fellows.

DIABOLOS.—That is the plan for our work. We need not be particular nor scrupulous about the means we employ. If there are no Masons in a community, or Odd Fellows, there may be Sons of Temperance. It will have the same effect, and do the work of ruin with equal success, to lead the preacher into an issue with these. Lead him to think that a Christian who joins them perjures his soul, forfeits his standing and should be excluded from the kingdom of God. Magnify it before his eyes, till he can see and think of nothing else. Lead him on till he thinks the whole Bible was written, the Lord sent from heaven, the Apostles sent into all the world, the gospel preached to every creature, the Christian ministry given and the church established on earth, to oppose the Sons of Temperance. Many preachers have I lead on in this way, thinking that they were, the only men in the world that had any sense, and everybody but themselves and a few carried away with the same delusion, could see at a glance that they were crazy.

LUCIFER.—I have a few men under my influence that are beautiful examples of this kind. I have lead some on till, they act as if they thought the only thing the Almighty had in his mind from the beginning of the world, the only design of the Bible, the Christian religion, the ministry and the church, was to prove that man is a material being—that he consists wholly of flesh, blood and breath, and when he dies he ceases to exist, and no more has a being than before he was created. I have frequently laughed to myself, to see one of this class of men start out to preach. He would no more perceive the Son of God than if he were not in the universe. He would no more think of converting and saving sinners than if there were no such work. His center of attraction is not the Lord. The Lord is not his ruler, nor his theme. His theme is soul-sleeping, and soon will he put the souls to sleep under his influence, or, what is worse, he will put them *spiritually to death.* I want no better instrumentality than such a man as this, if I can get the people to hear him, to kill religion in any community.

APOLLYON.—I have another class of men that do our work equally well. I allude, to Universalists. I have many of these poor ignorant dupes under my control so absolutely, that I frequently think they conceive the whole Bible designed to *prove that all will be saved.* Indeed, they appear to think that the eternal purpose of God, the promise to Abraham, the predictions of all the prophets, the preaching of John the Baptist, of Christ and all the Apostles, was intended to establish *the one idea that all will be saved.* Wicked men listen to a preacher of this description, laugh at his wit, sometimes at his want of sense, but appear to say to him, as the drunken man did to one in the midst of his argument, "Make it put if you can, for I am a gone sucker if you do not." Universalists administer the best opiate to sinners, to make them comfortable in their sins, of any class of men we have found.

LUCIFER—Infidelity serves the same purpose.

DIABOLOS.—You are widely mistaken, sir. Universalism paralyses all desire to serve God much better than open infidelity. It professes to be religion, and many of the vain talkers under its influence, work themselves into a partial security. It professes to reveal something good for man in the future. But infidelity lacks this. It simply involves all in uncertainty. For anything an infidel knows, or professes to know, there may be a hell and a heaven. A sinner cannot feel as secure, indifferent and unconcerned, in reference to the whole matter, if all the future is left in doubt, as infidels have it, as he can under the soothing influence of a system that leads him to deny all punishment in the world to come, and partly to believe that all will be happy in the future state.

APOLLYON—You are right, most worthy Diabolos; Universalism, serves our purpose in putting down religion, and easing the consciences of ungodly men, better than infidelity. Even Tom. Paine left sinners in trouble; for he admitted that there were future rewards and punishments, thus leaving the abominable and corrupt under the awful apprehension that they might, and be said he believed they would, suffer for their sins after death. This difficulty paused many to fall put with him and his doctrine and to seek repentance. But, Universalism takes away all this, and leaves a man without anything to lead him to repentance. Hence there is no repentance among Universalists.

DIABOLOS.—I amuse myself frequently in throwing a firebrand among professors of religion. I find a church pretty much departed from their first love, where the members have somewhat lost their attachment to Christ, only occasionally meet, never pray at home and consequently are prepared for a bone of contention. In an instance of this kind, if some man should come along, with his heart full of the love of Christ, of the Spirit of God, love to the brethren, and perceive their condition, and preach them a few affectionate discourses concerning Christ, his cross, his sufferings for our sins and their eternal allegiance to him, others would be added to their number and they would all be renewed in their minds. But, in all cases of this kind, if I can command a man whose soul feeds upon strife, whose element Is contention, whose cold heart has not contained one spark of the love of Christ for years, whose soul is not congenial with the cause, nor the brotherhood, among whom he prowls, whose mind is taken up with hobbies, and who is of so little consequence that he could gain no notice in any other way, I send him to preach to them against "the sin of our day"—"the giant sin of this generation"—"the great national sin of the American people." In a few months' wrangling, they fall out, abuse each other and cease to meet or worship. I have many examples of this kind now, and they are doing our work effectually.

REPORTER.

-----O-----

NOT A GENTLEMAN NOR A CHRISTIAN.

WE see, in the *Western Recorder,* the Baptist weekly of Louisville, Ky., an article from our quondam opponent, Rev. T. J. Fisher, pronouncing that we have *caricatured* him, in our description of him. We are free to confess, as we intimated at the time, that our picture is imperfect, incomplete, and only feebly represents him. It is not overdrawn, but falls far short of doing him full justice, especially in setting forth the ridiculous. We, however, did the best we could for him. He pronounces, further, that we have garbled the debate, but does not say wherein; and that, in *his* estimation, we are not a gentleman nor a Christian! Our case is then decided by the unquestionable authority of Rev. T. J. Fisher! Ain't we in a fix? Wonder if he knows what a gentleman or a Christian is? The trouble with him lies in a different direction. The *people decided* that he made the most perfect failure in the debate they ever knew. Here is one *sore place.* Another trouble he found in the estimate his brethren put upon his effort, in the *fine* contribution made for his services, of which, it appears, he has since had reason to complain. Let him come to Ghent and hold another meeting, and he can find out how highly he was, and is still, appreciated there, not only by those outside, but by the *Baptists;* if in no other way, by the remuneration he will receive. If we are not mistaken, he is beginning to. learn the meaning of the old adage—"Poor preach, poor pay."

He further pronounces, that those Baptist preachers who read the word of the Lord with us, and prayed for the blessing of Heaven upon us, during our protracted meeting in New Liberty, Owen Co., Ky., during which some twenty-one were added, acted very inconsistently, and he holds the rod of excommunication in *terrorum* over them. He has no relish for any such meetings as that was. Christ and him crucified was the theme on that occasion. All who desired to serve God were exhorted to follow the Savior, to love him, with all united in him. The preachers alluded to, we presume, love the Savior better than partyism, or party makers and propagators. When invited they cheerfully took seats with us in the pulpit, prayed with us and for us, that we might preach the truth, the whole truth and nothing but the truth. They did right in doing so, and knew they did right; and if party bigotry undertakes to exclude them, it will receive such a rebuke as will open the eyes of some men that no argument can enlighten. Let Rev. T. J.

Fisher try his influence in bringing about their exclusion, and see how they will make the matter tingle about his ears. What! exclude Baptist preachers, for going into the pulpit, praying with and for a man who claims to be trying to preach the gospel, and nothing but the gospel—praying that he may preach the truth as it is in Christ, and nothing but the truth! What! threaten them that if they preach the same, the gospel and nothing but the gospel—the truth, and nothing but the truth, they will be excommunicated from the Baptist church! Has it come to this, that Baptist preachers shall be held in awe, with the threat of excommunication for this? Are Baptist preachers thus to be lashed into party-ism by the rod of bigotry, with the boast of liberty, toleration and the right of private judgment upon their lips? Has it come to this, to talk about excommunication from the Baptist Church, with no other offence committed than accepting an invitation to a seat with us, reading the word of the Lord with us, praying with us and for us—that we may preach the truth, the whole truth and nothing but the truth; we say, speak of excommunication for this? or even for preaching the same themselves?—exclude them for this, while the history of the proscriptions, oppressions and persecutions of the first Baptists in America are fresh in their memories? Let men who thus talk never again mention toleration! Let them never again mention the price of liberty! They know nothing of the meaning of such expressions.

What if they did express their opinion of the debate! Are they bound to be bigots, partisans and despisers of those with whom they may differ in some respects? Why not exclude the Baptist Church in New Liberty for their kindness and liberality in granting us the use of their house? Why not exclude many of the members for coming to hear us? for giving the hand to the new converts in encouragement and congratulation, during our meeting? Why vent all this bitter feeling upon these preachers? Are they sinners above all other Baptists? Must they be published, implicated, as inconsistent, and deterred by talking of excommunication, for no other reason, than for manifesting common Christian courtesy to us while in their midst? Are Baptist preachers thus to be deterred from ordinary courtesies among preachers, by holding the rod of excommunication in *terrorum* over them! No, sir; there are many of them not to be driven into the little, narrow selfishness of partisan spirits. Their hearts have been expanded by a nobler philanthropy, a more exalted feeling and heavenly principle.

If, however, our quondam opponent determines upon excommunicating all Baptists and Baptist, *preachers,* especially those who, in any way, associate with us in worship, we propose that he send to us, and we will see Archbishop Purcell, and have him procure, from the Pope a bull of excommunication, prepared in due form, sequestering all heretics among Baptists, not only private members, but preachers, who in any way associate with Christians in worship, from the thresh-hold of the Baptist church, and from the only *true Baptist* faith, and calling upon all the hierarchies in heaven to thrust them down to bottomless perdition. Evidently *embryo* popes do not know how to prepare a bull in due form!   B. F.

-----o-----

SPIRITUAL INFLUENCE

Bro. Franklin:—In the July number of the Review is a criticism, by Bro. S. E. Pearre, on a discourse of mine, published in the previous number of your paper, which criticism calls for some reply. I have never received the Review which contained my discourse. It was lost in the mail I presume. I am sorry that I cannot give it another reading. There are many men, no doubt, who, after having their compositions reviewed critically, would change or qualify something.

Such *might* be the case with me in this instance, had I my composition before me. I do not, however, now recollect any sentiment that I would recall or qualify; at least I cannot adopt the views of Bro. Pearre, if I understand him correctly.

I agree with you, Bro. Franklin, in your remarks upon the impropriety of preaching discourses upon the influence of the Spirit—with some exceptions. There is no man whose judgment of propriety, in matters of Christianity, I value more highly than yours; still, I must dissent a little on this point. If the religious world had never abused their own minds and those of their hearers with erroneous and dangerous views upon spiritual influences, there would be no necessity for combating these errors. If the unscriptural practice of infant sprinkling had never been inculcated and followed, there would be no necessity for combating such a thing. But, as vital errors are taught and practiced, to combat them I hold to be allowable sometimes, at least.

I am pleased to see the kind of spirit in which Bro. Pearre urges his objections to what he conceives to be such fatal errors in me. In this I think he exercises the spirit of Christ; and I shall endeavor to follow his example the few remarks I may have to make in reply—intending, on my part, to carry the controversy no farther than the present communication.

Bro. P. says he deems the sentiments offered in my discourse "very untenable and very pernicious in their influence." I do not doubt that Bro. P. honestly entertains this opinion; yet he has failed to give me any convincing evidence of its truth. Perhaps more discerning minds may be able to see it as he does. He says "we are all in the habit of denying the charge so often made against us—that we do not not teach that the Spirit at present has any work to perform in the salvation of men—as a gross misrepresentation of our views. But when our enemies are able to turn to such sentiments as these, our mouths are closed." This is a saying I often hear urged in opposition to various views of our brethren—what will our enemies say—and I confess it has some weight with me, yet not enough to induce me to compromise, smother up, or swerve in the least from what I conceive to be the truth. Whilst I am not "one of those who reject everything that I cannot fully comprehend and explain," as Bro. P. seems to imply that I am; yet upon the subject of spiritual influences, many of our most learned and strongest brethren have been so "tender footed and indefinite, that they have been far from satisfactory to me, contending that there are but two kinds of powers—moral and physical; and that all the converting and sanctifying power is through moral means; that we are "begotten by the word of truth;" that the consoling and "comforting" evidence of our being heirs of God, and good and faithful servants, is found only in the word of God; and yet so quoting and applying the language of Christ to his Apostles, Paul to the Romans, Corinthians and Ephesians, and Peter to the Pentecostians, as to lead their hearers to expect the exercise of a physical power of the Spirit. So long as persons are taught to expect a physical operation of the Spirit, so long will they, as a general thing, substitute their imaginary operations of the Spirit for obedience to positive commandments. This is a fruitful source of error. The necessity for combating it lies in the fact that those who think themselves subjects of these special operations, deem their evidence of acceptability sufficient, and neglect what God requires them to do. It is our duty to teach people to believe all God says, and to do all he commands; and that all blessings—spiritual or otherwise—that God has promised in this age, will be conferred upon such persons. If this simple teaching could reach the minds of the people, there would be no occasion to stop and parley about spiritual operations; but some minds must first be disabused before they can be enlightened.

There are more of the "profound mysteries," of which Bro. P. speaks, out of the Bible than in it, and this same "personal indwelling" and physical operation of the Spirit is one of them. Does Bro. P. really think that God literally and physically dwells in and walks in every Disciple, as he would seem to argue by his quotation of II. Cor. vi. 16?

Bro. P. thinks the views advanced in my discourse are depriving the reformation of its moral power. If I believe and teach them, that people should faithfully and heartily do all that God requires of them, the reformation will not maintain its moral power, unless I believe and teach the physical operation and personal indwelling of the Spirit. Strange, indeed! Bro P. indicates that this teaching people to do all the requirements of God faithfully, is a merely logical religion. He says "a *merely logical religion* will *not* make a man any better." Will an *illogical* religion make men better, Bro. P.? A wiser man than either us, Bro. P., has said: "Let us hear the conclusion of the whole matter: fear God and keep his commandments; for this is the whole duty of man." Eccl. xii. 13. Yet Bro. P. argues that we must do more than this— believe in the personal indwelling of the Spirit.

Bro. P. says: Christianity has succeeded, because it does not recognize man's intellectual as his highest nature, and has ignored the maxim that, 'to educate is to reform,' but has dug deeper, and found a spiritual nature; and, by bringing it out in the warm sunshine of heaven, has made man strong against sin." To say nothing of this digging *deep* to get a *high* thing, I will simply remark, that I have never been able to separate man's, intellectual from his spiritual nature. Bro. P.'s view in this seems to be the same as J. B.. Ferguson & Co.'s.

Bro. P. says "all who obey the gospel are promised the gift of the personal spirit," as on the day of Pentecost, though in different measures. Here two difficulties present themselves in the reception of Bro. P.'s view. 1. The Spirit and the gift of the Spirit are different things. It is the *gift* of the Spirit Bro. P. says is promised and yet he contends I must have the personal *spirit itself.* 2. Bro. P. says we are promised the gift of the Spirit in different measures from what was promised anciently. We have no rule by which to graduate it; or, in other words, we cannot find the Scripture which teaches thus.

Again, Bro. P. says: "When God sent his Spirit to work miracles, it worked them; when He sent it to reveal truth, it did *that;* and when he only sent it to comfort the saint, it *comforted* them, and confined itself to the mission on which it was sent." Well, Bro. P., we must know *something* of the *how* of this comforting, in order that we may know we are com- forted; and this hope, you will let me inquire into without accusing me of "rejecting everything I cannot fully comprehend and explain." Does the Spirit comfort us through moral or physical means? or, in other words, is it by words addressed to our understanding, or is it by a personal indwelling? If the former, then we occupy the same ground; if the latter, we are as wide apart as the poles.

I do not see the difficulties in Rom. viii. 9-11, that Bro. P. seems to think he has presented. He says: "The identical spirit which raised Jesus from the dead was the spirit the Romans had in them; and if we simply have the disposition of Christ, then the disposition of Christ raised him up, and will be the agent that will raise us up." In the marginal reading we have, "shall also quicken our mortal bodies *because of his Spirit* that dwelleth in you." But, aside from the marginal reading, we have but to use the same "logic" that Bro P. uses himself to reconcile this passage of Scripture, and a host of others, with the views advanced in my discourse. That

Spirit was always confined to the mission on which it was sent. There is a diversity of missions, but the same Spirit. *The* Spirit was sent on a mission to instruct, comfort and console, and to beget in us *a* holy spirit. How can my body be *the* temple of *the* Holy Spirit? And this same Spirit, that by a metonymy of speech, we may be said to possess, because we possess the fruits of it, will be sent on a mission to raise us from the dead. So it is plain to be seen how it may comfort, console and instruct us, beget in us *a* holy spirit, be in us metonymically, create in us the disposition of Christ, quicken our mortal bodies and raise us from the dead; and still there be no literal personal indwelling or physical operation in our present state. And all this, too, without the great heresy that Bro. P. has conjured up, and without "the reformation losing its moral power over the world."

I have but little relish for anyone who rejects everything in Christianity because he cannot reduce it to the standard of his own reasoning; and less relish for one who ridicules reasoning upon matters of Christianity.

J. A. CLARK.
Midway, Texas, July, 1857.

-----o-----

BRACKEN ASSOCIATION OF UNITED BAPTISTS.
NUMBER IX.

ON page 6th of the Minutes of the Bracken Association, Elders Gardner, James, Hunt & Co. "distinctly and emphatically avow" that we teach "radical and *destructive errors,*" and that, therefore, a "union between the two bodies * * * would be suicidal to the Baptist denomination." Of course, gentlemen, you do not mean to be understood as saying, that if all our people, who were once Baptists, "renounce their errors and repent of their sins," and come into your congregations, that such a union would be "suicidal to the Baptist denomination!" Or, that if that other class of our people, who were "baptized for the remission of their sins," with-

without professing a "previous change of heart"—should sincerely renounce their errors and repent of their sins, and obtain a change of heart and pardon, and receive baptism at the hands of Baptist preachers, and thus unite with you, that such a union would be "suicidal to the Baptist denomination!" Certainly this is not what you mean. For a union upon such terms would add to your already very large sect, some two or three hundred thousand "United Baptists." This, so far from being suicidal to your cause, would add immensely to your denominational strength.

What, then, do you mean, when you so emphatically and distinctly avow that a union with us, would be "suicidal to the Baptist denomination?" Do you mean to say, that if you should take our position, and thus unite with us, that, as a *Baptist denomination, you would cease to be?* If this is what you mean, your conclusion is certainly true. For, unequivocally, union with us, upon the New Testament, sealed by the blood of Jesus, would be "suicidal to the Baptist denomination," and every other sectarian denomination in Christendom. In such a union the Christian would be saved, but the sectarian would be destroyed—the wheat would be gathered into Heaven's garner, the chaff would be blown away. If the erroneous impression, therefore, has been made, as the resolution affirms, that there is virtually no difference between us and the Baptists, I think it very likely the Baptists have made it themselves, to serve a purpose. Certainly no well informed man among us will deliberately affirm, that "there is virtually no difference between us and the Baptists." And while we would not say of them that they teach "destructive errors," yet the difference between them and us is sufficiently marked as utterly to forbid a union with them, as Baptists. And, therefore, while we concede that a union of the Baptists with us, upon our principles, would be suicidal to them, as a party, our union with them, on Baptist principles, would be equally suicidal to the great purpose of our organization, viz.: The union of all God's people, in one great New Testament, Christian organization. Let our Baptist brethren rest assured, then, we shall never stultify ourselves by seeking such sectarian union, and that, therefore, we can have no motive to make the "erroneous impression," that there is virtually no difference between the Baptists and us. Any one must see at a glance, that, having repudiated all sectarian names, creeds, etc., and having taken our stand upon the original foundation of the church of Christ, to unite with any sect in Christendom, would be to build again the things we once destroyed, and thus make ourselves transgressors against truth and consistency. Ours is a plea for the union of Christians "upon the foundation of apostles and prophets, Jesus Christ himself being the chief corner stone." Ours is a war of extermination against schism and schismatics—an effort to collect the sheep of the good Shepherd, that have been scattered by hirelings, false shepherds in the "dark and cloudy day," and immured in sectarian pens, and fed upon unwholesome food, until they are ready to perish. Ours is an effort to throw down these human barriers, that the saints may come out of these prison houses, into the green pasture of gospel grace, where flows the river of life, that they may grow up into Christ in all things; that the people of God may be one, according to the prayer of the Savior, as he and the Father are one, that the world may believe and be saved. Now, then, as in the presence of the Judge of all the earth, we declare, that the union of Christians upon the simple truth as taught by Christ and his Apostles, in order to the conversion of the world, is the great object of our labors, as a people. We have no party name to establish—no party creed and system of church government to set up, as tests of faith and practice. Thoroughly satisfied as we are, and as all the more pious and thoughtful, in Christendom, are, that the condition of the religious world is most unfortunate—that our corruptions and schisms (mutual causes and effects of one another) are promoting infidelity, and wickedness and alienation from God, we long to see these fearful fountains of death dried up, in the scriptural union of God's people. We appeal, therefore, to the good sense and piety of our Baptist brethren, and of the religious world, if ours is not a *most worthy, most benevolent, most necessary and most Christian object?* Did not our divine Master, in full view of the cross and all its agonies, pray most fervently to his Father that all who should believe on him through the word of truth, in all ages might be one, as he and his Father are one, that the world—that sinners might believe? And does not the fact, that the most intelligent and pious among all the sects mourn over our schisms, and pray for the union of God's people—proclaim in language loud as seven-fold thunder, that our divisions are wrong in their estimation? Do not the books and essays that have been written, the world's convention that met in London some years ago, and the many union meetings that have been held among the sects, all attest the fact, that the church, in her heart of hearts, feels the need of a union she has not realized for more than fifteen centuries? To talk, therefore, as some do, of union, as consistent with our present, distinct, sectarian organizations, is simply ridiculous, and not more inconsistent than to talk of sobriety in drunkenness, or chastity in lewdness!

All will concede, at once, that the union which existed among the apostolic churches, in harmony with the teachings of Christ and the Apostles, ought to exist among all organizations claiming to be Christian *now and forever.* This is a truism of great practical worth in Christianity.

Let us, then, look at the nature of that union, that we may see our wants in that regard. We must be brief. Let us state a few facts:

1. All who were worthy of the fellowship of the congregation of Christians at Philippi would be received into the fellowship and membership of any other Christian congregation, in apostolic times. What fitted an individual for membership in one church, fitted him for membership in every church.

2. Such evangelists as Titus and Timothy, were acceptable as such in all the churches of Christ in their day. These, to the Christian, are self-evident truths; and we might easily add to them, but these are sufficient for our purpose. How is it now?

1. That which fits a man to be an acceptable member of the Methodist Church disqualifies him for membership in any other distinct organization. He must cease to be a Methodist, before he can join a church of a different "faith and order." So of all the sects. Their tests of fellowship are different; and hence to leave any one of the parties, and go to another, is to renounce the peculiarities of the party left, and embrace those of the party joined. Here, then, there is no union among the sects.

2. How is it among the preachers? Will Baptist preachers circulate freely and acceptably among, all the other parties, and be sustained by them, as Titus and Timothy among the apostolic churches? Certainly not. Nor would it fare better with any of the others. The Episcopalians have their Ministerial Meetings; the Presbyterians their Presbyteries, Synods and General Assemblies; the Methodists their Quarterly, their Annual and General Conferences; the Baptists their Associations, etc. But the ministers of no one of all the sects will be regarded as having a right to a seat in a meeting of the ministers of any other sect. Evidently, then, there is no Christian union—no apostolic union among the leaders of the sects. He might well be esteemed as mad, who should pretend that there exists, among the religious teachers of the different sects, even of those called evangelical, such a union in faith, in feeling and effort as existed among the apostolic teachers. Allow me to introduce one more test of the union of the first Christians, and the want of union among us.

3. Such was the oneness of the faith, the feeling and the interests of the first churches, that the prosperity of one was the prosperity of all; that the success or triumphs of the principles of one was the triumph of the principles of all. If, therefore, one was honored, all rejoiced, because the honor was shared by all; and if one suffered, all sympathized with it. Such was the union of the original congregations of Christ. But, is such the state of things now? Certainly the farthest from it imaginable! Let Methodism take the world (as its friends sometimes say it will), and all the other sects would be swallowed up. Can the other parties then rejoice at the thought of the triumph of Methodism? While, then, the churches of Christ, in apostolic times, were sister organizations, having a common cause to support, and co-operating most cordially and lovingly to promote that common cause, and rejoicing in each other's success, the sects of these days are antagonistic in their names, their creeds, their interests; and hence no one of them could triumph, but by the downfall of all the rest. Let Episcopalianism take the world, and the Catholics, the Presbyterians, the Methodists, the Baptists, and all the rest of the sects, would be extinct. To dream of union, then, in the midst of such antagonisms as sectarianism contains, and has contained for many long centuries, is worse than useless.

Now, then, in such an emergency as this, when we come forward and propose an abandonment of all our sectarian strifes, and that we may all unite upon the plain and unequivocal teachings of Christ and his Apostles, ought we not to have the sympathies, the prayers and cordial co-operation of the good, the really pious among all parties? They see, and feel and know we are hopelessly divided; that in sectarianism there is no hope; that under its reign of terror we may grow worse—increase our divisions, but can never be united! We have looked at Elder Gardner's plan of union, which is simply that all parties shall become "United Baptists;" and have seen that it promises nothing but the establishment of one great mammoth sect upon the ruins of all the other parties. And that this is the only union Elder Gardner and his associates want, is clear from the general tenor of the circular, and especially from the resolution, on p. 6th of the Minutes, in which, after saying that, because we teach radical and destructive errors, a union between the Baptists and us would be suicidal to the Baptist denomination, they say, "we therefore cordially recommend to all brethren and churches *Campbellism Examined and Re-Examined,* by Dr. Jeter," etc. Observe, they do not recommend the word of God, the New Testament, as the means of showing the erroneousness of what they are pleased to call "Campbellism;" but Dr. Jeter's examination, or, rather, in many instances, misrepresentation of the views of Mr. Campbell. This work is much better suited to promote Baptist views and prejudices than the New Testament. As an offset to this, we might cordially recommend to our Baptist brethren Moses E. Lard's Review of Dr. Jeter's *Campbellism Examined and Re-Examined,* as a thorough refutation of his arguments against our views.

In our next, which, we think, will be our last, we propose to present some thoughts upon the scriptural basis of union and co-operation, and, perhaps, some other matters.

JOHN ROGERS.

ONE always receiving, never giving, is like the stagnant pool, in which whatever flows remains, whatever remains corrupts.—JAMES.

-----o-----

OSKALOOSA COLLEGE.

BRO. FRANKLIN Is it not indeed cheering to the contemplative Christian mind, to be cognizant of the late efforts of the disciples of our beloved Lord and Master, in the cause of rational Christian education? Not long since our ears were greeted with the news of the unparalleled success of "Bacon College" among the brethren and friends in Kentucky.

Indiana and Illinois have alike labored nobly in the same great cause, and Missouri is not far behind in her efforts at good works.

The brethren of Iowa, although less numerous and able to do as those of her sister States, have began likewise to show their faith by their works; and "Oskaloosa College" is not only fully born, but fast growing up to the full stature of a first-class educational institution.

It is to this effort I wish more particularly to call attention. This College is the first born of Iowa's literary and Christian Institutions under the immediate supervision of the Christian Church, and as such, claims the immediate and willing attention and assistance of the entire brotherhood of the State and elsewhere. Its location is in the suburbs of the large and flourishing town of Oskaloosa, the county-seat of Mahaska county, situated in the midst of a well cultivated, healthy and beautiful section of country.

A plan and engraving of the College, with a description of its aims and intentions was kindly given to the writer a short time since by Elder J. F. Rowe, who is at present, with others, traversing the State soliciting scholarships.

The main college building is of the *Italian* style of architecture, and, from the engraving, gives a large and imposing. and at the same time, from the peculiarity of its construction, a really beautiful appearance.

The exact dimensions, as to length, width and height, is not remembered, but are those of a large and first-class Institution. According to the provisions of the College rules and regulations, both sexes are to be admitted to its honors and privileges, upon terms of perfect equality. This is an important feature, and speaks much for the wisdom and intelligence of its founders and directors. Another and most important feature in its plan of education, is the happy arrangement by which the *whole* man or woman is to be developed in his or her three-fold nature of *body, soul* and *spirit*—and to this end, beside the *usual* literary, scientific and classical course developing the intellectual man—there is to be a *biblical department,* where the spiritual and moral nature may be fed; and also, a department of "Chemistry and Physiology," with the elements Of man's anatomy and hygiene, *a provision* of *immense importance,* in human education, yet entirely overlooked by 'the majority of educational institutions, Of the present day and age.

We need institutions of learning where the youth of our land, male and female, can be taught the truth of the declaration, uttered eighteen hundred years ago, that they are the temples of the living God, and that if those temples are abused and destroyed, that God will not overlook it.

The physiology of man should be taught, elucidated and enforced by appropriate ways and means, and the philosophy of human life, that interesting theme so closely connected with our .health and usefulness here, with all its facts, laws and analogies should be perfectly unfolded to view, and the anatomy and hygiene of the human economy should be as "familiar as household words" to the youthful ear.

The great principle, "a *sound mind in a sound body,"* should be one of the prominent jewels in the crown of a complete Christian education.

Thus a complete system is furnished, the whole human being is educated, and God's laws governing each and every nature of that being are understood and can be obeyed.

The body, soul and spirit, the grand triune, all so developed as to stand in perfect harmony with each other, with the laws governing, their respective nature and the whole economy, giving us; a being healthy, physically, intellectually and spiritually.

To "Oskaloosa College," then, so far as our knowledge extends, belongs the honor of bearing fruit in giving forth to the world such a system of rational education, and long may it live and flourish to show forth the practicability and the good and glory of such a scheme.?

We hope to see such an Institution meet with the sympathy and warm support of the entire brotherhood throughout the State, and, indeed, of all people who are interested in the welfare of mankind, and the advancement of the human race in science, health and spirituality. The work of endowment so far has been most successful, and, without a doubt, we predict a brilliant, successful and glorious future for "Oskaloosa College." A. J. C.,M. D.

Newton, Iowa, July, 1857.

-----o-----

THE DESIGH OF BAPTISM.

THE Lord says, "Whosoever shall break one of these least commandments, and teach men so, shall be called least in the kingdom of heaven." Again, he says to, his disciples,; "Except your righteousness shall exceed the righteousness of the Scribes and Pharisees, you shall in no case enter into the kingdom of God." In most solemn and admonitory style he says, "Strive to enter in at the straight gate, for many shall seek to enter in and shall not be able." Many admonitions of the same kind are found in the New Testament, going to show how important it is that men trifle not with the things of the kingdom of God. Nothing can be more manifest, than that any course of religious teaching that prevents men from obeying any commandment of God, is neutralizing, demoralizing and sinful. All preaching which inculcates disobedience or neglect of any commandment of God, is, in itself, whether intended or not, opposed to the gospel. The entire authority of God is in any one commandment. Not only so, but the same benevolent design of God in any one commandment, is found in his whole procedure. The ultimate design of God, or his eternal purpose, was the *salvation of man.* The same benevolent purpose was in his mind, and he was acting in reference to it, When he made the promise, to Abraham: "In thee and in thy seed shall all the families of the earth be blessed." The same design was in his mind when he loved the world. Hence it is said, "God so loved the world that he gave his only begotten Son, that whosoever believeth on Him should not perish, but have everlasting life." Here it is manifest, that the ultimate object is, that man may not *perish*, but have *everlasting life,* or *be saved.* The same is the object of the mission of Jesus Christ into this world—that the world, through him, *might be saved.* The same is the object of believing on him. He was lifted up, that whoever believeth on him might not perish, but have everlasting" life, or be saved. "He that believeth not the Son, shall not see life, but the wrath of God abideth on him." The design of God, in requiring man to believe, is the same as his design in sending the Savior into the world, viz.: *That man might be saved.*

No matter where you find faith mentioned, in the New Institution, it always has this ultimate design, that man might not perish, but have everlasting life or be saved. It is no difference how many immediate objects or designs faith may have, its ultimate design is that man may be saved. It never loses this design or object in our entire Christian life. Not only so, but whatever is connected with faith in the Christian Scriptures, has the same design. For instance, when the Lord says, "He that believeth and is baptized shall be saved," he makes the design of baptism and faith the same. He requires two things to be done, and sets one object before us to be gained in doing the things required. The object is *salvation.* The two things required, are to *"believe* and be *baptized.* Now to make faith here have one object, and baptism another, is out of the question. The Lord himself puts it with baptism, and gives it the same design, viz.; salvation. No matter, so far as the present investigation is concerned, what the precise import of the word *salvation* is. We may find the meaning of that afterward; but it is the design of baptism precisely as much as it is of faith, and that design is expressed by precisely the same words. No evasion in this universe can avoid it. Still, as men have their subterfuges, and are willing to risk their religious reputations upon them, we must notice them, no matter how weak or sophistical. One of this kind that we frequently met twenty years ago, from about third or fourth rate opponents, we heard mentioned a short time since by men who we had supposed to be better instructed and established in the truth. It runs in these words: "The Lord says, 'He that believeth and is baptized shall be saved, and he that believeth not shall be damned;' but he does not say, 'He that believeth not and *is not baptized* shall be damned.'" Here, it was urged, a distinction is made between the importance of faith and that of baptism!

We confess that we cannot approach this without feeling that the reader will say to himself, that is too weak—too manifestly "green"—to deserve attention. We should have thought so too, had it not come from too high a source for this. We must, then, approach it gravely, no matter what its appearance to us may be. The argument, if we may dignify it so much as to call if "argument." is this: that, inasmuch as the Lord said, "he that believeth not," and did not add, "and is not baptized," the whole rested upon the faith, and nothing upon the baptism. But this is not only a manifest sophism, but a miserably poor one at that. Where several conditions are contained in a covenant, what is proposed in it cannot be claimed, according to the covenant, till each one of the conditions are complied with. Complying with one or more of the conditions amounts to nothing, unless all are complied with. The failure to comply with any one condition, forfeits the whole. When you say to a plowman, If you will come to my farm, and plow my field, I will give you ten dollars; but if you do not come, I will not give you anything, it does not prove that the *coming* is all that is essential, or that *the plowing* is not essential. But as the plowing could not be done without *coming*, it is not necessary to mention the plowing when stating the negative part of the sentence. If the plowman does not come, it follows, as a matter of course, that he does not plow, and, therefore, does not get the pay. No man, who understands language, would say, "If you do not come and do not plow the field you will get the pay;" for the simple reason, that, if he does not come, as a matter of course, he does not plow the ground. As he cannot comply with the proposal without *coming*, this is all that is mentioned, when stating the negative part of the sentence. In precisely the same way, if a man does not believe, it follows, as a matter of course, that he does not repent, confess Christ, be baptized, pray or commune; and, in stating the negative part of the sentence, it is sufficient to say, "He that believeth not shall be damned." It follows, as a matter of course, that he is not baptized, or that he is a hypocrite, a mere pretender. Without faith a man cannot repent, confess Christ, be baptized, pray or do anything else acceptably to God; therefore, it is sufficient to say, "He that believeth not shall be damned." On the other hand, *with faith*, all faith, so that a man could remove mountains, without anything else, or even without charity, a man is nothing. The holy Apostle says, to the man with faith, without obedience, "Can faith save him?" and answers, "that faith without works is dead, being alone."

Scriptural baptism, repentance, confession or prayer, no man ever did, or ever can have, without faith, and, consequently, it is useless and senseless to add, to the sin of unbelief, that a man does not repent, confess, be baptized and pray, for his unbelief is sufficient ground of condemnation. But suppose we change this miserable, blind and stupid sophistry a little, and argue that repentance is not essential, for the Lord did not say, he that believeth not and *repenteth not* shall be damned, but simply he that *believeth not* shall be damned! Would this prove that repentance may be dispensed with, or that it is not essential? Not to men of sound minds. They would remind us, that the Lord elsewhere says, "Except ye repent, you shall all likewise perish." Suppose some man should say, the confession is not essential, for the Lord did not say, "He that believeth not and *confesseth not* shall be damned," but, simply, he that *believeth not*. Would this prove the confession not essential? Not with men sound in the faith. They would soon remind such a man, "That he that confesseth not that Jesus Christ is come in the flesh, is not of God." Such miserable, weak sophistries, from men of weak faith, to weaken the commandments of God, and weaken the desires of men to obey God, are a disgrace to the age in which we live, and must be exposed till men will forsake them from mere shame, if they cannot be induced to forsake them from conscience.

When baptism stands connected with repentance, as in the sentence, "Repent and be baptized every one of you, in the name of Jesus Christ for the remission of sins," repentance and baptism have the same design, or are for the same purpose, and no sophistry can evade it. What is the design of repentance in this passage? What is the repentance in order to?

Not because those addressed had been pardoned, nor for an evidence that they had *been pardoned;* for the Lord does not pardon men before they repent, or in impenitence, and then command them to repent because they are pardoned, or as an evidence that "they had been pardoned!" But the repentance is in order to pardon. Pardon is the object the believer is aiming at, and repentance is the road to it, and he cannot get to it by any other road, or, in other words, he cannot get to pardon without travelling over that part of the road called repentance. What is the immediate object, or design, of repentance? As found in the above passage, it is *"for the remission of sins;"* or as it is in another place, "That your *sins may be blotted out."* This is the immediate design. But is a passage already quoted, we have, "Except you repent, you shall all likewise perish." The object of repentance here appears to be, that men may *not perish.* This is the ultimate design. The immediate design of repentance, then, is pardon; but the ultimate design of pardon itself is, that we might not perish, or that we might have everlasting life. When baptism is placed with repentance, or in the same sentence, connected by the conjunction "and," it has the same design, or is for the same purpose, as stated by the holy Apostle, "for the remission of sins," or in order to the remission of sins. It is not the *procuring cause* of remission, but one step, and the last step, in the road to remission. In getting to any place, it is equally as important to take the last step as the first one. There is no getting there without both.

At the same time we heard some of the sophistry mentioned in the foregoing, we heard another that we must mention. It was observed, that we must look at the consequences of the doctrine of baptism for remission of sins. We were invited to think of the thousands who die without baptism, and without remission, if baptism is for remission. We were admonished to think what overwhelming *masses* were being lost at this rate, and how comparatively few would be saved. If this objector had met Noah, he would have overwhelmed him with the same objection, beseeching him to think what vast multitudes would be lost if his doctrine should prove true. He would have confronted our gracious Lord, in joining with the objectors of his time, inquiring, "Who then can be saved?" He would have confronted the angel of God who warned Lot out of Sodom, by admonishing him to reflect how few would be saved, if his doctrine should prove true. Such men neither know the Scriptures nor the power of God. Their eye is upon the world, and not upon the Almighty, maker of heaven and earth. But why, we ask, in God's name, are there so many who believe and are not baptized? Is not baptism accessible to all who believe? Why, then, are there so many who have faith, but not baptism? Why are there so many believers dying without baptism? Why are there so many honest souls mourning, grieving and in despair in the hour of death, because they have not been baptized? Why all this, we appeal to the ministry in God's name? *Because of untrue, unfaithful, cowardly, worldly and time-serving ministers, who cavil at the commandment of God, to " Repent and be baptized every one of you, in the name of Jesus Christ, for the remission of sins," whom God will call to account when he shall judge the secrets of men by Jesus Christ, according to the gospel.*

-----o-----

ANTI-REVISION SERMON.

We have before us one of the *literary* and *theological* curiosities of the second half of the nineteenth century, entitled "Anti-Revision Sermon, delivered at Warrensburg, Missouri, and subsequently called for by many friends, far and near, by Rev. W. W. Suddath, A. M., President of Chapel Hill College, Lafayette, Co;, Mo., June 15th, 1856." If the "Rev." had not been prefixed to the name, the idea of *reverence* for the author, certainly never would have entered into our mind, and if the "A. M." had not been affixed to the name which, our school-master taught us, stands for *Master of Arts,* we should never have thought of *arts* of any kind, to say nothing of "Master of Arts." As to *art* of any kind, this poor, stupid, miserable concern; contains none. We have seen sophistry that was brilliant, keen *artful,* but this, if to be admitted into the ranks of sophistry at all, is of the driest, fullest and most stupid order of sophistry. Its attempts at argument and reasoning are all backwards. It is the most perfectly and emphatically an *old fogy* document of anything we have had upon our table in twelve months. The idea of a man *calling himself* "Rev.," "A. M." "President of a College," and opposing the correction of all errors in translating the word of the living God, to be read by all nations of men, is so manifestly ridiculous and preposterous, and carries upon the surface such an air of inflated arrogance, pompous, conceit and empty vanity, that we confess our self incompetent to command language adequate to describe it. It is not enough, with him, to maintain the errors in his sectarian system of religion, with a human creed for a law, to govern those who cannot be governed by the law of God, his *sprinkling* for baptism, not even mentioned for the initiatory ceremony, in any translation under heaven, his religious establishment, the very name of which is not found in the whole revelation of God to man but he is determined to maintain, and have the people continued to read, as *the word of God,* the errors, of which he knows there are thousands, in our translation!

After this "Rev.," "A. M." and "President of a College," as *he announces himself,* makes a lengthy argument, in the regular old fogy style, to prove the competency of King James' translators, and that we have no men now possessing such qualifications as they had, he informs us that the "competent committee," appointed by the American Bible Society, had found variations, in the copies of the common version amounting to "but little short of *twenty-four thousand!*" How, then, even if he could succeed in proving the competency of the King James' translators, does that prove that we should not correct these *twenty-four thousand variations* in the version in common use? How, too, does he find scholars for this "competent committee," to point out these *twenty-four thousand* variations, since the learning of these times is so superficial and worthless? With him; a "competent committee, can easily be found, in the American Bible Society, to point out twenty-four thousand variations in the versions in use among the people, and this "competent committee" can correct such errors as may be corrected without conflicting with the errors in his church; but it will not do to call the attention of the piety and scholarship of the world to the work and correct *all the errors in translating* found in the whole Bible! This is commanding a little more piety, learning tad authority into the platter than he desired. He prefers that a "competent committee," with no authority but a party, without the knowledge of the learned men of the world, make such corrections as they please, and their corrections shall be counted sufficient!

But we are not done with this "Rev.," "A. M." yet. We have some still graver matters to which we wish to call his attention. We take no pleasure in calling in question the honor of men of distinction—men who claim to be preachers of the gospel and presidents of colleges, as well as "Master of Arts." Indeed, it is unpleasant to do so. But, in this instance, integrity to the Bible, to the cause of truth and righteousness demands, that one inflated pretender be humbled. He scraps together a few of the fulsome encomiums lavished upon the King James' translators, and then adds: "I fearlessly make the declaration, that there are not *now* men to be found in the whole wide world, so profoundly learned, so completely conversant in, and so entirely and thoroughly master of the languages in which the *will of* God was revealed to man." Now, that the reader may see what the declaration of this Rev. A. M., President of a College, is worth, we invite attention to what follows immediately after this inflated declaration. He says: "The last testimony, though not least, is Alexander Campbell, President of Bethany, and himself a translator." Reader, you must bear with us, as we are noticing an Anti-Revision Sermon, written by a Rev. A. M., President of a College, while we inquire who this "Alexander Campbell" is, that is "President of *Bethany.*" Bethany, if we understand the matter, is a little *town;* but we did not know it had a *President,* much less that "Alexander Campbell" was its President. But we must not always take a Rev. A. M. as he says, but as he means, if we can find out how that is. We take it, then, in this instance, that he did not mean President of Bethany, but of the *College* at Bethany. What, then, is he about to do with the testimony of Alexander Campbell? Why, sirs, make it sustain the competency of the King James' translators, of whom he is speaking! And pray, where does he find this testimony? Why upon the 7th page, he says, though we find the passage on the 6th page, of the New Testament, published by Mr. Campbell, in the preface; in words written concerning Drs. McKnight, Doddridge and Geo. Campbell, and saying nothing about the King James' translators! The following are the words:

"Yet it may so happen, that now and then (a rare thing, yet sometimes does happen), once or twice in a hundred years, an individual or two may arise, whose *literary acquirements, whose genius, independence of mind,* honesty and candor, may fit them to be *faithful* and *competent* translators, and of their honesty and faithfulness the greatest proof which can be presented, is their correcting the mistakes of their own party, and with impartiality censuring the errors in their own denomination, as they censure those of other denominations; and with cheerfulness commending the virtues, and acknowledging the attainments of those who are ranked under another name, as they do those of their own people. Such, *in a very eminent degree,* were the translators of this version."

The parenthesis in this quotation, is not in the passage, but inserted by our Rev. A. M. without the least sign, and the italics are also the work of his unsanctified fingers. Now, think of the morality of this opponent of Revision, in taking language spoken of one set of men and applying it to others, not in his mind at all, foisting a parenthesis into it, without any sign, and capitalizing portions of the quotation, to make it speak in strong terms of men not spoken of at all! This language is in the preface to the version published by Mr. Campbell, and is spoken of Drs. McKnight, Doddridge and Geo. Campbell, the translators of the version he was publishing and of which he was speaking. The words, "this version," at the close of the quotation, refer to the version published by Mr. Campbell and not to the King James' version. Sup- pose the Rev. A. M. had quoted seven lines immediately following those quoted by him, he would then have found the following:

It is much more likely, that we shall find that a faithful and perspicuous translation coming from individuals who, without concert, or the solicitations of a party, undertake and accomplish it, having no national or sectional cause to abet than to expect to find one coming from those summoned by a King, and his court, and paid for their services out of the public treasury—convened, too, from *one part* of those elements of discord, which had distracted and convulsed a whole nation." Why did not the Rev. gentleman quote these words of Mr. Campbell? Because they show that he was speaking of the "literary acquirement," in "an eminent degree," and "genius" of the translators of the version he was publishing, and against the college of translators summoned by King James. Recollect, these words are in the same connection, the very next words after those quoted by the Rev. Anti-Revisionist, and speaking on the same subject, and testifying precisely against the very thing he was trying to prove! But, at the close of his quotation, we find the following parenthetical sentence, "(our version)." Here is where we challenge the Rev. A. M. with telling what is not true. By "our version," he means King James' version. It was not "our version," or the King James' version, he meant, as we have abundantly shown. But, hear this Anti-Revisionist again, speaking of his quotation from Mr. Campbell: "I regard this testimony of the very highest authority, because it came from one whom I regard as the very soul and life of the Revision Association. Judas' testimony, in saying, 'I have betrayed the innocent blood,' was not stronger in attesting the innocency of the Savior than this testimony in establishing the competency of our translators to *be faithful and competent* in the work assigned them."

Here is insult added to injury, meanness added to meanness, provocation added to provocation. Mr. Campbell's words, spoken of the translators of the version he was publishing, perverted by this Rev. A. M. and applied to the King James' translators, and then his testimony compared to that of Judas! And what is all this for? To prove what he evidently knows nothing about, viz.: That the King James' translators were better qualified and more competent translators than any we can find now! What is to become of the people under the guidance of such men? The Lord pity them! They must act under the principle, "Let us do evil that good may come!" The plea must be, We must maintain the King James' version. To this end we must maintain the King James' translators. To do this effectually, and make the dupes of superstition, under our control, confide in them, we must tell a falsehood—that what Mr. Campbell said of McKnight, Doddridge and Geo. Campbell, he said of the King James' translators, which we know he never did say of them—and thus make the people believe in the King James' translators and hold on to the common version, right or wrong! What confidence can the public have in men who will do such things?

Someone, in mercy, may say this is a mistake—that he did not willfully make this perversion—that *he thought* Mr. Campbell was speaking of the King James' translators. This is equivalent to saying, that he had not common sense, or that he said it without examination, and in either case, that his word is wholly unworthy of regard. Our columns are open for him to extricate himself, if he is able.   B. F.

-----o-----

[From the Millennial Harbinger.]

STUDENTS ON HYMN BOOK AVAILS.

A NUMBER of students have been boarded as well as educated gratuitously at Bethany College, on the pledge that they devote their lives to the Christian ministry. It is not understood, nor on our part assented to, that they alienate their attention from the work of the Christian ministry to any secular employment, not even to teaching schools, or becoming professors in colleges, or any other business or calling, but the entire devotion of their lives to the Christian ministry and the work of the Lord. Any that have done so, or purpose doing so, are morally bound by every principle of Christian justice and honor to refund the amounts due on board and tuition. This is neither more nor less than simple honor *alias* honesty. The avails annually accruing on hymn book sales, gratuitously given to aid such, are, as a matter of course, annually diminishing, so many having been supplied. And we are sorry to learn that not unfrequently one or two bibles and hymn books supply a whole family, and that, too, for a long time. Such books, too, are usually so tough and hardy, that they are a long time in wearing out. Our funds, therefore, annually diminish, as a matter of course. We are, therefore, constrained to modify our expenditures in this department, and must henceforth select those from our own judgment and knowledge, whom we shall aid, and upon whom we shall feel ourselves justified in contributing more or less according to our means, and according to their promise and prospects of future usefulness. Indeed, our own horizon is more than large enough for all we can do in this particular field of Christian benevolence. Besides this, there are those now laboring in the field who have never been within the walls of a college, full as worthy objects of Christian charity and benevolence as those who have. We shall, therefore, henceforth exercise the right of private judgment, until we have made as full an experiment on this basis as will fully satisfy us that we cannot succeed better than we have hitherto done. Our business, *commercially* contemplated, like all such business, has its profit and loss accounts, and we presume to think that we have about as much experience in this department as generally obtains in any similar transactions—so much, at least, as, in all reason, should admonish us of the necessity of the contemplated change. We trust, then, that henceforth we shall be allowed, without any offence to Jew or Gentile, or to the church of God, to act in harmony with our own convictions, till we have made, another experiment, on which we may someday report progress, and ask leave to sit again.   A. C.

LEARNING makes a man fit company for himself as well as for others.

UPWARD TENDENCY—REFORMATION NOT A FAILURE—MISSIONARY WORK.

BUT few proverbs are more true than the one that says, "Like priest, like people." If the people, in any religious community, are wrong, it may not always be the case that the preachers have made them wrong; but it is certain that they have not made them right. If there is a radical wrong in any religious community, in nine cases out of ten the preachers are to blame for it. Still, from the time Aaron, the high priest, blamed the people for his making the molten calf, to this day, all priests, both high and low, have inclined to excuse themselves from all blame, in all the errors or wrongs of any kind that find way into the communities built up and directed by their own hands, and throw all the blame upon their flocks. But this is like parents blaming their children, complaining that they are the worst children in the world, etc. Their neighbors are apt to think they are unreasonable parents, complaining without occasion, or else they have failed to discharge their duty to their children, and that a considerable share of the blame rests upon the parents, The same is true in regard to complaining preachers. They are either unreasonable men, complaining without cause, or they have not discharged their duty in their respective communities.

We only speak now of some radical defect, some fundamental wrong, running through and effecting the body in general, and countenanced by the body, and not of mere individual defects. If a body of people imbibe and uphold an erroneous principle, in nine cases out of ten, the preacher is to blame for it. It may be that he did not inculcate it, but he did not counteract it. He did not apply the remedy in time to cure. If a preacher has no influence in a community, he is wrong in preaching for it, when he might find a place where he could have an influence. If he has an influence, and allows wrongs to work in without interposing his influence, much of the blame falls upon him. God gave him influence to be wielded for good, and he is responsible if he does not do it. No man, however, can wield his influence for good merely *by word*. His example must, in all cases, go before his word. The preacher must be an exponent of the doctrine, in his life, his example, his daily walk, for his brethren. Otherwise his words will have no force, and no one will regard them. Does he desire that his brethren shall be liberal and noble-minded, hating covetousness? Let him set an example, avoiding everything that is little, parsimonious and narrow-minded. He can act noble, no matter what his condition; show nobleness of soul, manliness of heart and greatness of spirit. In the same way, he can be parsimonious, narrow-minded and selfish, in the best positions in the world. Let him lead the way, showing an expanded benevolence, an enlarged heart and noble soul, thus showing the ennobling and exalted character of the religion he professes. This is the proper manner to commend Christianity to the world. Let men see in the lives of its public advocates something noble, exalted and excellent; and, if they receive the doctrine, they expect to live similar lives.

We cannot expect men of the world to believe the gospel we preach, or love it, if it does not have an influence upon our own hearts and lives. We must have a zeal, earnestness and devotion to the work, evincing that we esteem it above everything else, or we may not expect men of the world to believe the doctrine. A little sermon or two per week will not do the work, nor convince men of sense that we are useful men. Any preacher, thinking of doing good, on the lookout for an opportunity, having ordinary health and strength, will find places to preach, averaging a discourse for each day in the year. The people in the church, and out of the church, notice the man, that he is ever on the alert, looking out for an opportunity, pushing the cause ahead. You can see examples of this kind in all the parties around us. The notorious N. L. Rice, is an example in this respect. While many preachers, in the same fraternity, are content to read a pretty composition, called "the sermon," on the Lord's day, he would preach two extemporaneous sermons and then average one each day through the week. While his brethren in the ministry are lying idle all the week, or making "fashionable calls," passing off the time pleasantly and doing nothing for their cause, he is delivering spirited and powerful public addresses, thus making it tell for his cause. What is the result? Why, that he is doing more for his cause than a dozen others put together. He receives an independent support, which comes freely, all thinking that he deserves it, and his influence is extending throughout the ranks, and his fame is known throughout the nation. Though his cause is unscriptural, unphilosophical and self-contradictory, his indomitable energy and perseverance make it go.

We have the plain truth of heaven, the pure gospel of the blessed God, and have nothing else to carry or maintain. What is wanting now, is energy, perseverance, manly industry, to push the cause forward. Thanks to God, we have many men who are of this sort, who are in the field and making it tell for the good of man. God is with them, and his people will be with them, stand by them and support them, without thinking or feeling that it is a burden. Men who work for God, move his cause and do his will, shall purchase for themselves a good degree and great boldness in the faith. These will never be a burden, nor will good men ever think it a hardship to support them. A man who commends his doctrine by manly zeal and energy, by earnestness and faithfulness, by a diligent and unmitigated effort, to spread it in the world, will be believed and regarded. He shows that the doctrine has some force upon his own soul, upon his own heart; that he feels it, and esteems it worth pressing through the world. He shows that there is life and power in the system, giving him momentum, impetuosity and determination. He moves and keeps moving, with a spirit and animation that gives interest and motion to all around him. You do not hear him say that the cause is *going down,* for the good reason that it is *going up* wherever he goes.

Preachers of the gospel must be enterprising men, industrious and powerful men. There is no greatness only in doing something great; no usefulness only in doing something useful. A man that accomplishes nothing in the world, is neither great nor useful. In these times a man is not to wait for the world to bring him into notice. He need not wait for mere fortuity to make a man of him. He must go out into the world and do something manly, noble and commanding for the good of his race. It is his business to make the world feel that he is in it, that he is a part of it, a vital part of it, a moving part of it, and a part of it that moves the parts around him. Some young men seem to be waiting for the world to take them up and make men of them, bring them into notice and support them. But the world does not do this, especially in the Christian ministry. It will aid in putting a man down, if he is on the way; but it will not aid in elevating a man, at least till he has attained considerable distinction.

Nothing is so desirable or necessary to the advancement of the cause, as an active, energetic and industrious ministry, ever reading, ferreting out the insidious deceptions that surround us, enforcing and defending the truth. The work is triumphing wherever this is done. The cause is manifestly good, self-evidently right, and can be maintained, in defiance of all opposition. No partisan opponent can stand before him who preaches, Christianity, and nothing but Christianity; the truth, the whole truth and nothing but the truth. Such a one has attained to manhood—to. the fullness of Christ. He is not ever learning, and never able to come to the knowledge of the truth; but has the truth, is made free by it, and is free indeed. He has "the faith once delivered to the saints"—"the faith of Christ"—the "one faith," by which all are justified who come to God by Jesus the Christ. His own soul was justified by this faith, and he intends to maintain it to the end. Men of enterprise are rising, pushing out into the world and devoting themselves to the work, in all directions, whose labors are being crowned with success. They esteem Christ and his cause above all earthly considerations. They see men of the world leave their homes, wives, children and pursuits, for political fame, worldly gain and mere temporal objects. If men can sacrifice domestic happiness for these objects, how much more should they make sacrifices for Christ; for the souls of men; for the righteousness which is by the faith of Christ?

The requirement to go and preach is as strong, binding and urgent now as it was in the days of the Apostles, and the woe to him who *can go* and preach the word of life, but *will not,* is nothing less than it was then. Men are now being lost for the want of the preached gospel; they are perishing for the word of life; sinking in ruin and cannot be saved but by preaching Christ to them. Woe betides those who have the word and refuse to proclaim it to them. But, thanks to heaven, men are going in all directions, and young men are rising, with zeal, earnestness and *spirit,* who are carrying the work forward triumphantly. The missionary work is going on, in some form or other, in almost all directions. Go on, brethren, and again we say, go on in the noblest and best of all work. They who turn many to righteousness shall shine as the stars in the firmament forever and ever. We shall meet trials, embarrassments and afflictions; but we shall reap if we faint not. In the end of the harvest we shall return with many ripe sheaves. We shall see those brought to the kingdom of God by our humble instrumentality, walking the streets of the New Jerusalem, with palms in their hands, crowns upon their heads and songs of everlasting joy upon their lips. We shall hear them crying, "Blessing, and honor, and glory, and dominion and power unto the Lord our God!" And, again, we shall hear them shout, "Hallelujah to Him that sits upon the throne, and to the Lamb forever and ever." Press on, brethren, for great is your reward in heaven ! Push the victories of the cross to the ends of the earth, and make all men know our Emanuel!   B. F.

-----0-----

Editor's Table.

We are truly sorry that we could not attend the State meeting and the Great Missionary Meeting in Lafayette, Ind. We had intended, without fail, being there, but owing to a mistake we had made in the time when it would take place, we had made an engagement, covering the same time, that we could not countermand. By the Divine blessing, we will yet spend some two weeks in Lafayette and near there this fall. We hope the brethren will have a great meeting.

OUR PROSPECTS.—So far as known to us, our arrangement for issuing an enlarged and improved weekly meets universal acceptation. We are greatly encouraged, and trust the arrangement will work well. Some inform us that they are sorry to give up the pamphlet, as it can be preserved. But we think the advantage of having all things fresh every week will comport so much better with the spirit of the times, than waiting the tardy motion of a monthly, that all will be better satisfied. We intend, as far as possible, furnishing a complete report of the success of the gospel, in a condensed form, so that the brethren can have it at a glance. A column will contain announcements of important meetings, college commencements, sessions, changes in professors, changes in preachers, etc., etc. A department will be occupied with obituaries, marriages, etc. We aim to fill a column or two with important items of news, such as is desirable for a family, both home and foreign. A limited space will be occupied with prices current and business items, for the benefit of those who take no secular paper. But the main body of the work will be taken up by sermons, orations, essays, reviews, of a religious nature. In one word, we intend it to make as strong, bold and manly a defense of the faith of Christ as possible, yet in love and kindness. It will not contain more than four columns advertising, and that limited to books and educational institutions. We appeal to all our friends to make an effort for us, and give us an extended circulation. By the divine blessing, we will send them a sheet that will meet the wants of the brotherhood. Any person sending $2 any time between now and Jan. 1st, will be credited in full till January 1859, and receive the paper from time of subscribing till that time.

Will Bro. James Jones please send us his address?

Success of the Gospel.

ST. JOSEPH, MO., Sept. 18,1857.

BRO. FRANKLIN :—I have just returned from a meeting in Andrew county, where I saw twenty-two confess our Master. D. Z. ELLIS.

WAVERLY, Ill., Sept. 9, 1857.

BRO. FRANKLIN :—*We* have just closed a meeting of eighteen days at Union, in Greene county, and I think it was as interesting as any meeting I ever attended. We had the hearty co-operation of the Methodists and Baptists! We were assisted all the time by Elder Austin Sims, who is beloved by all who know him; and part of the time we had the assistance of Elder G. E. Sweeney—he had to leave, owing to ill health. The result of the meeting was ninety souls were added to the Disciples—eighty by confession and immersion, and ten otherwise. The Lord be praised.

Yours in Christ,

JNO. S. SWEENEY.

COLEMANSVILLE, KY., Sept. 21, 1857.

BRO. FRANKLIN :—We are thankful to be enabled to say to you that the good cause is still going onward and upward in this vicinity. I commenced a meeting at Pleasant Ridge, in Pendleton county, on Friday before the 4th Lord's day in July, which continued some five days. The result was four additions; three were immersed and one restored. We were aided, a portion of the time, at the above place, by Bro. Y. J Tharp.

I also commenced a meeting near Williamstown, in Grant county, on Friday before the 4th Lord's day in August, which continued six days. The result was eleven additions; nine were immersed, one of them was a Methodist; one restored. We were aided, at this point, by brethren Barnet and Reed. To the Lord be all the praise.

Yours in the good hope,

WM. JARROTT.

RUSSELVILLE, OHIO, Sept. 16, 1857.

BRO. FRANKLIN:—The cause in this region is still advancing. On the first Lord's day in this month, at my regular appointment in Hamersville, ten were added—all by confession and baptism. Lord's day before, in Bethel, in company with Bro. B. F. Sallee, we held a meeting of eight days and four were baptized. Several have been added at other points. In all I have baptized twenty-nine since I wrote you last; for which the Lord be praised.

Yours in the good hope,

JAMES WHITE.

LOUISVILLE, KY., Sept. 5, 1857.

BRO. FRANKLIN;—Yesterday I left Georgetown, where Bro. Jno. A. Gano and I had been conducting a meeting for the past seven days. There were nine confessions and baptisms. It was with deep regret I separated with the kind sisters and brothers and friends at this place, and particularly my dearly beloved Bro. Gano.

Affectionately your brother,

T. M. ALLEN.

P. S.—Yesterday (Sept. 7th) I preached twice in this city, in the meeting-house on Hancock street, and had three confessions. To-day I immersed them and at night spoke again, when those immersed took their membership. Brethren W. C. Rogers and Sewell were with me. Bro. Sewell expects to preach for the church on Hancock street the ensuing year. Bro. Rogers leaves to-morrow for southern Kentucky to evangelize there.

To-morrow I expect to leave Kentucky for Missouri, after a delightful, though laborious, sojourn of some ten or eleven weeks, during which time I have preached eighty-four sermons, and there have been one hundred and one additions at the different meetings I have attended. Praised be the Lord.

Affectionately your brother,

T. M. ALLEN.

CYNTHIANA, KY. Sept. 25, 1857.

BRO. FRANKLIN:—I have just returned from Colemansville with my father, our very promising Bro. Arnold, and our estimable fellow-laborer Bro. Parrott. We had a joyful time. Our joy was not greater in seeing many prodigals return to their Father's house, to receive a Father's blessing, than in witnessing demonstrations upon the part of the brethren of a deep devotional feeling, and a determination to be more interested in the cause of Christianity. We need revivals in the church everywhere; and when the Disciples begin to repent, we may hope to see sinners repenting.

Some two weeks ago we had the pleasure of laboring with the brethren at Indicutt's, some six miles east of this place, in connection with our dear Bro. Holton; my father and Bro. Wm. C. Rogers. My brother did much of the work, and (allow me?) it was well done.

Quite a number were added to the church. May the time soon come when Zion shall put on her clean garments—when Christians shall make the home above as much the theme of their conversation, and motive of their conduct, as they now do the home below.

JOHN ROGERS.

COLLINSVILLE, TENN., Sept., 21, 1857.

BRO. FRANKLIN:—I last Wednesday closed a meeting in North Mississippi, which resulted in twenty- four additions—thirteen by letter and eleven by immersion. I was assisted by our venerable Bro. Jas. E. Matthews. We are much encouraged and thank God for the success of our humble efforts;

Yours in hope,

GEO. PLATTEBURG

Obituaries,

PARIS, KY., Sept. 16, 1857.

BRO. FRANKLIN:—Our dear brother and relative, S. W. IRVIN, has gone to the home of "the pure in heart." On his way home from a laborious tour of preaching, the severity of his attack was so great, that he was compelled to stop at Maysville, where he died on Friday night last, after but a few days of severe suffering. I have just returned from the field of his labors, where almost every face seemed draped in mourning.

I have been told that the scene at his burial was mournful beyond description. Men, women, children and servants all overwhelmed with grief. Yes, Bro. Irvin had a deep, warm place in the heart of everyone who knew him.

I could wish he had lived to be as extensively known from the pulpit as he was from the press. For the eloquence of his pen was fully equaled by the eloquence of his discourse. I use the word eloquence in its true sense—that which melts the heart and enwraps the soul. I have known him and been intimately associated with him, from the little bright-eyed boy to the mature man—at home and abroad, in public and private, and I cannot tell in what particular position his brilliant talents and attractive graces shone brightest.

He has left a most interesting wife and a little son about nine months old to wander a little longer in the vale of tears. May God bless them and keep them to the great meeting.

Yours in haste,

J. I. ROGERS.

BRO. FRANKLIN:—I drop you this line to inform you of my loss. My beloved wife ELIZABETH died at Independence, Grant county, Ind., Sept. 20th., aged 36 years. She had been for eighteen years a faithful servant in the church of Christ. In her last sickness, which was five days, she suffered much, yet she died like a Christian, leaving six children and myself to mourn her loss. P. RIGDON.

THE AMERICAN CHRISTIAN REVIEW.

VOL. II.   CINCINNATI, NOVEMBER. 1857.   No. 11.

THE GOSPEL OF CHRIST—A DISCOURSE.
BY ELDER W. S. BROWN.

"For I am not ashamed of the gospel of Christ; for it is the power of God unto salvation to everyone that believeth; to the Jew first, and also to the Greek."—Rom. I. 16.

This was the language of the Apostle Paul, in his letter to the primitive Christians in Rome. The heroism displayed in the declaration, "I am not ashamed of the gospel of Christ," is worthy of the highest admiration; for of all things of which men in that day were most ashamed, and which they most despised, the gospel was the chief. The early followers of Christ, and the primitive Christians in general were, of all men in their day, the most despised and persecuted. Not that they were men deserving of such things; for of all men that lived, they were the most honest, peaceable and law-abiding; but because the great principles of truth, which made them Christians, were antagonistic in their nature and bearings to all the corruptions and wicked devices of the age—to all the philosophy and false religions that existed. "Men loved darkness rather than light," not that it was more attractive and beautiful, but "because their deeds were evil."

The Prince of Salvation, who knew no sin, neither was guile found in his mouth; who went about doing good, teaching as man never taught, working miracles and administering to the wants and necessities of men, was himself a continual object of persecution, "he was a man of sorrows and acquainted with grief," he was despised and rejected of men, he was reviled, yet he reviled not again. It was decreed that the disciple could not be above his Master, hence his disciples were objects of persecution after him. The bitterness of this decree, his apostles in carrying out the great commission, and the early Christians in general, realized to the fullest extent. The malice of their enemies was never appeased, nor their blood-thirsty, persecuting spirit ever satisfied, until they had heaped upon them every insult which could be devised, subjected them to every degradation and torture which it was possible for them to endure, and put them to death in the most ignominious and cruel manner possible. The Savior of the world had given them an example of suffering which had no parallel in the annals of either time or eternity (the foundations of his kingdom were laid in his death and cemented with his blood), and they, as true and loyal subjects, rejoiced that they were counted worthy to suffer persecution for his sake. Such Herculean labors as they performed, such zeal as they manifested, such resolution, unearthly fortitude and moral courage as they displayed, such humility and love as they exhibited, such miracles as they wrought, such matchless eloquence as fell from their lips, such heart-stirring appeals as they made, and, above all, such persecution as they endured, plainly showed that they were animated or inspired by a spirit not of earth.

But among all the ambassadors of Christ or apostles of our Savior, there were none in whose life and character these sublime and heavenly characteristics were more highly exemplified or brilliantly displayed than in the apostle Paul. The time was when he was considered an ornament to his country, and an honor to the land and city which gave him birth. He was of a high and honorable parentage, a citizen of no mean city, a Pharisee of the Pharisees, brought up at the feet of Gamaliel, one of the wisest doctors of the law, by whom, he was instructed in all the science and wisdom of the age in which he lived; hence, when he arrived at the age of manhood, he took rank amongst the highest dignitaries of State. Being extremely zealous of the law, and conversant with all its forms and ceremonies, together with the traditions of the fathers, he soon came to enjoy a more than ordinary degree of the confidence and esteem of his fellow men, and to be entrusted with the highest and most important offices within their gift.

But, notwithstanding all this, notwithstanding the high position which he occupied, and that he seemed to be traveling the high road to power and to fame, and was doing what he believed to be God's service, when Christianity was presented before him in all its pristine loveliness, when Christ, the now risen and coronated King of the heavens and the earth, spoke to him from off the eternal throne, exclaiming, "Saul, Saul, why persecutest thou me," and enveloped him in the brightness of his glory, he immediately resigned his commission, ceased his persecuting crusade, abandoned all his ambitious projects, changed his whole character and course of life, and became an humble and devoted Christian disciple and apostle. Was ever a change like this? He immediately sought the society of those whom he had been striving to persecute; he became obedient to their instructions, identified himself with them, and from thence to the day of his death, was what we here find him—a stern, uncompromising, zealous, untiring advocate of the truth as it is in Christ Jesus.

The Son of God, when upon earth, was not a guest at the court of kings, nor did he often visit the palaces of the rich; hence it followed that most of his disciples and of those who believed through their word were of the lowest class of society and from the humbler walks of life. To forsake posts of honor and influence and become identified with such a people, was by no means an alluring or attractive step to a worldly-minded or ambitious man. Nor did it comport with the design of the Founder of Christianity, nor with the nature of the institution itself, that men of such feelings and aspirations, should compose the living stone of Christ's earthly temple or kingdom. "My kingdom is not of this world," said the great Teacher. It was no part of his design to surround it with the paraphernalia of earthly majesty or glory. It was to be a spiritual kingdom composed of the newborn, regenerated, sanctified, adopted, reconciled, redeemed sons of men. Such was the apostle Paul and his illustrious compeers, the immortal twelve. Hence it matters not what were the circumstances that surrounded them, how great were the dangers or how appalling the terrors that threatened them—it mattered not whether they were in Jerusalem, Ephesus or Rome; whether in Athens, Corinth or Antioch; whether in chains arraigned before a Roman pro-consul, or incarcerated within the loathsome cells of some dark prison-house; whether exposed to the insults and menaces of an infuriated mob, or liable to apprehension at any moment by the bloody executioners of Nero, "the scourge of mankind," they were ever ready and never afraid to affirm, "*I am not ashamed of the gospel of Christ,*" and to seal their affirmation with their blood. What a glorious and noble example is here recorded for the imitation of all succeeding generations. Oh! would to God that the same Spirit of devotion and love, the same spirit of self-denial and self-sacrifice, the same heroic fortitude and high-toned moral courage, pervaded the hearts of God's people in this our day! How numerous and glorious would be the triumphs of the gospel in every land and country! Then would the word of the Lord run and be glorified; peace would flow throughout the earth as a mighty river, and righteousness spread abroad over the desert wastes of humanity as the waves of the sea.

The apostle Paul, up to this time in his history, had made every sacrifice in his power, and suffered almost every form of persecution which the relentless malice of his enemies could inflict upon him save scaling his testimony with his blood, and this he was ready to do whenever it was God's will that he should. In his own - language, he said: "Are they ministers of Christ? I am more; in labors more abundant, in strifes above measure, in prisons more frequent, in deaths oft. Of the Jews five times received I forty stripes save one; thrice was I beaten with rods, once was I stoned, thrice I suffered shipwreck, and a night and a day have I been in the deep. In journeyings often, in perils of waters, in perils of robbers, "in perils by mine own countrymen, in perils by the heathen, in perils in the city, in perils in the wilderness, in perils in the sea, in perils among false brethren. In weariness and painfulness, in watchings often, in hunger and thirst, in fastings often, in cold and nakedness."

Was ever such a catalogue of calamities enumerated in the history of one man?

And yet, in prospect of greater evils, in the face of death itself, the Apostle could fearlessly and triumphantly assert, "I am not ashamed of the gospel of Christ." Was ever heroism like this? He had suffered all these direful evils for the sake of the gospel; he had submitted to every indignity and insult; he had endured, in his zeal to propagate the gospel, every species of hardship and persecution, and yet his face had never crimsoned with shame, his courage had never failed him, his resolution had never faltered, his zeal had never abated, his faith in the sublime truths of the gospel had never been shaken.

But the Apostle gives a reason for the hope that is within him, or for the zeal for the gospel of Christ: "For," says he, "it is the power of God unto salvation." It is the great plan by which God, in his infinite wisdom and mercy proposes to save the world, to redeem man from his thralldom to sin and death. It is the way in which he exerts his infinite power and displays his boundless goodness in the salvation of men. Through its efficacy, or the efficacy of the blood of Christ, as exhibited therein, all the obstacles in the way of man's redemption are removed, and a door of mercy, a way of escape from the impending wrath of violated law and outraged justice, are opened unto him. "It is the power of God; hence it is no device of man. It is God's plan, and exists by his appointment. It did not originate with angels, nor was it devised by man, for whose benefit it was designed. It originated in the divine mind of the great *I am* of the universe, of him who is infinite in all the powers and attributes of his divine nature; hence we may rest assured that it is an efficacious plan, that it is adapted to the end proposed, that it is fitted to accomplish its purpose, viz.: The salvation of man. It is mighty; hence it is appropriately called power, not of man, but the power of God. It is not a feeble and ineffectual instrumentality, but is "mighty to the pulling down of strong holds." In the history of its progress throughout the nations of the earth, it had displayed a power as applicable to every degree of sin, and to every combination of wickedness. Like the little stone cut from the mountain's brow, it had continued to gather strength with its progress until it had acquired a momentum or power which the zeal and corruption of Jew and Gentile combined—which all the combinations of men and demons could not resist. Though contained in earthen vessels, though entrusted to the hands of a few illiterate fishermen, who of themselves were powerless—were perfect weakness; yet had it acquired an influence over the minds of men which no subsequent revolutions of nations and empires could eradicate. These men, panoplied in the gospel armor, and armed with the sword of the Spirit, or word of God, had traversed every nation, navigated every sea, visited every city of the Jewish and Pagan world, besieged every strong hold of Paganism, and upon the tottering battlements of the time-honored idolatrous temples and pagodas of the day, erected the golden standard of the cross. No power that existed could check this progress, no ear that listened could withstand the influence of their heart-stirring appeals. Were they persecuted?—the arrows of their persecution rebounded upon those who hurled them. Were they imprisoned and their feet made fast in the stocks?—they sung psalms and praised God until the prison walls were shaken to their foundation, and the heart of the cruel jailor meted into obedience, gentleness and love. Were they condemned to die a martyr's death?—they achieved a greater victory in the heroic fortitude and calm resignation displayed in their dying moments than they ever had or could have done by a life-time devoted to the cause which they plead. It mattered not what were the previous characters of men—whether they were scoffing Jews or idolatrous Gentiles—whether persecutors or blasphemers—whether illiterate fishermen or despised publicans—whether haughty Pharisees or worshippers of the great Diana—the gospel had the power to transform them into meek and humble followers of the Lamb, faithful and zealous soldiers of the cross. Despite their differences, national and sectional, religious and political, they become of one mind and one heart, as though members of one family, having a common parentage and a common destiny. Such a revolution in the thoughts and actions of men—such a reformation of life and character—such a regeneration of the hearts and consciences of both Jew and Gentile, was never witnessed in so short a time—was never effected by any other instrumentality.

As in the miracles wrought by the Savior and his Apostles, so in all the triumphs of the gospel, there was exhibited a power which was evidently of God. No one could contemplate it in all its grandeur and omnipotency, and not be convinced that it had God for its author; for surely no instrumentality not of divine origin could accomplish such wondrous works. This was the inevitable conclusion of every intelligent, sane, reflecting mind.

Such being the nature and power of the gospel of Christ, it becomes a matter of the deepest interest and highest importance to know in what that gospel consisted. "For," adds the Apostle, "it is the power of God unto salvation." There can, therefore, be no salvation without it. To this inquiry, fraught with so much interest and importance, would we desire to direct your attention for a time.

The term *gospel* is defined to signify precisely, "good news, glad tidings." Hence a proclamation of peace, proceeding from the proper authorities to a people overwhelmed with the calamities of war, might be appropriately denominated a gospel of peace to that nation. It is an authoritative proclamation of a definite and specific character, containing a message which all may understand, and which, being understood, causes the road of battle and the turmoil of war to cease, and carries joy to the heart of the nation.

The great King of the universe has not unfrequently issued proclamations and messages of a peaceful and joyous nature to his people on the earth. And wherever we find a proclamation or message of this kind recorded on the sacred page, we find it always accompanied by the most indubitable evidences of its divine origin, and expressed in language altogether insusceptible of misapprehension. God, in speaking to man or in giving revelations to the world, always spoke in the language of man. Even the immaculate Son, when the mouth-piece of the divine Father to the world, assumed our nature, or hid the beauties of his radiant countenance within the veil of mortality. Another marked and striking peculiarity of those divine proclamations is, that whatsoever overtures of mercy or of good they contain to man, are based upon certain conditions, or the faithful performance of certain positive duties, all of which are enumerated and defined in specific and positive terms. These duties may be of diverse character, depending upon the fact as to whether the message is addressed to a particular individual, to a chosen and peculiar people, or to the world at large. Yet the primary condition of pardon, or of blessing to man, is always the same; it is a never-varying, never-changing principle, and that is a faithful and implicit compliance with the specified requisitions of the King's proclamation. These proclamations, containing promises of grace, pardon and mercy, if based upon conditions with which the individuals addressed can comply, as is always the case in all God's messages to the world, may be appropriately denominated glad tidings or gospel, and not unfrequently do we find them thus denominated; hence it behooves man, in whatever age he lives, to search out the particular proclamation or gospel which relates to himself, or which embraces him in its promises and merciful provisions. When the original progenitor of our race, the first man—Adam—first discovered the enormity of his guilt and was made sensible of the direful consequences resulting there from in the sad calamity of the fall; when the light of God's favor was withdrawn and darkness impenetrable as the gloom of despair overwhelmed the future of his existence, and he was seemingly without hope and without God in the world, the merciful declaration of infinite goodness, that "the seed of the woman should bruise the serpent's head," contained a bright ray of hope that penetrated the innermost recesses of his perturbed soul, served to illuminate his dark pathway through the vale of his mortal existence, and to prompt him to a faithful discharge of his duty. This to him was gospel or glad tidings.

In the antediluvian age, when God looked forth upon the world and said that it was corrupt, and that all flesh had corrupted his way upon the earth, he said unto Noah, "The end of all flesh is come before me, for the earth is filled with violence through them, and, behold, I will destroy them with the earth. Make thee an ark of gopher wood, and with thee I will establish my covenant, and thou shalt come into the ark, thou and thy sons, and thy wife, and thy sons' wives with thee."

This declaration or promise to Noah of salvation, upon certain specified conditions, from this direful catastrophe, by which the earth was to be stripped of its entire population, was gospel or glad tidings to those who accredited the divine announcement. They immediately set to work to comply with the conditions specified, and though it required the labor of one hundred and twenty years to carry out the divine instructions in every particular, yet they ceased not their labors until their work was fully completed—until the ark was finished and freighted with its precious burden, the representatives of all the living beings of earth. It is recorded: "Thus did Noah; according to all that God commanded, so did he." By obedience—implicit, faithful, rational and persevering obedience, were the blessings of this gospel secured or the fulfillment of its promises realized.

The Apostle, from whose writings our text is chosen, records that to Abraham a gospel was preached, which affirmed that "in him all nations should be blessed." To one whose heart was burdened with a desire inherent in our nature, that our names should live after us, this was a promise fraught with the highest hopes, and the most pleasing anticipations. Innumerable are the devices which men have invented, and Herculean the labors they have performed to secure immortal fame; but here it is promised in its highest perfection, and clad in imperishable lustre. It is not only affirmed that his name should descend through all nations to the remotest posterity, but that being blessed in him, it would be held in the most grateful remembrance and esteemed with the highest veneration. That this gospel was not general, but exclusively personal in its application, none can pretend to doubt. It related alone to him to whom it was spoken, and could not possibly apply to any other. The glorious promise thus made to Abraham, has long since been fulfilled. From him nations have descended, and in him, or in the fulfillment of that promise, all nations of the earth are now being blessed.

To the Jews in Babylonish captivity, the royal proclamation of Cyrus, the renowned conqueror of mighty Babylon, authorizing them to return to their native land and to rebuild the city and temple of their God, was a gospel—it was glad tidings which caused their hearts to leap for joy. Many thousands accredited the announcement, readily complied with its requisitions, embarked in the hazardous enterprise, and were thus made instrumental in restoring their nationality, in re-establishing the sacred institutions of their fathers, and the worship of the true and living God.

The announcement of the Savior's birth by the angel to the devout shepherds, while holding nightly vigils on the plains of Judea, was a gospel. Said he, "Fear not, for, behold, I bring you good tidings of great joy, which shall be to all people. For unto you is born this day, in the city of David, a Savior, who is Christ the Lord." This was a grand and glorious announcement, one which caused a thrill of joy to rise from earth to heaven, bringing down a multitude of the heavenly host to join the sons of earth in a new chorus of praise to God and the Lamb. Yet this announcement alone, or the great fact upon which it was based, was not sufficient to accomplish the great work of human redemption. The birth of Christ was a sublime and glorious event—one which filled the hearts of men and angels with joy and amazement, yet it was only a prelude to the glorious drama of his eventful life, death, burial, resurrection and ascension on high, as the all-conquering Prince of Peace and Life.

The inspired Harbinger, John the Baptist, preached a gospel, when he said to his countrymen, "Repent ye, for the kingdom of heaven is at hand." This announcement his countrymen all understood, and rejoiced that they had lived to hear it announced. Our Savior, after having entered upon his public ministry, came into Galilee, preaching the gospel of the kingdom of God, and saying: "The time is fulfilled, and the kingdom of God is at hand; repent ye, and believe the gospel." But what was that gospel? It was, as he announced it in clear and specific terms, that "the time is fulfilled; the kingdom of God is at hand." To a people crushed to the earth by the weight of the foreign yoke to which they were subject—a people in the most abject bondage, sighing for liberty, and yet without hope, the announcement of even prospective deliverance was hailed with joy and reiterated with delight. Temporal, national deliverance from the galling tyranny of their Roman conquerors and oppressors, was what the

Jews vainly hoped to realize in the establishment of the kingdom of God. Hence they hailed with joy the announcement of its immediate coming, whether proclaimed by the inspired Harbinger, the humble Nazarene, or the seventy whom he commissioned to go to the cities of Israel and reiterate what they had heard him so often repeat. But, connected with this gospel or proclamation, there was no promise of future salvation. It had the same object in view, whether announced by John, Christ or the seventy, viz.: The preparation of the Jewish nation for the glorious advent of the Savior, or for the introduction of the spiritual reign of Christ on the earth.

To the halt, the blind and the dumb, the palsied and leprous hosts who flocked around the Son of Man, as he passed from city to city, during his sojourn upon the earth, the mandate which restored them to life and health, which gave them sight and made them whole, was a gospel—was glad tidings of great joy; but it was such only to them who were healed: for the whole needed not a physician. So were the eternal fiats which calmed the ocean's furious storm-king, and allayed the fears of the despairing mariner, which broke the slumbers of the unconscious dead and restored the lost loved ones to the fond embrace of disconsolate mourners, and which translated the penitent thief on the cross to the blissful bowers of Paradise; but they were so only to them—only to the few especially addressed, and not to the world at large. Neither these nor any of kindred import, that are found recorded in the sacred annals of revelation, from the creation to the resurrection of the Son of God from the tomb of Joseph, can be appropriately called "the power of God unto salvation," or contain general terms of pardon and redemption to man. But that of which the great Apostle affirms he is not ashamed, and which he dignifies with the name of "Gospel of Christ," differs as widely from all others, and is as much superior to every other exhibition of the divine goodness to man, as the immaculate Son, who is the brightness of his own transcendent glory, and the express image of his august person, by whom he made the worlds, and whom, he hath appointed heir of all things, is superior in all the godlike attributes of his divine nature to his ministering servants, be they faithful men, flames of fire, or blazing seraphs. To all the angels assembled around the eternal throne, he said, when he brought his first-begotten into the world, Behold your King, "worship him." The gospel which Paul preached was not the gospel of the kingdom, as proclaimed during the natural lifetime of our Savior, but it was that which the crucified, buried, arisen and glorified Prince of Peace, whilst standing upon the mount of ascension in Galilee, invested with all power both in heaven and earth, commissioned his disciples "to go into all the world and preach to every creature." "He that believeth," saith he, "and is baptized, shall be saved; he that believeth not, shall be damned." Here we discover that the conditions of the gospel, like those of every other ever vouchsafed to man, are as definite and specific as language could make them. There is left no room for caviling or misapprehension.

To those whom he then and there addressed, and constituted his apostles or plenipotentiaries upon the earth, invested with full power to go into all nations, and to proclaim the glad tidings of peace and salvation to every creature, must we appeal for a knowledge of the gospel. To them he committed the keys of his kingdom, and from them must require a knowledge of the way of life and of the great plan of salvation.

Said the apostle Paul, in his first letter to the Christian Church in the city of Corinth: "Moreover, brethren, I declare unto you the gospel which I preached unto you, which also ye have received, and wherein ye stand. By which also ye are saved, if ye keep in memory, what I preached unto you, unless ye have believed in vain. For I delivered unto you first of all, that which I also received, how that Christ died for our sins, according to the Scriptures; and how that he was buried, and how that he rose again the third day, according to the Scriptures, and how that he was seen of Cephas, or Peter, then of the twelve; after that he was seen of above five hundred brethren at once, of whom the greater part remain unto this present, but some are fallen asleep; after that, he was seen of James, then of all the apostles; and, last of all, he was seen of me also, as of one born out of due time," I Cor. xv.

The gospel, as preached by the apostle Paul, according to his own testimony, embraced these grand and sublime facts, the death, burial and resurrection of our Savior, all duly substantiated by living witnesses, none of which had not transpired and consequently could not have been preached during the natural life-time of the Messiah. To their refined, pleasure-seeking, idolatrous neighbors, the Athenians, the Apostle had introduced the gospel by striking a death-blow at their idolatry, in declaring unto them the unknown God, whom they ignorantly worshipped. He showed them that He was an infinitely greater being than were those imaginary deities with whom they professed to be intimately acquainted. He told them of his greatness, how that he had made the world and all things therein by the word of his power, that he is Lord of heaven and earth, that he dwelleth not in temples made with hands, as though he needed anything, but giveth life to all, and breath, and all things; that he had created all nations of men for to dwell on the earth, and had determined the bounds of their habitation. He then spoke of his boundless goodness, showing that, if possible, it far transcended his greatness, how that when man had sinned and forfeited all claims to divine mercy, when all was lost, and there was no eye to pity, and no arm to save, this same great, wise and beneficent being gave his only begotten Son a sacrifice for the sins of a lost and dying world. He assures them that this same immaculate Son of the most high God, had died—that he had died for their sins—that he had died for their sins according to the Scriptures, or in the manner set forth in the prophecies of previous ages. He also affirms that he was buried; and, more wonderful than all besides, that he rose from the dead on the third day. according to the Scriptures. Of these sublime and astounding facts, he assured them that he and his fellow-apostles, together with hundreds of others of equally undoubted veracity, were living witnesses, that they testified only of what they had seen and heard, or were eye and ear witnesses. And the sacred historian records that "the Corinthians, hearing these things, believed and were baptized." This was in strict harmony with the last declaration of Christ on earth: "He that believeth and is baptized shall be saved." The Apostle also affirms that this was the gospel which he preached, and which they received or believed, and by which they were saved."

Thus do we learn what was the gospel which Paul preached, and of which he was not ashamed, and which the ancient people of Corinth received, believed and obeyed. To them it became "the power of God unto salvation," even to as many as believed and obeyed.

But this is not the only exhibition of the gospel by the apostle Paul, recorded for the guidance of future generations. If we accompany him into Antioch in Pisidia, we find him in the Jewish synagogue, standing in the presence of a mixed audience of both Jews and Gentiles. After the customary exercises of reading the law and the prophets were performed, the rulers of the synagogue invited him to address the people. The Apostle responded to the call by proceeding to demonstrate from the word read and from the history of the Jewish nation, that the gospel which he preached was in strict harmony with the law and the prophets, and that of the seed of David, God had, according to promise, raised unto Israel a Savior—Jesus. To corroborate his declaration, he alluded to the testimony of John the Baptist, which was accredited by the Jewish nation as a people, and that, although they of Jerusalem and their rulers, in their blindness and ignorance of his true character and mission, and of the voices of the prophets, had condemned and executed him without cause, and had unconsciously fulfilled all that was written of him, by taking his mangled body down from the cross and laying it in the tomb of Joseph; yet had God raised him from the dead, without his seeing corruption, and he was seen alive during many days by them which came up with him from Galilee to Jerusalem, who are his witnesses unto the people. "Be it known unto you, therefore, men and brethren," says he, "that through this man is preached unto you the forgiveness of sins, and by him all that believe are justified from all things from which ye could not be justified by the law of Moses." Now it is evident that none were justified by the law of Moses, only those who were obedient to that law, for all disobedience it rigidly condemned and severely punished. And it is but rational to conclude that the same principle obtained in regard to the gospel or law of Christ, and that those who believed also obeyed or were baptized, as in other instances, and thus were justified or saved. This conclusion the sacred historian fully warrants in what he further records. "For," says he, "when the Jews were gone out of the synagogue, the Gentiles besought that these words might be preached to them the next Sabbath. And the next Sabbath day, almost the whole city came together to hear the word of God. But when the Jews saw the multitude, they were filled with envy, and spake against those things which were spoken by Paul contradictory and blaspheming. Then Paul and Barnabas waxed bold, and said it was necessary that the word of God should first have been spoken to you; but seeing ye put it from you, and judge yourselves unworthy of everlasting life, lo, we turn to the Gentiles; for so hath the Lord commanded us, saying, "I have set thee to be a light of the Gentiles, that thou shouldst be for salvation unto the ends of the earth. And when the Gentiles heard this, they were glad, and glorified the word of the Lord; and as many as were ordained, or disposed to eternal life, believed; and the word of the Lord was published throughout all that region, the unbelieving Jews continuing to oppose and persecute, whilst the disciples, and not the world, filled with joy, and with the Holy Spirit."

Thus, do we learn that the gospel, preached by the apostle Paul to the inhabitants, consisting of both Jews and Gentiles of Antioch in Asia, was the same as that preached to the refined citizens of Corinth in Europe—that it embraced the same great facts, viz.: The death, burial and resurrection of the Savior, according to the Scriptures, and that it was the power of God unto salvation to those only who heard, believed and obeyed, or glorified God. To them, through faith and obedience, it brought forgiveness of sins, salvation, joy, and the communion of the Holy Spirit; whilst to the unbelieving, blaspheming, persecuting Jews, it was a stone of stumbling and a rock of offence.

But the preaching of the gospel was not confined to the labors of the great Apostle to the Gentile world. The immortal Peter, who was first to conceive and give utterance to the great truth, that Jesus is the Christ, the Son of the living God, and to whom, by way of reward and distinction, were given the keys of Christ's earthly kingdom, also proclaimed the same gospel. On the memorable day of Pentecost, ten days after he and his fellow-apostles had seen their arisen Lord ascend to heaven from a mountain in Galilee, attended by a vast retinue of the heavenly host; when they were all assembled with one accord in one place, in the midst of the most sublime and awful, demonstrations of divine power which men or angels had ever witnessed; when the heavens and the earth seemed to have come together, and, in the presence of the awe-struck and mocking representatives of all the different nations and languages of earth, he stood up, and with a boldness which was characteristic only of the inspired ambassadors of Christ; hurled back the impious charge, that they were filled with new wine," into the teeth of those who made it, and proceeded to demonstrate from the same Scriptures, and from their; own personal-observation And knowledge, the same great facts in reference to the humble Nazarene, whose ignominious, yet wonderful, death, they had so recently witnessed, assuring the whole house or nation of Israel, that God had made the same Jesus; whom they had crucified, both Lord and Christ. When three thousand of his astounded auditory had listened to the wonderful words, as they fell from his lips, until their hearts were pricked or penetrated with the awfully solemn truths which he uttered, and they were overwhelmed with the enormity of their own guilt and that of their nation, and with the consequences of the just judgment and merited vengeance which awaited them, and cried out in the agony of despair, "Men and brethren, what shall we do?" Then answered Peter, "Repent and be baptized, every one of you, into the name of Jesus Christ, for the remission of sins, and ye shall receive the gift of the Holy Spirit."

Thus we learn, that to listening; convicted, trembling, believing Jews, the gospel, or terms of salvation, as announced by the apostle Peter, who held in his hands the keys of the kingdom, were repentance or reformation of life, and baptism into the name of Christ for the remission of sins; and as a prelude to the gift of the Holy Spirit, the historian adds, "that they that gladly received his word were baptized, and the same day there were added unto them about three thousand souls; and they continued steadfastly in the Apostles' doctrine and fellowship, and in breaking of bread and in prayers, praising God and having favor with all the people."

Did the rebellious sons of men ever give stronger evidence of conversion, of regeneration of heart and reformation of life than this? We know not. Yet it was the work of a day, and the legitimate result of the natural operation of truth upon the hearts and consciences of men. Nor do we ever see anything else exhibited in all the preaching of all the Apostles of our Savior. The word which they preached, the sublime and sacred truths which they uttered, were the vehicle, so to speak, by which the Spirit of God was conveyed to the heart of man. When the word was heard, and the truths believed, then began the Holy Spirit to soften and subdue the obdurate heart, even to the breaking down of strong-holds; and when the heart was melted into submission and obedience, then did it take up its abode and become the holy guest of the human soul.

But let us accompany this distinguished ambassador of Christ a little farther in his journeyings from house to house, and from city to city. Passing over many intervening events, we find him eight years; afterwards listening to a call of a distinguished, military Roman officer of the Italian band, stationed at Caesarea Philippi, the head-quarters of the Roman, army in Judea. Being instructed by a heavenly messenger, to obey the call, he went, nothing doubting. When he arrived at the house of Cornelius, he presented himself before him, to inquire the cause wherefore he had sent for him. The penitent and devout officer bowed at his feet and worshipped him, but Peter raised him up, saying; "Stand up, I, myself, am also, a man." After hearing Cornelius relate the vision which he had seen and heard four days previous, he opened his mouth, and said, "Of a truth I perceive that God is no respecter of persons, but in every nation, he that feareth him, and worketh righteousness, is accepted of him." He continued: "The word which God sent unto the children of Israel, preaching peace by Jesus Christ (he is Lord of all); that word, I say, ye know, which was published throughout all Judea, and began from Galilee, after the baptism which John preached; how God anointed Jesus of Nazareth with the Holy Spirit and with power: who went about doing good, and healing all that were oppressed of the devil; for God was with him. And we are witnesses of all things which he did, both in the land of the Jews and in Jerusalem; whom they slew and hanged on a tree: him God raised up the third day, and showed him openly: not to all the people, but unto witnesses chosen before of God, *even* to us, who did eat and drink, with him; after he rose from the dead. And he commanded us to preach unto the people, and to testify that it is he which was ordained of God *to be* the judge of quick and dead. To him gave all the prophets witness, that through his name whosoever believeth in him shall receive remission of sins. While Peter yet spake these words, the Holy Spirit fell on all them which heard the word. And the Jews, or they of the circumcision, which believed, were astonished, as many as came with Peter, because that on the Gentiles also was poured out the gift of the Holy Spirit; for they heard them speak with tongues, and magnify God. Then answered Peter: Can any man forbid; water, that these should not be baptized, which have received the Holy Ghost as well as we? And he commanded them to be baptized in the name of the Lord."

From this narrative we learn, that the gospel, as proclaimed by Peter to a Gentile audience, assembled at the house; of Cornelius, the Roman Centurion, was essentially and substantially the same as that proclaimed by himself to the Jews on the day of Pentecost, or by Paul to the Corinthians, Athenians and people of Antioch. We might continue our investigations until we had examined every recorded instance of the presentation of the gospel of Christ to the world, by the inspired Apostles of our Savior, and we would be forced to the same conclusion, viz.: that they were always harmonious, that each Apostle was consistent with himself; and that the teachings, of all harmonized with each individual. The same great facts were established by the same indubitable testimonies, and the same, plain, specific and positive duties enjoined, followed by the same marked, radical changes in the hearts and characters of men, whether Jew or Gentile, and accompanied by the same enjoyments of the Holy Spirit and hopes of immortality and eternal life. It would seem, there- fore, that enough were given to teach man a knowledge of the gospel, to show him what it is, and in what it does, and does not, consist. We learn, therefore, that it does not consist in the historical records of the Old or New Testament, or in bio- graphical notices of the elders or ancient worthies, in prophetical announcements of inspired prophets, in the songs of the sweet Psalmist of Israel, or the wise proverbs of the illustrious Solomon; it does not consist in the parables of our Savior, in the letters or epistles, sent to the churches, or in the apocalyptic visions of John the beloved on the isle of Patmos, nor in moral essays on religious subjects, in speculations concerning the trinity or divine essence, or in theories or systems of theology. All these have their appropriate design, and are wisely adapted to the accomplishment of that design, yet they are not "gospel" in the legitimate or apostolic use of that term. Says the Apostle: "The gospel of Christ is the power of God unto salvation." It is God's plan of redeeming or saving a lost and perishing world from the thralldom of sin and eternal death. It is a most wise and beneficent plan, the best which infinite wisdom and boundless goodness could devise; and, doubtless, like everything which ever came from the hand of Deity, perfect in every respect, and every way adapted to the accomplishment of its purpose. We arrive, therefore, at the irresistible conclusion, that the gospel of Christ, as referred to in the text, and as announced by the crucified, yet risen, Savior, from the, mount of ascension in Galilee, to his assembled and adoring disciples, and as proclaimed by them, in obedience to his instructions, to both Jews and Gentiles, throughout every nation and city of the habitable earth, was a special, personal and specific declaration of pardon, peace and salvation to man, upon certain plain and specific conditions, with which every son and daughter of Adam who hears and believes the divine announcement, may comply, and, complying from an honest heart, receive the promised blessing. It consist of facts, commands and promises—facts, sublime and awful, to be believed; commands, plain, simple and easy, to be obeyed; and promises, rich, full and glorious, to be enjoyed. In the boundless amplitude of its beneficence, it embraces all ranks and conditions, all races and castes of sinful, suffering humanity throughout the wide world of mankind. None are received except they possess the requisite qualifications of mind and heart, none are excluded save those who do themselves exclude. What a glorious exhibition of divine goodness, what a sublime fulfillment and realization of the promises made to the world during the Patriarchal and Jewish dispensations! Well might it be said of Abraham, that he rejoiced to see our day, and he saw it and was glad, yet he saw it only through the dim telescope of prophecy. We live in a glorious age, and to us are vouchsafed most exalted overtures of mercy, most sublime exhibitions of divine goodness. Less would have been inadequate to man's redemption, more would have been superfluous, as presenting more than man had the capacity to enjoy. As we contemplate the wondrous dealing of God with man as exhibited in the voluminous annals of the past, we are often overwhelmed with amazement at what we there find recorded. The goodness and long-suffering of God, as contrasted with the unfaithfulness, stubbornness and presumptuous rebellion of man, are matters of wonder and astonishment. On the one hand, we behold boundless goodness and infinite mercy, long-suffering and tender compassion; on the other, unbelief, stubbornness, rebellion and death. As we look at those things, we stand ready, not to excuse or commiserate, but to condemn and slay without mercy. We regard those declarations and messages, as made and sent to man through the instrumentality of angelic messengers and supernatural agencies, as full and complete, and attended by indubitable evidences of their divine origin, and expressed in terms clear and specific, so that those to whom they were addressed were left without excuse, if they mistook their meaning or failed to comply with their fully expressed requisitions. But surely no message or gospel ever vouchsafed by God to man, was ushered into existence enveloped in clearer light, or attended by more august and sublime evidences of its divine origin and heavenly parentage, or expressed in clearer or more explicit language, than the gospel of Christ. The evidences of its divine origin illuminate every page of heaven's sacred annals, envelope the whole history of the world, and span the great gulf that separates the heavens and the earth. They are the most overpowering and convincing which it was in the power of God to give, or within the heart of man to receive and comprehend. It comes to us heralded by the burning sons of light, substantiated by the accumulating evidences of unnumbered ages, and breathing the very spirit of its divine Author; and, although addressed to the world at large, to the whole Adamite race, past, present, and future, it is as much addressed to each individual of that race as though but the one existed. Had the first man who sinned been the only one that ever came into existence, his redemption and salvation would have cost the same sacrifice, the same life and blood, death and resurrection of the immaculate Son of God, that the redemption and salvation of the world has cost. Suppose this had been the case, and that after our first parent had sinned, by eating the forbidden fruit, by violating the only penal law of his existence, and rendered himself obnoxious to death and all its direful consequences; and that, upon contemplating his lost and undone condition, the glorious Son of God had, voluntarily, laid aside his regal robes and princely diadem, and came to earth to assume our nature, to live a life of unmitigated persecution and sorrow, to bleed, suffer and die the ignominious death of the cross for his redemption and salvation; and that, after all these, this man, the peculiar object of his boundless love and infinite compassion, had refused to accept the thus purchased and now proffered terms of salvation. What condemnation would have been too severe, what punishment too great for so vile, ungrateful and rebellious a wretch? Though imprisoned in the deepest caverns of hell, though suffering all the torments prepared for rebellious seraphs and blasphemous demons, yet must he, in contemplation of the atrocity and unreasonableness of his own conduct, his crimes and his ingratitude pronounce his condemnation just, and acquiesce in the miseries he endures. There is not a being in the wide universe of God capable of sitting in judgment on his conduct, that would not pronounce his punishment just, and declare it merited, But such a course of conduct, on the part of our first parents, would have been no more inconsistent and irrational than is that of each son and daughter of Adam, who hears the gospel proclamation and refuses to obey it. The man who thus acts, who hears the gospel of Christ and refuses to obey its requirements, is wholly without excuse in the sight of God and man, angels or demons. It comes to him clothed in light, and breathing the spirit of love; its appeals are based, upon the tender mercies of God, as exhibited in giving. His beloved and only begotten Son, to bleed and die for a lost and guilty world; it presents him the highest motives and principles of action known to men or angels; it conjures him by the fears of hell, and the hopes of a bright and blissful immortality, to lay down the weapons of his unnatural rebellion, and be reconciled to Christ, to accept the proffered pardon and fly to the outstretched arms of bleeding mercy. Could it do more? "The spirit and the bride, or church, say come; and let him that heareth say come; and let him that is athirst come; and whosoever will, let him partake of the water of life freely." "Now is the accepted time, and, behold, now is the day of salvation." Speak not of to-morrow, for it may never come. Say not, I will hear thee at a more convenient season. That expected season never arrived in the history of him who waited for it; nor will it ever arrive in the history of any whom we now address. For yourselves, personally and individually, separate and apart from the action of every other being in the universe of God, must you act, and upon that action is based your temporal and eternal happiness. Connected with the decisions of your own minds, the promptings of your own hearts, and the obedience or righteousness which you yourselves, each of you can render, is an eternity of bliss, a golden crown of immortality, or endless, irretrievable, unutterable torments, banishment interminable from the presence of God and the holy angels. Wait not, I beseech you, for a more convenient season, or for the miraculous promptings of some divine impulse; for, be assured, they will never come; but come *now,* whilst life, light and strength. combine to aid you, whilst the spirit and the bride, the eternal Father, the immaculate Son and the holy angels, bid you Welcome.

-----o-----

[From *the* Western Watchman.]
CAMPBELLISM AROUSED.

ON looking over a pile of exchanges, which had accumulated during our absence, a copy of the *Christian Age,* of Cincinnati, a paper devoted to the advocacy of Campbellism, fell under our eye, bearing date of August 18th. In that paper we find a lengthy editorial attack on an essay of ours, published in the *Christian Repository* of February, entitled, "The Order of Conversion."

Of the doctrine of that essay, this Campbellite editor says, he "has not seen anything more astonishing for a long time;" that it "contains the greatest amount of learned nonsense we have seen in the same space in twelve months;" repeats from half a dozen to a dozen times, that its doctrine is "a palpable absurdity;" declares that inquirers for the way of life might as well go to the "Book of Mormon, or the Koran of Mahomet" for light.

It is to be hoped that the writer paused to take breath and to adjust his senses, after he had relieved himself of this effusion. Like all writers of his class, of whom we have any knowledge, he confounds faith with a belief in the existence and attributes of God, and then makes a great outcry at the proposition that a man must be regenerated in order to the exercise of this sort of faith.

It is no cause of wonder to us, that such a person should find the doctrine of that essay all darkness and confusion. It is recorded of the cloud that stood between the camp of the Egyptians and the camp of Israel, that "it was a cloud and darkness *to them,* but it gave bright *to these."* Is it not strange that "the natural man understandeth not the things of the Spirit." We never supposed that a stranger to the spiritual exercises described in the essay, would perceive the truth of its conclusions, nor indeed that everyone who is truly begotten of the Spirit would be able to do so. It is only those who have their "senses exercised," and who are able to "discern between things that differ," who can see the beauty and glory of the plan of redemption by the grace of God.

As the writer of the article makes no effort nor pretense to confute the doctrine of the essay, his article calls for no reply. The essay may seem as dark and as full of "absurdities," to the writer as he says it does. We are bound to suppose that it does, and as he makes no attempt to reason or to analyze, we are equally bound to suppose him incapable of such exercises. He has, probably, done the best he could, in writing down his expressions of astonishment, of confusion, of trouble and of aversion. It is not probable that he can do better—or at least that he will do better—till he is made better. And that cannot be so long as he follows the blind guide of Bethany theology.

One, thing, however, is worthy of note. Our essay made no allusion to Campbellism, nor to the doctrines of Campbell, yet the Campbellite editors are exceedingly mad against it. One of their Reviews, as we are told, informed its readers that the devils had brought this same article of ours on "The Order of Conversion," before their infernal council, and that the prevailing opinion in that body of dark spirits, was, that it would help on their cause. Whether the reporter of this Campbellite periodical was present and reported the debates phonographically, we are not informed. If we had any evidence that the devils really entertain that opinion of the essay which he reports, we should have a meaner opinion of their intellectual acumen and theological attainments than we have before entertained As it is, we suspect that either the devils pulled the wool over the eyes of the Campbellite reporter, or that they said the opposite of what they really believe. They have, had too much experience in gulling Campbellite editors and reporters, to have their real opinions, divulged to their own disadvantage. We suspect, however, that the real "chief" who was "takin' notes" in that subterranean council, was a veritable imp of the pit, and that the editor got his information from him at second hand. The editor did the best he could, too; for as he could not find anything from above, to use against the essay, he could go nowhere else for help but beneath. And who should he expect would be so ready to help him out of his difficulty as his own cronies?

That a doctrine as old as orthodox theology should produce such contortions among Campbellites, is suggestive. It illustrates what we have long declared, that the real *virus* of Campbellism is its perverse and preposterous theology. The touch of truth is to Campbellism as the wand of Ithariel to Satan. Touch it with that wand, and it starts up in its true Satanic shape and proportions. It bears the same relation to the gospel that Ishmael did to the child of promise. If it cannot reason, it can mock.

-----o-----

REMARKS.

We clipped the above from the *Watchman*, a Baptist paper, published in St. Louis, and spread it before our readers, that they may see the piety and Christian spirit running through it. Rev. Crowell, the writer of this piece, is one that speaks of "discerning the things of the Spirit," being "born of the Spirit," and writes things so highly spiritual, that he never supposed one unenlightened, like ourself, would "perceive the truth of his conclusions!" What a valuable document for the enlightenment and conversion of the world, his long article on the "Order of Conversion" is! A man must be regenerated, born again, made acquainted with the spiritual exercises contained in it, before he can perceive the truth of his conclusions! Here, then, is a full concession, that what we said was true, when we said the unconverted had as well go to the Book of Mormon or, the Koran of Mahomet, to learn the way of salvation, as to this document. It is a cloud of darkness not only to *them*, but to *these* also. It contains not one ray of light for one soul of our race, either regenerated or unregenerated. The author of it is unenlightened, and his whole being entirely unadorned with the graces of the Holy Spirit. Hence his ill-natured and unlovely language.

We have made no complaint that we could not understand him. It was no trouble to understand him in his "Order of Conversion," nor is it any trouble, now to understand him in the above miserable evasion. We have sufficient spiritual discernment to see through all such empty pretenses and the men who make them, of such high attainments, that unfortunate persons, like ourself, who have not been born again, cannot understand them! We not only understand all this class of men and their empty pretenses, but the people can understand us, when we show up their inflated pretenses to superior illumination of the Spirit, while, they descend to the lowest cavils, most miserable evasions and unworthy subterfuges. His gospel on conversion, that the unconverted cannot understand, is not like that of Peter, which, when heard by his numerous auditory, "pierced, them to the heart." The good ground, in our Lord's parable of the sower, is "the man who receives the word into a good and honest heart, *understands* and obeys it." Rev. Crowell's gospel differs from this, in that it cannot be understood by unconverted men. Philip did not teach the Eunuch that he could not understand till converted, but asked him, as he was reading the fifty-third chapter of Isaiah, "Understandest thou what thou readest?" The preacher then proceeded to preach Jesus to him. After hearing the man of God preach Jesus, he inquired, "See, here is water, what doth hinder me to be baptized?" The preacher, in the place of telling him that he could not understand the gospel, said, "If thou believest with all thy heart, thou mayest." He answered, "I believe that Jesus Christ is the Son of God." Philip's gospel was not so highly spiritual that an unconverted man could not understand, believe and obey it; but, on the contrary, he did understand it, believe it, obey it and was forthwith converted. Not like this, the very spiritual things of Mr. Crowell. A poor, unenlightened Ethiopian could not understand his spiritual teachings till spiritually illuminated! Valuable teachings truly are those on conversion, that a man cannot understand till enlightened! He is not sent, as the Apostles were, to disciple all nations, but to teach them the "Order of Conversion," after they are converted. His gospel is not to enlighten sinners, for they cannot understand it, but for the enlightenment of spiritual-minded persons, who are already enlightened!

Our luminous divine tries to hide in the fog of the following: "Like all writers of his class, of whom we have any knowledge, he confounds faith with a belief of the existence and attributes of God, and then makes an outcry at the proposition, that a man must be regenerated in order to the exercise of this kind of faith." There is not smoke enough here to hide in, though here is a pretty attempt at it. But we can soon relieve him from all his trouble about *faith* and *belief.* Let us hear Paul: "Without faith it is impossible to please him; for he that cometh to God must believe." Heb. xi. 6. Here *faith* and *belief* are used to express the same thing. But what is it that must be believed? "For he that cometh to God must believe that he is, and that he is a rewarder of them that diligently seek him?" There can be no mistake here, as to what a man is to believe He must believe that God is, and that he is a rewarder of them who diligently seek him. Let Rev. Crowell hear again what a man is to believe, from Paul: "But what saith it? The word is nigh thee, even in thy mouth, and in thy heart; that is, the word of faith, which we preach; that if thou shalt confess with the mouth the Lord Jesus, and shalt believe in thine heart, that God hath raised him from the dead, thou shalt be saved." Here we find *faith* and *belief* used in reference to the same thing. We have also precisely what it is to be believed, and the object of the faith—salvation. It is, then, *saving faith.* To the same amount, the holy John says, "Many other signs truly did Jesus in the presence of his disciples, that are not written in this book, but these are written that you might believe." Believe what? "That Jesus is the Christ, the Son of. God." What is the object of that belief? "And that believing, you might have life through his name." "There is one faith." That set forth in the above Scriptures is the "one faith," "the faith once delivered to the saints," and the only faith that can save a sinner. No caviling can mystify this faith in our mind, and no man who understands even the elements of Christianity, will talk about loving God or repenting without this faith.

Rev. Crowell heads his article, "Campbellism Aroused!" What a wonder-working document his article is, not to rouse Campbellites, but Campbellism And what increases the wonder is, that it produces this effect without being understood! He never expected the unregenerate Campbellites to understand him! Still Campbellism is roused by an article they cannot understand! But the true state of the case is, that there is nothing about Campbellism or any other ism, except *Crowellism,* concerned in the case. This is what is roused up. The doctrine of Rev. Crowell, that in "the order of conversion," men love God first, repent secondly and believe thirdly, is what is called in question. We defy him to produce a single instance from the Bible, of any person loving God without faith, or repenting without faith, or in unbelief. We challenge the whole phalanx who agree with him, to produce a single instance from the volume of God, of one human being loving God, or repenting, without faith, or in unbelief. Such men as Mr. Crowell may show their anger, vent their malignity and offer insults, but produce an instance from the Bible, of any person loving God, or repenting, without faith, or, which is the same thing, in unbelief, they never can. We challenge them to the work; we will give them column for column in the AGE, or hour or half hour about in oral discussion. We have one advantage over him and all like him; the people can understand us, and we can make them understand that there is no light in them.

Not Crowellism, but *Crowell* is roused! His love to God before faith, without faith or in unbelief; or, in other words, his infidel love to God, in the "Order of Conversion," looks a little haggard. His repentance before faith, without faith or in unbelief; or, in other words, infidel repentance, looks him in the face, and his soul loathes it. He is ashamed of the miserable thing. What is to be done? He is too proud to confess that it is all wrong. He resolves to man up to the work, tell his readers that we cannot understand such highly spiritual things, and, what he knew to be false, that we made no attempt at argument! This is the way he disposes of things he cannot answer.

Come, Rev. Crowell, get in a good humor, and tell us if the love to God, which you teach in the "Order of Conversion," is before faith, without faith, or infidel love to God? And the repentance which you teach in the "Order of Conversion," is it before faith, without faith, or infidel repentance? Is that Baptist love to God and Baptist repentance, that is without faith or in unbelief? Is that love to God and repentance, that is before faith, without faith or in unbelief, a part of "*Christian* experience?"B. F.

-----o-----

THAT is respectable which is honest and sensible.

BRACKEN ASSOCIATION OF UNITED BAPTISTS.
NUMBER X.

HAVING seen that the union of Christians upon any party platform, is neither practicable nor desirable, we propose, in this number to look for the original basis of the church of Christ.

1, Paul says, "Other foundation can no man lay, than that is laid, which is Jesus Christ." "Upon this rock (says Messiah—addressing Peter—this grand truth you have confessed, that I am the Christ, the Son of the living God) "I will build my church, and the gates of hell shall not prevail against it." In harmony with this teaching, the great Apostle to the Gentiles says: "I am determined to make known nothing among you save Jesus Christ and him crucified "For I am not ashamed of the gospel of Christ; for it is the power of God unto salvation to every one that believes it; to the Jew first, and also to the Greek." "Moreover, brethren, I declare unto you the gospel which I preached unto you, which also you have received, and wherein ye stand; by which also ye are saved, if ye keep in memory what I preached unto you, unless ye have believed in vain: for I delivered unto you, first of all, that which I also received, how that Christ died for our sins according to the Scriptures; and that he was buried, and that he rose again the third day according to the Scriptures." Here, then, is clearly presented the basis of the church of God, in Christ Jesus. It is Christ born according to the Jewish Scriptures—teaching according to the Scriptures—healing the sick, cleansing the lepers, casting out demons, raising the dead, preaching the gospel to the poor, according to the Scriptures; it is Christ dying for our sins, and rising again for our justification, and exalted to the right hand of God, a Prince and a Savior, to give repentance and remission of sins." This, we repeat with emphasis, is the foundation of the church of Christ, and other foundation can no man lay than this. Let us now

2. In the second place, note the char

acter of the materials built upon this foundation.

John the Baptist, in the 3rd of Matthew, represents the Jewish state by wheat and chaff in one body, and by an orchard of trees, the fruitful and unfruitful standing together. But he says, in view of the new order of things to be established under the reign of Christ: "The axe is laid unto the root of the trees; every tree, therefore, that bringeth not forth good fruit, is hewn down and cast into the fire." And again: "His fan is in his hand, and he will thoroughly purge his floor, and gather the wheat into the garner; but he will burn up the chaff with unquenchable fire." How perfectly clear, then, that while under the Jewish institution, in the Jewish orchard, the fruitful and unfruitful trees were allowed to grow together, under the reign of Christ, or in the Christian orchard, none but fruitful trees are allowed to grow. And while, in the Jewish church or state, the wheat and the chaff were to be together, in the church of Christ, the wheat alone is to be garnered and the chaff blown away.

Again: When Christ, as the foundation of his church, is called a living stone, then the members are styled lively, or living stones. When the church is compared to a house, then it is said to be "built up a spiritual house, a holy priesthood, to offer up spiritual sacrifices, acceptable to God, by Jesus Christ." The members of the church of Christ, under the New Covenant, were to be distinguished from those under the Old, in that all of them were to know the Lord, from the least to the greatest. In the inscriptions of the apostolic letters to the churches, the members are described as "saints," as "faithful," as "in Christ Jesus." And Paul says, "If any man be in Christ, he is a new creature; and again, "Ye are all the children of God, by faith in Christ Jesus; for as many of you as have been baptized into Christ, have put on Christ: and if ye be Christ's, then are ye Abraham's seed, and heirs according to the promise." In the commission, it is said: Go, teach the nations, baptizing those discipled by teaching—Go, preach the gospel to every creature, and proclaim that he who believes the gospel you announce, and submits to baptism, is buried with Christ in baptism, shall be saved from his sins.

In view of these teachings of the word of God, and much more to the same effect, it is difficult to conceive how a proposition could be made plainer than these portions of scripture make the position, that none but truly penitent, converted, baptized and saved believers, were recognized as members of the apostolic churches. To talk of infants, or unrenewed persons, as members of the churches of God, in Christ, is to contradict the entire spirit and letter of the New Testament on this subject. Let us look now.

3. In the third place, look at the titles or designations of the New Testament church and its members. Upon this head we shall consume but little time. It is styled, "The Church of God—which is at Corinth,"—"The Church of the Thessalonians which is in God the Father, and in the Lord Jesus Christ." "Feed the Church of the Lord (evidently meaning Christ), which he hath purchased with his own blood." "We are bought with a price—not with silver and gold—but with the precious blood of Christ." The followers of Christ are styled "saints," or holy persons—"friends" of Christ—"disciples"—"Christians." The disciples were first called Christians at Antioch. The learned are divided as to the true import of this last passage. Some maintaining that they were called Christians by their enemies; others, that they called themselves Christians; and others, that they were called Christians by divine appointment. Now while, in view of all the criticisms of the learned I have seen, and my own readings of the Scriptures upon this question, I am very strongly inclined to the conclusion that the name was given by divine direction; still it is clear that whether it was given by divine direction

or not, it has been adopted by divine authority, which, in effect, is precisely the same. Peter was moved by the Holy Spirit to say to the followers of Christ, "If any man suffer as a Christian, let him not be ashamed, but let him glorify God on this behalf." And, by the way, I must think that the fact of Peter's using the name, is no mean proof that, at Antioch, it was given by divine direction. Now, while I have no objection to the titles, Friends, Saints, Disciples, still I greatly prefer the name Christian, as the family names of Christ's people, as much more definite, convenient and comprehensive than the others. There were *saints* under the former economies, and therefore this term does not necessarily indicate a follower of Christ; *friend* is entirely vague, as it may mean a friend of the devil as well as a friend of Christ. So the term *disciple* means simply a learner; it may be a learner of Christ or Voltaire; but the name Christian, of itself, indicates, signifies all we ought to be—all we are required to be. Christ was the anointed of the Father. The name Christian is derived from Christ, and signifies a saint, a friend and disciple of Christ, and an anointed one. The spirit was given to Christ without measure, but to Christians by measure. Let us now

4. In the fourth place, consider the Christian's creed. The distinguishing article of the Roman Catholic creed, is the great lie, that Peter is the basis or foundation of the church of Christ. Protestant creeds are mere abstractions, metaphysical deductions, as embodied in the thirty-nine articles of the Church of England—the articles of the Westminster Creed, or the twenty-five articles, of the Methodist Creed, or the sixteen articles of the Creed of the Bracken Association. But as distinguished from all these, the Christian's creed embraces one article only, and that is, that "Jesus is the Christ, the Son of the living God." This grand truth is the soul of the Bible, the antitype of all the types of former economies, the substance of all the shadows, the subject and object of all the prophecies, the truth of all truths. And while the tendency of human creeds for fifteen centuries has been to promote and build up sectarianism, Christians originally, under the administration of the Apostles, harmonized in their faith, in this one saving truth, and were perfectly joined together in the same mind and in the same judgment; and here the pious harmonize yet. We differ not about what the Scriptures say upon this or any other subject, but about our explanations of their sayings. And I reaffirm, that no man nor set of men has any right to set up their explanations of scripture propositions, as tests of orthodoxy or Christian fellowship. When the Eunuch said to Philip, who had been preaching to him Jesus, "See, here is water, what doth hinder me to be baptized?" Philip said, "If thou believest with all thy heart, thou mayest." And he said, "I do believe that Jesus Christ is the Son of God." And forthwith Philip immersed him; and the new convert went on his way rejoicing. If, then, an apostolic and an inspired teacher required only faith, with all the heart, in the proposition, that Jesus is the Christ, the Son of God, in order to baptism, what right have we to require more? And surely I need not say that they who are fit subjects of baptism, are, according to the New Testament, fit subjects for membership, in any Christian congregation.

But I have said that, in this fundamental—this all-embracing article of the Christian's creed, the really pious harmonize. They realize that they need just such a Savior, as the Scriptures declare Jesus to be. They feel that they are ignorant; and Jesus is the wisdom, of God, and is made unto them wisdom. They feel their need of righteousness; and he, of God, is made unto them righteousness. They deeply feel their need of personal holiness; and he is made unto them sanctification. They feel their need of redemption, deliverance from the bondage of the grave, and Jesus is made unto them redemption. They rest assured that in him all feeling dwells—the feelings of the Godhead; that he is, and ever will be, during his mediatorial reign, the author of eternal salvation to all them that obey him—that endure to the end. So that they are complete in him, without Jewish traditions, on the one hand, or Gentile philosophy, on the other; and equally complete without either Romish or Protestant traditions. We affirm, fearlessly, that faith in Jesus Christ, as the Son of God, and Savior of sinners, with the heart, resulting in submission to his government, in the ordinance of baptism, was all that was necessary to membership in the church of God; and that this faith evinced, and made perfect by a patient continuance in well doing, seeking for glory, and honor and immortality, is all that is necessary to the attainment of eternal life.

On the question of baptism, all the world concedes that immersionists have the vantage ground. Roman Catholics and Paedobaptist Protestants give it up, that the immersion of a proper subject, is Christian baptism. If anything is clear in the New Testament, these propositions are clear: That a penitent believer, only, is a proper subject of baptism; and that the immersion of such a subject, into the name of the Father, and of the Son, and of the Holy Spirit, only, is Christian baptism.

We cannot, therefore, conceive of the possibility of union, Christian union, without submission to this divine law of baptism. We have one Lawgiver, Christ; and for our lives, we cannot arrogate to ourselves the right to change his laws and ordinances. We may not add to nor take from them. Let us now

5. In the fifth place, take a brief survey of the organization of the church. But before we speak affirmatively, allow me to say that the New Testament knows nothing of such an organization of churches as Episcopalianism, either of the Church of England or of the Methodist Episcopal Church, contemplates; nor does it know anything of such an ecclesiastical establishment as Presbyterian Presbyteries, Synods and General Assemblies. It knows of no ecclesiastical organization above or beyond an individual Christian Congregation. "Tell it to the congregation," as the last resort, the highest ecclesiastical authority; and if he refuse to hear the church, there is an end to the matter, unless the church reconsider the matter in some way. Church history demonstrates that Christian congregations can only maintain their Christian freedom by cultivating a knowledge and love of truth, and by holding the reins of government in their own hands; by claiming their right to try even such as say they are apostles, but are not.

But our sheet is about full, and here, for the present, we shall conclude our review of the Minutes of the Bracken Association. We have rebuked our brethren sharply, but more in sorrow than in anger, that they may be sound in the faith. May the Lord lead us into all truth, and deliver us from all error, and make its all one according to his word, is the sincere prayer of

JOHN ROGERS.

-----o-----

PRESIDENT FANNING'S COURSE.

WE are at a loss how to take President Fanning's course. He appears determined to make himself not only a martyr for the truth, but the only martyr among the Christian editors of this continent. We have been looking at his course carefully, for some time, and while we have no respect, and never had any, for the higher-law principle, or the doctrine of revelations apart from those contained in the Bible, or inspirations to reveal religious truth, other than those that inspired the holy Scriptures, we respect several of the men who have fallen into this error, and regret the course pursued by Bro, Fanning, as much as we do that pursued by the most ultra among those whom he opposes. While we regard them as propagating an erroneous philosophy, which, if made the principle of action, would subvert the gospel, set aside the faith and delude the church, we have no confidence in, nor sympathy with, the course of President Fanning, in calling them "infidels." There is not the least doubt but the most of these brethren, and probably all of them, will abandon their theory or philosophy. The most of them are young men who have never done much thinking or reading, especially profound thinking and reading; nor have they a just appreciation of the New Testament. They are not infidels, nor have they any more intention of becoming such than Bro. Fanning or ourself. They have adopted some of the pretty expressions of an insidious philosophy and scattered them through some of their public teachings, as a kind of embellishment, like young Spurgeon has adopted Calvinism, without knowing what it is, and, as a matter of course, without its being his principle of action. No man need tell us that Prof. Robert Richardson is an infidel, till a more convincing evidence shall arise than the circumstance that in a question in philosophy, he has employed some cloudy expressions, unsound phrases and higher-law terms. He has as strong faith in our glorious Redeemer and in the word of his grace, as President Fanning or ourself. We must see something more than has yet appeared, before we shall hear that great and good man called an infidel, without our feelings shrinking and recoiling.

We invite Bro. Fanning to brush up his memory on another matter. We care nothing for priority and would say nothing for the sake of mere priority; but for the sake of Bro. Fanning, in view of his special pleading for *himself* as the only invincible defender of the faith, and the ado he makes about other publications refusing to publish his replies; we beg leave to call his attention to a few matters. Does he not remember writing us, soon after we had taken charge of the AGE, insisting that, as an article of Bro. Richardson's touching the question in dispute, had appeared in that paper before we had taken charge of it, we should publish his reply? Does he not know that, though the piece published, from Dr. Richardson made no allusion to him, and though we were not bound to involve ourself in the matters between him and a former editor, we did nevertheless, that he might have no *apparent* ground for complaint, publish his reply? Does he not know that he wrote us, inquiring where we stood, and that we answered in the most unequivocal terms, that we discarded all revelations or inspirations, except those through which the mind of God has been set forth to mankind in the Bible? Does he not know that we maintained this, when. he was saying nothing through the prints, in reply to Spiritualists? If he will look back through the CHRISTIAN AGE, during the defection of J. B. Ferguson, he will find more in quantity, and if not as good in quality, it was as good as we could furnish, maintaining that the Bible contains the only revelation from God to man—the complete and perfect revelation that nothing can be added to, or taken from, it. If he will now consult our publications, he will find that our voice has not been wanting.

It is true we have not suffered "deaths oft," nor thought of standing *alone* among our editorial brethren, or that we were entitled to any special consideration, or that our humble publications should have any special regard, on account of the little we had done, or might do. We still try to do what we can, and to do it right; but we never thought the fate of the cause hung upon our shoulders, that the brethren generally would run into infidelity, or that the great and good Professors of Bethany College would teach infidel philosophy, if we were stricken out of existence, nor do we now think so. We think that, in common with the brethren, especially the preachers and public men, we are doing some good, and we aim to do some more—but not by setting up exclusive claims, as if we were standing alone, among our editorial brethren, the only man sound in the faith, or who understands the tendency of things, and is saving the world.

We have regarded Bro. Fanning as one of our great and good men, and still so regard him, and we are as much opposed as he to all professions to revelation and inspiration aside from those made by Jesus Christ, the Prophets and the Apostles, inscribed upon the holy pages of the Bible. But we have no sympathy with him in pressing this matter to the injury of the great and good name of Bethany College or its Professors, or to make it the occasion to build up Franklin College or create a schism in the church of God. Franklin College stands high enough, and so does its distinguished President. He certainly thinks of no such thing as building upon the downfall of other men and institutions; yet it is strange that he does not perceive that his course has that appearance and, is making that impression, and the danger of causing offences among the children of God. We must think solemnly what we are aiming at, notice carefully whether what we do will have the effect we intend, and consider how things will be taken. Nothing we can do is more dangerous or sinful than creating schism, partyism and strife.

We confess that we felt grieved, afflicted and Wounded deeply, though we did not like Bro. Richardson's pieces, nor believe him right in some of his expressions, When he modified, explained and defined himself, as we thought, in the true spirit of reconciliation, harmony and unity, to find Bro. Fanning treating the whole procedure as a mere pretence and persisting in calling him an infidel. Our soul shrinks from this! If this is to be the course pursued, we may talk no more about union, harmony or love. Paul did not thus treat this disciples at Corinth, who had gone astray so far as to deny the resurrection of the dead. There is no necessity for such extravagant procedure, nor do we believe Bro. Fanning will find a party among the brethren that will sustain him in his course. Bro. Campbell has taken his pen in hand, and this matter will all be set right. The circumstance that Bro. Richardson has used a few of the mystic expressions of an unsound philosophy, and a few young men, graduates of Bethany College, have thought they were getting a little wiser, in resuscitating an exploded philosophy, is no evidence that Bethany College is not sound. There is no sounder college on this earth than Bethany College, nor are there any sounder men than its Professor's.

O! that we could follow the things that make for peace, love and harmony. There is room and work for us all, and God will bless us all, if we do his will.   B. F.

-----o-----

THE CONTROVERSY ABOUT THE SPIRIT.

THESE are emphatically *fast* times, and the people in them are *fast* people. In former ages men moved slowly, and it required years to produce much change in them. The general aspect of society did not change materially in a space of ten years; nor did ten years' time generally produce much change in individuals. But how different now! With what tremendous rapidity individuals and communities now change! When men now commence to change, especially for the worse, they pass with the rapidity of an express or lightning train. Six weeks' regular attendance and close attention in a "spirit circle," will pass a person in apparent ordinary good standing and fair Christian character, down to the icy regions and gloomy despondency of all the debts and uncertainties of infidelity. The next thing you hear from such an one, is clamoring about the "incongruities," "absurdities" and "contradictions" in the Bible —the book they never read—declaring that "geology contradicts the Bible," and ranting about the "incredibility of the account of the ark containing all the different species of animals said, to have been saved, in it," etc., etc. In a few weeks, he who once appeared the sound and consistent Christian, fully satisfied with the revelation of heaven contained in the Bible; confidently believing the word first spoken by the Lord, afterward confirmed by them that heard him; God also bearing them witness, both by signs and wonders, and with diverse miracles and gifts of the Holy Spirit, according to his own will; runs beyond Jerusalem, beyond all evidence, gets into the idle delusion that he is in some way inspired, and thinks that, when his delusion, which he calls "faith," becomes a little stronger, he will do miracles. Both the classes alluded to, with many others now operating, are loud in their clamor about *new light*, progression, advancement, and even talking of reformation. Some of these, who have said all they can say, but find that they cannot induce the people to believe their stupid theories and empty professions of supernatural illumination, complain merely of "proscription;" "tyranny of opinion," "unwritten creeds" and "iron bedsteads." These do not recollect that religious toleration has *two sides*—that their opponents have the same right to speak as themselves, and that the peoples have "the right of private *judgment*"—the right to believe that which they consider according to the oracles of God. It is no proscription for the people, who have heard a man, know what his doctrine is and all he can say in favor of it, to refuse to believe it, to hear him or employ him as their teacher. The people have rights—sacred rights—as well as public teachers, and one of these rights is to decide who shall be their instructors; who they will hear and what they will believe. He who imposes upon these rights and tramples them down, disrespects the dearest right. We would not proscribe a Mormon, Universalist, Deist or Atheist; but while we grant all such the same toleration we enjoy, we claim the right to decline hearing them, accepting them as our instructors or believing what they teach.

The threat of some such, that, upon certain contingencies; they might "bolt," alarms no one. That is a matter entirely dependent upon their allegiance to Jesus. They are under no head but him who sits upon the throne—"the way, the truth and the life." They have subscribed to no law but the law of God. They are identified with no church but the church of God, and have taken no name but that after which the whole family in heaven and upon earth is named. They have professed to be Christians, Disciples of Christ, Children of God and nothing else. They have nothing to "bolt," from but the Lord who purchased them with his own precious blood, his holy name, that fills heaven and earth, his infallible law, his church and their own solemn profession. The Lord has graciously received them, saved them from their sins and freely bestowed upon them all he promised them. They have received him, and, in him, all he has for the children of men in this world and the blessed, hope of eternal life in the world to come. Whether they will depart, or, to use one of their own expression, "bolt," depends wholly upon, their integrity to the Lord—their allegiance to the great King. The people of God are not bound to hear them preach, nor to believe them when they speak not according to the oracles of God, and if, on this account, they depart or "bolt." upon themselves falls the responsibility. It is too late now to make us believe the plainest matters in the Christian, religion are unsettled—that nothing is decided, fixed and immutable. To be set back now, "ever learning," and leaving everybody else ever learning and never able to come to the "knowledge of the truth," by men who have never carefully read the New Testament once through, comprehended its structure, nor the labors that have been done in the last thirty years, in simplifying the whole subject and rendering it plain and appreciable to the public mind, is out of the question. We are not now to become "clouds without rain," "wandering stars," nor "raging waves of the sea." "The faith formerly delivered to the saints"—the "one faith" of Paul, is something settled, fixed and immutable. It will stand when the present heavens and earth shall be no more. The children of God do not admit that all things are fluctuating, evanescent and changing. They know what it is to be established in the faith—rooted and grounded in the truth. With them everything is not open to philosophizing, metaphisicising and speculation. The plain truth, believed by so many thousands, on the first hearing, of all classes, anciently, is not now to be again entangled in the labyrinths of mystery, after the mighty struggle of this generation to make it again accessible to the whole people. Love to their opinions, their views and reasonings, with the Disciples of Christ, is not the bond of union. Love to the Savior of the world, respect to his authority and love to one another, binds them all in one delightful band.

"Love is the golden chain
That binds the happy souls above,
And he's an heir of heaven
That finds his bosom glow with love."

The children of God can conceive how they can consecrate themselves to their glorious Redeemer, devote their entire being to him and make it the great matter in their lives to glorify him. They love, admire and adore him who washed them from their sins in his own blood, and expect to ascribe their praises to him when they shall walk the streets of the New Jerusalem. They glory in him and walk hand in hand with those who love him. They delight to come after him, having found his word verified to them, that "his yoke is easy and his burden light." They are so enraptured with their leader, that they sing, as they follow him,

"Through floods and flames,

If Jesus leads, I'll follow where he goes." They have no taste for theories, philosophies, metaphysics and speculations of opinionated, vain and puffed-up men. After feeding upon the bread that came down from heaven and drinking of the water of which, if a man shall drink he shall never thirst, they have no relish for human theories, idle abstractions and cloudy mysticisms, that never were, and never will be, understood. All these, ever preached, never saved one soul of our race and never will.

The truth is, we have a few speculators aboard that have never read nor studied the investigations that the principal men among us have gone through, nor matured the topics contained in them. They are, we presume, in many instances without knowing it, dipping into some modern works that have appeared, such as Beecher's Conflict of Ages, Cousin, etc., which are nothing under the shining sun but the resuscitation of the main gist of the delusive vagaries discussed and exploded in the days of the Christian Baptist. This work contains a refutation of the whole train of mystics that never was, and never will be, answered. Not a man now among all the mystics, theorizers and philosophizers, agitating sundry communities, has advanced a single idea not advanced by the mystics of the days of the Christian Baptist, and exploded beyond contradiction in that work. Let any man name his item and demand of us to produce it.

But our readers wish to know what the new doctrine is. We shall, therefore, try and set it forth. It is not, then, in our estimation, that those who hold it are, in reality, more spiritual than other brethren, but they contend more for being spiritual. It is not that they really have more of the Spirit, than their brethren generally, but they contend more for having the Spirit. It is not that they really believe any more than their brethren generally, that Christians have the Holy Spirit, but they contend more for believing it. It is not that they really have more of the influence of the Spirit than their brethren, but they contend more for the influence of the Spirit. It is not that they really have more of the power of godliness than their brethren whom they oppose, but they contend more for the power. It is not that they do the work of conversion more effectually than their brethren generally, but they contend for doing it more effectually. It is not that they have more illumination of the Spirit than their brethren, but they contend more for illumination. It is not that they do any miracles, or come any nearer doing miracles than other brethren, but they contend more for doing miracles.

Now, be it distinctly understood, that we have no war with any of these brethren in reference to the truth, that Christians are spiritual—that the church is a spiritual building, a holy temple—an habitation of God through the Spirit, but We deny that Christians, or people of the world, were ever made spiritual by preaching the abstract theory, that *they should be spiritual.* There is neither philosophy—true philosophy—sense nor Bible in such a course. The Holy Spirit is not given by man. Theorizing on being spiritual has no more tendency to make a man spiritual, than theorizing on the effects of medicine has in curing the sick. A man as carnal as carnality itself, and evincing his carnality by his constant wrangling, can argue as stoutly as anybody, that *we must be spiritual.* The very lack of being spiritual, in some such instances, is the ground of their contention. If they were really spiritual, evincing the fruits of the Spirit, "love, joy, meekness, gentleness, fidelity, long-suffering," showing that their souls were under the dominion of the Son of God, all the brethren would be delighted. No church of Christ would have any aversion to this, but empty theories about being spiritual, from men evidently contentious, who obey not the truth, and have not the spirit nor the love of Christ in them, is disgusting, and loathsome.

We have no controversy with any man for *having* the Spirit. There is nothing new nor different from what we have undertook from the day we received the faith of Christ, in the teaching that the spirit of Him who raised up Jesus from, the dead dwells in Christians—that because they are sons, he has sent forth the spirit of his Son into their hearts, crying Abba Father—that if any man have not the spirit of Christ, he is none of his. But the Holy Spirit is not argued into men, reasoned into them, nor preached into them. Theorizing upon the Spirit, the manner of his reception or the mode of his operation, never imparted the Spirit to a human; being. One clear oracle of God is worth more, on a subject of this kind, than all the blind and stupid theories in this universe. We are not left in the dark as to who receive the Spirit, where they are to come and what they are to do, that they may receive, it. On the day when the keys of the kingdom of God were first used and the kingdom opened, in answer to the penitent seekers, who inquired, "Men and brethren, what shall we do?" the Holy Spirit of God answered, through Peter, "Repent and be baptized, every one of you, in the name of Jesus Christ, for the remission of sins, and *you shall receive the gift of the Holy Spirit."* Here is plain teaching, how these came to the point where they received the gift of the Holy Spirit. They heard the word preached by Peter, believed in Him revealed through the word, were pierced in their hearts, and inquired the way of salvation. The answer opened, to them the way to pardon and the impartation of the Holy Spirit. They received the directions given, confided in them, followed them and the Lord saved them from their sins, and he will do the same for all who come to him in the same way.

In Acts v. 32, after declaring that Jesus is highly exalted to the right hand of God, a Prince and a Savior, to give repentance to Israel and remission of sins, Peter says, "And we are his witnesses of these things, and so also is the Holy Spirit, *whom God hath given to them that obey Him."* It is not man who gives the Holy

Spirit; nor is it by preaching the Spirit, theorizing upon the Spirit, or his influence that gives the Spirit, or entitles a man to that gift. God gives the Spirit, not to the man who argues about the Spirit, theorizes upon him, or his influence, or the manner of his operation, but to "*them who obey him.*" This blessed promise is worth worlds upon worlds. It is worth more than all the nations of men on this earth. It is not a promise to those who believe a certain theory about the Spirit, his influence or operation; but his promise is to give the Holy Spirit to them who obey him. They ask him, obey him, come to him, in his own appointments, and he gives them his Spirit, and he continues his Spirit with those who abide in him. No preaching the Spirit, believing in the Spirit, contending for the Spirit or wrangling about the Spirit, can be any evidence that a man has the Spirit, who asks not according to the will of God, comes not to God in his appointments, obeys not the Savior and abides not in him. The Holy Spirit himself is received by "the hearing of faith." Gal. iii. 2. "The word is nigh thee, even in thy mouth and in thy heart; that is, the word of faith which we preach, that if thou shalt confess with thy mouth the Lord Jesus, and shalt believe in thine heart that God hath raised him from the dead, thou shalt be saved." Romans x. 8-9. Here is "the word of faith" preached by the Apostles, believed with the heart, confessed with the mouth; by the hearing of which the Holy Spirit has been received by everyone who has entered the kingdom, since the Lord ascended to heaven. The Spirit is not sent into the hearts of unbelievers to make them believers, but they are sealed by the Holy Spirit after they are believers. Hence the following most explicit statement from Paul: "In whom ye also trusted, after that ye heard the word of truth, the gospel of your salvation; in whom also, *after that ye believed*, ye were sealed with the Holy Spirit of promise."

The commission we are under says, "*Preach the gospel.*" Paul says, "I determined to know nothing but Christ and him crucified." Again, says he, "Preach the word." Our commission is to preach Christ. He who believeth on him hath everlasting life. Christ is to be preached. Christ is to be believed on. Christ is to be obeyed. Christ is to be loved. If any man love not the Lord Jesus Christ, he will be accursed when the Lord comes. O, brethren, let us keep our eye on him, confide in him, love him and obey him; for when he comes in flaming fire, he will take vengeance on them who know not God, and obey not the gospel of our Lord Jesus Christ, who shall be punished with an everlasting destruction from the presence of the Lord and the glory of his power. Let us pray more, be more devoted and fervent in the service of the Lord, that we may be accepted of him at his coming. B. F.

-----o-----

MESSRS. FORD, FISHER, JOHNSON & CO.

THE September number of the *Christian Repository* has just been handed us by a friend, a number not having been received in exchange for the last six months. On referring to our clerk, who has had the charge of mailing the REVIEW for the last two months, we learned that he had not found the exchange list, and, consequently, that he had not only failed to send the REVIEW to the *Repository,* but to all of its exchanges. This was certainly not only no design of ours, but we much regret it. The silly conceit, that we feared for anything we publish to come to the eye of Mr. Ford, is most ridiculous. We can unquestionably post him up. There is nothing in his writhing and twisting that alarms us, unless it be his "human depravity," from which arises his deliberate effrontery, in publishing that we deny "human depravity." We only deny, as he knows as well as he knows anything, *total he* reditary depravity, and not "human depravity," especially with such an example as he is before us.

Mr. Ford, being an *historian*, comes forward with a new history, not of the Baptists, nor the current reformation, but of the troubles of himself and his good Bro. Johnson with "Ben. Franklin!" The object of his effort appears to be to induce the Baptists to sympathize with him and his good brother, save them from ruin and the *Repository* from sinking, from the effects of a few paragraphs from the pen of the aforesaid "Ben. Franklin!" Hence the, following appeal: "Brethren, will you, each one, contribute your mite. Help me by remittances; for this, above all, I need to free me from all embarrassments. Help me, will you, by sending me a list of subscribers. By doing this, *you* will be doing your part towards the speedy completion of my plans. Baptists of Kentucky, will you enable me to defeat the plans and plots of our bitter foes? Shall these histories appear and speak for themselves in the *Repository?* If you say *yes*, let it come to cheer us in our efforts with the endorsement of subscribers names." (*Rep.* p. 580.) What histories are here spoken of? The "History of Baptists" and the history of the "Current Reformation." What "plans and plots" are here alluded to? Why, he would make the Baptists of Kentucky believe, that some mighty conspiracy and combination on our part, were employed against him! Dear me! What a man is he! that "plans and plots" are employed against him!

But what is the truth in the case? The truth is, that he is, and has been, all the time, the aggressor—the deliberate, cool, and premeditated assailant, in his unprovoked attacks. Messrs. Ford, Fisher and Johnson have been, all the time, the cool, meditated and deliberate aggressors and assailants—Mr. Ford, in his history of a people and work, such as he never had the fairness, honor or magnanimity to do justice, or the ability, if he had the will. Mr. Johnson in his persevering persecution of some of "the very best members" in the Baptist church in Ghent, for communing with the Disciples; his narrow-minded and churlish course with Disciples, especially in inviting Mr. Fisher to Ghent, against the expressed wish of some of the "very best members" in the Baptist church, and sustaining him, in declaring that the Disciples would "commune with Brigham Young and his harem," and publishing in the *Recorder*, that "some of the very best members" in the Baptist church were guilty *"of* most abominable heresy, in communing with the Disciples." This persevering, deliberate and determined aggressive, schismatical and belligerent course, on the part of these men, called forth our few paragraphs, which are now about to ruin Mr. Ford, and impel him to call for the Baptists of Kentucky to come to the rescue. Hear the poor man in his pitiable extremity! He cries, "Help me!" and again, he repeats, "Help me!" for, continues he, "above all, this I need to free me from all embarrassments." Again, cries he, pleading for assistance, "If you say *yes*, let it come to cheer us in our efforts." What is the object in all this urgent plea for *help?* He says, "To enable me to defeat the plans and plots of our bitter foes." Cannot the Baptists be induced to come, with the remittances, which, *above all,* he needs to defeat the *plans* and *plots,* consisting in a few paragraphs, from the pen of "Ben. Franklin!!!" Come! O, come! Help me! To your tents, O Baptists; the Campbellites are upon us! O Baptists, in Kentucky, come to the rescue! Help me! Help me! *above all,* not excepting the grace of God, I need subscribers! Cheer me! O comfort me, or I perish; for "Ben. Franklin" has pointed his aggravating questions at me!

On the same leaf where we find all this pitiful whining, is the following: "If B. Franklin will fully assert what he insinuates, and is responsible, and he or his friends wish to see him cleared from the charge of base, bloodless slander, it can be done in a civil court." There appears to be but one difficulty in the way of our suffering. That one is a ponderous "if!" Had it not been for that same embarrassing "if," both he and his Bro. Johnson would have made us suffer long since; for they *have the feeling.* Are we not in a precarious situation?—nothing but an "if" between us and the civil court! But these gentlemen have a higher guaranty to shield them from all danger from a civil court, on our part, on account of anything *they can say of us,* viz.: 1. That we would not hurt a hair on their heads, if we could. 2. That our reputation is beyond the power of anything they can say to impair it. They may, therefore, lay themselves liable to any kind of prosecution without any fear from us. We feel no disposition to prosecute them, and fear no prosecution from them or anything they *can utter about us.* We need no civil court to clear us of any charge made against us, for no charge is made by anybody that will be believed.

But if these gentlemen want something tangible, we will accommodate them as far as possible.

1. The *Western Recorder* inquired pressingly after the documents supposed to have been left, in manuscript, by Mr. Waller, when he died, implying that deep censure rested, certainly, upon someone.

2. Mr. Ford was publishing articles under similar titles, in the *Repository,* and upon similar subjects.

3. Mr. Ford was a co-editor with Mr. Waller when he died, and knew more about his documents than any other person.

4. After the inquiring of the *Recorder,* for the documents of Mr. Waller, Mr. Ford's histories ceased to appear in the *Repository,* not for the want of subscribers, for the *Repository* has been regularly published.

5. Mr. Ford is welcome to publish any private letters or anonymous letters he has in his possession. If he claims to have any, of either class, from us, or of our dictation, let them come. We will attend to them and him without any "civil court," simply by a few words of reply.

6. If Mr. Ford will confess, that what we have published has turned away his subscribers, and thus injured him, and show that the whole did not originate *in his own sins,* we will pay our proportion of the damage, *if* the *Recorder* will pay his.

We have yet a word for this very good Bro. Johnson.

1. Eld. Wm. Johnson retained his letter near two years, during which time he did not belong to any church, thus living in most manifest disorder.

2. Eld. Wm. Johnson and his lady, during the protracted meeting of Eld. T. J. Fisher in Ghent, joined the church there, for which he had been acting as pastor, and with which he had been communing, during the two years while he retained his letter, did not belong to any church, and thus was living in manifest disorder.

3. Eld. Wm. Johnson has not had the concurrence nor support, this year, of "some of the very best members" in the Baptist church in Ghent.

4. Mr. Ford says, referring to the words, "dismissed from us, when joined to another church of the same faith and order," "that important clause *is in the letter."* The gentleman holding the original, since seeing Mr. Ford's assertion, says, "it is not in it," We will see to this at another time. Somebody's veracity is at stake in this. Mr. Ford had better not have made this assertion.

5. Mr. Johnson has thought it needful to have some testimony from another State, to satisfy the people of his own section of country, in Kentucky, of his former good standing.

The following is *our opinion* of him: That he is a man of strong prejudices, a deeply dyed sectarian, a little meddlesome and contentious; but a *much better* man than Mr. Ford. *Our prediction* is, that the Baptist church in Ghent will not harmonize nor prosper till he leaves there.

Only one short sentence touching Mr. Fisher. He will not hold a respectable protracted meeting in Ghent in two years to come.

If Mr. Ford had taken our kind advice, and not published his "History of the Current Reformation," he would have saved himself from all this trouble. On his own head are the consequences. B. F.

-----o-----

UPWARD TENDENCY—REFORMATION NOT A FAILURE—MISSIONARY WORK.

We are, at present, more strengthened, encouraged and built up in the faith, the one faith of Christ, the soundness of the mind of the brotherhood and the position we occupy, as a religious community, than ever before. We, as a mighty religious body, have a mission from God, a great and good mission—a mission of benevolence to our race; and, with the divine blessing, we shall perform that mission. We are raised up by divine providence to do a great work—the greatest work done this side of the apostolic age, and we shall do that work. We shall not, as a people, prove recreant to him who called us, nor to his cause. We have the elements within ourselves, and are destined to be the greatest people, and do the greatest work on this continent, if not upon the globe. There should be no more hanging down of the head, fainting of the heart and feebleness of the knees. We are now, with one heart and one soul, as one man, to come up to the help of the Lord against the mighty. There is now no lion in the way, Philistines in the land, nor giants, that we should fear them. The invitation of the holy One of Israel is, "Come and possess the land." Never were the prospects brighter, the encouragements greater nor the way clearer for us, as a great religious community, to go forward, in the name of Israel's God, under our one Lord Jesus the Christ, our only Savior and Redeemer, than at the present time. We are past the crisis, and are now ready for work. Let us take a brief survey of the premises:

7.The main battle for the truth, the whole truth, and nothing but the truth, is over. The main battle for the position we occupy, as a religious community, in preaching the pure gospel of the grace of God, and nothing but the gospel; requiring men to believe the gospel and nothing else; to obey the gospel, and nothing besides; to be Christians, Disciples of Christ, and nothing more; to follow our blessed Savior as he has directed in his holy teaching, as well as to try to induce all good men to unite in the same good and holy work; we say the main struggle to gain this ground is over. The distracting war about doctrine, is being set aside by us. We have ascertained that we are under no obligation to settle many of the vain disputes now confusing the world; that we can be Christians, follow Jesus and get to heaven if they are never settled; that it would avail nothing if they could be settled. We have found that it amounts to nothing to settle controversies between Trinitarians and Unitarians, Calvinists and Armenians, Methodists and Presbyterians, Episcopalians and Lutherans, if it could be done. We have found, further, that it never can be done. We, therefore, ignore their whole field of controversy, take sides with none of them, and have nothing to do with their vain and empty disputes. We believe, simply, the plain truth of the Bible, precisely as we find it there, and demand of all men to believe the same. Here we have so fully defined ourselves and are becoming so well understood, that the main trouble in this matter is over.

We have had long controversies about faith alone, spirit alone and word alone; but these controversies are all passing away; and we, as a community, have no sympathy with faith alone, spirit alone, or word alone men. There is no faith without the spirit, nor spirit without faith;

nor is there any enjoyment among any people of the spirit or faith without the word. The Spirit, in the execution of his work, puts forth the sword of the Spirit, which is the word of God, that men may believe. How does the Spirit put forth the sword or the word? By publishing the gospel. "These things," says the holy writer, "are written that you might believe." "Faith comes by hearing, and hearing by the word of God." "God made choice among us," says Peter, "that the Gentiles by my mouth should hear the word of the gospel and believe." "How shall they hear without a preacher?" says the Apostle; and again, says be, "He hath committed unto us the ministry of reconciliation." The Almighty gave the Savior; the Savior gave the Apostles, went to heaven and sent to them the Holy Spirit to guide them into all truth. The Apostles, under the infallible influence of the Holy Spirit, spoke the word. It pierced the hearts of the hearers. They believed it and were saved by it.

3. God did his part of the work in giving Christianity to the world. The Lord and Savior did his part of the work. The Holy Spirit did his part of the work. The Apostles did their part of the work. All the numerous miracles done in the establishment and confirmation of Christianity, had their special place and work. But this was all work extraordinary, in the creation and establishment of a new order of things. It required creative power to bring a new order into existence, or a new species.

Without a miracle, we cannot have a new kind of tree, vegetable or animal. But, by the providence of God, in his ordinary supervision over his works and blessing upon them, all the different species given by miracle, in creation, at first, are propagated and perpetuated, without miracle or the direct exercise of creative power. In the same way, the Christian religion was a new species, given by miracle and confirmed by signs and wonders. The church was a new creation, established by miracle at the beginning, but not propagated and perpetuated by miracle. It came into existence by extraordinary means, but is propagated and perpetuated by ordinary means, in the gracious supervision, superintendence and providence of God. God works now as evidently as he did in the six days of creation, or the times of the creation and establishment of Christianity, but not at the same work. His work then was the work of *creation;* but his work now is his gracious superintendence, supervision and providence, in the propagation and perpetuation of that which was originally created and brought into the world by miracle. He works now in the saints, both to will and to do of his own good pleasure. Paul plants, Apollos waters, but God gives the increase. He cares for his people, is about them, a wall of fire. The everlasting arms are underneath them. His promise is, that he will never leave them nor forsake them. He will hear their prayers and answer them. The prayers of the poor, who have reaped down the fields of the opulent, their wages being kept back by fraud, enter the ears of the holy One of Israel, and he will redress their grievances. He is able to make all grace abound, to multiply seed sown, to do for us abundantly above all that we can ask or think; and we are exhorted to cast our care upon him, for he cares for us.

Does anyone inquire, *how* he does all this? We are free to answer humbly and reverently, that *we know not.* It may be by the ministration of angels; for we are clearly assured that they do minister for the heirs of salvation. Again, we say, we *know not;* or, if the question were put, as a similar one was to John in the Apocalyptic vision, by one of the august spirits before the throne, we should be compelled to say respectfully, as he did, "Sir, thou knowest." How the Infinite One, when he said, *"Let* there be light, and there was light," put forth physical power, in his fearful, awful and grand fiat, we humbly confess, before the wisdom of this world, and before him who made it, *we know not*. The expression—"Through faith we understand that the worlds were framed *by the word* of God," though it gives significance to *faith,* as was designed by the writer, and also to the *word of God,* relieves us not as to *how God made the world.* Nor is the wonder any less, when we consider the matter of which it is composed, how he preserves it, keeps it from ruin and makes it a secure habitation for man; or how he poised it upon its axis, gave its momentum in its daily revolutions, or its more incomprehensible momentum, in its annual revolution. How he made, upholds and manages that vast, overwhelming and incomprehensible structure, called the *universe,* we humbly and reverently confess we know not; yet we believe, most solemnly, that he did create, now upholds and manages the universe; nor need any skeptic laugh at our credulity, for our position, that the universe was made, is now upheld and managed by the Infinite One, is transcendently above his, who believes it made, upholds and manages itself, or that it came, is upheld and managed by chance, without any design or designer. We believe the Lord gives us food and raiment; that he sends the plague and pestilence, famine and war, sickness and health, adversity and prosperity; but how he does all this, we again meekly bow and confess we know not. Ten thousand times ten thousand things are done by him, for poor, weak and feeble men, many times, probably, when we know nothing of it, but essential not only to our happiness, but frequently to divert the most sad and disastrous calamity. How all this is done no man knows, and certainly no man of sense will try to tell.

5. *How* God may do all that he does, even in man's redemption, no man can tell. But he who has faith in God, believes that he will do all he has promised, all we need, and do it well—precisely as it ought to be done—whether we ever know how he does it or not. He who believes in our Lord Jesus Christ, believes that he will do his work—all he has promised—all man needs, and do it well—do it precisely as it ought to be done. Nor does any believer have the least distrust but the Holy Spirit will do his work, at the right time, for the right persons and in the right manner. The place where there may be danger, and the only place where there can be any danger, is on the part of man. Man may do wrong. He may do his part of the work wrong, or not do it at all. It is impossible for any mistake to arise any other place than on the part of man. Man is wrong, in his unconverted state, and the object of the gospel mission is to set him right. Never did the devil think of a more pretty device, than when he succeeded in turning the attention of the preacher from preaching to, expostulating with, and trying to reclaim the sinner, to idle speculations, touching how God does certain things not revealed, how the Savior does certain things, or how the Holy Spirit does them. The preacher will only proceed a short distance, till he will forget the question, What must poor, lost, fallen and sinful man do, that he may return and be accepted of his Creator?

We have rid ourselves of all commissions that read in the following style: "Go ye, therefore, and teach all nations *how* God does his work, *how* the Savior does his work, or *how* the Holy Spirit does his work." We are under the old commission *to man,* to disciple all nations, preach the gospel to every creature. Our commission is not to dictate how the heavenly Father should do his work; how our Lord should do his work, nor to teach the Holy Spirit how to operate, but to teach man how to operate so that he may be saved. We have no confidence in faith without works, systems of theory and empty talk. The time has now come for the affirmative and active principle—the principle of work. We have the work simplified down so that anybody can understand it. It consists in obeying the gospel ourselves and publishing it to all mankind. The only way we now know at once to stop the speculative questions that are going among us, is to push the missionary work upon the Disciples, so as to set them to thinking of it, talking of it, reading of it, preaching about it, praying for it and so busily engaged in it, that they will have no time to wrangle upon untaught questions. Let us enter the work in our congregations at home, in the District Co-operations, the State Missionary Societies, and the General Missionary Society, with the great work of man's salvation upon our hearts, and thus send the gospel throughout the world.

7. If any man approaches with any new doctrine, put the great evangelical work, of converting and saving mankind, at him and ascertain what he will do. No doctrine ever taught, or that ever will be taught, will save men who do nothing. Many of the speculative theories introduced, are simply the cogitations of empty talkers, who do nothing but talk, and are aimed simply as an apology for doing nothing. We aim to war upon one class of men wherever we find them, no matter what doctrine they hold. If they hold the truth in unrighteousness, so much the worse. The class we allude to, are those who do nothing, bearing any reasonable proportion to their ability. No matter how much truth these bold, how correct their views, nor how beautiful they can talk; it all amounts to nothing, so long as they do nothing. Men who do nothing, no matter whether preachers or private members, bearing any honorable proportion to their ability, need not think to annoy us with their fine theories, correct views and "evangelical doctrine." Preachers who are men of enterprise, pushing men, doing the work of evangelists, promoting peace, union, harmony and oneness among the Disciples and converting sinners, are men of God. They are doing the work of God, and should be esteemed for their work's sake. Congregations that meet, keep the ordinances, sustain the public worship, keep up the Sunday schools, persevere in trying to convert sinners both at home and abroad, are the people of God, whether they are very wise in doctrine or not. They are of God who work the work of God. God will render to every man according to his works, in the day of judgment. They who have *done good* will come forth to a resurrection of life. "Faith without works is dead, being alone." B. F.

TO THE BROTHERHOOD OF DISCIPLES.

DEAR BRETHREN:—Yielding to the urgent and oft-repeated solicitations of many whose judgment I am compelled to respect, I have very reluctantly consented to accept the Corresponding Secretaryship of the American Christian Missionary Society. It has been accepted with the assurance that the brethren generally are earnestly determined to do something in the missionary work, commensurate with its importance and grandeur, and with the ability which belongs to the 250,000 Disciples in the United States. Many brethren have pledged themselves to go to work to aid in spreading information, creating interest and raising money. We appeal to all who love our Lord Jesus Christ to come up to the help of the Lord against the mighty. The Barclay family are ready to return to Jerusalem to continue their missionary labors in a field which they love the more as they learn more of it, and to which they go back with great confidence in the ultimate success of their labors. Bro. David S. Burnet will probably go on a mission to Great Britain in the course of the year. Bro. J. O. Beardslee is in the field to solicit for a mission to Jamaica, and will go to that field as soon as the necessary funds can be raised. A correspondence will be opened with J. G. Oncken, relative to Germany as a missionary field. Other missions, domestic and foreign, are projected, of which the brethren will hear shortly through our periodicals. About $2,500 have been obtained in pledges and receipts during the sittings of the Convention. It is purposed to raise *twenty thousand* dollars this year for home and foreign missions. We humbly trust in God that the time has arrived when we shall rise up, as one man, and work in this most blessed enterprise. We ask the prayers, the sympathies and the assistance of every follower of Jesus, that this work may be prospered. We write this in haste, just as the paper goes to press. More anon.

All communications for the Corresponding Secretary must be addressed to him at Cincinnati, Ohio, care of H. S. BOSWORTH.

ISAAC ERRETT.

October 22, 1857.

The Church News, Obituaries, etc., were unavoidably crowded out of this number.

THE AMERICAN CHRISTIAN REVIEW.

VOL. II.   CINCINNATI, DECEMBER, 1857.   No. 12.

THE NECESSITY OF REGENERATION—A SERMON.
BY THE EDITOR.
TEXT.—"Blessed are the pure in heart, for they shall see God."—MATT. V. 8.

DEAR HEARERS: I have not selected the words just read as a text in the ordinary sense, but merely as a starting point. The theme I have selected is, *the Necessity of Regeneration;* or, simply, *the Necessity of Conversion.* I shall not attempt to discuss regeneration or conversion minutely, but shall simply argue the indispensible necessity of it. The Sermon on the Mount, as it is commonly called, being delivered some three and a half years before the full development of the gospel, or of Christianity, mainly contains general principles, to be more fully unfolded and literally detailed at and after the reign of Christ, then only at hand, should usher in. One of the great principles found in this preparatory discourse of our Lord to the commencement of his reign, is found in the expression, "Blessed are the pure in heart, for they shall see God." The Word "blessed," found here so repeatedly, is not considered, by the learned, as good a representative of the original as the word *happy*. Hence, in several versions of modern date, we have it, "*Happy* are the pure in heart." The Lord, then, in this preparatory and truly elementary discourse, lays down the divine law, "Happy are the pure in heart." This expression, to a man who understands language, equally explicitly declares, "Unhappy are the impure in heart." The principle is, that purity of heart and happiness go hand in hand. Impurity of heart and happiness go hand in hand.

No man can be happy with an impure heart. A man must be made pure in heart before he can be happy. Men may try to evade, cavil and equivocate as they please; but still, the law of Jesus will stare them in the face and thunder in their ears, "Happy are the pure in heart."

But, so far as we have now looked at this passage, it only relates to the present time. "Happy *are* the pure in heart." For a man's present happiness, peace and joy, he must be pure in heart. Those meditating fraud, blasphemy, corruptions, etc., are the impure in heart. Their designs, desires and aims are impure. Their thoughts meditations and impulses are corrupt. How transcendently are those whose hearts are pure above these! Their intentions are pure; their desires are pure. Their aims are holy. They have an abiding consciousness of the purest, holiest and highest designs. They are not perfect and do not think they are, but they know that they *desire to be*. They are *trying* for perfection. These are "pure in heart," and happy, *now*. But the latter part of the clause looks beyond the present—beyond what the pure enjoy, to what shall be in the future. It says, "For they shall see God." The word "see," here, is used in the sense of enjoy. It does not mean to look upon; for, in that sense, there is another passage that says, "Every eye shall see him." Even his enemies who pierced him shall look upon him in a coming day; but the pure in heart shall not only look upon him, but they shall *enjoy* him.

To those who carefully think, this passage establishes a connection between purity of heart in this life and enjoying God in the life to come. The law of the Lord is, "*Happy are* the pure in heart," *now,* or in the present state, for, or because, they *shall,* in the future state, *enjoy God.* We have listened not only by the hour but by the day, to those who maintain that all shall see or enjoy God, in the future state, whether they were pure in heart or not in this life; and we have noticed that they have immense trouble in explaining those passages that speaks of hell, the second death, punishment, torment, misery, lake of fire, the devil, Satan, etc., etc.; but if we could not find the words hell, punishment, misery, torment, lake of fire, devil, Satan, etc., etc., in the Bible, but were to find, as we do, in this solemn preparatory discourse of our Lord, the word's "Happy are the pure in heart, for they shall enjoy God," we should understand distinctly that the impure in heart were not to enjoy God. If Universalists could annihilate the devil and hell, still this passage eternally settles the matter, that the impure in heart are not now happy, and shall not in the future enjoy God. No reasoning in this universe can recover them from this dilemma.

But that we may not seem to suspend too much upon an isolated expression, we invite attention to another passage: "Follow peace with all men, and holiness, without which no man shall see the Lord;" Heb. xii. 14. This is a broader expression than the one we have been commenting upon. It not only includes the purity of heart, but the practice flowing from it, without which it unequivocally declares that no man shall see the Lord. The word *see,* here, is used in the same sense as before; that is, "without holiness no man shall *enjoy* the Lord." Proving that there is no hell, no lake of fire and no devil, if it could be done, but which no sound-minded man will attempt, does not evade this passage. It exhorts to the following of peace with all men, and holiness in this life, without which it declares no man *shall enjoy the Lord* in the future. No evasion, caviling or sophistry can get round this. It now stands, and will stand to the day of judgment, testifying that men must follow peace and holiness in this life, or they shall not, in the future, enjoy the Lord.

Being made "pure in heart," amounts to the same as being made holy; for it leads to following peace with all men, and holiness, without which no man shall enjoy the Lord. No man is regenerated, born again, or converted, according to the New Testament, who is not made pure in heart or holy; so that an argument in favor of being made pure in heart, or holy, is an argument in favor of regeneration, the new birth, or conversion; or a law requiring purity of heart, or holiness, is a law virtually requiring that a man be born again, regenerated or converted. We do not claim that these terms are precisely synonymous; but the man made pure in heart will follow peace with all men and holiness. In the same way, though being made pure in heart, is not the whole process of conversion or regeneration, it will lead to it. Hence the faith of Christ begins with the heart—corrects it—this leads to overt acts in correcting the life, resulting in righteousness and true

THE NECESSITY OF REGENERATION.

holiness. But no reasoning on a subject of this kind can be as satisfactory as an example. We, therefore, invite the attention of our auditory to an example—to an actual conversation between our Lord and unregenerate man. We allude to a no less distinguished personage than Nicodemus, a ruler of the Jews, who came to the Savior by night to have a personal interview. We admit that the circumstance of his coming *night*, shows a little want of manliness and boldness. We know not precisely the cause of his coming by night, but think probably that he was a little ashamed for it to be known that he had this interview, on account of the popular prejudice; or else he was under that precautionary policy so often seen on the part of religious rulers, or spiritual guides, that makes them careful about setting an example that might lead their weak brethren to hear something that might lead them from their wonted pasture and shepherd. We have frequently seen these cautious spiritual guides, who really desired to hear and could not rest without hearing, after advising their poor, weak and unsuspecting flocks not to hear some doctrine, which they pronounce dangerous before they hear it, slip into the meeting-house after the speaker had commenced, sit down in some dark corner, listen to every word to the close of the speech, and then leave, evidently desiring not to be seen. These valiant shepherds want to hear, but do not wish to lead their brethren to hear, lest they should be led astray. It may be said, That is not very polite. That is true; but we are not to expect politeness, or even common civility, from a man who becomes a blind devotee to party. Such men will do things that they would reprove an infidel for, if he were to do the like in their assemblies.

We do not know that Nicodemus was under so low and unworthy a feeling as this, but think very probably that some such influence caused him to make his visit at night. Be this as it may, he put on the best address he could command, and approached the Lord in what he considered the most respectful terms he could employ. He approached with the following address: "Rabbi, we know that thou art a teacher from God." He used the title *Rabbi,* in about the same sense as they do the titles Rev., Rt. Rev., Dr., etc., etc., as prefixes and affixes to names that have not sufficient weight to go without them. He thought the Lord would be pleased, as the Jewish rabbis were, to be addressed *Rabbi.* Hence, he said, "Rabbi, we know that thou art a teacher from God." This was probably making a broader concession than he was aware of. He not only speaks for himself, but for himself and others of the rulers, saying, "We know that thou art a teacher from God." He does not, either, speak in any doubtful terms, such as "we think," "we trust," nor even that *admit,*" but "we know that thou art a teacher from God." Not only so, but he was in advance of many in our time, for he could, tell *how* he knew, or give a reason *why* he knew; "For," says he, "no man can do these miracles which thou doest except God be with him." Certainly this was a good reason.

The Lord looked upon this man, upon the position which he occupied, and the very first sentence he uttered, struck from, under him his entire religious foundation. Hear his words: "Verily, verily, I say unto thee, except a man be born again, he cannot see the kingdom of God." This is all new to Nicodemus. He understood nothing of it, but, in confusion, inquired how a man would be born when he was old, thinking simply of a natural birth, or a birth of the flesh. The Lord responded, in language a little fuller,' "Except a man be born of water and of the Spirit, he cannot enter into the kingdom of God." The man stands in marvel, wonder and confusion. The Savior says: "Marvel not that I said unto thee, ye must be born again." Why did the Redeemer address this man in this style?

Why did he say, "Verily, verily, I say unto thee, except a man be born again, he cannot see the kingdom of God?" See how emphatic he is: "Verily, verily," is *most assuredly*. "Most assuredly, I say to thee, except a man be born again, he cannot see the kingdom of God." The word *see,* here, is used in the sense of *enjoy*—"Except a man be born again, he cannot *enjoy* the kingdom of God." Why, we ask again, does the Lord thus address this man? For the best reason in the world, viz: Because Nicodemus was basing his church membership, or his citizenship, in the kingdom, upon the flesh, and not upon the Spirit—upon a birth of the flesh, not a birth of the Spirit. It had never entered into the mind of Nicodemus that he must be born again, regenerated or converted, before he could enter into the kingdom of God or the church of Christ. From his earliest recollection, his fleshly birth-right, which gave him membership in the Jewish church, was that to which he had been directed as the basis of membership. He had never heard of a spiritual qualification for church-membership, a spiritual or a moral condition. He had never heard of a condition of church-membership that had anything to do with the heart. The only condition he knew anything about, was fleshly.

The basis of church-membership among the Jews, the only basis he knew anything about, was fleshly. It looked to the flesh and not to the Spirit. The descendants of Abraham, according to the flesh, were all church-members, by virtue of a fleshly relation, and not by virtue of a spiritual relation. A fleshly birth-right gave them membership without respect to the heart or character. This fleshly birth-right was the basis that Nicodemus was resting upon. He considered himself a member of the church of God, the true church and the only true church. All this rested upon the mere circumstance that he was born in Abraham's family, or upon a fleshly birth. This had to be dispersed from his mind the first thing. He had to be shown that he was unconverted, a man of the world, out of the covenant, out of the church, or kingdom of Christ, and that he could not enter it by virtue of a fleshly relation, his fleshly relation to Abraham, his first birth of the flesh. Hence the Lord placed before him, at the beginning, this hard point, saying, "Except a man be born again he cannot see the kingdom of God." This was a startling point to a Jew—setting his membership aside, putting him upon a level with the Pagan world and demanding of him to be born again before he could enter the kingdom of God. This was a main point, wherein Christianity was offensive to a Jew. It set aside his church-membership, his birthright, genealogy, as all nothing; admonished him not to say, "We have Abraham for our father," nor to depend upon the law. It declared that, by the deeds of the law, no flesh could be justified in the sight of God, and the advocates of Christianity, said, "We have no confidence in the flesh," that though we did know Christ after the flesh, or our fleshly relation to him, "yet now henceforth know we him no more" after the flesh. We know him now by our spiritual relation to him, by being begotten of him and born of the Spirit.

When Christianity came in its full glory, it set aside the fleshly basis of church-membership, and disregarded a man's nationality entirely. It made no difference what nation, tribe or tongue a man was of. It had no respect to the blood that coursed a man's veins, but declared to all alike, that except a man be born again, he cannot see the kingdom of God. It set aside the virtue of all fleshly birth-rights, as a basis of church-membership, declaring that "that which is born of the flesh is flesh." A birth of the flesh can only bring forth flesh; and, to be a citizen in a spiritual kingdom, a man must be born of the Spirit—born again—born from above—born of God. This doctrine is true yet, whether men believe it or not. No matter whose church-membership is affected by it, it is nevertheless true. When the Lord says, "Except a man be born again, he cannot enter the kingdom of God," it is no use for preachers to argue. No matter who it cuts off, there is not a human being in the church of God, proper, that has not been born again. There is not a greater cheat kept up on earth than the deception that a fleshly relation, or birth, can secure membership in the church of Christ. Thousands upon thousands of poor souls, to this day, are resting upon this same delusion, who would be converted if they had some honest teacher to assure them, as the Lord did Nicodemus, that, "except they be born again, they cannot see the kingdom of God."

Lift up your eyes to day, and cast your mind over Russia, at the innumerable swarms of men, women and children! What are all these? All church-members! How came they all to be church-members. By a birth of the flesh. The same birth that brought them into this world, brought them into the church. Not one in a thousand of them know what a birth of the Spirit is, or, indeed, that there is any such thing. Look, again, at the long lines of Jews, scattered among every nation under heaven? Who are all these? All church-members! How came they to be church-members? By being born again? by born above? by any preparation of heart? by any spiritual influence? No. By what means, then? By a birth of the flesh—the same birth that brought them into this world. The same birth that secures their interest in their father's inheritance, secures their interest in the church. Lift up your eyes again, and look at the long lines of Romanists spread over the world, men, women and children, and inquire how all these came to be church-members. Not in one case in a thousand by their own choice, their own action, any preparation or purification of heart or life.

Not by being born again—born from above—born of God, nor by any influence of the spirit of God or divine impression of any kind, but by the same birth that brought them into this world—a birth of the flesh! Nor is this all; would that it were. Look, again, at that quiet, peaceable and orderly people, called Friends, or Quakers! How came they in the church? Not by any act of their own, by their own choice, nor by any influence of the Spirit. Not by being born from above—born of the Spirit—born of God. No Friend would think of mentioning that he had been born again, as an evidence that he was in the kingdom of God. Nor would he think of referring you to the light within, or any preparation of heart, as an evidence that he was in the kingdom of God. To what would he refer to prove that he was in the church? To his birth-right—his fleshly birth-right—to the old family record, to show that his mother was in the church when he was born. How many thousands of poor, deluded souls are made to believe that they are in the church, entitled to ordinances and privileges by virtue of a birth of the flesh, who have not had the slightest preparation of heart, or influence of the Spirit!

No church that subverts regeneration deserves any consideration, any regard or respect, as Christian purification of heart—preparation of heart and life, and not a birth of flesh, prepares for induction into the church of Christ. The qualification for the ordinances of the New Testament are spiritual, and not fleshly. A "believing *parent*" is not a New Testament qualification, but a *believing heart,* on the part of the applicant, is the qualification for an ordinance of Christ. Christianity is a *profession;* hence we speak of "professors" and "non-professors." Professing is something the person does. The profession is chosen by the person, entered into and maintained, and not something that we are initiated into before we know anything about it. Hence the Apostle says, "To whomsoever you *yield yourselves* servants to obey, his servants you are." It is utterly useless to tell a man that he must be born again, up less he can *yield himself* to be born again. There is no regeneration, new birth, being born again, entering into ordinances, into the church, into a profession, etc., without the heart, the soul, the spirit of the person being in it. A religion that begins with the fleshly birthright, followed by ordinances and ceremonies, without the heart, the soul, the Spirit, the consent or knowledge of the person, is as perfect a subversion of Christianity as the man of sin can devise.

It is useless to debate infant baptism with persons under the influence of such a system. The simple matter for them to decide is, whether any religious rite can be acceptable to God unless the heart of the person is in it; whether any person can enter a profession acceptably before knowing that there, is a God, a Savior, a Holy Spirit, a church, a profession—in one word, before knowing anything; having any preparation of heart, change of heart, feeling on the subject, spiritual influence or holy impulse; without the heart, soul or spirit having anything to do with it. The main trouble is about the *heart,* and not about the *baptism.* Show me that the heart, the soul, the spirit, of those inducted into a church, a profession, and admitted to ordinances before they knew anything, was right, and I will not trouble them about baptism. The heart not being in it, not being right, not prepared, nothing else avails anything. All the ordinances of the New Testament, and the church to help, can never save one soul not right at heart, or whose heart is not in the work. All those, therefore, put into ordinances, churches or professions, by somebody else, before they knew anything, had any heart in it, or could even consent to it, had better, for themselves, yield to God, make a profession, be baptized and enter the church, *believing with all the heart,* and from that time forward, from the heart, serve God. Their profession will then be unquestionable.

We have advanced beyond the time in the world' for the continuation of a system of infant proselytism; inducting infants into churches before they know anything—before they are accountable. This system takes from them the right of private judgment. Indeed, it originated with people that do not believe in any such right, for their children or anybody else. It is a stealthy, insidious and cunningly devised scheme, for a ministry who know they cannot maintain their cause by fair argument, before intelligent and responsible people, to entrap, draw into their grasp and bind down under their power the unconscious infant before it can decide for itself. The device is to capture the souls of infants before they hear of Jesus, steal away their hearts from him and fasten them down in the shackles of some miserable, human system. Of all the wicked devices in this world, under the delusion of religion, there is not another equal to this. In the place of allowing the child to stand free, as God made it, an agent, and as soon as possible place the Lord before it, that *it may decide for itself, from the heart,* to serve God, there stands a priest, as soon as it is born, to throw a loop around its neck, bind down its soul and rivet the chains of party upon it, before it can think, act or know for itself! In the place of standing before the people, capable of thinking and acting for themselves, presenting their cause, arguing the case and appealing to the hearts of the people, and thus inducing them voluntarily to receive their doctrine, they are watching for the unconscious infant as soon as it is born, to involve its eternal fortune in a system, before it knows anything! What is all this based upon? Upon a fleshly relation—a fleshly birth of a believing parent!

All this our Lord sets aside. He sets aside

THE NECESSITY OF REGENERATION.

the first birth, or the birth of the flesh, and suspends the entrance into his kingdom upon the second birth or the birth of the Spirit. "Except a man be born of water and of the Spirit, he cannot enter into the kingdom of God." The *Spirit* is not to be set aside, and persons enter by a few drops of water, nor by any quantity of water. "Marvel not that I said you must be born again," says the Lord. How born again?"Born of water and of the Spirit," says Jesus. How is this done? Almost every preacher, of every party, for the last fifty years, quotes, "The wind blows where it lists, and you hear the sound, but cannot tell whence it comes nor whither it goes, so is every one born of the Spirit." What do they quote that for?"To explain the new birth," says one. Does it explain it? Who, in this audience, knows what that passage means. Not one in fifty, unless they are much more fortunate than we were for many years; nor do we believe it is generally quoted to explain the new birth, but to mystify it. No man, who has read nothing but the common version, we presume to say, can understand this passage. To start out, the common version turns the SPIRIT out of the passage, from the Greek *pneuma,* translated *spirit* near four hundred times in the New Testament, and inserts "wind," in its place; and then, to make it correspond, they make the wind *blow* where it pleases, or lists instead of "the Spirit, *breathes* where he pleases." If any man inquires how "the Spirit *breathes* where he pleases," we simply ask how Saul "breathed out threatnings." The answer manifestly is, that he *spoke* them. In the same way, "the Spirit breathes where he pleases" the words which the Father gave Jesus, Jesus gave the Apostles, and which the Spirit breathed through them, or uttered through them.

Then, to keep up consistency with the idea of the *wind blowing* where he pleases, they give us, and you "hear the *sound*" instead of hearing *his voice.* The Spirit speaks or breathes where he pleases, and you hear his voice, or his words, but cannot tell whence he comes nor whither he goes, so is every one begotten, who is begotten of God. The Spirit breathed, or spoke, through Paul and enabled him. to say, "I have begotten you through the gospel." These were begotten by the Spirit, through Paul and through the gospel. Thus, Peter was justified in saying, "Being begotten again, not of corruptible seed, but by incorruptible, *by the word of God,* which liveth and abideth forever." All begotten of God are begotten by the Spirit, who spoke through the Apostles, by the preachers of the word and by the gospel. For this we are indebted to Bro. Lard's Review of Jeter, though we have it not at hand, nor other works necessary to elaborate the subject. His book contains the first *interpretation of* this passage we ever saw. The amount of the matter is, that God, by his Spirit, through the Apostles, has spoken the word to man. When he hears it, receives it into a good and honest heart, and so confidently believes it as to repent and confess Christ, he is begotten by it, or begotten by the Spirit, and thus induced to be baptized, or born of water. Except thus born of water and of the Spirit, he cannot enter into the kingdom of God. Setting aside all dependence upon the first birth, or a birth of the flesh, the Lord says, "Marvel not that I said, You must be born *again.*

Having now seen that our Lord, when speaking of the process of turning to God, as a whole, declares it to be something that must be, we desire to spend a few minutes in looking at some of the parts of the process, to see if he speaks in the same unequivocal manner. Faith is a part of the process, the first part, that which makes the first impression upon us and that which leads to everything else. How, then, does the Lord speak of faith? Is it, to use a Babylonish phrase, indispensable? Let us hear the word of the Lord: "Without faith it is impossible to please him; for he that cometh to

God must believe that he is, and that he is a rewarder of them that diligently seek him;" Heb. xi. 6. He does not say it would be well to believe that men ought to believe, or that he should believe, but that "he that cometh to God *must* believe." That which *must be,* cannot be set aside. Let us look at another item. Is repentance indispensable? "Except you repent," says the Lord, "you shall all likewise perish?" "It does not say 'you *must* repent,'" says one. Do not be too certain of that. What does he mean by the words, Except ye repent, ye shall all likewise perish?" He says, "Except a man be born again, he cannot see the kingdom of God." A few words afterwards, referring to this same expression, he says, "Marvel not that I said unto you, You must be born again." He interprets his expression, "Except a man be born again, he cannot, see the kingdom of God," to mean that he "*must be* born again." In the same way, when he says, "Except ye repent, ye shall all likewise perish," it is the same as "you must repent or perish." The Lord does not trifle with men, but informs them what they *must* and what they *must not* do. There is no dispensing with repentance any more than with faith, "He who comes to God *must believe;*" and it is equally true that he must repent. There is no coming to God without these indispensable pre-requisites. Without these a confession, baptism, joining a church, prayer, the Lord's Supper, giving of alms, etc., would not be acceptable to God, would not avail anything.

"Well, says one, "I am glad that it does not say 'you *must be* baptized.'"

In that, my dear sir, you may be glad too soon. We think it does virtually say, "You must be baptized." Turn, if you please, to Acts ix. 6. Here you have an account of the Lord appearing to young Saul. The young man falls upon the ground and calls out, "Who art thou?" The Lord reveals himself to him in the following words: "I am Jesus whom thou persecutest." When Saul heard this and believed it, he said, "Lord, what will thou have me to do?" The Lord answered, "Arise and go into the city, and it shall be told thee what thou must do." He does not say it shall be told him his duty, or what would be well for him to do, or he might do, if it accorded with his way of thinking, or if *he felt like it,* but what *he must do.* The Lord, then appeared to Ananias, and told him to go to him and, tell him what he must do. Ananias says, "We have heard of this man? and learn that he is persecuting the saints." The Lord explains to him that he had appeared to Saul, called him to the ministry, and shown him how great things he should suffer for the name of Jesus, and that he was praying to him. He had prayed to Jesus, saying, "Lord, what will thou have me to do?" When Ananias heard this explanation he did not hesitate to go to him, to tell him, as the Lord said, what he *must do.* Acts xxii. 16, we learn what he told him to in the following: "Why tarriest thou? Arise and be baptized and wash away thy sins, calling on the name of the Lord."

Here he told him what he *must do,* and in the midst of what he *must* do, he is commanded to be baptized. Baptism is something, then, that *must be done.*

'This is no stranger than the Lord's own language—"Except a man be born of water, and of the Spirit, he cannot enter into the kingdom of God." "Born of water," here, undoubtedly, is baptism, and is quoted by Wesley and the Methodist Discipline, and applies to baptism. The same is true of all the principal authorities. The Lord gave significance and authority to this institution when he came to John the Baptist and demanded baptism of him. John excuses himself, saying, "I have need to be baptized of thee and comest thou to me?" when the Lord said, "Suffer it to be so now, for thus it becometh us to fulfill all righteousness."

THE NECESSITY OF REGENERATION.

John yielded to this exposition of the matter, and baptized him. The Lord still further shows the importance attached to baptism—even the baptism of John—when he said, "You rejected the counsel of God against yourselves, not being baptized of John." If, in refusing to be baptized of John, they were rejecting the counsel of God against themselves, what is it to reject the greater baptism, "into the name of the Father, and of the Son and of the Holy Spirit?"

But we shall detain you no longer to discuss the importance of baptism now. We have now seen that a man must believe. The reason of this is, that faith changes, purifies or prepares the heart for the service of God, and unless the heart is prepared, nothing good can follow. We have seen that a man must repent. The reason of this is, that repentance changes the life of a man—makes him right in life, or prepares him in character, or life, to servo God. When his heart and character are prepared, he is ready for induction. We have found that when Saul was informed what he *must do,* that he was commanded to be baptized. The reason that a man must be baptized, is that it is the initiation or induction of the person, whose heart has been previously prepared by faith, and whose life has been prepared by repentance, into the kingdom. Faith and repentance do not initiate or induct into the kingdom, but prepare the person for induction. Baptism does not prepare either the heart or life for induction, but initiates those already prepared in heart and life by faith and repentance. Nor is baptism the evidence of a previous pardon, or salvation, but the last step in the way to it. The pardon, or salvation, follows baptism. "He that believeth and is baptized shall be saved." "Except a man be born again he cannot see the kingdom of God," or enjoy the salvation, justification or pardon of God. "Except a man be born of water, and of the Spirit, he cannot enter into the kingdom of God," or into a state of justification, pardon or salvation.

"That doctrine is *unreasonable,*" says a man. No, sir; it is not unreasonable. There is nothing more reasonable than that a man must be born again before he can enjoy the kingdom of God, enjoy God himself or Jesus Christ. That the unregenerate, the unconverted, the man of the world, cannot enjoy God, is as evident as any proposition. Let us look at it for a few moments. Here is a gentleman who is moral, truthful, honest and honorable, as a man of the world. We admit that he stands far above the immoral,, lying, corrupt, debased and dishonest. This man says, "I am as good as many in the church. I speak the truth, deal honestly, live morally, and would not do many things that professors of religion do, and if I should die, I think I should be saved." Well, sir, suppose you come up here in front of the Lord's table, and take the front seat, as you are already so good, and join with us in celebrating the Lord's death. You, no doubt, will be happy in contemplating his sufferings for our sins, and partaking of the emblems of his body and blood. Come and view him, with an ignominious crown of thorns upon his head, great iron spikes driven through his hands and through his feet into the tree of the cross. Look at him, while his face is all in a gore of blood, all his muscles in a quiver, and he in the very agonies of death. View him; O! view him, till you see him breathe the last breath, and silently expire. See the thick darkness lower down over the whole land. O! try and realize that mighty throe of the earth when he expired. See the vale in the temple split in twain, and fall back against the wall! See the rocks rent asunder! Come here and sit with us, and commemorate this scene! Your heart responds "No." Again you say, "No; I cannot enjoy such a scene; I cannot come." You know your heart would revolt and shrink at the thought. You are as conscious as that you exist, that you would be miserable to attempt participation in such a scene. Your soul shrinks at the idea. You say, "No; let me have a seat more remote; or allow me to walk out of the house."

Every man who has never been converted or born again, knows this to be the case. Such an one is uncongenial with the whole spirit of Christianity, and could not be happy in singing the praises of God, the exhortations, the prayers, the reading of the Scriptures, the ordinances or the immediate mingling with the worshippers. Hence, you will always see those of the class alluded to, in a remote part of the house, or remaining outside. They feel much better at a distance. Suppose such an one were carried up into heaven and seated among those who have washed their robes and made them white in the blood of the Lamb. He lifts up his eyes, and runs them along the ranks of those who loved Jesus, worshipped him, talked about him and served him in this life, and hears them crying, "Blessing, and glory, and honor, and power, and dominion and thanksgiving unto him who sits upon the throne, and to the Lamb forever and ever." Again he looks, and sees Abraham, Isaac and Jacob, Enoch and Elijah, Job and Daniel, Isaiah and Jeremiah, with all the ancient worthies, arrayed in white, praising God and the Lamb. Again he lifts up his eyes, and beholds the Apostles of Jesus sitting upon twelve thrones. Still he looks, and beholds immense ranks of the holy martyrs of Jesus, as they walk the streets of the New Jerusalem! Once more he looks, and beholds long ranks of angels, in profound awe and subordination, praising God. He turns his eye to the throne, and sees Jesus seated upon the throne, his eyes as a flame of fire, and his feet as burnished brass. Yet once more he lifts his eyes, and beholds the face of the Almighty! Could he who could not come to the Lord's table, who took no pleasure in the worship of God, reading his word, associating with his saints, singing his praises, or calling upon his name, during a life-time, now turn round instantly, and chime in with the praises and joys of heaven? All that is rational, says No. The thought of never having loved Jesus, never having confessed him, nor made the least effort to serve him, would then thunder upon the soul with awful force. The reflection, then, that Jesus died for me; that he loved me; that he gave himself for me; that he most kindly, affectionately and earnestly invited me to come to him, would thunder home upon the conscience. When such an one would look upon him, all his kindness in his gracious invitations, would rush into the mind. Such language as the following would then rush upon the soul: "Come to me, all you that labor and are heavy laden, and I will give you rest"—"He that cometh to me, I will in nowise cast out"—"O, Jerusalem! Jerusalem! how oft would I have gathered your children, but ye would not"—"The Spirit says, come, and the bride says come, and whoever will, let him come and partake of the water of life freely." When these invitations flash through the mind, and the unregenerate think of having rejected all, disregarded and withstood all these kind and pressing invitations; when he would reflect that God loved him, but the love of God could not move him; that Jesus died for him, but the death of Jesus could not move him; the Lord poured out his blood for him, but the flowing blood of the Redeemer could not move him; that preachers reasoned with and exhorted him, but all their preaching and exhortations could not move him; that good people wept over him, and prayed over him, but could not move him; in one word, when he reflects that no charms that the kingdom contains could move him to love and serve God, can any man conceive of such a ridiculous idea, as that he would immediately turn round and unite in the anthems of heaven!

No; such a one would look for an oblivion in

which he could cover up and be hid forever. Such will call for rocks and mountains to fall upon them, and hide them from the face of him who sits upon the throne and from the wrath of the Lamb. We need something more to make us happy, than bare admission into a place of happiness. There are many in our glorious and happy Union who are not happy. They have as free admission here as anybody; but they are not prepared for happiness. They are not congenial to the country and people. They carry the seeds of misery in themselves, and could not be happy in paradise, unless they were changed. A man who has no love to God, no relish for the things of God, for the people of God and the praises of God, could not be happy if in heaven. Indeed, we cannot conceive where such an one would be much more miserable than in heaven. The reason is, he is not prepared for it. He must be changed, made acquainted with Christ, enlisted in his cause, a partaker of his Spirit and united with him. The cause of Christ must become his cause, so that he is happy in doing the will of God. He must be so transformed that he delights to be in the company of the Bible, the ordinances and the work of God, the people and worship of God, so that he can be happy with the people of God in this world, and he will be prepared to enjoy them in the world to come. But without being thus transformed, there is not a more idle chimera in this universe than to think of enjoying God, and heaven and the people of God in the world to come.

"Except you repent, you shall all likewise perish," says our blessed Lord and Master. "Except a man be born again, he cannot see the kingdom of God." Marvel not that I said, You must be born again." O that men would turn to the Lord! O that men would serve the Lord! Let us praise the Lord, that he has given repentance and remission of sins in the name of Jesus. God help us to honor and serve him!

MR. FORD IN TROUBLE.

Is IT So?—Is it a fact there is a tendency among Kentucky Baptists to Armenianism, Open Communion and "Reformationism?" If there is, it is time the lines were drawn, and every man and every church come out and show their hands. With all affiliation, compromise and compliance for peace sake, we, for ourselves, enter our solemn protest.

We claim no kindred, and ask no support of those, if such there be, who will sell the truth for the sake of peace. "If you continue that History of the Reformation," says a *Baptist,* in a recent letter and thus stir up strife with our brethren, the Reformers, I shall not continue to support you." Keep your support, *friend!* I would write it if all the Franklinites and their sympathizers among the Baptists combine and invent a thousand plots to ruin me. Let them show up one false statement, and I will yield to them. Are they ashamed of the facts of their own history? Then let them blush and bear it. Their whole organization sprung from the fanaticism of the Great Revival, guided by the light of experience. It was not, according to their own showing, the church Christ built, but was planned by unbaptized men, built of unbaptized materials, and by their own showing was established by unpardoned, unconverted, unchristian men. They cannot deny it.

Is *this Campbellism?*—"The spirit now dwells in the church by its moral presence, and in no other way. Physically it is not here; or if it is, one cannot know it, which amounts to the same thing. It is said of some of the ancient servants of God, that though dead they yet speak. They have their moral presence. Let me illustrate my meaning. Washington's Farewell Address breathes the spirit of Washington. In like manner we now have the spirit of God, and in no other way."

This is from a leading article in the *American Christian Review.* That something, nick-named Campbellism, has been hard to discover. *Is this it?* Is the spirit of God no more with us, or with his word, than the spirit of Washington is with his Farewell Address? Will Mr. Campbell answer *yes,* or *no?* Is this what people nick-name Campbellism, and which he properly names—something else? We respectfully ask Mr. Campbell himself to answer this. *Will he? Ah! will he?* We shall see.—*Christian Repository.*

-----o-----

REMARKS.

Mr. Ford has shown so much bitterness that we had pretty much failed to sympathize with him; but, since reading the above precious little article, our sympathies are almost moved in his behalf. How afflicting it is to him, to receive such a rebuke as the above from the more pious Baptists! We have known all the time that the more pious, enlightened and useful men among the Baptists did not approve his course. But we did not know that he was doing penance on as large a scale as now appears. He is suffering for his sins even in this world. Retribution is close upon his heels. Look at the above and see how imploringly he talks. He inquires, *"Is it so?"* Is what so? What is the matter with the dear brother? He proceeds, "Is it a fact there is a tendency among Kentucky Baptists to Arrnenianism, Open Communion and 'Reformationism?'" Apprehensive that there is, with tremendous determination and resoluteness, he proceeds, "If there is, it is time the lines were drawn." But here lies the trouble. Mr. Ford does not hold the lines. His patrons hold the lines, and when they begin to draw them a little tight, by the admonition, "I shall not continue to support you," they find him quite tender in the mouth. His begging for subscribers to aid him in bringing out his "History of the Current Reformation," shows that the good men among Baptists are drawing the lines pretty tight on him. They make him cry out lustily.

As to his silly conceit, that we dread for his history to come out, he need give himself no more trouble. We are in no danger from it. The Disciples know what estimate to put upon any history he can write. There is not the least danger of their being affected by anything he can write. Some honest, unsuspecting and pious Baptists may be prejudiced against us by reading his pieces; but even these will soon hear some good man preach, who will remove their prejudice, show them that they have been misled, and that Mr. Ford is in a bad spirit and that his *Repository* is deceiving them.

Mr. Ford and several other Baptist editors have a morbid appetite. They are not looking for something good to feed upon, but for putrid matter which will feed their morbid appetites, and which they suppose will feed Baptists in general, and in which they will frequently find themselves mistaken. Hence an unfortunate paragraph, which has been objected to by many brethren, and which we are satisfied would not be accorded with by one preacher in fifty among us, is culled from a sermon of Bro. Clark, of Texas, published in the *Review* several months ago, the main body of which is good and instructive, and the unfortunate paragraph peddled from paper to paper, and the question asked, "Is *this Campbellism?"* Their readers are all informed that it is a *leading* article in the *Review,* but not one of them informed that it is not editorial, nor, which is true, that the quotation is not a *leading* feature in the sermon, but an illustration of the writer's view of the manner of the indwelling of the Spirit. But did these gentlemen see the piece we published in reply and our remarks then and since, on the same subject? No; not they. Why not notice these? Because they do not want anything that will enable the people to understand us; but an isolated paragraph that will prejudice the people against us, they take pleasure in handing round.

Speaking of his History of the Current Reformation, he says, "I would write it if all the

MR. FORD IN TROUBLE.

Franklinites and their sympathizers among the Baptists combine and invent a thousand plots to ruin me. Let them show up one false statement and I will yield to them." We suppose he means "one false statement" in his History of the Current Reformation. We can show him several "false statements," in said history. But, for the present, we will only point out one "false statement," in his history of the Baptists. That is, simply the statement that *there was a Baptist church in America before the preaching of Roger Williams*. This statement is wholly without authority.

But that our readers and the Baptists may see that Mr. Ford is going down, and that he knows it, we insert the following just as it came to hand. It shows what kind of letters he is writing to Baptists to induce them to sustain him, in his wicked career. Had he gone on, in peace, kindness and love, publishing a valuable, manly and Christian paper, as Mr. Waller was doing when he closed his labors on earth, his doom would not have been to write such miserable, whining, pitiful and partisan appeals to prejudice the minds of his brethren, as the following, to keep from starving. But we let the following documents speak for themselves:

LIBERTY, Mo., Nov. 6, 1857.

Bro. Franklin:—You may think me cruel for warning you of your intended (of course it will be certain!) destruction; but then it may not be so cruel as it would seem to be, at first sight; for you will thus be allowed time to so reconstruct, change, or *abandon* your position, that you may escape the horrible end of such "Campbellites" as may not be blessed with the knowledge of the ruin speedily to overtake them; and which would have been upon them before this, it seems, but for the want of the necessary "material aid." It may be that the great pressure in financial matters will save us, and thus go far to prove that there is no wind that does not blow good to somebody.

As I am one of the doomed fraternity, I of course sympathize with you deeply, and would ask of you, as a great favor, that you advise me as to the best method of escape, if the information contained in the following epistle does not so far disturb your intellect as to render you incompetent to reason upon the subject. Would it not be well to join the Baptists immediately?!

The letter containing the dreadful intelligence (a copy of which I send) was sent to an old brother living in this county, whose name and address Mr. Ford had learned, I presume, from the list of subscribers for the *Baptist Banner,* for which paper the brother was a subscriber.

The following is a true copy of the letter to which I have alluded, as I am informed by the best authority.

Your friend and brother,
W. A. MARTIN.

LOUISVILLE, KY., Oct. 15, 1857.

Dear Brother:—Permit me to call your attention to the following facts. I have been gathering up, the past two years, the materials for writing the History of the Current Reformation at great labor and expense. I have collected a sufficient amount of materials to enable any one to write a most interesting and exact history of the Current Reformation. I have gone to their own congregations and obtained permission to see their records, when they had any, and have obtained from the Baptist churches, where splits took place, all the facts.

The history of Campbellism will be its death blow. They are aware of this, and oppose, by every effort, my undertaking; and sad is the fact, that some Baptists cooperate with them to defeat me.

The only difficulty in my way is the want of means. I fear that unless I keep traveling the subscription will not keep the *Repository* going. I am poor and I need support. Now, my brother, will you not give me a helping hand in this time of need? Will you take the *Repository,* if you do not, and send the subscription price, two dollars! Will you, if you are already a subscriber, present its claims to your church and friends, and send me a few subscribers, with the money? Do, my brother; *I need it.* And may the good Lord reward you.

My wife will commence in its pages soon a new work of historic character, adapted to the young—REBECCA BUNYAN; OR, THE DREAMER'S BLIND DAUGHTER. It will be commenced and finished in the *Repository*. But I will add no more. I need some assistance just now. I have no backer but my Master and my brethren, and cannot but hope that this appeal will not be in vain. Yours in hope,

 (Signed)   S. H. FORD.

-----o-----

[From the Christian Sentinel.]
ARE WE DISCIPLES?

As SOME doubt may, by implication, have been thrown upon this point of late, it may not be amiss to be made more certain—to use an idiom of the old Romans—respecting it. No religious body has made so much use of the term as we. No people have made more prominent the statement that whatsoever of Holy Scriptures was written aforetime was for our *learning*. All manner of conceivable changes have been rung, for more than a quarter of a century, upon the fact that Christianity was a matter to be learned, a thing adapted to man as a rational, intelligent being.

Now there was plausibility in this. It seemed, indeed, to savor of a becoming humility in a community, to be willing to take, as their distinctive appellation, a name pointing to Christ in his primarily relation to us—that of teacher. It seemed less like spiritual pride to call ourselves only learners of him, than to name us saints of his royal priesthood, or citizens of his heavenly kingdom. But it appears, at length, that we have indulged quite a superfluous modesty, and that we have outgrown the vestments of discipleship, and should don the scholar's gown, in token that we have finished our education, taken fellowships and are now residing about the halls of our former school-boyhood, as a kind of ornament to the institution, and for the sake of giving merely such attention to books as may farther beseem us as such. In a word, we are to let all men know that *we* are not of those who are "ever learning and never able to come to the knowledge of the truth." Not we. We have graduated. We were once disciples, mere pupils; now we are scholars.

Seriously, whither is this fast age leading? We have been astounded at the positions of some of our scribes, of late, on this subject. True, no one has quite asserted himself in the broad terms preceding. But if the bearing of certain prominent utterances is not in that direction, we know not whither they do tend. Has it come to pass, really, in a community boasting the largest liberty, that a man may not dare to think for himself, without being branded as a heretic? Is it to be shown to the world that the Reformation of the present century is as incapable as its predecessors of shunning the bigotry of stereotyping its views? Have a few religious teachers and expounders of scripture discerned the whole of its truth and meaning so that no man among us may say less or more than they without being branded as an "infidel?" Who shall tell us that we are bound to swear in the words of any man? Are we about to set up a something of the "iron-bedstead" order, analogous to the "tradition" of one people, or the "usage" of another? We shall see.

There is another note of the utterances alluded to, which, while not so preposterously bold and overbearing, insidiously tends in the same direction. It consists in questioning the truth of any teachings which all cannot or do not understand. It challenges the fitness of any man for a teacher, unless he make himself easy of comprehension to all. No matter what he discusses. If any man, in blindness or willfulness, hearing, misapprehends, and cries "infidelity!" the case is settled. Any teaching thus capable of being misunderstood is marked as spurious.

Now this is as contrary to all analogy as to the nature and fitness of things. Every well ordered school has its classes; and every judicious teacher adapts his instruction to those classes. He does not expect an abecedarian to understand a grammar and lexicon, will comprehend an abstruse lesson in mental philosophy. Should he carefully abstain from uttering anything except what every pupil in school could immediately fathom, His teachings would be speedily despised, and with good reason. But whoever heard an urchin in pinafore, tasked with the multiplication table, denouncing a geometrical problem for its false teaching? Or despising his instructor for not making Newton's Principia clear and luminous to his little brain?

Christ and his Apostles could not stand before such sweeping dicta. A few of their rudimental teachings were, of necessity, so simple and easy that all might understand. Of this character, most happily, are the directions about receiving Christ and entering into his school. But for those who have entered, lesson above lesson is arranged, so that a life-long study of them will not do more than take one through the primary school and fit him for the college above. And the same minister who can cause an inquirer in a few moments to understand the simple gospel—that particular "truth" to the knowledge of which some of old, ever learning of the wrong teachers, were never able to come—must yet labor with all diligence to lead his newly-made disciple into "all truth," but if he think to do it in a day, or a year, time will teach him better. For he will often find discourses, which he had certainly thought were easy, understood only by a few of his advanced hearers. Should he become discouraged at this, and so change his Choice of topics and his discussion of them as that everything should be comprehended instantly by all, he would soon find a woeful lack of interest and advancement both in knowledge and piety. No man is fit for a Christian pastor who dare not say anything to his flock except what he is sure they will all understand and believe. Nor is any man worthy such a post for whom "our doctrine" has terrors. Whoever added anything to the great fund of religious knowledge worth speaking of, without hearing the miserable barking and yelping at his heels—"Oh, beware! he does not preach *our doctrine!*"—?

Believing that the same rule applies to ministers and editors, we therefore speak, and shall speak, not as pleasing men, but as pleasing God. We dislike exceedingly, to turn aside from the more direct work of inculcating piety, to criticize the work of others. But with the name of this periodical, what it is, we cannot hold our peace forever. Truth should have guardians more vigilant than the fabled sentry of the golden fleece. One thing, however, we cannot afford to do; that is, to defend the good name of the *Sentinel,* or our own, against attacks or innuendoes; as brethren may satisfy themselves, if they choose, by still further experiment. We have chosen our work, and hope, by the blessing of God, to accomplish something for the good of souls and the glory of his blessed name. And we still confidently purpose to go on learning, and as confidently expect to find many others still willing to be *Disciples.*   I. N. C.

REMARKS.

It is true, the writer of the above calls no names, makes no quotations, save some very brief ones; is careful not to let his readers see any of the pieces that he speaks so kindly and piously about; is equally careful to form no issues with anybody directly, and advances no doctrine of any kind. He appears somewhat excited, annoyed and vexed with an expression from Paul, and comes nearer forming an issue with him than anybody else. He is troubled how to harmonize the Apostle's rebuke of those "ever learning and never able to come to the knowledge of the truth, with the name Disciple;" nor does he appear any better pleased with some editor who has approbatively quoted this same expression of Paul. He, therefore, for the information of Paul and the man who had the audacity to quote him, says that we have assumed the name *Disciples,* and that "no religious body has made so much use of the term as we." This name, he informs us, means *learner.* He then proceeds to defend the privilege of learning with great ability, and inquires, "Seriously, whither is this fast age leading?" If the *Sentinel* had thought and written *seriously,* in the place of the way he did think and write, he Would not have misconceived the whole scope of the Apostle's remark, and the intention of the man who quoted him. Had he not been so much excited that the "divinity within," "the inner consciousness," or "intuition," did not unfold to him the meaning of the Apostle, he would not have made his defense of the privilege of *learning*. He would have seen that such a defense was not called for. Neither Paul nor the man who quoted him, would debar the dear young brother the privilege of *learning*. Men in the habit of learning are not those reprimanded by Paul, nor those intended by the man who quoted Paul; but men "ever learning and *never able to come to the knowledge of the truth;*" or those who should have been men, able to digest strong meat, but yet have to be nourished at the breast; or, without a figure, those who need again to be taught which be the first principles of the oracles of God.

The foregoing pretty little piece of sophistry can never turn the matter now into the mere question whether Christians may advance in knowledge; whether the Scriptures were written for our learning, or whether the Disciples may advance in the truth. No mysticism can thus change the issue; no dodge can evade the point involved, nor can any evasion evade the true issue. We are not to be misled, decoyed nor intimidated by the charge of bigotry; nor are we, after having labored more than twenty years to present "the glorious gospel of the blessed God" clearly to the people of this country, and disentangle the public mind from mysticism, gloom and doubt, to be driven back by young men alleging that our language is "preposterously bold and overbearing," nor yet by speaking of the "insidious tendency" of what we say, nor the charge of "blindness" nor "willfulness." Nor are we to be represented as "questioning" or teaching others to question the truth of any teachings "which all cannot, or do not, at once understand," while we simply question the fitness of any man as a teacher who cannot make sensible men understand whether he is for Christianity or against it. No man is fit for a preacher of the gospel who cannot make himself understood; at least, so far that men of sense can decide whether he is for the gospel or against it. The truth is, the people can understand these wise young men in all their "lessons upon lessons," where they understand themselves. We have no use for that kind of learning which simply enables men to speak so that the *wise* and *learned* can understand them. Truly wise and learned men can understand anybody; but we had supposed that learning was intended to teach those ignorant and out of the way.

But we are not to be gulled by a little pomposity and inflated conceit about learning! It is not *learning* that troubles these brethren, but the lack of it. True learning enables a man to teach the people—the masses of the people—the way of salvation, in the simple and unadorned language of the New Testament. The great Apostle to the Gentiles had the grace of apostleship given him, to *make all men see,* and he wrote to the church at Ephesus—the whole church—that when they read, they *might understand* his knowledge in the mystery of

Christ. He was sent to the people to turn them from darkness to light and from the power of Satan to God. The idea of these young men claiming to have advanced so far, to have made such strides in knowledge, to have reached such a pinnacle in *learning*, that only the thinking few—those not addicted to "mental laziness"—can understand them, is simply a ridiculous and arrogant assumption. They are not so difficult to understand as they suppose. They will find, before they are aware of it, that the people understand them—the masses of the people—and will forsake them, if they do not shape their course differently.

"Mental laziness" is not to hinder a man from making himself thoroughly acquainted with the language of Jesus and the Apostles, nor is pride to hinder him from coming to the feet of Jesus and the Apostles, to learn of, and follow, them. No "mental laziness" is to lead the man of God aside from the unequivocal teachings of the Son of God, to "the inspirations of the inner consciousness"—the teaching of the "divinity within," or any other device to avoid the labor of reading and learning the word of God. Those preachers who can preach whole sermons and write *pious* books without scarcely a reference to Jesus or the Apostles, by mere "intuition," "the divinity within," or the "inner consciousness," have adopted a system of "mental laziness"—a labor-saving expedient—that they must abandon, or be unfit for preachers of Christ.

The admission that the rudimental matters of Christianity are simple or easily understood, is fatal to these brethren. Their new light does not relate to the details of Christianity, but to that which is emphatically *rudimental.* They strike at the question of inspiration, tamper with the foundation of the faith, the great principle lying at the basis of everything. Here, at the starting-point, is where they create distrust, unsettle public sentiment. It is not the detail of Christianity they are advancing in, learning abo-

ut, having "lesson upon lesson" in, but "inspiration," the foundation of the faith. This is what they are so hard to understand in reference to.

The opposition complained of, "the iron bedstead," "who shall tell them that they shall swear in the words of any man," is all mere cant. Who has questioned their right to think, to preach, or write, what they please? We question not their right to preach, write and think Mormonism, Swedenborgianism or Quakerism; but not at the same time to claim that is Christianity, and that we have no right to demur. If they have the right to preach a new doctrine concerning inspiration, we have a right to call it in question and the people have a right not to believe them, and they will exercise the right.

B. F.

-----o-----

SPECULATIVE QUESTIONS.

At the close of our discourse, on the 5th Lord's day in November, in North Middletown, Kentucky, a gentleman handed us the following, requesting that we should speak on it during our stay, at the same time assuring us that it came from a respectable source. We cheerfully yielded to the request, and spoke on it at night. At the close, nine persons made confession of their faith in their Savior, though we are inclined to think none of them from the party whence the document came. It has occurred to us, that a little notoriety for this document would be acceptable to its friends, and useful to others, and, therefore, we insert it here. It reads as follows:

"Do you believe in the fore-knowledge of God? that he knew, from the beginning, what would be the destiny of man? If so, can anything take place different from that fore-knowledge? and further, what agency has man in his own salvation, if the two first propositions be true?"

We learned, on the next day after speaking upon this document, that the gentleman who handed it in, said that we "never touched the main point in it," and, if we recollect, decided that he would not hear us again. How many he will find in that community who will agree with him, we presume not to say, further than that we think them "few and far between." We are not at all concerned on that point. We have been accustomed to receiving such slips of paper, at such times, so frequently, that we do not often misunderstand them; and we are very confident that we did not misunderstand those who cogitated this. We determined not to be foiled in our work, nor turned aside from the splendid prospects before us by any devices of this kind. We, therefore, read Eph. viii. 1-11; then read the document, and delivered our discourse, making it in our way to engross the main points aimed at in it, without making any direct criticism upon it, or the writer of it, though the temptation to do so was strong. The idea of men troubling themselves about the fore-knowledge of God, and man's agency, who cannot write six lines without involving so many absurdities as appear upon the face of this little paper, is ridiculous! The idea of men grappling with such subjects as the foreknowledge of God, the agency of man, and the destiny of man, who cannot discriminate between *questions* and *propositions;* or who call *questions, propositions,* and say, in reference to them, "Further, what agency has man in his own salvation, if the two first propositions be true?" is most preposterous and absurd. What is meant by the words, "If the two first propositions be true?" What *two propositions?* to say nothing about *"two first"* propositions, had been stated. None under the shining sun. Nothing had been affirmed, either true or false. Two *questions* had been asked, as follows: "Do you believe in the fore-knowledge of God? that he knew from the beginning what would be the destiny of man?"

Referring to these, he calls them "the two first propositions." There might be *one first* proposition and *one second one;* but not *"two first* propositions," certainly. But, in this case, there are no propositions at all, but simply two questions—a *first* and *second.*

Reader, what think you of explaining the fore-knowledge of God, man's agency and the destiny of man, to men who have not yet learned the difference between *questions* and *propositions*—men who ask, "Do you believe in the fore-knowledge of God? that he knew from the beginning what would be the destiny of man?" and then utter the following in reference to these two questions: "What agency has man in his own salvation, if the two first propositions be true?" If what two first propositions be true, in the name of common sense? The writer evidently does not mean any proposition stated or questions propounded; but he means, if we answer his questions affirmatively, or if the propositions that *God fore-knew all things*—that *he knew, from the beginning, what would be the destiny of man,* what agency has man in his own salvation? Our trouble is, how to teach men such mysterious, grand and awful matters as the fore-knowledge of God, human agency and man's destiny, who cannot state what they mean!

If such men would consent to be set back to the alphabet of Christianity—to the elementary matters—take a few humble lessons there first, and enter heartily into the practice of Christianity, no doubt they could understand, in a short time, all that is indispensable for a man to know, to serve God and make their way to a better world. Men may understand what they are required to believe, believe it, obey it and be Christians, whether they can understand the foreknowledge of God or not. In Christianity a man must begin at the beginning, keeping his duty distinctly in view, honestly doing as fast as he learns. But men who have never confessed

Christ, never made the first effort to give themselves to God, or serve him, may talk about the fore-knowledge of God till dooms-day and never understand that, or anything else in religion, right.

But, before we close, we will make an observation or two touching what we suppose to be the meaning of these questions. We do not believe that those passages in the New Testament, which contain the word "fore-knowledge," have any reference to how much or how little the Lord knew before. We, therefore, might say that we believe in the foreknowledge of God, without at all answering what was meant by the first question. That which is called "the determinate counsel and fore-knowledge of God," Acts 2nd, is called "those things which God had before shown by the mouth of his holy prophets;" Acts iii. 18. That which, in the New Testament, is called the "fore-knowledge; of God," is that which God has before revealed by the mouth of his holy prophets. But this is not the speculative question intended by our querist. His second question contains what he wants to get at: "Did God know, from the beginning, what would be the destiny of man?" We doubt not that he did—that he knew all things—that, with the Infinite One, it is neither fore-knowledge nor after-knowledge, in the common acceptation; but all is present and open to the eye of Him with whom we have to do. Nor does this, in the estimation of a man of clear head, in the least interfere with the agency of man. The Omniscient looking down from the beginning and seeing that the writer would propound the fore-going questions to us, had nothing to do in causing him to do it. Supposing him to have seen all things at all times, he saw them just as they were. He saw that the writer, an agent, free, or having power to write those questions, or not write them, to send them to us, or not send them, would voluntarily write and send them. Seeing that he would voluntarily do it, did not cause him to do it, and seeing that we could voluntarily notice them, as we are now doing, was not the cause of our doing it. We act just as free in doing it, as if the Lord did not know anything about it. There is no clearer proposition, to a man capable of looking at questions of this kind, than that fore-seeing what a man will do, acting freely, is not the cause of his action. The Lord fore-saw that Judas would hang himself, but the cause of his hanging himself was his terrible transgression, and not the Lord fore-knowing what he would do.   B. F.

-----o-----

DISAPPOINTMENT, DELUSION AND DECEPTION.

It is amusing to see with what self-complacency, inflated; conceit and arrogance our opponents can talk of "dangerous doctrine," "delusion," "deception," etc., etc. They appear to think that they have but little to do but stand and make objections to our procedure, interpose difficulties and throw obstructions in the way. They appropriate to themselves, in a very comforting way, the appellations, "evangelical," "orthodox" and "popular denominations," and assume that all is right with themselves. The-, policy is to put us, and keep us, in the defensive. This saves. them from many severe examinations, exposures and mortifications which they would otherwise suffer. All the opposing parties around us; have shielded themselves in this way. No skeptic could ever, have made anything of a defense, had his position been brought into examination. But allow him to make the attack, demand of the Christian to defend, explain and answer difficulties, and quite an ignorant and; stupid skeptic, that has never read the Bible once through, nor ten other books, in his life, can make quite a show and bluster. He can inquire where Cain got his wife, how you account for the people of God making slaves of those taken in war, or how you justify the command to destroy the Canaanites, etc., etc. But put him in the defensive; and demand of him to account for the creation of the world, and he is dumb; or, if not entirely, dumb, one man says, "It came by chance." Another yet, says, "I do not know anything about it." Demand of him whence came man, and you obtain a similar answer. He knows nothing about it. Inquire of him whence came death, and he is dumb; or, which is the same thing, or more perplexing, he says: "It is natural to die?" But who made such a nature? He knows nothing about it. Demand of him whence came murders, robberies, thefts, adulteries, etc., and he is again dumb. He knows nothing about it, and can give no satisfaction to anybody. Inquire of him, Is death the end of man? He is again speechless; or, if he speaks, it is without knowledge. He knows nothing and answers nothing that can afford any relief. Shall he, then, who can answer nothing, has nothing to stand upon, nothing to offer, and can make no explanation of anything, stand and interpose difficulties and make objections? Turn the matter upon him, and demand of him to answer his own stupid questions, and you will find him dumb. The man who thinks he can never be a Christian till he can understand all these matters, if he acts upon the same principle, will starve to death before he will sow seed or plant.

In the same way, our opposers can stand and demand of us, in reference to the New Testament plan of pardon, if this doctrine be true, what will become of all the good people who did not understand it, and did not come to God in that way. This is not a matter for us to account for. If we have the New Testament way of it, all we have to do is to maintain and practice it, and leave those who have not understood and practiced it in the hands of a wise and merciful God. But turn the matter round, and demand of them if their practice of calling persons to the mourner's bench, to pray and be prayed for, is the right way, what will become of those good people who died without coming in this way, and they are dumb. Coming to the mourner's bench to pray and be prayed for, as a part of the process in conversion, is a modern invention. The whole thing is unknown to the Bible. Not a man in the world can quote a reference to it from all that God has said to man. If the Lord were to come down and stand before the preacher engaged in the practice alluded to, and demand of him, Where is your authority for this? he would stand speechless. Not a man on earth can give any more authority for it than a Romanist can for counting beads. Not a preacher among all who now engage in the practice, thinks of finding a reference to it in all history till the present and the century before it. If this mourner's bench process is the way of coming to God, what of all in the days of the Apostles and all others down to John and Charles Wesley? They never came to the mourner's bench, and never heard of such a thing. Are they all lost? "No," exclaims a good friend to the mourner's bench, "we do not claim that *there is no other way*. We believe that thousands have lived Christians; died happy and gone to heaven, who never came to the mourner's bench." That cannot be, if this mourner's bench way is the way of the Lord; for he says, "I am the way, the truth and the life; no man cometh to the Father but by me," or by the "way which I teach." No man can come to the Lord only by the way of the Lord. When it is, therefore, admitted that a person can come in some other way, it is granted that coming by the mourner's bench is not coming by the way of the Lord; for it will not be pretended that any can come only by the way of the Lord.

But we are not done with this mourner's bench practice, or calling sinners forward to pray and be prayed for, as a part of the process in their conversion, or bringing them to God. It is not only without one particle of authority from God, from Scripture, or any precedent in all antiquity, which should forever set it aside; but there are other objections to it, which we demand of its friends to answer to, or admit that they cannot. It is a fact, that all who came to the Apostles, inquiring the way to salvation, or pardon, were forthwith shown the way, and submitted to the appointments of God. Not a single inquirer, so far as we are informed, ever came to the Apostles, or, any preacher of Christ, in their day, without being forthwith shown the way; and not one, that we have any account of, that followed their directions, and did not find pardon or salvation. But the practice, at the mourner's bench, is as different from this, as day is from night.

Look at the honest souls that come there, seeking pardon or salvation! Hear the preachers give them directions what to do! See them, in deep contrition, solemnly and honestly do all the preachers require; and what is the result? Do they find pardon? No; not one out of ten profess to have obtained salvation! What are these to do who have come inquiring the way, been directed what to do, have done it, and have not found salvation? What, we demand of all who maintain and countenance the practice, are these to do, who have come—who know they have come honestly, sought earnestly and solemnly, received directions, followed them sincerely, but *failed to find,* been disappointed; deceived and deluded? What are these to do now, after being thus disappointed once? What does the preacher then tell them to do? Why, he hardens his face, and tells them to come again the next night, or the next day, as the case may be. They go away mourning, disappointed and discouraged; but determine to try again. Again they come; but only again to be disappointed. They pray, seek, mourn and agonize. The preacher comes along, but without any light upon the subject. He knows no more how to solve the problem than the mourner. They are all in the dark together— the blind leading the blind. He repeats over the same directions, like the doctor who has prescribed the only, thing he knows, saying, "Try again; it may be that you will obtain relief."

These honest souls come again and again, night after night; hear sermon after sermon; go to the mourner's bench, time after time, but are disappointed again, and again, and again. They are received into the church as *seekers,* and continue to seek, week after week, meeting after meeting, month after month, and, in a number of instances, year after year, without one ray of light, or one additional encouragement. We have known them to continue in this condition for years—we have known many as well disposed, honest, sincere and desirous to serve the Lord as the world contains, thus to seek and fail, seek and fail; thus to suffer one disappointment after another for many years, and die without even professing to find salvation! The whole land abounds with persons who have, to a greater or less extent, been thus treated, disappointed and discouraged, as sincere and honest souls as are to be found in this world. Who is to answer for these poor souls, thus disappointed, disheartened and discouraged, by being kept seeking, mourning and striving in a blind way, not having a promise of God in it, for years, and, in many instances, dying without finding God. Thousands upon thousands, if they were so disposed, could say to those who practice in this way, "We came to you with flowing tears, broken hearts, inquiring what should we do to be saved. You told us what to do. We did what you told us, honestly, solemnly, from the bottom of the heart. You told us to come and try again. We came again and again, inquiring and seeking solemnly, and did all you told us to do, but did not find. We have thus continued for years, but have not found, and cannot find, salvation."

Some that are dead, can meet these teachers, and say, "We came to you, seeking God, followed your directions for years; and died trying your way, but *failed to find.*" Who is to answer for all this? Who is to account for their disappointment, discouragement and failure to find salvation? B. F.

-----o-----

GOD TO BE FOUND IN HIS APPOINTMENTS.

WE have two distinct classes of men now-a-days. Indeed, we are not certain but there have long been the same two classes, viz.: 1. Those who believe God may always he found in his appointments. 2. Those who believe God may be found out of his appointments, or where he has not appointed. The first class go directly to the Bible, and have no trouble in showing that, in all ages, those who come to God, or seek him in his appointments, sincerely, without a single exception, find him. This is undeniable. The other class, generally, in the abstract, or theoretically, admit this; but they insist that the Lord may be found, and actually is found, in many instances, where he has not appointed, or where men have appointed. For this, the former class maintain, there is no evidence. Thus the issue stands, in the first place. But it ends not here. Those who maintain that the Lord may be found where he has not appointed, soon fall into the habit of directing the seeker where the Lord has not appointed invariably for salvation. They soon give the way not appointed the decided preference over the way appointed. The way not appointed soon becomes the way almost universally practiced. The party going in the way not appointed, become the large party, the popular party and the strong party. With all these, the question, whether a man can come to the Lord and find him, *in a way which he has not appointed,* becomes an all-engrossing question, upon which their entire religious claim depends. Their all is at stake. If it cannot be proved that a man can come to God in a way which he has not appointed, their entire claim is forfeited. No wonder that they should be somewhat excited in the examination of the question, especially if they should find themselves likely to fail in the argument. On the other hand, those who come to God according to his own appointments, or in his own appointments, not only know that they are right, that they are safe, but their opponents admit that those who come to God in his appointments are right, that they find God and are safe. These have nothing at stake in the controversy. They are upon sure footing, as all admit. They can afford to be magnanimous, generous and fair. Their investigations are not for their own sake, as they are admitted right, but for the sake of others, whose position is doubtful. These are difficult to assail. They feel their strength, and others feel it. Their opponents have looked at every conceivable place where an attack might be made. No sophistry, that, we know of, has proved more effectual than the old, the one they have so frequently employed, that the doctrine that men must come to God in his appointments, *cuts off so many good people.* They begin by speaking of the large number that have never come to God in his appointments, and are consequently lost, if none can come to God only in his appointments, or if men cannot come to God in a way not appointed. They speak at large of the exclusiveness and uncharitableness of such a doctrine. They want you to tell what you think will become of all the good people who have died without coming to God in his appointments! What is the intention of all this? Is it to prove anything? to enlighten anybody? to show any one the truth? or only to prejudice the mind against any light, any reasoning or argument that may be offered?

The first thing to look at is the fact that all have taken a doubtful, in the place of an unquestionable, course, to say the least of it, who have attempted to come to God by a way which he has not the appointed. If they had come to God in way which he has appointed, there could have been no doubts started in their case. But as it is; to say the least of it, their case is in doubt, dispute and uncertainty, Who is to blame for this? Their religious instructors, unquestionably, their editors and preachers, undoubtedly, who have directed them in the way not appointed, instead of the way appointed. They could just as well have directed them to the appointments of God, where all the promises would have met them fairly and plainly, and where they would have been involved in no doubt. Those converted on Pentecost were left in no doubt, for they were directed to the appointments of God, in which they found the salvation of their souls, and the infallible promises of God. Those converted in Solomon's portico were left in no doubt, and uncertainty, because they came to the Lord in his own gracious appointments and met his never failing promise.

This was an end to all doubt, dispute and uncertainty. The same was true of all converted under the Apostles and early evangelists. These holy men directed him to the appointments of God; in which everyone, who came honestly and sincerely, found the Lord, without a doubt and uncertainty. But how different all those who come in some way not appointed. Therein constant doubt, dispute and uncertainty hanging over it. Who is to blame for all these, many of them as sincere as the world contains, being left in doubts, disputes and uncertainty? Who is to blame for their being placed in a questionable position? Nobody but their religious guides. These have involved them in this doubtful predicament, by directing them to appointments not of God, when they could just as well have directed them to God's appointments.

It is of no avail to talk of exclusiveness, as a shield for guiding men to appointments not of God; nor will it amount to anything to speak of uncharitable doctrine. No charity can make it right to depart from the plain appointments of Heaven, and make it safe to adopt the appointments of men; or save him from uncertainty who does it. If men would listen, to the proper dictates of charity, they would be careful to direct honest inquirers to the plain appointments of God, where all agree he may be found. In the popular sense, Christianity is a system, perfect and distinct in itself, from everything else. It inquires nothing about what will suit one man or another, one party or another, one nation or another. It is a system such as it *pleased* God to give, and such as man must accept, if he would have God accept him. As to exclusiveness, it admits nothing else to be right or acceptable to God but itself. As to the law of Moses, Christianity sets it aside by the one sweeping statement, that, by the deeds of the law, no flesh can be justified in the sight of God." Respecting those under the law, and all others, the great Apostle says: "We have before proved all in unbelief;" and, says he, "God has concluded all under sin, that he might have mercy upon all." As to the law, the Apostle says, "It is abolished." The first institution was taken away to make room for the second. As to Pagan deities, institutions and worship, Christianity sets them all aside, and declares them all nothing. The religion of Jesus Christ lifts itself up above everything else, and pronounces all else inefficacious, displeasing and detestable to God. It equally pronounces against all perversions of Christianity, corruptions or mutilations of it, and pronounces favorable to nothing but *itself,* in its native and original purity. It matters nothing about the number who do not practice it, who do not receive it or oppose it. Its Author can judge, condemn and punish a large number of opposers just as conveniently as a few, and will just as certainly do it.

If every Jew under heaven had departed from Jerusalem, where the name of God was recorded, and gone to Gerazim, where his name was not recorded, God would not have gone there, would not have heard a prayer offered there, nor acknowledged a single worshipper there. If Naaman, the Assyrian leper, in the place of dipping himself seven times in Jordan, as God appointed, had dipped himself seventy times seven in the Euphrates or Nile, he would have been a leper still; he would not have been healed; but, in the simple appointment of God, the Lord healed him. If, when Moses lifted up the serpent in the wilderness, that whoever looked upon it might be healed, the people had lifted up a thousand other serpents and looked a thousand times at them, and offered ten thousand prayers, with fasting, God would not have heard nor healed them. They could not come to God only through his appointments. If, when the Lord commanded the Israelites to march round the walls of Jericho seven days, once each day, then seven times on the seventh day, then blow the trumpet and shout, the bad marched twice as far in some other direction, instituted a band of music in the place of the trumpet, and a dance in the place of a shout, the walls would not have fallen, and the blessing of God would not have attended. The circumstance of His appointing anything, gives it a preference, and designates the place where he may be found. Whoever seeks him where he has appointed, finds him. His appointments may appear to man very simple in some instances. Such appointments as anointing a man's eyes with clay, and requiring him to wash, is an appointment of that description; but the man for whom this appointment was prescribed, found the blessing of God in it. The dying thief on the cross, who could not do anything, but appealed to Jesus, was not required to submit to any appointment, and simply received the response, "To-day shalt thou be with me in paradise." But when the Lord had ascended to heaven, was coronated, crowned Lord of all, had commenced his regular administration, having sent the Holy Spirit to guide the Apostles into all truth, and the first full and clear announcement of the gospel was made, three thousand inquirers cried out, in intense solicitude, "Men and brethren, what shall we do?" Here follows the appointment of God: "Repent and be baptized, every one of you, for remission of sins, and you shall receive the gift of the Holy Spirit." Here is the clear appointment of God. These inquiring souls sought God in his appointments and found him. No doubt was left over their conversion. Nor were there any among them who did not find. Why was there no doubt left over their case? Because they came to God in his appointments, where all admit he may be found. The doubts are on the part of those who try to find God, or to come to him, in some way which he has not appointed. Doubts will forever hang over these. Why do so many seek God at the mourner's bench and do not find? Simply because there is not a promise of God that they should find him there; and because, furthermore, there is not an evidence that any man ever did find God at the mourner's bench. The preachers themselves never promise anything certain at this place, but tell the people to *try it. Maybe they will find the Lord!* But the Lord says, "He that believeth, and is baptized *shall be saved.*" B. F.

-----o-----

FORE-KNOWLEDGE AND HUMAN AGENCY AGAIN.

As we have before stated, with the Infinite One, there is, in the common acceptation, neither fore-knowledge nor afterknowledge. With Him, who "sees the end from the beginning," all things are present. All things are open to the eyes of Him with whom we have to do. There is nothing of the past, present or future hid from Him. But, as we have before said, the mere fore-seeing that an event will come is not the cause of its coming.

Anybody can foresee that a debt contracted will come due, but fore-seeing that it will come due, is not the cause of its coming due. It would come due just the same if no one fore-saw that it would come due. The omniscience of God is only the more wonderful and overwhelming to us, when we consider that he can fore-see what an agent will do—one that acts freely—that exercises that wonderful something that we call the *will* or volition—that chooses, decides or determines his own actions. But to say that God decreed these actions of men, and that he only fore-saw them because he decreed them, is to destroy the chief glory of the divine prescience, and let it down from the wonderful and overwhelming ability to fore-see what a being, acting entirely free, will do, to the mere circumstance of fore-seeing that a machine which God had made, set in motion, and to which he had applied the necessary power to perform a certain revolution, would perform the revolution which he had decreed. Those who make God fore-see certain things, or all things, because *he decreed* them, only make him a wise machinist who has made a fine machine, decreed it to a certain work, applied to it the power necessary to perform that work, and fore-sees the work that it will do. This is a small affair, compared with Omniscience looking down through the immense cycles of the eternal ages, upon the countless multitudes of men and angels all acting free, deciding themselves what they will do, and fore-seeing all their actions.

But one of the sage questions that troubles those who study more to find and present some speculative questions, intricate subtleties and unanswerable difficulties, than how to perform their duty to God or man, is to the following amount: "If God fore-saw the actions of man, could they have been otherwise than he fore-saw they would be?" We answer that *they could have been otherwise.* There was no necessity upon the agent. He was perfectly free and could have acted in some other way; but had he done so, the Lord would have fore-seen that he would have acted in that other way. The fore-seeing how he will act, lays no necessity upon him who acts. He acts just as freely as if no being in the universe fore-saw how he would act.

In our estimation, the devil never thought of a more stupid device than to put into a man's head the silly conceit that he cannot determine his own actions, and, therefore, is not accountable. All law, both human and divine, has its very foundation in the self-evident truth that man acts freely. All blame and praise, all vice and virtue, all our ideas of good or bad are founded in the self-evident principle that a man acts freely, determines his own actions, can do good or bad. Hence, if a man does an injury by accident, he is not punishable. The reason is, he did not intend it, or had not the power to have avoided it. If a man falls into poverty by manifest misfortune, when making manly exertions of an honorable and noble character, he is pitied, and has the sympathy of the community generally. But if a man falls into poverty by manifest indolence, no one pities him, for the simple reason that he could have avoided it. If a locomotive runs against a man and knocks him down, he feels no resentment towards it and does not make battle with it. Why? For the simple reason that it had no volition in the case; that it did not act freely, or did not control its own action. But suppose the injured man perceives that the engineer run it against him purposely; resentment rises in one moment, and he feels like seeking some kind of redress. Why does he blame him? For the manifest reason that he acted freely; that he did it of choice—that he willed it when he could have acted otherwise. He acted *freely,* but the engine by *necessity.* The free action is accountable, but the action from necessity is not.

An insane man kills a man, but no one

thinks of punishing him for murder. Why? Because his action is not free. He is not capable of controlling his action. We think proper to confine him, so that he may not kill another man; but no one thinks of holding him accountable, for the simple reason that he is incapable of controlling his own actions. Some men, who talk about *reason* and *consistency,* insist that God will put them, and that preachers of Christ should put them, and all men, upon the same footing with insane persons—that is, upon the ground that they cannot act otherwise than they do, or that they are not free, do not and cannot control their actions, and cannot, therefore, be held responsible. To this we cannot consent. We are free to admit their *perversity,* but not their *insanity,* and the Lord makes a difference between perversity and insanity. He will not treat a perverse person as he will an insane person; neither will the civil law or the community. The perverse man is to be held free and responsible; but the insane man is neither free nor responsible. Of all the little, pitiful and childish places through which men—full-grown men, who profess to be men of reason, consistency and manliness—have attempted to crawl to escape responsibility to God, there is none, that we know of, so weak, cowardly and unmanly as to come before God and man, and plead to be dealt with upon the same principle as all laws, both human and divine, and the common sentiment of mankind deal with the insane—that is, the principle that they are not free in their actions, have no volition, cannot resolve and do this or that, and, therefore, the Almighty cannot hold them to an account for their sins! Or, perhaps, they prefer to be put upon the list with infants. If an infant child should break or destroy anything—if it should set a house on fire, no one would think of punishing it, for the simple reason that it knows no better, can do no better, is incapable of any better action; therefore neither God nor man think of holding it accountable. If anyone should think of punishing the child, the plea would resound through all the land, that the inoffensive creature knew no better, and was not capable of acting otherwise, and could not be held responsible.

How infinitely little, weak and childish for full-grown men to put up the same plea for not being held to an account as would be made for an infant. Their plea amounts simply to this: That *they are not men,* that they are not free, do not decide what they will do, determine their own actions as intelligent, rational and accountable beings. For all this class of men, if, as their doctrine makes them, they are not free, rational and accountable men, there should be a special provision, and a very extended one at that. They are not eligible to any office. Who would vote for a man, to fill any office, if it were known of him that he could not determine his own course of action, that was not free, but acted like an insane person, or an infant, from necessity, and could not be held accountable! Such persons are not eligible voters at our polls. How can a man vote that has no volition? that cannot determine his actions? that cannot decide, or, which is the same thing, make choice who he will vote for? Such a man is incompetent to transact the ordinary business of life, because in that there is accountability and responsibility. It is impossible to deal with a man who is not free, who cannot control his own actions, decide what he will do, and what he will not do. If his reason why he cannot be responsible to God for his actions is, that he is not free, and could not have done otherwise, he has the same reason why he cannot be responsible for his actions and transactions between him and his fellow-men.

Such men are wholly incompetent to act as physicians. Who would take medicine from a man not free, not capable of controlling his actions, determining what the disease is, or deciding what the treatment should be? and who, if he should administer medicine that would kill your wife or child, would tell you that God fore-saw that he would do it, and that he could not have done otherwise? Who would trust an important law case in the hands of a lawyer who is not free, has no volition, cannot decide upon his own course of action, and, therefore, is not responsible? Such men might be fit subjects for an asylum, or objects of charity and pity, but not for any useful stations in life. Some of them might he regarded as infants, inoffensive, innocent and unoffending, but not accountable, from the fact that they have no ability. This, we again say, is one of the very least of all the little places men ever attempted to creep through to escape accountability to their Creator. It is to *unman themselves,* to escape the responsibility of *men,* and put in the pitiful plea, before God and the world, that they could not determine their actions, could not have acted otherwise, and, therefore, must be treated as insane persons, or an infant who does an injury—*not be held responsible!* God pity the man thus deluded! B. F.

-----o-----

[From the Western Watchman.]
CAMPBELLISM UNCHANGED.

SEVERAL Baptist writers, especially since the affiliation of Baptists and Campbellites in Bible revision, have declared that Mr. Campbell had renounced his most glaring errors, and was really on the road to sound doctrine. In this, however, it seems that they were woefully mistaken. The Christian world would hardly believe that a religious teacher could be found, in this age of the world, who teaches that it is wrong for a sinner to pray for the forgiveness of his sins before he has been baptized.

Our readers have been informed that a book has been published, as a reply to Dr. Jeter's "Campbellism Examined," by a Mr. Lard, of Missouri. We have not noticed this book, because no copy has been sent to us. Nor have we ever possessed the book, though we turned over a few pages of a copy which happened to fall in our way a few moments, To this book Alexander Campbell has given his fullest endorsement. In this book, Mr. Lard, referring to Dr. Jeter's charge, that the Campbellites had, formerly, taught that unbaptized persons ought not to pray, yet gave them credit for having changed or modified their views on this point, very emphatically denies it, and says:

"We assert now, as we have ever done, that there is not one passage in the Bible which, during the reign of Christ, makes it the duty of an unbaptized person to pray. Mr. Jeter is greatly mistaken if he supposes that we cherish not this as a capital item. We do not say the sinner may not pray; and, when he does pray, we do not say it is wrong. Let us be understood. We do say, with singular emphasis, that it is *not the duty* of the sinner, the unbaptized, *to pray for the remission of his sins;* that it is not made his duty to do so by the Bible—not even by implication. It is against this practice, or, rather, fiction, that our objection is specially pointed.

"The sinner is taught by *orthodox* preachers—blind guides in this case, certainly—to pray for the remission of his sins; nay, more, that God will give him a *feeling sense* of remission when it occurs."

But should any one, with a false charity, still maintain Campbellite orthodoxy, here is more from Lard and Campbell:

"Of all the gross and fatal delusions of Protestants, there are few we can deem worse than this. It is a shame to the Baptist denomination—of which we can truly say, 'With all thy faults, I love thee still'—that it should hold and teach this error. Were a sinner, in a moment of deep distress, to pray the Lord to forgive his sins, we could not find it in our heart to chide him for the deed; but we should certainly endeavor to teach him the way of the Lord more perfectly. But one thing we should never do: teach him what the Bible does not teach him—to expect the remission of his sins merely because he prayed for it. Why pray for a blessing which our heavenly Father has never promised to confer in this way, and for this reason, but which he certainly does confer in another way, and for a different reason? Where is the advantage of the prayer unless the Lord has promised to heed it?

"Consequently, since there is *no law* (we state it with emphasis) defining the sinner to be obliged *to pray for the remission of his sins,* we hence conclude that this is not duty, and therefore will avail him nothing."

For these extracts, we are indebted to one of our exchanges. We copy them, not to confute, for no intelligent believer can need help to confute such a monstrous absurdity. Our object is, to let our readers see what opinions come forth from the (American) Bethany of our age! *That* is the Campbellism of 1856, without disguise! What Mr. Campbell's Lard brands of the "shame of the Baptist denomination," we esteem as our glory.

-----o-----

REMARKS.

If the reader please, he will look carefully what Mr. Crowell asserts, and then examine his proof, and he will find his assertion wholly unsupported; nay, more, positively contradicted. What is his assertion? It is that the Disciples, whom he glories in nick-naming "Campbellites," teach "that it is wrong for a sinner to pray"—"that unbaptized persons ought not to pray." Does his proof say "it is wrong for sinners to pray?"—"that unbaptized persons ought not to pray?" or anything equivalent? It does not; but, on the contrary, it does say, "We do not say the sinner may not pray; and, when he does pray, we do not say it is wrong." Mr. Crowell's proposition is, that we "teach that *it is wrong* for a sinner to pray"—"that unbaptized persons *ought not to pray;*" and his proof is, that "we do not say *the sinner may not pray;* and, when he does pray, we *do not say it is wrong.*"

Bro. Lard does say that it is not the duty of the sinner, the unbaptized, to pray for the remission of sins. Does Mr. Crowell quote any Scripture showing that it is his duty? No, not he; that is not the easy way to dispose of the case. Those who change baptism from the initiatory ordinance, through which the believing penitent enters the house of God, to the practice or duty of one *in the* house, or from the duty of the penitent alien, in which he is baptized *into Christ,* to the duty of a Christian—one *in* Christ. —could not easily take prayer, the duty and practice of a Christian—one already *in* Christ—*in* the house of God—and transform it into a part of the process in converting sinners. The question with us is not whether the penitent sinner, who believes with all the heart, as he goes forward in making confession of his faith in Christ and obedience in being baptized, *may call upon the name of the Lord* for his blessing in his surrender to God. This is precisely the way to come to obtain the promise: "Whosoever shall call upon the name of the Lord shall be saved." But the simple question with us is, whether prayer can be made into a converting institution, through which sinners can enter into Christ, into the kingdom of God, or a state of justification, without their confessing Christ and being baptized. Or, if possible, to state the matter more clearly, will God be more likely to hear the prayers of sinners who simply come to a mourner's bench and pray, without confessing Christ and obeying his command, "to repent and be baptized," than those who, like Saul, are commanded to "arise and be baptized and wash away their sins, *calling* on the name of the Lord?"

Mr. Crowell and many occupying the same position, on this point, will one day render a serious account. It is no small offence to take the institution of Heaven, appointed for the believing penitent, to induct him into Christ, into the kingdom, and make it an item of Christian practice in the house of God; and take prayer, an item of practice for saints, as long as they remain in this world, and turn it into a converting ceremony, at the same time setting aside confession and baptism. If baptism is an item of Christian practice, a duty for those in Christ, in the body, in a justified state, why is it never to be repeated? Christians are to continue to pray, commune, etc., because these are items of practice after induction. Baptism is to be performed but once, because it is the initiatory ceremony to a proper subject; and when initiated, he is done with it. Bringing persons to a bench to pray and be prayed for, as a part of the process in their conversion, as practiced by some Baptists, has no more authority than infant baptism, sprinkling for baptism or Romish penance. All any honest man has to do, to satisfy himself of this, is to examine every case of conversion found in the New Testament; and all any Disciple need do, to confute Mr. Crowell in this practice, is to demand one passage authorizing it. They will find him speechless. B. F.

-----o-----

A GENEROUS PROPOSITION.

THERE are three parties in this country that have had much trouble with us as a religious body, have denounced us long, loud and bitterly, as not orthodox, evangelical or sound in the faith, but most dangerous and damnable heretics. These three parties are Baptists, Methodists and Presbyterians. Our proposition is not to give them column for column, paragraph for paragraph, sentence for sentence and word for word in our sheet, provided they will do the same with us, though this would be a fair, just and equitable proposition. We are well aware, and think they are equally well aware, that they cannot safely venture to meet us upon terms of mere fairness and equality. They have long since demonstrated that they will not allow their readers to see *both sides*. This they cannot *safely risk*. We know it is useless to ask this of them. We, therefore, propose to them the following fair and generous opportunity to point out to us our danger, show us our errors and reclaim us: *Each one of the parties alluded to shall have two columns per week in our enlarged sheet, commencing January first,* 1858, *and extending through the entire year, and we will only occupy the same space in reply.* We only require of the writers that they be men of sufficient note to enable us to accept them without any endorsement, or to come endorsed by the publications of their own party.

From present prospects, we shall have an extended circulation, and this proposition will contain a fine opportunity to convince us, if, indeed, we are in error. We desire to be convinced, and for all men to know it, if we are wrong. Who will undertake this benevolent work? We want men of ability, and who, at the same time, have the confidence of the people, that what they say may labor under no disadvantage from an unacceptable advocate. Come, gentlemen, we shall all give an account to God, and we had better examine the matter well and prepare ourselves for that great account. May we all find the good and right way, unite and walk in it and ultimately attain to the glory to be revealed at the revelation of Jesus Christ! B. F.

-----o-----

OURSELVES AND OUR SAVIOR.

O! did we but know ourselves and our Savior! We are poor, but he is rich—we are dead, but he is life—we are sin, but he is righteousness—we are guiltiness, but he is grace—we are misery, but he is mercy—we are lost, but he is salvation. If we are willing, he never was otherwise. He ever lives, ever loves, ever pities, ever pleads. He loves and saves to the uttermost, all who come unto Him.

A GENEROUS PROPOSITION.

Editor's Table.

TO THE READERS OF THE MONTHLY REVIEW.

DEAR READERS: We have gone pleasantly through another year and now come to you in the closing number of the volume, kindly thanking you for your patronage and encouragements in our feeble efforts to maintain the greatest and best of all causes—that cause in which is the hope of all nations. Truly are we grateful to all our agents and friends, who have taken such an active part and afforded us such valuable assistance, in extending our circulation. We are under lasting obligations to many who have done us great service, without receiving any reward, save the satisfaction of circulating the work. Nor are we under less obligation to those who have received the small percentage which we have allowed agents, as the amount was so small as to be scarcely any inducement, and therefore we regard their efforts simply aimed to extend the circulation of the REVIEW. The principal preaching brethren have generally co-operated with us and aided us beyond our power to reciprocate. Thanks to all—our most sincere thanks to all; but especially to God, who put it into their hearts to aid us. This year has been the most laborious, most happy and most successful year of our life, in each of the departments of our labor. 1. In resuscitating the missionary work; 2. In publishing; 3. In preaching. The Lord has been with us and abundantly blessed us in all our efforts. Blessed be His name forever and ever.

We must now take an affectionate farewell, for this year, of all the patrons of the REVIEW. We bid them all adieu. Whether our relation shall be continued, as editor and subscribers, is not in our power to decide. We are in the field for re-election. Indeed, we are re-elected *now* for another year. But each man has the privilege to decide whether we shall edit *for him* or not. His voting for us this year, does not bind him for next. We shall not presume to edit for any man who does not vote for us. The voting is done by subscribing for another year, or refusing to subscribe. All who subscribe for our enlarged weekly and send the pay according to terms, vote for us. Those who do not subscribe, vote against us. Now is the time to send in your votes We intend sending our first enlarged sheet to all the patrons of the REVIEW, that they may see it, and if they do not subscribe, it will stop.

OUR PROSPECTS.

WE are now in some two weeks of the commencement of our enlarged weekly, called "THE AMERICAN CHRISTIAN REVIEW." The monthly pamphlet and the weekly CHRISTIAN AGE, both stop at the end of this year, and will be succeeded by the enlarged weekly. Those who are subscribers to the AGE, and have paid into next year, after January 1st, will receive the enlarged weekly in the place of the AGE till their time is out. Some few have paid in advance for the monthly. These will receive the weekly till they have the worth of their money. Now is the time to make up clubs, obtain subscribers and make up a large list, for a weekly that shall be a general medium of communication for the brotherhood. We now have about seven thousand subscribers for the two publications. The time for which a majority of these subscribers expires January 1st. Will our friends, everywhere, see to it, and renew the lists? So far as we can see, our prospect is beautiful. Large clubs are being made up in all directions. Brethren, our cause is in your hands, as we are all in the hands of the Lord. Send on the names as soon as possible.

AMERICAN BIBLE UNION.

THIS Institution was never in a better condition than at present. The hand of Divine Providence has been seen in its regular progress from the commencement. The scholars composing the Final Committee, or Board of Revisers, are not excelled by any men living. Everything is now permanently arranged, and progressing systematically, regularly, on to completion; but it is a work that cannot be hastened. Time must be taken, *all the time necessary*. While we are anxious to see the work out, and for the people to have the benefit of it, we hope that no desire to hasten, or gratify friends who are anxious to see the work, will prevent the Final Committee from having the last minute of time they may desire. When the work appears, we hope to have an *English Bible* that we can quote as *authority*, and one that will challenge the criticism of the world. Time must be had for this, and we know that the men now engaged will take the time, and the anxious public must have the *patience to wait for the work till it can be done right.*

BOOK NOTICE.

A BRIEF VIEW OF MISSIONS. By ELD. ISAAC ERRETT.

A neat pamphlet, of the foregoing title, written by Eld. Isaac Errett, now Corresponding Secretary for the American Christian Missionary Society, and published by said Society, is now before us."This pamphlet originated within a resolution passed at the General Missionary Meeting at Macomb, Ill., last May, requesting us to prepare, or have someone else prepare, such a pamphlet. We preferred that Bro. Errett should prepare it, and wrote him, making the request. He prepared it accordingly, and read a considerable portion of it as a Missionary Address. It was, as far as known to us, universally esteemed as an able, interesting and valuable address. The portion not read is mainly statistical and contains an amount of information on the subject of Missions not to be found in any work of the same size that we are acquainted with. It contains sixty-four pages, closely printed, of common book size, and ought to be circulated everywhere among the brethren. It will suit State Missions as well as the General Missionary Society. It is put down at something near cost, so that churches, or persons friendly to missions, can buy and circulate gratis.